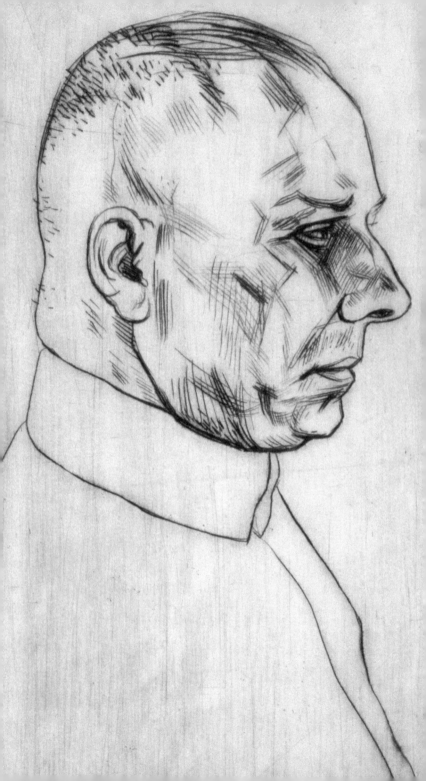

My Favorite Films

By

Cyrus Ghani

MAGE PUBLISHERS
WASHINGTON, DC
2004

The images in this book are by Frank Martin and are used by permission:
Cover and spine painting of Greta Garbo;
page ii, drawing of Erich von Stroheim;
page vi, drawing of Marlene Dietrich;
page viii, gouache of Carole Lombard;
page xiv, drawing of Dolores del Rio;
page 208, drawing of Louise Brooks;
page 458, sketches of Jean Harlow.
All are from the author's collection

Library of Congress in Cataloging Data

Ghanī, Sīrūs
My favorite films / by Cyrus Ghani. -- 1st ed.
pc.cm
includes bibliographical references and index
ISBN 0-934211-87-6 (hard. : alk paper) -- ISBN 0-934211-86-8 (pbk. : alk. paper)
1. Motion pictures--Plots, themes, etc. 2. Motion pictures--Catalogs. 1. Title.
PN1998.G525 2004
791.43'75--dc22
2004003364

HARDCOVER ISBN 0-934211-87-6
PAPERBACK ISBN 0-934211-86-8

Mage Publishers books are available at bookstores,
through the internet, or directly from the publisher.
Call 202-342-1642, or e-mail *info@mage.com* for our catalog,
or visit *mage on the web* at
www.mage.com.

For Laila and Roya,
a third generation of movie lovers

CONTENTS

PREFACE

Along with many other interests, I've had a lifelong fascination with movies. One result has been a collection of some 1,200 books on the subject as part of a sizable library on a variety of subjects. Some of these movie books date back to the forties when only a few commentators were writing about the industry. They sit beside my collection of videocassettes containing nearly 3,500 films. I have met a wide array of people "in the business," including producers, directors, actors, designers and cameramen. Thus the seeds of this book were, in some ways, sewn many years ago. But the immediate impetus was a list that I came across while going through some of my papers not too long ago. It consisted of my favorite one hundred films which I had compiled at the request of George Stevens, Jr., then president of the American Film Institute, whom I had met in Miami in July 1972. I decided to bring my list up to date, and from there it seemed to grow of its own accord.

Let me offer a brief summary of my background, which is a little out of the ordinary. I was born in a small city in northeastern Iran. When I was five years old my family moved to the capital, Tehran. I have loved movies ever since my first exposure at age nine, late by today's standards but not at that time and place. Soon I was allowed to see one film a week. They were mostly Buster Crabbe's *Flash Gordon* serials and Buck Jones and Ken Maynard cowboy films, the space fiction and Westerns of the day. But shortly there was a Ministry of Education regulation, far ahead of its time even in the Western world, prohibiting anyone under age fourteen from seeing films not specifically made for children. For almost a year only a handful of films were available to me. I remember having seen *Snow White and the Seven Dwarfs* several times during this period of drought. There were, however, two exceptions brought about by my father. He was a distinguished physician who was educated abroad and was conversant in several languages. He left his practice when I was twelve and began a career as a writer, a scholar, and later as a diplomat. I went with my father and some of his friends to see *The Story of Louis Pasteur* and later *The Life of Emile Zola*. My father, who had seen very few films during his entire life, wanted me to see these two films for their historical content. Although I enjoyed the occasion, in truth, both the subjects and the language were beyond me. It was not until years later that I appreciated what good films they were.

At age fourteen I was sent to the preparatory school of the American University of Beirut. From there I was sent to England to Millfield School in Somerset, and I finished my secondary education at Cheshire Academy in Connecticut. In each of these schools I was free to see movies on the weekends. During half terms and holidays, whether in Beirut, London, Cheshire and Waterbury, Connecticut or New York City, I was able to pursue my interest, seeing one or more films a day. I then proceeded to the University of Southern California in Los Angeles.

My father had been a delegate to the founding of the United Nations in San Francisco in 1945 where he made many friends, including Dr. Jesse Marmorston, who was married to the film producer Lawrence Weingarten. Later, when my father came to Los Angeles to visit me, he became their frequent guest. I would chauffeur him to and from their parties at their home and elsewhere and get glimpses of or brush shoulders with the likes of Louis B. Mayer and his successor

Dore Schary, Buddy Adler, Sid Grumann, Katharine Hepburn, Gail Patrick and even Charlie Chaplin and Groucho Marx. My only formal invitation to the Weingarten home was a Thanksgiving dinner in 1949 when I met Spencer Tracy and his family. My father introduced to the Weingartens my girl-friend, Lailee Bakhtiar, an Iranian girl who had come to study in the U.S. and who ultimately became a prominent Los Angeles physician. They had two young daughters, Lizzie and Norma, and invited Lailee to stay with them. She remained for many years and became a member of their family. Once she was given a small part in the film *Kim*, and I went to the pre-mier with the Weingartens. I was an extra in *Pat and Mike*, produced by Lawrence Weingarten. Alas, I wound up on the cutting room floor.

In 1952, after the death of my father, I moved to New York where I continued my education at Wagner College, followed by graduate studies in English literature at Columbia Univer-sity and then law school at New York University. It was during that time I met Caroline, my future wife. She, too, was a law student. The only time we had for movies was Saturday nights when starting early in the evening and ending past midnight we saw two and, with precise timing, sometimes three movies as we raced from one movie house to another having prese-lected the best half of each double feature.

In 1958 we went to live in Tehran. The Iranian film industry had not yet matured and only a few theaters showed undubbed foreign films. Movie houses began to proliferate with special evenings for undubbed versions. But it was when I made visits to Europe and the U.S., in a professional capacity or for pleas-ure, that I resumed my old habit of seeing as many films as I possibly could. Caroline and I had two children, Ali and then Vida, who also grew to know and enjoy films.

Because of my reputation in Tehran as a film buff, most British and Americans who came to make films in Iran were referred to me through my law firm or were given social introductions. Some frivolous lawsuits were also referred to me. A well-known bald actor sought to stop a shampoo manufacturer from using his name and image in their advertisements. An aging glamor girl wanted to stop the use of her name by a cosmetics manufacturer for a new shade of lipstick because she considered the color too dark. Some with whom I spent much time socially discussing their films were Frederic March, Florence Eldridge, Loretta Young, Curt Jergens, and the director Jean Negulesco among others.

In December 1968 I came to Washington, D.C., as a member of the prime minister's party on a state visit at the invitation of President Johnson. Among the cities in which we were hosted was Los Angeles, where a lunch was given at Warner Bros. The studio had invited most of the producers, directors and actors who were currently engaged in filming at Warner Bros. The following night there was a dinner at the home of Charlton Heston, who was then president of the Screen Actors Guild, where there were many Hollywood guests. I asked the State Department protocol officer if I could see several directors privately. Meetings were arranged with Elia Kazan, Billy Wilder and William Wyler. Most of the people I met on this visit were just fleeting encounters. My lengthy conversations were with Kazan and Wyler, both of whom I saw on further occasions in Tehran or New York.

There was a revolution in Iran in 1979, and my family and I came abroad. We lived in London and then in New York.

In the course of my varied life I have met a wide range of film people. Those whose frequent company I have enjoyed and with whom I have had many lengthy discussions are but a few: John Huston, Irene Selznick, Richard Burton, Richard Silbert, Adolph Green, Kenneth Hyman, Frank Capra, George Roy Hill, Robert Mitchum, F. Benjamin Fisz and Andrew McLaglen. There are a few close friends of long standing who have contributed to my knowledge and enjoyment of films. Farrokh Ghaffari, a French stage actor, film director, and foremost Iranian film historian; Ebrahim Golestan, writer, director and producer; Fereydoun Hoveyda, prolific writer, artist and film critic of *Cahiers du Cinema*; Arthur Schlesinger, Jr., a foremost historian and erstwhile film critic. Kitty Carlisle Hart, actress and soprano; the late Jean Negulesco, artist and director; Leslie Linder, actor, agent and producer; and Joe Morgenstern, former *Newsweek* film critic now with *The Wall Street Journal* and National Public Radio.

From all I have gained valuable insights into films, filmmaking and history. This, coupled with the vast number of films I have seen over the years, makes me feel that I may have something worthwhile to say about my favorite movies.

Cyrus Ghani
January 2004

INTRODUCTION

My selection of films for this book is purely personal. They are those I have enjoyed seeing again and again, some more often than others. Certain of them will be well recognized. Others may be less so to the moviegoing audience of today. They are from many countries. Some are in black and white, which many current filmgoers may find unappealing. As a movie lover I could have included three to four hundred more films; however, that would have made the book unwieldy. I am reasonably certain that there are very good films that I have omitted. A number of my comments may appear to be more critical than complimentary. That is because even some of my favorites have blemishes that in no way diminish their stature. The mere fact that they are included indicates that I think they have considerable merit and are enjoyable.

There are more past than contemporary films. Since my list starts from the early twentieth century that is numerically inevitable. Also, in recent years the perfection of photographic techniques and special effects has created a trend that I feel is detrimental to filmmaking. Technical panegyrics for their own sake often upstage or replace the story and acting. For the most part I share the view of the director and film historian Peter Bogdanovich who said in his film *Targets* that all the good movies have already been made. To paraphrase Shakespeare's "I want my books well bound and to speak of love," I want my films well made and to speak intelligently. It is regarded by some filmmakers as heresy to say that a good film must have good plot and dialogue. I am principally influenced by the script, the acting and the direction. Although the role of the cinematographer is crucial, good movies are made by good directors as a rule. That is why in my top films the names of the same directors appear again and again. I did not begin by seeking out their works but my favorite films just naturally come from outstanding directors.

There are two categories of films that I have chosen not to include in this book: made-for-television movies and documentaries. They are by no means of lesser value. It was more a question of time and space. How can one dismiss such great documentaries as *Night Mail* (1936), written and directed by Basil Wright from a poem by W. H. Auden with music by Benjamin Britten, about the London to Glasgow mail train; or *The River* (1937), written and directed by Pare Lorentz, a poetic hymn to the Mississippi; *Olympia* (1936) directed by Leni Riefenstahl, a record of the 1936 Berlin Olympics marred by propaganda lauding the Nazi regime. *The Sorrow and the Pity / Le Chagrin et la Pitie* (1970), directed by Marcel Ophuls, an examination of the behavior of the French people under German occupation; *Point of Order* (1963), directed by Emile de Antonio, the editing of TV footage of the 1954 U.S. Senate Army/McCarthy hearings; *Hotel Terminus: The Life and Times of Klaus Barbie* (1987), directed by Marcel Ophuls, about Barbie's arrest in Bolivia and his being sent to France to face a war crimes tribunal; *Roger and Me* (1989), directed by Michael Moore, about the closing of the General Motors truck plant in Flint, Michigan, putting 40,000 employees out of work, among many others. Or such television films as John Le Carré's *Tinker, Tailor, Soldier, Spy* and *Smiley's People*.

Very few films are free of flaws, but in my opinion those in this book are all superior. Of course, tastes differ. I sincerely hope my selection will match the readers' for the most part and that I will be forgiven if some of their favorites are not included.

ACKNOWLEDGMENTS

I wish to acknowledge and thank those who have helped in the creation of this book. First and foremost is my wife, Caroline, supporter, editor and girl Friday who in many ways should be considered a co-author of this book. Bahram Chubin, an established novelist, gave of his valuable time to comment on parts of my first drafts and offer valuable and insightful professional advice. My profound thanks to Kate O'Neill who typed and retyped the manuscripts written in my barely legible hand and all the various subsequent drafts. I am grateful to the British artist Frank Martin for his kind permission to use some lithographs of his work from my collection to adorn the cover and inside the book. I also thank my patient publisher and friend Mohammad Batmanglij for all his personal attention. Many thanks also to Hugh MacDonald who so ably assisted him, and to the staff of Mage Publishers.

GUIDE & GLOSSARY

The organization of this book falls into three categories:

100 of my very favorites, which I consider to be the greatest films
200 other favorites, which I consider to be great films
363 more favorites, which I consider to be near-great films
Throughout the reviews I have also made various references to more than 100 other films not reviewed.

In instances where the foreign film is better known in English, it is listed under that title followed by the foreign title in italics in the description and credit paragraph that follows the title. When films in English are known by more than one title, the alternate title follows, designated a.k.a., "also known as."

The description and credits that follow the titles are listed in the following order and employ the following abbreviations:

Title
(a.k.a. alternate title) *translation*.
Year of release.
Running time.
Color or b.w. (black & white)
Country of origin.
Prod.—producer;
Dir.—director;
Scr.—screen writer;
Cin.—cinematographer;
Ed.—editor;

Prod. D.—production director;
Art D.—art director;
Mus.—music;
Cast:

Some further explanations are called for. Running times often vary from one source to another. They should be taken as being close approximations. Dates of release also vary. Some sources use the date when released in the country of origin, others when released in the U.S. Cast lists are limited to those important to the plot but not in strict order of importance. Awards are not always mentioned. These explanations hopefully will help the reader through this book.

THE GREATEST

The African Queen

1951. 105 min. color. U.S. **Prod.** Sam Spiegel; **Dir.** John Huston; **Scr.** James Agee, John Huston (based on the novel by C. S. Forester); **Cin.** Jack Cardif; **Ed.** Ralph Kemplen; **Mus.** Allan Gray; **Cast:** Katharine Hepburn, Humphrey Bogart, Robert Morley, Peter Bull, Theodore Bikel.

It is late 1914 in an unnamed East African territory. World War I had begun in August. Both Germany and Britain have colonial possessions in East Africa and a conflict is inevitable. Charley Allnut (Humphrey Bogart), a Canadian blacksmith, had come to East Africa some time ago to work on a British railroad project as a mechanic of sorts. He had stayed after completion of the project and with his wages had bought a dilapidated steamer that he named *African Queen*. He has begun trading with the villages on the banks of a river. At one of his regular stops he warns Reverend Samuel Sayer (Robert Morley), a British Methodist minister, and his spinster sister Rose Sayer (Katharine Hepburn) that they should leave as German soldiers may soon occupy all the villages along the river. The reverend and his sister have come to Africa to make Christians of the natives and they are determined to stay put. A good shepherd does not abandon his flock. On his next trip Allnut finds that German soldiers have already raided the village and burnt all the native huts, forcing the villagers to leave. Reverend Sayer has died of an injury from a blow by a rifle butt and sunstroke. Allnut buries the reverend and pleads with his shocked sister to come somewhere safe as the Germans may be back. Rose gathers her meager belongings and the boat heads down the river, which empties into a large lake. The pair must pass a German fort and then navigate deadly rapids. The lake itself is controlled by a large German steamship, The Louisa, which prevents Britain from sending troops to any of the outlying villages.

The film, which up to now appeared to be merely an adventure story, takes on other dimensions. Allnut and Rose begin to change each other. Rose throws away Allnut's gin bottles and convinces him that it is their duty as subjects of the British Empire to do their share for the war. They could, if Allnut put his mind to it, fashion a torpedo from the oxygen tanks and explosives on the boat. Allnut thinks she is out of her mind. Soon, however, they begin to fall in love. They become "Charley" and "Rose." He becomes a Christian soldier and she becomes aware of the beauty of nature. They gain a new purpose and commitment. They devise a crude torpedo, but a fierce storm throws them overboard and they are picked up by *The Louisa*. They are judged to be spies and the captain orders them to be hanged. However, the captain grants their last wish and marries them. Just before they are to be hanged there is a massive explosion and *The Louisa* is sunk in the most unexpected way. Charley and Rose swim to safety.

The African Queen is a well-directed and well-photographed film, and the acting is superb. If the film had been made in the eighties or nineties the emphasis would have been on the storm, the rapids and the explosion. Huston made it a story of Charley and Rose. Just the two people in the boat bring a vibrant energy to the film. Bogart won his first and only Academy Award for best actor.

All About Eve

1950. 138 min. b.w. U.S. **Prod.** Darryl F. Zanuck; **Dir.** Joseph L. Mankiewicz; **Scr.** Joseph L. Mankiewicz (based on the story The Wisdom of Eve by Mary Orr); **Cin.** Milton Krasner; **Ed.** Barbara McLean; **Art. D.** Lyle Wheeler, George W. Davis; **Mus.** Alfred Newman; **Cast:** Bette Davis, Anne Baxter, George Sanders, Celeste Holm, Gary Merrill, Thelma Ritter, Marilyn Monroe, Hugh Marlowe, Gregory Ratoff.

Margo Channing (Bette Davis) is appearing on Broadway in *Aged in Wood*, written by Lloyd Richards (Hugh Marlowe) and directed by Bill Simpson (Gary Merrill), all well established in the theater. Simpson is romantically involved with Margo. One night, Karen Richards (Celeste Holm), the wife of the playwright, brings Eve Harrington (Anne Baxter) to Margo's dressing room. Karen has seen Eve night after night near the stage door. Eve has seen every one of Margo's performances for the past six months and considers Margo the greatest actress in the world. Eve talks of her difficult childhood, her struggle to make a living and losing her husband in the war. Nearly everyone in the room is reduced to tears. Birdie Coonan (Thelma Ritter), Margo's devoted personal maid and dresser, however, feels the story is too pat. Eve's tale, she says, "had everything but bloodhounds snapping at her rear end." Margo reprimands her for her insensitivity and takes Eve in as her companion. Soon she becomes Margo's efficient secretary.

Margo is vain and obsessed about growing old. She has just turned forty and is insecure, especially about her relationship with Simpson, a younger man. Birdie warns Margo that the young Eve appears to be studying her every gesture and mannerism, apparently in an attempt to model herself on Margo. To be rid of Eve, Margo convinces the producer, Max Fabian (Gregory Ratoff), to give Eve a job in his office. In no time at all Eve manages to become Margo's understudy. Karen, annoyed at Margo's treatment of the apparently simple, hard-working Eve, wants to teach Margo, her best friend, a lesson in humility. Karen arranges for Margo to miss a performance and Eve substitutes for her. Eve, knowing that she will go on stage that day, invites Addison De Witt (George Sanders), the most influential critic in New York, to view the show. Addison gives her performance a glowing review that suggests the time has come for younger actresses to play roles written for younger women. Eve's career in the theater is launched and Margo contentedly decides to retire and marry Bill Simpson. After having made no romantic headway with Bill, Eve goes after Lloyd Richards, who is in a position to write plays for her. Meanwhile, Addison checks into Eve's background and discovers that she is a calculating liar who has fabricated everything about her past. With one of the best pieces of dialogue in the film Addison makes his move, telling Eve: "You're an improbable person Eve, and so am I. We have that in common. Also, an inability to love or be loved…. We deserve each other." The scene is cathartic. It allows the viewer to vent all the hostility built up towards the scheming, unprincipled Eve. Her flight of fantasy has come to an end. From here on she belongs to Addison. The final scene in which an admiring young stage-struck girl will surely become Eve's companion hints far too obviously that history is about to repeat itself.

The film belongs to George Sanders. He walks away with every scene he is in and he has the best lines with which to work. At a party at Margo's apartment, he brings an aspiring actress (Marilyn Monroe) and introduces her as "a graduate of the Copa Cabana school of acting." It is also Bette Davis' best role. As a rule, Davis was too mannered an actress. In broadly playing a Broadway star, though, she fits perfectly. Thelma Ritter, Celeste Holm and Gregory Ratoff are well cast, but the other performances are uneven. Anne Baxter, an overrated actress, is only passable. *All About Eve* is one of the more literate films to come out of Hollywood. It debunks the myth that Broadway is gentler than Hollywood and that talent is more readily recognized with no need for hype or manipulation. Joseph Mankiewicz has been underrated, especially by critics in Europe, because he made literate films with no unusual camera angles or cinematic storytelling. He was always a competent director and made some fine films: *A Letter to Three Wives* (1948), which he also scripted, and *Julius Caesar* (1953). There are well-photographed scenes in *All About Eve*, but the script transcends the visual artistry. It won six Academy Awards, including best picture, director, screenplay and supporting actor (George Sanders).

All Quiet on the Western Front

1930. 105 min. b.w. U.S. **Prod.** Carl Laemmle, Jr.; **Dir.** Lewis Milestone; **Scr.** George Abbott, Maxwell Anderson, Dell Andrews (based on the novel by Erich Maria Remarque); **Cin.** Karl Freund, Arthur Edeson; **Ed.** Edgar Adams, Milton Carruth; **Art D.** Charles D. Hall, William R. Schmidt; **Mus.** David Broekman; **Cast:** Lew Ayres, Louis Wolheim, John Wray, Slim Sommerville, Ben Alexander, Beryl Mercer, Arnold Lucy.

The film recounts the story of one German soldier, Paul Baumer (Lew Ayres), who together with fellow students in a gymnasium (secondary school) are goaded into enlisting by the exhortations of a war-mongering teacher who advocates military glory for the "fatherland." We follow their training by a seasoned veteran, Corporal Katczinsky (Louis Wolheim), who becomes a father figure to the boys. Barely ready, they are thrust onto the front lines in 1916 and their platoon is slowly decimated. This gradual but relentless disintegration is symbolized by a pair of soft leather boots that passes from one soldier to the next as they are killed.

There are a number of memorable scenes. One is the encounter of Paul with a young French soldier whom he bayonets in a foxhole. As the Frenchman lies dying, Paul begs his forgiveness. Another is Paul carrying the wounded Katczinsky on his back, talking nonstop about the future when the war ends, not knowing that Katczinsky is already dead, killed by a shell fragment. The most moving is the closing scene. Paul is in a trench and suddenly sees a butterfly. He extends his hand and slightly raises his head to catch it. There is the sound of one shot and we see his hand go limp. The image of the butterfly amidst the carnage and slaughter is profoundly moving.

One of the greatest and most vivid antiwar films, the battle scenes have a documentary-like realism that is emotionally draining. Made during the early advent of sound in 1930, *All Quiet on the Western Front* broke ground in other respects as well. War films of the silent era, with the possible exception of *The Big Parade* (1925), depicted war as a great and noble adventure that featured bravery, manliness and camaraderie. This film delineates the horrors of war. We see the scale of suffering of the ordinary soldier and the ultimate futility of his sacrifices. The film is a faithful version of Erich Maria Remarque's novel, albeit in a more concise form. It was a daring enterprise at the time, especially given the fact that it sympathetically depicts the ordeal of a German soldier barely ten years after the end of a war in which the United States fought against Germany. The force of the novel and the excellent innovative direction of Milestone make us feel the same sorrow for the German as we do for the French soldier, both of whom are nothing more than pawns in a senseless war, a catastrophe the world allowed itself to stumble into in 1914. The film was banned in Germany, France and Poland, and was also badly received in certain quarters in the U.S. for its pacifist content. Acting honors go to Louis Wolheim who creates a memorable character with a minimum of dialogue. The rest of the cast, including the novice Lew Ayres, competently handle their roles. The film received Academy Awards for best picture and best director, and nominations for its screenplay and cinematography.

All the King's Men

1949. 109 min. b.w. U.S. **Prod.** Robert Rossen; **Dir.** Robert Rossen; **Scr.** Robert Rossen (based on the novel by Robert Penn Warren); **Cin.** Burnett Guffey; **Ed.** Al Clark; **Mus.** Louis Gruenberg; **Cast:** Broderick Crawford, Joanne Dru, John Ireland, Mercedes McCambridge, John Derek, Shepperd Strudwick, Anne Seymour, Raymond Greenleaf, Will Wright, Ralph Dumke.

The story recounts the rise and fall of a ruthless politician, Willie Stark (Broderick Crawford), who is modelled on Huey Long, the King Fish, who served as governor of Louisiana from 1928 to 1931 and senator from 1932 to 1935. Having built one of the most dominant political machines in the nation's history, Long continued to run the state, even while serving in Washington. He was assassinated in 1935 by a 29-year-old physician whose sister may have been raped by Long. (Long was killed when he was a senator but the film's main character is assassinated while governor). The political dynasty Long established dominated Louisiana for over three decades after his death, into the early seventies. His son, Russell, served several terms in the U.S. senate and his brother, Earl, was governor. Huey Long ran a populist campaign of "share the wealth" that gained a national following. Had he lived, he may well have formed a third party to challenge Roosevelt for the presidency in 1936.

The film is set in a southern state and is told through the eyes of Jack Burden (John Ireland), an aimless former journalist who starts off as Stark's press agent and ends as his chief hatchet man. We first see Stark as a poor but honest country boy who has become a lawyer by attending night school. After the collapse of a school building with many casualties he begins a campaign against the crooked politicians who had been bribed by unscrupulous building contractors. His success and popularity bring him to the attention of state politicians who put him up as a candidate for governor in a three-man race. Their hidden agenda is to have Stark split the vote with the reformist candidate, enabling their crooked candidate to be elected. By the time Stark realizes he is being used, it is too late. Four years later, however, he runs again for governor, this time on his own. He is elected by the votes of the poor and downtrodden. As governor he starts massive public projects; roads, bridges, schools, hospitals and irrigation schemes. The result is an accumulation of such power that soon he is in a position to control the press and radio, and to silence all who oppose him. These changes spill over into his private life. He ignores his wife and uses his son. Sadie Burke (Mercedes McCambridge), a campaign manager, becomes his first mistress. She is soon discarded and he takes up with Anne Stanton (Joanne Dru), Jack Burden's fiancée. When threatened with impeachment for crooked dealing, Stark blackmails Anne's father, a distinguished and influential judge, to use his influence on Stark's behalf, driving the judge to suicide. He soon has national ambitions that are brought to an abrupt end when he is assassinated by Anne's brother, Adam (Shepperd Strudwick). Stark's last words are "God, don't let me die. I have so much to do."

All the King's Men is based on the 1946 Pulitzer Prize-winning novel by one of America's important literary figures—the poet, novelist and literary critic Robert Penn Warren. Warren learned the intricacies of Louisiana politics as a professor of English literature at Louisiana State University (LSU) during the height of Long's power. LSU was backed financially by Long against the more prominent Tulane University. The novel has biblical allusions to original sin. Rossen's film is less concerned with theology than the corrupting influence of power; not just those who possess it, but those on its periphery as well. Stark is a brutal political animal who creates a semi-fascist state. There are no sympathetic characters either in the novel or the film. The novel is as much about Jack Burden, the man who loses his idealism, as it is about Willie Stark, but the film blurs Burden's fall. Everyone soon compromises and sells out; Jack Burden, Anne and Adam Stanton and Sadie

Burke. Rossen also depicts the instability and volatility of the elec-
torate and how the voter can be swayed and deceived.

The acting is superb. Broderick Crawford, a "B movie" actor,
got the role of a lifetime in this film and gives one of the great
performances of American movies—a performance he never
equaled. Mercedes McCambridge in her film debut is very good.
John Ireland and Raymond Greenleaf, as Judge Stanton, are more
than competent. Will Wright and Ralph Dumke are perfect as
rural political bosses. The film was shot in Stockton, in northern
California, and Rossen used hundreds of townspeople as extras
and bit players. This, coupled with the excellent cinematography
of Burnett Guffey, gave the film realism. Rossen never matched
his work on this film. He had difficulties with the House Un-
American Activities Committee throughout the fifties, and only
much later, in 1961, did he make a superior film: *The Hustler. All
the King's Men* won Academy Awards for best picture, best actor
(Crawford) and best supporting actress (McCambridge).

Amarcord

1974. 127 min. color. Italian. **Prod.** Franco Cristaldi; **Dir.** Federico Fellini; **Scr.** Federico Fellini, Tonino Guerra; **Cin.** Giuseppe Rotunno; **Ed.** Ruggero Mastroianni; **Art D.** Danilo Donati; **Mus.** Nino Rota; **Cast:** Magali Noel, Bruno Zanin, Pupella Maggio, Armando Brancia.

Set in Romagna on the Adriatic Coast of Italy in the mid-thirties,
the film is a recollection some forty years later of a year in the life of
Titta (Bruno Zanin), a boy in his late teens. It is a plotless film comprised of dreamlike episodes that had made a deep impression on
the young boy. His father, Aurelio (Armando Brancia), is a construction foreman with a volatile temper. He is hard working and
supports some six people. He is a staunch socialist opposed to the
fascist regime of Mussolini. Titta's mother, Miranda (Pupella Maggio), is a cheerless and melancholic woman who is always quarreling
with her husband. She has two brothers: one is in an insane asylum,
the other lives off Aurelio. Titta's grandfather is a jolly old man who

still enjoys pinching and chasing women. Titta also has a younger, undisciplined brother. Titta's father is disappointed in him because he has yet to find a job. The focus of Titta's life is sex, whether vicarious or self-gratified. He is taken by his mother to confession. The priest asks him if he masturbates and Titta begins to drift off, visualizing all the desirable women in town. The most attractive is Gradisca (Magali Noel), the hairdresser. In the early evenings she and two friends walk along the main street, provocatively swinging their hips. Gradisca is madly in love with Gary Cooper and sees all his films. We get glimpses of other women in the town, typical Fellini circus-like characters: the tobacco shop owner who weighs close to 250 pounds, and the mad Volpina who gives herself freely to any man. We see scenes of Titta's school where, again, the object of his daydreams is a buxom teacher.

We also witness a year in the life of the town. The film begins with the end of winter and celebration of the coming spring with a huge bonfire in the main piazza. The summer is marked by the sailing of a transatlantic ocean liner, Rex, off the coast of Romagna. Autumn brings the death of Titta's mother, which devastates his father. It also includes the marriage of Gradisca, not to Gary Cooper but to a local policeman. We witness suffocating political conformity and the mass hysteria of fascist rallies. There are few voices of dissent, but Titta's father insists on wearing his socialist tie. He is taken to the Fascist headquarters where he is forced to drink a bottle of castor oil.

Fellini was born in Rimini, a seaside town much like the one in the film, and left in 1938 at the age of eighteen. *Amarcord*, which means "I remember" in the Romagna dialect, is partly autobiographical. Most of Fellini's films, beginning with *I Vitelloni* (1954), have a confessional element. In *La Dolce Vita* (1962) the main character is modeled on himself and *8 1/2* (1963) is unmistakably autobiographical. All these confessional and autobiographical films deal with elements of personal guilt. There are many glorious scenes in this film. The radiantly lit ocean liner becomes real through the beautiful photography of Giuseppe Rotunno and the art direction of Danilo Donati. There is also a haunting musical score by Nino Rota.

The Asphalt Jungle

1950. 112 min. b.w. U.S. **Prod.** Arthur Hornblow; **Dir.** John Huston; **Scr.** Ben Maddow, John Huston (based on the novel by W. R. Burnett); **Cin.** Harold Rosson; **Ed.** George Boemler; **Art D.** Cedric Gibbons, Randall Duell; **Mus.** Miklos Rozsa.; **Cast:** Sterling Hayden, Louis Calhern, Jean Hagen, James Whitmore, Sam Jaffe, John McIntire, Marc Lawrence, Marilyn Monroe, Barry Kelly, Anthony Caruso, Brad Dexter.

Aging master criminal Irwin "Doc" Riedenschneider (Sam Jaffe), just released from prison, has one last job in mind—the robbery of an upscale jewelry company in a midwestern city. His first contact is Cobby (Marc Lawrence), a bookie who introduces him to Alonzo Emerich (Louis Calhern), a prominent but shady lawyer who agrees to bankroll the job and fence the jewels, giving Doc and his gang one million dollars in cash. Unknown to the others, Emerich is broke and plans to steal the jewels after the robbery. He convinces the unsuspecting Cobby to finance the job. Doc assembles his assistants methodically: Louis Ciavelli (Anthony Caruso), a professional safecracker, for $25,000; Gus Ninissi (James Whitmore), who operates a small diner, as the getaway car driver for $10,000; and Dix Handley (Sterling Hayden), an aimless petty hoodlum who dreams of buying back his father's Kentucky horse farm, for $15,000. Doc has planned the robbery meticulously and his assistants know precisely what they have to do. His plan works perfectly until Ciavelli is shot in a freak accident and later dies. Still later, Emerich's bodyguard (Brad Dexter) is killed and Doc's perfect plan begins to unravel.

Huston, working with a first-rate script prepared by Ben Maddow and himself, develops some ten characters incisively in a 112 minute film without affecting the pace. There are numerous examples. In a thirty-second scene at the very beginning of the film we see Doc carefully examining a girlie calendar at Cobby's betting shop, preparing us for his arrest in the last scene as a result of his voyeurism. At one point early in their meeting, Emerich asks Doc, "What is it like for a man with your tastes behind bars for seven years?" Doc answers, "It is a matter of temperament."

Emerich says, "I couldn't take it." The scene prepares us for his
suicide at the end of the film. Cobby is shown to be weak, and
later when arrested, he predictably breaks down and names the
participants in the robbery. Gus, on the other hand, has been loyal
to his friends throughout, and doesn't break when arrested. Dix
owes some gambling debts to Cobby. Though given an extension,
he feels humiliated. He borrows the money from his friend Gus
and repays Cobby in full. Dix also shows his sense of honor in the
way he treats Doll (Jean Hagen), a chorus girl out of a job with
no place to stay. The thieves are better people than Emerich, who
neglects his invalid wife, keeps a mistress (Marilyn Monroe), and
intends to double-cross the people who trust him. Huston's sympathies are clearly with the thieves. At one point, Emerich
explains to his unsuspecting wife that he occasionally has to represent criminals, adding, "Crime is only a left-handed form of
human endeavor." Huston attempts to tell us that there is only a
fine line separating a big-time lawyer and a big-time criminal,
and that the personal ethics of the latter may be preferable.

Acting honors go to the entire cast. Hayden, Calhern, Jaffe and
Whitmore are excellent. Jean Hagan, who was wasted at MGM
(she was given only one decent role in her career, the 1952 *Singin' in the Rain*), gives a very good performance. Even Marilyn
Monroe handles her brief role well. The cinematography is excellent. Most of the film takes place in a dirty, overcast city. Only in
the very last scenes when the mortally wounded Handley and
Doll have left the asphalt behind and are driving in the Kentucky
countryside does the sun come blazing through. The score by
Rozsa is excellent. Although a much copied film, none come
anywhere near this almost perfect film noir.

Bad Day at Black Rock

1955. 81 min. color. U.S. **Prod.** Dore Schary; **Dir.** John Sturges; **Scr.** Don McGuire, Millard Kaufman (based on a story by Howard Breslin); **Cin.** William Mellor; **Ed.** Newell P. Kimli; **Art D.** Cedric Gibbons; **Mus.** Andre Previn; **Cast:** Spencer Tracy, Robert Ryan, Anne Francis, Dean Jagger, Walter Brennan, John Ericson, Ernest Borgnine, Lee Marvin, Walter Sande, Russell Collins.

Late in 1945, with the war over in Europe and the Pacific, a one-armed stranger gets off the train at Black Rock. No train has stopped at this isolated small desert town for several years, and everyone from Mr. Hastings (Russel Collins), the telegraph clerk at the railroad station, to Pete Wirth (John Ericson), the hotel clerk, becomes nervous and cannot figure out why a stranger has gotten off the train. Hector David (Lee Marvin), a local tough guy, is the first person to talk to him, saying "You look like you need a hand." The pervading hostility even extends to the town's drunken sheriff, Tim Horn (Dean Jagger).

John J. MacReedy (Spencer Tracy) has come to Black Rock to see Komoko, a Japanese farmer who lives in Dobe Flat, some ten miles from the town. No one is willing to give him directions or offer any help, except Doc Velie (Walter Brennan), the mortician, who at least has a civil conversation with him. MacReedy finally gets to Dobe Flat in a rented jeep and sees a partially burnt place, a water well and evidence of an unmarked grave. Black Rock is dominated by a rancher, Reno Smith (Robert Ryan), who tells MacReedy that Komoko was relocated after Pearl Harbor to some alien detention camp and no one has heard from him since. MacReedy soon learns that Reno Smith had sold the worthless, arid land to Komoko but became insanely angry when Komoko discovered water on it. One night after Pearl Harbor, Smith and his henchmen became "patriotically" drunk and, together with Hastings, Pete, Hector, Coley (Ernst Borgnine) and Sam (Walter Sande), who runs the local diner, drove to Komoko's farm, burnt the place, and murdered Komoko. MacReedy had come to Black Rock to present Komoko with a medal posthumously awarded to his son by the U.S. Army. He had been killed in the Italian campaign while saving MacReedy's life.

The film is exceptionally well directed by John Sturges. There is sustained suspense. Who is MacReedy? Why has he come to Black Rock? Why is the town so hostile towards him? What has happened to Komoko? The entire story takes place in a brief twenty-four hours. It is a lean film that runs eighty-one minutes and in that short time about seven characters are developed enough for us to know what motivates them. There is not one wasted frame. Two superb scenes are the fight between MacReedy and Coley at the diner, and the climactic scene when MacReedy improvises a Molotov cocktail. The camera work of William Mellor is excellent. There are several stunning shots, most notably one of four men, Reno Smith and three of his henchmen, standing on the railroad tracks discussing what to do about MacReedy. This was the first film to deal with the treatment of Americans of Japanese descent after Pearl Harbor. Tens of thousands were "relocated" in hastily built detention camps in the deserts of southeastern California and Nevada. The movie is not just about prejudice and bigotry but also about mob mentality and greed. Tracy, one of the great screen actors, gives his role the subdued self-assurance the character requires. Robert Ryan is well cast as the dominating overlord of the town. The tension always present in his voice serves him well. The overall acting is more than competent. The only weakness is the pretentiousness of some of the lines spoken by Dean Jagger as the sheriff of Black Rock and more especially Walter Brennan as its mortician.

The Best Years of Our Lives

1946. 172 min. b.w. U.S. **Prod.** Samuel Goldwyn; **Dir.** William Wyler; **Scr.** Robert E. Sherwood (based on the blank verse novella *Glory for Me* by MacKinlay Kantor); **Cin.** Greg Toland; **Ed.** Daniel Mandell; **Art D.** George Jenkins, Perry Ferguson; **Mus.** Hugo Friedhofer; **Cast:** Fredric March, Myrna Loy, Teresa Wright, Dana Andrews, Virginia Mayo, Harold Russell, Hoagy Carmichael, Gladys George, Roman Bohnan, Steve Cochran, Ray Teal, Cathy O'Donnell.

World War II is over and three servicemen, Al Stephenson (Fredric March), Fred Derry (Dana Andrews) and Homer Parrish (Harold Russell) are at an air force base together with hundreds of other returning GIs waiting to catch a plane back to their hometowns. Al, the elder of the three, had been a minor officer in a small bank and as an army sergeant had seen action in the Pacific. Fred who came from a poor family, had worked as a drug store soda jerk before enlisting in the air force and had been promoted to captain. Just before being shipped overseas he had married a girl he barely knew (Virginia Mayo). He still has nightmares about his bombing missions over Germany. The third, Homer, had been in the navy and lost both arms from the elbows down in a training accident. He had been a superb athlete in high school and was engaged to his childhood sweetheart (Cathy O'Donnell). He, even more than the other two, is facing an uncertain future. These three are from the same town and share space on a bomber. The film is about how they try to adjust to civilian life. Each has been changed by his wartime experience. The services had given them security and a feeling of belonging. Now, coming back, there is a sense of alienation.

Samuel Goldwyn got the idea for the film from a *Life* magazine article about returning veterans. Robert E. Sherwood wrote an excellent script based on a lengthy poem by MacKinlay Kantor. The film is neither maudlin nor sentimental. What distinguishes it is the very high standard of acting, the magnificent cinematography of Greg Toland and the steady directorial hand of William Wyler. This collaboration produced several scenes that rank among the best ever on film. There is a scene at a bar and grill owned by Butch (Hoagy Carmichael). Fred has been told by Al to stop seeing his daughter, Peggy (Teresa Wright). He doesn't want his daughter courted by a married man. We see Fred in a telephone booth near the entrance to Butch's bar calling Peggy to tell her he would not see her again. Al is standing in the foreground, one eye on Homer and his uncle Butch playing chopsticks on the piano, and the other transfixed on the phone booth, which is in deep focus. Another scene is when Fred has given up hope and is on the verge of leaving town. He passes by an airplane graveyard with row upon row of air force bombers stripped bare, waiting to be sold as scrap metal. He climbs into the nose of a B-17 and painful memories come back. The last scene at Homer's wedding at which Fred is the best man is also outstanding. He is at the near end of the room. Peggy, whom he has not seen since the fateful telephone call, is at the other end. The camera scans the gathering and probes every corner of the room, while its main focus is on Fred and Peggy, whose eyes meet from a distance. There are many other memorable scenes: Al unexpectedly returning home after four years; Homer's mother at the first sight of her son's hooks where his hands had once been; Fred's father (Roman Bohnan) proudly and tearfully reading to his wife (Gladys George) the citation his son has received from the air force. The film won numerous Academy Awards, including best picture, actor (March), director, screenplay and editing. Fredric March is excellent, but Dana Andrews had the more difficult role and merited a prize. Andrews, an underrated actor, never received the recognition he deserved. The nonprofessional Harold Russell, who was actually a veteran who had lost his hands, won the best supporting actor award. Myrna Loy as Al's wife, Virginia Mayo as Fred's unfaithful wife, Roman Bohnan and Gladys George are all very good, but Teresa Wright stands out among them.

The Bicycle Thief

Ladri di Biciclette. 1948. 90 min. b.w. Italian. **Prod.** Umberto Scarparelli; **Dir.** Vittorio De Sica; **Scr.** Cesare Zavattini (based on a novel by Luigi Bartolini); **Cin.** Carlo Montuori; **Ed.** Eraldo da Roma; **Art D.** Antonio Traverso; **Mus.** Alesandro Cicognini; **Cast:** Lamberto Maggiorani, Lianella Carell, Enzo Staiola.

A deceptively simple film, *The Bicycle Thief* tells the story of Antonio (Lamberto Maggiorani), a poverty-stricken man in Rome shortly after the end of WWII unable to find employment. He finally runs across an opening for a job as a billboard poster hanger, but the prerequisite for the job is a bicycle. Having pawned his bicycle some time ago, he now needs money to retrieve it. His wife pawns the family bed sheets, the last of her dowry, to raise the money. On the very first day his bicycle is stolen while he is hanging a poster. He gives chase, but the thief disappears among the street crowds. The poor workman goes to the police who explain to him it would be next to impossible to find his bicycle. With his young son Bruno in tow, he begins an odyssey along the streets and back alleys of Rome. The search gets nowhere. After an argument with Bruno, they are briefly separated and the man is beside himself. But soon he sees his son safely standing on the top of some steps. To make up, he takes Bruno to a restaurant and orders him a dish, although he can barely afford to pay for it. The search for the bicycle continues and Antonio spots the thief. He chases him to a bordello, but he can do nothing. The thief turns out to be a poor epileptic, and in any case Antonio cannot prove the theft. The girls at the bordello protect the epileptic. Soon the neighbors also take the thief's side, and threaten Antonio. The last episode is Antonio's desperate attempt to steal a bicycle outside a sport stadium. As he tries to ride off, he is knocked down and caught. His son wordlessly pleads with the owner, who decides not to press charges. The father is humiliated, and at that moment Bruno takes his father's hand in a gesture of solidarity and the two walk away.

Filmed in black and white, *The Bicycle Thief* has the look of a documentary. All the actors are nonprofessionals and the screenplay by Zavattini has a minimum of dialogue. Nevertheless, the film is rich in its vivid depiction of the lives of ordinary Italian people, with the story of the bicycle being a commentary on their condition, their suffering at the end of the war, and how economic circumstances turn a victim into a thief. It is one of the finest achievements of the Italian neorealist cinema. De Sica left a lasting imprint on the history of cinema with this, his best film.

The Bridge on the River Kwai

1957. 161 min. color. British. **Prod.** Sam Spiegel; **Dir.** David Lean; **Scr.** Carl Foreman and Michael Wilson (both uncredited), and Pierre Boulle (based on his novel); **Cin.** Jack Hildyard; **Ed.** Peter Taylor; **Mus.** Malcolm Arnold; **Cast:** William Holden, Alec Guinness, Jack Hawkins, Sessue Hayakawa, Geoffrey Horne, James Donald, Andre Morell, Ann Sears.

The film is set in Siam (Thailand) and Burma (Myanmar) in late 1942 when Japan dominated the region. By the time of the fall of Singapore and the Malaysian peninsula, Japan had some 130,000 British war prisoners with which to contend. A battalion of these prisoners under the command of Colonel Nicholson (Alec Guinness) is being relocated to a large camp where the Japanese army is in the process of building a Bangkok to Rangoon railroad line. The 250-mile route traverses the river Kwai and a bridge has to be built. When the officers of the British battalion are ordered to work alongside the men, Colonel Nicholson, citing the Geneva Convention, refuses to allow his officers to do manual labor. The camp commander, Colonel Saito (Sessue Hayakawa), has Nicholson imprisoned in the infamous "punishment hut." The Japanese army falls far behind schedule and the skill of the British army, which had built numerous bridges in India and Southeast Asia, is now needed even more. Nicholson is released, having won a moral victory. In order to restore the men's morale, however, he orders both men and officers to faithfully cooperate in building a durable bridge. To show the indomitable British spirit he drives his men ruthlessly, oblivious to the fact that he is aiding the enemy. As the bridge nears completion, British high command becomes alerted and plans to dispatch a commando unit led by Major Warden (Jack Hawkins) to destroy the bridge. Shears (William Holden), an American sailor who had made a miraculous escape from Saito's camp a few months earlier, is to be part of the unit. He had been rescued by British forces and, in order to enjoy officers' amenities, had passed himself off as a navy lieutenant. The British had checked his record and, under threat of court-martial by the U.S. navy, blackmailed him into guiding the commando unit through the jungle from which he had escaped. The unit reaches the camp just as the bridge is completed and Colonel Nicholson has nailed up a plaque commemorating the British army's role in building the bridge. In a convoluted ending, the bridge is blown up as the first trainload of Japanese soldiers are crossing it.

The Bridge on the River Kwai is an extremely well-made film with fine cinematography, editing, acting and a rousing score, principally "Colonel Bogey's March." It is Lean's first film in color. The opening shot of a hawk freely soaring above the jungle and an immediate cut to the brutal prisoner of war camp where Shears is the head gravedigger of perished prisoners is magnificently photographed. Equally well done are the scenes of the jungle, mountains and rivers that the commandos must cross to get to the camp. Most of the major characters are developed well. Alec Guinness has one of his best roles as the class-conscious and arrogant colonial officer enamored of India. His standing up to Saito, besides demonstrating his courage, highlights his sense of superiority. He has to educate the primitive oriental about the Geneva Convention. Tragically, once he wins his point he forgets he is in effect giving aid to the enemy. Colonel Saito is also racist. He cannot comprehend Nicholson's stubborn courage, nor his subsequent collaboration. We get to know Major Warden, a Cambridge don who taught Eastern languages. He is not a military man, but he has a job to do. Hawkins handles this role well. The only character not developed sufficiently is Shears. He is too

smooth and witty for an ordinary sailor, and we never learn anything of his background.

What could have been one of the greatest antiwar films fails by
a deliberately contrived ending. The irony of Colonel Nicholson,
wounded, stumbling and accidentally falling on the plunger that
demolishes the bridge is both deceitful and spurious. The last
scene, which has the battalion doctor (James Donald) who has
witnessed the chaos shouting "madness, madness," is intended to
compensate for what Lean, a very skilled director, has failed to
portray clearly. In most of Lean's films the scripts are not on a par
with the direction and cinematography. *Kwai* won Academy
Awards for best picture, best actor (Alec Guinness), director,
adapted screenplay, cinematography, editing and musical score.
Sessue Hayakawa was nominated for best supporting actor. It
should be noted that no bridge was built on the Kwai River. The
bridge in question was farther north and was destroyed by U.S.
bombers in 1944.

Casablanca

1942. 102 min. b.w. U.S. **Prod.** Hal B. Wallis; **Dir.** Michael Curtiz; **Scr.** Julius J. Epstein,
Philip G. Epstein, Howard Koch (based on the play *Everybody Goes to Rick's* by Murray
Burnett and Joan Alison); **Cin.** Arthur Edeson; **Ed.** Owen Marks; **Art D.** Carl Jules Weyl;
Mus. Max Steiner; **Cast:** Humphrey Bogart, Ingrid Bergman, Paul Henreid, Claude Rains,
Conrad Veidt, Peter Lorre, Sydney Greenstreet, Dooley Wilson, Marcel Dalio, S. Z. Sakall,
Madeleine Le Beau, Curt Bois, Leonid Kinsky.

So much has been written about *Casablanca* that a recounting
of the plot serves little purpose. The story begins sometime in late
November or early December 1941, probably just before the
Japanese attack on Pearl Harbor on December 7, but definitely
before December 11 when Germany and Italy declared war on
the U.S. since Rick would have been interned as an enemy alien
any time after that. *Casablanca* is one of those very rare films in
which almost everything is just right. The very few lapses in the
plot narrative can be easily overlooked. The film was charmed

before work on it even began. The studio initially had wanted George Raft, Hedy Lamar and Herbert Marshall for the three leads, and Lena Horne for the Dooley Wilson part. Even Ronald Reagan's name had been mentioned as the lead. Fortunately they were either unavailable or declined. The film opened on Thanksgiving Day 1942, three weeks after U.S. forces landed in North Africa. Then in January 1943 Roosevelt and Churchill met in Casablanca, soon joined by Generals Charles de Gaulle and Henri Giraud, from which the film garnered name recognition and enormous publicity.

Not to detract from either the excellent leads and one of the best supporting casts with the most gifted group of character actors ever assembled (Claude Rains, Sydney Greenstreet, Peter Lorre, Marcel Dalio, S. Z. Sakall, Dooley Wilson, Madeleine Le Beau and Leonid Kinsky), it is above all Michael Curtiz who controls the film to perfection in close-ups in key scenes and the economical and smooth narrative flow. More than three-quarters of the film takes place on one set, Rick's café, with a few scenes in the marketplace, in Renault's office and on the airstrip. Yet the film is not stagy. *Casablanca* evokes the noblest dreams in us all. Few of us can hold back a tear or two when midway in the film the "Marseillaise" is played in the café after Rick gives a go ahead nod to the band leader: the close-ups of the singer forcefully strumming her guitar and belting out "marchon, marchon"; the French tart making amends for her liaisons with German officers by singing the anthem as loudly as she can with tears flowing down her cheeks; and the quick shot of Elsa showing her pride in her husband for having told the orchestra to play the French national anthem and exhorting the crowd to sing. Dooley Wilson's "As Time Goes By," now a classic, is so well interwoven into the story. The editing of the beautiful last scene at the airport, the close-ups of Bogart and Bergman, and Bogart and Claude Rains walking off into the fog are magic.

The film also has some of the sharpest and wittiest dialogue ever written. Koch injected the politics and the anti-Nazi bite, and the Epsteins brought the Broadway brand of humor. There are some oddities in the plot. At the very beginning of the film a British tourist and his wife are having a drink at an outdoor café when the man's wallet is stolen. What are British tourists doing in Casablanca in November and December 1941 when war is raging at home and in North Africa? Then there is the fog-bound airstrip in the middle of a desert. These do not intrude because of the fairytale quality of the film. *Casablanca* has not dated at all and remains spellbinding.

Chinatown

1974. 131 min. color. U.S. **Prod.** Robert Evans; **Dir.** Roman Polanski; **Scr.** Robert Towne; **Cin.** John A. Alonzo; **Ed.** Sam O'Steen; **Prod. D.** Richard Sylbert; **Mus.** Jerry Goldsmith; **Cast:** Jack Nicholson, Faye Dunaway, John Huston, Perry Lopez, John Hillerman, Darrell Zwerling, Roy Jenson, Roman Polanski.

The year is 1937 and the place is Los Angeles. Private eye J. J. Gittes (Jack Nicholson) is hired by Mrs. Mulwray to investigate her husband's affair with a young woman. Gittes has some photos taken and delivers them to his client. Somehow the photographs are published the next day in a tabloid. Later Mr. Mulwray's corpse is found in a water reservoir. Gittes learns that the woman who introduced herself as Mrs. Mulwray has been murdered too. The real Mrs. Evelyn Mulwray (Faye Dunaway) shows up, and Gittes is served with notice of an impending lawsuit by her. Later she drops the lawsuit, opting instead to hire Gittes to find out who murdered her husband. He discovers that Hollis Mulwray (Darrell Zwerling) and one Noah Cross (John Huston), now a powerful and wealthy man, had once been partners. They had owned the Los Angeles water supply, sold their rights to the city, and then parted. Mulwray had become the Water Commissioner of Los Angeles and Cross a wealthy land owner. Cross had lobbied for the building of a dam to bring more water to Los Angeles and the surrounding areas that he owned. Mulwray had opposed the dam project, believing there were other priorities for the water supply. Soon Gittes and Evelyn become lovers. One night he follows her and sees her going into a house and arguing with a young girl in her early teens who happens to be the girl in the photograph with Hollis Mulwray. Evelyn finally confesses to him that the girl is both her sister and her daughter as a result of rape by her father, Noah Cross. She is hiding the young girl because Noah claims her as his daughter. Further investigation by Gittes turns up conclusive evidence that Cross murdered Mulwray. At the end of the film, Evelyn resists Cross' attempt to take her daughter, wounding him with a gun. When she tries to drive away with the girl, the police, who are beholden to Cross, order her to stop. As she drives on, they open fire and kill her.

The acting by the entire cast is convincing; Huston gives a chilling performance as a ruthless, amoral land speculator who would stop at nothing. He represents the pioneers who built Los Angeles. But the film is made notable by the tight direction of Polanski in this, his best work; Robert Towne's intricate screenplay; and the photography of John A. Alonzo, who captures the color of the women's makeup and clothes of the era, plus his use of diffused indoor lighting to great effect. Probably more important is the superb production design by Richard Sylbert who chose evocative locales that gave the film authenticity. Los Angeles is displayed in all its bright sun, bright colors, and class privilege. There is also a beautiful jazz score by Jerry Goldsmith. The ending is all Polanski, who insisted that Evelyn Mulwray be killed by the police to emphasize the immense power of Noah Cross over the city of Los Angeles. The title *Chinatown* likely refers to the L.A. Police Department's cynical way of describing unsolved murders.

Citizen Kane

1941. 119 min. b.w. U.S. **Prod.** Orson Welles; **Dir.** Orson Welles; **Scr.** Herman J. Mankiewicz, Orson Welles; **Cin.** Greg Toland; **Ed.** Robert Wise, Mark Robson; **Art D.** Van Nest Polglase; **Mus.** Bernard Herrmann; **Cast:** Orson Welles, Joseph Cotton, Everett Sloane, Agnes Morehead, Dorothy Comingore, Ray Collins, George Coulouris, Ruth Warrick, William Alland, Paul Stewart, Erskine Sanford, Fortuna Bonanova, Philip van Zandt, Alan Ladd.

Welles adopted an ingenious approach in telling the story of *Citizen Kane*. John Foster Kane, a prominent man, dies. His last utterance is, "Rosebud." A newspaper editor sends his ace reporter to find out what Rosebud means. The reporter, Jerry Thompson (William Alland), then traces the story of Kane's life. It is told in flashbacks through the eyes of five people: Walter Parks Thatcher (George Coulouris), Kane's guardian and trustee; Bernstein (Everett Sloane), general manager of Kane's first newspaper, the *New York Enquirer;* Jedediah Leland (Joseph Cotton), Kane's closest friend since college; Susan Alexander (Dorothy Comingore), his second wife; and Raymond (Paul Stewart), Kane's butler at his estate, Xanadu. As a boy, Kane inherits sixty million dollars and acquires complete control at age twenty-five. He buys a newspaper that goads the U.S. administration into the Spanish–American War. In 1900 he marries Emily Norton (Ruth Warrick), the President's niece, and subsequently takes a mistress, Susan Alexander. He runs for governor, but a crooked political boss, J. W. Gettys (Ray Collins), exposes the love nest and Kane loses the election. Shortly thereafter his wife and son are killed in a car crash. He marries Susan, a mediocre singer, and builds an opera house for her in Chicago. She flops miserably, but Kane refuses to allow her to quit, and she attempts suicide. He gives in and agrees to her retirement. He builds a castle on a 49,000 acre estate in Florida that he calls Xanadu, with the biggest private zoo in the world and a sizable museum. Susan leaves him. He dies alone at age seventy-six whispering "Rosebud." which brings us back to the beginning of the film.

Twenty-five-year old Orson Welles, the boy wonder of Broadway and radio, was given a contract by RKO Studios to direct
three films with complete control. Welles had become a sensation
on Broadway with a black version of *Macbeth*, and an equally
impressive modern dress version of *Julius Caesar* in which the
Caesar crowd wore the Fascist black shirts and the conspirators,
the senators, wore white shirts. Then, in October 1938, he broadcast on radio an adaptation of H. G. Wells' "War of the Worlds" in
which Martians attack the earth. It was so credibly made that it
sent thousands of listeners fleeing from their homes. Welles came
to Hollywood in August 1939 with several projects in mind. No
actor except Erich von Stroheim had ever before directed a full-
length feature film. Welles decided on a manuscript by Herman J.
Mankiewicz, titled *The American*. Soon the name was changed to
Citizen Kane, which became the greatest first movie of a director,
and probably the most important film of the sound era.

Welles was fortunate to work with the cinematographer Greg
Toland. Both were willing to take risks and created a landmark
film with a variety of innovative techniques: odd-angle and deep-
focus shots; bizarre lighting; creative use of sound such as the
echoes in Xanadu's cavernous rooms; and dissolves and freeze
frames in the editing. There are many examples of jump cuts,
sharp transitions or fades, which were copied for decades thereafter. Almost every scene is a masterpiece. In the very opening, the
camera focuses on a wire fence with the initial K and a "No Tres-
passing" sign, then pans the grounds where one sees a castle,
Xanadu, on top of a hill. The camera next zooms in on a single
lighted window. Inside is a dying old man. There is a close shot of
his lips as he utters one word, "Rosebud," and dies, and the camera
follows a crystal ball as it falls from his hand and shatters. In a later
scene, there is a sharp cut from the newspaper editor's instructions
to interview Kane's second wife, to an electric sign atop a nightclub in Atlantic City advertising the appearance of Susan
Alexander against torrential rain and a flash of lightning. The
employees' party at the offices of the *New York Enquirer* has odd
angles and deep focus. The erosion of Kane's marriage is seen
through a succession of shots of Kane and his wife at the breakfast

table, each representing the passage of several years. In each sequence their chairs are farther and farther apart and their conversation changes from argument to a few words to, at the end, silence. A masterpiece of cinematography by Greg Toland occurs after Susan's opera debut when Kane goes to the newspaper office to see what Leland, his theater critic, has written. The camera captures the scene in close-up and sharp focus.

The film has a first-rate script by Mankiewicz and Welles with some memorable lines: Bernstein, an old man now, reminiscing about the glimpse of a girl some forty-six years earlier; or commenting on old age, "It is the only disease you don't look forward to being cured of." Leland on Kane: "He never gave anybody anything. He just left you a tip," or, "He was disappointed with the world, so he built one of his own, an absolute monarchy." There has been controversy as to how much of the script is Welles' work. Welles always said the lion's share belonged to Mankiewicz, and his own name in the screen credits is both after Mankiewicz's and smaller. There are also some grand performances, foremost that of Welles. Most of the actors came from radio and theater. They had been with Welles in his Mercury Theater group and almost none had previously appeared in a film. Welles brought them to Hollywood and extracted superb performances from Cotton, Sloane, Coulouris, Collins and the very brief appearance by Agnes Morehead. The score by Bernard Herrmann is very good. The editing was done by two young men who went on to become noted directors: Robert Wise and Mark Robson. However great the contribution of others, *Citizen Kane* is almost entirely Orson Welles' film. There were attempts to stop the distribution of the film which fortunately failed. At William Randolph Hearst's urging, Louis B. Meyer offered RKO $842,000, the cost of the film, to destroy the negatives. Miraculously RKO refused. *Citizen Kane* is still relevant. It is not simply about a bygone era. Only the scale has changed. There are publishers today with multimedia empires who make Kane/Hearst look frail and ineffectual.

City Lights

1931. 86 min. b.w. Silent. U.S. **Prod.** Charles Chaplin; **Dir.** Charles Chaplin; **Scr.** Charles Chaplin; **Cin.** Roland Totheroh; **Ed.** Charles Chaplin; **Mus.** To accompany the film, Charles Chaplin; **Cast:** Charlie Chaplin, Virginia Cherrill, Harry Myers, Hank Mann.

A tramp is mistaken for a millionaire by a blind girl who sells flowers. The tramp, evading police who are chasing him, steps through a parked limousine. The blind girl hearing the car door close thinks a rich man has gotten out and tries to sell him a flower. The tramp gives her his last dime and becomes her friend. There is a real rich man (Harry Myers), an alcoholic who is drunk every night. When drunk, he befriends Charlie, takes him home and tells him he is his best friend. The next morning when sober, he does not recognize him and orders his valet to throw him out. This goes on for several days and nights. Meanwhile, the tramp learns that the girl's sight can be restored by an expensive operation. He tries to raise money. He becomes a street cleaner, but a circus is in town and the elephants make cleaning the streets a hopeless job. Next he agrees to fight a professional boxer and if he stays on his feet for a few rounds he will be given the purse. In the ring he does everything to avoid the boxer; he dances and hides behind the referee. But the money from the fight is not enough. Somehow through coincidences he gets the money from thieves who had broken into the rich man's house. The police think he is the robber and chase him. Before they catch up to him he gets to the girl and gives her the money. Some time later after his jail sentence has been served he is reduced to a beggar walking the streets. The blind girl with her sight restored has opened a flower shop that he happens to pass. She presses a coin into his hand and recognizes her benefactor by the mere touch. She asks, "You?" He says, "You can see now?" She says, "Yes, I can see now." They don't move and look at each other. The camera moves from face to face in close-ups. The tramp, out of embarrassment, puts a rose in his mouth. We can see in Chaplin's face joy and also hopelessness and despair. He is aware that now that she can see him, a tramp, any chance of romance is over.

Along with The Gold Rush (1925), this is Chaplin's best. It has one of the greatest endings, even though it reeks with sentimentality. Virginia Cherrill is much better than Georgia Hale in *The Gold Rush* and Paulette Godard in *Modern Times* (1936) and *The Great Dictator* (1940). Harry Myers is excellent as the millionaire, the representative of the idle rich that Chaplin has in most of his films. Chaplin chose to remain with the tramp in a silent film though the film was made three years after the advent of sound.

Cries and Whispers

Viskningar Och Rop. 1972. 106 min. color. Swedish. **Prod.** Ingmar Bergman; **Dir.** Ingmar Bergman; **Scr.** Ingmar Bergman; **Cin.** Sven Nykvist; **Ed.** Siv Lundgren; **Art D.** Marik Vos; **Mus.** Frederic Chopin, Johann Sebastian Bach; **Cast:** Harriet Andersson, Liv Ullmann, Ingrid Thulin, Erland Josephson, Kari Sylwan, Georg Arlin, Henning Moritzen.

The film is set in a country mansion in Sweden at the turn of the twentieth century. Agnes (Harriet Andersson), a spinster in her late thirties, is in the terminal stages of stomach cancer. She is in unbearable pain and is cared for by Anna (Kari Sylwan), the housekeeper and the person closest to her. Agnes questions her suffering and her abandonment by God. Anna, who had lost her only child some years ago, has come to terms with death and she tries lovingly to comfort Agnes. Karin (Ingrid Thulin) and Maria (Liv Ullmann) have come to see their dying sister. Through a series of flashbacks we gain insight into each of the sisters and their relationships with one another. Agnes had worshipped her mother (also played by Liv Ullmann), but she had not returned Agnes' love, showering her attention on Maria, who was light-hearted and prettier. Agnes never married as she was considered too serious by suitors. Maria had had a lengthy extramarital affair that had driven her husband to attempt suicide. The elder sister, Karin, an intense guilt-ridden woman, married a diplomat. She was frigid, with suicidal tendencies, and to deny her husband intimacy she had mutilated her genitalia. Agnes finally dies a horrible painful death, but she has found faith. The sisters do not appear to have been particularly moved, nor do they seem to have understood what Agnes had been through. After a brief memorial service, in which the pastor barely mentions Agnes' short and tragic life, dwelling instead on the glory of God, the sisters are ready to leave. Totally oblivious to Anna's devotion to Agnes and her years of service to the family, they dismiss her and give her only a few weeks' extra pay.

A bleak film, even for Bergman, about dying, pain and faith. *Cries and Whispers* is also his most beautifully photographed film. Not even *Fanny and Alexander* (1982), with its rich texture and color, can compare with *Cries and Whispers*. The color is predominantly dark red, the color of blood. The film is also notable for its use of silence as a substitute for sound. There are scenes in which nothing is said. The silence is broken at key moments by a mournful cello playing Bach, the ticking of clocks, and soft cries and whispers in the background. The entire cast is excellent, with Thulin giving one of her best performances. Karin and Maria are very much like the two sisters in an earlier Bergman film, *The Silence* (1963). There is no communication between them. As in many of Bergman's films, women are the main characters, which gives testimony to his expressed belief that women are more expressive than men.

The Dead

1987. 83 min. color. U.S. **Prod.** Wieland Schulz-Keil, Chris Sievernich; **Dir.** John Huston; **Scr.** Tony Huston (based on the story by James Joyce); **Cin.** Fred Murphy; **Ed.** Roberto Silvi; **Prod. D.** Stephen Grimes, J. Denis Washington; **Mus.** Alex North; **Cast:** Anjelica Huston, Donal McCann, Rachael Dowling, Cathleen Delany, Dan O'Herlihy, Donal Donnelly, Helena Carroll, Ingrid Craigie, Marie Kean, Frank Patterson.

The story is set in Dublin on the night of 6 January 1904, the Feast of Epiphany. Two spinster sisters, Kate (Helena Carroll) and Julia (Cathleen Delany), together with their unmarried niece, Mary Jane (Ingrid Craigie), are hosting their annual dinner and dance party. Their guests include their nephew, Gabriel Conroy

(Donal McCann), a newspaper editor, and his wife Gretta (Anjelica Huston); an elderly Protestant, Mr. Browne (Dan O'Herlihy); an unemployed drunk, Freddy Malins (Donal Donnelly), and his widowed and somewhat embarrassed mother (Marie Kean); a young professional singer, Bartell D'Arcy (Frank Patterson); and a few other young guests, some of whom had been the sisters' music students. Before dinner there is a piano recital by Mary Jane, some dancing and a song by Julia. She had been a singer once, but now her voice is gone and her memory is fading. The only genuine, uncondescending admirer of her performance is the drunken Freddy who extravagantly compliments her. There is more spirited dancing followed by dinner with lively discussion on past and present tenors. This is followed by a thank-you speech by Gabriel, which he had prepared with great effort. After most of the guests have left, D'Arcy is finally prevailed upon to sing. Gretta is deeply moved by the song, "The Lass of Aughrim." In the cab ride back to their hotel Gretta is silent and totally withdrawn. Only when they reach their room does she tearfully explain to her husband that the song had brought back poignant memories of her first young love, Michael Fury, who had often sung that song. Michael was a delicate, consumptive youth of seventeen in Galway who had left his sickbed on a cold winter night to see her before she was to leave, and had died a week later. "I think he died for me," she says. In a powerful last scene Gabriel is hopelessly shattered. He can do nothing to compete with Gretta's revived memories of her first love, especially as the beloved had died for her. This is a crisis with which the self-assured Gabriel cannot cope. He goes to the window; the falling snow covering everything leads Gabriel to think of death and the transience of life. There is a common end to all of us. The snow falls on everyone. It was falling on the churchyard where Michael Fury lay buried.

In a way Joyce is saying that they are all dead. Gretta ceased to "live" after Michael's death. Gabriel, himself, is too fearful and repressed to live. The spinster sisters have long since ceased to live and just relive old memories. The niece, Mary Jane, will doubtless remain a spinster, and the drunken Freddy will never reform. "The

Dead" is the longest story in the collection of fifteen Joyce short stories, *Dubliners*. As in most of the other stories, such as "Araby" and "Clay," nothing appears to have happened, but profound changes have taken place within the characters. Gretta and Gabriel will never be the same.

The Dead is one of the most beautiful and delicate films ever made. It was a labor of love for Huston. He was a great admirer of Joyce and had toyed with the idea of making *The Dead* from the late fifties but could never get the financial backing. He directed the film at age eighty from a wheelchair, suffering from emphysema breathing from an oxygen mask. It was shot in California as he could not travel to Ireland where he had been a long-time resident. However, he assembled an excellent cast, some from Dublin's Abby Theatre, and extracts very good performances from them all. O'Herlihy and Donal Donnelly stand out. The two sisters, especially Cathleen Delany, and Anjelica Houston, are also outstanding. Huston's eldest son wrote a fine screenplay that is totally faithful to Joyce's story. The film is beautifully photographed and the control Huston exercises over every detail of the dinner scene is a marvel, a truly meaningful and moving epitaph for one of the greatest directors in the history of cinema. He is the only major director to have dared to direct three literary classics, all of which had been considered unsuitable and too difficult: *The Red Badge of Courage* (1951), *Moby Dick* (1956) and his last film, *The Dead*.

Dr. Strangelove: Or How I Learned to Stop Worrying and Love the Bomb

1964. 93 min. b.w. Columbia U.K. **Prod.** Stanley Kubrick; **Dir.** Stanley Kubrick; **Scr.** Stanley Kubrick, Terry Southern, Peter George (based on the novel *Red Alert* by Peter George); **Cin.** Gilbert Taylor; **Ed.** Anthony Harvey; **Prod. D.** Ken Adam; **Art D.** Peter Murton; **Mus.** Laurie Johnson; **Cast:** Peter Sellers, George C. Scott, Sterling Hayden, Slim Pickens, Keenan Wynn, Peter Bull, James Earl Jones, Tracy Reed.

General Jack D. Ripper (Sterling Hayden), who has lost his sexual prowess, is convinced the Communists are behind a master plan "to sap and impurify all our precious body fluids." The Russians, he believes, are contaminating the water supply with chemicals (fluoride). "They don't care because they drink vodka." General Ripper is commander of Burpelson Air Force Base. One day he decides to end the evil empire and dispatches his bomber wing to attack targets in the USSR with nuclear weapons. U.S. president Merkin Muffley (Peter Sellers) is informed of the mission by General "Buck" Turgidson (George C. Scott), the air force chief of staff. The president convenes an emergency meeting of his National Security Council. In addition to senior members of the cabinet, presidential aides and heads of all military services is the wheelchair-bound ex-Nazi rocket scientist, Dr. Strangelove (also Sellers). The president is told the planes are near the point of no return and the code for aborting the mission is known only to General Ripper, who has cut all communications with his base. The president, much to the dismay of General Turgidson, orders an attack by the army on Burpelson. General Turgidson seizes on the crisis as an opportunity to push for the total destruction of the Soviet Union and argues for an all out nuclear attack. He concedes that there will be retaliation and heavy U.S. civilian casualties: "I won't say we won't get our hair mussed. No more than ten to twenty million killed top, depending on the breaks." The president rejects the idea.

Meanwhile, British Royal Air Force Group Captain Lionel Mandrake (also Sellers), who is assigned temporarily to General

Ripper, tries to reason with and convince him to recall the planes. He fails. General Ripper is killed when the base is overrun by the army. Mandrake deciphers the code but communications with the outside have been cut. He manages to get change for a pay phone but is stopped by Colonel Bat Guano (Keenan Wynn), the officer who has liberated the base. Colonel Guano, baffled by Mandrake's uniform and British accent, accuses him of being "some kind of prevert [sic]." Mandrake finally gets through with the code but it is too late. The planes nearing their targets have cut off radio contact. The Soviet ambassador (Peter Bull) is called to the war room. He tells President Muffley that the USSR has perfected a doomsday device that will automatically trigger buried atomic missiles to target all major U.S. cities if their country is bombed. The president gets on the phone with the Soviet premier, Dimitri Kissoff, and much to the dismay of the joint chiefs informs the premier of the exact location of the U.S. planes and gives permission to shoot them down. Eventually, all but one of the planes are downed. The surviving plane is commanded by Major T. J. "King" Kong (Slim Pickens), an experienced pilot who evades Russian missiles as he heads to his target inside the USSR sitting astride his released bomb. The film closes with the mushroom cloud and Vera Lyn, the most popular British singer of World War II, singing her signature song, "We'll meet again, don't know where, don't know when..."

The film opens with what is probably its most original scene, the midair refueling of a bomber in a procedure amounting to copulation with the background music of "Try a Little Tenderness." The attack on Burpelson, the war room conference and the action on Major Kong's B-52 are masterfully intercut. The cinematography and production design are excellent. The main credit belongs to Terry Southern, who wrote one of the best of the black comedies of the era. Sellers is magnificent in two of his three roles, as President Muffley and Group Captain Mandrake. There is fine acting by Sterling Hayden, Keenan Wynn, Slim Pickens, and especially George C. Scott. This is another depiction in a series of films by Kubrick in which mad men rule the world:

George Macready in *Paths of Glory* (1957), the people who invented Hal in *2001* (1968), and the mad doctor in *A Clockwork Orange* (1971). Here we have the Turgidsons, the Rippers and an ineffectual President Muffley.

Duck Soup

1933. 70 min. b.w. U.S. **Prod.** Herman Mankiewicz; **Dir.** Leo McCarey; **Scr.** Bert Kalmar, Harry Ruby, Arthur Sheekman, Nat Perrin; **Cin.** Henry Sharp; **Ed.** LeRoy Stone; **Art D.** Hans Dreier, Wiard Ihnen; **Mus.** Bert Kalmar, Harry Ruby; **Cast:** Groucho, Harpo, Chico and Zeppo Marx, Margaret Dumont, Louis Calhern, Edgar Kennedy, Leonid Kinskey, Raquel Torres.

The Duchy of Freedonia has two important ministries: the Ministry of War, and the Ministry of Finance and Parking. Freedonia is bankrupt. Mrs. Teasdale (Margaret Dumont), a dowager millionairess, will give the Duchy twenty million dollars on the condition that it appoints Rufus T. Firefly (Groucho Marx) its president and dictator for life. Firefly makes his appearance and the first thing he does is to insult Trentino (Louis Calhern), the ambassador from neighboring Sylvania. Trentino lets the insult pass because he has bigger plans. He hires a vamp, Vera Marcal (Raquel Torres), to romance, seduce and discredit Firefly, while he sets about courting Mrs. Teasdale. His intention is to marry her, get her money and have Sylvania annex Freedonia. Trentino also hires Chicolini (Chico Marx) and Brownie (Harpo Marx) as spies to report Firefly's every move. They give their first report to Trentino: "Monday we watcha Firefly's house, but he no come out. He wasn't home. Tuesday we go to the ball game, but he fool us, he no show up. Wednesday, he go to the ball game. We fool him, we no show up. Thursday was a doubleheader, nobody show up. Friday it rain all day. There was no ball game. So we stay home and listen to it on the radio."

The vamp gets nowhere with Firefly. Mrs. Teasdale, despite being exasperated by Firefly's repeated insults, remains very fond of him and continues her support. Firefly to the portly Mrs. Teasdale: "You cover a lot of ground…I see you standing over a stove, except I can't see the stove." Mrs. Teasdale to Firefly: "Your Excellency." Firefly: "You ain't so bad yourself." Firefly, who claims his ancestors came over on the *Mayflower*—"The *Mayflower* was full of Fireflies"—is insulted when Trentino calls him "an upstart." Firefly starts a war against Sylvania. Chicolini, who had been a spy for Sylvania, changes sides and becomes Minister of War of Freedonia. Just when things look bleak for Freedonia, Trentino is captured and pelted with oranges. Freedonia is victorious. When the overjoyed Mrs. Teasdale begins to sing Freedonia's national anthem, she too is pelted with oranges by Firefly, Chicolini and Brownie.

This superb, irreverent comedy depicts the absurdities of war. Dictators go to war on the flimsiest pretexts. The sole justification is sung: "We got guns. They got guns. All God's chillun got guns." Patriotism is ridiculed as Chicolini changes sides because "the food is better in Freedonia." Religion, patriotism and everything deemed respectable and proper is pilloried and pelted with oranges.

The Earrings of Madame De…

Madame De… 1953. 105 min. b.w. French. **Prod.** H. Baum, Ralph Baum, **Dir.** Max Ophuls; **Scr.** Marcel Achard, Annette Wademant, Max Ophuls (based on the novel by Louise de Vilmorin); **Cin.** Christian Matras; **Ed.** Borys Lewin; **Mus.** Oscar Straus, Georges Van Parys; **Cast:** Charles Boyer, Danielle Darrieux, Vittorio De Sica, Mireille Perrey, Jean Debucourt, Lea di Lea.

The film is set toward the end of the nineteenth century. Countess Louise De (Danielle Darrieux), whose last name is never given, is in debt and she must raise money. In a beautifully and concisely photographed scene she searches through her belongings for anything she could sell. We see furs, rings, a necklace and finally a pair of diamond earrings she had received as a wedding gift from her husband, General Andre De (Charles Boyer). She takes the earrings to her jeweler, M. Remy (Jean Debucourt), and sells them. Later at the opera with her husband, she feigns losing them. When an item in a newspaper reports the theft of some diamond earrings at the opera, the jeweler, conscience stricken, takes them to the general who buys them back and gives them as a parting gift to his mistress who is traveling to Constantinople. The mistress, Lola (Lea di Lea), loses them gambling at the casino. Some time later they are purchased by an Italian diplomat, Baron Fabrizio Donati (Vittorio De Sica). The baron, posted to Paris, meets Louise at a social function and soon a passionate affair develops. He gives her the earrings without any knowledge of their history. She is ecstatic. The general is jealous, but thinking this is one of his wife's usual flirtations sends her to Italy to forget the baron. When she comes back the affair is renewed with greater passion. She tells the Baron that during her time away, "The earrings were my only consolation." In Paris she wears the earrings and tells her husband she had found them hidden in her gloves. The general, now very upset, forces her to make a gift of the earrings to her niece who had just given birth. The niece sells them to M. Remy, but this time the general refuses to buy them back. Feeling rejected and humiliated the general challenges the baron to a duel. Louise begs the baron to go away, but he stays and is killed. She collapses and dies. In the last scene we see the diamond earrings next to candles on the altar of her church with the inscription, "In Memory of Madame De."

As the film develops Ophuls subtly shows the transformation of a rather shallow woman who grows and matures through her love for the baron. The best acting is of Boyer and Danielle Darrieux. De Sica is magnificent, but he was to give an even better performance in *General Della Rovere* (1959). This story is from a novel by Louise de Vilmorin, with the ending changed. In the novel there is no duel. Madame De dies of illness and the general gives one of the earrings to the baron. Ophuls visually rounds out the story in the dancing scenes between Louise and the baron in which we see the intensity of their relationship develop. The first time we see them dancing in a crowded ballroom with no close-ups. Beautiful tracking shots dissolve into the next scene of the pair dancing, then a cut to the lovers all alone on an empty dance floor. Ophuls adds a dark footnote. When their last dance is over, a footman puts out the candles in the ballroom one after another and puts a cover on them. The scene ends in darkness. It is one of the most elegant and delicate movies ever made and probably Max Ophuls' most fully realized film. As in *Letter From an Unknown Woman* (1948), *La Ronde* (1950), and *Le Plaisir* (1951), there are similar recurrent themes on the transitory nature of pleasure, love, and the illusion of happiness.

8 1/2

Otto e Mezzo. 1963. 135 min. b.w. Italian. **Prod.** Angelo Rizolli; **Dir.** Federico Fellini; **Scr.** Federico Fellini, Ennio Flaiano, Tullio Pinelli, Brunello Rondi; **Cin.** Gianni De Venanzo; **Ed.** Leo Catozzo; **Art D.** Piero Gherardi; **Mus.** Nino Rota; **Cast:** Marcello Mastroianni, Claudia Cardinale, Anouk Aimée, Sandra Milo, Rossella Falk, Mario Pisu, Guido Alberti, Madeleine Le Beau, Jean Rougeul, Barbara Steele.

This film has one of the most dazzling opening scenes. A man appears trapped in his car in the middle of a huge traffic jam. He tries desperately to escape by banging and kicking at the doors and windows. Just as he is about to give up he is miraculously able to get out through the roof of his car and fly away. It is a fantasy in the mind of forty-three-year-old Guido Anselmi (Marcello Mastroianni), a famous filmmaker on the verge of a nervous breakdown who has developed a mental block. He cannot complete his script and is indecisive about casting the picture. He begins to think of his childhood, his dead parents, and his relationship with his mistress, wife, friends and collaborators. In his world of fantasy he somehow resolves his difficulties and concocts scenes for his film. Soon his doubts are cast aside and he is ready to begin work. In the last scene of the film all of his friends and colleagues parade and sing on the seaside sand. He joins them.

Marcello Mastroianni was one of the very good actors of his generation who never received sufficient international attention because he spoke no language other than Italian and thus appeared only in Italian films. The film has its usual collection of Fellini circus clowns and bizarre women. As in *Amarcord* (1974), the movie is partly autobiographical, hence self-centered, and at times even self-indulgent. However, the sheer cinematic virtuosity and a very good score by Nino Rota raise the film out of the ordinary.

Fanny and Alexander

1983. 197 min. color. Swedish. **Prod.** Jorn Donner; **Dir.** Ingmar Bergman; **Scr.** Ingmar Bergman; **Cin.** Sven Nykvist; **Ed.** Sylvia Ingemarsson; **Art D.** Anna Asp, Susanne Lingheim; **Mus.** Daniel Bell, Benjamin Britten, Frans Helmerson, Robert Schumson, Marianne Jacobs; **Cast:** Pernilla Allwin, Bertil Guve, Gunn Wallgren, Allan Edwall, Erland Josephson, Harriet Andersson, Boerje Ahlstedt, Christina Schollen, Ewa Froeling, Jarl Rulle, Jan Malmsjo.

The film takes place in the Swedish town of Uppsala shortly after the turn of the twentieth century and it is mostly through the eyes of a ten-year-old boy that we follow the story. The film begins joyously at the home of the widowed grandmother Helena Ekdahl (Gunn Wallgren) on Christmas Eve. It is beautifully photographed and Bergman's attention to detail is astounding. Helena's three sons, their wives, and their children are present. The household servants also are seated at the long dining table. The focus is on the eldest son, Oscar (Allan Edwall), his pretty wife, Emilie (Ewa Froeling,) and their two children, Fanny (Pernilla Allwin), age six, and Alexander (Bertil Guve), age ten. Oscar is a theatrical manager and lead actor of his own company. Oscar has a stroke during a performance and dies. Some time later Emilie accepts the offer of marriage of the bishop of Uppsala, who appears benign and considerate, and moves with Fanny and Alexander to the bishop's home. The fundamentalist bishop turns out to be a sadistic monster. The bishop's sister and mother also live in the house and closely resemble the witch burners of Carl Dreyer's *Day of Wrath* (1943). The children are given the blandest of food in the smallest quantities and are punished for the slightest infractions. When they complain to their mother they are imprisoned in the attic by the bishop. Emilie is prevented from seeing any of her relatives or those of her dead husband. She secretly visits Helena and reveals her own and the children's sordid experiences in the bishop's household. The children's two uncles call on the Bishop who has some unpaid debts. He is offered money and then threatened, but the haughty Bishop, with his status in the church and the community, refuses to free the children. Through a clever plot, the children are finally smuggled to freedom by old Isac (beautifully acted by a Bergman stalwart Erland Josephson), a Jewish antiques dealer, an old friend of the Ekdahl family and a long-time lover of widowed Helena.

Initially a five-hour television play, it was later reduced to a 188-minute movie. While the story concentrates on Fanny and Alexander, there are several subplots involving the two uncles and their wives, the pregnancy of a maid, and the bishop's dead first wife. Bergman, whose films are marked with anguish and despair, made this totally atypical film with a redemptive ending. It is beautifully photographed by Sven Nykvist. Bergman wrote the original story and screenplay which are partly autobiographical. It is Bergman's last film, and when everyone expected a farewell rage against a distant God, he made this gentle and loving film.

Forbidden Games

Les Jeux Interdits. 1951. 87 min. b.w. French. **Prod.** Robert Dorfmann; **Dir.** Rene Clement; **Scr.** Rene Clement, Jean Aurenche, Pierre Bost (based on the novel *Les Jeux Inconnus* by Francois Boyer); **Cin.** Robert Juillard; **Ed.** Roger Dwyer; **Art D.** Paul Bertrand; **Mus.** Narciso Yepes; **Cast:** Brigitte Fossey, Georges Poujouly, Lucien Hubert, Suzanne Courtal, Jacques Marin, Laurence Badie, Amedée.

It is May 1940 and the German invasion of France has begun. Refugees are fleeing the city in droves. German planes strafe the escaping civilians on a bridge, some in cars, some in carts and some on foot. The father and mother of Paulette (Brigitte Fossey), a five-year-old, are killed when their car is hit. Paulette, who had left the car to run after her small dog, is spared. The dog was also killed and someone throws the dead dog over the bridge. She runs along the river's edge and retrieves its body. She meets Michel (Georges Poujouly), a boy of eleven who takes her to his parents' farm. They also are drawn to the distraught little girl and decide to take care of her. Paulette sees graves with crosses and wants her dog to be buried with a cross. Thus begin their "games." They bury chickens, moles and even insects, and they steal crosses to put on the graves. From the very beginning, Michel senses Paulette's yearning for her dead parents, and the ritual of burial and stealing crosses diverts her melancholy. The games become a way of dealing with the death of her parents. Some time later the local authorities learn of the presence of the girl and gendarmes are sent to take her to an orphanage. Michel is devastated. He screams and kicks and breaks all the crosses. The last scene of the film is one of the most moving. In a crowded railroad station turned into a refugee center, the terrified Paulette, with hundreds of distraught people all around, is being comforted by a nun. Then she hears someone call out the name Michel. Her eyes brighten. She jumps from her chair and starts running in the direction from which the voice had come. She does not find her Michel but an older man. She begins to cry frantically and quietly repeats the name, "Michel, Michel," over and over again. There is a crane shot that rises as the cries of Paulette recede. The poignant strains of Narciso Yepes' guitar, the musical background throughout, ends the film.

Clement cast nonprofessionals and tested hundreds of children for this acclaimed antiwar film. Fossey was with her parents in Nice on vacation and he selected her to play Paulette. He wanted an eight-year-old for the part but fortunately settled on the five-year-old girl. Her parents played themselves. Poujouly was found in a holiday camp for underprivileged children. *Forbidden Games* is one of the great films; an unexpected attainment from a highly unexpected source. Rene Clement, basically a documentary filmmaker, had directed some ten shorts including Jaques Tati's screen debut. After the war he made four films, none notable. Then he made this masterpiece. Thereafter he reverted to form and made mediocre films. His biggest failure was *Is Paris Burning?* in 1966. However, he will be remembered for having made *Forbidden Games*.

The Four Hundred Blows

Les Quatre Cents Coups. 1959. 99 min. b.w. French. **Prod.** Francois Truffaut; **Dir.** Francois Truffaut; **Scr.** Francois Truffaut, Marcel Moussy; **Cin.** Henri Decae; **Ed.** Marie-Josephe Yoyotte; **Art D.** Bernard Evein; **Mus.** Jean Constantin; **Cast:** Jean-Pierre Léaud, Patrick Auffay, Claire Maurier, Albert Remy, Guy Decombie, Georges Flament, Yvonne Claudie, Robert Beauvais, Jean Moreau, Jean-Claude Brialy.

Antoine Doinel (Jean-Pierre Léaud) is a healthy twelve-year-old schoolboy. He is not a good student and his teacher is dissatisfied with him. When school is over he becomes exuberant, and runs and plays in the streets of Paris and in amusement arcades. He lives in a tiny apartment but is content as long as his bickering parents are not there. One day he sees his mother kiss a strange man in the street and she doesn't come home until late that evening. He hears his parents quarrel loudly. The next day when his teacher asks him why he had missed class a few days earlier he says it was because his mother had died. His parents are called to school. His father slaps him in front of the class and Antoine is deeply humiliated. A while later he is expelled from school when the teacher discovers he has lifted long passages from Balzac in one of his essays. Next, Antoine is caught stealing a typewriter from his father's place of work. Although he swears he was actually returning it, his father takes him to the police station where he spends a night in jail. He is now totally alienated. He is sent to a succession of reform schools, one harsher than the other. He escapes and heads north to the sea. After several days he reaches the shore and is unable to run any more. In one of the most powerful film images Antoine turns around with his back to the sea to face the camera and the viewer. With a look of despair, he appears to be pleading with us to tell him where to go now. The camera freezes and the movie ends.

This was Truffaut's first film. He had been a reviewer at *Cahiers du Cinema* and deeply involved in movie history. At the urging of his father-in-law he made this semi–autobiographical film for which he also wrote the script. Truffaut had had a difficult childhood and adolescence and had been sent to reform schools.

There is not, however, an ounce of sentimentality in the film, although Truffaut treats the troubled boy with compassion. Part of the success of the film is the natural acting of Jean-Pierre Léaud and the black and white photography of Henri Decae that gives the film its realism. It was photographed on the streets of Paris with a very limited budget. The year 1959 was the beginning of a revolution in French filmmaking and the birth of the New Wave. Alain Resnais's *Hiroshima Mon Amour* and Jean-Luc Godard's *Breathless* soon followed *The Four Hundred Blows*. The term four hundred blows is a French expression for the limit of what one can bear.

The General

1927. 74 min. b.w. Silent. U.S. **Prod.** Joseph M. Schenck; **Dir.** Buster Keaton, Clyde Bruckman; **Scr.** Buster Keaton, Clyde Bruckman, Al Boasberg, Charles Smith; **Cin.** J. Devereaux Jennings, Bert Haines; **Ed.** Sherman Kell; **Cast:** Buster Keaton, Marion Mack, Glen Cavender.

It begins in 1861 in Marietta, Georgia soon after Fort Sumter has been fired on and the Civil War has started. Hundreds of men line up to enlist. Keaton, a railroad motorman, is one of the applicants. The recruiting officer rejects him saying he is of more value as the driver of the Western Atlantic train. His girl (Marion Mack) does not believe him and says she will never talk to him unless he is in uniform. A year goes by and she has a new beau. The Yankees send spies to Marietta to steal the train. Their plan is to hijack it, take it north and burn all the bridges behind them. They stage the takeover during the train's dinner stop. Keaton sees the train pulling away. It is loaded with ammunition, but what he doesn't know is that his former fiancée is on the train. He shouts to his coworkers to give chase, but they don't hear him. He is all alone running after the train in the classic Keaton awkward run. He soon finds a hand-operated rail trolley and when that breaks down he steals a bicycle. He catches up, rescues his girl and takes the train back. He then plays a crucial role in alerting the Southern commanders of an impending attack. He is made a lieutenant and gets the girl.

The film has the usual Keaton struggles with machines. Throughout, the actor contains his emotions and maintains the stoic expression that heightens the comedy. The man, who during his entire film career smiled perhaps only once or twice argued that, "There wasn't much to smile about." This is the essential Keaton and his best film. It also has one of the great comic chases in movie history. It is not the direction (Keaton was codirector) or the story that make the film memorable. It is Keaton's persona and presence.

The Godfather

1972. 175 min. color. U.S. **Prod.** Albert S. Ruddy; **Dir.** Francis Ford Coppola; **Scr.** Mario Puzo, Francis Ford Coppola (based on the novel by Mario Puzo); **Cin.** Gordon Willis; **Ed.** William Reynolds; **Prod. D.** Dean Tavoularis; **Art D.** Warren Clymer; **Mus.** Nino Rota; **Cast:** Marlon Brando, Al Pacino, James Caan, Richard Castellano, John Cazale, Diane Keaton, Talia Shire, Robert Duvall, Sterling Hayden, John Marley, Richard Conte, Al Lettieri, Abe Vigoda, Al Martino, Gianni Russo.

The film begins with an elaborate wedding party in the late summer of 1945. It is being held at the large compound of the Godfather, Don Vito Corleone (Marlon Brando) whose only daughter, Connie (Talia Shire), is being married to Carlo Rizzi (Gianni Russo), a small-time bookie. The senior members of the five New York crime families, as well as the heads of families in other parts of the country, are among the guests. In about forty minutes most of the key characters are developed. The Don has three sons. The eldest, Sonny (James Caan), the heir to the Don's title, is headstrong and impulsive, unlike his shrewd and methodical father, who is given to patience and thoughtful pause before acting. The second son, Fredo (John Cazale), is not very bright and has no position of substance in the family. The youngest is Michael (Al Pacino), a college-educated, highly decorated Marine captain who has only recently been discharged after serving with distinction in World War II. He is engaged to Kay Adams (Diane Keaton). In the opening scenes we also are given brief glimpses of others who will play important parts. These include Tom Hagen (Robert Duvall), a non-Italian orphan adopted by the Don, who became a lawyer and is the consigliere or legal advisor to the family; and Don Barzini (Richard Conte), the head of another family and, as we soon learn, Don Corleone's principal rival. The Don is approached by Sollozzo (Al Lettieri), a gangster who has the backing of yet another New York family. He seeks to purchase and distribute heroin but needs additional financial backing and the Don's extensive influence with local politicians. The Don declines to help. He is satisfied with his family's operation of prostitution and gambling, and is fearful of losing his political contacts if he becomes involved in the sale of heroin. There is an attempt on the Don's life. He survives but is hospitalized. Sonny in turn plots the killing of Sollozzo. Michael, who so far has distanced himself from his father's business, volunteers to do the job and, in one of the best-photographed scenes, kills Sollozzo and his bodyguard, a police captain (Sterling Hayden). Michael is immediately sent to Sicily for his own protection. The other families plot and murder Sonny with the help of Connie's husband. The Don is released from the hospital and makes peace with the heads of the families. Michael's safety is guaranteed and he returns. The Don appoints Michael as his successor and advises him on how to get revenge. When the Don dies, Michael begins an orgy of killings. All the heads of the New York families and their top lieutenants are killed simultaneously throughout the city and other parts of the country. Michael is the unquestioned Godfather.

The film is a story of greed and vengeance. The film historian David Thomson aptly called *The Godfather* a film noir in color. There is not one sympathetic character in the film other than Kay and Don Corleone's wife. The Don is deceptively soft-spoken and is sentimental toward his immediate family, but he is clearly ruthless and carries all the hatred stored in him over the years. The scenes in which he coaches Michael on getting revenge stand out. Michael knows no loyalty except to his parents, and by the end of the film he, too, becomes a ruthless killer.

The family's henchman, Clemenza (Richard Castellano), despite his jovial appearance is a cold-blooded murderer; and a remorseless lack of loyalty is shown by the lugubrious Tessio (Abe Vigoda). It is also a study of the criminal warlord's business and private life. The emphasis on the Don's family gives strength to the film. Most important, the film influences the viewer's perception of organized crime. There are telling implications that the career and goals of a gangster are not much different from those of a businessman, nor a criminal empire that diverse from the operation of a large corporation or conglomerate. Both are part and parcel of the free enterprise system.

The Godfather is one of the most significant movies—flawlessly directed, acted, edited, photographed, and rooted in an excellent script. Foremost is the virtuoso performance of Marlon Brando, the greatest actor of his generation. Paramount had wanted Laurence Olivier, who would have been miscast. Brando vigorously lobbied and auditioned for the part. Other outstanding members of the cast are Robert Duvall, Richard Castellano, Sterling Hayden, Richard Conte, James Caan, John Marley, Diane Keaton in one of her best roles, and Al Pacino who went on to shine brighter still in *The Godfather Part II*. Coppola was also fortunate in his choice of cinematographer Gordon Willis. Most of the scenes are photographed with diffused lighting, and the colors of Los Angeles and Las Vegas are more vibrant than New York. The film far surpasses the novel in artistry. The superb opening wedding scene and the last masterfully juxtaposed scenes of the church baptism and the orgy of killing are well done. It is a three-hour film that moves at a deliberate pace and yet we don't want it to end. It won Academy Awards for best film, best actor (Brando), best supporting actor (Caan), and best adapted screenplay; and received Academy Award nominations for best supporting actor (Duvall and Pacino), director and editing.

The Gold Rush

1925. 82 min. b.w. Silent. U.S. **Prod.** Charles Chaplin; **Dir.** Charles Chaplin; **Scr.** Charles Chaplin; **Cin.** Rollie Totheroh; **Ed.** Harold McGhean; **Art D.** Charles D. Hall; **Mus.** to accompany film, Charles Chaplin; Max Terr for 1942 release; **Cast:** Charlie Chaplin, Georgia Hale, Mack Swain, Tom Murray.

The tramp has suffered many hardships in his films, but here he is up against his greatest adversary, nature. He is a prospector in the freezing mountains of the Alaskan Klondike. We first see him in his usual tramp's clothes and cane walking a narrow path on the edge of a snow-covered mountain. He is pursued by a hungry bear, but he makes it to a cabin that is inhabited by a fierce prospector, Big Jim (Mack Swain), who has struck gold. They are snowed in with no food. The starvation scene, one of Chaplin's best, has him boil an old shoe and carve it as if it were a turkey, portioning it between himself and Big Jim. The tramp treats the boiled shoelaces as spaghetti and the nails as juicy bones. Fortunately, just before Big Jim, hallucinating, could cause injury to the little fellow, he shoots a stray bear and both are saved from starvation and death. They part, but later Big Jim is hit on the head in a fight and suffers loss of memory. The tramp makes his way to a mining town and gets by doing odd jobs. He falls hopelessly in love with a barmaid and invites her and her two friends to a New Year's Eve dinner. In one of the most imaginative scenes displaying the essence of Chaplin's talent there is the famous dance of the bread rolls. He stands forks in two rolls with his face above the forks, making them appear as his dancing legs and feet. The three girls, having forgotten the invitation, do not show up until well after the New Year by which time the tramp has left his cabin. In the next part, the tramp runs into Big Jim in the tavern. Big Jim has recovered from his injury but still cannot remember where his gold mine is located. The tramp takes him to the cabin, but a severe storm has moved it to the edge of a precipice. Somehow they survive before the cabin falls into the ravine and with Charlie's help they find the mine. They both have become millionaires and take an ocean liner to Europe. The former barmaid is a passenger in the third-class section of the ship. Charlie and his love are reunited.

Along with *City Lights* (1931), this is the best of Chaplin's full-length feature films. There are, as always, some overly sentimental scenes, but that is a small price to pay to see Chaplin at work.

The Gospel According to St. Matthew

Il Vangelo Secondo Matteo. 1966. 135 min. b.w. Italian. **Prod.** Alfredo Bini; **Dir.** Pier Paolo Pasolini; **Scr.** Pier Paolo Pasolini (based on the Gospel of Matthew); **Cin.** Tonino Delli Colli; **Ed.** Nino Baragli; **Art D.** Luigi Scaccianoce; **Mus.** Luis Bacalov, Bach, Mozart, Prokofiev, Webern; **Cast:** Enrique Irazoqui, Margherita Caruso, Susanna Pasolini, Marcello Morante, Mario Socrate.

The film is the life of Christ based entirely on the Book of Matthew. It opens with Joseph, a middle-aged man, looking very despondent and disturbed with his young pregnant wife Mary. He is close to striking her but thinks better of it. With his head bowed he goes to the hills. An angel appears and delivers a message and disappears. He returns and smiles radiantly at his wife. Mary gives birth and the people adore the child, which pleases her. The film continues with events in Christ's life: the temptation by Satan; his baptism; Jesus' recruitment of disciples beginning with the two fishermen, Peter and Andrew; the Sermon on the Mount; going to the temple to drive out the money changers, offending priests and scribes; charges of blasphemy by the Pharisees; trial by Pontius Pilate; crucifixion and resurrection.

Pasolini depicts Jesus as a highly motivated political figure who cares deeply about justice, the poor, and the brotherhood of man. He is full of anger and his Sermon on the Mount is not a plea but authoritarian in tone. He does not appear close to his disciples and keeps his distance. Pasolini's Jesus bears no resemblance to the Hollywood spectacles that depict him as passive and in total serenity. It is a highly original and remarkable film by a Marxist Christian. It lags toward the end and Pasolini uses too many close-ups, which slow the film. The entire cast is nonprofessional. Pasolini cast his mother as Mary, and as Jesus he cast a Spanish student who resembles a figure from an El Greco painting. The score is very effective. There is Bach, Mozart and Prokofiev's "Alexander Nevsky" as well as spirituals. In a lovely scene, the birth of Jesus is accompanied by the background music of "Sometimes I Feel Like a Motherless Child," sung by Odetta.

Grand Illusion

La Grande Illusion. 1937. 117 min. b.w. French. **Prod.** Raymond Blondy; **Dir.** Jean Renoir; **Scr.** Jean Renoir, Charles Spaak; **Cin.** Christian Matras; **Ed.** Marguerite Renoir; **Art D.** Eugene Lourie; **Mus.** Joseph Kosma; **Cast:** Jean Gabin, Pierre Fresnay, Erich von Stroheim, Marcel Dalio, Dita Parlo.

During the latter stages of WWI Captain de Boeldieu (Pierre Fresnay) and Lieutenant Marechal (Jean Gabin) are shot down by German ace Captain Von Rauffenstein (Erich von Stroheim). They survive a crash landing, and before being sent to a prisoner of war camp are invited by Rauffenstein to the officers' lunch. From the outset, Rauffenstein and Boeldieu appear to have a great deal in common. Both are refined and members of the military elite. Marechal, on the other hand, is a plebeian who has little in common with either. After lunch they are taken to the prison camp. They meet and befriend Rosenthal (Marcel Dalio), a Jewish French officer and scion of a Paris banking family. Together they plot their escape. Because of an Allied offensive, the prisoners are transferred to a camp farther east. The commandant of the new camp is Rauffenstein, the former pilot who, in the interim, has been retired from active duty due to battle injuries. He now wears an iron corset and neck brace. Rauffenstein treats the prisoners with deference, but warns them that the camp is escape-proof and anyone caught attempting to flee will be shot. Later, in conversation with Boeldieu, he laments the fact that this war will bring an end to the gentleman class of officers and the existing social order.

Soon there is an escape attempt. Boeldieu creates a noisy diversion on the roof of the prison to distract Rauffenstein and the guards while Marechal and Rosenthal escape. Having warned and even pleaded with Boeldieu, Rauffenstein has no choice but to shoot. He aims for Boeldieu's legs but by accident mortally wounds him. A moving scene has Rauffenstein trying to explain to the dying Boeldieu that he had only meant to wound him slightly. Meanwhile, there is a heavy snowfall and Rosenthal cannot keep pace with Marechal, who begins to taunt him cruelly. Marechal walks away, leaving Rosenthal behind, but comes back to lift his exhausted companion and continue the journey at a slower pace. They reach a remote farmhouse and are sheltered through the winter by a German peasant woman (Dita Parlo) who has been widowed by the war. A romance develops with Marechal, but spring comes and they leave the generous, lonely woman with a promise by Marechal to return after the war. As they approach the Swiss border, they are spotted by a German patrol that is about to shoot at them. The German corporal orders his men to hold their fire and they escape to Switzerland.

The acting of Fresnay, Gabin and Dalio is superb. There is also the inspired casting of Stroheim, who couldn't find employment in Hollywood and had gone to France. He suggested touches that added a certain panache to the character of Rauffenstein. It was his idea to have the injured Rauffenstein wear the iron corset and neck brace. The script by Renoir and Charles Spaak is excellent. Renoir had been a pilot in WWI but said that, "I made this film because I am a pacifist." He makes a plea for peace and highlights the absurdities of war. As a member of the Popular Front, a collection of leftist, labor and center parties headed by Leon Blum from 1936 to 1937, Renoir also weaves a proletarian theme through the film. Division of people by nationalities and religions is artificial. The film is about relationships that transcend manmade conventions, boundaries, and religions. Marechal, a working-class fellow, comes to love Rosenthal, a wealthy Jew, as a brother, and falls in love with a German widow. At the end the German corporal holds his fire because he recognizes another poor pawn like himself. Renoir the realist, however, tells us that the end of wars and the creation of an egalitarian society may just be an illusion.

The Grapes of Wrath

1940. 129 min. b.w. U.S. **Prod.** Darryl F. Zanuck, Nunnally Johnson; **Dir.** John Ford; **Scr.** Nunnally Johnson (based on the novel by John Steinbeck); **Cin.** Gregg Toland; **Ed.** Robert Simpson; **Art D.** Richard Day, Mark-Lee Kirk; **Mus.** Alfred Newman; **Cast:** Henry Fonda, Jane Darwell, John Carradine, Charley Grapewin, Russell Simpson, John Qualen, Ward Bond, Dorris Bowdon, O. Z. Whitehead, Eddie Quillan, Zeffie Tilbury, Frank Darien, Grant Mitchell.

The film begins in 1934–1935, the height of the Great Depression, when a severe drought led to banks and mortgage companies repossessing farms and homesteads. Tom Joad (Henry Fonda), just released from prison after serving a four-year sentence for manslaughter, is trying to hitch a ride on a road in the dry Oklahoma landscape. A truck with a "no riders" sign stops for him. Tom's character is established by his very first words to the driver: "A good guy don't pay no attention to what some heel makes him stick on his truck." He is dropped off at a feeder road near his family farm. He comes across Casey (John Carradine), a former preacher who has lost the call and no longer ministers. Together they make their way to the Joad farm only to find it abandoned. They run into Muley (John Qualen), a neighboring farmer. He, like the Joad family, is a victim of foreclosure. The Joads are all in an uncle's house nearby. Pa (Russell Simpson) has seen a handbill offering thousands of jobs in California for fruit pickers. Despite doubts, the entire Joad family of twelve load their meager belongings on an old dilapidated truck and head west with $150 to their names. Ma Joad (Jane Darwell) is heartbroken. In a beautifully photographed scene she leaves behind her old letters and photos. Casey accompanies the family. When Grandpa dies en route, he is buried by the roadside and Casey delivers some brief words: "If I was to pray, I'll pray for the folks that is alive and don't know which way to turn. Old Grandpa here, he ain't got no more trouble like that." California turns out to be far different from what they had envisioned. There are perhaps one thousand jobs for over ten thousand migrants and even if they get work, the orchard owners pay only starvation wages. There are armed guards who will beat up anybody who so much as complains or talks back. There is a fight with the armed guards and the police arrest Casey. The Joads finally get to one of the government-run camps recently established under the New Deal. The accommodations are clean, and the Joads are treated decently and given work picking fruit. Casey, now released from prison, has become a union organizer. Vigilantes raid the strikers' camp and one of them kills Casey. A few nights later Tom retaliates and kills Casey's murderer. In the confrontation his face is cut. He knows the police will be after him and his wound will make him easy to find. He leaves the family and his famous last words to his mother are, "I'll be everywhere…." He, too, will be a union organizer.

Gregg Toland, the photographer, was greatly influenced by Pare Lorentz's 1936 documentary, *The Plow That Broke the Plains*. *The Grapes of Wrath* has the same documentary feel and it is one of Toland's best works. There is much use of shadow and all is gray except the New Deal camp, which is mostly white. The film is flawlessly directed by Ford and he has given us one of the most unforgettable scenes on film. John Carradine squats, contemplating the arid ground. The light is clear and he casts a long shadow. In addition to the sheer drama of the image, it has the composition of a painting. Except for "Red River Valley" sung over the credits, there are none of the sentimental folk songs which are the staples of John Ford films. The cast is excellent. Zanuck, the head of Fox Studios, wanted either Don Ameche or Tyrone Power as Tom Joad. Ford, who had made *Young Mr. Lincoln* with Fonda in 1939, insisted on Fonda. Zanuck agreed provided that Fonda sign a multi-picture contract with Fox. Fonda gave one of the very best performances of his career, but he suffered greatly under the contractual arrangement. Other than *My Darling Clementine*

(1946), again with Ford, he was assigned to some silly movies. Jane Darwell is also magnificent. Her soliloquy at the very end of the film is exceptionally moving. Nunnally Johnson added the soliloquy, which is not in Steinbeck's novel. This is one of the rare Hollywood films that takes an uncompromising stand on the plight of the poor and dispossessed.

Great Expectations

1946. 118 min. b.w. British. **Prod.** Ronald Neame; **Dir.** David Lean; **Scr.** David Lean, Ronald Neame, Anthony Havelock-Allen, Cecil McGivern, Kay Walsh (based on the novel by Charles Dickens); **Cin.** Guy Green; **Ed.** Jack Harris; **Art D.** Wilfred Shingleton; **Mus.** Walter Goehr; **Cast:** John Mills, Valerie Hobson, Bernard Miles, Francis L. Sullivan, Finlay Currie, Martita Hunt, Jean Simmons, Alec Guinness, Torin Thatcher, Anthony Wager.

In one of the most effective openings of any film a young boy is running across the salt marshes of a vast plain in southeast England on Christmas Eve to visit his mother's grave in a desolate churchyard. The only sound we hear is the howl of the wind and the shaking of bare trees. The boy kneels beside his mother's tombstone. As he rises to leave he runs into the towering figure of an escaped convict, still in chains, who places an enormous hand over the boy's mouth. So begins *Great Expectations*, set in 1830, which chronicles the story of Pip Pirrip (Anthony Wager as a child and John Mills as an adult), an orphan raised by his shrewish sister and her kind husband, a blacksmith named Joe Gargery (Bernard Miles). The boy takes some food, water and metal files to the convict, Magwitch (Finlay Currie), who shortly thereafter is captured and sent to a penal colony in New South Wales. Some time later the boy is summoned to come and play at the decaying mansion of an eccentric and reclusive old maid, Miss Havisham (Martita Hunt). He becomes immediately enticed by her beautiful and arrogant ward Estella, a girl his own age (Jean Simmons as a child and Valerie Hobson as an adult). Years pass. Pip has grown to manhood and has become an apprentice to his brother-in-law. He is visited by a lawyer from London, Mr. Jaggers (Francis L.

Sullivan), who tells him an anonymous benefactor has left a considerable sum of money to him and he must go to London to
make his way as a gentleman of "great expectations." Pip assumes
the benefactor is Miss Havisham. In London Pip shares a flat with
a boy he had met in his youth at Miss Havisham's, the upper-class
and slightly eccentric Herbert Pocket (Alec Guinness). He learns
the manners of a gentleman, visits all the right places, goes to parties, and meets the grown-up and beautiful Estella, who naively
leads a very busy life in society. She would soon be taken advantage of and jilted by an adventurer. Pip's life is further
complicated by the unexpected arrival of Magwitch, who has
escaped from New South Wales to see Pip. Magwitch tells Pip he
is the anonymous benefactor. Pip and Pocket attempt to help him
escape, but an old enemy of Magwitch alerts the police and Magwitch is seriously injured in an accident while escaping. Before
dying he tells Pip that Estella is his daughter. Miss Havisham also
dies when a piece of coal from the fireplace sets her clothes on
fire. Estella, who since her abandonment by the rogue suitor has
lived a secluded life in Miss Havisham's mansion, is reunited with
Pip and the two of them set out to begin a new life.

Despite the elimination of several characters, the film is faithful
to and captures the tone of the novel. If there is any weakness to
the film it is the happy ending which seems counter to everything that has gone before. Very well directed and visually
flawless, Lean creates suspense throughout, from the identity of
the benefactor to the attempted escape of Magwitch. The cast of
Mills, Hobson, Currie, Guinness, Sullivan and Simmons is first
rate. Martita Hunt gives one of her great performances. This is by
far the best of Dickens on film; better than *Oliver Twist* (1951),
also by Lean, and Cukor's *David Copperfield* (1935).

Greed

1925. 140 min. b.w. Silent. U.S. **Prod.** Erich von Stroheim; **Dir.** Erich von Stroheim; **Scr.** June Mathis, Erich von Stroheim (based on the novel *McTeague* by Frank Norris); **Cin.** Ben F. Reynolds, William H. Daniels; **Ed.** Frank Hull, Joseph W. Farnham; **Cast:** Gibson Gowland, ZaSu Pitts, Jean Hersholt, Chester Conklin.

The film is set around 1910 (the novel by Frank Norris was published in 1899). It begins at a California gold mine where McTeague (Gibson Gowland), an uneducated clod, works as a miner and his mother as a cook. The mother, ever hopeful that her son could rise above a common laborer, pleads with a quack dentist to take her son on as an apprentice. McTeague soon opens his own practice. One day his friend Marcus (Jean Hersholt) brings his cousin Trina (ZaSu Pitts) who has a toothache. McTeague, who has been shielded by his mother from temptation, immediately falls in love with the girl. They soon become engaged and married. They host a gaudy wedding dinner where the guests, who are as primitive as McTeague, gorge themselves on huge quantities of food and drink. Later in the bedroom he goes after his frightened bride like an animal, until his passions are satisfied. Their marriage begins to disintegrate from the start. Soon thereafter she wins a $5,000 lottery prize and their lives change forever. She becomes a miser, begins to hoard and save every cent and puts her husband on a pitiful allowance. She taunts him for his poverty and dim wits. He is allowed to go one night a week to the local bar. On a night of torrential rain she refuses to give him car fare. She cheats and scrounges to save money. One night McTeague runs into his friend Marcus who has become resentful that McTeague has married a woman with five thousand dollars. They have a brutal fight and part as enemies. Marcus informs the authorities that McTeague is practicing dentistry without a license and soon thereafter his shop is closed. McTeague takes menial jobs but can't hold them due to his drinking. He walks out on his wife. Months later he runs across her working as a charwoman in a school. After a night of heavy drinking he goes home and demands money. When she refuses he kills her and steals the money. He escapes and goes south, pursued by a posse. Marcus is a member of the posse and follows him to Death Valley. Both men are trapped without water. They are sustained by their mutual hatred and greed. They fight like animals and McTeague finds himself chained to Marcus. He beats Marcus to death but knows his own end is very near.

The film deals with moral decay. What helps make *Greed* outstanding is von Stroheim's details in scenes of Northern California and Death Valley. Although a silent film, von Stroheim wrote complete dialogue and made his actors rehearse the lines and speak them during filming. Erich von Stroheim, one of the great film directors, had planned a ten-hour film, but Irving Thalberg, the head of production at MGM, and others at the studio cut it to under two hours. A 1999 reconstructed version has added some forty-five minutes, which greatly enhance the picture. Stroheim's insistence on detail and authentic background made him unemployable. Forced to retire he only appeared in a few films as an actor, the most notable being Renior's *La Grande Illusion* (1937) as a Prussian officer, Billy Wilder's *Five Graves to Cairo* (1943) as Rommel, and *Sunset Boulevard* (1950) as a failed director.

The Heiress

1949. 115 min. b.w. U.S. **Prod.** William Wyler; **Dir.** William Wyler; **Scr.** Ruth Goetz, Augustus Goetz (based on their play and the novel *Washington Square* by Henry James); **Cin.** Leo Tover; **Ed.** William Hornbeck; **Art D.** John Meehan, Harry Horner; **Mus.** Aaron Copland; **Cast:** Olivia de Havilland, Ralph Richardson, Montgomery Clift, Miriam Hopkins, Vanessa Brown, Mona Freeman, Ray Collins.

Set around 1850 in New York City in a townhouse at 16 Washington Square. Catherine Sloper (Olivia de Havilland) lives with her father, Dr. Austin Sloper (Ralph Richardson), an eminent physician, and her widowed aunt, Lavinia Penniman (Miriam Hopkins). Catherine is plain looking, withdrawn, and lacking in social graces. She is twenty years old but has had no suitors. Her mother, who was beautiful and charming, died during childbirth.

Dr. Sloper adored his wife and unconsciously blames Catherine for her death. He is condescending toward his daughter and has never given her the love she deserves. Catherine has inherited $10,000 a year from her mother and will inherit a much larger annuity upon her father's death. At a wedding party, Catherine is stranded with no one asking her to dance. She is approached by Morris Townsend (Montgomery Clift) and dances with him. Morris has just returned from Paris where he, has lived for the past few years, having squandered all of his meager inheritance. He begins to court Catherine. Dr. Sloper suspects from the outset that he is a fortune hunter. He questions him and later arranges to meet Morris' widowed sister. He finds out Morris spent the entire family inheritance and never helped his sister and her three children. He warns Catherine and takes her to Paris hoping she will forget Morris. On their return Dr. Sloper becomes ill. He loses his temper when Catherine still insists on marrying Morris and inadvertently makes several unkind comments. He tells Catherine that she is plain and Morris is only after her money, and if she insists on marrying him she will be cut off from her inheritance. Angered, Catherine arranges to elope with Morris. Morris, having learned of her possible disinheritance, does not show up. Shortly thereafter Dr. Sloper dies and Catherine inherits everything. Morris now calls on her apologizing for his behavior and again professes his love. She asks him to come back that night to elope. Morris shows up this time. She, however, bolts the door leaving him to pound and entreat.

The Heiress is based on the 1881 novel *Washington Square* by Henry James. It is the best screen adaptation of a Henry James work. With the exception of Montgomery Clift, of whom a better performance would be expected, Wyler extracted superb efforts from the other two leads. It is by far the best role and best performance by Olivia de Havilland. She changes from a sweet docile girl into a cold decisive woman. She will be a spinster, but she will be independent with her integrity intact. When her father repeats that Townsend does not love her, she changes from a tongue-tied dull-witted girl answering her father, "I lived with you for twenty years and you didn't love me." Richardson as the magisterial father

gives one of his very best screen performances. He may unconsciously resent the loss of his wife as a result of Catherine's birth,
but he is genuinely concerned about his daughter's future and
knows Morris is rotten. Miriam Hopkins also has one of her best
roles. As a woman she instinctively feels it is better for Catherine
to marry a rogue than to spend a lifetime in solitude. Wyler had
wanted Greg Toland, who had been the cinematographer on three
good Wyler films: *Wuthering Heights* (1939), *The Little Foxes* (1941)
and *The Best Years of Our Lives* (1946). Paramount assigned Leo
Tover. *The Heiress* would have been a better film with Toland. It
was nominated for Academy Awards in several categories, including best picture, and won awards for de Havilland as best actress
and best score by Aaron Copland. Leonard Bernstein, in conversation, when complimented for his score for *On the Waterfront*
(1954), modestly said that the best film score ever was Copland's
for *The Heiress*.

Henry V

1945. 137 min. color. British. **Prod.** Laurence Olivier; **Dir.** Laurence Olivier, Reginald
Beck; **Scr.** Alan Dent, Laurence Olivier (based on the play by William Shakespeare); **Cin.**
Robert Krasker; **Ed.** Reginald Beck; **Art D.** Paul Sheriff; **Mus.** William Walton; **Cast:** Lau-
rence Olivier, Robert Newton, Leslie Banks, Renee Asherson, Leo Genn, Ernest Thesiger,
Felix Aylmer, Esmond Knight, Ralph Truman, Harcourt Williams.

Henry V is sometimes played as a king goaded into war with
France by the Archbishop of Canterbury. This Henry is also bent
on overcoming his notoriety as an unruly young man during the
reign of his father Henry IV and proving himself worthy of the
crown. He does, in fact, consolidate his power at home and prove
himself a worthy king. At other times Henry V is played as a born
leader who inspires men by his eloquence. This Henry is a man of
destiny who fights for the glory of God and England. When filming was to begin Olivier sought the advice of the great actor
Charles Laughton, who had played Henry VIII in a 1933 film, as
to how he should play Henry V. Laughton unhesitatingly and
unequivocally answered, "Be England." It was an inspired piece of

advice as Britain was in the midst of one of the most difficult periods of World War II. The Germans had made the pilotless V-1 and V-2 rockets, which rained destruction on southern England. Furthermore, as the Allies were preparing for the invasion of mainland Europe, most likely through German-occupied Normandy, the victory of England at Agincourt, in Normandy, in 1411 by the twenty-eight-year-old King Henry made excellent propaganda. Olivier, therefore, played down the role of the church and the nobility and entirely eliminated the part of the plotters.

Olivier, not the best of directors, still fashioned a beautiful and rousing film. There are some memorable scenes. The film begins and ends with a performance of the play at the Globe Theatre in 1603. The chorus at the outset tells us to "piece out any imperfections with your thoughts." Then gradually the proscenium of the theater fades and the cinematic scenes begin.

There is an outstanding scene of the night before the great battle. Henry's army has been depleted after a number of bloody battles and it is now besieged at Agincourt. The French outnumber his forces by five to one. Henry moves incognito through his camp. He salutes an old warrior and moves on to a group of youngsters who are frightened and uncertain of their fate. They question the purpose of the war. Henry has resolved in his own mind the justice of his cause and imparts his confidence to the men. There are also the early-morning scenes on the day of battle, St. Crispin's Day, when everyone is preparing for the fray. Some are planting stakes in the ground as barriers against French horsemen; some are sharpening their swords, stretching their bows and checking the tips of their arrows; some are operating derricks to lift the knights onto their horses. The contrast with the leisurely pace of work at the French camp is striking. The heavily armored chevaliers polish their armor and raise their wine glasses in toasts. The overconfident French are certain the battle will be short. One charge and the English will be routed. The king of France is shown as senile, the dauphin arrogant and dismissive of the English. After Henry mounts his horse and gives his St. Crispin's Day speech—"We few, we happy few, we band of brothers"—the battle is joined. The English longbows decimate the French horsemen with a rain of arrows. The battle is won and Henry prays, "Not unto us, O Lord, not unto us but unto Thy name give glory."

Henry V is a jingoistic film, but the intensity of the patriotism is somewhat alleviated by Henry's romantic and humorous encounters with the demure French Princess Catherine. The scene of the maid giving Catherine an English lesson on the battlements is charming. The entire cast is excellent. Leo Genn as the sardonic constable of France is first rate. Robert Newton as Pistol overacts, as always, but gets away with it. Renee Asherson as Princess Catherine and Leslie Banks as the chorus are very good. But the film belongs to Olivier in this, his best Shakespeare film.

High Noon

1952. 84 min. b.w. U.S. **Prod.** Stanley Kramer; **Dir.** Fred Zinnemann; **Scr.** Carl Foreman (based on the story "The Tin Star" by John W. Cunningham); **Cin.** Floyd Crosby; **Ed.** Elmo Williams, Harry Gerstad; **Prod. D.** Rudolph Sternad; **Art D.** Ben Hayne. **Mus.** Dimitri Tiomkin; **Cast:** Gary Cooper, Thomas Mitchell, Lloyd Bridges, Katy Jurado, Grace Kelly, Otto Kruger, Lon Chaney, Jr., Harry Morgan, Lee Van Cleef, Sheb Wooley, Ian MacDonald, Bob Wilke.

High Noon is one of the two or three great Westerns in film history. Will Kane (Gary Cooper), a retiring marshal, is marrying Amy Fowler (Grace Kelly), a Quaker. After the ceremony, as they are about to leave, word arrives that Frank Miller (Ian MacDonald), a killer whom Kane had put behind bars, has been pardoned and is on his way back to town to settle the score with Kane. Three of Miller's gang, his brother (Sheb Wooley) and two gunmen (Bob Wilke and Lee Van Cleef), are already at the train station waiting for him to arrive on the noon train. Even though it will be a few days before the new marshal arrives, Kane's wife and everyone at the wedding urge him to leave. The couple drive away in a carriage, but a few minutes later he realizes the uselessness of his flight and turns back. He now attempts to enlist deputies but he is turned down by everyone. His young deputy, Harvey (Lloyd Bridges), harbors a grudge because the town eld-

ers didn't appoint him marshall and he thinks Kane may have had
something to do with it. Kane's old friend and mentor, Martin
Howe (Lon Chaney, Jr.), is bitter because after a lifetime as a lawman he has nothing to show for it and is crippled by arthritis.
William Fuller (Harry Morgan), an influential merchant, hides
and won't even see Kane. The judge who convicted Miller, Percy
Mettrick (Otto Kruger), is packing up his law books and running
away. As parting advice he warns Kane that he will be abandoned
by everyone and that he too should leave. Kane decides to go to
church where the town's more prosperous families have gathered
for service. Kane pleads his case and some men offer halfhearted
suggestions. The minister only offers platitudes. Kane's face shows
his mounting desperation and disappointment until Jonas Henderson (Thomas Mitchell), the town's leading merchant and
seemingly Kane's most ardent supporter, stands up. At first, he
appears to be saying that everyone owes a debt of gratitude to
Kane who tamed the town and made it safe to live in, but he ends
by saying that unless Kane leaves town, everyone will suffer
financial reverses. Having been abandoned by all the people he
had depended on, Kane is now alone. His isolation is reflected in
a very well done scene in which he goes to the livery stable and
stares at his horse, trying to decide whether to stay or go. His
deputy, who has followed him, asks, "Are you scared?" "I guess
so," Kane replies. The immature deputy knocks Kane unconscious and puts him on the horse, thinking he would then be in
charge. But Kane revives and finally knocks out the deputy. This
encounter dispels all his doubts. He will remain and meet his fate.
Kane goes back to his office and prepares to write his will, but in
the end tears up what he has written. In perhaps the best scene of
the movie, Zinnemann cuts to a close-up of the face of each of
the townspeople who has deserted Kane. After a few seconds we
see the clock at noon and hear the train whistle.

The casting of Cooper was inspired. At fifty-one, with his face
seasoned by time, he was ideal for the part. Cooper was always at
his most effective when he had a minimum of dialogue. In *High
Noon* he says little, perhaps twenty-five lines, but he carries the story
with his body movements, facial expressions and mannerisms. He

has been deeply hurt by his friends, and his pain is clearly evident on his face. It has been said that Cooper was in fact in physical pain, suffering from a bleeding ulcer during the filming. There is also fine acting by Mitchell, Chaney and Kruger. The only uneven performances are by Grace Kelly, Lloyd Bridges and Katy Jurado, who seems to be reciting her lines. The script by Carl Foreman and the much imitated score by Tiomkin are excellent. The theme song "Do Not Forsake Me, Oh My Darling," written by Ned Washington with music by Tiomkin, is interwoven with the action. However, the film really belongs to Zinnemann. There is not a frame wasted and the editing is superb. It is eighty-five minutes long, roughly the time span of the story itself.

When released, the film sparked a variety of reactions. One of the great writers on film, Robert Warshow, did not consider it a true Western because the bulk of the film dealt with social drama. Two other diametrically opposed but equally fallacious arguments came from the communist *Daily Worker,* which considered it anti-proleteriat because it glorified one person when collective action was called for, and from Howard Hawks and John Wayne, who argued that a sheriff would never beg for help, and who in turn responded with *Rio Bravo* (1959). *High Noon* is now generally accepted as one of the best films to come out of Hollywood.

How Green Was My Valley

1941. 118 min. b.w. U.S. **Prod.** Darryl F. Zanuck; **Dir.** John Ford; **Scr.** Philip Dunne (based on the novel by Richard Llewellyn); **Cin.** Arthur Miller; **Ed.** James B. Clark; **Art D.** Richard Day, Nathan Juran; **Mus.** Alfred Newman; **Cast:** Walter Pidgeon, Maureen O'Hara, Donald Crisp, Anna Lee, Roddy McDowall, John Loder, Sara Allgood, Barry Fitzgerald, Patric Knowles, Rhys Williams, Arthur Shields, Ann Todd.

Set at the beginning of the twentieth century in a small Welsh mining village, this is the story of the devastation of a family and a community. The focus is on the family of Gwillym Morgan (Donald Crisp), an authoritarian father of seven with a loving wife (Sara Allgood). Morgan and five of his sons work in the coal mine. There is peace and contentment in the valley until the

mine owner announces a wage reduction. The Morgan boys talk
to their father about forming a union. Morgan rejects the idea as
"socialist nonsense." Soon there is talk of a strike. The boys argue
with their father, but when he adamantly rejects the idea they
pack their belongings and move to a boarding house. The
youngest, ten-year-old Huw (Roddy McDowall), and his unmarried sister, Angharad (Maureen O'Hara), remain with their
parents. The strike continues into its sixth month and the villagers
become further divided. The village pastor, Mr. Gruffydd (Walter
Pidgeon), and Angharad fall in love, but he will not marry her
and subject her to a life of poverty. Angharad will eventually
marry the mine owner's son in a loveless match. The striking
miners lose their fight and go back to work at the lower wages.
Morgan and one of the sons are killed in mining disasters due to
neglect by the owner. Huw leaves school and goes to work in the
mine. The remaining older boys immigrate to America.

Through the fate of the Morgan family the film deals with the
human cost of industrialization, its ecological effects and the
insensitivity of the mine owners. *How Green Was My Valley* is a
tender film, but the characteristic sentimentality of John Ford is
controlled. There are several scenes that compare with the best of
Ford: a former boxer, now blind, teaching Huw to defend himself
against a school bully, and later the boxer himself getting revenge
on Huw's sadistic teacher. The best is when the mine owner
comes to the Morgan cottage to ask for Angharad's hand in marriage to his son. The scene is greatly enhanced by Donald Crisp's
quiet dignity.

The film was to have been made in Wales, but with the advent
of WWII Fox built an entire Welsh village and coal mine in the
San Fernando Valley and painted the rocks black to simulate a
mining community. The great cinematography of Arthur Miller
furnished the details which furthered the realism. To lend authenticity to the speech patterns of the cast, Ford brought over the
Welsh actor Rhys Williams to teach them the intonations and
inflections of the Welsh. Williams also played the role of Dibahn-
Doh, the blind prize fighter. All the actors are excellent, especially
Donald Crisp, Sara Allgood, and Walter Pigeon. The film won

Academy Awards for best picture, director, supporting actor (Donald Crisp), cinematography and art direction; and received some five other nominations.

Ikiru

To Live. 1952. 143 min. b.w. Japanese. **Prod.** Shojiro Motoki; **Dir.** Akira Kurosawa; **Scr.** Akira Kurosawa, Hideo Oguni, Shinobu Hashimoto; **Cin.** Asakazu Nakai; **Art D.** So Matsuyama; **Mus.** Fumio Hayasaka; **Cast:** Takashi Shimura, Nobuo Kaneko, Kyoko Seki, Miki Odagiri, Kamatari Fujiwara, Makoto Koburi.

The film begins most economically and concisely. We see an x-ray machine and hear a doctor tell a nurse offscreen that the patient has incurable colon cancer. The second scene has Kanji Watanabe (Takashi Shimura), a civil servant, being told of his cancer at the doctor's office. Watanabe is the head of a Tokyo municipality bureau. He has recently been given an additional department to run, the Citizens Committee. A group of women petitioning for a playground on the sight of a refuse dump have called on him. Watanabe, who does his job mechanically, tells the women to send their petition to the Public Works Department. The project must then be reviewed by the Sewage, Fire and Education Departments. It will then be sent on to the deputy mayor for approval. The deputy mayor will, in all likelihood, send it to Watanabe's Citizens Committee. Kurosawa, with a single camera shot, demonstrates Japan's tangled and hopeless bureaucracy. Watanabe is shown cleaning his desk with a discarded cover page of a 1930 report, which he had probably written in his first years on the job, titled "Improving Office Efficiency."

The film now deals with Watanabe's coping with the realization that he has no more than six months to live. His initial reaction is despair and self-pity. He has no one to talk to. His wife died some years ago, and he does not have a close relationship with his son and daughter-in-law. Watanabe decides to use his savings to pursue a hedonistic life in his remaining months. He goes to several of the hostess clubs and bars in Tokyo, which he soon realizes offer no solace. Next he attempts to establish a Platonic friendship with a young girl who works at his office. Both he and the girl, however, realize it is a fruitless relationship. He is now totally despondent. Then, on the brink of death, he finds his calling. The petition for the playground inevitably has been sent back to his Citizens Committee. The petitioning women now have come full circle. He pursues the project to help the children and beautify the ugly city. There are brief scenes showing what he has to confront. He fights the entrenched bureaucracy, the land speculators and their gangster henchmen.

The last third of the film starts with a wake for Watanabe attended by coworkers and his son, his only relative. The deputy mayor, in his brief talk, minimizes Watanabe's role in the playground project. He says Watanabe was a dying man with nothing else to do, so he pursued the building of the playground. He leaves and there is silence. As the wake continues and the guests have had some sake, tongues loosen and someone recounts the magnitude of what Watanabe was able to accomplish in the face of the forces arrayed against him. Slowly, the others begin to acknowledge Watanabe's feat. There is a flashback to the completed playground. Watanabe is alone in the park at night. He is sitting on a child's swing. As snow falls, he quietly and contentedly sings. One of the refrains is "there will be no tomorrow." The next day, a policeman finds Watanabe dead on the swing. The end of the movie is set at the municipal office. A new chief has taken over the Citizens Committee. We hear him say, "Send it back to the Public Works Department." An employee gets up to disagree but thinks better of it and sits down. We next see the playground full of mothers and children.

One of Kurosawa's great films, Ikiru is about an "everyman" trying to find some meaning to his life before it ends. There is a pronounced existentialist strain in the story: anguish and choice. It is a well-controlled film and depicts Japan in the aftermath of its devastating defeat in World War II: the frenzied nightlife of people trying to forget the war experience, and the attempt to reconstruct the city of Tokyo. We get a sense of the city's crowdedness, from its offices, streets and nightclubs. The most open space in the film is the playground. Acting honors go to Shimura, one of Kurosawa's favorite actors, and to Miki Odagiri as Toyo, the joyous young girl who briefly befriends Watanabe.

I Know Where I'm Going

1945. 91 min. b.w. British. **Prod.** Michael Powell, Emeric Pressburger; **Dir.** Michael Powell, Emeric Pressburger; **Scr.** Michael Powell, Emeric Pressburger; **Cin.** Erwin Hillier; **Ed.** John Seabourne; **Art D.** Alfred Junge; **Mus.** Allan Gray; **Cast:** Wendy Hiller, Roger Livesey, Finlay Currie, Pamela Brown, Nancy Price, John Laurie, George Carney, Petula Clark.

From an early age Joan Webster (Wendy Hiller) knew where she was going. At five she wrote to Santa Claus, "I want silk stockings." At eighteen she wanted to have dinner at the best restaurant in town even if only once a month. At twenty-five she invites her father (George Carney), a bank manager, to dinner at a very posh restaurant where the management is most deferential toward her. Her father tells her he shouldn't be seen there. People will think he is squandering the bank's money. She tells her father she is going to marry Sir Robert Bellinger, the industrial tycoon who owns Consolidated Chemical Industries and is one of the wealthiest men in England. She shows her father her sizable diamond engagement ring. She is going to meet him at the island of Kiloran in the Hebrides and is taking the sleeper train that very evening. Her father accompanies her to the train and the only thing he says is, "Bellinger must be as old as I am." Bellinger's men are there to send her off, make her comfortable and give her the itinerary. The song "I Know Where I'm Going" is the background music for the train journey. She reaches the small Isle of Mull, where she is to take the boat to Kiloran, but there is a fierce storm and crossing is impossible. She meets Torquil MacNeil (Roger Livesey), a former naval officer who also wants to get to the island. In fact, he is the lord and owner of the island, but needing money he has given a long lease to Bellinger.

Joan and Torquil both stay at a boarding house owned by Catriona Potts (Pamela Brown). Joan finds there will be no crossings for several days. Torquil takes her to an abandoned castle where there is a curse on the MacNeil family. Neither will enter it. He also takes her to a Scottish dance and we sense they are attracted to each other. She is still after fame and fortune, however, and before the storm abates she bribes a young inexperienced boatman to take her across to Kiloran. At the last minute Torquil jumps in the boat. The storm has created a deadly whirlpool and they are saved from drowning by Torquil's boatmanship. Back on shore Torquil chides her selfish underhandedness. Next day the sea is calm. Joan is going to the island and asks Torquil for a farewell kiss and they part going in opposite directions. She then turns around and follows Torquil to the castle. He tells her no member of his family has set foot in the castle for centuries. A MacNeil had been in love with a Killanin and they had gone to the castle with tragic results. The curse says that any MacNeil who sets foot in the castle will be chained to the person who enters with him. Joan follows Torquil in and the two will be chained together for life.

One of the simplest and most beautiful films. The direction of Michael Powell and the high-contrast photography of Erwin Hillier make it an enchanted fable. The scenes of the sea with the black mist and the tiny boat at the edge of the whirlpool are magnificently photographed. All of Powell and Pressburger's films are visually stunning. The script is excellent and the cast of Hiller, Livesey, Brown, and Finlay Currie, in a minor role, represents the cream of British filmdom.

Intolerance

1916. 178 min. b.w. Silent. U.S. **Prod.** D. W. Griffith; **Dir.** D. W. Griffith; **Scr.** D. W. Griffith; **Cin.** Billy Bitzer, Karl Brown; **Ed.** James E. Smith; **Mus.** to accompany film, Joseph Carl Breile; **Cast:** Lillian Gish, Robert Harron, Mae Marsh, Constance Talmadge, Bessie Love, Eugene Pallette, Miriam Cooper, Alfred Paget, Elmo Lincoln, Walter Long, Seena Owen.

The success of *Birth of a Nation* (1915) made D. W. Griffith think of an even more ambitious film both in cinematic terms and story line. Also, stung by criticism that *Birth of a Nation* was racist, Griffith sought to demonstrate that he was free of any prejudice. The result was *Intolerance,* a film that was improvised as he went along without any prepared script. *Intolerance* is longer and more complex in construction than *Birth of a Nation. Birth of a Nation* told a story in a single country at a certain time in history. *Intolerance* has four separate and unrelated stories, all of which are cinematically interwoven. One is set in 538 B.C., another at the time of Christ, a third in sixteenth-century France, and the last in contemporary America. Griffith's great innovation is the convergence of all four strands in one epic, with an intertwined climax in the last reel.

The first story is the account of the conquest of Babylon and overthrow of Belshazzar by the armies of Cyrus, the king of Persia, through the treachery of Babylonian priests—the most imaginative of the four episodes. It has spectacular sets, battle scenes and erotic harem settings, all of which were much copied later, most especially by Cecil B. DeMille. The highlight is the "mountain girl" racing in her chariot to warn Belshazzar that he has been betrayed. The second story is about the persecution of Huguenots during the reign of Charles IX and the vengeful queen, Catherine de Medici. Its cinematically outstanding moment is the St. Bartholomew's Day massacre of Protestants with the heroine's fiancée struggling in crowded Paris streets to reach her home before the mob. The third story chronicles the conflict of Jesus with the Pharisees and his road to Calvary. The last has a girl speeding in a car to catch up to a train carrying the governor in order to get a pardon for her innocent husband who is about to be hanged. There is a great deal of intercutting among the four tales to create a unified depiction of social, political and religious injustice throughout history.

Intolerance was far in advance of its time in terms of cinematography, production design, editing and control of the massed crowd scenes. Two gifted future directors were assistant directors, Erich von Stroheim and W. S. Van Dyke. Griffith's talent, as with all great directors, lay in his attention to detail. The film, however, has its drawbacks. The title cards are verbose and pedantic, and the acting is primitive. More important, Griffith attempted to do too many things. The mixture of the social realism of the modern episode does not blend well with the escapist, pseudo-historical spectacular.

Kind Hearts and Coronets

1949. 104 min. b.w. British. **Prod.** Michael Balcon; **Dir.** Robert Hamer; **Scr.** Robert Hamer, John Dighton (based on a novel by Roy Horniman); **Cin.** Douglas Slocombe; **Ed.** Peter Tanner; **Art D.** William Kellner; **Mus.** Mozart; **Cast:** Dennis Price, Alec Guinness, Valerie Hobson, Joan Greenwood, Miles Malleson, Hugh Griffith, John Penrose.

Set at the turn of the twentieth century in the Edwardian era, Louis Mazzini (Dennis Price), now the tenth Duke of Chalfont, awaits execution for a murder he did not commit. He is to be hanged the next day. While in prison he has completed his memoirs from birth to dukedom. The prison governor and hangman are most deferential to their esteemed prisoner. In a biting comment on class distinction, the hangman (Miles Malleson), who has never hanged a duke before, is most interested to learn how to address him. He is relieved to find the correct form of address, "your grace," which he practices several times before being introduced.

The story unfolds with Louis Mazzini as a young man far down the line to the dukedom. He is an outcast because his mother, the sister of the ninth duke, married an Italian opera singer, Louis' father. To add further insult, at her death, permission to bury her in the family cemetery was denied. Louis vows revenge and decides to remove all obstacles to his ascent to the dukedom. He methodically goes about eliminating those senior to him. Some meanwhile die natural deaths. At the end only his uncle, the ninth duke, remains, whom he also dispatches. Things become complicated when he falls in love with Edith D'Ascoyne (Valerie Hobson), the widow of one of his victims, while conducting an affair with his childhood sweetheart, the married Sibella (Joan Greenwood). Sibella's husband, in dire financial straits, commits suicide. Sibella out of spite hides her husband's suicide note and Louis is arrested for the one murder he did not

commit. At the last minute Sibella turns up with the suicide note
and Louis is released. He does not realize that he has left his
memoirs behind wherein he has detailed the murders of the
D'Ascoyne family. We are left in suspense as the film ends. Will
Louis choose Sibella or Edith? Will the obsequious governor turn
over the manuscript to the authorities or give it back to him?

This black comedy was immensely popular and put Ealing Studios on the map. Although one of the most cynical movies ever
made it does not offend the viewer for two reasons: the D'As-
coynes are a most unsympathetic lot, and no violence is shown.
Alec Guinness played eight members of the D'Ascoyne family
and became established as a major actor. The acting by Dennis
Price, Joan Greenwood, Miles Malleson and Valerie Hobson is
outstanding. The film is more literary than pictorial. It is well
edited but it will be remembered more for Guinness and Price
and the superb screenplay, which has some of the wittiest lines in
filmdom. Some samples: "Tradition of the landed gentry was to
send the fool of the family to the clergy." The D'Ascoyne bishop
exudes over his stained-glass windows, "My west wing has all the
exuberance of Chaucer without happily the concomitant crudi-
ties of his period." Regarding Sibella it is said, "Pretty enough in
her suburban way." It is director Robert Hamer's best film, but he
will also be remembered for his great episode of "The Haunted
Mirror" in the film *Dead of Night* (1945).

La Femme Infidéle

The Unfaithful Wife. 1969. 98 min. color. French. **Prod.** Andre Genoves; **Dir.** Claude
Chabrol; **Scr.** Claude Chabrol; **Cin.** Jean Rabier; **Ed.** Jacques Gaillard; **Art D.** Guy Littaye;
Mus. Pierre Jansen; **Cast:** Stephane Audran, Michel Bouquet, Maurice Ronet, Serge
Bento, Michel Duchaussoy, Stephane Di Napoli.

Charles Desvallees (Michel Bouquet) is a successful insurance
broker who lives with his beautiful wife, Helene (Stephane
Audran), and ten-year-old son Michele in the affluent Paris suburb of Versailles. Suspecting his wife of infidelity he employs a

private detective who reports that she regularly visits one Victor Pegala (Maurice Ronet) at his apartment in Neuilly. He also provides a photograph of Pegala, who is apparently well off with no recognizable source of income, although he dabbles in writing. Charles visits the lover and they have a conversation about his wife. When he pretends that he and his wife lead separate lives, each with his and her own lover, Victor becomes elated at Charles' open mind and lifestyle and takes him on a tour of his apartment. In the bedroom Charles sees the cigarette lighter he had given to his wife some time ago for their third wedding anniversary. As Victor, feeling more relaxed, continues talking about his affair with Helene, the mild-mannered Charles can no longer control his passion and wounded pride. He picks up a statue and strikes Victor on the head. When he regains his senses he cleans the blood-stained carpet, wraps the corpse in a blanket and throws it in a pond some miles away. Having found her name in Victor's address book, two detectives call on Helene and question her. Later Helene finds a photograph of her lover in Charles' coat pocket. Realizing what may have happened, which impresses upon her the intensity of her husband's love for her, she destroys the photo. Further police enquiries connect Charles with the disappearance of Pegala and they come to his home to arrest him. As he is led away he says to Helene, "I love you madly." It had been a passionless marriage, but now Helene has acquired new respect and a new love for Charles.

Although we don't learn the outcome of Charles' trial, we presume he is convicted on some charge of murder. What is not ambiguous is that he has gained the respect and love of his wife. *La Femme Infidéle* is, in the end, a story of rekindled love with no moralizing or sentimentality. That is what makes it so powerful and affecting. The film is beautifully photographed, starting with the opening tracking shot of Charles and Helene's beautifully kept garden and grounds to the last scene of Helene's expression of longing. There is great emphasis on detail. Victor's apartment is studied. It is a very visual film with a minimum of dialogue. Its leisurely pace does not detract from the suspense, which is sustained throughout. The acting of the three principals is excellent.

Chabrol and Eric Rohmer had written a book on Hitchcock in 1957 and Hitchcock's influence is clearly apparent. This is Chabrol's best film and a minor masterpiece.

La Ronde

Circle of Love. 1950. 97 min. b.w. French. **Prod.** Sacha Gordine; **Dir.** Max Ophuls; **Scr.** Max Ophuls, Jacques Natanson (based on the play *Der Reigen* by Arthur Schnitzler); **Cin.** Christian Matras; **Ed.** Leonide Azar; **Art D.** Jean D'Eaubonne; **Mus.** Oscar Straus; **Cast:** Anton Walbrook, Serge Reggiani, Simone Signoret, Simone Simon, Daniel Gelin, Danielle Darrieux, Fernand Gravet, Odette Joyeux, Jean-Louis Barrault, Isa Miranda, Gerard Philipe.

A merry-go-round of desire and sex, lovers change partners until the carousel has come full circle. Set in Vienna toward the end of the nineteenth century, a young street walker (Simone Signoret) has a quickie under a bridge with a soldier (Serge Reggiani) who has to rush back to his barracks. The soldier next sleeps with a maid (Simone Simon). The maid initiates the virgin son of her employer (Daniel Gelin) who is later seduced by a worldly married woman (Danielle Darrieux) whose husband (Fernand Gravet) has a young shop girl as his mistress (Odette Joyeux) who has a mad crush on a poet (Jean-Louis Barrault) who is in love with a well-known actress (Isa Miranda). The actress, however, is after a dashing cavalry officer (Gerard Philipe) who brings the carousel full circle with a brief fling with the street walker of the first episode.

One of the best films of director Max Ophuls who returned to France after an absence of ten years. This was the first of four films he made in France before his untimely death in 1957. All four, as well as his 1948 *Letter from an Unknown Woman,* made in the U.S., deal with variations on the same theme of desire and illusions of love. As always in Ophuls' films there is great thought given to set detail, costumes and delicate touches of photography. Christian Matras photographed some scenes through a lens covered with sheer silk, giving the film a dreamlike quality. Ophuls linked the episodes with lyrical ease. The picture never stalls despite the ten separate stories. There are some fine pieces of acting, most notably by the veteran Anton Walbrook as the ringmaster and commentator. Walbrook was probably the only major actor to have been fluent in German, English and French, and acted in each with equal ease. He is a world of charm with a smile and a meaningful pause here and there. He says at the onset, "J'adore le passe." There are very good performances from the women: Signoret, Darrieux and Miranda. Among the men Reggiani and Gelin are good, but Barrault and Gravet are somewhat disappointing. Based on the Arthur Schnitzler play, which explored the follies of sex and transmittable diseases, the film stays away from the theme of venereal disease. Ophuls directed it more as a satire on the follies of desire. The U.S. censors, however, still alarmed by the casual sex in the film, delayed its release until 1954.

La Strada

The Road. 1954. 115 min. b.w. Italian. **Prod.** Carlo Ponti, Dino De Laurentis. **Dir.** Federico Fellini; **Scr.** Federico Fellini, Tullio Pinelli, Ennio Flaiano; **Cin.** Otello Martelli; **Ed.** Leo Catozzo, Lina Caterini; **Art D.** Mario Ravasco, E. Cervelli; **Mus**; Nino Rota; **Cast:** Anthony Quinn, Giulietta Masina, Richard Basehart, Aldo Silvani, Marcella Rovere.

Zampano (Anthony Quinn) is a traveling strongman whose act consists only of hooking a chain around his chest and with the expansion of his muscles breaking it open. We are never sure how strong he is and whether any tricks are involved. He makes a meager living by being thrown a few coins. To improve his act he wants a girl to bang a drum and toot a horn to announce his entrance. He buys a slow-witted girl, Gelsomina (Giulietta Masina), for a nominal sum from her indigent mother, who has too many children to feed. She accompanies him from village to village, becomes his mistress and slave. He abuses her and treats her as property, but Gelsomina, with her heart of gold, follows him blindly and enjoys her work. Soon Zampano and Gelsomina join a small circus and meet Il Mato, "The Fool" (Richard Basehart), a clown and high wire performer. The fool treats Gelsomina kindly and through him she discovers a whole new world. He tells her "everyone serves a purpose." She begins to believe that her purpose is to serve Zampano. Zampano intensely dislikes the clown from first sight. The stupid brute cannot understand the free-spirited and mirthful clown and resents his attention to Gelsomina. After being teased by the clown he goes after him with a knife. The police arrest him and he serves some time in jail. Gelsomina who has waited for him continues to be his dutiful slave. Zampano now is consumed with hatred for the clown and holds him responsible for his imprisonment. He leaves the circus and they take to the road again. Some time later they see the clown stranded on a deserted road. When he playfully taunts Zampano, the stupid strongman beats and kills him. Even Gelsomina has a limit to her endurance. She is horrified by the murder and for days she is unable to speak. Zampano has no further use for her. One day when she is sleeping he abandons her. She is taken in by nuns from a nearby convent. Some years later Zampano is by the seaside close to where he had abandoned Gelsomina. He hears a girl singing the song Gelsomina often sang. He is told by the singer that she learned the song from Gelsomina who is now dead. Zampano walks forlornly on the beach, apparently becoming aware of what he has lost.

Although the film is set in the aftermath of World War II and shows devastation and rampant poverty, a major theme in neorealist films, *La Strada* was the first major break with Italian neorealism. There is a poetic and dreamlike quality, especially in the scenes between Masina and Basehart. It is only when the clown is killed that the background scenery becomes harsh, with snow and ominous clouds. Fellini had established his name in Italy with *I Vitelloni* (1953). *La Strada* gave him an international reputation. Fellini had written the story with his wife, Masina, in mind but had difficulty finding backers. He resisted the casting of Silvana Mangano and Burt Lancaster as his backers demanded. He was able to get Basehart, who was married to the Italian actress Valentina Cortesa, and Anthony Quinn, who was making a film in Europe. Quinn's characterization of Zampano could have had more depth and we are not entirely prepared for the overly sentimental scene at the end. Basehart, an underrated actor who had given excellent performances in *He Walked By Night* (1948) and *Fourteen Hours* (1951), was an inspired choice. This was the second collaboration of Fellini and Nino Rota, and the score is one of Rota's best. But it is really Masina's outstanding performance that gives the picture its lyrical beauty.

The Last Command

1928. 88 min. b.w. Silent. U.S. **Prod.** Joseph Bachman; **Dir.** Joseph von Sternberg; **Scr.** John F. Goodrich, Herman J. Mankiewicz; **Cin.** Bert Glennon; **Art D.** Hans Dreier; **Mus.** Max Steiner; **Cast:** Emil Jannings, Evelyn Brent, William Powell.

Hollywood director Leo Andreyev (William Powell) is making a film on the Russian Revolution and needs a large number of extras. The casting director brings him photographs of suitable faces. He comes across a photograph which he immediately recognizes. It is a picture of Grand Duke General Sergius Alexander Dolgruki (Emil Jannings), who had been the head of the czar's army in 1917. They had both been in love with the same woman and Andreyev once had been imprisoned by the general. The former commander of the czar's army is now a pitiful figure who lives in a cheap rooming house under an assumed name, waiting for a call from the studios for an extra at $7.50 a day. He receives a call to report the next morning at six. There are more than fifty extras waiting, all much younger and more fit. He is singled out and given a general's uniform and is mocked by the other extras. He has kept a medal given to him by the late czar and pins it on his chest. The other extras think the old man has made up his story.

There is now a lengthy flashback to Russia at war in 1917. The Grand Duke is inspecting the army. The soldiers are given rotting food. He pays no attention and is haughty toward both officers and soldiers. Andreyev, a former director of the Kiev Theater, and Natalie (Evelyn Brent), a beautiful actress, are brought before him. They are there to entertain the troops, but in fact they are both revolutionaries and have come to the front to incite the soldiers to rebel. The Grand Duke tells them there is a war and the army does not need actors now. He orders Andreyev to be put into uniform. When Andreyev makes a disparaging remark he is imprisoned. Natalie is asked to have dinner with the Grand Duke. She accepts the invitation intending to shoot him, but changes her mind. He seduces her and the next day asks her to accompany him to the front on a special train. Mutineers and revolutionary mobs attack the train, kill the guards and beat the general senseless. Natalie saves him from further beatings by throwing him out of the train. Natalie herself is killed when the train is derailed. He escapes from Russia ill and palsied.

The movie he is to be in has a scene where he is to face the rebellious soldiers who are on the verge of desertion and order them to hold the line. He becomes his old self and performs magnificently. The strain of playing himself and the revival of old memories are too much for him. He collapses and dies. The assistant director says, "It is a shame. He was a great actor." Andreyev adds, "And a great man," and drapes him in a Russian flag.

The Last Command is one of the outstanding silent films. There is a common strain with Sternberg's later film *The Blue Angel* as they both deal with degradation and humiliation. Visually *The Last Command* is a marvel. Both films display well Sternberg's characteristic use of shadows and fog. Extremely well acted, it is enhanced by imaginative sets and stylish camera work. It is also rich in its depiction of Hollywood at the time. The idea for the film came from Ernst Lubitsch. He passed it to Sternberg who was better able to handle Emil Jannings, who gives a magnificent performance.

Last Year at Marienbad

L'Anneé Dernière à Marienbad. 1961. 94 min. b.w. French. **Prod.** Pierre Courau, Raymond Froment; **Dir.** Alain Resnais; **Scr.** Alain Robbe-Grillet; **Cin.** Sacha Vierny; **Ed.** Henri Colpi, Jasmine Chasney; **Art D.** Jacques Saulnier; **Mus.** Francis Seyrig; **Cast:** Delphine Seyrig, Giorgio Albertazzi, Sacha Pitoeff, Francoise Bertin.

The entire film takes place in a huge baroque hotel with endless corridors, reception rooms and manicured geometric gardens. A handsome man, "X" (Giorgio Albertazzi), who is the film's narrator, approaches a beautiful, stunningly dressed woman, "A" (Delphine Seyrig), and asks if she remembers him. He tells her they met a year ago at Fredericksbad and that she had promised to meet him again the following year and run away with him. "A" denies ever having been to Fredericksbad or having met "X" anywhere before. "X" says perhaps it was Marienbad and possibly even here at this hotel. "A" persists in denying they have ever met. "A" is with an older man, "M" (Sacha Pitoeff), who may be her escort or husband. "M" spends most of his time gambling, playing a no-win game with his opponents. "A" is gradually drawn to "X" but wonders what would happen if she went away with him. There are several imagined scenes; the hypothetical likelihood of a jealous and enraged "M" shooting "X," and other similarly bizarre situations. The film ends with "A" undecided as to what she may do. She asks for another year's delay. "A" promises they will meet next year and go away together.

The viewer is left to decide what the future holds. Perhaps "X" is dreaming or perhaps the hotel is an asylum where "X" and "A" are patients and "M" is a psychiatrist. As in Resnais' *Hiroshima Mon Amour* (1959) the film is about the complexity of thought and why and how we remember. Do we deliberately forget and when we remember, do we retrieve from our memory only what we want to remember? *Last Year at Marienbad* is an original film, influencing serious filmmakers over the years. It is beautifully photographed by Sacha Vierny with long tracking shots of the gardens and corridors. The sets designed by Jacques Saulnier are

imaginative and the details of the costumes are also splendid. The
acting is impersonal as the film demands. The actors make us
remember they are playing roles. The film has not dated as it was
a unique effort. Alain Resnais was the most original of the New
Wave directors and although he made only fifteen films in forty
years, several of them are outstanding.

Lawrence of Arabia

1962. 216 min. color. British. **Prod.** Sam Spiegel, David Lean; **Dir.** David Lean; **Scr.**
Robert Bolt, Michael Wilson (based on the book *The Seven Pillars of Wisdom* by T. E.
Lawrence); **Cin.** Freddie Young; **Ed.** Anne V. Coates; **Prod D.** John Box; **Art D.** John Stoll;
Mus. Maurice Jarre; **Cast:** Peter O'Toole, Alec Guinness, Anthony Quinn, Jack Hawkins,
Claude Rains, Anthony Quayle, Arthur Kennedy, Omar Sharif, José Ferrer.

The film begins with the death of Lawrence (Peter O'Toole) in
1935 in a motorcycle crash. After a memorial service at St. Paul's
Cathedral in London, a reporter briefly interviews Field Marshal
Allenby (Jack Hawkins), the wartime commander of British
forces in the Middle East. There is then a lengthy flashback that
covers Lawrence's life beginning in 1916 as an undisciplined lieutenant at British army headquarters in Cairo. He catches the eye
of Dryden (Claude Rains), a senior Foreign Office diplomat in
Egypt who heads the Arab Bureau. As someone conversant in
Arabic and Arab culture, Lawrence is sent to Arabia to make contact with Prince Faisal (Alec Guinness), who is leading the Arab
revolt against the Ottomans. On his way, his guide is shot and
killed at a water hole in the desert by Sharif Ali (Omar Sharif), a
key supporter of Prince Faisal. Lawrence learns that the guide
was killed merely because he was a member of another tribe that
did not have the right to use the well. With Sharif Ali and some
fifty of Faisal's men, Lawrence traverses the "uncrossable" Nefud
Desert. They join forces with the leaders of other tribes, most
notably with Auda Abu Taye (Anthony Quinn). They attack the
port of Aqaba and decimate the Turkish forces occupying the
port. Lawrence unites additional tribes and organizes a guerrilla
force that attacks Turkish columns. In these massacres, Lawrence

comes to realize that he enjoys killing. Later, on a reconnaissance mission to a Turkish-held town, he is captured, sodomized and tortured. His exploits are glorified by journalists, most notably the American Jackson Bentley (Arthur Kennedy), who is loosely modeled on Lowell Thomas. Lawrence is promoted to the rank of colonel. His last attempts to unify the Arabs fail. With the war over, he is sent home to England.

The film represents one of cinema's greatest achievements. There are scenes and images that are stunning for their composition, color and cinematography: a lighted match becomes the sun; a black dot on the desert horizon slowly becomes the figure of a man on a horse; Lawrence climbing on top of a captured train, flaunting his white tunic; his entry into the segregated officer's bar in Egypt with an Arab boy who has crossed the desert with him. It is one of the best-directed and best-edited films with a great cast and an exceptional musical score. A confusing script, however, introduces serious flaws in a supposedly historical and biographical film. There is not one mention of World War I, which had engulfed most of Europe and Ottoman Turkey. The film makes it appear as if Britain were merely standing on the sidelines, cheering the Arabs on to defeat the Turks. Field Marshall Allenby's role in the defeat of the Turks is only marginally mentioned and nothing is said of British colonial interests and aims in that part of the world. In reality, Britain divided up the Ottoman Empire and created countries, kings and rulers.

In his earlier, well-made film *Bridge on the River Kwai* (1957), Lean opted for a confusing ending. We never find out whether Colonel Nicolson was a hero or merely a fool. Similarly, the character of Lawrence is not explicitly defined. Was he just another agent of British colonialism? What were the sources of his attraction to the Arabs and the desert? O'Toole, a virtual unknown at the time, is excellent in the title role. Omar Sharif, Claude Rains and Jack Hawkins are also first rate. *Lawrence of Arabia* won Academy Awards for best picture, director, cinematography, editing, musical score, sound and art direction; and received nominations for best actor, supporting actor and screenplay. A 1989 version restored twenty minutes of the film cut by Lean and Sam Spiegel, the producer. Another twenty minutes cut by Spiegel and Columbia Studios appear to have been lost. Lean's greatest success was with Lawrence. He faltered with his last three films: *Doctor Zhivago* (1965), the embarrassing *Ryan's Daughter* (1970) and even his last film, *A Passage to India* (1984). While displaying much of Lean's talents, they do not match his earlier works.

Love Me Tonight

1932. 96 min. b.w. U.S. **Prod.** Rouben Mamoulian; **Dir.** Rouben Mamoulian; **Scr.** Samuel Hoffenstein, Waldemar Young, George Marion, Jr. (based on the play *Tailor in the Chateau* by Leopold Marchand and Paul Armont); **Cin.** Victor Milner; **Ed.** William Shea; **Art D.** Hans Dreier; **Mus.** Rogers and Hart; **Cast:** Maurice Chevalier, Jeanette Mac-Donald, Charlie Ruggles, Myrna Loy, C. Aubrey Smith, Charles Butterworth, Elizabeth Patterson, Ethel Griffies, Blanche Frederici.

In a virtuoso opening, way ahead of its time, director Rouben Mamoulian plays with sound and images. It is early morning and total silence. A Paris street is waking up to a chorus of sounds. The first is a wheelbarrow; then picks and shovels of workers repairing the street; the camera goes to a window and we hear a snore; an old lady sweeps leaves off the pavement; puffs of smoke rise from a chimney; a baby cries, an alarm clock rings; the knife grinder starts work as do two cobblers; a shutter goes up; a housewife beats her carpets. Soon the ensemble of noises creates a musical rhythm. The rest of the film is a romantic fairy tale. Maurice (Maurice Chevalier) is the best tailor in Paris. Vicomte Varez (Charlie Ruggles), a playboy, has ordered dozens of suits but continues to delay payment. Maurice has no choice but to travel to the Vicomte's ancestral chateau to collect. When he gets there, the Vicomte, afraid that his uncle the duke (C. Aubrey Smith) may cut his allowance, introduces Maurice not as a tailor but as a baron. He promises to pay Maurice in just a few days. Maurice wins over the entire family, including three elderly aunts and a young widowed princess (Jeanette MacDonald). Everyone says she should marry again, but there are no eligible men of high enough rank. Count de Savignac (Charles Butterworth), an old fool, is after her but he is rejected. Maurice begins to court her. When the Princess needs a riding habit, Maurice is more than happy to create one. She is surprised by his talent and he admits he is a tailor. She is deeply disappointed, but in a very spirited ending the two lovers come together.

Love Me Tonight is one of the most original and one of the very best musicals. There is innovative use of natural off-camera sound. The score by Rogers and Hart is outstanding and several of their best songs are in the film. "Isn't It Romantic" is introduced very imaginatively. First one of Maurice's happy customers sings a few bars. The tune is picked up by a taxi driver. A passenger in the cab, a composer, hears the driver and writes down the notes. While the composer is on a train, some soldiers pick it up and sing it during their maneuvers. Gypsies hear the song and one of them plays it on the violin. The princess hears the violin through an open window and sings it. Another song, "Mimi," sung by Maurice, is picked up by the old duke. Elizabeth Patterson, one of the elderly aunts, sings it, imitating Maurice. Mamoulian integrated music, movement and dance to develop the characters and form the plot narrative. Further examples are Myrna Loy playing a man-crazy, sex-starved relative singing "Mimi" in her suggestive transparent negligee, and the three aunts (who serve as the chorus in Greek drama) singing "The Son-of-a-Gun Is Nothing But a Tailor." What a surprise it is to hear C. Aubrey Smith, the dean of British actors in Hollywood, and the venerable Elizabeth Patterson sing. The one drawback is the casting of Jeanette MacDonald, who doesn't do justice to the witty script. It is Mamoulian's most charming film.

M

Morder. 1931. 99 min. b.w. German. **Prod.** Seymour Nebenzal; **Dir.** Fritz Lang; **Scr.** Fritz Lang, Thea Von Harbou, Paul Falkenberg, Adolph Jansen, Karl Vash (based on an article by Egon Jacobson); **Cin.** Fritz Arno Wagner, Gustav Rathje; **Ed.** Paul Falkenberg; **Art D.** Emil Hasler, Karl Vollbrecht. **Mus.** Edvard Grieg; **Cast:** Peter Lorre, Otto Wernicke, Gustaf Grundgens, Theo Lingen, Theodor Loos, Ellen Widmann, Inge Landgut.

The film is set in Berlin in 1931. We see a group of children playing in a schoolyard. The film cuts to a woman cooking lunch for her daughter who should be home soon. School is over and all the children leave in one direction. Only Elsie goes in an opposite direction. As she walks she bounces her ball on a wall with a wanted poster for a child murderer. Suddenly a man's shadow falls across the poster. The man buys Elsie a balloon from a blind street vendor. He whistles a few bars from Grieg's "Peer Gynt" and the film cuts to Elsie's ball rolling and her balloon floating away. So begins Fritz Lang's first sound film, about a child molester who kills little girls. Berlin is terror-stricken. Police have raided dozens of locations and made scores of arrests but cannot find the killer, who has sent them a letter: "I have not finished yet." The raids and arrests have upset the activities of petty criminals as well as organized crime, and word goes out from underworld leaders to catch the killer at any cost. Lang intercuts between police conferences and underworld meetings showing the underworld to be more resourceful. Underworld agents are finally able to capture the killer, who is identified by the blind balloon seller by his voice and whistling of the Grieg theme. There is a mock trial. The pathetic murderer pleads for his life and shouts that he is sick and cannot help himself. He cannot even remember what he has done until he sees his wanted posters. An appointed "defense attorney" pleads that even the head of the "tribunal" is wanted by the police for three murders, but this man is sick and they cannot kill a man who is not responsible for his actions. The mothers of the murdered children are among the "jurors" One of them speaks out and sways the kangaroo court to convict him. The murderer is about to be lynched when the police arrive and take him away.

M is based on the actual case of one Peter Kurten, who was arrested in 1930 for a series of murders around Düsseldorf. The film established the cinematic world of Fritz Lang—a world of criminals and psychologically wounded people with preordained fates. Lang, who was a pioneer of German expressionist films, tells the story in shadows and claustrophobic sets. He shows Berlin in its squalor and corruption during the Depression. The editing is extremely well done. The cross-cutting between the girl walking away from school, the mother waiting and then the newspaper boy shouting of another murder is very well integrated. The most telling scene is at the end of the film when the police enter the cellar in which the murderer is being tried. Everyone raises his hands with instinctive submission to authority, a foretelling of things to come in Nazi Germany. The film captures the last days of the Weimar Republic and its degeneration, which leads to the Nazi laws to eliminate social undesirables and misfits. Lang also shows mob mentality and hysteria. *M* is Lang's most powerful film. There is also excellent camera work and virtuoso acting by a young Peter Lorre.

The Magnificent Ambersons

1942. 88 min. b.w. U.S. **Prod.** Orson Welles; **Dir.** Orson Welles, Freddie Fleck, Robert Wise; **Scr.** Orson Welles (based on the novel by Booth Tarkington); **Cin.** Stanley Cortez, Russell Metty, Harry Wild; **Ed.** Robert Wise, Jack Moss, Mark Robson; **Art D.** Mark-Lee Kirk; **Mus.** Bernard Herrmann, Roy Webb, **Cast:** Joseph Cotton, Tim Holt, Dolores Costello, Anne Baxter, Agnes Moorehead, Ray Collins, Erskine Sanford, Richard Bennett, Donald Dillaway.

"The magnificence of the Ambersons began in 1873…The streetcar, too slow for us nowadays, because the faster we are carried the less time we have to spare. In those days they had time for everything." Orson Welles' voiceover sets the tone for this nostalgic saga of bygone days. It is set between the turn of the century and the years preceding World War I. Isabel Amberson (Dolores Costello), the daughter of a socially prominent land-rich family in

Indianapolis, had been courted by Eugene Morgan (Joseph Cotton), a struggling inventor and designer of automobiles, whom she loved. Her family had felt Morgan's bourgeois background made him an unsuitable suitor for an Amberson. She marries Wilbur Minafer (Donald Dillaway), the scion of another wealthy land-owning family, but it is not a happy marriage. She has one child, a spoiled boy, George (Tim Holt). Eugene meanwhile marries someone else. The story resumes some twenty years later with George's homecoming from college. There is a large and elaborate party for him, a beautifully photographed scene some fifteen minutes long in which we are introduced to all the key characters: George's beautiful mother Isabel, the elderly and frail Wilbur Minafer, Isabel's bitter unmarried sister Fanny Amberson (Agnes Moorehead), her brother Jack (Ray Collins), and her father Major Amberson (Richard Bennett). Among the guests are Isabel's old beau, Eugene Morgan, now a widower and successful manufacturer of automobiles, and his attractive daughter, Lucy (Anne Baxter). Shortly thereafter Wilbur Minafer dies, leaving Isabel with her son, father, sister and brother to live in the Amberson mansion. Eugene begins to court Isabel who has fallen in love with him again. George, attracted to Lucy, begins to court her. After his father's death, George, ever the spoiled boy, takes command of the family, and their fortunes begin to decline. He browbeats his mother, abuses his aunt Fanny, and generally ruins the lives of all those around him. When Eugene Morgan calls on Isabel, he drives him away. George really likes no one. In addition he believes Morgan is after their money to finance his automobile projects. "We are Ambersons, mother," he tells her. By closing the door on Morgan, he not only ruins his mother's life, but his egotism leads to the end of his courtship of Lucy. Eugene is the complete antithesis. He is gentle and kind, and never acts vindictively against George. Isabel meekly submits to her son's order not to see Eugene anymore. Isabel's father dies and she soon follows him. George, Aunt Fanny and Uncle Jack, the only survivors, are now impoverished. They have to make the painful adjustment of leaving the mansion, and George and Fanny take rooms in town. To make ends meet George takes on a "dangerous occupation" in a high-explosive munitions factory. As the townspeople had hoped from the very beginning, George finally has gotten his "comeuppance."

The Magnificent Ambersons is a story of the gradual decline and isolation of the landed upper class and the emergence of a new bourgeoisie; the conflict between the landed gentry and the industrial entrepreneurs. When filming finished, Welles went to Brazil to make *It's All True* (never completed), and the final editing of *The Magnificent Ambersons* was taken out of his hands. Forty-five minutes from the latter segments were arbitrarily eliminated. Welles always claimed they were "the whole heart of the picture." Welles had already cut the film from 148 minutes to 131. Studio head George Schafer instructed Robert Wise, the film editor, to shorten it to eighty-eight minutes, and he added a happy ending in which George and Lucy are reunited. Wise has been held responsible for having ruined the film by his editing. It was something he had to do as his job was at stake. More important, had he not done it, the picture would have faced a worse fate in the hands of RKO executives. Even with the cuts and the artificial ending, it is a remarkable film. Welles wrote an imaginative screenplay of Booth Tarkington's 1919 novel. George Minafer is not much different from the central characters of most of Welles' films. The egotistical George belongs to the scorpions of the world very much like Charles Foster Kane, Mr. Arkadin and Hank Quinlan. The cinematic style bears close resemblance to *Citizen Kane* (1941). The whole alphabet of cinematography introduced by Greg Toland in *Citizen Kane* is replicated by Stanley Cortez. The homecoming party for George is magnificently directed and photographed. The outing through the snow-covered road in Eugene's primitive automobile, everyone under blankets, laughing and singing "The Man Who Broke the Bank at Monte Carlo," is an outstanding achievement in sight and sound. Many soft-focus shots give the look of faded photographs. The device of overlapping dialogue introduced in *Citizen Kane* is carried further here. Excellent performances are given by Joseph Cotton and Agnes Moorehead of Welles' old Mercury Theater troupe.

The Maltese Falcon

1941. 100 min. b.w. U.S. **Prod.** Henry Blanke; **Dir.** John Huston; **Scr.** John Huston (based on the novel by Dashiell Hammett); **Cin.** Arthur Edeson; **Ed.** Thomas Richards; **Art D.** Robert Haas; **Mus.** Adolph Deutsch; **Cast:** Humphrey Bogart, Mary Astor, Peter Lorre, Sydney Greenstreet, Ward Bond, Gladys George, Barton MacLane, Elisha Cook, Jr., Jerome Cowan, Lee Patrick.

The film opens as an attractive sophisticated woman, Miss Wunderly (Mary Astor), calls on Sam Spade (Humphrey Bogart), a private investigator, at his office in San Francisco. She wants him to locate a man called Thursby who lured her sister to San Francisco from New York under false pretenses. She gives Spade an advance of two hundred dollars. Spade's partner, Miles Archer (Jerome Cowan), is killed by an unknown assailant while following the mysterious Thursby. Later that night Thursby himself is murdered. The police have no clues and suspect Spade of murdering Thursby in revenge for the killing of his partner. Next day Spade receives a call from Miss Wunderly, who now calls herself Miss Leblank. She confesses she made up the story about her sister because she was afraid Thursby might kill her. Spade says, "We didn't exactly believe your story, Miss, but we believed your two hundred dollars." Miss Leblank now also admits her real name is Brigid O'Shaughnessy. For an additional five hundred dollars Spade agrees to continue helping her. Then a Joel Cairo (Peter Lorre) calls on Spade and offers him five thousand dollars to recover what he vaguely describes as a certain object. Soon Spade discovers he is being followed by Wilmer (Elisha Cook, Jr.), a nondescript little hood whom Spade refers to as a "gunsel." He is led to the head of the ring, Kasper Gutman (Sydney Greenstreet), who offers ten thousand dollars if Spade can deliver a statue of a falcon encrusted with priceless jewels. The falcon had been a gift in 1539 from the crusading Knights of Malta as a tribute to King Charles V of Spain. The ship carrying the object had been attacked by pirates and nothing had been heard of the falcon until several centuries later. The first time Gutman learned of it was in 1923 and ever since has devoted his life to getting his hands on it. Now, some seventeen years later, he has finally located the falcon in Hong Kong and it is being shipped to San Francisco. The ending of the film is not dissimilar to John Huston's later films: *The Treasure of the Sierra Madre* (1948), *The Asphalt Jungle* (1950) and *The Man Who Would Be King* (1975).

Huston wrote the screenplay from the fine novel of Dashiell Hammett, who had been a private detective and knew the milieu he was writing about. This was Huston's directorial debut. Nevertheless, it has all the marks of a great filmmaker, starting with Huston's impeccable casting. As in his later *The Asphalt Jungle* (1950) some ten characters are well developed in a hundred-minute film without slowing the narrative drive. Sam Spade is basically a cynical man with many instincts of a gangster. Despite his audaciousness, he has the wit to stay just within the parameters of the law. He trusts no one, not his client, not the police, not even his partner. There is little sentiment in him. He changes the name of his agency from "Spade and Archer" to "Sam Spade" just a day after his partner is murdered. He also has a streak of sadism. The only person he respects and takes seriously is the Fat Man, Gutman. He finds him as clever and daring as himself. Gutman is literate and enjoys conversation. "I am a man who likes talking to men who like to talk." Joel Cairo is prissy and emotionally unstable. Wilmer is splendid with his oversized heavy coat. Miss O'Shaughnessy is also well drawn. She cannot stop lying until the very end, when circumstances force her to confess. The impeccable casting extends to the secondary actors: Gladys George as the widow of Miles Archer, and Lee Patrick as Effie, Spade's loyal and clever secretary. Acting honors go to Bogart who dominates every scene except those with Greenstreet, which are standoffs. The film is one of the forerunners of what later came to be known as "film noir."

The Man in the White Suit

1951. 84 min. b.w. British. **Prod.** Michael Balcon; **Dir.** Alexander Mackendrick; **Scr.** Roger MacDougall, John Dighton, Alexander MacKendrick (based on the play by Roger MacDougall); **Cin.** Douglas Slocombe; **Ed.** Bernard Gribble; **Art D.** Jim Morahan; **Mus.** Benjamin Frankel; **Cast:** Alec Guinness, Joan Greenwood, Cecil Parker, Michael Gough, Ernest Thesiger, Vida Hope.

The film opens with a voice-over narration by Alan Birnley (Cecil Parker), the owner of a large textile mill mentioning a recent turbulent period in the textile industry that has now fortunately passed. The narration leads to a long flashback. Birnley is being shown a small neighboring mill by its owner, Michael Corland (Michael Gough), his prospective son-in-law, who is eager for Birnley to invest in his mill. He is taken to the laboratory and notices a Rube Goldberg-type apparatus making odd gurgling noises. No one can explain its function and the man operating it is seen quietly slipping out. We later find out that he is Sidney Stratton (Alec Guinness), a trained chemist and inventor. Stratton is next seen working at Birnley's mill as a menial cleaner. When the mill takes delivery of a recently purchased electron microscope, Stratton accompanies the delivery man. He is the only one who has any idea of how the microscope works. The lab manager mistakes him for the manufacturer's representative and asks if he would stay a few weeks until his people learn to operate it. Stratton now has his chance to work in a larger and better-equipped lab. He again constructs the gurgling apparatus and begins his experiments. Nobody understands what he is doing but the staff allow him to proceed believing it is somehow related to the microscope. After weeks of experiments he is able to produce a chemical compound he has been after for most of his life. He is exultant and rushes to the office of the lab manager who thinks Stratton is hysterical and calls the factory nurse. He runs away and goes to Birnley's home. He gains entry and explains his discovery to Birnley's daughter Daphne (Joan Greenwood), who is intelligent enough to know what it means. Later, even Birnley is convinced that a revolutionary invention is in the making. All the necessary equipment and unlimited resources are placed at Stratton's disposal. After a series of mishaps in the lab he creates an indestructible white synthetic material that is dirt and stain repelling, never needing to be mended, washed or cleaned. Soon the owners of other large mills are alerted and seek the advice of the elder of the industry, Sir John Kierlaw (Ernest Thesiger), who warns the manufacturers that Stratton must be stopped at any price and his invention destroyed, otherwise there will be no need for anyone to buy more than one set of clothing in a lifetime. Sir John proposes to buy and destroy the formula. When Stratton refuses to sell they attempt to imprison him. Stratton manages to escape wearing a suit made of his new all-white fiber. The workers at the mill realize their jobs are at stake and join the management in pursuing him. As Stratton is running the suit begins to disintegrate and he is left only in his underwear. In a moving scene an old washer woman whose sole income is derived from washing dirty clothing admonishes him, "Why can't you [scientists] leave things alone?" In the last scene we see Stratton leaving the mill. The voice-over of Birnley concludes that "The news of Stratton's failure brought relief to the world." But Birnley may have been too hasty. As Stratton is walking away, we see him pause and a smile comes to his face.

Alec Guinness gives a superb performance and we see the range of his talent even early in his career. Cecil Parker, a very good actor of light comedy, and Joan Greenwood with her unique velvety voice are magnificent. The introduction of the ageless Ernest Thesiger as the textile tycoon was a clever choice. Seldom has sound played as important a part in heightening a comedy. The bubbling, gurgling and hiccupping of the chemicals passing through the elaborate apparatus will be remembered as one of the most original sounds in film. The literate script is rich in social and political issues including the conspiracy between management and labor to impede progress. The underrated Alexander MacKendrick, who is better known for his biting and acerbic *Sweet Smell of Success* (1957) and the dark comedy *The Ladykillers* (1955), shows he is equally competent in fashioning a bright comedy. *The Man in the White Suit* received an Oscar nomination for best original screenplay.

McCabe and Mrs. Miller

1971. 121 min. color. U.S. **Prod.** David Foster, Mitchell Brower; **Dir.** Robert Altman; **Scr.** Robert Altman, Brian McKay (based on the novel *McCabe* by Edmund Naughton); **Cin.** Vilmos Zsigmond; **Ed.** Lou Lombardo; **Prod. D.** Leon Ericksen; **Art D.** Philip Thomas, Albert J. Locatelli; **Mus.** Leonard Cohen; **Cast:** Warren Beatty, Julie Christie, Keith Carradine, Rene Auberjonois, John Schuk, William DeVane, Shelly Duvall, Bert Remsen.

At the very beginning of the twentieth century in the far northwest a small-time gambler, John McCabe (Warren Beatty), comes to a small settlement called Presbyterian Church. He is boastful and people are convinced he is an experienced gunfighter. Presbyterian Church is a miserable cold place, raining or snowing the whole time. The men are miners or lumberjacks and there are very few women. There is not much to do except drink and gamble or go with one of the three or four whores around. With his winnings from gambling McCabe buys three women with the idea of starting the first whorehouse in the community. He doesn't do very well until he meets Constance Miller (Julie Christie), a London prostitute who has worked in whorehouses in Seattle and still has contacts there. She becomes the senior whore as well as the madame of the new establishment. The business that had started in tents moves to a small building with several rooms and a bathhouse. There is no love affair between McCabe and Mrs. Miller. She is an opium addict who treasures her opium above all else. The whorehouse and the bath become the center of activity and the two are making money. They both want to make enough to move to San Francisco where the real action is. Soon the mine owners become interested in the thriving business and send representatives to buy the enterprise for $6,250. Despite Mrs. Miller's advice to take the offer seriously, McCabe rejects it and asks for $15,000. The mine owners get three hired guns against whom McCabe has no chance.

McCabe and Mrs. Miller is Robert Altman's most fully realized film. The story of the confrontation between the small man and big business is told in understated terms. It debunks the hero myth of countless Western movies. Vilmos Zsigmond's cinematography is magnificent. Leonard Cohen's mournful ballads sung throughout the film accentuate the desolate surroundings. Altman has gathered a very good supporting cast. As the leads, Julie Christie is fine but an actor older than Warren Beatty would have made a better McCabe.

M. Hulot's Holiday

Les Vacances de M. Hulot. 1953. 86 min. b.w. French. **Prod.** Jacques Tati, Fred Orain; **Dir.** Jacques Tati; **Scr.** Jacques Tati, Henri Marquet, Pierre Aubert, Jacques Lagrange; **Cin.** Jacques Mercanton, Jean Mousselle; **Ed.** Suzanne Baron, Charles Bretoneiche, Jacques Grassi; **Prod. D.** Henri Schmitt; **Art D.** R. Brian Court, Henri Schmitt; **Mus.** Alain Romans; **Cast:** Jacques Tati, Nathalie Pascaud, Michelle Rolla, Louis Perrault, Lucien Fregis, Valentine Camax, Raymond Carl.

The film has no conventional plot and no dialogue. It is a series of events, or mishaps, that are created without intent by the central character, M. Hulot. We know nothing of his background. All we know about him is that he is an unmarried, early-middle-aged Frenchman. He is an awkward character. He has an unusual bouncy walk, with his body tilted forward and his chin jutted out. Throughout the entire film he wears a hat and a light rain-coat and has an unlit pipe in his mouth. He is shy and timid, polite and deferential towards everyone, especially women. He is totally oblivious to the fact that his mere presence creates mishaps. Hulot is on a holiday in early July at a seaside resort in Brittany, northern France, where it is windy and without sun for the most part. The hotel hosts vacationers who take their holidays seriously and try too hard to relax and enjoy themselves. There is the businessman with his family who is always making telephone calls or sending telegrams. There is a former military man who thinks he is still leading his troops. There are the husband and bossy wife who are always the first in the dining room. We also have an attractive young woman (Nathalie Pascaud), who is amused by Hulot and his shy reticence. Then there are the over-worked manager of the hotel and the surly waiter. Neither have ever run into a guest like Hulot before. He leaves the main doors open so that gusts of wind wreak havoc inside. When he is not opening doors, he is playing jazz records on his gramophone as loud as he can, with no ill intent. One of the most amusing incidents is when, on a trip to a neighboring village in his old beat-up car, Hulot has a flat tire. While he is trying to replace it, the spare rolls down the road picking up fallen shrubbery and flowers. He chases it and catches up at the entrance to a cemetery where a funeral for a village notable is in progress. Those attending think he must be either a close relative or an important person to have come with so large a wreath and offer their condolences, which he bemusedly accepts. Hulot plays the most unorthodox and awkward tennis, but defeats a younger player with his ferocious and unreturable serve. Later, Hulot is accidentally locked in an unlit cabin that houses fireworks for the Bastille Day celebration. He lights a match and all the fireworks explode.

Hulot makes sounds but never says a word. His face and body express it all. From the very beginning of the film, when weary travelers are told by a garbled voice on a loudspeaker to go from one train platform to another, to the sound of the swinging doors of the hotel dining room that becomes the theme music at feeding time, Tati makes ingenious use of sound. Tati made five full-length films in twenty-five years plus three shorts and a TV film, *Parade* (1974). He always had difficulty getting financial backing. *M. Hulot's Holiday* is his best, followed by *Mon Oncle* (1958), and two others, *Playtime* (1968) and *Traffic* (1971). His first feature, *Jour de Fête* (1949), introduced a Hulot-like character. By *M. Hulot's Holiday*, his second film, the character of M. Hulot had taken full shape. In all five films Hulot is unambitious and, unlike Chaplin and Keaton, never sets out to get the girl or achieve anything. Tati said, "I invented him because I wanted to find a man who would be simple and honest and also a little bit out of control." Andre Bazin has said, "Hulot is all gracefulness…a scatterbrained angel."

Mon Oncle

My Uncle. 1958. 126 min. b.w. French. **Prod.** Jacques Tati; **Dir.** Jacques Tati; **Scr.** Jacques Tati, Jacques Lagrange, Jean L'Hote; **Cin.** Jean Bourgoin; **Ed.** Suzanne Baron; **Art D.** Henry Schmitt, Pierre Etaix; **Mus.** Alain Romans, Franck Barcellini; **Cast:** Jacques Tati, Jean-Pierre Zola, Adrienne Servantie, Alain Bercourt, Lucien Fregis.

Hulot (Jacques Tati) lives in a picturesque, charming working-class neighborhood. His sister, Madame Arpel (Adrienne Servantie), and her husband (Jean-Pierre Zola) and nine-year-old son Gerald (Alain Bercourt) live in an upscale neighborhood in an ultramodern house run by push-button gadgetry. M. Arpel owns a plastics factory. The Arpels decide to get Hulot a job in the company and a wife so he will settle down. Both attempts are disastrous failures. Hulot establishes a very warm relationship with Gerald who has an absentee father and a mother who is obsessed with cleaning and showing off her house. The Arpels are disapproving and they finally arrange for Hulot to be sent away as a representative of the Arpel Company somewhere in the provinces.

Mon Oncle is Tati's third feature film and second with the character of M. Hulot. It is Hulot's first battle with the modern world of technology and gadgetry, a subject Tati would pursue in his next three films. He is the same "scatterbrained angel" with the same raincoat, hat and umbrella. As in *M. Hulot's Holiday* (1953) there are many funny situations from which Hulot extricates himself with great difficulty. Despite his awkwardness he emerges as the only sane person in a modern antiseptic world. There are also amusing episodes involving his nephew and mischievous classmates after school hours. When cars are stuck in a traffic jam the boys simulate the sound and jolt of a car being bumped from behind, and get the two drivers involved in a fierce argument. Another game the boys play is to hide somewhere in the street and wait until some innocent passerby is very close to a lamppost, then one of the boys whistles loudly so the passerby turns his head and collides with the post. There is a street sweeper who never works, just engages any passerby in lengthy heated discussion. There is the man who is on the street every morning ostensibly to walk his dog. Instead he heads to the local bar for a few stiff drinks and returns home drunk. The contrast between the lively neighborhood of Hulot and the hygienic, automated Arpels household is beautifully contrasted. There is no dialogue but a very creative use of sound in the Arpel house and a background of accordion music in Hulot's neighborhood. There are a couple of scenes that are too long: Hulot's first venture in the Arpel offices and the party at his sister's house. Tati, as always, was faced with raising money, and *Mon Oncle* took two years to be completed. Coming after *M. Hulot's Holiday*, it established Tati as one of the great film comedians.

My Darling Clementine

1946. 97 min. b.w. U.S. **Prod.** Samuel G. Engel; **Dir.** John Ford; **Scr.** Samuel G. Engel, Winston Miller (based on a story by Sam Hellman from the novel *Wyatt Earp, Frontier Marshall* by Stuart N. Lake); **Cin.** Joseph MacDonald; **Ed.** Dorothy Spencer; **Art D.** James Basevi, Lyle Wheeler; **Mus.** Cyril J. Mockridge, David Buttolph; **Cast:** Henry Fonda, Linda Darnell, Victor Mature, Walter Brennan, Cathy Downs, Tim Holt, Ward Bond, Alan Mowbray, John Ireland, Jane Darwell, Grant Withers, Don Garner, Roy Roberts.

On their way to California in 1882 to sell their herd of cattle the four Earp brothers, Wyatt (Henry Fonda), Morgan (Ward Bond), Virgil (Tim Holt) and James (Dan Garner) have driven their recently purchased herd from Mexico to the outskirts of Tombstone, Arizona. They run into old man Clanton (Walter Brennan) who offers to buy their cattle for a song. Wyatt rejects the offer and heads to town with two of his brothers, leaving the youngest to guard the herd. In Tombstone Wyatt disarms a rowdy drunken Indian who is shooting up the town. The grateful townspeople offer him the job of sheriff but he declines. Returning to camp he finds his young brother murdered and the cattle stolen. He returns to Tombstone and accepts the job with his two brothers as deputies. Wyatt meets and strikes up a friendship with Doc Holliday (Victor Mature). Despite a rocky beginning they acquire mutual respect. Wyatt also meets the former fiancée of Holliday, Clementine (Cathy Downs), who has come all the way from the East but is again rejected by Holliday. Later another of Wyatt's brothers is murdered by the Clantons, which leads to the famous shootout at OK Corral.

None of the characters are fully developed. The dialogue is frugal, but the film is developed visually. There is a simple plot as Wyatt Earp the legendary ex-marshal of Dodge City tames another lawless town, Tombstone. The story is not much different from some ten or twelve films made about the exploits of the famous marshal. Here it is the orchestration of a series of incidents so lovingly put together by John Ford that elevates the film to the status of a near masterpiece. There is a lyrical nostalgia about the American past in almost all of his Westerns. This is the most poetic of Ford's films and there are scenes that speak volumes. There is the scene of the drunken touring Shakespearean actor (Alan Mowbray) who is harassed and prevented from performing by the neanderthal Clantons. At the urging and protection of Holliday and Wyatt he recites the best-known Hamlet soliloquy that in his drunken stupor he cannot continue. Doc Holliday movingly completes it, "To die, to sleep no more." Then there is the scene of the operation by Holliday to remove a bullet from Linda Darnell, his mistress, shot by one of Clanton's sons. Both these scenes are lighted by a kerosene lamp. And the classic scene of Wyatt and Clementine at the site of the yet to be built church where we see him awkwardly dance with her. Wyatt has fallen in love with Clementine but won't tell his brothers nor admit it to himself. We learn of his love in a short conversation with the local bartender. Wyatt asks him, "Ever been in love?" "No," he replies, "I've been a bartender all my life."

In *The Grapes of Wrath* (1940) and in this film, Fonda established himself as one of the great motion picture actors. The surprise is the fine acting by Victor Mature. He is perfect as the tormented, doomed, tubercular Doc Holliday. As in a later film, Henry Hathaway's *Kiss of Death* (1947), Mature demonstrated that under a competent director he could give a compelling performance. Walter Brennan played a part unlike most of the roles in his long career, as the autocratic, vicious and cold-blooded head of the Clanton clan. As in most Ford films there is no sustained musical score but variations on Western folk songs, and here we have the ballad "My Darling Clementine." There is a lyrical beauty to this film unmatched in any of Ford's others.

Napoleon

1927. 235 min. b.w. Silent. **Dir.** Abel Gance; **Scr.** Abel Gance; **Cin.** Jules Kruger, Leonce-Henry Burel; **Ed.** Abel Gance, Marguerite Beauge, Henriette Pinson; **Mus.** Special score composed by Arthur Honegger to accompany film; **Cast:** Albert Dieudonné, Antonin Artaud, Pierre Batcheff, Wladimir Roudenko, Annabella, Armand Bernard, Alexander Koubitsky, Gina Manés, Edmond Van Daële, Abel Gance.

This cinematic epic follows Napoleon from the age of twelve in 1781 to the Italian campaign to drive out the Austrians in 1797. The film opens with Napoleon as a student at the military school of Brienne. A number boys are in the midst of a huge snowball fight. Napoleon and his team are defending a snow fort against heavy odds. Napoleon stays calm and directs his team to hold back until the invading boys are at the very edge of the fort. He then orders massive volleys of snowballs and the invaders are driven back. For the first time Napoleon smiles. He is a lonely boy and his only companion is his pet eagle. In revenge the defeated boys release the eagle. Years later in 1790, Napoleon has completed his schooling and is visiting Paris as an officer. The revolution has begun. Danton, Robespierre and Marat are the leaders. Napoleon attends a revolutionary assembly where a young officer brings a recently composed song, "La Marseillaise," which will be the anthem of the Republic. In a stirring scene, he joins in the singing. The revolutionary fervor has inspired Napoleon. He goes back to Corsica to bring it to the side of the revolution. He fails, and in danger of his life he escapes in a small boat using the tricolor of the Republic as the sail. Amidst a fierce storm he reaches mainland France. In one of the great scenes in movie history, the storm at sea is juxtaposed with the political turmoil in Paris where the revolution reaches its frenzied heights. The revolution has begun to devour its own children.

As commander of a contingent of revolutionary troops, Napoleon distinguishes himself by defeating British forces that had laid siege to Toulon. He returns to Paris, which is in the grip of terror. Marat has been stabbed to death by Charlotte Corday, and a Committee of Public Safety has been established by Robespierre, Saint-Just and Couthon. Hundreds of people are guillotined every day. Napoleon himself is imprisoned for a short time. Danton is beheaded. However, by the summer of 1794, Robespierre and Saint-Just are deposed and guillotined and the Reign of Terror ends. Napoleon takes command of the army of the Republic, defeats the royalists and foreign armies that had attacked France from several directions, and the Republic is saved. Next Napoleon is planning to invade Italy and drive out the Austrian forces. The film ends when we see the eagle hover over Napoleon's army and we know it will be victorious.

This was Gance's only great film and was technically far ahead of its time. He experimented with split screens, triptych screens, handheld cameras (one camera was strapped to a horse's back), superimposed images, color tinting, and some daring montages. There are several scenes in which he cuts from a long shot to a close-up. Many sets and scenes were modeled on the paintings of David and Delacroix. The prints cut by Gance were mutilated by various distributors and exhibitors. Kevin Brownlaw, the film historian and director, spent years assembling a 270-minute version from Gance's original 360 minutes. Francis Ford Coppola was instrumental in having it exhibited in the U.S. in 1981. The film is far from perfect. The acting generally, and especially Napoleon played by Albert Dieudonné, is wooden. Gance's own portrayal of Saint-Just is overdone. It is purely visual storytelling: basically a hero-worship saga told in lyrical cinematic language. Napoleon clearly was a military genius. Gance gives him other dimensions, elevating him to a man of destiny.

A Night at the Opera

1935. 92 min. b.w. U.S. **Prod.** Irving Thalberg; **Dir.** Sam Wood; **Scr.** George S. Kaufman, Morrie Ryskind, Al Boasberg, Bert Kalmar, Harry Ruby (based on a story by James Kevin McGuinness); **Cin.** Merritt Gerstad; **Ed.** William Le Vanway; **Art D.** Cedric Gibbons, Ben Carre; **Mus.** Herbert Stothart; **Cast:** Groucho, Harpo and Chico Marx, Kitty Carlisle, Alan Jones, Margaret Dumont, Sig Rumann, Walter Woolf King.

Otis B. Driftwood (Groucho Marx) is a hustler trying to con wealthy Mrs. Claypool (Margaret Dumont), who has cultural pretensions, into investing in an opera company. Herman Gottlieb (Sig Rumann), an impresario, is also after Mrs. Claypool's money. There is controversy over the lead singers. Gottlieb wants a pompous Italian tenor. Groucho and his allies, Chico and Harpo, want to help two attractive aspiring young singers (Kitty Carlisle and Alan Jones). The film becomes an unceasing attack on grand opera and high society. There are three or four very funny scenes that are among the best of the Marx brothers. There is a five-minute scene in Groucho's particularly small ship's cabin. It eventually accommodates Groucho, three hungry stowaways, Chico, Harpo and Alan Jones, two chamber maids, an engineer and his assistant who have come to turn off the heat, a manicurist, a girl looking for her aunt Minnie, one or two cleaning women, and two stewards with dinner trays. When Mrs. Claypool calls on Groucho and opens the door, the crowd explodes from the cabin. Another of these scenes involves contract negotiations between Graucho and Chico. They end up tearing up the whole contract because there is a sanity clause and everyone knows there is no "Sanity Clause." When the ship docks, the mayor of New York has arranged a ceremony at City Hall honoring three Russian aviators who have flown across the Atlantic. Chico, disguised as one of the aviators, responds to the mayor's greeting describing their flight: "The first time, we get halfway across when we run outta gasoline and we gotta go back. Then, we take twice as much gasoline. This time we just about to land, maybe three feet, when whadda ya think? We run outta gasoline again and we go back to getta more...(finally) we take the steamship."

The film ends in one of the best scenes with the three brothers demolishing the opening night presentation of *Il Trovatore*.

The Marx brothers were lured away from Paramount by MGM, which insisted that their comedy be interspersed with set pieces of music and dance. It worked well in *A Night at the Opera*, but from then on their movies lost the pace and spontaneity of their earlier work. The only blessing of the later films was that they were not burdened with the untalented presence of the fourth brother, Zeppo. Groucho is the central character in all Marx brothers films. He has the best lines and the best barbs and insults. Chico and Harpo have relatively smaller parts but they bring their own brand of comedy. Margaret Dumont is essential as the butt of all Groucho's insults. The Marx brothers made fourteen movies. *Duck Soup* is their very best, followed by *A Night at the Opera*.

The Night of the Hunter

1955. 93 min. b.w. U.S. **Prod.** Paul Gregory; **Dir.** Charles Laughton; **Scr.** James Agee (based on the novel by Davis Grubb); **Cin.** Stanley Cortez; **Ed.** Robert Golden; **Art D.** Hilyard Brown; **Mus.** Walter Schumann; **Cast:** Robert Mitchum, Shelley Winters, Lillian Gish, James Gleason, Evelyn Varden, Peter Graves, Billy Chapin, Sally Jane Bruce, Don Beddoe.

One of the most original and intriguing films, it is the first and only directorial effort of the great actor Charles Laughton. It opens with the angelic face of a smiling old lady against a starlit sky. It cuts to the rural South during the Great Depression, where the body of a woman is found, then cuts again to a preacher on horseback leisurely singing a hymn. Harry Powell (Robert Mitchum), a deranged preacher with the word "love" tattooed on the knuckles of his right hand and "hate" on the left, is a serial killer of women. While in jail on a different charge, his cellmate is one Ben Harper (Peter Graves), who has been condemned to death for killing a guard during a bank robbery. No money was found on Harper when he was arrested at his home shortly thereafter. Powell is certain that the stolen ten thousand dollars must have been hidden by Harper somewhere in his house or left with his wife. Harper is

6₂

...ted and Powell, after completing his sentence, tracks down ...rper's widow, Willa (Shelley Winters). When he offers her both marriage and salvation, the gullible Willa accepts. She has two children, John (Billy Chapin) and Pearl (Sally Jane Bruce). John knows that his father had hidden the stolen money in Pearl's doll and senses that the preacher has married his mother for the money. Powell soon murders Willa and goes after the children. But John and Pearl take the doll and flee to the countryside. Powell follows a distance behind them on horseback. The children are sheltered by Rachel Cooper (Lillian Gish), a spinster who has devoted her life to caring for homeless and orphaned children. She realizes John and Pearl's desperate plight and protects them. Powell traces the children to Rachel's house and threateningly insists that she hand them over. Rachel holds her own against Powell. She stays awake all night on her porch, rifle in hand, waiting for Powell to make his move. In an extraordinary scene, Powell, from the shadows, sings the hymn "Leaning on the Everlasting Arms." To show she is not afraid or intimidated, Rachel begins to sing with him in harmony. There is a showdown and the next day the police take the wounded Powell away.

The film is an allegory of the struggle between good and evil for the soul of innocent children. As a secondary theme, it also deals with the vigilante justice endemic to the rural South at the time. The couple who operate the local diner, once so taken with Powell that they had introduced him to Willa, are the first to rouse the townspeople into a frenzied mob intent on lynching the imprisoned Powell. The local hangman, who earlier had grown so weary of his profession he had decided to retire, now considers it a "privilege" to hang Powell. It is a dark film, which also has some of the most beautiful, lyrical scenes. In making this film, Charles Laughton used a variety of techniques of the Hollywood silent-era masters and of German expressionists. Laughton was fortunate to have the great cinematographer Stanley Cortez of *The Magnificent Ambersons* (1942) fame. The film reaches lyrical heights in the flight of the children downriver in a rowboat. They are watched from the banks by animals in close-up, with a starlit sky reflected in the river. The journey conveys similarities with the story of Moses in the bulrushes. Other symbols of innocence include the children reaching shore and sleeping in a stable. Laughton, himself one of the greatest actors of the twentieth century, gets a masterful performance from Mitchum. The inspired casting of the ageless Lillian Gish gives further weight to the film. The secondary cast, including the juveniles through whose eyes the story is told, are also very good. *The Night of the Hunter* was a financial disaster and Laughton was never given another chance to direct. Despite the directorial setback, Laughton continued acting in films, giving outstanding performances in *Advice and Consent* (1962) and *Witness for the Prosecution* (1957), and memorable stage readings of Shaw's *Don Juan in Hell* and Stephen Vincent Benét's *John Brown's Body*.

Ninotchka

1939. 110 min. b.w. U.S. **Prod.** Ernst Lubitsch; **Dir.** Ernst Lubitsch; **Scr.** Charles Brackett, Billy Wilder, Walter Reisch (based on a story by Melchior Lengyel); **Cin.** William Daniels; **Ed.** Gene Ruggiero; **Art D.** Cedric Gibbons, Randall Duell; **Mus.** Werner R. Heyman; **Cast:** Greta Garbo, Melvyn Douglas, Ina Claire, Sig Rumann, Felix Bressart, Alexander Granach, Bela Lugosi.

The film opens with the caption "Set in Paris in those days...when a Frenchman turned off the lights, it wasn't for an air raid." Three mid-level Soviet functionaries arrive in Paris: Ironoff (Sig Rumann), Buljanoff (Felix Bressart) and Kopalski (Alexander Granach). They carry in their suitcase jewels that had once belonged to Grand Duchess Swana (Ina Claire) but had been expropriated by the Soviet government in the aftermath of the revolution. Their task is to sell the jewels and buy farm machinery with the proceeds. They were to stay at the modest railroad hotel, but one look at the lobby of the elegant Hotel Clarence changes their minds and they book the royal suite. Grand Duchess Swana, who now lives in Paris, is informed and immediately assigns her lover, Count Leon (Melvyn Douglas), to keep ₒf the Soviet arrivals. Leon gets a court injunction that stops ₑ sale of the jewels and the court must now determine the question of legal ownership. In the meantime Leon entertains the three functionaries very lavishly and introduces them to wicked Parisian life. The Ministry of Trade in Moscow is alerted to the impasse in Paris and sends the steely, dedicated, beautiful young commissar Nina "Ninotchka" Yakushova (Garbo) to Paris to consummate the sale of the jewels. The playboy Leon is immediately struck by her and follows her all over the city. Their conversations are among the wittiest in movie annals. Ninotchka: "The last mass trials were a success. There are going to be fewer but better Russians." Or Leon, saying "I have been fascinated by your Five Year Plan for the last fifteen years."

In the meantime a valet at the hotel, at Swana's instructions, steals the jewels. Swana realizes Leon has fallen in love with Nina and offers a deal. If Nina were to take the next plane back to Moscow, the Soviets would be given back the jewels. Nina is also in love with Leon, but being a loyal Soviet citizen she leaves. On the strength of what Moscow regards as a successful job the three functionaries are sent to Istanbul to sell furs. Leon is informed and he too goes to Istanbul to tempt and corrupt the three in the hope that Nina again will be sent to save the day. This time they open a Russian restaurant. The trade commissar sends Nina to get them back. When Nina and Leon meet, he asks her to marry him. Now she accepts.

Although this is Garbo's best role it is really Ernst Lubitsch who made the film one of the most original comedies to come out of Hollywood. We see Lubitsch's skill in the camera work and his way with actors. Garbo had not played a twentieth-century woman since *Mata Hari* (1931) and *Grand Hotel* (1932). Although there are traces of the Garbo intensity, she plays here a straightforward, sensible woman. Melvyn Douglas is perfect. Garbo never had a more witty, charming and urbane lover in any of her films. Rumann and Bressart are excellent as always. The famed Lubitsch touch is apparent everywhere. In the scenes with the maids at the Paris hotel, we know what goes on behind the closed doors without being shown; Nina and Leon's first meeting on the streets of Paris at night; the love scenes at Leon's apartment and Ninotchka meeting Leon's butler, "Little father"; and their lunch at a workingman's restaurant. The script by Brackett, Wilder and Reisch is one of the best. Nevertheless, the film was not very popular. It was released in November 1939 when war had already broken out in Europe. Also, people were not used to seeing Garbo in a comedy. The film slows down in its last fifteen minutes and the sparkle evaporates slightly. It received Academy Award nominations for best picture, best actress, best original story by Melchior Lengyel, and best screenplay by Brackett, Wilder and Reisch.

North by Northwest

1959. 136 min. color. U.S. **Prod.** Alfred Hitchcock; **Dir.** Alfred Hitchcock; **Scr.** Ernest Lehman; **Cin.** Robert Burks; **Ed.** George Tomasini; **Prod. D.** Robert Boyle; **Art D.** William Horning, Merrill Pye; **Mus.** Bernard Herrmann; **Cast:** Cary Grant, Eva Marie Saint, James Mason, Leo. G. Carroll, Martin Landau, Jessie Royce Landis, Philip Ober.

Roger O. Thornhill (Cary Grant) is a successful advertising executive in New York City. He is a heavy drinker, twice divorced. He is glib, inconsiderate and selfish. His character is established in the very opening scenes of the movie. He is on his way to a lunch appointment, rushing for a taxi as his secretary runs beside him taking notes. He commandeers a taxi hailed by another couple by pretending his secretary is ill. Once inside, he justifies his action by telling her that he has done a good deed by making the couple "feel like good Samaritans." At the Plaza Hotel restaurant he appears to answer a page for someone else and is mistaken for a Mr. George Kaplan. He is threatened by two goons and is forcibly taken to a house in the suburbs. There he is questioned by a Mr. Phillip Vandamm (James Mason). Despite Thornhill's protestations, Vandamm is convinced he is George Kaplan, a U.S. intelligence agent. Vandamm and his goons decide to do away with him in a "drunk-driving accident." He is forced to gulp down nearly a bottle of bourbon and put in a car. This time his heavy drinking habit saves him. He manages to stay awake and keep the car on the road and is arrested by the police for drunk driving. No one at the police station believes his story. Even his mother Clara Thornhill (Jessie Royce Landis), knowing his history of drinking, does not believe him. He is released the next day on bail. Accompanied by his skeptical mother, he checks the house to which he was taken. The maid denies ever having seen him or heard of Vandamm. The house is owned by a Mr. Townsend who works at the United Nations. Next, they go back to the Plaza Hotel where they check Kaplan's room, but Kaplan had never been seen by anybody. On the way down in the elevator they run into the two goons who had tried to kill him. When Thornhill points them out to his mother she doesn't believe him. In one of the best scenes in the movie his mother turns to the two killers and says, "You gentlemen aren't really trying to kill my son, are you?" Everyone in the elevator laughs uproariously, the goons look confused and Thornhill looks on hopelessly. Next Thornhill goes to the U.N. building to see Mr. Townsend, who is killed by a knife thrown by one of Vandamm's goons and intended for Thornhill. Thornhill is now wanted for murder also. He eludes the police and escapes on a train headed west to Chicago. In the dining car he is seated at a table with an alluring woman, Eve Kendall (Eva Marie Saint). She befriends him and even hints at casual sex. He spends the night in her compartment and the next day she helps him leave the train undetected. He is puzzled. He knows she recognizes him from his pictures in all the papers. Why isn't she afraid of him? Hitchcock keeps us guessing. Thornhill has several more encounters with death, including one of the greatest chase scenes in movie history as he is attacked by a crop-dusting plane in the middle of nowhere. The last segment of the film takes place across the face of Mount Rushmore in South Dakota.

North by Northwest has the essence of all good Hitchcock films, and the "wrong man" theme of many. The fact that we never find out what and for whom Vandamm has stolen U.S. Government secrets is irrelevant. From the excellent opening credit scenes punctuated by Bernard Herrmann's captivating musical score, to the last phallic symbol of a train entering a dark tunnel the viewer's interest is sustained. The film resembles Notorious

(1946), a better film, in the sexual exploitation of women by U.S. intelligence agencies. In addition to this dark side, there is the fine humor of a witty script. The auction room scene, although lifted from *All Through the Night* (1942) in which Humphrey Bogart and William Demarest are the bidders, is well done. The crop-dusting plane chase is a masterpiece. The usual film site of an assassination would have been a dimly lit street corner. Here Hitchcock moves it to the open spaces of farmland alongside a country road on a bright and sunny afternoon. The Mount Rushmore scenes are implausible and forced, but they also work nonetheless.

The acting is more than satisfactory. Jessie Royce Landis steals every scene she is in, and Eva Marie Saint is a better actress than Hitchcock's other sexy cold blondes. James Mason and Martin Landau as the effeminate gunsel are perfect for their parts. This was Cary Grant's fourth and final film for Hitchcock. He was still dashing although he was the same age (fifty-four) as Jessie Royce Landis who plays his mother. The title of the film is from *Hamlet*, "I am but mad north by northwest."

Notorious

1946. 101 min. b.w. U.S. **Prod.** Alfred Hitchcock; **Dir.** Alfred Hitchcock; **Scr.** Ben Hecht; **Cin.** Ted Tetzlaff; **Ed.** Theron Warth; **Art D.** Albert S. D'Agostino; **Mus.** Roy Webb; **Cast:** Cary Grant, Ingrid Bergman, Claude Rains, Louis Calhern, Leopoldine Konstantin, Moroni Olsen, Reinhold Schunzel, Ivan Triesault, Alexis Minotis.

The film begins in Miami in 1946. A court sentences John Hubermann to twenty years for treason. His daughter, Alicia Hubermann (Ingrid Bergman), is first seen as a dissipated drunkard who has invited some equally decadent people to her bungalow. An uninvited guest is Devlin (Cary Grant), a hard-bitten cynical agent with a U.S. government agency. Devlin and his superiors know through secret recordings and taped conversations that Alicia hates the Nazis, strongly disapproves of her father and has remained loyal to the U.S. Devlin recruits her as an espionage agent. She reforms and stops drinking. They are ordered to Rio de Janeiro. In Rio, Devlin learns that Alicia's assignment is to

renew her acquaintance with Alexander Sebastian (Claude
Rains), a wealthy German who once had been an ardent admirer
of Alicia. Sebastian lives in an elegant mansion and often entertains a circle of former Nazi functionaries and scientists. Alicia's
job is to find out what the group is up to. Devlin, who is now
involved with Alicia, tells his boss, Prescott (Louis Calhern), that
she is new in her job and not equipped to handle such a delicate
mission. He is overruled, however, and it is soon arranged for Alicia to run into Sebastian, seemingly by chance. Sebastian, once
again taken by her, starts courting her. Alicia is soon invited to
dinner at the mansion to be formally introduced to Sebastian's
mother (Mme. Konstantin), an overpowering lady who dominates her son. Alicia reports on the guests and especially on their
preoccupation with some bottles of wine of a specific year. Over
the objections of his mother, Sebastian proposes marriage. Devlin
objects once again, but his superiors are delighted as Alicia would
not only have complete access to the house but she would be
apprised of all the goings-on. She marries Sebastian.

The Hitchcock "MacGuffin" in this movie borders on the
absurd. The Nazis in Brazil, a year after the total defeat and devastation of Germany, are shipping enriched uranium to Germany
in preparation for the next war. Hitchcock uses this ludicrous
plot for a cruel and sick tale of love. Alicia is made by her government bosses, and tacitly by the man she loves, to grant sexual
favors to and marry a Nazi to get information. Yet it is one of
Hitchcock's best films. He was under contract to David O.
Selznick who needed money for his next film, *Duel in the Sun*
(1946), and sold the Notorious project to RKO. Hitchcock was
freed from Selznick's interference and had complete control. He
was a very meticulous director who planned each shot totally, far
in advance. There are several scenes that equal anything Hitchcock has done. One is the elaborate reception given by Sebastian
and Alicia. The camera mounted on a high crane begins at the
top of a grand staircase showing the guests from above, then gradually pans down to the floor below, ending in an extreme
close-up of a key clutched in Alicia's hand. Having secured the

key to the wine cellar, we see Devlin and Alicia examining wine bottles. One of the bottles accidentally falls and breaks revealing its contents to be uranium ore. Sebastian and the butler, needing more champagne, unexpectedly come to the cellar. Hitchcock extracts every ounce of suspense from this short scene. An equally effective scene is Sebastian's confessing to his mother that his new wife is a spy. In an excellent close-up we see how the mother revels in the news. She has been vindicated for her earlier objections, but what is more important, she will now be in complete control of her son without interference. In a kissing scene between Alicia and Devlin that appears to last for an eternity, Hitchcock overcame the Hays office rule that touching lips cannot exceed four seconds by dividing the duration with tender whispers and movements of the heads. This technique, together with the excellent photography of Ted Tetzlaff, stretches the kiss to well over four minutes. The final scene in which Devlin saves Alicia from certain death and the large door of the house closes, is a very Hitchcock ending. *Notorious* is also a very well-acted film. Bergman, as the exploited girl who has accepted a humiliating assignment to atone for her father's treason, is very good. Her scenes of being slowly poisoned by her mother-in-law are among the best in her career. Grant's role is also one of his best. He loves the woman, yet his professional code forces him to have her marry someone else. As in *None But the Lonely Heart* (1944), this was one of the very few non-sympathetic roles Grant accepted.

One Flew Over the Cuckoo's Nest

1975. 133 min. color. U.S. **Prod.** Saul Zaentz, Michael Douglas; **Dir.** Milos Forman; **Scr.** Lawrence Hauben, Bo Goldman (based on the novel by Ken Kesey and the play by Dale Wasserman); **Cin.** Haskell Wexler, William A. Fraker, Bill Butler; **Ed.** Richard Chew, Lynzee Klingman, Sheldon Kahn; **Prod. D.** Paul Sylbert; **Art D.** Edwin O'Donovan; **Mus.** Jack Nitzsche, **Cast:** Jack Nicholson, Louise Fletcher, Brad Dourif, William Redfield, Michael Berryman, Peter Brocco, Scatman Crothers, Will Sampson, Christopher Lloyd, Danny DeVito.

Randle Patrick McMurphy (Jack Nicholson) is transferred from a prison farm to a mental asylum after serving two months of a six-month sentence for statutory rape. McMurphy also had four prior arrests for assault and battery. He had convincingly pretended to be "crazy" and in need of psychiatric help believing he would have an easier time at the asylum in the remaining four months of his prison term. What McMurphy had not counted on is Head Nurse Mildred Ratched (Louise Fletcher). She is a woman in her forties, an authoritarian although well-meaning person who believes in strict adherence to the asylum routine of taking tranquilizers, warm baths and group therapy sessions. McMurphy's fellow inmates, other than two or three who are seriously ill, appear to McMurphy to be "no crazier than the average asshole walking the streets." To escape the monotonous routine, McMurphy introduces three or four of the inmates to the game of blackjack with pornographically illustrated cards, and he organizes basketball games between inmates and guards. Nurse Ratched does not allow them to watch the World Series on television. McMurphy simulates the commentary on the game to the howling delight of the inmates. He takes a group of them fishing by hijacking a bus and then a boat. The price he pays for his disobedience and infractions is a session of shock treatment. Soon thereafter he goes a step too far. He arranges for two hookers to come to their dormitory by bribing the night watchman, Turkle (Scatman Crothers). Billy Bibbit (Brad Dourif), a patient whose problems stem from his relationship with a domineering mother, idolizes McMurphy. Billy has never had sex and McMurphy arranges for one of the hookers to whom Billy is attracted to initiate him. The next day Ratched finds the dormitory in shambles with most of the patients drunk and Billy in bed with the hooker. Nurse Ratched tells Billy she will tell his mother what had happened. Billy slashes his wrists and dies. McMurphy now cannot control his rage and tries to strangle Nurse Ratched, which spells his doom.

A difficult movie to have made and a tribute to director Forman. It is a comedy set in an insane asylum that turns into an unforgivable tragedy. On the surface, the film deals with the inadequacy of mental institutions that appear to rely on a regimen of pills and shock treatment irrespective of the nature of the patient's illness. The hospital staff, including the nurses and psychologists, are depicted as well meaning but inept, and they treat patients impersonally. Both Head Nurse Ratched and especially the repressed assistant nurse appear incapable of communicating with the patients. The film's power derives from the character of McMurphy, a rebel, and his struggle against suppression. It also raises questions as to who is "mad" and who is "sane." This is a rare film in which the entire cast is magnificent. Director Milos Forman has selected some of the most expressive faces. Nicholson, has his best role, which appears made for him and he plays the non-conformist character he had played before: Robert Dupea in *Five Easy Pieces* (1970) and Buddusky in *The Last Detail* (1973). Louise Fletcher as the enigmatic Nurse Ratched is excellent. The film won the top five Oscars: best picture, actor, actress, director and adapted screenplay, and received nominations in four other categories.

On the Waterfront

1954. 108 min. b.w. U.S. **Prod.** Sam Spiegel; **Dir.** Elia Kazan; **Scr.** Budd Schulberg; **Cin.** Boris Kaufman; **Ed.** Gene Milford; **Art D.** Richard Day; **Mus.** Leonard Bernstein; **Cast:** Marlon Brando, Karl Malden, Lee J. Cobb, Rod Steiger, Pat Henning, Eva Marie Saint, Leif Erickson, Tony Galento, Tami Mauriello.

The gangster boss of the dockworkers' union in New York City is Johnny Friendly (Lee J. Cobb). His number two man is "lawyer" Charley Malloy (Rod Steiger) who has had a year or two of college. Friendly's immediate entourage also includes petty hoods who run his loan shark operation, goons who force union members to kick back part of their wages, and hit men. Charley's brother, Terry (Marlon Brando), does errands for Johnny and in return is given handouts and the easy, less taxing jobs on the docks. Terry had been a professional boxer with promise, but in his most important match his brother had asked him to throw the fight. From then, it was all downhill for Terry. Now he is little more than a bum. His only love is the pigeons he keeps on the roof of his tenement building. Johnny Friendly tells Terry to ask one of the dockworkers who is holed up in his apartment to meet Terry on the roof. The worker shows up and two of Johnny's goons push him off to his death. Terry, in a state of shock, tells some of Johnny's men, "I thought they were going to lean on him a little." Later, Terry meets Edie (Eve Marie Saint), the murdered man's sister. Her innocence and simplicity heighten his sense of guilt and he begins to feel responsible for her brother's murder. She introduces him to Father Barry (Karl Malden), a crusading priest whose parish is near the docks. He tells Terry that Edie's brother was killed because he had been scheduled to appear before a crime commission investigating racketeering on the docks. He had been the only dockworker willing to defy Johnny and his henchmen. Father Barry convinces Terry to provide the crime commission with the information they are seeking; information that will put the dock racketeers in jail.

On the surface, *On the Waterfront* is about the exposure of corruption and racketeering on the New York docks. It is also the story of a simple man's redemption through the love of a woman and a dedicated priest. On another level, it is an intensely emotional and personal film for Elia Kazan, the director, and Budd Schulberg, the screenwriter, who used the film to justify their "naming names," informing on friends and colleagues before the House Un-American Activities Committee in 1951. When Terry agrees to testify against his bosses, he pleads, "Who am I ratting on?" In Terry's case it is racketeers; in Kazan and Schulberg's case, it was former communists and fellow travelers. What mars this extraordinary powerful film, however, is the attempt by Kazan and Schulberg to turn Terry into a Christ-like figure. The real power of the film stems from the acting of the entire cast and most especially Brando, who turns in a memorable performance. Kazan was an actor's director. He himself had been an actor in the early thirties in theater groups in and around New York, and in the mid-thirties he gave a number of unremarkable performances as gangsters in several Hollywood films. He got his first chance to direct a movie in 1945's *A Tree Grows in Brooklyn*. He returned to Broadway and his reputation as an actor's director was enhanced by the performances he extracted from Brando in *A Streetcar Named Desire* and Lee J. Cobb in *Death of a Salesman*.

The film is beautifully photographed. Boris Kaufman, in his first American film (he had photographed all of Jean Vigo's pictures before settling in the U.S. in 1942), gave it a grainy semidocumentary look. There are some scenes that will stand out in movie history. The most celebrated is the taxi scene in which Terry tells his brother, "I coulda had class. I coulda been a contender...instead of a bum...It was you Charley." Equally powerful is Terry's confession to Edie in the bar and later outside that he was unintentionally involved in the murder of her brother. The outdoor scene is filmed against the background of ships on the river. One cannot hear his words over the deafening sound of a ship's horn, but Brando always used his body to great effect. The musical score is also legendary. It was Leonard Bernstein's first venture in composing for the movies, and he received an Academy Award nomination. The film won eight Academy Awards including best actor, supporting actress, director, screenplay and cinematography. Lee J. Cobb, Karl Malden and Rod Steiger were nominees.

The Passion of Joan of Arc

Le Passion De Jeanne D'Arc. 1928. 77 min. b.w. Silent. French. **Dir.** Carl Theodor Dreyer; **Scr.** Carl Theodor Dreyer, Joseph Delteil; **Cin.** Rudolph Maté; **Ed.** Carl Dreyer; **Art D.** Hermann Warm, Jean Hugo; **Cast:** Renée Maria Falconetti, Eugene Sylvain, Maurice Schutz, Michel Simon, Antonin Artaud.

The film is set in Rouen, northern France, on 30 May 1431. Joan of Arc (Renée Maria Falconetti), a country girl of seventeen, having been inspired by heavenly visions and voices, had dressed as a boy and led French soldiers in lifting the siege of Orleans and defeating the English forces that had invaded France. Some six months later she was captured by the Burgundians, allies of the English in France. At this time all of France north of the Loire River was held by the English and Burgundians who also dominated the king and his court. The film begins with Joan's trial for witchcraft and heresy by an ecclesiastic court presided over by the Bishop of Cauchon (Eugene Sylvain). It has compressed the lengthy proceedings, which took about eighteen months, into one day in which Joan undergoes repeated sessions of interrogation. She is ridiculed and questioned for her claim that Saint Michael appeared to her and that she had taken inspiration from him. She then is questioned in her cell. Her interrogators tell her that she has insulted the church and must make a public apology. Joan's only answer is that she simply serves God and will only obey her voices. The next interrogation takes place in the torture chamber. She is subjected to mental torture and told she will be burned as a witch if she does not disavow her claims. Joan yields. She is condemned to life imprisonment and her head is shaved. Once alone, she realizes she has disobeyed her

voices and betrayed God. She recants her confession and is
burned at the stake in the town's marketplace. Her last word
before dying is "Jesus" and we see a flight of birds overhead. The
surrounding crowd begins to murmur that Joan is a saint. They
are beaten by the soldiers and a large number are massacred.

Dreyer based his film on the transcripts of the actual eighteen-
month trial. Dreyer's Joan, unlike George Bernard Shaw's *Saint
Joan,* is not concerned with nationalism or nationhood. Nor is
Dreyer concerned with the salvation that awaits Joan in heaven.
He simply shows us the suffering of a mortal being. Rudolph
Maté's camera employs a very effective use of close-ups to show
the travails of Joan. The entire cast performed without any
makeup, making the fleshy, corpulent clergy look more cruel and
corrupt while the Joan's suffering is accentuated. Dreyer had considered casting Lillian Gish but then found Falconetti, a young
French stage actress for whom this was a first and only screen
appearance. She proved ideal for the part. For the role of the
Bishop of Cauchon, he cast one of the leading actors of the
Comédie Francaise. The Archbishop of Paris demanded many
scenes be cut, which mutilated the film. It was a failure in France
and was not allowed to be shown in Britain for several years.

Paths of Glory

1957. 86 min. b.w. U.S. **Prod.** James B. Harris; **Dir.** Stanley Kubrick; **Scr.** Stanley
Kubrick, Calder Willingham, Jim Thompson (based on the novel by Humphrey Cobb);
Cin. George Krause; **Ed.** Eva Kroll; **Art D.** Ludwig Reiber; **Mus.** Gerald Fried; **Cast:** Kirk
Douglas, Ralph Meeker, Adolph Menjou, George Macready, Wayne Morris, Timothy
Carey, Richard Anderson, Joseph Turkel, Suzanne Christian.

It is 1916, the Western Front in World War I. After initial gains
by the German army in 1914 and 1915, the French army holds
and prevents any further advances. Both armies have dug in at
heavily fortified positions under ceaseless artillery barrage. Army
Corps Commander General Broulard (Adolph Menjou) has
decided to launch an all-out attack to dislodge the Germans from

an impregnable high ground. The orders go to General Mireau (George Macready), the division commander, and to an infantry regiment commanded by Colonel Dax (Kirk Douglas) who is to head the assault and capture the enemy position in forty-eight hours. Dax's regiment has suffered heavy casualties and has been subjected to incessant artillery fire. He had hoped they would be relieved. The assault is a failure and the French are driven back to their trenches with further heavy casualties. Generals Broulard and Mireau now need scapegoats for the failure and order the court-martial of three men chosen at random to set an example. The incompetent and cowardly Lieutenant Roget (Wayne Morris) selects the three victims. One is a dying man, Private Arnaud (Joseph Turkel), suffering from a non-combat injury. The second is Private Ferol (Timothy Carey) who is considered a misfit. The third is Corporal Paris (Ralph Meeker), who is chosen solely because the lieutenant has a personal grudge against him. Colonel Dax is charged with the defense of the three. Despite his passionate defense, they are convicted of cowardice and executed. General Mireau is disgraced by his failure and relieved of his command. Broulard, totally unmoved by recent events, routinely offers Dax a promotion and the post of division commander and refers callously to the executions: "There are few things more stimulating than seeing someone else die." Dax calls Broulard a sadist and walks out. The film ends with a young German girl, a prisoner, forced to sing for a crowd of French soldiers in the mess hall. She sings a song of separation, longing and love, and the rowdy soldiers become silent and a few have tears in their eyes. Colonel Dax witnesses the event and his expression reveals his hope that there is still some humanity left in most of us.

The film is from a book by Humphrey Cobb that was partially based on an actual incident. In World War I a French general ordered a captain to fire at some of his men who would not move out of the trenches. The captain refused and the high command selected several men who, after a perfunctory court-martial, were executed. The whole incident was hushed up. The subsequent book and film were banned in France for many years. *Paths of Glory* is not an antiwar film like *All Quiet on the Western Front*

(1930). It is more an attack on the high brass, their conduct of war and their utter disregard for the soldiers who serve under them. The film deals with the incompetence of the commanders and their refusal to accept responsibility for their ill-advised actions and needless sacrifice of lives. It is Kirk Douglas' best acting, ably supported by Menjou and Macready. It is also one of Kubrick's finest films. His camera moves through the battle scenes with tracking shots of the squalor of the trenches contrasted with the luxury and magnificence of the officers' chateau, well out of range of enemy fire.

Persona

1966. 81 min. b.w. Swedish. **Prod.** Ingmar Bergman; **Dir.** Ingmar Bergman; **Scr.** Ingmar Bergman; **Cin.** Sven Nykvist; **Ed.** Ulla Ryghe; **Art D.** and **Prod. D.** Bibi Lindstrom; **Mus.** Lars-Johan Werle; **Cast:** Bibi Andersson, Liv Ullmann, Gunar Bjornstrand, Margareta Krook.

Actress Elizabeth Vogler (Liv Ullmann), after a performance of *Electra*, stops speaking. During a brief stay in a hospital, it is determined there is nothing wrong with her vocal chords. The psychiatrist sends her to her own seaside cottage to be looked after by an experienced nurse, Alma (Bibi Andersson). As Elizabeth continues her silence, Alma takes over and chats about herself and her background. Soon Alma reveals her most intimate experiences. She relates an unhappy love affair and her current engagement to a decent but uninteresting fellow. She also tells Elizabeth about a sexual encounter she and her girlfriend had with two young boys they met on a deserted beach. The experience gave her the greatest satisfaction of her life, but it had led to an abortion about which she still feels guilty. Elizabeth listens with sympathy but does not utter a word. As Alma pours her heart out we realize she too is a troubled person. We begin to feel and see that the two women resemble each other in many ways. Alma reads a letter Elizabeth has asked her to mail to her husband. She finds that Elizabeth considers her as lightheaded and ordinary. Alma becomes very angry and begins to abuse Elizabeth. There is shouting and displays of anger that eventually subside. Nevertheless, Alma takes a bus from the seaside cottage back to town.

Persona is one of Bergman's most difficult films. One of his perennial themes is accentuated—the difficulty of meaningful communication between human beings. The causes of Elizabeth's withdrawal and silence are not even hinted at. Could it be the horrors of the twentieth century? There is a scene of Elizabeth in the hospital watching TV news showing monks in Vietnam burning themselves. Could it be an unhappy marriage? Or is it simply that Elizabeth is preparing for her next role on stage. One of the best acted of Bergman's films, Ullmann handles a difficult role well and conveys everything with facial expressions and body movements. Bibi Andersson is also excellent. Using shadows, Bergman and Nykvist accentuate the resemblance between Elizabeth and Alma, and there is a highly original shot as their faces begin to merge.

Potemkin

(a.k.a. *Battleship Potemkin*) *Bronenosets Potyomkin*. 1925. 65 min. b.w. Silent. Russian. **Dir.** Sergei Eisenstein; **Scr.** Sergei Eisenstein; **Cin.** Edouard Tisse; **Cast:** Alexander Antonov, Vladimir Barsky, Grigori Alexandrov.

We see the czarist fleet anchored in the Black Sea and indications of unrest among the sailors of the cruiser, *Potemkin*. Their disquiet comes to a head when the meal of the day is a soup with rotten meat. The ship's doctor claims to see nothing wrong, although maggots are clearly all over the meat. The sailors refuse the soup, but the ship's captain orders them to eat. When some still refuse, the captain orders that they be hanged. The mutiny begins and some officers are thrown overboard. The sailors take over the ship, but in the struggle their leader is shot. His body is taken by a small boat to shore and placed on the pier. The people of Odessa come to pay their respects and soon cries of "Down with the tyrants" are heard. A contingent of mounted Cossacks appear and as they descend a large outdoor staircase they open fire shooting at everyone indiscriminately. In one of the greatest scenes in movie history, a woman with a baby carriage is killed. The carriage rolls down the steps, bouncing over dead bodies. After the massacre, other ships of the fleet converge around the *Potemkin,* whose sailors prepare to defend their ship. As the vessels draw closer we see their crews cheering. They have joined the rebellion.

After his first feature film, *Strike* (1924), Eisenstein was assigned to make a propaganda film on the twentieth anniversary of the 1905 mutiny by the sailors of the battleship *Potemkin* and the ensuing uprising by the people of Odessa. Eisenstein delivered the propaganda film but turned it into something much more. He re-created the events in a lean narrative using nonprofessionals for all of the parts and employing the most innovative photographic techniques. Eisenstein used over 1,400 separate shots in a mere sixty-five-minute film, repeating an image from different angles and in close-up. The masterful editing and cutting reflects Eisenstein's belief that rapid transition of visual images creates greater emotional impact. It is said that when Max Reinhardt, the great stage impresario and director, saw the film, he said, "I am willing to admit now for the first time that the stage will have to give way to cinema."

Pygmalion

1938. 95 min. b.w. British. **Prod.** Gabriel Pascal; **Dir.** Anthony Asquith, Leslie Howard; **Scr.** George Bernard Shaw, W. P. Lipscomb, Cecil Lewis, Ian Dalrymple, Anthony Asquith (based on the play by George Bernard Shaw); **Cin.** Harry Stradling; **Ed.** David Lean; **Art D.** Laurence Irving; **Mus.** Arthur Honegger; **Cast:** Leslie Howard, Wendy Hiller, Wilfrid Lawson, Marie Lohr, David Tree, Scott Sunderland, Jean Cadell, Esme Percy.

Professor Henry Higgins (Leslie Howard) spends time at Covent Garden studying and identifying various English accents. He meets Colonel Pickering (Scott Sunderland), a scholar of Sanskrit-based languages, who has just returned from India. The two bachelors soon form a friendship and Pickering accepts an invitation to stay with Higgins for the duration of his stay in

London. Higgins is approached by a flower girl, Eliza Doolittle (Wendy Hiller), urging him to buy some flowers in an atrocious cockney accent. As a lark, Higgins bets Pickering that he can transform and alter her accent within three months whereby not even an expert could guess her background. He then induces Eliza, whom he calls a "squashed cabbage leaf" and an "incarnate insult to the English language," to come to his house the next day. The inconsiderate, selfish Higgins works Eliza day and night and pushes her to the limit. Part of the elocution lessons entails Eliza talking with marbles in her mouth. When she swallows one, Higgins' only comment is, "That is all right, we have plenty more." Higgins and Pickering plan to take her on her first outing to the home of Mrs. Higgins (Marie Lohr), the professor's mother, who has a weekly tea party. Higgins' instructs Eliza to stick to the weather: "In Hartford, Hereford and Hampshire hurricanes hardly ever happen." She hits each "H" perfectly, but soon she is bored and turns the subject to her aunt "who drinks gin like mother's milk" and was finally "done in." Eliza is then made ready for her grand test. Accompanied by Higgins and Pickering she attends an embassy ball in honor of the country's visiting archduchess. She passes the test easily. Her demeanor, poise and measured speech impress Count Aristid Karpathy (Esme Percy), a former student of Higgins who now considers himself an expert on languages. He confides to the Archduchess that Miss Doolittle is not even British. She is a European princess of royal blood as her English is too perfect. Higgins has molded a common Covent Garden flower girl into someone fit to converse with royalty.

The ending of the film was altered for commercial reasons by Pascal, the producer, who had exclusive film rights to all of Shaw's plays. He made Eliza and Higgins finally get together. Despite his agreement with Shaw not to tamper with his plays, Pascal also eliminated most of the social commentary of Alfred Doolittle (Wilfred Lawson), Eliza's father, which embodied Shaw's socialist beliefs. Shaw had used the mythical tale of the sculptor Pygmalion and his creation, Galatea, to advance his thesis that language and accents are sources of power by the wealthy and wellborn to oppress the weak and the poor. As Shaw sets out in his preface to the play, Eliza is a "life force" like many of Shaw's heroines, such as Candida, St. Joan and Major Barbara. Wendy Hiller is superb in a very difficult role. Leslie Howard as a Pygmalion has one of his best roles. Wilfrid Lawson and Marie Lohr are very good. The only weakness is the bland Scott Sunderland as Pickering. The first two-thirds of the film move along handsomely, but the film creaks a little toward the end. The direction and cinematography are ordinary and there are too many freezes without any camera movement. David Lean as the editor had little room to exert his mastery of editing. But it is, after all, a charming and highly enjoyable film. *Pygmalion* is the best screen adaptation of a Shaw play. Director Asquith was one of the founders of the British Film Society along with Shaw, H. G. Welles and Julian Huxley.

Rashomon

1950. 88 min. b.w. Japanese. **Prod.** Jingo Minoura; **Dir.** Akira Kurosawa; **Scr.** Shinobu Hashimoto, Akira Kurosawa (based on the short story "Yabu no Naka" and the novel *Rasho-Mon* by Ryunosuke Akutagawa); **Cin.** Kazuo Miyagawa; **Art D.** So Matsuyama; **Mus.** Fumio Hayasaka; **Cast:** Toshiro Mifune, Machiko Kyo, Masayuki Mori, Takashi Shimura, Minoru Chiaki, Kichijiro Ueda.

The story is set in eleventh-century Japan. A fierce rainstorm forces three people to seek shelter in an abandoned temple. The three—a beggar (Kichijiro Ueda), a young priest (Minoru Chiaki) and a wood gatherer (Takashi Shimura)—reflect on the recent violence which has taken place in the nearby woods. A merchant has been murdered, his wife has been raped, and the alleged killer has been apprehended and brought before a magistrate. There is a dissolve and a series of flashbacks. The bandit, Tajomaru (Toshiro Mifune), accused of murder, gives his testimony at the inquest. He had been taking a nap in the forest when he was awakened by the passing of a merchant (Masayuki Mori) and his wife (Machiko Kyo) on a horse. In a beautifully photographed scene with the sun shining through the trees, a gentle breeze lifts the woman's veil.

The bandit is aroused and follows the two. He lures the husband away by claiming he has a treasure of fine swords that he wants to sell. He ties up the husband and returns to rape the wife. He claims she yielded to him without much struggle. He then unties the husband and challenges him to a sword fight. When the husband is killed the wife flees. Next we hear the wife's version. She recounts the rape and the flight of the bandit afterward, leaving her alone with her contemptuous husband. She cuts him loose, offers him a dagger and begs to be put out of her misery. He refuses. She realizes that he has lost all respect for her and, overcome by the trauma, she faints. When she regains consciousness she sees "my dagger in my husband's heart." Through a medium the dead husband testifies that after the rape his wife begged the bandit to kill him and take her away. Seeing his wife running away with the bandit, the husband committed suicide. At the temple the bandit's story is retold by the beggar, and the wife's version is recounted by the priest, both of whom had been at the inquest. The wood gatherer, who had been silent throughout, shouts that he had been in the forest that day and had witnessed the entire event: After the rape, the wife had run to her husband, cut the ropes binding him, and implored him to avenge her dishonor. The husband and the bandit had a long struggle at the end of which the husband was killed, and the wife ran away.

The film demonstrates the ambiguity and relativity of truth. Each individual's story differs from the others. The bandit says the wife yielded willingly and he subdued the husband in a fair fight. The woman says she was raped in the presence of her bound husband and, after he refused forgiveness, she killed him while in a state of shock. The husband's medium says he committed suicide after his wife had willingly fled with the bandit. The wood gatherer who had witnessed the incident says that no one behaved honorably. Having dealt with human weakness throughout, the film ends on a discordant optimistic note concerning a baby found abandoned at the temple and taken by the poor wood gatherer, who has several children of his own to feed. This leads the priest at the end to say, "I have regained my faith in man." This masterpiece is beautifully photographed with a poetic quality

Rear Window

1954. 112 min. color. U.S. **Prod.** Alfred Hitchcock; **Dir.** Alfred Hitchcock; **Scr.** John Michael Hayes (based on the story "It Had to Be Murder" by Cornell Woolrich); **Cin.** Robert Burke; **Ed.** George Tomasini; **Art D.** Hal Pereira, Joseph MacMillan Johnson; **Mus.** Franz Waxman; **Cast:** James Stewart, Grace Kelly, Wendell Corey, Thelma Ritter, Raymond Burr, Judith Evelyn.

A news photographer, L. B. "Jeff" Jeffries (James Stewart), has broken his leg and is confined to a wheelchair in his Greenwich Village apartment. His work has taken him all over the world, sometimes on dangerous assignments. Now, being immobile, he is restless and bored. He has nothing to do but gaze through his rear window and watch what goes on in the courtyard and in the apartments across from him. This has become his routine and he enjoys being a voyeur. He watches his neighbors with binoculars, occasionally switching to a camera. They are unaware of his peeping. Among these neighbors are a newlywed couple whose shades are always drawn; a composer hard at work attempting to complete his composition; a lonely woman, whom Jeff dubs "Miss Lonelyhearts," who sets her dining table for two every night and entertains an imaginary lover; an energetic young dancer who does nothing but practice the entire day; and a middle-aged childless couple who sleep on the fire escape with their dog to relieve the summer heat. Then there is Lars Thorwald (Raymond Burr), a dour man who is constantly bickering with his wife. Later, Jeff sees part of a struggle between the two. The continued absence of Mrs. Thorwald, coupled with the fact that she had left behind her handbag and wedding ring, leads Jeff to suspect that she has been murdered by Thorwald. Soon Jeff's beautiful fiancée, Lisa Carol (Grace Kelly), a fashion model, shows up. She does not believe what he tells her and chides him for looking through other people's windows. Even Stella (Thelma Ritter), Jeff's nurse/housekeeper, doesn't believe him and admonishes him, "We have become a race of peeping Toms." While continuing to monitor Thorwald, Jeff suddenly realizes that he, himself, is being watched. In a well-done series of scenes of mounting suspense we discover that there was, indeed, a murder and Jeff's hunches were on the mark. In the process, Jeff is rewarded with another broken leg, as a result of which he will continue to be wheelchair -bound for some time. Jeff, who had always shied away from any commitment to Lisa, finds himself harboring a newfound love and respect for her. He had not given her credit for the courage and determination she showed during the unraveling of the mystery.

Rear Window is one of Hitchcock's near-perfect films. He succeeds in making us all voyeurs. The film covers three days and three nights, during which time we share everything that Jeff sees, with the exception of one brief but crucial scene. While Jeff is taking a nap, we see Thorwald leave his apartment with a woman. She could possibly be Mrs. Thorwald, and hence there is no murder. This single scene adds to the suspense. The film is well acted. James Stewart, Grace Kelly, Raymond Burr and Wendell Corey are all good. Thelma Ritter gives the film a needed touch of humor. The film ends with typical Hitchcock tongue-in-cheek. The dancer's boyfriend comes home; the composer completes his work; Miss. Lonelyhearts has a beau; and the new-lyweds still have their shades drawn.

The Remains of the Day

1993. 135 min. color. British/U.S. **Prod.** Mike Nichols, John Calley, Ismail Merchant; **Dir.** James Ivory; **Scr.** Ruth Prawer Jhabvala (based on the novel by Kazuo Ishiguro); **Cin.** Tony Pierce-Roberts; **Ed.** Andrew Marcus; **Prod. D.** Luciana Arrighi; **Art D.** John Ralph; **Mus.** Richard Robbins; **Cast:** Anthony Hopkins, Emma Thompson, James Fox, Christopher Reeve, Peter Vaughan, Hugh Grant, Michael Lonsdale.

The film tells the intertwined stories of the head butler, Stevens (Anthony Hopkins), and the housekeeper, Miss Kenton (Emma Thompson), and their employer, Lord Darlington (James Fox), who has pronounced sympathies for Nazi Germany. Lord Darlington, who had served in World War I and had witnessed the carnage, believes war against Germany must be stopped at any cost. "We imposed harsh terms on Germany," he states, referring to the Treaty of Versailles, and he believes that Germany should be allowed to rearm. He arranges meetings at his sumptuous mansion among Chamberlain, Lord Halifax and Von Ribbentrop, the German Ambassador to the Court of St. James, who later became foreign minister. As a result, Britain and France allow Germany to annex Czechoslovakia. Stevens is ignorant of the world and barely aware of the significance of what goes on in the mansion. He has been a butler his entire life, as has his father. He is a pathologically repressed man who devoutly believes people of his class have no function other than to serve. He is also a lonely man who has never allowed anyone to get close to him. Miss Kenton, an orphan who had always worked as a maid and now has become a housekeeper, frankly admits she cannot go out in the world to seek any other type of employment. Miss Kenton has a difficult time with Stevens but gradually comes to admire him for his selfless service and dedication to his work. She even begins to care for him and finally brings herself to make mild advances. Poor Stevens, however, is incapable of responding. Soon Miss Kenton accepts the offer of marriage of a junior butler and gives her notice. The repressed Stevens cannot bring himself to ask her to stay.

Some twenty years pass. Lord Darlington dies. His mansion, with furnishings and art work, is purchased by an American multimillionaire, Mr. Lewis (Christopher Reeve). Lewis, as a congressman, had been a guest of Lord Darlington in 1937–8 when Darlington had convened what amounted to an appeasement conference. Lewis had admonished the group that as amateurs they should not meddle in serious political issues. The film ends with Stevens going to the West Country to lure Miss Kenton to return as housekeeper. Miss Kenton, who has divorced her husband, declines the offer because she has to look after her pregnant, married daughter. Stevens still is incapable of professing his love or admitting that the job offer was merely an excuse to meet and ask for her hand in marriage. They part in a pouring rain.

The Remains of the Day is by far the most ambitious and best film to come out of the Merchant/Ivory collaboration, which dates from 1963. The direction, as always, is very straightforward.

There is beautiful cinematography by Tony Pierce-Roberts and magnificent acting by Hopkins and Thompson. Anthony Hopkins has never been better. He captures every nuance of a butler who devotes his life to his master. In the scene where Emma Thompson slowly reveals her feelings for him, Hopkins' face, with its ticks and twitches, is a marvel to watch. Emma Thompson does equal justice to her part. The rest of the cast, especially James Fox, Michael Lonsdale, Peter Vaughan and Christopher Reeve, are also very good. The film is based on the 1989 Booker Prize-winning novel by Kazuo Ishiguro, which is in part based on the receptions hosted by Lord Astor at his county seat at Clivedon for Ambassador Von Ribbentrop and assorted British Nazi appeasers.

The Rise of Louis XIV

La Prise de Pouvoir par Louis XIV. 1966. 100 min. color. French. **Prod.** Pierre Gout; **Dir.** Roberto Rossellini; **Scr.** Philippe Erlanger, Jean Gruault; **Cin.** Georges Leclerc; **Ed.** Armand Ridel; **Art D.** Maurice Valay; **Mus.** Betty Willemetz; **Cast:** Jean-Marie Patte, Raymond Jourdan, Silvagni, Katherina Renn, Dominique Vincent, Pierre Barrat, Fernand Fabre, Francoise Ponty.

The film begins in 1661 as Cardinal Mazarin (Silvagni), who has been the power behind the throne, is dying. The physicians give up hope and retire. A priest is called to hear his confession. When the priest leaves, Colbert (Raymond Jourdan), Mazarin's associate and protégé, calls on him. Colbert informs him that since his illness there has been more intrigue at court. The Queen Mother, Ann of Austria (Katherina Renn), favors the corrupt Fouquet (Pierre Barrat) as the first minister to run the country. Mazarin tells Colbert to ask the king for an audience. A delegation calls on the twenty-three-year-old King Louis (Jean-Marie Patte). In a well-done scene the king is dressed and groomed, and the film cuts to Mazarin preparing himself with rouge on his pale cheeks and powder on his face, and cuts then to the audience. The king next calls on his mother to tell her that Mazarin is very near death. His mother who had always disliked Mazarin now openly attacks him. Louis says Mazarin loved him and kept his enemies at bay. He saved him from the fate of his late cousin Charles I of England. The king leaves and the Queen Mother tells her entourage that her son is interested only in hunting, playing cards and dancing. He will soon tire of running the state and then she will rule.

The king realizes that in the absence of Mazarin power will be shared by too many hands and his transformation from a disinterested and frivolous young man to an omnipotent ruler begins. He convenes the council of advisors and decides to have the mourning ceremony for Mazarin held at the court, where previously only royal funerals were held. Colbert is appointed as the senior advisor and the king asks him to report to him every morning. The Queen Mother's favorite, Fouquet, a dishonest scoundrel, and the Queen Mother herself are removed from the council. Intrigues at court continue, however, since the general belief is that Louis will soon tire and revert to his old ways. Fouquet is exiled and forced to sign over his entire estate to the Treasury. Louis begins an era of change. He orders Colbert to start building an infrastructure for the country and to initiate a shipbuilding industry. Taxes will be levied not only on the poor but on the wealthy and aristocrats. Louis strengthens his rule in a variety of other ways. In some of the best scenes in the film we see his decision to change his wardrobe. The material must be the best with the finest laces. He orders larger wigs so as to appear taller. It is he who must set the fashion, not the nobles. He orders the building of Versailles. The nobles must live in various quarters in the palace where he can keep an eye on their activities. Louis also sets the style for eating, drinking and music. He eats alone on an elevated table. When finished he asks his brother, seated at a lower table, to eat, and then the nobles. He will arrange the rituals for funerals, state occasions, banquets, personal audiences and cabinet meetings. His transformation from playboy to the "Sun King," who gives nourishment and life to his subjects is complete. Louis XIV occupied the throne for seventy-three years, longer than any monarch in the history of Europe.

It is an extremely well-made film with superb performances, imaginative use of color and a well-researched script. Although it is set in an era that lends itself to spectacle and gaudy indulgence, Rossellini created a subdued document of a king and his time.

The Searchers

1956. 119 min. color. U.S. **Prod.** Merian C. Cooper, C.V. Whitney; **Dir.** John Ford; **Scr.** Frank S. Nugent (based on the novel by Alan LeMay); **Cin.** Winton C. Hock; **Ed.** Jack Murray; **Art D.** Frank Hotaling, James Basevi; **Mus.** Max Steiner; **Cast:** John Wayne, Jeffrey Hunter, Vera Miles, Ward Bond, Natalie Wood, John Qualen, Harry Carey, Jr., Olive Carey, Ken Curtis, Henry Brandon, Dorothy Jordan, Walter Coy, Hank Warden, Pat Wayne

It is 1868 and Ethan Edwards (John Wayne) has returned home to Texas. No one has seen him since the Civil War ended. In a magnificent opening scene, a cabin door opens on an arid landscape. A woman comes out of the doorway and sees a distant figure on horseback slowly approaching. Ethan comes to the small ranch of his brother Aaron (Walter Coy), his wife Martha (Dorothy Jordan) and their three children, Lucy, Ben and Debbie (Natalie Wood) and adopted son Martin (Jeffrey Hunter). Ethan is wearing a Confederate coat with sergeant's stripes and carries a saber he had refused to surrender at the armistice. He also has a sack full of gold coins and he gives some to his brother to cover his keep at the ranch. One wonders what he has done in the three years since the end of the war. A few days later Reverend Samuel Clayton (Ward Bond), captain of the local Texas Rangers, calls at the Edwards ranch accompanied by some of his men. It appears some marauding Indians have stolen cattle from the neighboring Jorgensen (John Qualen) ranch. Clayton needs more men to go after the Indians and asks Ethan and Martin to join him. After riding a distance they find the stolen cattle, slaughtered. They instantly realize the theft was merely a ruse to lure away the settlers from their ranches. Ethan, Martin and an old Indian scout, Mose Harper (Hank Warden), race back to the Edwards ranch, but they are too late. The ranch is on fire, and

Aaron, Martha and Ben have been killed and mutilated. Lucy, who was to be married to Brad Jorgensen (Harry Carey, Jr.), and eight-year-old Debbie have been taken away. Ethan, Martin and Brad follow the trail of the Indians with the Rangers. Before long the trail becomes cold and the Rangers turn back, but the three continue. Ethan soon discovers Lucy's body. She has been raped and murdered. Brad becomes so unnerved that he rides shooting into the Indian camp and is cut down. Ethan and Martin continue their search for Debbie for a year. They return temporarily to the Jorgensen ranch. The owner of a trading store, Futterman, tells Ethan that he has information on the tribe that had kidnapped Debbie. Futterman has a piece of Debbie's dress traded by an Indian from a Comanche tribe headed by Chief Scar. Ethan leaves and Martin follows despite pleas from the Jorgensen daughter Louise (Vera Miles), who has loved Martin since childhood. The second year of the seven-year search commences.

Martin begins to see Ethan's fanatical hatred of the Indians. Even Martin, who is one-eighth Cherokee, is taunted and regarded with disdain. "He is as dark as a half-breed." The intensity of Ethan's feelings is also shown when they run into a herd of buffalo and Ethan shoots as many of the animals as he can in order to deny food to the Indians. Martin is convinced that even if Debbie is found, Ethan will kill her. She will be tainted by having become a squaw and disgraced in Ethan's eyes. Finally Scar is found. A cavalry attack, led by Clayton's Rangers, Ethan and Martin, overruns his camp and Debbie is rescued. It is Martin who shoots Scar dead, but Ethan gets his own revenge by scalping him. Ethan, who moments earlier had been ready to kill Debbie, now feels cleansed and lifts her and says, "Let's go home Debbie."

It is an abrupt and difficult climax for us to accept and one that is not entirely satisfactory. In an earlier scene, when Ethan learned that Debbie had become one of Chief Scar's many wives, Ethan's hatred of Scar and contempt for Debbie is all too apparent. Yet we are asked to believe that once Scar is killed, ironically by Martin, Ethan's thirst for vengeance and revulsion toward Debbie have been quenched and that he has rid himself of his demons. In a very effective ending, Debbie is delivered by Ethan and Martin to the Jorgensens. Martin follows them into the cabin but Ethan, ever the outsider, stays behind as the door closes. The film gains further depth by the intimation an earlier love between Ethan and Martha, who later married Ethan's brother. Several scenes establish the relationship. In a very delicate scene at the beginning of the film we see Martha caress and fold Ethan's coat with a look that seems to betray her feelings for him. A ballad accompanies the opening credits: "What makes a man to wander? What makes a man to roam?" The question is never answered, but we can guess it may have been Ethan's love for Martha. He has become a hate-filled loner who can find neither inner peace nor acceptance.

John Ford's heroes are almost always quiet men who don't say very much. He maintained the same visual style in all his films and where possible used the same locations and the same actors. As in most Ford films there are many scenes of intended humor, but not all of them work. The scenes depicting the incompetence of the cavalry, which is almost revolutionary for Ford who always lauds the cavalry, are most welcome. The light touches provided by John Qualen, Hank Warden, and Pat Wayne as a novice lieutenant, lighten an otherwise very dark film. The wedding for Martin's forced marriage to a squaw is too long; Ken Curtis' courting of Vera Miles is not that funny and the fight over her between Curtis and Hunter is overlong. Despite the complexities and unanswered questions, *The Searchers* is one of John Ford's greatest films.

The Set-Up

1949. 72 min. b.w. U.S. **Prod.** Richard Goldstone; **Dir.** Robert Wise; **Scr.** Art Cohn (based on the poem by Joseph Moncure March); **Cin.** Milton Krasner; **Ed.** Roland Gross; **Art D.** Albert S. D'Agostino, Jack Okey; **Mus.** Constantin Bakaleinikoff; **Cast:** Robert Ryan, Audrey Totter, George Tobias, Alan Baxter, James Edwards, Wallace Ford, Darryl Hickman, Percy Helton, Hal Baylor.

A realistic and merciless portrayal of the world of professional boxing, *The Set-Up* is the story of one fight in the career of Stoker

Thompson (Robert Ryan). Stoker has been in the ring for almost twenty years. He may have been a promising newcomer but when we see him he is regarded as a "has-been," although still a draw for his punching power. He has lost his last several fights. In a telling line early in the film when his crooked manager Tiny (George Tobias) enquires about his whereabouts just before the fight, he is told Stoker is taking a nap. Tiny comments, "Don't that guy get enough shut-eye in the ring?" On this night he is up against a young newcomer who is sponsored by the local gangsters. We first see Stoker in a cheap run-down hotel a few hours before the fight having an argument with his wife Julie (Audrey Totter) who wants him to quit boxing and open a small candy store. Stoker argues that he feels he is just "one punch away" from bigger things. What Stoker doesn't know is that his manager has made a deal for fifty dollars with a gangster, Little Boy (Alan Baxter), for Stoker to throw the fight. Tiny and the trainer believe Stoker will be knocked out in the first or second round in any event so they feel there isn't a need to tell him and share the fifty dollars. During the fight Stoker learns about the deal that was made behind his back. Out of sheer pride he refuses to go down, and knocks out his opponent. After the fight Little Boy and his men corner Stoker, give him a severe beating and break his fingers.

This tight and concise story takes place in seventy-two minutes, the exact running time of the film. The details distinguish it as probably the best boxing film. A short scene before the fight in the locker room shows the boxers' last-minute preparations before they are called to the ring—a youngster in his first fight and a punchy fighter going through the motions. Later the film focuses on some of the typical spectators, as well as a blind man who is being told how the boxers are punishing each other and a hysterical sadistic woman who just screams "Kill him, kill him!" These scenes are enhanced by the excellent cinematography of Milton Krasner. The manager and trainer are well-sketched, credible characters. The film highlights both the dirty and seamy side of the boxing establishment and the illusory hopes of boxers. Ironically the film is set in a town called Paradise City and Julie finds her husband beaten in a dark alley under a neon sign that reads "Dreamland Dance Hall." *The Set-Up* is the best work of the talented director Robert Wise, who began his career as an editor. Unfortunately he made only one great film after *The Set-Up*, *The Day the Earth Stood Still* (1951). Thereafter he became known as a reliable director and was assigned several large-budget films that are technically proficient but lack the inspiration of his earlier work. Robert Ryan is superb as the weary boxer past his prime and the entire secondary cast is excellent.

The Seven Samurai

1954. 204 min. b.w. Japanese. **Prod.** Shojiro Motoki; **Dir.** Akira Kurosawa; **Scr.** Shinobu Hashimoto, Hideo Oguni, Akira Kurosawa; **Cin.** Asakazu Nakai; **Ed.** Akira Kurosawa; **Art D.** So Matsuyama; **Mus.** Fumio Hayasaka; **Cast:** Takashi Shimura, Toshiro Mifune, Yoshio Inaba, Ko Kimura, Seiji Miyaguchi, Minoru Chiaki, Daisuke Kato, Kuninori Kodo, Kamatari Fujiwara, Yoshio Tsuchiya.

The setting is seventeenth-century Japan. The film opens as a gang of bandits prepares to attack a village. Their chief tells his men that they had pillaged the same village only a few months before and taken what they wanted; better to wait for the next harvest. The bandits are careful not to take all the produce when they raid a village, so that they leave enough for the farmers to survive, assuring themselves of a steady supply. They move on to another village. The conference of the bandits is overheard by a peasant hidden in the bushes. He reports what he hears to a gathering of the frightened farmers. Knowing now that the bandits will be back in less than three months, they debate as to what to do. Some argue for submission as before, while a few, especially the younger farmers, argue resistance. They decide to consult the village elder. He tells them that many years ago he had heard of one prosperous village that had hired samurai and beaten off the bandits. The once powerful samurai have descended to the nadir of their former proud and noble status. They no longer have wealthy warlords to serve in territorial battles. The village elder says that there are many idle and hungry samurai and they should seek them out in the nearest town. He also warns them that their village is poor and can only afford to offer the samurai three bowls of rice a day and a roof over their heads.

Three farmers travel to the town and stay at a flophouse. They go hungry in order to save their rice rations for any samurai who may accept their offer. They approach everyone who carries a samurai sword, but none are interested. By chance they witness a dramatic rescue. A cornered thief has taken a child hostage and fled to a barn. No one dares try to retrieve the child until an aging samurai, Kambei (Takashi Shimura), volunteers for two bowls of rice. He disguises himself as a priest, goes in unarmed, slays the thief with his own sword and frees the child. Kambei, who has fallen on hard times, becomes the first samurai to accept the farmers' offer. He also becomes their recruiter. By questioning the three farmers as to the exact location of the village and its access lanes, he determines that he needs six others to defend the village. Kambei looks over likely candidates, tests each one and finally recruits five. Each of them has a short scene that tells us who he is and what his expertise is. Kambei is also approached by an eccentric, if not a madman, who pretends to be a samurai and desperately wants to join the group. We find out he is in fact a farmer's boy who goes by the name of Kikuchiyo (Toshiro Mifune). He is rejected but refuses to give up. He follows the group until they reach the village, where he is finally accepted. We soon learn that he is ingenious, strong and fights like a lion. Now they are seven. They are first viewed with suspicion by the villagers who hide their women and surplus food. But soon their suspicions dissipate as they witness the dedication and fearlessness with which the samurai prepare to face the bandits. The farmers are trained and become an important element in Kambei's plan to defend the village. The samurai's passion for battle inspires the villagers and they exert themselves even more. The bandits number forty. They are well armed, some with guns, and ride swift horses, a combination that makes them appear invincible. Kambei, however, has studied the contours of the land around the village, and has placed obstacles. After the harvest he orders all the farmland surrounding the village to be flooded, leaving only one access lane. His battle plan is to let in two bandits at a time and then close in on them. Soon the bandits, who had looked indomitable, are decimated piecemeal. The village is saved but only three of the samurai survive.

The battle scenes are as good as any ever filmed. The hand-to-hand combat in pouring rain is magnificently choreographed by Kurosawa who had a painter's eye for composition. The acting is superb. Two of Kurosawa's favorites, Shimura and Mifune, appear again in this film. This 204-minute film is so well edited that, despite its length, it moves quickly, keeping us engaged. The comic relief by Mifune and a love affair between one of the samurai and the daughter of a villager soften the plot. The photography is excellent. The wooded surroundings, the morning mist and especially the downpour of rain, so difficult to capture, are perfectly depicted. The film is the masterpiece of one of the twentieth century's greatest film directors—a period piece with contemporary themes of dignity and courage.

The Seventh Seal

1957. 105 min. b.w. Swedish. **Prod.** Allen Ekelund; **Dir.** Ingmar Bergman; **Scr.** Ingmar Bergman (based on his play Tramalning); **Cin.** Gunnar Fischer; **Ed.** Lennart Wallen; **Mus.** Erik Nordgren; **Cast:** Max von Sydow, Gunnar Bjornstrand, Nils Poppe, Bibi Andersson, Bengt Ekerot, Ake Fridell, Inga Gill, Maud Hansson, Gunnel Lindblom, Inga Landgre.

The setting is fourteenth-century Sweden in a forested area not far from the sea. The region is engulfed by the bubonic plague, the Black Death, where tens of people are dying every day. A knight, Antonius Block (Max von Sydow), and his squire, Jon (Gunnar Bjornstrand), are returning from the Crusades on their way to the knight's castle when at the seashore the knight is visited by a pale-faced figure in a black robe who announces himself as Death (Bengt Ekerot). The knight asks where he has come from and the black-robed figure says, "I have been walking by your side for a long time." Death had not expected the knight to return alive from the wars. It is now his time to submit to Death as there are many others he must visit. The knight proposes a bargain. He offers to play chess with Death on the condition that he may live as long as he is not checkmated and remain alive if he wins the game. The film now cuts back and forth to the chess game in progress and what the knight and his squire see during this grace period. They witness acts of cruelty and horror one after another. They see self-flagellation by a long line of people, others carrying heavy crosses at the prodding of the clergy. They witness a girl about to be burned as a witch for having started the plague on the orders of Satan. When the knight has given up all hope, he comes across a juggler, Jof (Nils Poppe), his serene wife and their infant child in a nearby valley. Jof confesses that he sees visions of the Virgin Mary, angels and occasionally the devil. The knight assists Jof and his family to escape the area. After they are safe, the chess game resumes and Death checkmates the knight. He travels to his ancestral castle. Death soon knocks at the door and the knight submits to him.

The knight, who was disillusioned by the slaughter he had witnessed in the Crusades and the indifference of a loveless God, represents Bergman himself, who in nearly all his films is in search of a loving God. The only people who survive are the symbols of the holy family—the juggler, his wife and their child— because they have never questioned God's love. They are the "pure in heart." *The Seventh Seal* is one of Bergman's most personal films. The knight at the outset says he seeks knowledge, not belief, but at the end we are left in doubt as to what he has learned. It is also one of Bergman's greatest and most ambitious films. The stark imagery reinforces the absence of a loving God. Max von Sydow has one of his best roles as the lonely knight in search of a meaning to life. Bjornstrand as the down-to-earth and irreverent squire and the rest of the cast are all very good. The film's title is from the Book of Revelations: "The Lamb opened the Seventh Seal, there was silence in Heaven."

Shane

1953. 118 min. color. U.S. **Prod.** George Stevens; **Dir.** George Stevens; **Scr.** A. B. Guthrie, Jr., Jack Sher (based on the novel by Jack Schaefer); **Cin.** Loyal Griggs; **Ed.** William Hornbeck, Tom McAdoo; **Art. D.** Hal Pereira, Walter Tyler; **Mus.** Victor Young; **Cast:** Alan Ladd, Jean Arthur, Van Heflin, Jack Palance, Brandon de Wilde, Ben Johnson, Edgar Buchanan, Emile Meyer, Elisha Cook, Jr., Paul McVey.

Set in Wyoming territory in the 1870s, Shane (Alan Ladd), a lone weary rider on his way to nowhere in particular, stops at the small farm of Joe Starrett (Van Heflin) and asks for a cup of water. Starrett lives with his wife, Marion (Jean Arthur), and their nine-year-old son, little Joey (Brandon de Wilde). To make amends for an initial misunderstanding, Shane is asked to stay for dinner. Later, when he helps Starrett remove a large tree stump from the yard, the farmer offers Shane a job. Little Joey takes an immediate liking to Shane with his buckskin jacket and pearl-handled gun in a studded holster. Shane is a man of few words. He is a gun-fighter, but he is tired and wants to settle down. The next day he puts away his gun and wears cowboy work clothes. The home-steaders have formed a small community that is threatened by the local cattle baron, Ryker (Emile Meyer), and his cowhands. Ryker knows Starrett is respected by the other farmers and offers to buy him out, thinking the others will follow suit. Starrett refuses. Later, when Ryker's men start a fight with Shane and Starrett in the saloon and are roundly beaten, Ryker sends for Wilson (Jack Palance), a hired gun from Cheyenne. Wilson is to provoke one of the homesteaders into a gunfight and kill him. The rest then will leave, abandoning their farms. The victim is a hot-headed former Confederate soldier, Torrey (Elisha Cook, Jr.), who draws his gun first and is "lawfully" killed by Wilson. When news of Torrey's murder reaches the farmers, most decide to leave the valley but Starrett convinces them to stay. To lure Starrett to the saloon he is sent a message that Ryker is willing to talk. Shane knows Starrett is no match for Ryker and Wilson. In an attempt to stop him, there is a fight and Shane is forced to knock out Starrett with his pistol butt. Shane tries to explain his action to

Marion, then rides to the encounter wearing his gunfighter clothes and gear. He is unaware that little Joey and his dog are following on foot. In a beautifully staged scene, the ritual of the gunfight is enacted. As the noted film critic Robert Warshow observed, "The moment of violence must come in its own time according to special laws or else it is valueless." Shane enters the dimly lit saloon and tells the gunfighter, "I've heard about you, Wilson." "What have you heard, Shane?" replies Wilson. "I've heard you are a low-down Yankee liar." Shane is faster and Wilson is killed. Shane is ambushed by Ryker and his brother and is forced to kill them as well. He has been shot in the arm but comes out alive thanks to Joey's warning cry. He knows that Joey has become too attached to him. Shane tells him "Go home now and tell your mother there are no guns in the valley," and rides off. With tears running down his cheeks, Joey shouts after him to come back until he is almost out of sight.

The film is shown through the eyes of little Joey as he remembers it years later. The scene of Shane trying to teach Joey to shoot, and the anger that comes to Shane's face when he draws his gun, is extraordinary. There are several subplots, the most touching of which is Marion and Shane's unspoken love, evidenced in many ways. When Shane is about to leave for the showdown she asks, "Are you doing this for me Shane?" He answers, "For you, Joe and...little Joey." Earlier, Joe Starrett had told his wife that he knows Shane will take care of her and little Joey if anything were to happen to him. And finally, little Joey trying to persuade Shane not to leave shouts, "Come back Shane, my mother wants you to come back."

The cast is very interesting. Van Heflin, a fine actor, gives an excellent portrayal of a plodding farmer who is a tower of strength for his family and neighbors. Jean Arthur, who had retired from the movies after Billy Wilder's *A Foreign Affair* (1948), gives a touching performance with her cracking, husky voice. She had appeared in two previous George Stevens films, *The Talk of the Town* (1942) and *The More the Merrier* (1943). Shane was to be her last film. Brandon de Wilde is ideal as little Joey. The supporting cast is very good: Elisha Cook, Jr. and Edgar Buchanan as homesteaders, Paul McVey as the frontier storekeeper and Ben Johnson as a cowhand with a conscience. The choice of Emile Meyer as the villain, made up to look like a vengeful Old Testament prophet with a pronounced eastern accent, is jarring. Jack Palance as evil incarnate is a little too mannered, but convincing. Alan Ladd was not a good actor. He had some excellent roles in a fairly long career but was unconvincing in all of them: *This Gun for Hire* (1942), *The Glass Key* (1942), *The Blue Dahlia* (1946) and *The Great Gatsby* (1949). In *Shane* he somehow fits the part and great acting was not required. He is a fairy tale hero who comes out of nowhere as a deus ex machina. He eliminates all the guns in the valley and rides off into nowhere. The outdoor cinematography is matchless: the Grand Teton range, the storms, the glorious sky and the ugly miserable little town. Most of George Stevens' post-World War II films have dated, but Shane retains its elegance and beauty.

Shoeshine

Sciuscia. 1946. 93 min. b.w. Italian. **Prod.** Paolo W. Tamburella; **Dir.** Vittorio De Sica; **Scr.** Cesare Zavattini, Sergio Amidei, Adolfo Franci, Cesare Viola, Vittorio De Sica; **Cin.** Anchise Brizzi; **Mus.** Alessandro Cicognini; **Cast;** Rinaldo Smordoni, Franco Interlenghi, Aniello Mele, Bruno Ortensi.

The story of two shoeshine boys in Rome, one a twelve year old streetwise kid, Giuseppe, and the other younger, Pasquale. They long for the day when they will have enough money to buy a white horse they had seen in a stable outside of Rome. Their only source of income in post-war Rome of 1946 are the American GIs who can afford a few lira to have their boots shined. Giuseppe's older brother, who is involved in the black market, talks the two boys into taking delivery of a few woolen blankets. They now have enough money to buy their dream horse. They are in heaven and spend all the time they can with their horse, and even sleep in the stable. They are abandoned by the men they helped and soon are arrested and sent to a reformatory. To elicit information, the authorities trick the boys into turning against one another. Slowly they become alienated and divided and join rival prison gangs with tragic results. It is a tender and poetic film that deals with the loss of innocence, but it is also a critique of the brutal Italian penal system. It is a fine example of the neorealist Italian cinema, although some of the scenes were shot in a studio. The actors were nonprofessionals.

Singin' in the Rain

1952. 102 min. color. U.S. **Prod.** Arthur Freed; **Dir.** Gene Kelly and Stanley Donen; **Scr.** Adolph Green, Betty Comden; **Cin.** Harold Rosson; **Ed.** Adrienne Fazan; **Art D.** Cedric Gibbons, Randall Duell; **Mus.** Nacio Herb Brown; **Cast:** Gene Kelly, Debbie Reynolds, Donald O'Connor, Jean Hagen, Cyd Charisse, Millard Mitchell, Douglas Fowley, Rita Moreno, Madge Blake.

Don Lockwood (Gene Kelly) and Lina Lamont (Jean Hagen) are stars of silent films. *Singin' in the Rain* opens in 1927 on the night of the premier of their latest silent swashbuckler and they are being interviewed by a Louella Parsons-type reporter. The studio publicity department has put out press releases that the two are madly in love and marriage is in the offing. Lina has begun to believe the publicity. Don, on the other hand, doesn't even like the selfish Lina who has a shrill voice and is not particularly bright. Among her typical remarks is, "I make more money than Calvin Coolidge put together." Don had been in vaudeville and burlesque as a hoofer. When he and his best friend Cosmo Brown (Donald O'Connor) came to Hollywood the only jobs they could find were as stuntmen specializing in hazardous stunts. Through a series of flashbacks we see some of their burlesque routines and chores as stuntmen which eventually led to a director giving Don a chance to act. Now he has become the leading man in Lina's pictures. In interviews, however, Don insists that he had been a classically trained actor and musician. A few months after the premier, the sound era arrives with *The Jazz Singer* (1927) and every studio rushes to produce sound pictures. Lina's voice and diction prove hopeless despite rigorous coaching. Lina has many fans and the producers don't want to lose her. Don meets a chorus girl with acting aspirations, Kathy Seldon (Debbie Reynolds). She has a pleasant speaking and singing voice. The producer and director agree, without Lina's knowledge, that Kathy will dub Lina's voice in their next picture, *The Dancing Cavalier.*

Singin' in the Rain is one of the best musicals. It has a witty script by Adolph Green and Betty Comden. It also gives us a whole range of characters involved in the early days of the "talkies"; the daring stuntmen, the aspiring pretentious starlets, the tough director, and producers who think it is prestigious to be addressed by their initials. The recycled musical numbers, most of them written by the lyricist Arthur Freed and songwriter Nacio Herb Brown years earlier, are made more memorable than when they were first introduced. Donald O'Connor's classic "Make 'em Laugh" from the Cole Porter song "Be a Clown" is one of the funniest numbers in musical comedy. Then there is the classic "Singin' in the Rain," where an exuberant Gene Kelly dances, kicks and stomps in puddles and climbs a lamppost. The supporting cast is excellent. Jean Hagen could have been another Judy Holliday had MGM cast her in better roles. The only weaknesses of the film are the pretentious "Broadway Ballet" number with Gene Kelly and Cyd Charisse, which has no relation to the rest of the movie and is obviously forced, and the limited acting range of Debbie Reynolds. An amusing irony is the fact that Debbie Reynolds' singing voice was dubbed by Betty Royce.

Some Like It Hot

1959. 119 min. b.w. U.S. **Prod.** Billy Wilder; **Dir.** Billy Wilder; **Scr.** Billy Wilder, I. A. L. Diamond; **Cin.** Charles Lang; **Ed.** Arthur Schmidt; **Art D.** Ted Haworth; **Mus.** Adolph Deutsch; **Cast:** Jack Lemmon, Tony Curtis, Marilyn Monroe, Joe E. Brown, George Raft, Pat O'Brien, Nehemiah Persoff, George E. Stone, Mike Mazurki, Joan Shawlee, Billy Gray.

Set in Chicago during prohibition, two musicians—Joe (Tony Curtis) a saxophone player and Jerry (Jack Lemmon) a bass player—play in a speakeasy owned by big-time bootlegger Spats

Columbo (George Raft). The speakeasy is fronted by a funeral parlor, but the police are alerted by Toothpick Charley (George E. Stone), a rival gangster, and the club is raided. Spats is arrested and the club closed. None of the workers in the club, including Joe and Jerry, is paid his back wages. Joe, who is a compulsive gambler, has lost all of his own and Jerry's money. They go to a garage to pick up their car and witness the cold-blooded murder of seven gangsters, including Toothpick Charley, by Spats and his gang. Joe and Jerry get away but their only way of getting out of town is to impersonate girls and join an all-girl band that has a three-week engagement in Florida. They become Josephine and Daphne. On the train they befriend Sugar Kane (Marilyn Monroe), the band's singer, and Joe/Josephine falls in love with her. Osgood Fielding III (Joe E. Brown), a millionaire resident at the Florida hotel, with a yacht anchored nearby, becomes attracted to Jerry/Daphne. Osgood has been married seven or eight times. Joe meanwhile assumes yet another guise as a millionaire bachelor and invites Sugar Kane to Osgood's boat and makes love to her. Osgood gives a diamond bracelet to Daphne. Josephine pinches it and makes a gift of it to Sugar Kane who in her best line says, "It must be worth its weight in gold." After a beautifully staged tango by Osgood and Daphne the two become engaged. About that time there is a convention of gangsters who have come to Florida from all parts of the U.S. At an elaborate banquet hosted by Little Bonaparte (Nehemiah Persoff), the don of dons, Spats is given a huge cake for his birthday. Bonaparte asks for a minute of silence for the Chicago seven. Then Spats and his entire gang are gunned down. It was not even Spat's birthday.

Wilder and Diamond wrote a witty script, but filming proved difficult. Monroe, who had begun to take herself too seriously, was either absent or late or forgot her lines. Three years earlier, she had formed her own company to produce *The Prince and the Showgirl* (1957) with herself and Laurence Olivier, determined to show the world she could hold her own even against Olivier. Wilder, worried about Monroe, decided to have the movie end with Jack Lemmon and Joe E. Brown and it proved a blessing.

Daphne finally tells Osgood that he is a man. Osgood, in the most memorable line of the film, replies, "Well, nobody's perfect." Of the supporting cast Raft, replaying his persona from *Scarface* (1932), and Persoff are excellent. Curtis was not one of the best actors of his time, but his imitation of Cary Grant's accent in his wealthy bachelor guise fits well. Jack Lemmon has one of the best roles of his career. *Some Like it Hot*, however, is essentially Wilder. After talking all his life about his idol Ernst Lubitsch's touch, Wilder had perfected his own touch.

Spartacus

1960. 184 min. color. U.S. **Prod.** Edward Lewis; **Dir.** Stanley Kubrick, Anthony Mann; **Scr.** Dalton Trumbo (based on the novel by Howard Fast); **Cin.** Russell Metty, Clifford Stine; **Ed.** Robert Lawrence, Robert Schulte, Fred Chulack; **Prod. D.** Alexander Golitzen; **Art D.** Eric Orbom; **Mus.** Alex North; **Cast:** Kirk Douglas, Laurence Olivier, Jean Simmons, Tony Curtis, Charles Laughton, Peter Ustinov, John Gavin, Nina Foch, Herbert Lom, John Ireland, Charles McGraw, Woody Strode.

Set in the first century B.C., Batiatus (Peter Ustinov), the owner of a gladiator training school in Capua south of Rome, examines a caravan of slaves. He purchases a number of them, including Spartacus (Kirk Douglas), a third-generation Thracian slave. The first scenes detail the selection process. They are examined thoroughly for any physical defects. They will be rigorously and brutally trained with every type of weapon and sold to the operators of the Roman colosseum as gladiators. All they are told is that if they fight bravely and survive they may become free men after a number of years. They are fed well and allowed conjugal visits once a month by female slaves. Unexpectedly, Marcus Licinius Crassus (Laurence Olivier), a wealthy Roman general traveling through Capua, stops at the gladiator school and orders a fight to death by four gladiators whom his capricious female companions choose for their entertainment. In the first contest one gladiator kills the other. In the second a black man, Draba (Woody Strode), is matched against Spartacus. Draba defeats him, but, refusing to break the bond of brotherhood and kill Spartacus, he turns instead on Crassus. Draba is killed by the guards and his throat is slit open by Crassus. Deeply moved by Draba's heroic gesture and longing for a slave girl, Varinia (Jean Simmons), Spartacus begins a revolt. All the guards and trainers are killed. The gladiators then raid the neighboring estates and free the slaves. Within two years their number swells to 90,000. They hold the Roman legions at bay for four years but are finally defeated by Crassus. The survivors, Spartacus among them, are crucified.

Spartacus is based on a novel by Howard Fast, with an intelligent script by Dalton Trumbo who finally was given a screen credit after years on the black list. The story has some basis in historic fact. The film is rich in characterizations and subplots. There is Gracchus (Charles Laughton), a Roman senator and an active opponent of Crassus' quest for total power. As a patrician, Crassus believes Rome belongs to him and his class and wants to impose order on the rest. Olivier plays him as a flamboyant bisexual. There is also Varinia (Jean Simmons), a slave from Britannia who becomes the wife of Spartacus and mother of his infant son. Both are granted their freedom by Gracchus shortly before his forced suicide. The film is well photographed by Russell Metty and very well acted. Charles Laughton is magnificent as the senator of the masses. Peter Ustinov as the greedy and calculating owner of the now bankrupt gladiator school matches Laughton in one of the best scenes in the movie in which they both scheme to deny Crassus victory and pride themselves on their corpulence. Laurence Olivier, as the arrogant, wealthy patrician general, has one of his best film roles. There is, however, some miscasting, especially Tony Curtis as a slave minstrel and John Gavin as the young Julius Caesar. Spartacus is by far the best of the Hollywood Roman epics, but what prevents it from being a truly great film is the excess of sentimentality in the second half, most especially the crucifixion of Spartacus. The film suffers when it shifts its focus away from the machinations at the Roman senate to the joyous celebrations of the freed slaves. Stanley Kubrick came to the film after Anthony Mann had been fired. He had no hand in

the script but did a masterful job of direction. Spartacus was the
brainchild of Kirk Douglas who was the executive producer. He
has been involved in a number of socially conscious films during
his long career.

The Spy Who Came in from the Cold

1965. 112 min. b.w. British. **Prod.** Martin Ritt; **Dir.** Martin Ritt; **Scr.** Paul Dehn, Guy Tro-
sper (based on the novel by John Le Carré); **Cin.** Oswald Morris; **Ed.** Anthony Harvey;
Prod. D. Hal Pereira, Tambi Larsen; **Art D.** Edward Marshall; **Mus.** Sol Kaplan; **Cast:**
Richard Burton, Claire Bloom, Oscar Werner, Peter Van Eyck, George Voskovec, Sam
Wanamaker, Cyril Cusack, Michael Hordern, Bernard Lee, Robert Hardy, Rupert Davies.

Alex Leamas (Richard Burton) is an MI6 agent in charge of
British agents in East Germany. When one of his men is killed by
East German Intelligence he goes back to London and tells his
immediate superior, Control (Cyril Cusack), that he wants to retire.
Control explains that he has worked out a plan to get even with the
head of East German Intelligence, Dieter Mundt (Peter Van Eyck),
and asks him to undertake one last assignment. Leamas, deeply upset
over the loss of one of his men, accepts. Leamas ostensibly retires
and gets a job at a neighborhood public library. He has an affair with
the young assistant librarian, Nan Perry (Claire Bloom), an innocent
idealistic member of the Communist Party. Soon his behavior
becomes erratic. He begins to drink heavily, beats up a defenseless
shopkeeper and is imprisoned for a short term. The bait has been
taken and on his release he is approached by people working for
East German Intelligence. He is offered a large sum if he were to
defect to the East. He is taken to a remote house in a wooded area
in East Germany and interrogated ceaselessly by the deputy head of
Intelligence, Fiedler (Oscar Werner), who has suspected for some
time that Mundt was double-dealing. Leamas cleverly incriminates
Mundt by drip-dropping information. Fiedler takes it all in and
brings charges against Mundt for treason. At the trial Leamas
becomes aware that he has been used. He realizes that the aim of
MI6 has been to discredit Fiedler who was getting close to finding

out that Mundt was in fact a double agent. Mundt easily refutes the phony information Leamas had fed Fiedler and turns the tables on Fiedler who is arrested and charged with treason. Leamas is helped by Mundt to escape to the West but at a great sacrifice.

The film is based on what is probably the best work of John Le Carré who questions the morality of all spy agencies. The film lashes out at how these agencies will even dupe their own agents as well as innocent bystanders. When Nan, who had been dragged into the trial, asks Alex to tell her what it is all about, Alex says, "Spies are a bunch of seedy, squalid bastards like myself." The film has the best screen performance of Richard Burton, who could have been one of the greatest actors of his time. It is also Claire Bloom's best performance on film. Oscar Werner is another fine actor who wasted away his talents. The film has some shortcomings. The trial of Mundt and the decisions of the judges are too perfunctory. A three-minute scene would have tied up all the loose ends. Directors have been remiss in bringing Le Carré's books to the screen. This is by far the best. Only the BBC productions of *Tinker, Tailor, Soldier, Spy* and *Smiley's People* do the works full justice.

Stagecoach

1939. 96 min. b.w. U.S. **Prod.** Walter Wanger; **Dir.** John Ford; **Scr.** Dudley Nichols (based on the story "Stage to Lordsburg" by Ernest Haycox); **Cin.** Bert Glennon; **Ed.** Dorothy Spence, Walter Reynolds; **Art D.** Alexander Toluboff, W. Franke Harling, Louis Gruenberg, Leo Shuken, John Leipold; **Mus.** Richard Hageman; **Cast:** Claire Trevor, John Wayne, Andy Devine, John Carradine, Thomas Mitchell, Louise Platt, George Bancroft, Donald Meek, Tim Holt, Berton Churchill.

Set in the 1880s, a stagecoach is taking six passengers from Tonto, a small town in New Mexico, to Lordsburg, Arizona. Among the passengers is Doc Josiah Boone (Thomas Mitchell), a drunken physician given to misquoting Shakespeare. He is being kicked out of town for malpractice. Dallas (Claire Trevor) is a saloon girl of questionable morals whom the sheriff, at the behest of the righteous ladies of Tonto, has forcibly put on the stagecoach. She is the quintessential independent woman of hundreds of Westerns. With a heart of gold, she is the only one who understands the hero. Major Hatfield (John Carradine), who may have been an officer in the Confederate army, is now a professional gambler. He has the manners of a Southern gentleman but whether he is a cheat and cardsharp we never learn. Lucy Mallory (Louise Platt), also a Southerner, is the pregnant wife of a cavalry officer on her way to a reunion with her husband stationed at a military fort in Lordsburg. She is haughty, treats Dallas with disdain and refuses to talk to the others. Samuel Peacock (Donald Meek), a whiskey salesman, carries a sample case that becomes the object of attention of Doc Boone who helps himself to several sample bottles. The last passenger is Mr. Henry Gatewood (Berton Churchill), a pompous, overbearing Tonto bank president who stops the coach and boards on the outskirts of town. He carries a small valise which he clutches tightly the entire trip.

Riding on top is the driver, Buck (Andy Devine), a friendly, likeable but not too bright fellow who is deadly afraid of the marauding Apaches and wants to make the trip in the shortest time possible. Riding shotgun is Sheriff Curly Wilcox (George Bancroft). Before long they are stopped by the Ringo Kid (John Wayne). He has broken out of jail and has a warrant out for his arrest but must board the stage because his horse went lame. The fair-minded sheriff who knows and likes the Kid lets him come on board but warns him not to try to escape. The Kid only wants to get to Lordsburg to settle a score with the three Plummer boys who murdered his brother. The stagecoach stops at a way station for the midday meal. In deference to the banker and Mrs. Mallory, the Kid and Dallas are given their meals at a separate table. When Mrs. Mallory goes into labor, Doc Boone sobers up and with help from Dallas delivers the baby who is cared for by Dallas for the rest of the trip. With everyone busy, the Kid considers escaping, but he sees Apache smoke signals and decides to stay with the vulnerable passengers. The stagecoach starts out but soon is attacked by some thirty Apaches. The driver, Buck, is injured and loses the reins. The Kid jumps between the galloping horses and gathers the reins. As the Apaches begin closing in, the cavalry comes to the rescue. The stagecoach reaches Lordsburg, wife and baby are delivered to the husband, the banker who had absconded with bank funds is arrested and the injured driver is attended to. There is a shoot-out between the Kid and the Plummer gang. In the end the Kid and Dallas ride off together.

Stagecoach is the first modern Western in terms of the sheer number of characters and the introduction of several social themes: hypocrisy, duplicity and greed. Although the characters are somewhat developed by Dudley Nichols' tight screenplay, they remain stereotypes for the most part. Still, the film made its lasting imprint as a classic manual on how to direct, photograph and edit a film. Orson Welles, who had never made a movie when he signed with RKO, has said he saw *Stagecoach* some twenty or thirty times in preparation for his filming of *Citizen Kane*. There is also the breathtaking work of Yakima Canutt, the legendary stuntman who, doubling for John Wayne, throws himself between the wagon wheels and the galloping horses' hooves to retrieve the reins. This was the first film Ford shot in Monument Valley on the Arizona-Utah border, a site that enriched many of his later films. The beautiful landscape is contrasted with the confined space on the stagecoach. This was also the first time the U.S. Cavalry was used by Ford as a deus ex machina to rescue the threatened passengers.

Stalag 17

1953. 120 min. b.w. U.S. **Prod.** Billy Wilder; **Dir.** Billy Wilder; **Scr.** Billy Wilder, Edwin Blum (based on the play by Donald Bevan and Edmund Trzcinski); **Cin.** Ernest Laszlo; **Ed.** Doane Harrison, George Tomasini; **Art D.** Hal Pereira, Franz Bachelini; **Mus.** Franz Waxman; **Cast:** William Holden, Don Taylor, Otto Preminger, Robert Strauss, Harvey Lembeck, Richard Erdman, Peter Graves, Neville Brand, Sig Rumann.

The story is set sometime in 1944, two years after the Allies had begun the heavy bombing of Germany. The U.S. 8th Air Force, which had the task of dangerous daylight bombings, suffered heavy casualties. Countless U.S. planes were shot down or forced to crash-land in German-controlled territory and the survivors were imprisoned. Stalag 17, somewhere near the banks of the Danube River, is one of the prison camps to which they were sent. It holds 630 prisoners—all Americans, all in the air force and all sergeants. There is also a compound close by that houses Russian women prisoners of war. Stalag 17 is run by the sadistic Prussian-type Oberst (colonel) Von Scherbach (Otto Preminger). The focus of the film is on Barracks Four, the responsibility of Sergeant Yohan Sebastian Schultz (Sig Rumann), a gregarious but uncanny guard. He speaks English, which he had learned as a professional wrestler in Cincinnati before the war. He hopes to resume his career in America when the war ends. The most interesting prisoner of Barracks Four is Sergeant Sefton (William Holden) who had failed officers training school and is bitter. On his first day at the camp some of his belongings were stolen, but he has more than compensated for that loss. He has decided to sit out the war and live as comfortably as he can. He looks with disdain on fellow prisoners who are plotting to escape and fight again. He has become an entrepreneur without equal. He stages games and attractions and accepts bets on everything. He arranges gambling sessions, produces homemade alcohol, trades in cigarettes, and even offers vicarious sex through a telescope trained on Russian women prisoners taking their weekly showers. He trades with the German guards: stockings and watches for a telescope or a radio and extra rations of food. The Nazis are also capitalists and eager to trade. He openly admits trading with the enemy. He says, "I'm trading, everybody is trading, I'm just trading sharper." As the film unfolds, we see Sefton is more intelligent than most of the other prisoners. He incurs the enmity of his fellow prisoners when two of them are about to make a break and he makes bets that they won't make it. No one has yet been able to escape from Stalag 17. The two are killed before they reach the outer perimeter. There is a newcomer to the camp, an officer, Lieutenant Dunbar (Don Taylor). The Germans find out that he was responsible for blowing up a munitions train while he was in custody at the train station on his way to Stalag 17. Dunbar is interrogated mercilessly as to how it was done. The entire Barracks Four becomes certain Sefton is the rat who squealed. They give him a severe gang beating and confiscate his trading goods. Sefton's life has become miserable and the only way to escape further persecution is by uncovering the spy. There is a catharsis at the end. The informer/spy is discovered to be a planted Kraut and a plan is devised for him to be killed by his own side.

The film is really a whodunit, but Wilder adds a running commentary on capitalism. Sefton's enterprise and free marketeering make him a winner. The losers are the barracks chiefs Hoffy (Richard Erdman) and Duke (Neville Brand) who waste their time plotting escapes. Wilder also touches on other elements of Americana, one being vigilantism. Duke would be right at home in a lynch mob. At one point he says of Sefton, "Hanging him makes my mouth water." Wilder gave maximum emphasis to the mystery aspect of the plot. The looped electric light cord signaling that the spy has put a message in a hollow chess queen is very well done. Wilder also broadens the visual horizons of the film, which is based on a stage play. He moves back and forth among the confines of the barracks, the prison yard, the outer perimeter, the Russian women's prison, the colonel's office, and even a water tank. There is also fine acting. Otto Preminger, obviously influenced by Stroheim's portrayal of a German officer in *Grand Illusion* (1937), gives a superb performance. Neville Brand, a fine character actor who usually portrayed criminals and psychotics, is first rate. Brand was actually the third-highest decorated U.S. soldier of World War II. *Stalag 17* is also a very good comedy, and Sig Rumann, Harvey Lembeck and Robert Strauss are perfectly cast. William Holden, a distinctively American actor and one of the best of his generation, finally received his due in this role. He had been in films since 1937 but was not established until *The Dark Past* (1948) and Billy Wilder's *Sunset Boulevard* (1950). For his performance in *Stalag 17* he won the Academy Award for best actor.

Sullivan's Travels

1941. 91 min. b.w. U.S. **Prod.** Paul Jones; **Dir.** Preston Sturges; **Scr.** Preston Sturges; **Cin.** John Seitz; **Ed.** Stuart Gilmore; **Art D.** Hans Dreier, Earl Hedrick; **Mus.** Leo Shuken, Charles Bradshaw; **Cast:** Joel McCrea, Veronica Lake, Robert Warwick, William Demarest, Margaret Hayes, Porter Hall, Eric Blore, Franklin Pangborn, Robert Greig.

John L. Sullivan (Joel McCrea) is an established Hollywood director with box office hits that include such fluff as *So Long Sarong, Hey, Hey in the Hay* and *Ants in Your Pants.* Now, after separating from his wife and facing a midlife crisis, he is tired of making escapist movies and wants to make a "real" film, O *Brother Where Art Thou?* It is about human suffering and poverty, showing how capital and labor are destroying each other. The studio bosses (Robert Warwick and Porter Hall) adamantly object, but since he is their top moneymaker, they try to humor him. They argue that he has lived a privileged life and knows nothing of poverty. Sullivan decides to go into the real world and learn how the poor live. As a compromise with the bosses, he agrees to have some studio people accompany him. They immediately turn it into a publicity stunt for Sullivan's next film. They place at his disposal a land cruiser with beds, a kitchen, a chef, his own valet and butler (Eric Blore and Robert Greig), followed by the studio publicity agent (William Demarest) and photographers. The trip is a failure and Sullivan convinces the studio to let him go out on his own. In his first job he is employed by a widow to wash windows. She indicates amorous intentions and Sullivan flees. He meets an aspiring, out-of-work actress (Veronica Lake) who accompanies him on his next venture, which is also a failure. He decides to give it one last try. Feeling sorry for the tramps and hobos he has encountered, he takes a thousand dollars in five-dollar bills to distribute among them. The money attracts the attention of a tramp who knocks Sullivan out with a blunt instrument, steals the money as well as his shoes and shoves him into an empty freight car about to leave the rail yard. The tramp, while trying to get away, is hit by a passing train and his body and face are mangled beyond recognition.

Everyone believes Sullivan is dead as the tramp had been wearing Sullivan's shoes in which Sullivan had hidden his identity papers.

Sullivan comes to on the moving train suffering from amnesia. He is questioned by a railroad guard but can't identify himself. When threatened by the guard he assaults him and is arrested. He is sentenced to six years of hard labor in a southern state prison and forced to work in a chain gang. While in prison he witnesses wanton brutality and human degradation. He begins to lose all hope. One night the prisoners are given an exceptional treat. They are taken in chains to a country church where they are shown an old Mickey Mouse cartoon. The prisoners, who had been sullen the whole time, erupt with laughter and shout with joy. They are grateful for the outing and the opportunity to laugh. They identify with the tiny mouse and its besting of the large Pluto, a symbol of prison authority. In this most moving scene, the film comes into its own. The black minister in his sermon to his all-black parishioners, who are as downtrodden as the prisoners, says, "We are all equal in the sight of God. The lame shall lead and the blind shall see." They sing the spiritual, "Go down Moses, way down in Egypt land, and tell old pharaoh to let my people go." Sullivan soon thereafter regains his memory. He has to let his former associates know that he is not dead. He finds a way to get his picture in the newspapers by confessing to the murder of Sullivan. Veronica Lake, now a successful actress, sees the picture. The studio bosses come to the rescue and he is released. They all think that after the hardship he has suffered he is going to direct *O Brother Where Art Thou?* However, he tells them he is going back to making his old comedies. He explains, "There's a lot to be said for making people laugh. It isn't much, but it's all we have in this cockeyed world."

Sturges began as a screenwriter. He wrote and directed several other fine films: *The Great McGinty* (1940), *The Lady Eve* (1941), *The Miracle of Morgan's Creek* (1944) and *Hail the Conquering Hero* (1944). His contract with Paramount ended in 1944 and he made only one good film thereafter, *Unfaithfully Yours* (1948). His heavy drinking appears to have taken its toll. *Sullivan's Travels* is the most personal of Sturges' films. Like Sullivan, he came from well-to-do parents and had attended several elite boarding schools in Europe and the U.S. This film has been read as a defense of Hollywood escapist movies and there is reason to support that contention. Sturges believed that it is very difficult to deal with serious social issues in films, and that writers should stay away from themes of poverty, justice and equality. This touching film from one of the most original filmmakers in Hollywood is dedicated "To all the funny men and clowns who have made people laugh."

Sunset Boulevard

1950. 110 min. b.w. U.S. **Prod.** Charles Brackett; **Dir.** Billy Wilder; **Scr.** Billy Wilder, Charles Brackett, D. M. Marshman, Jr. (based on the story "A Can of Beans" by Charles Brackett and Billy Wilder); **Cin.** John Seitz; **Ed.** Doane Harrison, Arthur Schmidt; **Art D.** Hans Dreier, John Meehan; **Mus.** Franz Waxman; **Cast:** Gloria Swanson, William Holden, Erich von Stroheim, Nancy Olson, Fred Clark, Cecil B. Demille, Anna Q. Nilsson, Lloyd Gough, Jack Webb, Buster Keaton, Hedda Hopper.

In an extraordinary opening, narrator Joe Gillis (William Holden) lies dead, face down in a swimming pool. In a lengthy flashback, Gillis recounts the events leading to his murder. Heavily in debt with his last chance to sell a movie script a failure, Gillis can't afford to remain in Los Angeles and is thinking of going back to Dayton, Ohio. While trying to make up his mind, he sees two repossession men in their car. He speeds away and, trying to elude them, turns into the driveway of a large mansion on Sunset Boulevard. It belongs to Norma Desmond (Gloria Swanson), a great star of the silent screen who has not appeared in movies for more than twenty years. Gillis is mistaken for an undertaker summoned to bury Norma's dead chimpanzee. When she learns Joe is in fact a scriptwriter, she offers him a job to rewrite *Salome,* the script she has been working on for her comeback. Desperate for money and with creditors at his heels, Joe accepts. Norma insists that he live in the mansion for the duration of his work. The only other person living there is Max (Erich von Stroheim), the butler, who once had been a noted silent film director. He had discovered Norma and had become the first of her three husbands. He knows she has no chance of making a comeback, but still loyal and devoted to her he nurtures her illusions and is determined to protect her from reality. Max tells Joe of the admirers and worshipers Norma had in the old days, and of a maharajah who "came all the way from India to beg for one of her silk stockings. Later he strangled himself with it." Joe becomes a virtual prisoner and kept man. Later, when Norma senses she may lose him, she slashes her wrists and Joe, for the first time, shows some true tenderness and confesses, "You are the only person in this stinking town who's been good to me." Soon thereafter, however, Joe decides to leave with tragic consequences.

Sunset Boulevard is Wilder's greatest film. It is the only truly radical film about Hollywood itself. It is amazing how Wilder makes the story work despite the weird opening in which the fate of the hero is revealed. From its unorthodox structure we get some of the great scenes in the movie: the burial of the chimpanzee in a solemn ceremony; Norma screening her faded silent films, including *Queen Kelly*, which was actually directed by Stroheim; Norma's imitation of Charlie Chaplin; her New Year's Eve party with an elaborate buffet, an orchestra, Max the butler and just Norma and Joe as guests; and the last scene where Max directs Norma down the stairs as she is being taken away by the police. These and other outstanding scenes are enhanced by John Seitz's "noirish" camera work and Swanson's extraordinary acting. Interestingly, she was not Wilder's first choice. Other silent stars including Mary Pickford, Pola Negri and Mae Murray were considered, but Swanson was perfect for the part. She brought to it her experience in silent movies and perhaps personal memories of the loneliness of forgotten film actresses. She is most convincing when she says, "We didn't need dialogue in those days, we had faces" or, "I'm big…the pictures got small." Another crucial choice Wilder made was to cast Stroheim as Max. Stroheim was highly regarded by both Wilder and Charles Brackett, the cowriter, and was given free reign on the interpretation of the character. He was allowed to add certain touches to embellish his role, but when he wanted a scene in which he would be ironing

Norma's clothing, including her underwear, Wilder refused. He was afraid it would not get past the censors. For the male lead, Wilder wanted Montgomery Clift, who was not available. William Holden was a better choice. He handled the ambiguity of the character well. Wilder's heroes and heroines are never paragons of virtue. In *Double Indemnity* (1944), *Stalag 17* (1953), *The Apartment* (1960) and *Ace in the Hole* (1961) they are all flawed; those on-the-keep and those on-the-make.

The film contains some pointed jabs at Hollywood: Gillis recounting a script he had written about the victims of the Great Depression, which was turned into a war movie; and Cecil B. Demille, who made his name with biblical epics, turning down Norma's *Salome* while busy shooting *Samson and Delilah*. *Sunset Boulevard* is far better and more honest than any of the half-dozen or so films Hollywood has made about itself and self-destructive movie stars. In *Sullivan's Travels* (1941), *The Bad and the Beautiful* (1952) and *Two Weeks in Another Town* (1962) there are upbeat endings. In *What Price Hollywood?* (1932) and *A Star Is Born* (1937, 1954, 1976) the self-destructive star's place is taken over by a younger actor. The ending of *Sunset Boulevard* is all darkness.

The Third Man

1949. 104 min. b.w. British. **Prod.** Carol Reed; **Dir.** Carol Reed; **Scr.** Graham Greene (based on his novel); **Cin.** Robert Krasker; **Ed.** Oswald Hafenrichter; **Prod. D.** Vincent Korda, Joseph Bato, John Hawkesworth; **Mus.** Anton Karas; **Cast:** Orson Welles, Joseph Cotton, Alida Valli, Trevor Howard, Bernard Lee, Wilfrid Hyde-White, Paul Hoerbiger, Ernst Deutsch, Erich Ponto, Siegfried Breuer.

Post-World War II Vienna in 1948 is divided into four sectors: Russian, British, American and French. Holly Martins (Joseph Cotton), an American writer of Western pulp fiction (e.g. *The Lone Rider of Santa Fe)* comes to Vienna to take a job with his long-time friend Harry Lime (Orson Welles) who has paid for his trip from the U.S. When he arrives he is stunned to find that Lime is dead having been hit by a truck and killed a day earlier.

Martins rushes to the cemetery in time to see Lime's coffin lowered. A few of Lime's friends and associates are there, including
Anna Schmidt (Alida Valli), an actress and Lime's devoted companion. Also present is a British officer, Major Calloway (Trevor
Howard) of the military police. Calloway bluntly tells Martins
that Lime was a ruthless crook and a murderer. Martins is so upset
that he tries to hit the major but is restrained. He decides to look
into the accident and Lime's death. He arranges to meet two of
Lime's associates who recount how Lime was hit by a truck as he
stepped out of his apartment building and crossed the street without looking. The two claim they picked up Lime's body and
carried him to the nearby square. Martins next meets Anna
Schmidt. She confirms the account of Lime's death. He also talks
to others who had known Lime, including the doctor who had
pronounced him dead. Martins gradually becomes suspicious, as
all the witnesses were close associates of Lime and there were no
strangers or passersby. The porter at Lime's apartment building
says he witnessed the entire event from a window, but there were
three people, not two, who carried the body to the square. The
next day the porter is found dead. Later, as Martins goes out he
sees the outline of a figure hiding in the doorway across the
street. In a magnificent scene we see a shot of the dark doorway,
then a shot of shiny black shoes, then Lime's sardonic face and in
a second he is gone. Martins informs Calloway and the police dig
up the grave. They find the body of a Joseph Harbin, a medical
orderly who had informed on Lime. It is now obvious that Lime
was the third man who had carried the body of the murdered
Harbin. He had staged his own death to throw the police off his
trail. Martins is told that in this depressed city Lime had made
large sums of money trafficking in diluted penicillin on the black
market, which brought agonizing death to scores of children.
Martins is taken by Calloway to hospitals where Lime's maimed
and disfigured young victims have been sent. Next Martins
secretly arranges a meeting with Lime at a deserted amusement
park. Lime shows up with a smile and a hearty greeting. At Lime's
suggestion they go "for privacy" up the elevator of a giant ferris

wheel. Martins asks Lime if he had seen any of his victims. Lime by sheer sophistry tries to justify his racket. "Look down there. Would you really feel any pity if any of those dots stopped moving forever? If I offered you £20,000 for every dot that stopped…" Then in one of the most memorable lines in movie history (written by Welles himself), Lime says, "In Italy, for thirty years under the Borgias they had terror, murder and bloodshed, but they produced Michelangelo, Leonardo da Vinci and the Renaissance. In Switzerland they had brotherly love, five hundred years of democracy and peace, and what did they produce? The cuckoo clock." Martins by now is thoroughly disillusioned by his old friend. He arranges another meeting with Lime and informs Calloway. Lime is hunted down in the streets and killed in the sewers of Vienna.

The Third Man is basically a mystery story. It has an excellent script by Graham Greene, with the lines at the amusement park about the Borgias added by Welles to bolster his meager role. Welles still ended up with the shortest role of any billed costar in movie history. The cinematography and acting are exceptional. The camera work of Robert Krasker is among the most memorable in films. He captures grim postwar Vienna with its dark, menacing alleys. There are some outstanding individual scenes throughout the movie: the first appearance of Lime in the doorway; the hunt for Lime in the sewers; and finally the fade-out ending on a road lined with leafless trees and Anna ignoring Martins as she walks past him. She cannot forgive him for the betrayal of a friend.

Reed had turned out two very good films after the war, *Odd Man Out* (1947) and *The Fallen Idol* (1948). *The Third Man*, however, is Reed's most original work. He made some outstanding choices in addition to the selection of Krasker. The music was probably the most inspired choice any director has ever made. A zither became a commentator on the action. Reed's choice of Orson Welles was equally fortunate and Welles gave one of his bravura performances. David O. Selznick had a small holding in the film and he pressured Reed to have Noel Coward for the Lime role. Fortunately Reed resisted and Welles, who was not interested as he was working on his own projects, finally relented. Joseph Cotton and Alida Valli were contract players with Selznick's studio. Joseph Cotton, one of the best actors of his generation, gave the character of Holly Martins added dimensions. Martins is the ordinary "innocent" American out of his depth in Vienna, but Cotton gave him a certain charm and decency. His scene at the British Council meeting where he is mistaken as a serious writer of fiction and asked about Joyce and Proust is amusing. He is horrified when Lime, in order to justify his evil, babbles, "Nobody thinks in terms of human beings. Governments don't. Why should we? They talk about the people and the proletariat. I talk about suckers and mugs…" Martins finally sees Lime as the fascist killer that he is and it is obvious he will turn in his old friend. Alida Valli, badly used by Selznick, gave her best performance in an English-speaking role. Equally good were Trevor Howard, Bernard Lee and the Austrian and German cast. Selznick had several other recommendations that were fortunately turned down by Reed. He suggested the name of the film be changed to *Night in Vienna*, he wanted some anti-communist scenes and also wanted a happy ending. In 1999, the film was restored to its original cut and eleven minutes that had been cut by Selznick were restored.

The 39 Steps

1935. 87 min. b.w. British. **Prod.** Michael Balcon, Ivor Montagu; **Dir.** Alfred Hitchcock; **Scr.** Charles Bennett, Alma Reville, Ian Hay (based on the novel by John Buchan); **Cin.** Bernard Knowles; **Ed.** Derek Twist; **Prod D.** Otto Wendorff, Albert Jullion; **Mus.** Louis Levy; **Cast:** Robert Donat, Madeleine Carroll, Lucie Mannheim, Godfrey Tearle, Peggy Ashcroft, Wylie Watson.

Richard Hannay (Robert Donat), a mild-mannered, urbane Canadian, is in London on holiday. One night he goes to see a music hall variety show. The featured attraction is Mr. Memory, a man who can correctly answer any question asked by the audience. During his act there is a commotion, a gun is fired and soon there is a riot. A frightened veiled woman, Margaret (Peggy Ashcroft), tells Hannay her life is in danger and begs him to allow her to spend the night at his place. Hannay agrees, and in the middle of the night she staggers to his room with a knife in her back. With her last few breaths she tells him she is a counter-espionage agent trying to expose a sinister spy ring, and that his life is now in danger. She asks him to go to Scotland and gives him a map with the name of a village circled. She doesn't know the name of the spymaster he is to find there. In fact, all she knows about him is that he has a missing finger on his right hand. Before dying she also says something about thirty-nine steps. Shortly thereafter, Hanney becomes the prime murder suspect and the police are after him. He takes the train to Edinburgh. On board he sees a beautiful girl, Pamela (Madeleine Carroll), who recognizes him and immediately alerts the police. He jumps from the train and makes his way to the village marked on the map. There he meets Professor Jordan (Godfrey Tearle) and soon notices his missing finger. When Hannay attempts to escape, Jordan shoots him and leaves him for dead, but a Bible in his stolen overcoat has stopped the bullet. He eludes Jordan's men and goes to the town hall where a Liberal Party meeting is in progress. He is mistaken for the speaker who is to nominate the parliamentary candidate. He talks in generalities and is wildly applauded. He again runs into Pamela, who once again reports him to the police. The two are handcuffed together, and it becomes clear that the policemen actually are Jordan's henchmen posing as police. Hannay and Pamela escape and spend the night at an inn. There he finally convinces her of the truth of his story. They head to London where Pamela goes to the police and Hannay to the music hall. Mr. Memory is used by the spies to transmit government secrets. The police close in and the spies are caught.

The 39 Steps, together with *The Lady Vanishes* (1938) are the best of Hitchcock's British films, before coming to America in 1940. The film has most of the elements of his later films. There is the "wrong man" caught in a conspiracy not of his making, the cool blonde, witty dialogue and mounting suspense. There is little violence and the protagonist is unarmed. It is the first film in which

Hitchcock abandons any attempt to make the story plausible. He also introduced his famed MacGuffin formula. What the spies are stealing and transmitting to the enemy is never explained. Is the thirty-nine steps a spy organization, or is it the blueprint for a new weapon design? As in later Hitchcock films, the logic of the plot is not of much importance. What happens to the central characters and how they change is Hitchcock's chief concern. There is much humor in the film, and the relationship between Hannay and Pamela is handled with a great deal of charm. The beautiful Madeleine Carroll was one of the best of Hitchcock's cool blondes. She also appeared in his *Secret Agent* (1936) a year later. Robert Donat was a fine actor both on stage and screen. Lawrence Olivier believed him to be the consummate cinema actor and when making *Wuthering Heights* (1939) he had intended to fashion his acting on Donat's style, but was dissuaded by William Wyler. Donat was plagued by chronic asthma which curtailed his career. He had a well-modulated, pleasing voice and his recordings of poetry and plays are of the highest order.

Top Hat

1935. 99 min. b.w. U.S. **Prod.** Pandro S. Berman; **Dir.** Mark Sandrich; **Scr.** Dwight Taylor, Allan Scott (based on the musical *The Gay Divorcee* by Dwight Taylor and Cole Porter and the play *The Girl Who Dared* by Alexander Farago and Aladar Laszlo); **Cin.** David Abel; **Ed.** William Hamilton; **Art D.** Van Nest Polglase, Carroll Clark; **Mus.** Max Steiner, songs by Irving Berlin; **Cast:** Fred Astaire, Ginger Rogers, Edward Everett Horton, Helen Broderick, Eric Blore, Lucille Ball, Eric Rhodes.

This, the fourth of the nine films Fred Astaire and Ginger Rogers made together, is their best. As usual it has a silly plot about mistaken identity which is similar to their previous film, *The Gay Divorcee* (1934). Astaire pursues Rogers until at the end the reluctant Rogers gives in. The story takes place in London and Venice, but it was all filmed on studio sets. As in most Astaire/Rogers films there are some lusterless numbers, but they are more than compensated by some great Irving Berlin songs, including the two best numbers in the film:"Isn't It a Lovely Day" and "Cheek to Cheek."There is also the excellent supporting cast of Edward Everett Horton, Helen Broderick and Eric Blore, who were among the best Hollywood comedians of the time.

The Astaire and Rogers movies were escapist fare for Depression audiences, but a few of them, including *Top Hat,* have not dated at all. As Katharine Hepburn commented, Ginger Rogers brought sex and Fred Astaire brought class to their partnership, an unbeatable combination. Astaire had no more than a pleasant singing voice and was not much of an actor, but he was the best dancer in films. Mark Sandrich was a competent director of musicals.

The Treasure of the Sierra Madre

1948. 124 min. b.w. U.S. **Prod.** Henry Blanke; **Dir.** John Huston; **Scr.** John Huston (based on the novel by Berwick Traven Torsvan); **Cin.** Ted McCord; **Ed.** Owen Marks; **Art D.** John Hughes; **Mus.** Max Steiner; **Cast:** Humphrey Bogart, Walter Huston, Tim Holt, Bruce Bennett, Barton MacLane, Alfonso Bedoya, John Huston.

Fred C. Dobbs (Humphrey Bogart), an apparently decent fellow, is down on his luck and has been reduced to begging in the streets of Tampico, Mexico. He befriends another struggling American, Curtin (Tim Holt). A fast-talking shady contractor, McCormick (Barton MacLane), offers them work at reasonable wages and takes them to a remote oil field. They work long, brutal hours. They can't be paid until the end of the job when McCormick himself is paid. When work is completed, they return to Tampico and McCormick asks them to wait while he goes to pick up the payroll. He gives a few dollars to Dobbs and Curtin, the only Americans among the workers, and leaves. Dobbs and Curtin take beds in a flophouse, where they meet a garrulous old man, Howard (Walter Huston), a long-time gold prospector. He regales them with stories, recounting how he had made several fortunes and wasted them. He ends up by saying greed is the undoing of all prospectors. McCormick is nowhere to be found and Dobbs and Curtin learn that he has a long history of running out on his workers. They are again penniless and hungry. Some days later they run into McCormick who tells them he is still unpaid and can't pay them their wages. In an ensuing fight the half-starved Dobbs and Curtin beat him senseless and take what be owes them from his wallet. They know the money won't last long and they seek out Howard to ask if he would be interested in one last venture to find gold. A partnership is formed. They take a train to the base of the Sierra Madre Mountains, purchase the prospecting equipment and head up the mountain. Howard finds a likely place at the top and they begin mining for gold. The first sign of trouble comes when Dobbs insists that the gold dust be divided at the end of the day and each person be responsible for the safe keeping of his own "goods." Although Curtin saves Dobbs' life after the collapse of a tunnel, the increasingly unstable and paranoid Dobbs accuses him of attempting to steal his sacks of gold dust. Howard, who had maintained peace between the two, knows it can come to no good. A few days later an interloper, Cody (Bruce Bennett), comes to their camp and asks to be made a partner in any gold found thereafter, otherwise he will report them to the authorities. They reject his proposal and decide to kill him. At that moment Cody sights a party of bandits and warns them to take cover. He is killed by the outlaws before they are finally driven off. They learn from Cody's papers that he was a fruit farmer with a family. Howard has had enough. He is able to convince his two partners that the mountain has given up all the gold it had and it is time to leave. They had made the fortune they were after. They load their donkeys with the bags of gold dust and start to descend.

In addition to bandits, the Sierra Madre are also home to indigenous Indians. They have no knowledge of gold and lead simple, peaceful lives. A young boy from an Indian village has nearly drowned and is unconscious. Needing help, a group of Indians intercept Howard and his partners. They have respect for age, and Howard is the only one who speaks Spanish. They ask him to come and save the boy. Once Howard leaves, Dobbs, who has by now become psychotic, shoots Curtin and leaves him for dead. Dobbs takes the donkeys with the bags of gold and heads for the train. With the bandits not far behind his own fate is sealed. At the end of the film, Howard and Curtin, who has been found and saved by the Indians, pursue Dobbs' trail with the help of their Indian friends. Dobbs has been killed and the bandits have taken the donkeys and thrown away the bags of gold dust, which is now being scattered by a fierce sandstorm. In an effective and memorable ending, Howard laughs hysterically and says to Curtin, "It's a great joke. The gold has gone back to where we found it." Curtin joins in the laughter as the camera pans the storm-swept landscape and we see the empty bags flapping in the wind.

Huston's cast gave the performances of their careers: Bogart, Huston, Holt, Bennett, and Bedoya as the leader of the bandits. We also get short scenes that strengthen the film. The hard work of sifting and cleaning the gold is shown cinematically with no need for dialogue. The film's greatness lies, however, to a large extent, in Huston's attention to detail. He went so far as to convince his father, Walter Huston, it would be more effective if he acted without his false teeth. Early in the film, when the train is attacked by bandits, we see that the boastful Dobbs is a hopeless shot. His poor marksmanship is further shown when the bandits attack the mountain hideout. Thus, when Dobbs fires three or four shots at Curtin without killing him, we are prepared to accept it. Howard was an environmentalist ahead of his time. Before leaving the mountain he insists upon restoring it to the way it was found. His decency is shown in his relations with the Indians to whose village he returns to live out his days in peace and tranquility. Curtin is also a decent fellow who comes out of his experience a better man. He plans to see Cody's widow and children to tell them of Cody's death and help with the fruit harvest, as he had long dreamed of being a farmer. The film won Academy Awards for best supporting actor (Walter Huston), best director and best screenplay by John Huston, and received a nomination for best picture.

To Be or Not To Be

1942. 99 min. b.w. U.S. **Prod.** Ernst Lubitsch; **Dir.** Ernst Lubitsch; **Scr.** Edwin Justus Mayer; **Cin.** Rudolph Maté; **Ed.** Dorothy Spencer; **Prod. D.** Vincent Korda; **Mus.** Miklos Rozsa; **Cast:** Jack Benny, Carole Lombard, Robert Stack, Lionel Atwill, Felix Bressart, Sig Rumann, Tom Dugan, Stanley Ridges.

The film opens on the streets of peacetime Warsaw, Poland in the late summer of 1939. The shopkeepers and passersby cannot believe their eyes as they see Adolph Hitler taking a leisurely, unaccompanied walk. We soon find he is an actor, Bronski (Tom Dugan), who with proper makeup bears an uncanny resemblance to Hitler. Bronski is with the Joseph Tura Theater Group, which is putting on an anti-Nazi play. The group has competent actors and all the proper Nazi uniforms and paraphernalia, and has rehearsed the play countless times. At the last minute government censors order the project to be abandoned as it may inflame the Germans. A production of *Hamlet* is to replace the anti-Nazi play. The lead actors of the group are Joseph Tura (Jack Benny) and his beautiful wife Maria Tura (Carole Lombard), two exceptionally vain actors who are constantly bickering, and neither is above stealing scenes from the other. On September 1, Poland is invaded by Germany and occupied within a few weeks. Some Polish Air Force officers flee to London and form the nucleus of the Polish Squadron of the R.A.F. One such young officer is Sobinski (Robert Stack), a great admirer of Maria Tura. Sobinski soon becomes aware that their mentor, the patriotic Professor Siletsky (Stanley Ridges), is in fact a Nazi agent who has gathered the names of prominent resistance fighters in Poland and is on his way back to give the names to the local Gestapo chief, Colonel Ehrhardt (Sig Rumann). Siletsky has to be stopped from seeing Colonel Ehrhardt at any cost. Sobinski himself is secretly parachuted into Warsaw and alerts Joseph and Maria Tura. The film, which until this point has had an element of intrigue and suspense, now becomes basically a farce, and it is by far the best part of the film. Jack Benny impersonates Colonel Ehrhardt and later Professor Siletsky. The theater group succeeds in humiliating the Germans and in the end the actors impersonate Hitler and his entourage. They even steal Hitler's plane and escape to London. Joseph Tura achieves his ambition to play Hamlet on the London stage.

It is Lubitsch's funniest film but it was beset by misfortune from the beginning. Shooting began in late 1941 when Germany had swallowed Poland and overrun the Low Countries and France, and the fall of Moscow seemed imminent. The film was released some two months after the attack on Pearl Harbor, and Japan was on the road to the conquest of Southeast Asia. Before the film's release its star, Carole Lombard, was killed in a plane crash while on a tour selling war bonds. No one was in a mood to laugh. The film was bitterly attacked by critics who accused Lubitsch of bad taste and it fared badly at the box office. A difficult film to appreciate when first shown, with the passage of time it shines much brighter. Chaplin opened the door with *The Great Dictator* (1940) for filmmakers to ridicule Hitler. *To Be or Not To Be* is in the same mould. The Lubitsch touch gives substance even to a farce. The Shylock plea delivered by Felix Bressart near the end is genuinely moving and as good as any rendition of those famous lines. There are also some gems in the dialogue. Professor Siletsky: "Shall we drink to a Blitzkrieg?" answered by Maria Tura: "I prefer a slow encirclement." Joseph Tura in the guise of the spy Siletsky says to Colonel Ehrhardt, "The great, great Polish actor Joseph Tura, you must have heard of him." Ehrhardt replies, "Oh yes. What he did to Shakespeare, we are now doing to Poland." The acting of the supporting cast is excellent, except for Robert Stack who remained somewhat wooden throughout his entire career. Lionel Atwill playing a ham actor is very good, as is Dugan and Bressart. Sig Rumann, one of the great comedians, steals every scene he is in. The beautiful Carole Lombard gives one of her best performances. She was at the height of her career as a comedienne. Jack Benny, one of the best stand-up comics, carries his part, but his pauses and measured delivery so effective on radio do not work as well here.

Tokyo Story

1953. 134 min. b.w. Japanese. **Prod.** Takesha Yamamoto **Dir.** Yasujiro Ozu; **Scr.** Yasujiro Ozu, Kogo Noda; **Cin.** Yushun Atsuta; **Ed.** Yoshiyasu Hamamura; **Prod. D.** and **Art D.** Tatsuo Hamada, Itsuo Takahashi; **Mus.** Takanobu Saito; **Cast:** Chishu Ryu, Chieko Higashiyama, So Yamamura, Hanko Sugimura, Kuniko Miyake, Setsuko Hara, Kyoko Kagawa.

An elderly couple (Chishu Ryu and Chieko Higashiyama) who live with their youngest daughter in the southern coastal city of Onomichi are to take their first trip to Tokyo. They are to visit their married son who is a doctor in suburban Tokyo and their married daughter who operates a beauty salon. They had another son who was killed in the war and left a widow (Setsuko Hara) who also lives there. Their youngest son lives in Osaka and is too busy to make the trip to Tokyo. The son and daughter in Tokyo are also too busy to spend time with their parents. The beautician houses them for their first two nights. There are some excellent touches that develop the characters early. The daughter buys the least expensive food for her parents, saying they won't know the difference. Her young son of ten or eleven who is upset over having to give his room to his grandparents barely greets them. They are made to feel unwelcome from the start. To be rid of the parents for a few days they send them to a resort that is frequented by young people. After a sleepless night in the noisy resort, they return to spend two more nights in Tokyo. The father spends a night with some old drinking comrades whom he had not seen in years, and comes home drunk. He is severely reprimanded by his daughter. The mother spends a night with her widowed daughter-in-law who is the only person to make them feel welcome. The couple, convinced that their children have little time for them and that they are a burden, decide to leave. On the train back to Onomichi, the mother, who had not felt well from the start of the journey, becomes ill. The children are summoned and she dies shortly after their arrival. The sons and the daughter now regret their neglect of their parents but nonetheless are anxious to get back and resume their lives. The gracious daughter-in-law stays the longest, but she has a job in Tokyo and must return. Her father-in-law gives his wife's watch to her. In the end the old man sits on the porch alone looking at the ocean. He has come to terms with age and death.

The film is realistic and bleak. There is no sentimentality. The parents are dignified during their ordeal in Tokyo. The film becomes a sad commentary on parenthood and children. There is only the daughter-in-law whose kindness gives solace to the old couple and softens their melancholy. The film deals with these questions, but the focus is on the generation about to leave the world. Ozu, the most traditional of Japanese filmmakers, made over fifty films, beginning in the silent era. Many of them have been lost or destroyed and only a few were ever exhibited in the West. Most of his films deal with problems in twentieth-century Japan and several deal with parents and children. As a traditionalist Ozu uses very few fades or dissolves and even fewer self-conscious camera shots. His camera, however, often lingers after his characters have left the scene and slowly pans the surroundings. His technique suits the contemplative nature of his films. *Tokyo Story* is deceptively simple film.

Touch of Evil

1958. 111 min. b.w. U.S. **Prod.** Albert Zugsmith; **Dir.** Orson Welles, Harry Keller; **Scr.** Orson Welles (based on the novel *Badge of Evil* by Whit Masterson); **Cin.** Russell Metty; **Ed.** Virgil Vogel, Aaron Stell, **Art D.** Alexander Golitzen, Robert Clatworthy. **Mus.** Henry Mancini; **Cast:** Charlton Heston, Orson Welles, Janet Leigh, Joseph Calleia, Akim Tamiroff, Marlene Dietrich, Dennis Weaver, Ray Collins, Victor Millan, Mercedes McCambridge, Zsa Zsa Gabor, Joseph Cotton.

The film opens with a car entering the U.S. border town of Los Robles from Mexico. Behind the wheel is a middle-aged man with a young blonde floozy. The car, rigged with dynamite, explodes a few seconds after it enters U.S. territory. A cop, Hank Quinlan (Orson Welles), is dispatched to investigate the case. Mexican narcotics agent Ramon Vargas (Charlton Heston), who is

vacationing with his bride Susan (Janet Leigh), witnessed the
explosion and joins in the investigation. Quinlan immediately has
a suspect, Sanchez, the Mexican boyfriend of the murdered man's
daughter. In his long career as a policeman, Quinlan has acquired a
reputation for unusually well-honed instincts when it comes to
criminal investigations. To be certain to secure a conviction against
Sanchez he plants some sticks of dynamite in a box in Sanchez's
bathroom. Vargas, who had been to the same bathroom some ten
minutes earlier and had seen an empty box, accuses Quinlan of
planting evidence. A bitter argument ensues and Quinlan threatens to resign because his integrity has been called into question.
Quinlan will now go to any length to discredit Vargas. Vargas, with
the help of the local D.A., searches Quinlan's record of past arrests
and finds that in many cases Quinlan had fabricated evidence to
secure a conviction. A gangster, Joe Grande (Akim Tamiroff), who
is involved in drugs and whose brother has been imprisoned in
Mexico by Vargas for drug running, pounces on the opportunity
to "persuade" Vargas not to continue his investigation into drug
running in Los Robles. He orders his people to harass Vargas' wife
who is staying at a motel, but his orders are carried too far. Susan is
shot full of heroin and dumped in the bedroom of a cheap run-
down hotel. Vargas now has to salvage his own reputation. There
will be another murder, ending with Quinlan's death as well. The
irony is that Sanchez has confessed to his crime and Quinlan's
intuition has been proven right once again.

Touch of Evil is a masterpiece of cinematography. It starts with a
highly acclaimed opening scene, a three-minute tracking crane
shot of the car crossing the border and exploding. The film continues with each scene being a monument to Orson Welles'
mastery of the medium. The murder of Grande begins with the
ritual of Quinlan putting on his gloves, the only light in the room
coming from the flashing neon street sign, and the placing of the
dead body next to the drugged and unconscious Susan Vargas, the
neon light now flashing squarely on the grotesque face of the
strangled Grande. The final scene has the dying Quinlan sink into
the filthiest beach ever photographed. Welles and his photographer, Russell Metty, were not only inventive, but they utilized

every photographic trick to great effect. Over half of the movie takes place in the dark or with only low-key lighting. The grossly fat Quinlan is photographed from a very low front angle, emphasizing his bulk. Welles rewrote a discarded script based on a mediocre novel, embellished it and created several additional roles. Quinlan's wife had been murdered some thirty years earlier and the murderer had been set free for lack of evidence. Quinlan himself had been crippled by a gangster's bullet. There is a connection between these events and his planting of evidence. In Welles' script Quinlan becomes a more complex and tormented figure. The movie hosts a bizarre array of characters. Foremost is Quinlan himself, weighing some three hundred pounds. Akim Tamiroff, even with his absurd wig, is more menacing than funny. There are a blind woman shopkeeper, Mercedes McCambridge as a lesbian leader of a motorcycle gang, Dennis Weaver as a deranged motel clerk, and Zsa Zsa Gabor as the owner of a strip joint. Joseph Cotton as a doctor and Ray Collins, both unbilled, are favorites of Welles from his Mercury Theater and his first two films. There is also the inspired casting of Marlene Dietrich as the madam of a bordello. Welles asked her to appear in the same clothes and makeup she had worn as a gypsy in *Golden Earrings* (1947) and to use her natural accent. Dietrich literally steals the two scenes in which she appears. When she first sees Quinlan after the passage of many years in which his weight had ballooned, she tells him, "You're a mess honey. You've been eating too much candy." Heston as the self-righteous cop gives one of his better performances. He was asked by Welles to forgo imitating a Mexican accent and his natural speech works much better. Joseph Calleia gives a touching performance as Quinlan's deputy who owes his life to Quinlan and yet has to betray him. Janet Leigh has a limited part.

Welles was originally approached only to act in the film. Charlton Heston accepted his role assuming that Welles would be the director as well. The producer and Universal Studios needing Heston's name had to agree. Welles accepted the directorial assignment barely three weeks before shooting was to start. This was Welles' first return to Hollywood after a ten-year absence and he had his usual difficulty with the studios. Universal denied him the final cut. The film was released in a mutilated ninety-five-minute version. In 1978 some thirteen minutes were added and in 1998 the film was restored to 111 minutes, which brought into sharper focus its themes of justice versus the law, and loyalty and betrayal.

The Tree of Wooden Clogs

L'Albero Degli Zoccoli. 1978. 185 min. color. Italian. **Prod.** Giulio Mandelli; **Dir.** Ermanno Olmi; **Scr.** Ermanno Olmi; **Cin.** Ermanno Olmi; **Ed.** Ermanno Olmi; **Mus.** Bach; **Cast:** Luigi Ornaghi, Francesca Moriggi, Omar Brignoli, Antonio Ferrari, Teresa Brescianini, Giuseppe Brignoli, Carlo Rota, Pasqualina Brolis, Massimo Fratus, Francesca Villa.

The story is of one year in the lives of four sharecropping families on the estate of an absentee landlord in the province of Lombardi in 1896. There is no central plot. Their lives are revealed through a series of small incidents: the cultivation of fully ripe tomatoes by an old farmer before they are seasonally due, and the illness and recovery of the only cow in the compound. The death of the head of one family with six children forces his widow to plead with the local priest to place at least two of her children in an orphanage as she will be unable to feed them. The priest can only make arrangements for one. The kind and thoughtful priest is shown to be most helpful to the peasants. There is the courting and marriage of a young couple who take a boat trip to Milan for a two-day honeymoon at a convent. They witness violent street demonstrations broken up by the police but take no interest. The priest convinces one family to send their bright young son to the elementary school despite the parents' argument that they need the boy to do chores on the farm. The school is six kilometers away and within a few months his shoes are worn out. In the incident that gives the film its title the father cuts a tree and makes a pair of clogs for his boy. The manager of the estate discovers the remains of the tree and as punishment the entire family including the old grandfather and pregnant wife is expelled and some of their belongings confiscated.

The peasants are portrayed realistically, not romanticized or patronized. There is a political element in the film depicting the vast gulf between the lives of the peasants and the managers and owners. Each farm family lives in one or two bare bleak rooms. The estate manager's house is shown as fully furnished with all the amenities of a middle-class household. The absentee land-lord's mansion is seen while he is hosting a piano recital. The cruel treatment of an entire family for the loss of a tree is shown without any moralizing or touch of sentimentality. The film is scripted, directed, photographed and edited by Ermanno Olmi and it is a near-perfect effort. There is beautiful camera work and magnificent use of color in depicting the change of seasons. The cast is entirely nonprofessional, which gives the film added real-ism. Olmi himself came from the town of Bergamo in Lombardi. Born of peasant parents and having a feel for depicting peasant life and characters, he created a masterpiece.

---

12 Angry Men

1957. 95 min. b.w. U.S. **Prod.** Henry Fonda, Reginald Rose; **Dir.** Sidney Lumet; **Scr.** Reginald Rose; **Cin.** Boris Kaufman; **Ed.** Carl Lerner; **Art D.** Robert Markell; **Mus.** Kenyon Hopkins; **Cast:** Henry Fonda, Lee J. Cobb, Ed Begley, E. G. Marshall, Jack Klugman, Jack Warden, Martin Balsam, John Fiedler, George Voscovec, Robert Webber, Edward Binns, Joseph Sweeney.

New York City on a hot summer's day. The trial of a young Latino slum kid accused of knifing his father to death has con-cluded. The all-white jury is instructed by the judge and retires to the jury room to deliberate on the verdict. The twelve jurors elect as their foreman a high-school assistant football coach (Martin Balsam). Among the jurors there is an architect (Henry Fonda), an old, mellow and deferential man (Joseph Sweeney), a Madison Avenue advertising executive (Robert Webber) who has difficulty making up his mind, a watchmaker (George Voscovec) who has

recently immigrated to the U.S. and is proud to live in a democracy, a house painter (Edward Binns), a wisecracking marmalade
salesman (Jack Warden) who wants to get the whole thing over as
quickly as possible as he has tickets to the Yankee's night game, a
garage owner (Ed Begley) who has strong feelings against blacks
and Puerto Ricans, the owner of a messenger service (Lee. J.
Cobb) who has had a stormy relationship with his son, and a very
calm and methodical stockbroker (E. G. Marshall). To most of the
jurors it is an open and shut case. Even the boy's court-appointed
attorney had not made a vigorous defence. Within about ten
minutes of entering the jury room, a vote is taken and it is eleven
to one for conviction. The lone dissenter, the architect, argues
that there is a reasonable doubt in his mind as to the boy's guilt.
All he asks for is some more talk before another vote is taken.
Through a review of the evidence and pure logic, he gradually
persuades the rest of the jury that the prosecution has not made
its case and there is more than reasonable doubt.

   12 Angry Men is an intelligent and literate film. The motivation
and the thinking process of each of the jurors is revealed,
although there are a few stock characters among them: Ed Begley, the old-fashioned bigot; Robert Webber, the glib advertising
executive; and Jack Warden, an apparently successful marmalade
salesman who feels himself superior for being an ardent fan of the
champion Yankees. It is also among the best films in terms of
directing, photography and acting. It had been a teleplay that Sidney Lumet had directed. This was Lumet's first film, but his
familiarity with the script allowed him to shoot it in twenty days.
Lumet, as he was to demonstrate in countless later films, was a
master of confined interiors. The entire film, other than a one-
minute scene at the outset in the courtroom and a two-minute
scene at the end on the courthouse steps, is shot in the jury
room. Lumet punctuates the story with as much action as the set
permits: fussing over a fan, opening windows, and reenacting the
testimony of key witnesses. He builds suspense in several ways.
There is a great deal of vote switching in the early ballots and the
audience becomes involved in who will change his vote. About

two thirds into the film the jurors have solidified into an eight to four acquittal vote. What brings suspense thereafter is our anticipation of who next will break the ranks of the entrenched guilty votes. The film was an eye-opener for the wealth of talent present on the New York stage and in television. The director had never directed a movie and, but for five actors in the cast, the rest were unknown to movie audiences. The film has dated a little with an all-white all-male jury, and the blatant racism of Ed Begley that now has been replaced by more subtle prejudices.

The Wages of Fear

Le Salaire de la Peur. 1952. 156 min. b.w. French. **Prod.** Henri-Georges Clouzot; **Dir.** Henri-Georges Clouzot; **Scr.** Henri-Georges Clouzot, Jerome Geronimi (based on the novel by Georges Arnaud); **Cin.** Armand Thirard, Madeleine Gug, Etiennette Muse; **Prod. D.** Rene Renoux; **Mus.** Georges Auric; **Cast:** Yves Montand, Charles Vanel, Peter Van Eyck, Folco Lulli, Vera Clouzot, William Tubbs, Joe Dest.

The opening shot of four beetles strung together by a child prepares us for the filth and poverty of a Central American village. Set around 1950 in Las Piedras in an unnamed country, the first fifty minutes sets the tone and introduces us to four expatriates who, for various reasons are stranded with little hope of being able to leave. They are the unemployed Corsican, Mario (Yves Montand), with probably a shady background; his roommate, the jolly Italian, Luigi (Folco Lulli); a German, Bimba (Peter Van Eyck); and Smerloff (Joe Dest). Then there is Linda (Vera Clouzot), a native woman who works in the only café in town. She is the mistress of the café owner, but is after Mario who does not return her affection. Soon Joe (Charles Vanel), an aging Paris hoodlum on the run, arrives at the nearby airport. Mario is impressed with Joe's background and tales of his exploits in the Paris underworld and they take to each other quickly. There is an implied homosexual relationship between Mario and Luigi, who immediately forms a resentment toward Joe.

The only employer in these parts is Southern Oil Company, an American firm managed by Bill O'Brien (William Tubbs). A fierce fire breaks out in the oilfield, which is some three hundred miles away. O'Brien decides to send two trucks with nitroglycerine to the area to blow up the burning wells. It is a perilous journey through jungles and mountains on unpaved roads with hairpin curves. The smallest jolt or spark will detonate the nitro. Each truck will have two drivers who will take turns. Each driver will be paid $2,000 upon their arrival. Although the risks are over-whelming, $2,000 means freedom and escape. Finally Mario, Luigi, Bimba and Smerloff are selected. Joe, despite the fact that he had known O'Brien before, is rejected because of his age. But at departure time Joe appears in lieu of Smerloff, whom we presume has been killed by Joe. Joe and Mario are paired and they are in the lead truck. There is unbearable tension from the beginning of the journey and Clouzot handles it masterfully. Mario executes a 180-degree turn on a dilapidated wooden platform suspended over a deep ravine that collapses just as he pulls off. Bimba, who has been paired with Luigi, has passed Mario's truck and gets to a huge boulder on the road. In one of the most tense scenes he successfully blows it up with two or three drops of nitro. Soon Joe's nerves are shattered and he refuses to go on with the journey. Mario has to slap the once-boastful French hoodlum to prevent him from deserting. When their journey is resumed, Mario and Joe hear a faint noise in the distance. In a skillfully devised scene we see a cloud of smoke on the horizon and instantly know that Bimba and Luigi have been blown up. The explosion has damaged the pipeline and created a crater. Oil is rapidly filling it. Mario sends Joe into the oil spill to measure the depth and guide him through. Joe slips and falls. Mario has no recourse but to continue, driving over Joe's leg in the process, and it is crushed and later turns gangrenous. By the time they reach the oilfield, Joe is dead. Mario gets the $4,000 and starts back the next day. Intoxicated by his success and the money, he drives recklessly and hurtles down a ravine to his death clutching a memento, a Paris metro ticket. The deafening siren of the truck ends the film.

The Wages of Fear is much more than an adventure story. There are layers of political undertones. It is never explained how a French hood had come to know the manager of an American oil company. There is an implied criticism of the U.S. for its exploitation of Central American countries. The four drivers, all Europeans, are taking a deadly risk for a U.S. oil company, which could be read as an allegory on NATO. Clouzot is clearly on the side of the drivers. Although taking unnecessary risks, their choice is preferable to their slow decay in Las Piedras. The Georges Arnaud novel on which the film is based is more explicit regarding the homosexuality of the Mario-Luigi-Joe triangle; the locale is identified as Guatemala; Mario is the pimp for the whore Linda; and the characters are nastier. Clouzot had wanted Jean Gabin for the lead. When he turned it down, Clouzot cast Yves Montand, a very popular music hall singer whose career as a film actor was launched. At the first U.S. showing, one hour was cut and the film was mutilated. It has since been restored to the original 156 minutes. The suspense is unrelenting. It is on a higher pitch than even the best of Hitchcock. This was Clouzot's sixth feature film. He made only one good film after *The Wages Of Fear—Les Diabolique* (1954). His health later deteriorated.

White Heat

1949. 114 min. b.w. U.S. **Prod.** Louis F. Edelman; **Dir.** Raoul Walsh; **Scr.** Ivan Goff, Ben Roberts; **Cin.** Sid Hickox; **Ed.** Owen Marks; **Art D.** Edward Carrere; **Mus.** Max Steiner; **Cast:** James Cagney, Virginia Mayo, Edmond O'Brien, Margaret Wycherly, Steve Cochran, John Archer.

Cody Jarrett (James Cagney) is a psychotic killer with a mother fixation. He and his mother, Ma Jarrett (Margaret Wycherly), head a gang of train robbers. After the last robbery, in which two people were murdered, the Treasury agents are certain that it was Jarrett's gang that pulled the job, but they can't make it stick. Cody has gotten himself convicted and jailed on a minor robbery charge in another state, showing that at the time of the robbery he was out of state. The Treasury Department plants one of its own men, Vic Pardo (Edmond O'Brien), in the same prison cell as Cody hoping to get more information about the gang's members and operations. Pardo gains Cody's full confidence when he helps to revive him from one of his frequent seizures. When Cody finds out his mother has been killed by Big Ed Somers (Steve Cochran) who wants to take over the gang, he goes into an uncontrollable rage and soon thereafter escapes with Pardo. Once out he kills Big Ed and plans his next job, which is the payroll office of a large chemical plant in Torrance, California. Pardo alerts the Treasury men and all the gang members are killed in a shoot-out. Cody himself dies on top of a large oil storage tank engulfed in flames.

White Heat is one of the best crime movies ever made. It was also one of the very first explorations of gangsters as psychotics. The thirties gangster movies set against the background of the Depression were more socially oriented and the gangster was often depicted as the victim of social injustice and economic deprivation. This film also deals tangentially with the theme of betrayal. Cody is ultimately defeated not by his homicidal bent and psychotic behavior but by the people he trusted—his wife who allied herself with Big Ed, and Pardo, who filled the void left by the murder of Ma Jarrett. Margaret Wycherly, a great actress, is excellent as Cody's mother. Virginia Mayo as the voluptuous and disloyal wife and Edmond O'Brien as the Treasury plant both handle their roles well. Among the supporting cast neither Steve Cochran nor John Archer as the senior Treasury agent give convincing portrayals. The film's only blemish is the urge by the director and the producers to exhibit and dwell at some length on the latest police technology and gadgetry that was unnecessary and now embarrassingly dated.

Director Raoul Walsh was involved with movies for almost fifty years. He was an actor in *Birth of a Nation* (1915), becoming a journeyman director and a good storyteller. This is by far his best film. It is very well paced, but it is the sheer power of Cagney's acting that raises the film above the ordinary. There are several scenes that demonstrate Cagney's professionalism. After one of his seizures he staggers toward his mother who cradles him in her lap. Later when he hears the devastating news of his mother's death he becomes frenzied and with quick and supple movements succeeds in punching several prison guards. There is also the famous last scene in which he is on top of the huge burning storage tank, firing his gun indiscriminately and shouting, "Made it Ma! Top of the world!" Cagney was the most imitated actor of his day and is considered by several directors, including Orson Welles, to be the finest Hollywood actor. He was the first actor to receive the Lifetime Achievement Award of the American Film Institute in 1974.

The Wild Bunch

1969. 134 min. color. U.S. **Prod.** Phil Feldman; **Dir.** Sam Peckinpah; **Scr.** Walon Greene, Sam Peckinpah; **Cin.** Lucien Ballard; **Ed.** Lou Lombardo; **Art D.** Edward Carrere; **Mus.** Jerry Fielding; **Cast:** William Holden, Ernest Borgnine, Robert Ryan, Edmond O'Brien, Warren Oates, Ben Johnson, Jaime Sanchez, Strother Martin, L. Q. Jones, Albert Dekker, Bo Hopkins, Emilio Fernandez, Dub Taylor.

Set in 1913, a band of outlaws led by aging Pike Bishop (William Holden), whose primary targets have been trains, railroad payroll offices and banks, now have in their sights a railroad bank in San Rafael, a small Texas border town. Their numbers have been reduced to eight by bounty hunters employed by the railroads. This is to be their last job before they go their separate ways. They enter the town wearing stolen U.S. army uniforms. What they don't know is that Harrigan (Albert Dekker), a ruthless railroad executive who owns the town, is aware of their plan and has hired a band of cutthroat bounty hunters led by Deke Thornton (Robert Ryan) who once rode with Pike. Thornton had been serving time in prison, but Harrigan had him freed temporarily with the understanding that his complete freedom depended upon his elimination of Pike. The other bounty hunters are scum and can't even shoot straight. In the ambush, two of the outlaws are killed but six others escape with the loot from the bank. One of them has been wounded and blinded and

Pike is forced to put him out of his misery. Some bounty hunters are killed, as well as innocent townspeople caught in the crossfire. Pike now has four men: the loyal Dutch Engstrom (Ernest Borgnine); the always quarrelsome Gorch brothers, Lyle (Warren Oates) and Tector (Ben Johnson), who are undisciplined and don't like anybody; and a young Mexican, Angel (Jaime Sanchez). They meet up with an old outlaw, Sykes (Edmond O'Brien), who joins them. On opening the bags stolen from the bank, they find they are filled with metal washers instead of gold. They now have to plan another job. Knowing that Thornton and his men are not far behind, they cross over to Mexico, a country torn by civil war. In the north, there are troops led by a cruel and vicious bandit calling himself General Mapache (Emilio Fernandez) who is up against the forces of Pancho Villa. The gang spends its first night at Angel's village. The next day they reach Agua Verde, the base of Mapache and his troops. Mapache strikes a deal with them. In return for payment in gold, Pike and his men are to rob an American train carrying rifles and ammunition to a U.S. military camp, and turn them over to Mapache. The robbery goes well, and they deliver the rifles, ammunition and even a machine gun. Angel had arranged with Pike to forgo his share of the gold in exchange for one box of rifles, which he gives to his people who are fighting Mapache. The gang is paid but Angel is kept behind and tortured. The gang abandons him and leaves, but they have second thoughts and turn back to save him. After spending a night with some local whores, four of them (Sykes had been wounded by the bounty hunters and is being cared for by Angel's people) stride into Mapache's camp. In one of the bloodiest scenes in movies to that date, they are all killed, but not before Mapache's army is decimated. Except for Thornton, the rest of the bounty hunters pursuing the gang are killed by Angel's people. Thornton and Sykes remain in Mexico and join Angel's rebels to rid northern Mexico of other outlaw generals.

The Wild Bunch is Sam Peckinpah's masterpiece. He had not directed for several years when Warners agreed to produce *The Wild Bunch*. Producers and distributors had a penchant for mutilating his previous films. His only film that had been relatively spared was *Ride the High Country* (1962), which is itself a minor masterpiece. They cut much of this film as well, not for content but to shorten it to a commercially viable two hours. It has now been restored to the director's cut. *The Wild Bunch* is not just important cinematically; it also changed the mythology of the Old West that John Ford and other directors had created over the years. The U.S. Cavalry is shown as a band of untrained youngsters. The railroad, which in previous films had been depicted as the vehicle that brought civilization to the West, is shown to have been operated by unscrupulous businessmen who employed mercenary killers. Almost all of Peckinpah's films deal with people who have, in essence, become dinosaurs and who refuse to adapt to suit the new order. Peckinpah's world has no good people, only the evil and the less evil. Men, women and even children are cruel. It is a boy and a woman who shoot and kill Pike at the film's end. The only lesser evil people in this film are the characters of Pike, Dutch, Angel and probably Thornton. In the film's opening we see a group of laughing children who have put a scorpion into an ant colony. The scene is Peckinpah's vision of the Old West. The ants will devour the scorpion in time. The film is also a masterwork of Lucien Ballard's photography. In scene after scene he outdoes himself. During the robbery, one of the robbers is shot and spectacularly crashes with his horse into a shop window, spewing shattered glass. Later, Pike, who had suffered a leg injury at some stage in the past, falls off his horse, remounts with great difficulty and without looking back rides into the desert, disappearing over the horizon. Other superb images are a bridge being blown up with men and horses tumbling down into the river below; the scene of the whore and her baby; the shot of a large woman soldier in full military uniform breast-feeding her baby; the choreographed drama of the wild bunch's last march to confront Mapache; the death of each of the bunch's four members; and the shot of a vulture sitting on one of Mapache's dead soldiers. As with most masterpieces, however, there are some small flaws. In *The Wild Bunch*, a few scenes are either too short or too long. The flashback of Pike and Thornton in a bordello and their ambush is too short and the character of

Thornton is not fully defined. The torture of Angel is a minute or so too long. So too is the scene of the Gorch brothers and their whores bathing. The gang leaving Angel's village to the strains of "La Golandrina" is a bit sentimental; and the presence of the two Germans in Mapache's camp can be deemed unnecessary.

The film has two very fine performances by William Holden and Robert Ryan, both outstanding actors. Borgnine, the loyal and only political revolutionary in the gang who wants a free, unified Mexico, has one of his best roles and some of the best lines in the film. He is proud, and considers himself a better person than the Mapache and railroad crowd, claiming, "We don't hang people." In the attempt to save Angel, knowing that he is going to certain death, he says, "I wouldn't have it any other way." The film also has the outstanding performance by Edmond O'Brien as Sykes, resembling Walter Huston in *The Treasures of the Sierra Madre* (1948). *The Wild Bunch* was a groundbreaking film for graphic violence and the deglamorization of the West.

Wild Strawberries

1957. 90 min. b.w. Swedish. **Prod.** Allan Ekelund; **Dir.** Ingmar Bergman; **Scr.** Ingmar Bergman; **Cin.** Gunnar Fischer, Bjorn Thermenius; **Ed.** Oscar Rosander; **Art D.** Gittan Gustafsson; **Mus.** Erik Nordgren; **Cast:** Victor Sjostrom, Ingrid Thulin, Bibi Andersson, Gunnar Bjornstrand, Jullan Kindahl, Folke Sunquist, Bjorn Bjelvenstam.

Events take place on a Saturday in June 1957. Seventy-eight-year old widower Isak Borg (Victor Sjostrom), professor emeritus of bacteriology in Stockholm, lives with his old housekeeper, Agda (Jullan Kindahl), who worships and spoils him. He has one child, Evald (Gunnar Bjornstrand), who is pressing his pregnant wife, Marianne (Ingrid Thulin), to have an abortion. Evald is angry at the whole world and does not want to bring a child into a chaotic and meaningless environment. Marianne has come to her father-in-law hoping he will talk to Evald and resolve their difficulties. Isak is not on the best of terms with his estranged son. They have had a difficult relationship. When his son had needed some money, Isak, instead of making an outright gift, had lent him the money at a high interest rate. Isak is to receive an honorary degree the next day from his alma mater, Lund University, on the occasion of the fiftieth anniversary of receiving his doctorate. He has had a disturbing nightmare the night before. In the dream he walks through an abandoned city and is approached by a faceless man. He sees a clock without hands and watches a passing hearse. Suddenly a coffin falls out onto the street and its lid comes loose. He looks inside and recognizes himself. The corpse's hand tries to drag him into the coffin. He resists and is awakened. Still upset over the dream he decides to make the three hundred-mile journey by car and forgo the flight he had arranged with his housekeeper. Marianne, who wants to talk to him, volunteers to drive. Barely on their way Marianne begins telling him of her difficulties with Evald and his insistence on an abortion. Isak listens attentively but offers no advice. Marianne is terribly upset and accuses him of being an aloof, cold and selfish man incapable of giving or receiving love. Isak is amazed at his daughter-in-law's estimate of him.

They pick up three students, a girl and two boys, who are hitchhiking to Italy for their summer vacation. One of the boys is an atheist medical student, the other a theology student. They argue the whole time and the girl, Sara (Bibi Andersson), plays the peacemaker. They all become impressed when they find that Isak is an eminent scientist on his way to receive an honorary degree. Sara has an uncanny resemblance to a girl Isak had been in love with in his youth and had wanted to marry. They stop to rest near a patch of wild strawberries and he begins to daydream, remembering his youthful romance. Even in his youth he had been too proud and serious. The girl had lost interest and married his brother, a much more easygoing person. He had married someone else and had never been happy. Marianne and Isak resume their journey and they pick up a married couple who are stranded because of a car accident. Their constant vicious attacks on each other remind Isak of his own marriage. The couple become more abusive and Marianne asks them to get out of the car. Isak and Marianne reach Lund. The honorary degree is bestowed on Isak in an archaic ceremony. He becomes more responsive toward Marianne and later talks to Evald. It appears that he may soften his relationship with Marianne. She kisses Isak and says she loves him. When he falls asleep he dreams of his childhood and sees his parents wave to him.

The film is a study of old age, lost opportunities of youth and the imperative for forgiveness between children and parents. It is as much about the relationship between Isak and his mother as it is about Isak and his son. In a dream sequence, Isak's much-respected mother is shown to be cold and indifferent to her children, especially Isak. Bergman himself has written that in making the film he wanted to justify himself to his dead parents. A difficult film with its combination of reality, dreams and nightmares, but Bergman gives it coherence. The acting of Sjostrom, himself a successful director of silent films, is very good, as is the acting of Thulin. The three students are cardboard characters and no attempt is made to develop them. In another Bergman film, *The Seventh Seal* (1957), wild strawberries were the symbol of human kindness. In this film they are symbols of lost opportunities.

Woman in the Dunes

Suna No Onna. 1964. 123 min. b.w. Japanese. **Prod.** Kiichi Ichikawa, Tadashi Ohono; **Dir.** Hiroshi Teshigahara; **Scr.** Kobo Abe (based on his novel); **Cin.** Hiroshi Segawa; **Ed.** F. Susui; **Mus.** Toru Takemitsu; **Cast:** Eiji Okada, Kyoko Kishida, Koji Mitsui, Hiroko Ito.

Entomologist Niki Jumpi (Eiji Okada) has come to a beach not far from the city to collect insect specimens. He misses the last bus back and is stranded. Some helpful villagers offer him a place to spend the night. He is taken to a shack located at the bottom of a sandpit, the only access being by rope ladder. The shack is owned by a widow (Kyoko Kishida) whose husband and child died during a sandstorm. He spends the night and the next day there. As he is about to leave, he notices the ladder has been removed. The woman is busy shoveling sand into buckets that are then lifted by rope by the villagers above. He spends hours trying to climb the sand dune and each time he slides back. He becomes exhausted and by nightfall he gives up. He realizes that in return for the sand buckets, the widow receives water and food. The next day, he sees the shifting winds have filled part of the room with sand and he joins the woman in sending up buckets. In time, a close relationship develops with the woman. She becomes pregnant and can't do her share of work. To avoid being engulfed by sand he works twice as hard. He gives up any idea of escaping. He has now become totally devoted to her and realizes how self-less and brave she is. One day he notices the rope ladder has been lowered and he could climb out. He chooses to stay.

The film could be read as an allegory on the nature of free-dom and liberty. In his enslavement Jumpi has found his freedom. There is also a similarity to the myth of Sisyphus, whom the Gods punished for his transgressions by having him roll a boulder up a mountain. When Sisyphus reaches the moun-tain top the boulder rolls down and he must repeat his labor—for eternity. While descending, he has the freedom to contemplate his condition and rises above his predicament. *Woman in the Dunes* is a great film, often overlooked. Okada, as the scientist who has grown tired of living in an impersonal city, wants solitude. Kishida, as the selfless inarticulate woman who has had a tragic past, accepts her fate. In coming together, they both find their freedom.

Wuthering Heights

1939. 103 min. b.w. U.S. **Prod.** Samuel Goldwyn; **Dir.** William Wyler; **Scr.** Ben Hecht, Charles MacArthur (based on the novel by Emily Brontë); **Cin.** Gregg Toland; **Ed.** Daniel Mandell; **Art D.** James Basevi; **Mus.** Alfred Newman; **Cast:** Merle Oberon, Laurence Olivier, David Niven, Flora Robson, Donald Crisp, Geraldine Fitzgerald, Leo G. Carroll, Cecil Kellaway, Miles Mander, Hugh Williams, Rex Downing.

Set in Yorkshire during the early years of Queen Victoria's reign, a kindly widowed father of two children, Mr. Earnshaw (Cecil Kellaway), brings home a dark gypsy-like orphan boy named Heathcliff (played as an adult by Laurence Olivier) to be a companion to his motherless children. Soon a bond develops between Heathcliff and Cathy (played as an adult by Merle Oberon), while the son Hindley (played as an adult by Hugh Williams) hates the strange intruder from the very outset. When Mr. Earnshaw dies Hindley becomes master of the house and begins to abuse Heathcliff mercilessly. He makes a servant of him and sends him from the house to live in the stable. Heathcliff comes close to leaving several times but his love for Cathy keeps him there. When Heathcliff hears that Cathy may marry their wealthy neighbor, Edgar Linton (David Niven), he is devastated and finally decides to leave. He returns after several years as a polished man of means but consumed by hatred for everyone, especially Cathy for having married. Out of spite he marries Edgar's younger sister Isabella (Geraldine Fitzgerald) with a tragic outcome for all.

The film covers the first fifteen chapters of the Brontë novel and the story is narrated by the housekeeper Ellen (Flora Robson). The film is made memorable by a combination of the direction of the under-appreciated William Wyler, the beautiful photography of Gregg Toland and the set designs by James Basevi of *The Ox-Bow Incident* (1943) and *The Searchers* (1956). Goldwyn spent a good deal of money and with the help of Basevi converted a 450-acre tract of land near Ventura, California into the Yorkshire moors, complete with heather shipped from England. The moody cinematography of Gregg Toland, which won an Academy Award, stands out. The Earnshaw house is bright, but once purchased by Heathcliff becomes bleak and somber. Olivier had appeared in some fifteen films between 1930 and 1939, both in Britain and the U.S., and never did anything outstanding. He was to have appeared opposite Greta Garbo in *Queen Christina* (1933), but Garbo insisted on John Gilbert and Olivier returned to England very bitter. He was somehow persuaded to come to the U.S. for *Wuthering Heights* and under the direction of Wyler established himself as an accomplished film actor. For the first time in his movie career he showed a passion that had been absent from his earlier films. The acting of the entire supporting cast is excellent, especially Cecil Kellaway, Donald Crisp, Geraldine Fitzgerald (as Isabella Linton caught in a loveless marriage) and Flora Robson (as the housekeeper who in the novel is unknowingly in love with Heathcliff). Merle Oberon who could not bring any intensity to her role as Cathy lets the film down. Goldwyn did not like films that ended with the death of the star. Over Wyler's objection he had a scene added to the end in which ghosts of Heathcliff and Cathy are seen on the moor.

—

Z

1969. 127 min. color. French. **Prod.** Jacques Perrin, Hamed Rachedi; **Dir.** Constantin Costa-Gavras; **Scr.** Constantin Costa-Gavras, Jorge Semprun (based on the novel by Vassili Vassilikos); **Cin.** Raoul Coutard; **Ed.** Francoise Bonnot; **Art D.** Jacques d'Ovidio; **Mus.** Mikis Theodorakis; **Cast:** Yves Montand, Irene Papas, Jean Louis Trintignant, Charles Denner, Marcel Bozzufi, Jacques Perrin, Francois Périer, Pierre Dux, Julien Guiomar, Bernard Fresson, Renato Salvatori.

In an unnamed country an organization called Friends of Peace is holding a rally that is to be addressed by its leader, referred to as the Deputy (Yves Montand). The meeting is expected to draw a crowd of several thousand. At the last minute the government rescinds its permission to stage the rally in a large meeting hall and the group is allotted a very small auditorium instead. The organizers decide to have the meeting outdoors. As the Deputy begins to address the crowd, the police allow a small van to pass through and someone in the van clubs the Deputy on the head, killing him. The Deputy's death is declared an accident. However, in order to silence the opposition, the government appoints an examining magistrate (Jean Louis Trintignant) to conduct a cursory review of the incident. To the surprise of all, the magistrate decides to wage a thorough investigation. The government, through the public prosecutor, makes a futile attempt to halt the proceedings. One witness is killed before he can testify and there is an attempt on the life of another witness, Manuel (Charles Denner). Soon a photojournalist (Jacques Perrin) helps uncover a secret neo-fascist organization that is backed by the army Royal Fighters for a Christian West. One of its members, Yago (Renato Salvatori), had driven the van and another, Vago (Marcel Bozzufi), clubbed the Deputy. The two hoodlums, along with several high-ranking army officers, are arrested and sentenced to terms of imprisonment. In an epilogue we are told there was a coup d'état by the army shortly thereafter. All the imprisoned men were freed and a neo-fascist government was installed. The examining magistrate and judge were removed and imprisoned. A long list of prohibitions were promulgated by the army junta including freedom of the press, peace movements and long hair on men.

Z is based on the 1963 murder of Gregorios Lambrakis, a professor of medicine and a member of parliament who, as a leader of the peace movement, was opposed to the installation of nuclear missiles in Greece. He was the victim of a conspiracy by right-wing colonels. The murderers were tried and sentenced in October 1966. There was a military coup d'état on 21 April 1967 that came to be known as the colonels' coup. The absolute dictatorship that followed lasted seven years. One of the signs of protest by the followers of Lambrakis against the colonels' regime was the scrawling on walls of the letter Z, which stands for the Greek "*zei,*" meaning "he lives."

The film is magnificently directed by Constantin Costa-Gavras, a relative newcomer in his third film. He later made other fine films, but *Z* is by far his best. There is excellent camera work by Raoul Coutard, Jean-Luc Godard's cameraman. The film moves at a breathtaking pace. Costa-Gavras cuts frequently from one character to another and sustains the suspense to the end. The music of Theodorakis, who was in jail in Greece at the time, blends perfectly with the film and, in some scenes, it even becomes an integral part of the narrative. The acting by the entire cast is very good. We are taken by Montand's long suffering face, with dedication written all over it. Irene Papas is magnificent as the Deputy's grieving wife. *Z* is one of the very best political thrillers ever made. Hollywood stopped making such films with the advent of the Cold War, opting instead for some embarrassingly bad films in the early fifties. It was not until the early 1960's that Hollywood managed to make some good political thrillers: *The Manchurian Candidate* (1962) and *Seven Days in May* (1964). The mid-seventies brought *The Parallax View* (1974), *Chinatown* (1974), and *All the President's Men* (1976). *Z* still holds its own as among the very best. It received rare recognition by being nominated for Academy Awards for both best film and best foreign film. It won for best foreign film and best editing.

THE GREAT

The Adventures of Robin Hood

1938. 102 min. b.w. U.S. **Prod.** Henry Blanke; **Dir.** Michael Curtiz, William Keighley; **Scr.** Norman Reilly Raine, Seton I. Miller (based on the novel *Ivanhoe* by Sir Walter Scott and the opera *Robin Hood* by De Koven-Smith); **Cin.** Sol Polito, Tony Gaudio; **Ed.** Ralph Dawson; **Art D.** Carl Jules Weyl; **Mus.** Erich Wolfgang Korngold; **Cast:** Errol Flynn, Olivia de Havilland, Basil Rathbone, Claude Rains, Eugene Pallette, Alan Hale, Melville Cooper, Ian Hunter.

This film is based on the often-filmed legend of King Richard the Lion-Hearted who is captured on his way back from the Crusades by Duke Leopold of Austria. Richard's brother, Prince John, is unwilling to pay the demanded ransom and appoints himself regent. Prince John imposes ever-higher taxes on the Saxons who are near revolt against their Norman conquerors. Sir Robin Locksley (Errol Flynn) becomes an outlaw, and robs the rich to raise enough money to pay King Richard's ransom. The people win and King Richard returns triumphant.

One of the best adventure films, it still holds up. Warners put everything into it. There is the expert direction of Michael Curtiz who stepped in after the initial choice, William Keighley, fell ill. There is a rousing score by Erich Wolfgang Korngold, and lush color. Flynn has his best role supported by an excellent cast of Claude Rains as the deceitful Prince John; Basil Rathbone, the perfect villain, as Sir Guy of Gisbourne; Alan Hale as Little John; Eugene Pallette as Friar Tuck; and Olivia de Havilland as Maid Marion. The film won Academy Awards for best editing, art direction and musical score.

The Adventures of Robinson Crusoe

1952. 90 min. b.w. U.S. **Prod.** Oscar Danciger, Henry Ehrlich; **Dir.** Luis Buñuel ; **Scr.** Hugo Butler, Luis Buñuel (based on *The Life and Strange Surprising Adventures of Robinson Crusoe* by Daniel Defoe); **Cin.** Alex Phillips; **Ed.** Carlos Savage, Alberto Valenzuela; **Mus.** Anthony Collins; **Cast:** Dan O'Herlihy, Jaime Fernandez.

The film is set in the early eighteenth century. The well-born son of a prosperous family, Robinson Crusoe (Dan O'Herlihy), runs away to sea. His ship is wrecked in a fierce storm and he is the only survivor, swept to the shore of a tropical island. He returns to the sinking ship and retrieves a cat, a dog, some tools, muskets, pistols, gunpowder and other necessities. He crawls into a cave and after a bout with fever he explores the island. He plants seeds, learns to fish, shoots birds, and covers himself with tree bark. One day, after eighteen years of solitude, he sees a band of natives from a neighboring island come ashore. They are cannibals and are about to slaughter a prisoner. He shoots one of them and the rest escape with their boats. The intended victim, whom he saved, he names Friday (Jaime Fernandez). He is elated that after all these years he has a companion and can escape his loneliness. At first he treats Friday as a servant, but soon a strong bond develops between them. They spend another ten years on the island, until a ship anchors nearby and Crusoe and Friday are rescued and taken to England.

The film was made by Buñuel during his self-exile in Mexico and it is his only film in English. *The Adventures of Robinson Crusoe* and *Los Olvidados* (1950) rank as his only notable films of that period. There is little of the surrealist flourishes of his 1930 masterpiece *L'Age d'Or*. Crusoe's story is told in a straightforward manner with only a very brief surrealistic dream sequence depicting his sexual deprivation. There is also an absence of Buñuel's customary attack on the church and middle-class morality. Defoe, the author of the 1719 novel, was also a religious dissenter who wrote several satirical pamphlets attacking the church. But in *Robinson Crusoe* the thrust of his story is on faith and belief, which enabled Crusoe to survive. Buñuel does not go that far. There is, however, a magnificent scene when Crusoe, all alone on the island, goes to a hilltop and shouts the twenty-third Psalm into an echoing valley to overcome his loneliness and affirm his faith. Dan O'Herlihy, a fine actor with a booming voice, gives a great performance in a difficult role. *The Adventures of Robinson Crusoe* is Buñuel's warmest and most life-affirming film.

All the President's Men

1976. 138 min. color. U.S. **Prod.** Walter Coblenz; **Dir.** Alan Pakula; **Scr.** William Gold-man (based on the book by Carl Bernstein and Bob Woodward); **Cin.** Gordon Willis; **Ed.** Robert Wolfe; **Prod. D.** George Jenkins; **Mus.** David Shire; **Cast:** Robert Redford, Dustin Hoffman, Jack Warden, Martin Balsam, Hal Holbrook, Jason Robards, Jr., Jane Alexander, Ned Beatty, Robert Walden.

This film examines the break-in at the Democratic National Headquarters offices in the Watergate building on 19 June 1972 and its aftermath, leading to the resignation of President Nixon. Based on the 1974 Carl Bernstein and Bob Woodward book, with an excellent script by William Goldman, it constitutes Alan Pakula's finest directorial effort. Pakula brings tremendous suspense to a story of which every viewer knew the outcome. With Gordon Willis' cinematography the film becomes as good a thriller/detective story as ever made. There are scenes of tremendous power that capture a conspiracy in the making. Even the streets of Washington, D.C. look menacing. The very brightly lit offices of the Washington Post are contrasted with the shadows of a deserted garage where the sound echoes ominously. The film has a superb cast. Hoffman and Redford are good, but it is the members of the supporting cast who are tailor-made for their roles. Jason Robards as Ben Bradlee, the executive editor of the Washington Post; Jack Warden and Martin Balsam as metropolitan and managing editors respectively; and Hal Holbrook as "Deep Throat." Probably the best nuanced acting in the film is by Jane Alexander who plays a bookkeeper at "Creep" (Committee for the Re-election of the President). Jason Robards received the Academy Award for best supporting actor and William Goldman for best adapted screenplay. The film was nominated for several awards, including best picture, best director, best supporting actress, editing and art direction.

Amadeus

1985. 105 min. color. U.S. **Prod.** Paul Zaentz; **Dir.** Milos Forman; **Scr.** Peter Shaffer (based on his play); **Cin.** Miroslav Ondricek; **Ed.** Nena Danevic, Michael Chandler; **Prod. D.** Patrizia von Brandenstein; **Art D.** Karel Cerny, Francesco Chianese, Joseph Svoboda; **Mus.** Mozart, Salieri, Pergolesi; **Cast:** F. Murray Abraham, Tom Hulce, Elizabeth Berridge, Simon Callow, Jeffrey Jones.

Based on an imaginative play and scripted by the playwright himself, Peter Shaffer, the film strongly suggests that Mozart was driven to his death in 1791 by a mediocre composer, Antonio Salieri (F. Murray Abraham). It opens in 1823 with Salieri near death in an insane asylum making a deathbed confession to a novice priest that he caused Mozart's death. There is then a lengthy flashback to 1780s Vienna when Mozart (Tom Hulce) has gained a degree of recognition and has come to the attention of Emperor Joseph II, who considers himself a good amateur musician. Mozart's growing fame and his genius turn Salieri into a hate-filled madman who will do anything to discredit Mozart.

The film becomes a study of the intense jealousy of mediocrity toward genius. It is expertly directed and beautifully photographed. F. Murray Abraham is magnificent in his first starring role. He plays a near-tragic figure who realizes he and Mozart have little in common and that Mozart is on a different plane. What affects one's full appreciation of the film is the casting of Tom Hulce as Mozart. Hulce is too contemporary and his high-pitched voice exaggerates Mozart's idiosyncrasies. He too often plays for laughs. The film received Academy Awards for best picture, best actor (Abraham), best director, adapted screenplay, art direction, sound and costumes; and a best actor nomination for Tom Hulce.

American Graffiti

1973. 110 min. color. U.S. **Prod.** Francis Coppola, Gary Kurtz; **Dir.** George Lucas; **Scr.** George Lucas, Gloria Katz, Willard Huyck; **Cin.** Ron Everslage, Jan D'Alquen; **Ed.** Verna Fields, Marcia Lucas; **Art D.** Dennis Clark; **Mus.** Karin Green; **Cast:** Richard Dreyfuss, Ron Howard, Paul LeMat, Cindy Williams, Candy Clark, Charles Martin Smith, Harrison Ford, Bo Hopkins.

The film is set in a small town in central California in the spring of 1962. It is the story of a group of friends and their adventures during a single night. Steve (Ron Howard), a good solid boy, is to leave for college in the East the next day. His possessive girl Laurie (Cindy Williams) is upset that Steve has chosen a college so far away. By the end of the evening they make up. Curt (Richard Dreyfuss), more cerebral, with something of a poet in him, is also leaving for college in the East the next day. He is in search of romance and intrigue. While driving, he sees a beautiful blonde in a white Thunderbird who smiles, and he believes she says something like "I love you" as she pulls away. The rest of the evening he searches for the elusive goddess, never finding her. There is Terry the Toad (Charles Martin Smith), an awkward figure who wants to be as cool as the rest of his high-school friends. Terry unexpectedly meets his ideal, the attractive and "experienced" Debbie (Candy Clark), and has an evening he had not bargained for. John (Paul LeMat) is "Mr. Cool" and drives the fastest car in the valley. A newcomer, Alfa (Harrison Ford), challenges him to a race and John comes very close to losing. In a written postscript we are told that John was killed by a drunken driver in 1964, Terry is MIA in Vietnam, Steve sells insurance in Modesto, California, and Curt probably evaded the draft and is a writer living in Canada.

This semi-autobiographical film by George Lucas is far from faultless. Some scenes are unnecessarily long, like Terry and Curt's encounter with the Pharaoh gang. The film's depiction of teenagers coming of age is warm and compassionate with no sentimentality. The title appears to refer to the transient nature of life. The boys and girls in the film do not leave an indelible mark but merely graffiti. It is very well edited and moves smoothly from one episode to the other. The art direction and set designs are excellent. The actors, all unknown at the time, are convincing and this film launched their careers. The movie that cost about $850,000 grossed over $100 million and started Lucas in a new direction.

The Americanization of Emily

1964. 117 min. b.w. U.S. **Prod.** Martin Ransohoff; **Dir.** Arthur Hiller; **Scr.** Paddy Chayefsky; **Cin.** Philip Lathrop; **Ed.** Tom McAdoo; **Art D.** George W. Davis; **Mus.** Johnny Mandel; **Cast:** James Garner, Julie Andrews, Melvyn Douglas, James Coburn, Joyce Grenfell, Keenan Wynn, Edward Binns.

Set in London on the eve of the Normandy landings, Lt. Commander Charles Madison (James Garner) is the personal aide to two-star Admiral William Jessup (Melvyn Douglas), one of the planners of the invasion. Madison is dubbed "Dog Robber" because one way or another he will procure whatever the admiral wishes: rare delicacies in food, the best suites in luxurious hotels, and companions for dinner. The admiral has not been the same since his wife died a few months earlier and sometimes is given to erratic behavior. In order to boost the Navy's morale and image, the admiral decides that the first casualty at the Omaha Beach landing must be a navy man and orders Madison to join the navy demolition team going to Omaha Beach. Madison believes that life is worth living and that "dead heroes are simply dead men," paraphrasing Falstaff's definition of a hero, "he who died o' Wednesday." Emily (Julie Andrews) is a widowed English motor pool driver who has become involved with Madison. Madison tells her he is an avowed coward and there is nothing honorable or noble in getting oneself killed.

What could have been a very original and witty antiwar film is impaired by an artificial ending that goes against everything the film stood for to that point. James Garner, a fine actor especially in light comedy roles, is very good. The reliable Melvyn Douglas also plays his role mostly for laughs. Julie Andrews, James Coburn, Edward Binns, Joyce Grenfell and Keenan Wynn round out an excellent cast. The direction of Arthur Hiller, however, has little merit.

Anatomy of a Murder

1959. 160 min. b. w. U.S. **Prod.** Otto Preminger; **Dir.** Otto Preminger; **Scr.** Wendell Mayes; **Cin.** Sam Leavitt; **Ed.** Louis Loeffler; **Mus.** Duke Ellington; **Cast:** James Stewart, Lee Remick, Ben Gazzara, Arthur O'Connell, Eve Arden, Kathryn Grant, George C. Scott, Murray Hamilton, Brooks West, Joseph N. Welch.

Set in a small community on the upper peninsula of northern Michigan, young Lieutenant Frederick Manion (Ben Gazzara) has turned himself in to the police and is charged with first-degree murder. He had found his wife, Laura (Lee Remick), badly bruised and hysterical. She had been raped by a restaurant/bar owner. Without pause he had taken his gun and gone to the lakeside restaurant and shot the owner. A trial date is set and Laura hires Paul Biegler (James Stewart), a middle-aged confirmed bachelor, who once had been a prosecuting attorney and now has a small practice. He has a passion for jazz piano and fishing. He has a good friend, Parnell McCarthy (Arthur O'Connell), an aged and experienced lawyer who is drunk most of the time, and a devoted secretary, Maida (Eve Arden), who is often owed back wages. Manion's case appears open and shut. Having committed a premeditated murder, there can be no defense of justifiable homicide. Biegler asks his friend McCarthy to sober up and help with the case. They search the state records for days and discover a case in which the accused was acquitted on the grounds that he had acted on an "irresistible impulse." They still, however, have many hurdles. The prosecution is being handled by an experienced and wily assistant district attorney (George C. Scott) from Lansing, the state capital. Although Laura has passed a lie detector test, it is inadmissible as evidence, and her medical exam is inconclusive. Since the rape has yet to be confirmed, the only thing the defense has to go on is the seldom tested principle of "irresistible impulse." They unexpectedly are saved by the forceful testimony of the murdered man's illegitimate daughter, Mary Pilant (Kathryn Grant), who found the torn panties worn by Laura on the night of the rape. The lieutenant is acquitted. He and his wife skip town without paying the lawyer's fee, leaving a note saying they had to leave on "an irresistible impulse."

An extremely well made film that despite its two hours and forty minutes length sustains the suspense to the end. Both principals and minor characters are developed in short strokes: the loyal bartender (Murray Hamilton), the incompetent local D.A. (Brooks West) and the principled illegitimate daughter of the victim. The photography makes the northern Michigan setting come to life. The screenplay by Wendell Mayes is sharp and literate. The courtroom scenes and the battle of wits between the defense attorney and the Lansing D.A. are extremely well done, containing gripping drama and effective humor. The self-centered and arrogant lieutenant and his pretty but sluttish wife stand in contrast to the warmth and charm of James Stewart and Arthur O'Connell. Preminger was lucky to have Lee Remick, a very competent actress. Originally Lana Turner was to have played Laura Manion. In a well-known incident, she got into an argument with the autocratic, no-nonsense Preminger and slapped him. Preminger slapped her back and she never returned to the set. The casting of Eve Arden, who had been absent from the screen and television (*Our Miss Brooks*) for some time, as the loyal but sharp-tongued secretary was an excellent choice. Having the amateur Joseph N. Welch as the judge was inspired. He had achieved public recognition as the gentle and soft-spoken senior counsel for the United States Army in the televised Army-McCarthy senate hearings of 1954. After having listened to the endless rantings of the demagogic Senator Joseph McCarthy, he demolished the senator in soft but intense tones with what has become the famous line, "Have you no sense of decency, Sir? At long last have you no decency?" *Anatomy of a Murder* together with *Laura* (1944) are Preminger's best films. An important element of the film is the score by Duke Ellington.

Another Woman

1988. 84 min. color. U.S. **Prod.** Robert Greenhut; **Dir.** Woody Allen; **Scr.** Woody Allen; **Cin.** Sven Nykvist; **Ed.** Susan E. Morse; **Prod. D.** Santo Loquasto; **Cast:** Gena Rowlands, Mia Farrow, Ian Holm, Gene Hackman, Blythe Danner, John Houseman, Sandy Dennis.

Marion Post (Gena Rowlands) is a professor of philosophy nearing her fiftieth birthday and is married to a physician, Ken Post (Ian Holm). She is presently working on a book on German philosophers and, in order to be undisturbed, has rented a small apartment to complete her writing. Her next-door neighbor is a psychiatrist. Through an air-conditioning vent she overhears a young pregnant woman (Mia Farrow) baring her soul in a therapy session. The young woman's confessions have a profound effect on Marion and she begins to question her own life. She has lived a self centered, secluded and barren existence and has avoided any emotional entanglements. Her professional work has dominated her life. She now begins to retrace her early years.

Another Woman is more than just another Woody Allen film about relationships in Manhattan. It is a highly intelligent film where complex characters and their equally complex relationships are developed. It is also one of the best acted of Allen's films. Gena Rowlands, a fine actress, gives a highly effective performance. Sandy Dennis, after an extended absence from films, and John Houseman, in his last film, are also perfect. Of all Woody Allen's Bergmanesque films, this comes closest to his aspiration.

The Apartment

1960. 125 min. b.w. U.S. **Prod.** Billy Wilder; **Dir.** Billy Wilder; **Scr.** Billy Wilder, I. A. L. Diamond; **Cin.** Joseph La Shelle; **Ed.** Daniel Mandell; **Art D.** Alexander Trauner; **Mus.** Adolph Deutsch; **Cast:** Jack Lemmon, Shirley MacLaine, Fred MacMurray, Ray Walston, Edie Adams, Jack Kruschen.

C. C. Baxter (Jack Lemmon), a bachelor, is a clerk at a large New York insurance company. When his superiors find out he lives alone in a one bedroom apartment in the city there are demands by company executives that he lend it out to them for a few hours in the evenings for trysts with their mistresses or one-night stands. Baxter receives a promotion for his services. J. D. Sheldrake (Fred MacMurray), a senior executive who is head of personnel, is carrying on with the neurotic elevator girl, Fran (Shirley MacLaine). He uses the apartment several times a week. Baxter is soon made vice president with unspecified duties. Around the Christmas holidays, Sheldrake, who had deceitfully promised to divorce his wife and marry Fran, breaks off their relationship. Fran attempts suicide in Baxter's apartment, and Baxter has to nurse her back to health. Inevitably, a romance develops between them.

Of the three Wilder films that can be considered "serious," only *Sunset Boulevard* (1950) returned its initial investment. *Ace in the Hole* (1951) and *The Spirit of St. Louis* (1957) were commercial failures. *The Apartment* was intended as another "serious" movie. It is sardonically saying that ingratiating oneself with bosses is the key to success. Wilder chose to sugarcoat the film with the romance to make it more appealing to audiences. Other than the forced romance and the contrived ending, the film is engrossing and in many ways ahead of its time in dissecting the corporate ethos. There is some fine acting, especially by Jack Lemmon and Fred MacMurray, who has his best role since *Double Indemnity* (1944). Jack Kruschen as Dr. Dreyfuss, Baxter's next-door neighbor who saves MacLaine, was an excellent choice. Fran is miscast. The film is too long and the last third creaks here and there. Alexander Trauner's sets stand out, especially the huge office with row upon row of uniform desks with hundreds of employees cramped together.

Assault on Precinct 13

1976. 90 min. color. U.S. **Prod.** J. S. Kaplan; **Dir.** John Carpenter; **Scr.** John Carpenter; **Cin.** Douglas Knapp; **Ed.** John T. Chance; **Art D.** Tommy Wallace; **Mus.** John Carpenter; **Cast:** Austin Stoker, Darwin Joston, Laurie Zimmer, Martin West, Tony Burton, Nancy Loomis.

A violent multiracial gang lays siege to a police station that is about to be closed down and has only a skeleton staff. Telephone and electric lines are cut and the station is repeatedly attacked by kamikaze assaults. The gang is held off for over seven hours by only a policeman, a secretary and two convicts headed for death row.

A frugal film in which there is not one unnecessary frame, *Assault on Precinct 13* was made on a minuscule budget by twenty-eight-year-old John Carpenter in his second film. Carpenter also scripted and wrote the synthesizer score which is used very effectively. The cast was totally unknown, most of them in their first film. Suspense is maintained to the very last scene and social commentary on youth gangs is avoided. The action sequences are as good as any experienced director has put on the screen. There are some extremely well-made scenes: the eerie silence before each attack; the sounds of bullets hitting venetian blinds, and cabinets; and a piece of paper floating about as it is repeatedly hit. The film is Carpenter's homage to Howard Hawks and is modeled on Hawks's *Rio Bravo* (1959).

Au Revoir, Les Enfants

Goodbye Children. 1987. 103 min. color. French. **Prod.** Louis Malle; **Dir.** Louis Malle; **Scr.** Louis Malle; **Cin.** Renato Berta; **Ed.** Emmanuelle Castro; **Mus.** Schubert, Saint-Saens; **Cast:** Gaspard Manesse, Raphael Fejto, Francine Racette, Philippe Morier-Genoud, Francoise Negret.

The film is set in a Jesuit boarding school near Paris in January 1944, when France was still under German occupation. The headmaster, Father Jean (Philippe Morier-Genoud), agrees to accept a twelve-year-old Jewish boy under the assumed gentile name of Jean Bonnet (Raphael Fejto). Jean is an exceptionally bright and literate youngster who plays the piano beautifully. He arrives at the school with a suitcase full of books. Returning to school from Christmas holidays is Julien Quentin (Gaspard Manesse), an equally intelligent boy who is intellectually far superior to his classmates. He comes from a privileged background and is very attached to his doting mother. Julien does not especially enjoy the school. He cannot relate to his loutish classmates who are mostly bullies and have no interests other than in childish antics. Being the same age, Julien and Jean are housed in the same dormitory. Julien is puzzled by the mysterious new boy who is interested in reading books and indifferent to the taunts and insults of the other boys. He is also baffled as to why the headmaster protects him. Julien begins to resent Jean and sees him as a rival in class. Soon, though, their common interests and passion for reading draw them together. Julien, however, is still perplexed by Jean and goes through his locker, finding that Jean's last name is really Kipplestein. Late one night he hears Jean say his prayers in Hebrew. Julien makes nothing of his discoveries and keeps silent about them. Their bond of friendship continues, even deepening. Soon the French police come for an inspection. Father Jean hides young Jean and the police leave. Shortly thereafter the Gestapo show up and Jean, Father Jean and another priest are taken away. The informer was Joseph (Francoise Negret), a slimy character who works in the kitchen. Jean is sent to Auschwitz and killed. Father Jean and the other priest are sent to a forced labor camp. The school is closed and not reopened until October 1944, when France is liberated and cleansed of the Nazis.

Louis Malle's earlier film *Lacombe Lucien* (1974) explored the nature and circumstances of how and why a French teenager becomes a collaborator. *Au Revoir Les Enfants*, however, is a more personal film. Malle had attended a Jesuit school in Fontainbleu, near Paris, in 1944 as a twelve-year-old and had befriended a Jewish boy who had been protected by the headmaster but ultimately was sent to his death at Auschwitz. Malle had been deeply moved by the experience and forty years later wrote, produced and directed this film. The story takes place within the space of several weeks. It is an extremely moving and humane film without any sentimentality. Neither boy is depicted as wholly loveable. There are no special pleadings. All the film deals with is responsibility, to friends and to society. It also illuminates the collaboration with the Nazis and the anti-Semitism of the sons of the upper class by remarks such as, "Better Pétain than the Jews." The acting of the entire cast is excellent, most especially the two boys and the betrayer, Joseph. The direction is straightforward, free of any technical wizardry.

Babette's Feast

Babettes Gaestebud. 1987. 102 min. color. Danish. **Prod.** Just Betzer, Bo Christensen; **Dir.** Gabriel Axel; **Scr.** Gabriel Axel (based on the Isak Dinesen short story); **Cin.** Henning Kristiansen; **Ed.** Finn Henriksen; **Mus.** Per Norgard, Mozart; **Cast:** Stephane Audran, Birgitte Federspiel (older Martine), Vibeke Hastrup (young Martine), Bodil Kjer (older Filippa), Hanne Stensgard (young Filippa), Jarl Kulle (older Lorenz Lowenhielm), Gudmar Wivesson (young Lorenz), Jean-Philippe Lafont, Bibi Andersson.

The year is 1871, after the defeat of the French by the Germans, the ensuing upheavals of the Paris commune, and the abdication of Louis Napoleon. Babette (Stephane Audran), a distraught young woman traveling from Paris, comes to a remote fishing village on the Danish coast of the Jutland peninsula. We later learn that her husband and son were killed and her own life had been in danger. She seeks refuge with two middle-aged sisters, Martine (Birgitte Federspiel) and Filippa (Bodil Kjer), who run a small Calvinist-type religious community. Offering her services for a nominal sum, she becomes their housekeeper and cooks for the ascetic sisters their constant diet of bland boiled fish soup with crumbled bread. Their father, a widowed parson who founded the sect, had been a strict religious man who had raised his daughters accordingly. In flashbacks we see the sisters in their youth, both beautiful. Martine (Vibeke Hastrup), the older of the two sisters, had been proposed marriage by an aimless nobleman in the army, Lorenz Lowenhielm (Gudmar Wivesson). Martine's father had felt she had a higher calling and Martine turned down his offer. The younger sister, Filippa (Hanne Stensgard), had been blessed with a beautiful voice and had taken lessons from a famous French tenor, Achille Papin (Jean-Philippe Lafont), who was traveling in the region. Papin had been so taken by her beauty and voice that he asked her to come to Paris for a career in opera. Filippa rejected the offer for the same reasons as her older sister. Papin had left dejected, but we learn subsequently that it was he who had advised Babette to seek refuge with the sisters.

Babette works devotedly for the sisters for fourteen years. She leaves them when she wins a lottery prize of 10,000 francs, but soon she is back with a small boat full of fish, fowl, fruit and other delicacies, along with many bottles of wine. She intends to cook a sumptuous dinner for the sisters and the elders of the congregation to honor the hundredth birthday of the late pastor. At first the sisters are reluctant to host a dinner unbecoming to their ascetic ways, one that is perhaps even sinful, but they relent. Among the guests is Martine's former suitor, Lorenz Lowenhielm (Jarl Kulle). He has reformed and is now a general who lives near the village with his aged mother and is a faithful member of the congregation. Now comes the multicourse dinner. It begins with turtle soup followed by caviar and blini with champagne. Then there are quail in pastry shells and vintage wine. Then salads and cheese are served, and the meal ends with desserts and rare tropical fruits. The guests are transformed. The camera catches their reactions after tasting each course. The sisters' response is muted but one can see the delight in their faces. We are also taken to the kitchen where Babette is in her element, preparing the food. The general's carriage driver, a gruff fellow, takes some morsels and becomes friendly and all smiles. A young servant boy who is helping Babette is equally happy. The general reminisces that the only place that served a meal matching tonight's dinner was a Paris restaurant, Café Anglais, which had a female chef. It is revealed to the viewer that Babette was that celebrated chef. The general then toasts the two sisters with a look of nostalgia and speaks of righteousness and mercy. He and his mother leave and the other guests, who seldom talk to each other or have a kind word, are so happy with good food and wine they form a ring outside the house and sing in praise of the Lord. Babette has spent her entire prize winnings on the dinner. She tells the sisters she will stay on. The sisters say, "You will be poor the rest of your life." Babette answers, "An artist is never poor."

From a short story by Isak Dinesen, the film is competently directed and photographed. Stephane Audran is sublime. She surpasses her performances in *La Femme Infidèle* (1969) and *Le*

Boucher (1969). Jean-Phillipe Lafont as Achille and Jarl Kule as the general are excellent. There is also great humor in a film that is essentially about self-sacrifice and generosity.

The Ballad of Cable Hogue

1970. 121 min. color. U.S. **Prod.** Phil Feldman, Sam Peckinpah, William Faralla; **Dir.** Sam Peckinpah; **Scr.** John Crawford, Edmund Penney; **Cin.** Lucien Ballard; **Ed.** Frank Santillo, Lou Lombardo; **Art D.** Leroy Coleman; **Mus.** Jerry Goldsmith; **Cast:** Jason Robards, Stella Stevens, David Warner, Strother Martin, Slim Pickens, L. Q. Jones.

The film is set at the turn of the twentieth century. Prospector Cable Hogue (Jason Robards) is left to die in the desert by his two partners, without food or water. He crawls on his hands and knees and finds an abandoned water well. Once he recovers, he gets a title deed for the area and establishes a rest stop for stagecoach travelers. He prospers and even finds love with an ambitious former whore. He runs into his former partners but comes out of the encounter safely. He meets an untimely and unexpected death when he is run over by a new contraption called an automobile. It is very much a Peckinpah ending, representing the demise of the old West. A well-told and well-photographed story by Peckinpah in his only humorous and gentle film. It is also well acted by Jason Robards and Stella Stevens.

The Band Wagon

1953. 112 min. color. U.S. **Prod.** Arthur Freed; **Dir.** Vincente Minnelli; **Scr.** Betty Comden, Adolph Green; **Cin.** Harry Jackson; **Ed.** Albert Akst; **Art D.** Cedric Gibbons, Preston Ames; **Mus.** Adolph Deutsch; songs Howard Dietz, Arthur Schwartz; **Cast:** Fred Astaire, Cyd Charisse, Oscar Levant, Nanette Fabray, Jack Buchanan.

The plot is simple. The moviegoing public has lost interest in Hollywood dancer Tony Hunter (Fred Astaire). He has been offered a leading role in a Broadway musical comedy written by Lily and Lester Marton (Nanette Fabray and Oscar Levant), costarring Gaby Gerard (Cyd Charisse), a prima ballerina, and directed by the biggest name on Broadway, Jeffrey Cordova (Jack Buchanan). Tony accepts and leaves for New York. What he doesn't know is that Cordova, an eccentric and pretentious director, is determined to turn the musical into the story of Faust and Mephistopheles. In time, however, Cordova realizes he "has to change his plans" and the musical comedy written by the Martons is left basically intact.

Fred Astaire at age fifty-four is still nimble and has a much better script than the RKO films with Ginger Rogers. He has several highly enjoyable dance numbers: "A Shine on Your Shoes," "Dancing in the Dark" and the charming duet with Jack Buchanan "I Guess I'll Have to Change My Plans." Just as Comden and Green made fun of Hollywood in *Singin' in the Rain* (1952), *The Band Wagon* is a satire on Broadway and its pretentious directors, although it lacks the bite of the earlier film. Cyd Charisse is as beautiful as ever and her jazz ballet with Astaire, "Girl Hunt," is not as pretentious as some ballet-like sequences in other MGM musicals. Oscar Levant is more controlled and less hammy than usual and Nanette Fabray as a Betty Comden type is fine. The unexpected star of the movie is Jack Buchanan, the English music hall star who had not appeared in a Hollywood film since *Monte Carlo* (1930). He was in his early sixties but as charming and elegant as ever. His duet with Astair is the best number in the film. Vincente Minnelli's direction is smooth and professional, as always.

The Bank Dick

1940. 74 min. b.w. U.S.; **Dir.** Eddie Cline; **Scr.** W. C. Fields; **Cin.** Milton Krasner; **Ed.** Arthur Hilton; **Art D.** Jack Otterson; **Mus.** Charles Previn; **Cast:** W. C. Fields, Cora Witherspoon, Una Merkel, Franklin Pangborn, Russell Hicks.

This is W. C. Fields' best film and has the essence of his brand of humor. He plays Egbert Souse, an unemployed henpecked man with a shrewish wife and mother-in-law, and a daughter who is engaged to Ug Oggilby, whose name "sounds like a bubble in a bathtub." He accidentally captures a would-be bank robber and is rewarded with a job as a guard. He is drunk most of the time, insults the bank customers and goes as often as he can to the nearby Black Pussy Cat Cafe bar for a few stiff drinks. He captures the same robber a second time, after a wild car chase modelled on the chases of silent films. He sells his story to a movie studio for $10,000. His shares in an abandoned gold mine appreciate and he becomes a man of wealth. Fields wrote the script himself under the absurd nom de plume Mahatma Kane Jeeves. Fields, one of the great comedians, is known for his cynical and incisive comments: His remedy for insomnia is "Get plenty of sleep." On ambition, "If at first you don't succeed, try, try, again. Then quit. No sense making a damn fool of yourself." There is also his denigration of Philadelphia at every opportunity simply because bars there were closed on Sundays.

Bashu—The Little Stranger

Bashu—Gharibe-ye Kouchak 1989. 120 min. color. Iranian. **Prod.** Alireza Zarin—Institute for the Intellectual Development of Children and Young Adults; **Dir.** Bahram Baizaee; **Scr.** Bahram Baizaee; **Cin.** Firouz Malekzadeh; **Prod. D.** Fathollah Dalili; **Cast:** Susan Taslimi, Adnan Afravian, Parviz Pour Hosseini, Azam Rahbar, Akbar Doudkar.

A young boy, Bashu (Adnan Afravian), from Khuzestan, a southern province of Iran, loses his entire family in an Iraqi artillery barrage during the Iran-Iraq war. He hides in a truck and falls asleep. When he wakes up he is hundreds of miles north in the lush farmlands of Gilan province. He gets off the truck near a farmhouse. The husband of the family there had been drafted and the only people left are Naeejan (Susan Taslimi) and her two young children. At first they have difficulty communicating as they speak different dialects, but soon Naeejan learns Bashu has been orphaned by war. A bond develops among them and they accept him as a member of the family. There is some difficulty with the attitudes of the villagers who attempt to dissuade her from feeding a stranger. The husband returns from the war having lost an arm. He too accepts Bashu into the family.

The film clearly has an antiwar message and was not allowed to be shown until 1993, almost four years after production. A minor theme is the brotherhood of man. The film tells a touching story and is finely acted, especially by the beautiful Susan Taslimi who gives a well modulated sensitive performance. It is also well photographed and directed, and despite its length of two hours moves smoothly at an even pace. *Bashu* was the first postrevolution Iranian film that found an international audience and was shown at several film festivals. In the last fifteen years Iranian films have come into their own. They have made great advances in cinematography, realistic acting and credible story lines. Fine, internationally recognized directors have emerged such as Abbas Kiarostami, Amir Naderi, Bahram Baizaee, Mohsen Makhmalbaf, and Jafar Panahi among others.

Battleground

1949. 118 min. b.w. U.S. **Prod.** Dore Schary; **Dir.** William Wellman; **Scr.** Robert Pirosh; **Cin.** Paul C. Vogel; **Ed.** John Dunning; **Art D.** Cedric Gibbons, Hans Peters; **Mus.** Lennie Hayton; **Cast:** Van Johnson, John Hodiac, Ricardo Montalban, George Murphy, Marshal Thompson, Denise Darcel, Don Taylor, James Whitmore, James Arness, Jerome Courtland, Douglas Fowley, Leon Ames.

In December 1944 the German High Command had devised a plan to cut off U.S. troops in Luxembourg, Belgium, and eastern France, drive them to the sea and recapture the vital strategic supply port of Antwerp. The fallacy of the plan was that even if it had succeeded it would merely have prolonged the war a few months. The key to the German offensive was the capture of the city of Bastogne, which was held by the Americans. The attack started on December 16 along a wide front. What helped the Germans initially was a heavy fog in the Ardennes Forest that did not lift for twelve days. During that time, the overwhelming Allied air superiority was rendered ineffective.

Battleground tells the story of the ordinary soldiers of the Second Squad, Third Platoon, T Company, of the 101 Airborne Infantry Division who were cut off from all other units. They know nothing of the big picture or the grand strategy devised by the top brass. Some ten to twelve characters are well developed. There is Holley (Van Johnson), a light-hearted soldier who seeks romance and was scheduled to go to Paris on leave. Jarvess (John Hodiac) is a small town newspaper reporter with a social conscience. Roderigues (Ricardo Montalban), a Mexican-American from Southern California is beside himself when he sees his first snowfall. There is Pop Stazak (George Murphy) who is to be discharged from the service because of age and dependants. Abner Spudler (Jerome Courtland) from the Kentucky mountains takes his boots off before sleeping, even in trenches. The key person in the squad is Kinnie (James Whitmore), a tough and experienced sergeant.

This story of the Second Squad is one of the handful of good films about World War II. It succeeds because of an abundance of detail and character development. Robert Pirosh, who had been in Bastogne during the actual siege, wrote an excellent screenplay. There is no sentimentality or glorification of war. It is a rare film that captures the misery and boredom of the foot soldiers. The entire movie was filmed on the MGM back lot, but Wellman's direction gives it authenticity. The art direction of Cedric Gibbons also helped transform the back lot into a credible battleground. The musical score is very effective, especially the infantry marching song, "Sound Off." It begins the film and ends it when the soldiers are finally relieved and led by James Whitmore limping on frostbitten feet, the squad marching off singing lustily. Dore Schary, who brought the project from RKO to MGM, cast most of the MGM leading men. Van Johnson was a much better actor than the studio gave him credit for, always casting him as the juvenile. James Whitmore was one of the best character actors of his day. This was Schary's first film at MGM. It was a great commercial success and received Academy Award nominations in six major categories. For L. B. Mayer, who had opposed the production, this was the beginning of his decline as MGM chief. A little over a year later he was gone from the studio.

The Battle of Algiers

La Battaglia Di Algeri. 1965. 123 min. b.w. Italian/Algerian (in French). **Prod.** Antonio Musu, Yacef Saadi; **Dir.** Gillo Pontecorvo; **Scr.** Gillo Pontecorvo, Franco Solinas; **Cin.** Marcello Gatti; **Ed.** Mario Serandrei, Mario Morra; **Mus.** Gillo Pontecorvo, Ennio Morricone; **Cast:** Yacef Saadi, Jean Martin, Tommaso Neri, Brahim Haggiag.

The film opens in 1957 as French paratroopers, under the command of Colonel Mathieu (Jean Martin), have extracted under torture the whereabouts of Ali La Pointe (Brahim Haggiag), the last surviving senior member of the Algerian Liberation Front (FLN). The apartment building where La Pointe is hiding is blown up, killing and maiming scores of other tenants. There is a flashback, and the film shifts to 1954, the initial stages of the Algerian revolution against the French colonialists, when the FLN recruited thousands of revolutionaries and created a pyramid of cells. France then dispatched paratroopers who launched a systematic attack on the FLN from its lowest cells. The film focuses on the key events and personalities that fueled the final uprising.

Although the film's sympathies are clearly with the revolutionaries, Pontecorvo observes a measure of balance. He shows the unspeakable methods of torture used by the paratroopers as well as the indiscriminate acts of terror committed by the revolutionaries, including the bombing of a sidewalk café filled with teenagers dancing to a jukebox and a child licking an ice cream cone. The struggle lasted until 1962, when Algeria finally gained independence. Other than a short scene at the end of the film showing the rising up of the population in 1962, the film concerns itself with the events of 1957. It does not show or deal with Charles de Gaulle's crucial role when he withdrew support from the colonists and ordered all military personnel to mainland France.

The cast is almost all nonprofessional. Only Jean Martin, as the colonel, was a professional actor. Yacef Saadi, the film's producer, plays an FLN leader. About fifteen minutes of the film, the more graphic sequences of French torture, were cut from prints shown in the U.S. The photography, in a gray-muted black and white, gives it a documentary look. It is heavily influenced by Eisenstein's *Potemkin* (1925), both in the re-creation of events and the novel editing techniques. One of the great political films and one of the most ingenious semidocumentaries in the history of cinema.

Belle De Jour

1967. 100 min. color. French. **Prod.** Robert Hakim, Raymond Hakim; **Dir.** Luis Buñuel; **Scr.** Luis Buñuel , Jean Claude Carriere (based on the novel by Joseph Kessel); **Cin.** Sacha Vierny; **Ed.** Walter Spohr; **Art D.** Robert Clavel; **Cast:** Catherine Deneuve, Jean Sorel, Michel Piccoli, Genevieve Page, Pierre Clement.

A frigid young girl of twenty-three, Severine Serizy (Catherine Deneuve), with strong masochistic tendencies, is married to a successful Parisian surgeon, Pierre Serizy (Jean Sorel). While she appears content, her daydreams reflect her true state of mind. In the opening scene, she fantasizes that they are in a carriage and her husband orders the driver and the footman to drag her to the woods, tie her to a tree and violate her. In another daydream, she is again bound and has mud thrown at her. Either in her dreams or in reality she goes to work in a brothel where she can satisfy her desire for abuse. A young gangster takes to her. When she stops working there, he finds her home and shoots her husband, believing him to be the obstacle, and leaves him paralyzed. In the end, Pierre learns about the brothel and has tears in his eyes. In an alternate ending, we see Pierre in perfect health discussing a vacation they are planning, and Severine appears to have shed her demons and erotic fantasies and is content with her life and marriage.

Based on a 1928 novel by Joseph Kessel, a psychological study of a repressed, masochistic woman who decides to humiliate herself by working several afternoons a week in a brothel, hence the name "Belle De Jour," given to her by the madam. Buñuel, with his cowriter Jean Claude Carrier, moved the setting to contemporary times and turned the film into a surrealistic account of

Severine's sexual fantasies. By juggling scenes, Buñuel leaves it to our imagination as to whether certain events actually occur or are merely daydreams. Ultimately reality and dreams merge, and it is unclear where one begins and the other ends. Buñuel 's life-long enmity toward the bourgeoisie is clearly present; however, the film lacks both his usual bite and his sardonic view of the Catholic church. *Belle De Jour* may not be one of Buñuel's masterpieces; nevertheless, it is a very well-made and imaginative film. Catherine Deneuve as the ice-cold woman has her best role. Genevieve Page, the brothel madam, and Michel Piccoli, a lecherous friend of the family, are excellent as epitomes of the degenerate bourgeoisie.

The Big Heat

1953. 90 min. b.w. U.S. **Prod.** Robert Arthur; **Dir.** Fritz Lang; **Scr.** Sydney Boehm (based on a magazine serial by William P. McGivern); **Cin.** Charles Lang; **Ed.** Charles Nelson; **Art D.** Robert Peterson; **Mus.** Daniele Amfitheatrof; **Cast:** Glen Ford, Gloria Grahame, Jocelyn Brando, Alexander Scourby, Lee Marvin, Carolyn Jones Jeanette Nolan.

Police detective Lieutenant Dave Bannion (Glen Ford) is assigned to investigate the suicide of fellow officer Captain Tom Duncan who has left no suicide note. It is revealed early that Duncan had kept a daily journal that detailed the operations of a criminal empire headed by Mike Lagana (Alexander Scourby) and listed officials of the city on its payroll, including Duncan himself. Mrs. Duncan (Jeanette Nolan) places the diary in a bank safe that can only be opened in the event of her death. She blackmails Lagana and is placed on his payroll. Bannion is ordered by the police commissioner to stay away from the case. He resigns from the force but continues the investigation privately. His wife is killed by a car bomb intended for him. With unexpected help from Debbie Marsh (Gloria Grahame), the girlfriend of gangster Vince Stone (Lee Marvin) whom Vince had disfigured, Lagana's criminal empire is destroyed. All the corrupt officials are removed and Bannion returns to his desk.

An ordinary gangsters and cops story that was made into a first-rate thriller by the master director Fritz Lang. The film moves very fast and in eighty-nine minutes all loose ends are tied up. The acting, especially Grahame and Marvin as a sadistic gangster, is first rate. *The Big Heat* is a very violent film. The scene of Marvin throwing a boiling coffee pot at Gloria Grahame's face still sends shivers down the spine. The theme of revenge often surfaces in Lang's American films, *Fury* (1936) and *Rancho Notorious* (1952).

The Big Sleep

1946. 114 min. b.w. U.S. **Prod.** Howard Hawks; **Dir.** Howard Hawks; **Scr.** William Faulkner, Jules Furthman, Leigh Brackett (based on the novel by Raymond Chandler); **Cin.** Sid Hickox; **Ed.** Christian Nyby; **Art D.** Carl Jules Weyl; **Mus.** Max Steiner; **Cast:** Humphrey Bogart, Lauren Bacall, Martha Vickers, John Ridgely, Jean Louis Heydt, Regis Toomey, Dorothy Malone, Bob Steele, Elisha Cook, Jr. Charles Waldron.

Philip Marlowe (Humphrey Bogart), an experienced private detective, calls on his new client, General Sternwood (Charles Waldron), at his large estate. The general has two spoiled daughters. The elder, Vivian (Lauren Bacall), is an addicted gambler; and the younger, Carmen (Martha Vickers), is a drug addict with nymphomaniacal tendencies who is often in trouble. Marlowe is asked to investigate Geiger, a blackmailer who owns a Hollywood bookshop, a front for pornographic books. Geiger has compromising photographs of Carmen. Marlowe goes to the bookshop, but the elusive Geiger can't be found. Marlowe learns his address and goes to his home where he finds Geiger murdered and Carmen drugged. He manages to retrieve Carmen's photographs and get her out of Geiger's house before the police arrive. He soon finds out that General Sternwood has other things in store for him. The general's confidante and aide has disappeared and he wants Marlowe to locate him. The plot thickens, and by the end some fourteen people are killed, including one person who does not even appear on screen, and there is one unresolved murder. Marlowe learns that much more than blackmail was involved. The principal villain is one Eddy Mars (John Ridgely), owner of a fashionable gambling casino, and Marlowe knows he ultimately will have to have a showdown with Mars and his henchmen.

Despite all the murders, *The Big Sleep* is not a violent film. The plot is so confusing and convoluted that one doesn't care after a while who did what to whom. It is the individual scenes, meticulously directed by Hawks, that make the movie so satisfying. For example, Marlowe's seduction of Dorothy Malone, the owner of a shop, in the shortest time possible; Marlowe assuming an effete pose at the Geiger bookshop and asking, "Would you happen to have a Ben Hur 1860?" The assistant, "First edition?" Marlowe, "No, no, no, the third, the one with the erratum on page 116." Furthermore, there is the suggestive dialogue. Marlowe to Vivian: "You got a touch of class, but I don't know how far you can go." Vivian responds, "A lot depends on who is in the saddle," somewhat echoing Cleopatra's longing, "O happy horse, to bear the weight of Antony." Most of the film takes place at night and ironically the shadows and fog, basically used to hide Warners' notoriously cheap sets, give the film character and reflect the lurid demimonde of Chandler. As for the acting, Bogart, now with some four or five starring roles behind him, is at his most confident and dominates every scene.

Black Narcissus

1947. 99 min. color. British. **Prod.** Michael Powell, Emeric Pressburger; **Dir.** Michael Powell, Emeric Pressburger; **Scr.** Michael Powell, Emeric Pressburger (based on the novel by Rumer Godden); **Cin.** Jack Cardiff; **Ed.** Reginald Mills; **Art D.** Alfred Junge; **Mus.** Brian Easdale; **Cast:** Deborah Kerr, David Farrar, Sabu, Jean Simmons, Flora Robson, Kathleen Byron, Jenny Laird, Judith Furse.

The ruler of a province in northern India during British governance makes an arrangement with the Catholic Church in England to establish an elementary school and infirmary in a remote Himalayan village. Five nuns headed by Sister Clodagh (Deborah Kerr) arrive and begin their work of teaching and tending to the sick. They occupy an old palace that had housed the harem of a maharajah, built on a ledge some eight thousand feet high in the mountains. This is Sister Clodagh's first assignment in a position of authority, and she seeks help from Mr. Dean (David Farrar), the local agent of a British commercial company, who is familiar with the area and its people. Their work becomes complicated when Mr. Dean asks the sisters to look after an attractive young Indian girl for a few months. Soon thereafter, the ruler sends his young son (Sabu), already made a general by his father, to stay with the nuns and learn English. The young general, who wears a strong perfume called Black Narcissus, is attracted to the girl. The strain of work in the rarified air of the Himalayas, the suggestions induced by living in a former harem, the unexpected arrivals of the young girl and the amorous general, and the presence of Mr. Dean who is always in shorts begin to take their toll. It unbalances young Sister Ruth (Kathleen Byron). In an hysterical frenzy she decides to leave the order and offers to live with Mr. Dean. When she is rebuffed by Dean she has a dramatic and tragic end. The other nuns realize the hopelessness of their situation and decide to return to England.

Black Narcissus is one of the greatest and most beautiful feats of color cinematography, for which it won an Oscar. The film was shot entirely at the Pinewood studio, outside London, with superimpositions of the Himalayas. There is very convincing acting by Deborah Kerr and Flora Robson as another of the nuns. The greatest performance, however, comes from Kathleen Byron who is overwhelming. In one of the odd vagaries of fortune, when everyone expected the emergence of a great actress, Byron was offered only a few minor roles and then faded away. But major credit goes to the Powell and Pressburger team, which had the courage to produce, direct and script highly original and unorthodox films such as *The Life and Death of Colonel Blimp* (1943), *I Know Where I'm Going* (1945), *A Matter of Life and Death* (1946) and *Red Shoes* (1948). *Black Narcissus* ranks among the best of them. A most unusual film both for its location and subject matter; a group of English nuns in the foothills of the Himalayas containing suggestive scenes of temptation.

The Blue Angel

Der Blaue Engel. 1930. 103 min. b.w. German. **Prod.** Erich Pommer; **Dir.** Joseph von Sternberg; **Scr.** Robert Liebmann, Karl Vollmoeller, Karl Zuckmayer (based on the novel *Professor Unrat* by Heinrich Mann); **Cin.** Gunther Rittau, Hans Schneeberger; **Ed.** S. K. Winston; **Mus.** Friedrick Hollander; **Cast:** Marlene Dietrich, Emil Jannings, Kurt Gerron, Rosa Valetti, Hans Albers.

Professor Immanuel Rath (Emil Jannings) teaches English in a gymnasium (high school). When we first see him in class, he is cruel and insensitive toward his students. Lola Frohlich (Marlene Dietrich) is the star attraction at the Blue Angel cabaret. Her posters are everywhere and the students carry her photographs. Rath decides to visit the Blue Angel and see for himself the object of his students' adoration. He is immediately captivated and begins to frequent the cabaret. His weakness for alcohol and sex makes him easy prey. He resigns from the school and marries Lola. He tries hopelessly to preserve his dignity while following her and the troupe from one town to another. He is induced by the manager and Lola to join the show as a clown. We see him five years later when the manager brings the troupe back to Rath's hometown for an extended stay at the Blue Angel. Posters highlight Rath as a member of the troupe and capitalize on his having been a professor at the local school. His act includes his crowing like a rooster. An audience of his former students taunts him as a cuckold. Lola is in the wings in an amorous embrace with her new lover, the escape artist. Rath can no longer take the taunting and the humiliation. He attacks the new lover and tries to kill him. He is restrained and put in a straitjacket. After calming down, he is released. He staggers through the streets to his old classroom and kills himself.

The film is a study of human degradation and sadism. The sadism of Rath toward his students, as he was less interested in teaching than in exercising authority; the sadism of the boys in destroying their hated teacher; the troupe manager and Lola in their degradation of the haughty professor; and Lola, who in her debasement of Rath gives vent to her hatred of the bourgeoisie who look down on her. Sternberg, an Austrian, was one of the great screen directors. After making some ten films in Hollywood, he went to Germany to make this, probably his best film. *The Blue Angel* was filmed simultaneously in German and English. There is a minimum of dialogue. Sternberg's lighting and shadows, and the use of silence as sound enhanced the film. Emil Jannings was an outstanding silent era actor and his performance here is essentially a silent one. This was the first film Dietrich made with Sternberg. They subsequently made six films together, a collaboration that was very important in the development of Dietrich's screen persona.

Body and Soul

1947. 104 min. b.w. U.S. **Prod.** Bob Roberts; **Dir.** Robert Rossen; **Scr.** Abraham Polonsky; **Cin.** James Wong Howe; **Ed.** Robert Parrish; **Art D.** Nathan Juran; **Mus.** Hugo Friedhofer; **Cast:** John Garfield, Lilli Palmer, Anne Revere, William Conrad, Joseph Pevney, Canada Lee, Lloyd Goff, James Burke, Art Smith, Hazel Brooks.

Most of the film is told in flashbacks. Charlie Davis (John Garfield), a lower eastside New York boy is an amateur boxer hoping to become a professional. His mother, Anna (Anne Revere), wants him to forget boxing and go back to school. When his father, who runs a small candy store, is killed by a bomb explosion in a turf war between rival gangsters and his mother is forced to live on charity, Charlie turns pro. As he wins his first fights an influential fixer/gambler, Mr. Roberts (Lloyd Goff), becomes interested in him. Charlie abandons his manager and trainer and signs with Roberts who got into promoting fights because he "likes boxers better than horses." He wins all his bouts and becomes the middleweight champion of the world. He abandons his girl Peg (Lilli Palmer) and takes up with a floozy (Hazel Brooks). He starts drinking, slowly dissipates and falls heavily in debt to Roberts. When he is challenged by a young contender, Roberts has the fight fixed and Charlie is to go the distance and lose on points. Charlie agrees and bets all the money he has against himself. Roberts has now decided he would make more money if Charlie, the favorite, loses by a knockout. In the twelfth round his opponent is told to knock him out. Charlie barely survives the round. He is badly battered and stays away from his opponent in the next round but goes after him in the last two rounds.

Body and Soul is among the two or three most exciting boxing films. Although it is cliché-ridden, the cinematography of James Wong Howe makes it outstanding. Howe wore roller skates to shoot the boxing scenes as close as possible. John Garfield was one of the best actors of his time but died at the height of his career at age thirty-nine. The rest of the cast are all fine actors. Unfortunately Lilli Palmer is miscast. She was too worldly and sophisticated for the part. The film was well directed by Robert Rossen, assisted by his ideological ally, scriptwriter Abraham Polonsky. To highlight the corruption in the system, the script has probably over fifty references to money, which dominates the film. Mr. Roberts says at one point: "Everything is addition or subtraction. The rest is conversation."

Boomerang

1947. 88 min. b.w. U.S. **Prod.** Louis B. Rochemont; **Dir.** Elia Kazan; **Scr.** Richard Murphy (based on an article by Anthony Abbott); **Cin.** Norbert Brodine; **Ed.** Harmon Jones; **Mus.** David Buttolf; **Cast:** Dana Andrews, Jane Wyatt, Lee J. Cobb, Arthur Kennedy, Sam Levene, Robert Keith, Ed Begley, Karl Malden, Taylor Holmes.

The film is based on an actual unsolved murder of an elderly and popular priest in Bridgeport, Connecticut in the 1920s. A vagrant, John Waldron (Arthur Kennedy), is picked up by the police and charged with the murder. The state's attorney, Henry L. Harvey (Dana Andrews), is to prosecute the case. The evidence against Waldron seems conclusive. Several eyewitnesses claim to have seen someone very much like him leaving the scene of the crime. Waldron is subjected to unceasing grilling and after a few days breaks down and confesses. But now the prosecutor who has thoroughly reviewed the evidence and interviewed the witnesses becomes convinced Waldron is not guilty. It was too dark for any of the witnesses to get even a glimpse of the accused. The primary witness, a waitress, is bent on revenge as Waldron had walked out on her some time ago. Finally, the presumed murder weapon, a pistol, could not have been fired at the angle from which the priest was shot. Waldron is released. The hearings are intercut with the intense pressure put on Harvey by the mayor, the head of the city council as well as the influential owner of the local newspaper. They all have a vested interest in prosecuting the vagrant, which will divert the attention of the public from the corruption at city hall. Harvey is offered the gubernatorial nomination if he pursues the case.

The film is a modest gem. It is a lean movie directed in a semi-documentary style by Elia Kazan, in his third film. What also elevates the film is the excellent cast of Andrews, Kennedy, Lee J. Cobb as the police detective, Jane Wyatt as Harvey's wife, Ed Begley as the head of the city council and Taylor Holmes as the newspaper owner. When the residents of Bridgeport objected to the filming it was shot in the neighboring city of Stamford. *Boomerang* was one of the first Hollywood movies to be filmed outside the studio and led to a series of more realistic films shot on location. State prosecutor Henry L. Harvey is a pseudonym for Homer S. Cummings who later gained further prominence as President Roosevelt's first attorney general from 1933 to 1939.

Born Yesterday

1950. 103 min. b.w. U.S. **Prod.** S. Sylvan Simon; **Dir.** George Cukor; **Scr.** Albert Mannheimer (based on the play by Garson Kanin); **Cin.** Joseph Walker; **Ed.** Charles Nelson; **Mus.** Frederick Hollander; **Cast:** Judy Holliday, William Holden, Broderick Crawford, Howard St. John.

Harry Brock (Broderick Crawford), a ruthless scrap metal tycoon who himself is an uneducated boor, decides that his mistress, Billie Dawn (Judy Holliday), a former chorus girl, is an embarrassment. Now that he has come to Washington on business and must entertain senators and congressmen, he decides that Billie needs a tutor to teach her social graces and smooth her rough edges. He hires Paul Verrall (William Holden), a newspaperman, to educate her. Verrall does an excellent job, but what the tycoon had not counted on is for Billie to fall in love with her teacher. The film is all Judy Holliday who had played the part on Broadway. The rest of the cast is overshadowed by her mere presence. It is also very smoothly directed by George Cukor. Some preachy segments date the film. Judy Holliday won a debatable Academy Award for best actress, beating Gloria Swanson in *Sunset Boulevard* and Bette Davis in *All about Eve.*

Brief Encounter

1945. 85 min. b.w. British. **Prod.** Noel Coward; **Dir.** David Lean; **Scr.** Noel Coward, David Lean, Anthony Havelock-Allan (based on the play *Still Life* by Noel Coward); **Cin.** Robert Krasker; **Ed.** Jack Harris; **Mus.** Sergei Rachmaninov; **Cast:** Celia Johnson, Trevor Howard, Stanley Holloway, Joyce Carey, Cyril Raymond, Margaret Barton.

Laura Jesson (Celia Johnson), a housewife, and Dr. Alec Harvey (Trevor Howard), a physician, live in the suburbs of a fairly large town. Laura comes to town each Thursday for weekly shopping. Alec commutes daily to the hospital. They meet at the train station café when he removes a cinder from Laura's eye. A week later, they meet again by chance at a restaurant in town. They learn that both are happily married and Laura has a small boy. They begin to see one another every week. Soon their relationship develops into something much deeper. One early evening, Alec takes Laura to the flat of a friend to which he had been given the key. Almost immediately his friend unexpectedly shows up. Laura hastily leaves and his friend asks for his key. Alec runs after her and finds her sitting on a park bench. Both are deeply ashamed and decide not to see one another again. Their last moments together in the railroad café are interrupted by one of Laura's talkative friends. Alec leaves to take his train. For an instant Laura contemplates throwing herself in the path of an oncoming train but decides to go back to her husband and small boy. There are two minor subplots, but they are connected thematically to the main story. The manageress of the railroad café, Myrtel (Joyce Carey), is assiduously being chatted up and courted by Albert (Stanley Holloway), the station manager; and Myrtle's teenage help, Beryl (Margaret Barton), is being wooed by a young fellow.

Brief Encounter, an expanded version of a Noel Coward one-act play, is one of the simplest films ever made. David Lean, at the beginning of his directorial career, shows his skill and control. The cinematography of Robert Krasker, who later became Carol Reed's favorite, brings a sense of realism to an austere postwar England with its quaint tea shops, railroad station cafés, and local cinemas. Krasker also captures the atmosphere of the dimly lit train station with its dark shadows and connecting underground passages. David Lean opens up the film and moves the story outside to the streets, restaurants and the cinema. The casting of Johnson and Howard was most appropriate. As neither is beautiful or handsome, the realism is heightened. The secondary cast, especially Joyce Carey and Stanley Holloway, is also very good. Their flirtations and teasing adds humor. The Rachmaninov Second Piano Concerto, often played fortissimo, could be too much, but it works here.

The film, however, reflects its age, as attitudes towards sex and marriage have changed since 1945. It also suffers somewhat from Noel Coward's attitude towards sex and the British class system. He seems to be saying that sex is for the lower classes. Myrtle and Albert flirt outrageously and obviously will soon be involved. We can be equally certain that Beryl will sleep with her boyfriend, if she hasn't yet. On the other hand, we have Alec's upper-class friend telling him, "I'm disappointed in you," and demanding his key back. Despite these reservations, the film holds up well and the themes of guilt and loyalty have not dated.

Broadway Danny Rose

1984. 86 min. b.w. U.S. **Prod.** Robert Greenhut; **Dir.** Woody Allen; **Scr.** Woody Allen; **Cin.** Gordon Willis; **Ed.** Susan E. Morse; **Prod. D.** Mel Bourne; **Cast:** Woody Allen, Mia Farrow, Nick Apollo Forte, Sandy Baron.

The film begins with a group of Catskills comedy writers and comics having coffee at the Carnegie Deli and reminiscing or telling stories about some unusual people in the business. Someone mentions a former comic turned agent, Danny Rose (Woody Allen), who represented clients with weird acts: wine glass players, a bird trained to play the piano, a one-legged dancer, a one-armed juggler, a blind xylophonist, etc. He also represented an overweight alcoholic crooner, Lou Canova (Nick Apollo Forte), who was getting nowhere. Danny started to pick his songs with new arrangements and Lou began to fare better. He sang on cruise ships and occasionally appeared on TV. Finally Danny had Lou booked to sing at a charity extravaganza at the Waldorf-Astoria with a number of well-known performers. Canova, although married, was having an affair with a Mafia widow, Tina Vitale (Mia Farrow). He told Danny he couldn't perform unless she was with him. Tina was mad at Lou because he had been seen with other girls and refused to attend. Danny, afraid Lou would start drinking and miss his big chance, went to see Tina. She wouldn't let Danny explain and left to attend a Mafia wedding. Danny followed her. Everyone there thought Danny was Tina's new boyfriend. The local don was in love with Tina. She turned down his marriage proposal and the love-stricken don committed suicide. There was talk of revenge and a couple of Mafia hoods followed Danny and Tina. They smashed his car and tried to kill him. Somehow Tina and Danny made it back to the city and Lou sang at the charity event. In a postscript we find that Lou gave a successful performance but dumped Danny and got a new agent.

Shot by Gordon Willis in black and white, as in *Manhattan* (1979), *Broadway Danny Rose* is one of the very best of Woody Allen. It is not as ambitious as his preceding film, *Zelig* (1983), where he experimented with new film techniques, but it is much more charming. The jokes come naturally and are part of the plot narrative. It is a portrait of a sweet, loyal and gentle loser. It is one of the best-acted Allen films, and has Mia Farrow's best performance. Equally good is Nick Apollo Forte who is a natural as the boozy, two-timing, mediocre crooner.

Broken Blossoms

1919. 95 min. b.w. silent. U.S. **Prod. D.** W. Griffith; **Dir.** D. W. Griffith; **Scr.** D. W. Griffith (based on the story "The Chink and the Child" by Thomas Burke); **Cin.** Billy Bitzer, Hendrik Sartor, Karl Brown; **Ed.** James E. Smith, Rose Smith; **Art D.** Charles E. Baker; **Mus.** to accompany the film, Louis Gottschalk, D. W. Griffith; **Cast:** Lillian Gish, Richard Barthelmess, Donald Crisp, Arthur Howard.

This is the story of an unspoken romance of an abused, motherless girl (Lillian Gish) who is beaten routinely by her drunkard father (Donald Crisp), a sadistic professional boxer. After one beating too many she runs away and is given shelter by a gentle young Chinese man (Richard Barthelmess) who has come recently to London to teach Chinese traditions to the English. He treats her as a newly found flower and nurses her back to health. The enraged father finds out and takes her home. In another drunken rage he beats his daughter to death. The Chinaman takes revenge and kills the father. He carries her body back to his room, kneels beside her and commits suicide. A restrained and poetic film, finely acted, asking for tolerance among races and religions. As in almost all of Griffith's films the title cards are mawkish and awkwardly phrased. Nevertheless, a very well made film and one of the master's greatest.

Bullitt

1968. 113 min. color. U.S. **Prod.** Philip D'Antoni; **Dir.** Peter Yates; **Scr.** Alan R. Trustman, Harry Kleiner (based on a novel by Robert L. Pike); **Cin.** William A. Fraker; **Ed.** Frank P. Keller; **Art D.** Albert Brenner; **Mus.** Lalo Schifrin; **Cast:** Steve McQueen, Robert Vaughn, Jacqueline Bisset, Don Gordon, Simon Oakland, Norman Fell, Victor Tayback, Robert Duvall.

One of the best thrillers of the past several decades, the film tells the story of a principled San Francisco cop, Bullitt (Steve McQueen), assigned to safeguard a former Mafia treasurer turned state's witness, and an ambitious politician who hopes to use the publicity of the crime hearings to advance his career. A typical sixties glossy movie made memorable by some great scenes: the search for a hired killer in a hospital rehab center; the final scenes at the San Francisco airport; and the most spectacular car chase ever filmed. The hilly streets of San Francisco are the perfect venue for the exciting hazardous chase. The film is well photographed with some fine acting. Steve McQueen has a minimum of lines and acts mostly with his face and body. Robert Vaughn as the politician, Simon Oakland as a police captain, and Norman Fell as a political type in the police department handle their roles very well. *Bullitt* is a forerunner of Clint Eastwood's *Dirty Harry* films and is an attack on liberal politicians.

Burn

a.k.a. *Queimada*. 1969. 112 min. color. French/Italian. (in English) **Prod.** Alberto Grimaldi; **Dir.** Gillo Pontecorvo; **Scr.** Gillo Pontecorvo, Franco Solinas, Giorgio Arlorio; **Cin.** Marcello Gatti; **Prod. D.** Piero Gherardi; **Mus.** Ennio Morricone; **Cast:** Marlon Brando, Evaristo Marquez, Renato Salvatori.

The story begins in 1845. England covets a Portuguese West Indies island with the fictitious name of Queimada for its rich sugar crop, but does not want to go to war with Portugal. Instead it sends Sir William Walker (Marlon Brando), an agent provoca-

teur, to stir discontent and foster a revolt to dislodge the Portuguese rulers. Three centuries earlier, the Portuguese had wiped
out the native people who had rebelled, and populated the island
with black slaves from Africa to work on the sugar plantations.
Walker incites the blacks led by the intelligent José Dolores
(Evaristo Marquez) to rebel and wage war. The Portuguese are
either killed or flee the island. Dolores, however, is denied the
presidency promised to him, and a docile mulatto, Teddy
Sanchez, is declared the ruler. Dolores retires to his village and
works on the plantations. Some ten years later Dolores leads the
oppressed blacks in a second revolt and is on the verge of winning. Walker, who had returned to England, is sent again to quell
the revolt. This time Walker employs a scorched earth policy, forcing the blacks to come out in the open where they are massacred.
Dolores is captured and given a chance of freedom if he will side
with the British. He chooses martyrdom. Walker is assassinated on
the docks as he is about to leave.

The film was beset with a host of problems from the outset.
Spain, which had adopted similar strategies in the Caribbean, now
objected to the Spaniards being portrayed in a bad light and
warned it would ban the import of the film to Spain. The producers and United Artists, the distributors, relented and the film title
was changed to *Burn* and the colonial power to Portugal, a smaller
film market. Some scenes had to be reshot and Brando, after having worked nine months on the film, left the location. Some
twenty minutes were awkwardly cut and the film, having been
denied any publicity, was shown for only a few weeks in a limited
number of movie houses. Despite the flaws it remains an important political film. There are hints of an analogy with the U.S.
involvement in Vietnam; the U.S. having replaced France as a
colonial power. It may not be one of the greatest of Brando's roles
as the clever, deceitful and foppish English gentleman, but he is
convincing. The film is beautifully photographed and there are
some fine images, including the black slaves on white horses ready
for battle. There is also an excellent score by Ennio Morricone.

Call Northside 777

1948. 111 min. b.w. U.S. **Prod.** Ray Stark; **Dir.** Henry Hathaway; **Scr.** Jerry Cady, Jay Dratler (adapted from *Chicago Times* articles by Quentin Reynolds and Leonard Hoffman); **Cin.** Joseph MacDonald; **Ed.** J. Watson Webb; **Art D.** Lyle Wheeler; **Mus.** Alfred Newman; **Cast:** James Stewart, Richard Conte, Lee J. Cobb, Helen Walker, Moroni Olson, Bettty Garde, E. G. Marshall.

Chicago, 9 November 1932. There is a murder at a candy store that operates a numbers racket and is also a front for a speakeasy. A cop who had come in for a drink is shot by two robbers. Frank Wiecek (Richard Conte) and another man who live in the neighborhood are arrested. They are identified as the robbers by the shopkeeper, Wanda Skutnick (Betty Garde), and sentenced to ninety-nine years. The case is forgotten until October 1944 when an ad is run by Frank Wiecek's mother, Tillie, in the *Chicago Times* offering a reward of $5,000 for any information that would clear her son's name and free him from prison. The editor, Brian Kelly (Lee J. Cobb), sends his reporter, Jim McNeal (James Stewart), to interview the woman. Tillie works as a scrubwoman in a large office building and has saved money over the years for the reward. McNeal is skeptical and advises Tillie that it is a hopeless case. Tillie counters that she will work another twelve years and the higher reward may interest someone. McNeal is about to drop the assignment but his editor publishes the interview as a human-interest story. The public reaction is very favorable. McNeal digs deeper and finds a police coverup, perjury and missing evidence. There had been a mayoral race and the police were pressed to get a conviction. Wiecek is exonerated.

Call Northside 777 is an excellent film noir/documentary/thriller. It is shot mostly in the Polish neighborhoods of Chicago and the cinematography of Joseph MacDonald lends great authenticity to the film. It is based on the actual story of Joe Majczek of Chicago. The reporter was Jim McGuire who won a Pulitzer Prize for his series of articles. There is fine acting by the entire cast. After the war years Stewart began to select his films wisely and no longer limited himself to comedies. Here he very effectively plays a cynical

reporter changing gradually into a crusader. Lee J. Cobb and Betty
Garde as the shady criminal are excellent. Richard Conte was not
recognized as the fine actor he was. He came to films when all lead-
ing men had to be handsome. There is a magnificent final scene.
Wiecek is released from prison. His wife had divorced him and
remarried in order to give their infant son a father to care for him.
The husband, played by E. G. Marshall in one of his earliest roles,
the wife, the son and Wiecek's mother are all there to embrace
Frank. James Stewart is the outsider in the far background. John
Ford, a good friend of Henry Hathaway, used a similar closing in
The Searchers (1956). Hathaway made several other excellent films
shot on actual locations: *The House on 92nd Street* (1945), *Kiss of
Death* (1947), and *Fourteen Hours* (1951).

Cape Fear

1962. 105 min. b.w. U.S. **Prod.** Sy Bartlett; **Dir.** J. Lee Thompson; **Scr.** James R. Webb
(based on the novel *The Executioners* by John D. MacDonald); **Cin.** Sam Leavitt; **Ed.**
George Tomasini; **Art D.** Alexander Golitzen; **Mus.** Bernard Herrmann; **Cast:** Gregory
Peck, Robert Mitchum, Polly Bergen, Lori Martin, Martin Balsam, Jack Kruschen, Telly
Savalas.

Max Cady (Robert Mitchum), a vicious sex offender, is
released from prison after serving an eight-year sentence for
aggravated assault and attempted rape. He returns to the small
southern town where he was convicted. He seeks revenge against
a local attorney, Sam Bowden (Gregory Peck), who had witnessed the assault and whose testimony led to the conviction.
Cady makes his intentions known to Bowden but uses no violence nor makes any overt threat against Bowden, his wife or
their teenage daughter. The police pick up Cady for vagrancy, but
he shows he has a bank account and he is released. He beats up a
local girl he has picked up at a bar, but she refuses to bring
charges. When Bowden's dog is poisoned, he devises a plan in
which Cady will follow Bowden's wife and daughter which will
be deemed an overt threat by the police. He sends his wife and

daughter to a moored houseboat on the lake and he stays behind to follow Cady. By using his wife and daughter as bait the consequences are more harrowing than anticipated.

What makes *Cape Fear* work so well are a combination of factors: the menacing presence of Robert Mitchum, seedy locations like the bars and the bowling alley, the equally menacing score by Bernard Herrmann and, more important, the direction and pacing of the film by J. Lee Thompson. It moves very fast until the last fifteen minutes when Thompson deliberately slows it down. He shows details of the lake, the beach and the wooded area around the lake, getting maximum suspense from these scenes. Gregory Peck's underacting does not work in this film. For someone whose family is threatened, he shows too little emotion. Mitchum dominates every scene in this very nasty film. The supporting cast is excellent except for Telly Savalas who seems out of place as a Southerner. Thompson had made his reputation with *Guns of Navarone* (1961). *Cape Fear* is a superior film that he never equaled. An unnecessary remake by Martin Scorsese in 1991 is vastly inferior.

Carnival in Flanders

La Kermesse Héroique. 1935. 115 min. b.w. French. **Dir.** Jacques Feyder; **Scr.** Jacques Feyder, Charles Spaak; **Cin.** Harry Stradling; **Ed.** Jacques Brillouin; **Art D.** Lazare Meerson; **Mus.** Louis Beydts; **Cast:** Francoise Rosay, Louis Jouvet, Jean Murat, Alfred Adam, Bernard Lancret, André Alerme, Micheline Cheirel.

The story takes place in a small Flemish town on 17 September 1616, the date of its annual festival. Jean Broughel (Bernard Lancret), a young painter, is in love with Siska (Micheline Cheirel), the daughter of the burgomaster (André Alerme), and they intend to be married on that day. Her father refuses permission. He sees no future for painters and wants his daughter to marry the local butcher. An envoy sent by the invading army of Spain rides furiously into town and informs the frightened burgomaster and other notables that a battalion of Spanish soldiers led by the Duke of Olivares (Jean Murat) will be quartered in town for that night. Having heard of the brutal treatment given the people of other towns, the town elders are very agitated. The burgomaster devises a plan. He will play dead and the rest of the elders will go into hiding. The Spanish troops will respect a town in mourning. Cornelia (Francoise Rosay), the burgomaster's wife, is disgusted by the men's cowardice and rallies the wives to show that they can save the town by their courage. Cornelia and the women lead a welcoming committee for the Duke of Olivares. She informs the duke of her husband's death. The duke sympathizes but says his horses must rest. He promises to leave at dawn the next day. The officers are to spend the night at the houses of the notable women and the duke is a special guest of Cornelia. Cornelia asks the duke for a favor, to command the wedding of her daughter Siska to Broughel. After having spent a memorable night and having been entertained in every way the Spanish battalion leaves very happy early the next morning as promised. After they leave, Cornelia summons the joyful populace and tells them that it had been solely through the burgomaster's wisdom and bravery that the town was spared. She further gives them the good news that her husband had declared a tax exemption for one year. The film ends with Cornelia caressing a necklace the duke had given her.

The very charm of the film is that it is coy and ambiguous. We never find out why the Spanish officers departed so happily. Was it just in response to friendly, attractive faces and good food and wine, or were other favors also bestowed? The story is inspired by Aristophanes' play *Lysistrata*, in which Athenian and Spartan women join forces and deny their husbands conjugal rights as long as they wage war against each other. Jacques Feyder, a Belgian-born director who worked in Hollywood briefly in the late twenties before returning to France, researched Flemish and Dutch paintings and used the works of the masters—Bruegel, Hals and Vermeer among others—as inspiration for many scenes. Cornelia's dress is copied from a Frans Hals portrait. Harry Stradling, one of the great cinematographers, made the scenes come alive. Women always played prominent roles in Feyder's films. The renowned French actress, Francoise Rosay, the wife of Feyder, here has her great film role. Jean Murat is charming and elegant as the duke.

Charade

1963. 114 min. color. U.S. **Prod.** Stanley Donen; **Dir.** Stanley Donen; **Scr.** Peter Stone (based on the story "The Unsuspecting Wife" by Marc Behm, Peter Stone); **Cin.** Charles Lang; **Ed.** James B. Clark; **Art D.** Jean d'Eaubonne; **Mus.** Henry Mancini; **Cast:** Cary Grant, Audrey Hepburn, Walter Matthau, James Coburn, George Kennedy, Ned Glass, Jacques Marin.

On returning to Paris after a short holiday in the French Alps, Regina Lambert (Audrey Hepburn) finds her apartment ransacked and torn apart. She is informed by the police that her husband has been murdered. She learns that her husband, while a soldier in World War II, had stolen $250,000 in gold belonging to the U.S. government which had never been recovered. She has no clue as to what he had done with the money or who has murdered him. The only person she turns to is Peter Joshua (Cary Grant) whom she had casually met at the ski resort. But she soon loses trust in him when she finds his name is not really Peter Joshua. She seeks the help of the CIA man at the U.S. Embassy, Bartholomew (Walter Matthau), who advises her to search for the money and return it to the embassy—otherwise her life would be in danger. Soon she is threatened by three menacing people who claim to have served with her husband in the army.

The film successfully blends hideous murders with romantic comedy. The viewer is teased almost to the very end as to the identity of the murderer. Stanley Donen, known as a choreographer and later as codirector of musical comedies such as *On the Town* (1949) and *Singin' in the Rain* (1952), skillfully directed this, his first "mystery" movie. He is helped with a witty script and the veteran cinematographer Charles Lang, who captures some beautiful scenes of Paris. Cary Grant, as young as ever at sixty, is perfect for the part. He was to make only two more films before retiring. Hepburn with her Givenchy chic brings a great deal of charm to the film. Walter Matthau's flair for comedy somehow interferes with his portrayal. The film shows Hitchcock's influence, especially in the early parts.

Charley Varick

1973. 111 min. color. U.S. **Prod.** Don Siegel; **Dir.** Don Siegel; **Scr.** Dean Riesner, Howard Rodman (based on the novel *The Looters* by John Reese); **Cin.** Michael Butler; **Ed.** Frank Morriss; **Art D.** Fernando Carrere; **Mus.** Lalo Schifrin; **Cast:** Walter Matthau, Joe Don Baker, Felicia Farr, John Vernon, Andy Robinson, Sheree North, Norman Fell.

Former aerial circus pilot turned crop duster Charley Varick (Walter Matthau) is now a small-time bank robber. He holds up a little bank in Tres Cruces, New Mexico, hoping the heist will net ten to fifteen thousand dollars. His wife is the driver and his accomplice is a young punk named Herman (Andy Robinson). During the robbery his wife is killed in a shootout with the police. They later discover the take is more than $750,000, which was money the Mafia-controlled bank was laundering. Charley knows there will be trouble and tries to convince his partner to give the entire money back, but the greedy and arrogant young man insists they divide the take. Soon a sadistic Mafia hit man, Molly (Joe Don Baker), is on their trail. Charley through his wit and resourcefulness comes out of it alive, but others are not so lucky.

The film has little substance, but under the master director Don Siegel and with the superb actor Matthau the film works to perfection. From the very first scene we see Varick is not just a thief—he is a man of great common sense and cunning and a survivor. His touching farewell to his dead wife in a funeral pyre and his removal of her wedding ring establishes him also as a person of sensitivity. Molly, his adversary, is a sadistic, bigoted animal who destroys everyone in his path. The film is well photographed by Michael Butler mostly in Nevada with some excellent action scenes.

Chimes at Midnight

1966. 115 min. b.w. Spanish/Swiss. in English. **Prod.** Emiliano Piedra; **Dir.** Orson
Welles; **Scr.** Orson Welles (based on Shakespeare's *Henry IV* Parts I and II, *Henry V,
Richard II* and *The Merry Wives of Windsor,* and Holinshed's *The Chronicles of England*);
Cin. Edmond Richard; **Ed.** Fritz Muller; **Prod. D.** Gustavo Quintana; **Mus.** Angelo Francesco
Lavagnino; **Cast:** Orson Welles, Jeanne Moreau, Margaret Rutherford, John Gielgud,
Marina Vlady, Keith Baxter, Norman Rodway, Ralph Richardson, narrator.

Prince Hal (Keith Baxter), the son of King Henry IV (John
Gielgud) and heir to the throne of England, is an irresolute young
man who spends most of his time in the company of Sir John Falstaff (Orson Welles), a bawdy drunkard who is always in debt.
Falstaff lives in Eastcheap at the Boar's Head Tavern run by Mistress Quickly (Margaret Rutherford), where Prince Hal takes part
in Falstaff's neverending revelry. The king is disappointed in his
son's behavior and choice of friends. The guilt-ridden King
Henry's throne is shaky as he has come to power through the
murder of his predecessor, Richard II. His rule is soon threatened
by an uprising led by Henry Percy, Earl of Northumberland, and
his son the hot-tempered warrior Hotspur (Norman Rodway).
There is a crucial battle at Shrewsbury in which the king's army is
triumphant. Prince Hal leads the king's forces and in man-to-man
combat slays young Hotspur. "O Henry, thou hast robb'd me of
my youth." Falstaff sits out the battle much to the dismay of Prince
Hal. The king dies shortly thereafter and Prince Hal is crowned
Henry V. Falstaff believes his old friend, now king, will appoint
him to some high office, but instead he is banished from the court.
"I know thee not old man, fall to thy prayers." Later as Henry prepares to lead his army against the French, news comes that the
heartbroken Falstaff has died.

For over twenty years Welles had wanted to make a film of Falstaff. In his Hollywood days no studio was interested. By the early
fifties, having earned enough money as an actor mostly in Fox
films, Welles began to prepare a script largely based on *Henry IV*
Parts I and II and *The Merry Wives of Windsor* in which Falstaff has
a prominent role. He also relied on *Richard II* and *Henry V* to

round out the lives of the kings, Henry IV and Henry V. Filming began in Spain, but as always Welles soon ran out of money. The film was not completed until early 1966. Welles believed Falstaff was the very essence of a good man and that his vices were minor. He is presented as a tragic figure whose friendship is betrayed by the cold and ambitious Henry V. Falstaff is a pragma-tist who does not believe in military heroism or valor. He thinks courting death foolish: "What need I be so forward with him that calls not on me." The film is marred by one of the worst voice synchronizations by sound technicians. In the first ten minutes, as well as some very short sequences thereafter, the sound and images do not match at all. But this is more than compensated for by some extraordinary scenes. The battle of Shrewsbury is staged as well as any of the great movie battles. Welles fashioned these scenes after the paintings of Uccello. There is fine acting by Welles, Gielgud and Keith Baxter, but Jeanne Moreau as Doll Tearsheet and Margaret Rutherford are wasted. *Chimes at Mid-night* is Welles' most ambitious film and it is a near masterpiece.

Cinema Paradiso

Nuovo Cinema Paradiso. 1988. 123 min. color. Italian. **Prod.** Franco Cristaldi; **Dir.** Giuseppe Tornatore; **Scr.** Giuseppe Tornatore; **Cin.** Blasco Giurato; **Ed.** Mario Mora; **Prod. D.** Andrea Crisanti; **Mus.** Ennio Morricone; **Cast:** Philippe Noiret, Jacques Perrin, Salva-tore Cascio, Marco Leonardi, Leopoldo Trieste.

This film is mostly told in a flashback that begins soon after the end of World War II in a small town in Sicily. A ten-year-old boy, Toto (Salvatore Cascio), lives with his mother and small sister. His father has not returned from the war and is presumed dead. Toto visits the local movie house, Cinema Paradiso, almost every day and is befriended by the childless projectionist, Alfredo (Philippe Noiret), who teaches him how to run the film projector. Toto saves Alfredo from being burned to death when the projection booth catches fire. Alfredo is blinded and there are no other pro-jectionists in town. The cinema owner falsifies Toto's age and, through his contacts in the municipality, Toto becomes the pro-jectionist for several years. When Toto finishes school and military service, Alfredo talks him into leaving Sicily for Rome to make a name for himself. The film opens with Toto (Jacques Perrin) as a grown man who has become a successful film director. He receives a message from his mother that Alfredo is dead, and the flashback begins. Then, the adult Toto travels to Sicily for the funeral. His mother gives him a package that Alfredo had left for him. On returning to Rome he opens the package to find film clips—cut from the movies shown at Cinema Paradiso by order of the local priest—which Alfredo had saved for him.

The film was originally three hours, later cut to two and a half hours for export within Europe, and pared to two hours and a few minutes for the U.S. Tornatore, who wrote and directed the film, appears not to have been aware of the gem he had in the very basic story. Further paring would have produced a near mas-terpiece. In its U.S. cut the film is still at least five minutes too long, especially the sentimental middle parts involving the teenage Toto's romancing of the local banker's daughter, and his military service. Despite these unnecessary scenes, the movie is revitalized by the last ten minutes, which are pure magic. Toto watches Alfredo's censored clips, which are all kissing scenes, with a touching smile. The film has an excellent cast. Philippe Noiret, a fine actor who was briefly absent from the screen, reestablishes himself. Salvatore Cascio, a first-time actor, is especially strong. The set designer, Andrea Crisanti, did a marvelous job with the local cinema and the square in which it is located. The lovely musical score by Ennio Morricone reinforces the nostalgia.

Closely Observed Trains

Ostre Sledovane Vlaky. 1966. 89 min. b.w. Czech. **Prod.** Zdenek Oves; **Dir.** Jiri Menzel; **Scr.** Jiri Menzel, Bohumil Hrabal, Vaclav Nyvlt (based on the novel by Hrabal); **Cin.** Jaromir Sofr; **Ed.** Jirina Lukesova; **Art D.** Oldrich Bosak; **Mus.** Jiri Sust; **Cast:** Vaclav Neckar, Josef Somr, Jitka Bendova, Vladimir Valenta, Vlastimil Brodsky, Jiri Menzel.

The film is set during World War II and the German occupation of Czechoslovakia. The story centers on the coming of age of Milos (Vaclav Neckar), a boy in his late teens who has been hired by the railroad as a platform guard. He is sent to a remote station for training. Hubicka (Josef Somr), the dispatcher, takes him under his wing and teaches him the intricacies of his job. As Milos is still a virgin, Hubicka, a womanizer, also teaches him the way with women. Milos is introduced to sex by the wife of the stationmaster. Still giddy from his discovery of heretofore unknown pleasures, Milos decides impulsively to become a hero and impede the German war effort, for which he pays with his life. This early comedy/tragedy, the first solo effort by Jiri Menzel, is probably his best picture and won an Academy Award for best foreign film.

The Conformist

Il Conformista. 1971. 115 min. color. Italian. **Prod.** Maurizio Lodi-Fe; **Dir.** Bernardo Bertolucci; **Scr.** Bernardo Bertolucci (based on the novel by Alberto Moravia); **Cin.** Vittorio Storaro; **Ed.** Franco Arcalli; **Prod. D.** Ferdinando Scarfiotti; **Mus.** Georges Delerue; **Cast:** Jean-Louis Trintignant, Stefania Sandrelli, Dominique Sanda, Pierre Clementi, Enzo Tarascio, Gastone Moschin.

Marcello Clerici (Jean-Louis Trintignant) comes from an upper bourgeois family. His father has a mental disorder and has voluntarily committed himself to an asylum. His mother, a morphine addict, has a lover and thinks of herself as still young and desirable. The film is set principally in 1938, with some flashbacks and a short flash-forward. As a thirteen-year-old, Marcello had been raped by the family chauffeur whom he shot to death shortly afterward. There are strong indications that he had led on the chauffeur. Now in his late twenties and still plagued by the memory of the traumatic experience, he is desperate to show his sexual orthodoxy and obliterate any hint of homosexuality. He marries the dull and ordinary Giulia (Stefania Sandrelli), a girl from a petit bourgeois family, and soon thereafter joins the Fascist party to show his masculinity and conformity. He is ambitious and knows that in order to rise in the party hierarchy he must volunteer for special tasks. He sees a high-ranking functionary who tells him that in order to prove his absolute loyalty he must be ready to perform any assignment. He is instructed to help assassinate an anti–Fascist professor who had been his mentor at the university and now lives in Paris. He travels to Paris with Giulia and arranges a dinner with Professor Quadri (Enzo Tarascio) and his wife Anna (Dominique Sanda). Marcello remembers Anna, a lesbian former prostitute whom he had met some time ago. Anna, however, is more interested in Giulia. In a virtuoso scene, the best in the film, Anna and Giulia dance a teasing and seductive tango on the empty dance floor of the restaurant. Marcello's attraction to Anna delays the fulfillment of his assignment, and he is warned to get on with his duty. He lures the professor and Anna to the woods where the assassins are waiting. The professor and his wife are killed in an orgy of bloody stabbings. There is a brief flash-forward to the post-Mussolini era in which Marcello berates and chases an older man making sexual advances to a young boy.

The film explores the interconnection between repressed sexual desires and the attraction to totalitarian politics. Marcello will do anything to erase the memories of his homosexual past and assert his "manhood." In his desperate search for orthodoxy he becomes a Fascist goon. As in an earlier Bertolucci film, *The Spider's Stratagem* (1970), the film pictures Fascist Italy and one individual's experience. The acting is competent. The script is a bit facile and nothing is delved into with any depth. However, *The Conformist* is a fascinating film, and is well directed and beautifully photographed. The use of flashbacks and the one flash-forward are extraordinarily well done.

The Conversation

1974. 113 min. color. U.S. **Prod.** Francis Ford Coppola; **Dir.** Francis Ford Coppola; **Scr.** Francis Ford Coppola; **Cin.** Bill Butler; **Ed.** Walter Murch, Richard Chew; **Prod D.** Dean Tavoularis; **Mus.** David Shire; **Cast:** Gene Hackman, John Cazale, Allen Garfield, Frederic Forrest, Michael Higgins, Cindy Williams, Teri Garr, Harrison Ford, Michael Higgins, Elizabeth MacRae, Robert Duvall (unbilled).

Harry Caul (Gene Hackman) is a professional surveillance and wiretap expert who is regarded by many as the best in the business. He is an intensely private person with no friends. He has a mistress he sees occassionally—purely for functional reasons. He is a good saxophone player and his only moments of relaxation are when playing his sax in his apartment. He is also a devout Catholic and regularly goes to confession. We first see him in San Francisco's crowded Union Square during the lunch hour where with his two assistants, Stan (John Cazale) and Paul (Michael Higgins), as he is tracking and recording a young couple, Ann (Cindy Williams) and Mark (Frederic Forrest). When enough has been recorded and photographed, he goes back to his lab and plays the tapes over and over again. He dubs out the other sounds of the square until what is left is several minutes of clean conversation between the couple. His employer for this job is a powerful businessman who is known only as the Director (Robert Duvall in an unbilled cameo role). Ann is the wife of the Director and Mark an employee. It appears to Caul that Ann is having an affair with Mark. Caul delivers the tapes and photographs to the Director, thinking his job is over. There are lingering doubts in his mind, however, so he goes to his lab and painstakingly listens to the tapes, adjusting and readjusting the sound. It finally dawns on him that it is not a simple case of marital infidelity. Ann and Mark are afraid for their lives and believe the Director is out to have them murdered. Some years earlier when Caul's assignment had led to the murder of three people, his attitude had been, "I'm not responsible for the outcome of my work." Now he cannot overcome his guilt and decides to do something to prevent the murder. What he does not realize is that much more is involved.

Although a murder has been planned he is wrong about the perpetrator and the victim. Still worse, the surveillance expert himself has been bugged, and even when he turns his apartment upside down, almost demolishing his rooms in the process, he cannot locate the bug.

Coppola made *The Conversation* after *The Godfather* (1972) and while he was working on *The Godfather, Part II* (1974). It is a bleak film about a lonely and forsaken man. It is a difficult and ambitious film to bring off as very little can be shown visually and, by its very nature, the subject matter restricts the pace. Still, it is most imaginative. Seldom has ordinary sound been used to such great effect. Gene Hackman is excellent in a very difficult role, and is ably supported by Allen Garfield and John Cazale.

The Court Jester

1956. 101 min. color. U.S. **Prod.** Norman Panama, Melvin Frank; **Dir.** Norman Panama, Melvin Frank; **Scr.** Norman Panama, Melvin Frank; **Cin.** Ray June; **Ed.** Tom McAdoo; **Mus.** Vic Schoen; **Cast:** Danny Kaye, Glynis Johns, Basil Rathbone, Angela Lansbury, Cecil Parker, Mildred Natwick, Robert Middleton, John Carradine, Michael Pate, Herbert Rudley, Noel Drayton.

This is the story of how the destiny of a nation was changed by a birthmark, "a royal birthmark on the royal backside." The throne has been usurped by King Roderick (Cecil Parker). The rightful infant king is cared for by the followers of the Black Fox, who is determined to overthrow Roderick and place the baby on the throne. Hawkins (Danny Kaye) is the valet to the Black Fox and it is through his ingenuity that Roderick is overthrown. The baby becomes king once his backside is shown to the people. *The Court Jester* is the best and most enjoyable of Danny Kaye's films. It has a couple of good songs by Sylvia Fine and Sammy Cahn, and the best of tongue twisters: "The vessel with the pestle has the pellet with the poison. The chalice from the palace has the brew that is true." Which then becomes, "The chalice from the palace has the pellet with the poison. The flagon with the dragon has the brew that is true." The cast is first-rate. Glynis Johns as Maid Jean is the ideal medieval maid, Basil Rathbone is the slimy snake he was in *The Adventures of Robin Hood* (1935), and Angela Lansbury, Cecil Parker and Mildred Natwick are the same consummate pros of countless films.

Crossfire

1947. 86 min. b.w. U.S. **Prod.** Adrian Scott; **Dir.** Edward Dmytryk; **Scr.** John Paxton (based on the novel *The Brick Foxhole* by Richard Brooks); **Cin.** J. Roy Hunt; **Ed.** Harry Gerstad; **Art D.** Albert S. D'Agostino, Alfred Herman; **Mus.** Roy Webb; **Cast:** Robert Young, Robert Mitchum, Robert Ryan, Gloria Grahame, Sam Levene, Steve Brodie, Paul Kelly, Jacqueline White, George Cooper, William Phipps.

The film is set during the demobilization period after WWII when a group of soldiers are about to be discharged. Montgomery (Robert Ryan), a brutal Jew-baiting soldier, goes to a bar with two of his buddies. There they meet Joseph Samuel (Sam Levene), a recently discharged wounded veteran, and his girlfriend. Samuel invites a lonely, confused soldier to his apartment. Montgomery, learning that Samuel is a Jew, goes to the apartment uninvited with his buddy Floyd (Steve Brodie) for the free liquor. Now drunk and seething with his hatred of Jews, Montgomery beats Samuel to death. Later, Floyd, who had witnessed the killing, is also murdered. Police detective Finlay (Robert Young), with the help of a level-headed G.I. (Robert Mitchum), lays a trap for the killer.

Crossfire was the first Hollywood film that openly dealt with anti-Semitism in the U.S. It was also daring to portray a vicious bigot as a member of the armed forces. The film was based on a novel by the future director Richard Brooks that dealt with homosexuality, itself a controversial subject at the time. The producer changed the subject to anti-Semitism. *Crossfire*, under the very able direction of Edward Dmytryk with his claustrophobic sets and bizarre lighting, is also a first-rate mystery. The acting of all three Roberts is excellent, but Robert Ryan, one of the best

actors of his generation, is by far the dominant actor. The only
flaw in the film is a lengthy scene in which Finlay sermonizes
about prejudice and bigotry. Not only does it slow the pace, but it
in no way answers the viciousness or the intensity of Montgomery's hatred. Still, the film picks up quickly, aided by one final
plot twist. It was released a few months earlier than *Gentleman's
Agreement,* which also dealt with anti-Semitism in U.S. society.
However, *Crossfire* is by far the better film. Adrian Scott, the producer, and Dmytryk were brought before the House
Un-American Activities Committee as communists. Scott's
career ended in 1947 when he refused to testify. Dmytryk
recanted and was allowed to continue working in Hollywood.
None of Dmytryk's subsequent films equaled *Murder My Sweet*
(1944), *Cornered* (1945) or *Crossfire.*

Dark Eyes

Oci Ciornie. 1987. 118 min. color. Italian. **Prod.** Silvia D'Amico Bendico, Carlo Cucchi;
Dir. Nikita Mikhalkov; **Scr.** Alexander Adabachian, Nikita Mikhalkov, Suso Cecchi D'Amico
(based on the stories "The Lady with the Little Dog," "The Name-Day Party," "Anna
Around the Neck" and "My Wife" by Anton Chekhov); **Cin.** Franco Di Giacomo; **Ed.** Enzo
Meniconi; **Art D.** Mario Garbuglia, Alexander Adabachian; **Mus.** Francis Lai; **Cast:** Mar-
cello Mastroianni, Silvana Mangano, Marthe Keller, Elena Sofonova, Pina Cei, Vsevolod
Larionov.

The film is set at the beginning of the twentieth century. It
tells the story of a promising young Italian architect, Romano
(Marcello Mastroianni), who marries a banker's daughter and
soon abandons his ambitions. He spends his time seducing
women, keeping mistresses and staying at various spas. At one spa
he meets and seduces a young Russian married woman who,
afraid of falling in love, departs hastily to Russia. The balance of
the film is his search for the Russian girl, the one love of his life.
He poses as a rich capitalist who will bring industry to the hin-
terland. He is hailed as a hero by all except a seeming madman
who wants no factories as they will ruin rivers and forests. The

film is too glossy. It is Mastroianni's film and the best parts are when Romano goes to Russia. It is based on four Chekhov stories, but mainly "The Lady with the Little Dog." It has some of the same themes of director Mikhalkov's earlier *Oblomov* (1950) which depicts indolence.

Day for Night

La Nuit Americaine. 1973. 120 min. color. French. **Prod.** Marcel Berbert; **Dir.** Francois Truffaut; **Scr.** Francois Truffaut, Suzanne Shiffman, Jean-Louis Richard; **Cin.** Pierre-William Glenn; **Ed.** Yann Dedet, Martine Barraque; **Mus.** Georges Delerue; **Cast:** Jacqueline Bisset, Jean-Pierre Aumont, Valentina Cortese, Francois Truffaut, Jean-Pierre Leaud, Alexander Stewart, Nathalie Baye, David Markham, Graham Greene.

Ferrand (Francois Truffaut), a director, is shooting a feature film, *Meet Pamela*, in the south of France. It is a banal story, a variation of *Bonjour Tristesse*: a son brings his bride home only to have his father fall in love with her. It is now the last seven days of shooting and the film is beset with problems. The cast includes an immature and spoiled young actor, Alphonse (Jean-Pierre Leaud), who thinks "woman are magic" and can't live without them. He plays the son. The bride is played by Julie (Jacqueline Bisset), a beautiful actress recovering from a nervous breakdown. She is accompanied by an elderly man who turns out to be her husband and doctor. There is Alexandre (Jean-Pierre Aumont) as the father, a debonair, handsome actor who has played similar parts in many films. Alexandre is known to be a closet homosexual. There is also Severine (Valentina Cortese), a veteran of many films who is now an alcoholic and can't remember her lines. She plays Alphonse's mother. Things begin to go wrong when a bit player, whose pregnancy begins to show, causes the reshooting of her scenes with a double. The script girl, who was sleeping with Alphonse, decides to leave him and go away with the stuntman. Alphonse is despondent and wants to leave the picture. Julie, feeling sorry for him and wanting the picture completed, sleeps with Alphonse and his confidence is restored. Alexandre and his lover

are killed in a car crash. There are budget overruns and the producer and the insurance company are at loggerheads. Things
eventually fall into place. A double for Alexandre is found, the
film is completed and the cast and crew go their separate ways.

Day for Night is a lighthearted and immensely enjoyable film
and the least pretentious of films about how movies are made. In
addition to its humor, we gain insight into the characters
involved in making a film. The acting is uniformly good.
Valentina Cortese is excellent in her brief scenes. Graham Greene
appears in the film as the British insurance executive. At the time,
he lived nearby in Antibes and volunteered for the part.

At one point, the lovesick Alphonse asks the director Ferrand,
"Are movies more important than life?" Truffaut answers the question in a dream sequence in which a young boy, about ten, with a
cane in his hand walks toward a closed movie house showing *Citizen Kane*, and steals all the still photographs. The scene also shows
three posters of films of Truffaut's favorite directors, Dreyer, Welles
and Hitchcock. The final crane shot, showing how a film is put
together, to the accompanying strains of semi-religious music, is
excellent. The only minor flaw is the depiction of the director as the
embodiment of self-restraint and serenity. Truffaut's penultimate
film, *The Man Who Loved Women* (1977), is more indicative of his
attitude toward women. The French title of the film, *La Nuit Americaine*, refers to scenes shot at daytime with diffused light and
underexposed film, giving the appearance of night. In one of his
later films, *The Last Metro* (1980), set in Paris during the German
occupation, Truffaut deals with methods of staging a play. The film
is, however, better remembered for its political content than for the
its portrayal of the mechanics of stage production.

The Day of the Jackal

1973. 141 min. color. British/French. **Prod.** John Woolf, David Deutsch; **Dir.** Fred Zinnemann; **Scr.** Kenneth Ross (based on the novel by Frederick Forsyth); **Cin.** Jean Tournier; **Ed.** Ralph Kemplen; **Art D.** Willy Holt, Ernest Archer; **Mus.** Georges Delerue; **Cast:** Edward Fox, Alan Badel, Cyril Cusack, Michel Lonsdale, Delphine Seyrig, Derek Jacobi.

A group of former French officers with some former French residents in Algeria, all with thwarted vested interests and all members of a secret organization, the OAS, have held General de Gaulle wholly responsible for the "sellout" in Algeria. They have made several unsuccessful attempts to assassinate the general. After the last attempt in 1963, French security forces rounded up most of their senior members. Some were sentenced to long prison terms and a few were executed. When the film begins there are only three senior members left, hiding under assumed names in Rome and Vienna. They decide to hire a professional assassin, and select the best—an Englishman who had carried out the 1961 assassination of Trujillo in the Dominican Republic, and had taken part in the murder of Patrice Lumumba in the Congo the same year. The Englishman goes by the name of Jackal and demands $500,000, one half at the start and the other half when he has completed the job. He leaves no address and will contact his employers as and when necessary. To raise the money, the OAS embarks on a series of bank robberies.

The Day of the Jackal was a difficult movie to bring off. Almost everyone knew that de Gaulle was not assassinated. To hold the viewer's interest and create suspense, Zinnemann concentrated on the minutely detailed preparation by the assassin and the countermeasures by the alerted French security forces to identify the would-be assassin and foil his plot. The Jackal's every step is meticulously depicted. He forges and steals several passports and identity papers. He has a gunsmith design a very compact collapsible rifle that fires a single explosive bullet. In the course of the planning, the Jackal ruthlessly murders three people. He selects 25 August, Liberation Day, for the deed. On that day de Gaulle will be laying a wreath on the tomb of the Unknown Soldier. The efforts of the security forces are equally well detailed. What keeps one's interest piqued is the race against time that Zinnemann carefully crafts.

There is an interesting selection of actors in this film. For the Jackal, Zinnemann wanted a lesser-known face and chose the relatively unknown Edward Fox, who gives an icy portrait of an assassin. The presence of four very good actors, though not well known to U.S. audiences, contributes greatly to the film: Cyril Cusack as the emotionless gunsmith who asks, "Would you be going for a head or chest shot?"; Michel Lonsdale as the key French detective; Derek Jacobi as Lonsdale's assistant; and the elegant Delphine Seyrig in a brief liaison with the Jackal. Zinnemann had a talent on par with Kazan in getting the best performances from his actors. An erudite and literate director, Zinnemann had not made a film since *A Man For All Seasons* (1966). He had spent some four years preparing a script for André Malraux's *Man's Fate*, a highly ambitious project which never came to fruition. After *The Day of the Jackal* he made only two films, the more notable being *Julia* (1977).

The Day the Earth Stood Still

1951. 92 min. b.w. U.S. **Prod.** Julian Blaustein; **Dir.** Robert Wise; **Scr.** Edmund H. North (based on a story by Harry Bales); **Cin.** Leo Tover; **Ed.** William Reynolds; **Art D.** Lyle Wheeler; **Mus.** Bernard Herrmann; **Cast:** Michael Rennie, Patricia Neal, Hugh Marlowe, Sam Jaffe, Billy Gray, Frank Conroy.

Klaatu (Michael Rennie), an emissary from another planet in human form, lands his single spacecraft on the Mall in Washington, D.C. He is accompanied by Gort, a ten-foot-tall robot. They are met by a contingent of U.S. military with tanks and artillery. When a nervous soldier takes a shot and wounds Klaatu, Gort reacts by wiping out all the weapons assembled on the mall with a laser beam. Klaatu is taken to a military hospital and recovers within minutes. He tells a presidential aide who has called on him that he represents a federation of planets sent to warn all governments on Earth to cease nuclear testing on land, sea and in outer space. Klaatu says there have been too many wars on Earth already, but now with the advent of nuclear weapons the inhabitants of other planets are concerned. If mankind continues, the federation is prepared to blast Earth out of the universe. He asks the White House aide to arrange a meeting with all heads of state. When he is told that is not feasible, Klaatu escapes from the hospital and takes a room at a boarding house run by a war widow, Helen Benson (Patricia Neal). He meets and listens to the other guests. He learns of the fears and anxiety of ordinary people, especially their fear of nuclear war with the Soviet Union. He befriends the landlady's twelve-year-old son Bobby (Billy Gray) and sees the famous monuments in Washington. With the boy's help he meets the most eminent scientist in the U.S., Dr. Bernhardt (Sam Jaffe). Klaatu gains his confidence by completing an equation in a matter of minutes that Dr. Bernhardt has been working on for several years. A meeting is arranged with some of the outstanding scientists in the world where Klaatu repeats his warning. To demonstrate the capabilities of the federation he has all sources of power cut off for a half hour all over the globe and everything comes to a standstill. Wounded again, Klaatu departs Earth. The film ends on a hopeful note. Klaatu has acquired a certain amount of affection for Earth people and believes his advice will be heeded.

An intelligent, and one of the very best, science-fiction films. It moves at great speed and is very well directed by the skilled Robert Wise. The scenes at the boarding house are especially well done and the worries of humans are believable and realistic. There are also some subtle touches. Klaatu and Bobby go to the mall where the spaceship has landed and Gort stands guard. A radio reporter is interviewing the spectators and Klaatu is asked about his reaction to the space invader. He answers that people's fears are unfounded. In a telling commentary on the media, the reporter cuts him off and engages at length someone else who makes dramatic alarmist comments. The Bernard Herrmann score is original and perfectly suits a film relating to outer space. The art direction of Lyle Wheeler is deliberately played down. *The Day the Earth Stood Still* is the only pacifist science-fiction movie. What is

remarkable is that it was made and released at the height of the
Korean War. The Department of Defense refused to provide jeeps
and artillery for use in the film. Fortunately, the California
National Guard agreed. An interesting footnote is that Spencer
Tracy wanted to play the role of Klaatu because of the film's pacifist content. Robert Wise argued that a known face would ruin
the movie. Another difficulty was that Sam Jaffe who plays the
Einstein figure had been blacklisted. Zanuck took all the risks, and
the movie was a great commercial success.

Dead of Night

1945. 102 min. b.w. British. **Prod.** Michael Balcon; **Dir.** Alberto Cavalcanti, Basil Dear-
den, Robert Hamer, Charles Crichton; **Scr.** John Baines, Angus Macphail, T. E. B. Clarke
(based on stories by H. G. Wells, E. F. Benson, John Baines, Angus Macphail); **Cin.** Jack
Parker, Harold Julius; **Ed.** Charles Hasse; **Art D.** Michael Relph; **Mus.** Georges Auric; **Cast:**
Mervyn Johns, Roland Culver, Mary Merrall, Frederick Valk, Renee Gadd, Sally Ann
Howes, Anthony Baird, Googie Withers, Miles Malleson, Michael Redgrave, Basil Radford, Naunton Wayne.

An architect (Mervyn Johns) has been asked to remodel a
country house. When he pays a visit to the house, the owner has
some ten guests for afternoon tea. He is taken aback when he
realizes that although he had never met any of them, they have all
been characters in his dreams and nightmares. At first the guests
are dubious of his claims but as the architect relates his dreams,
they realize he has uncanny powers. One of the best surreal/hor-
ror films, it tells its story in five brief segments directed by four
separate directors. Two of the tales stand out. "The Haunted Mirror," directed by Robert Hamer, is very well done. But the best is
the last segment, "The Ventriloquist's Dummy," directed by
Alberto Cavalcanti. Michael Redgrave plays the ventriloquist
who comes to believe the dummy has assumed his personality
and he has become the dummy.

The Deer Hunter

1978. 183 min. color. U.S. **Prod.** Barry Spikings, Michael Deeley, Michael Cimino; **Dir.** Michael Cimino; **Scr.** Deric Washburn; **Cin.** Vilmos Zsigmond; **Ed.** Peter Zinner; **Art D.** Ron Hobbs, Kim Swados; **Mus.** Stanley Myers; **Cast:** Robert De Niro, John Cazale, John Savage, Meryl Streep, Christopher Walken, George Dzundza, Chuck Aspegren, Shirley Stoler, Rutanya Alda.

The film is set in the late sixties in the small steel mill town of Clairton, Pennsylvania, and in Vietnam. It is about three close friends who work in the mill and are drafted or volunteer for military service. The film begins with the wedding of Steven (John Savage) to a local girl in a Russian Orthodox church, followed by a half-hour of their wedding party. Steven's closest friends are Michael (Robert De Niro) and Nick (Christopher Walken). Later the three, along with a few other friends, drive to the mountains for deer hunting. The film then cuts to the three friends in Vietnam. They all are taken prisoner by the Viet Cong. They are tortured and in one of the most brutal scenes they are forced to play Russian roulette against each other while their captors bet on the outcome. Through the ingenuity of Michael, they kill their captors and escape. Steven is a paraplegic and is sent home. Nick is mentally wounded and remains behind. Only Michael returns without injuries. After a time Michael goes back to Saigon to bring Nick home.

The Deer Hunter is a beautifully photographed movie with some of the most stunning scenes ever filmed. There are memorable performances by the entire cast. Credit also goes to the director, Michael Cimino, for having made a powerful and intense film. Despite its length of three hours, it maintains its pace. It is not, however, an accurate depiction of the American presence and experience in Vietnam.

Dersu Uzala

1975. 140 min. color. Japanese. **Prod.** Eiti Mattsue; **Dir.** Akira Kurosawa; **Scr.** Akira Kurosawa, Yuri Nagibin (based on the journals of Vladimir Arseniev); **Cin.** Asakazu Nakai, Yuri Gantman, Fyodor Dobronavov; **Ed.** V. Stepanovoi; **Prod. D.** Yuri Raksha; **Mus.** Isaak Shvarts; **Cast:** Maxim Munzuk, Yuri Solomine, Schemeiki Chokmorov, Svetlana Danielchanara.

In the early twentieth century, a military contingent commanded by Captain Areniev (Yuri Solomin) is conducting a topographical survey in unexplored regions of eastern Siberia. They run into an old trapper, Dersu Uzala (Maxim Munzuk), who becomes their guide and teacher in the ways of nature. He shows them how to survive in the treacherous uncharted region. The captain and Dersu become friends and the captain convinces Dersu to retire and come to the city to live with him and his family. Dersu reluctantly accepts, but after a few weeks he realizes he cannot adapt to city life and goes back to the wilds. The film begins with the captain wanting to find Dersu. He finds Dersu's grave and learns that he had died some time ago. There is then a flashback to his first encounter with the old trapper. The film is some twenty minutes too long, but there is a great extended scene of an approaching storm that elevates the movie. Dersu's knowledge of nature saves himself and the captain. He senses the coming of the storm and with the captain's help constructs a shelter with available dead wood and brush. There is a poetic strain through the entire film. In addition to Dersu's natural dignity and the bond of friendship between the two, it shows how man has disfigured the wilds.

Kurosawa had been unable to start a film in nearly three years. He had been in a deep depression and had even contemplated suicide. Then came the offer from the Russian Mosfilm. Kurosawa accepted, provided he could have his own cinematographer, Asakazu Nakai. *Dersu Uzala* is basically a survival story, but it shines with the love of nature. The completion of this film revived Kurosawa's spirits and he went on to make several very fine films.

The Discreet Charm of the Bourgeoisie

Le Charme Discret De La Bourgeoisie. 1972. 100 min. color. French. **Prod.** Serge Silberman; **Dir.** Luis Buñuel; **Scr.** Luis Buñuel , Jean-Claude Carriere; **Cin.** Edmond Richard; **Ed.** Helene Plemiannikov; **Art D.** Pierre Guffroy; **Mus.** Galaxie Musique; **Cast:** Fernando Rey, Delphine Seyrig, Stephane Audran, Jean-Pierre Cassel, Michel Piccoli, Bulle Ogier.

Six middle-aged respectable, bourgeois characters are never able to manage to have dinner together. After receiving an invitation they show up, but on the wrong night. They go to a restaurant where they do not stay because the owner has died and his corpse is still in the middle of the room. At another restaurant they are told the establishment has run out of all beverages, including water. They are frustrated at another household when the host and hostess prefer to make love and have run out of the house. On another occasion, just as they are about to start dinner, an army contingent sequesters the house. Finally, when they secure a reservation at the private room of a restaurant, the curtain goes up and they realize they are actors in a play. We also learn that one of them is the ambassador from Miranda, a Latin American country, and he and his cohorts are involved in smuggling heroin via the diplomatic pouch. This wittiest of all Buñuel films hosts the commanding presence of Fernando Rey, a Buñuel favorite, and two elegant women, Delphine Seyrig and Stephane Audran. No Buñuel film is complete without the master's barbs and ridicule of the clergy and the bourgeoisie. It is interesting how the daring themes that run through his films have become accepted by the film-going audience.

D.O.A.

1950. 83 min. b.w. U.S. **Prod.** Leo C. Popkin; **Dir.** Rudolph Maté; **Scr.** Russell Rouse, Clarence Green; **Cin.** Ernests Laszlo; **Ed.** Arthur H. Nadel; **Art D.** Duncan Cramer. **Mus.** Dimitri Tiomkin; **Cast:** Edmond O'Brien, Pamela Britton, Luther Adler, William Ching, Neville Brand, Beverly Garland, Lynne Bagget, Laurette Luez.

Frank Bigelow (Edmond O'Brien) walks up to a police station in Los Angeles and reports his own murder. He then collapses and dies. A lengthy flashback follows. Bigelow, an accountant in a small town in northern California, wants to get away from his possessive fiancée Paula (Pamela Britton) for a few days and goes to San Francisco. He spends a night on the town. Next day he feels sick and sees several doctors who tell him that he has been poisoned with something for which there is no antidote, and that he will be dead in two or three days. He runs away horrified, but slowly he gathers his wits and retraces his steps. He remembers he had unknowingly notarized a bill of sale for the purchase of a deadly substance for someone in Los Angeles. He travels to Los Angeles and soon finds out that he is the only person who can provide the evidence that could put away a gang of criminals. Before he can unravel the plot, he has to confront a slimy corrupt businessman and a psychopathic killer.

Maté, a cinematographer and then director from the mid-twenties in both Germany and the U.S., fashioned a first-rate thriller. From the bar scene in San Francisco to the police station in Los Angeles, the film moves at a breathtaking pace. Indoor scenes are followed by scenes on the city streets with striking effect. Edmond O'Brien is on screen for almost every scene. His acting and presence exude an unusual energy. Luther Adler as the criminal mastermind and Neville Brand, in one of his early roles, as the psychotic killer are both very good. The title is the police abbreviation for "dead on arrival," which is stamped on Bigelow's file in the final shot of the film. One of the great sleepers of the early fifties.

Dodsworth

1936. 101 min. b.w. U.S. **Prod.** Samuel Goldwyn; **Dir.** William Wyler; **Scr.** Sidney Howard (based on the novel by Sinclair Lewis); **Cin.** Rudolph Maté; **Ed.** Daniel Mandell; **Art D.** Richard Day; **Mus.** Alfred Newman; **Cast:** Walter Huston, Ruth Chatterton, Paul Lukas, Mary Astor, David Niven, Maria Ouspenskaya, Spring Byington, Odette Myrtil, Gregory Gaye, John Payne.

Middle-aged industrialist Sam Dodsworth (Walter Huston), an automobile tycoon, sells his entire holdings in Dodsworth Motors and decides to retire. He plans to travel and gain "some insight into himself" and better understand his wife, Fran (Ruth Chatterton). Fran has social pretensions and is tired of life in a Midwestern city. She wants to meet and socialize with upper-class Europeans. They have a daughter who just married and Fran is afraid of aging and becoming a grandmother. On board a luxury liner to England, they meet a British playboy, Lockert (David Niven). Fran immediately wants everyone to know she had been to Europe and attended a Swiss boarding school. She chides Sam who had never been out of the U.S. for saying "bourgeois things." She leads Lockert on but when he makes advances, she becomes embarrassed and frightened. Lockert admonishes her: "You are not a woman of the world as you pretend." Fran learns nothing from the humiliating experience. She asks Sam to cancel their stay in London and they go directly to Paris where she becomes involved with a calculating banker, Arnold Iselin (Paul Lukas). She travels with him, but when she realizes he is only after her husband's money she leaves.

Sam, thoroughly bored by the social scene, travels alone to Italy. He meets an attractive American, Edith Cartright (Mary Astor), whom he met briefly on the ocean liner. She has been recently widowed and had decided to settle in Italy. He is taken by her and they find they have many mutual interests, but they remain merely friends. Fran now has become involved with an Austrian baron, Kurt Von Obersdorf (Gregory Gaye), who proposes marriage. Fran asks Sam for a divorce and he reluctantly agrees. The baron, however, must have his mother's approval. The mother,

Baroness Von Obersdorf (Maria Ouspenskaya), and her son call on Fran. After brief greetings the baroness tells Fran outright: "You are older than my son.... He must have children. Can you give him children?" She walks out, followed by her son. Fran now withdraws her request for a divorce. She has become a grand-mother but begs Sam not to talk about it. Sam takes her back to the U.S. but realizes the hopelessness of their situation and leaves her intending to seek a divorce. He returns to Italy to renew his relationship with Edith.

Based on a play by Sidney Howard (adapted from the Sinclair Lewis novel), Wyler expands on the theme of middle-age marital problems. Walter Huston as the idealistic American businessman, an incongruity, gives a magnificent performance. Mary Astor and Ruth Chatterton are also very good. Chatterton's performance, although more suited to the stage, is well controlled by Wyler. Maria Ouspenskaya, an actress with the Moscow Arts Theatre at the turn of the twentieth century, dominates her brief scene. It is a masterful film by William Wyler, but it has dated somewhat. It received Academy Award nominations in every major category.

Dog Day Afternoon

1975. 130 min. color. U.S. **Prod.** Martin Bregman, Martin Elfand; **Dir.** Sidney Lumet; **Scr.** Frank Pierson (based on an article by P. F. Kluge, Thomas Moore); **Cin.** Victor J. Kemper; **Ed.** Dede Allen; **Prod D.** Charles Bailey; **Art D.** Douglas Higgins; **Cast:** Al Pacino, John Cazale, Charles Durning, James Broderick, Chris Sarandon, Sally Boyar, Penny Allen, Susan Peretz.

The film depicts an actual attempted robbery of the First Sav-ings Bank of Brooklyn by three incompetent would-be robbers on the hot afternoon of 22 August 1974. The getaway car driver backs out at the last minute. Of the remaining two, Sonny (Al Pacino), is the mastermind. He is bisexual, married with children, and has fallen in love with a transvestite, Leon (Chris Sarandon), who wants to have a sex change. Sonny has planned the robbery to pay for the operation. His accomplice is dimwitted Sal (John

Cazale). Both are Vietnam war veterans. They burst into the bank
fully armed, to find only $1,100 in the safe. The collection van
has already come and taken all the cash. As they rifle the tellers'
booths for small bills and coins, the police spot them and sur-
round the building. The two robbers take hostage the bank
staff—the manager, the guard and six women tellers. It soon
appears that the entire Brooklyn police force, headed by Lieutenant Moretti (Charles Durning), has surrounded the bank. A
crowd of passersby gather. Sonny releases the guard, an elderly
man who has had a heart attack. As the guard comes out, the
police, seeing a black man, rush to arrest him assuming he is one
of the robbers. The swelling crowd begins to boo and heckle the
police. TV cameras arrive and the crowd of onlookers grows
larger still. Later, when Sonny releases one of the women he
comes out and shouts, "Attica! Attica!," the name of a prison in
upstate New York where the guards killed more than forty riot-
ing inmates who had taken over the prison. The crowd picks up
the chant, and the police nearly lose control of the mob, which
has become totally sympathetic to the robbers. Inside the bank,
the tellers fraternize with their captors. Sonny begins to receive
and make dozens of phone calls: TV reporters, the police, the
FBI; his wife and his lover, who both complain of neglect; and his
mother who consoles him, "The FBI understands why you did
this. It is all the fault of your wife." Sonny negotiates with an FBI
agent and is promised one million dollars and a plane to fly him
and Sal to a distant country. In a masterful ending, Sonny and Sal
armed with a shotgun and surrounded by the remaining hostages
are taken to the airport to a waiting plane, but with an unexpected outcome.

Dog Day Afternoon together with *12 Angry Men* (1957) are Sidney Lumet's best directorial efforts. Lumet is peerless when the
story is confined to a claustrophobic indoor setting where he
captures minute details that give the picture intense realism. The
cast is excellent. As the uneducated, not very bright hoodlum
who is totally out of his league, Al Pacino gives one of his finest
performances. John Cazale and Charles Durning are superb. Sally
Boyar as Mulvaney the bank manager, Penny Allen as the senior

teller and James Broderick as Sheldon, the senior F.B.I. agent, are equally good. Lumet and the cast were working with a first-rate, witty script by Frank Pierson. In the very opening scene, when the getaway driver asks to be let go, Sonny tells him, "OK, but don't take the car, take the subway." When Sonny asks Sal what country he wants to be taken to, Sal answers, "Wyoming."

Don't Look Now

1973. 110 min. color. British. **Prod.** Peter Katz; **Dir.** Nicolas Roeg; **Scr.** Allan Scott, Chris Bryant (based on a story by Daphne du Maurier); **Cin.** Anthony Richmond; **Ed.** Graeme Clifford; **Art D.** Giovanni Soccol; **Mus.** Pino Donaggio; **Cast:** Julie Christie, Donald Sutherland, Hilary Mason, Clelia Matania, Massimo Serato.

John Baxter (Donald Sutherland) is a restorer of mosaics, tiles and stained glass in England. While he repairs some stained glass assisted by his wife Laura (Julie Christie), their daughter rides her bicycle outside. She runs over some broken glass. John clearly senses some imminent danger. He rushes out, but is too late. His daughter has fallen into a pond and drowned. John and Laura are shattered by the loss. The incident, however, brings about the realization that he has some sort of psychic powers, but he does not confide in anyone for fear of ridicule. Some time later, the couple travels to Venice for a church restoration. The city is disturbed by the presence of a mass murderer and the police are helpless. Two strange English sisters, Heather (Hilary Mason) who is blind and Wendy (Clelia Matania), tell him they are in contact with his dead child. They also say they have a premonition that something horrible will happen. Later on, he sees a childlike figure with the same red raincoat as his daughter in the back alleys of Venice, but he is never able to catch up to it. He also has a vision of a funeral boat with his wife seated next to a coffin. After a harrowing experience in the church, when the scaffolding collapses, he begins another search for the figure in the red coat with a tragic end.

Don't Look Now is one of the eeriest films ever made. The very choice of Venice in autumn as the locale for most of the film adds to the mystery. A deserted and decaying Venice in the off-season can be an eerie place. Nicolas Roeg uses the myriad back alleys and the Grand Canal, itself, to maximum effect. The film also has some potent scenes: John Baxter's near fall from a high scaffold; his prevision of his own funeral; and the last ten minutes of the film when he is pursuing the darting, red-cloaked figure. There is also one of the most magnificently filmed love scenes: John and Laura having sex, which is intercut with their post-coital activity of getting dressed to go out to dinner. There is excellent acting by the two leads, and it is by far the best effort of Roeg as a director. What prevents the viewer from embracing the movie fully, however, is the meaninglessness of the story and the fact that the central characters are too distant and aloof. Nevertheless, it has great visuals and is filmmaking at its best.

Do the Right Thing

1989. 120 min. color. U.S. **Prod.** Spike Lee, Monty Ross; **Dir.** Spike Lee; **Scr.** Spike Lee; **Cin.** Ernest Dickerson; **Ed.** Barry Alexander Brown; **Prod. D.** Wynn Thomas; **Mus.** Bill Lee; **Cast:** Danny Aiello, Ossie Davis, Ruby Dee, Richard Edson, Giancarlo Esposito, Spike Lee, Bill Nunn, John Turturro.

The story is set on one block of a black and Latin neighborhood in the Bedford Stuyvesant area of Brooklyn on a single sweltering summer day. The only whites are Sal (Danny Aiello) and his two sons, Pino (John Turturro) and Vito (Richard Edson), who own and operate the local pizzeria and commute every day. An unenthusiastic young black, Mookie (Spike Lee), is the deliveryman. Sal and his younger son Vito are even-tempered, but Pino is a hotheaded fellow who has pleaded unsuccessfully with his father to move out and relocate in another area. Sal has argued that most people there are friendly and it would be foolish to move. The stifling heat begins to take its toll and one minor incident after another heightens tensions. The local activist is angry that only photographs of Italian-Americans are on the walls of the pizzeria and there is not one black man amongst them. A retarded neighborhood postcard seller is insulted and kicked out, which angers some residents. There is an altercation with a customer playing a boom box very loud and the police are called. They use excessive force and soon there are rumors that the customer had been choked to death. Rumors are enough for a full-scale riot and the pizzeria is set on fire.

The film, rich in detail, is almost a textbook on the anatomy of a riot. Spike Lee, the producer, director and writer, dissects the conditions, circumstances and spark that set off a riot. The film is equally rich in characterization. Three idle elderly black men serve as the chorus. They sit around arguing and complaining and observe how soon the Koreans have succeeded in adjusting in the U.S. and have become successful small grocery store owners. There is the peacemaker in the community (Ossie Davis) who is self-titled "Da Mayor." He is rendered helpless once the riot begins. There are Mother Sister (Ruby Dee) who is listened to by youngsters, Pino who blames the blacks for his lowly status and Sal who believes he is free of prejudice but is insensitive. He could have put up photographs of Jackie Robinson or Hank Aaron as well as Sinatra and Joe DiMaggio. *Do the Right Thing* is an original contribution and has immense power. It shows the poverty of the ghettos and the idle men and women in the streets going nowhere. There is no sentimentality or preaching and the film has no heroes or villains. There is fine acting by Aiello, Turturro and Davis. The commentary by the disc jockey at the end of the film is unnecessary and is the film's only minor blemish.

Double Indemnity

1944. 106 min. b.w. U.S. **Prod.** Joseph Sistrom; **Dir.** Billy Wilder; **Scr.** Raymond Chandler, Billy Wilder (based on a story by James M. Cain); **Cin.** John Seitz; **Ed.** Doane Harrison; **Art D.** Hans Drier, Hal Pereira; **Mus.** Miklos Rozsa, Cesar Frank; **Cast:** Barbara Stanwyck, Fred MacMurray, Edward G. Robinson, Porter Hall, Tom Powers, Fortunio Bonanova, Jean Heather.

Walter Neff (Fred MacMurray), a thirty-five-year-old unmarried insurance salesman bleeding from a gunshot wound, barely makes it to his empty office building at night. He gets to his private office and begins speaking into a Dictaphone. As he speaks, there is a long flashback. A Mr. Dietrichson (Tom Powers) is behind on his car insurance installments. Dietrichson is not at home and Neff meets his young and seductive wife, Phyllis (Barbara Stanwyck). He is immediately attracted to her. The car insurance payment is made and he leaves. He remembers, "It was a hot afternoon and I can still remember the smell of honeysuckle all along that street. How could I have known that murder sometimes smells like that." He cannot stay away and at his next visit Phyllis convinces him to help have her husband buy a life insurance policy, then murder him and collect the proceeds. Walter is intrigued and plots the murder in such a way as to qualify Phyllis for double indemnity (i.e. having Mr. Dietrichson "accidentally" fall from a moving train). They execute the murder perfectly and it is only a matter of time before they can collect. Though they have to contend with the claims adjuster Barton Keyes (Edward G. Robinson) who is a marvel at calculating statistical odds of accidents, they still could get away with it. But their suspicions of one another, the urge to dominate the other and their guilt begin to emerge and a bloody end awaits them.

Double Indemnity was Billy Wilder's third movie as a director and he controls this outstanding film with his passionless, analytical approach. John Seitz's shadow and light photography captures Los Angeles of the late thirties. There is also an excellent terse script by Raymond Chandler from the James M. Cain novel. The only weakness of the film is some of the acting. Edward G. Robinson is superb and dominates every scene he is in. Although Fred MacMurray's character is not fully developed—he falls for Phyllis and the murder plot much too quickly—he does a competent job. It is Barbara Stanwyck's performance even with platinum blonde hair, tight sweaters and anklets that is not convincing. The supporting cast, other than Porter Hall as a passenger on the train, is also weak.

The Dresser

1983. 118 min. color. British. **Prod.** Peter Yates; **Dir.** Peter Yates; **Scr.** Ronald Harwood (based on his play); **Cin.** Kelvin Pike; **Ed.** Ray Lovejoy; **Prod. D.** Stephen Grimes; **Art D.** Colin Grimes; **Mus.** James Horner; **Cast:** Albert Finney, Tom Courtnay, Edward Fox, Zena Walker, Eileen Atkins, Michael Gough.

The film is set in wartime Britain in late 1940. Albert Finney, who is referred to as "Sir" during the entire film, is an aged actor/manager of a repertory company touring small provincial towns. Shakespeare's plays are the troupe's forte. Sir is a boozing tyrant, nearing senility, who cannot remember what play he is doing that night. But once on stage the words come naturally and the lines flow. He has performed all the better-known Shakespeare plays dozens of times—*King Lear* in particular some 227 times. The actors in his troupe are either too old for military service or have some physical defect. The only person who can prepare Sir for a performance is his middle-aged gay valet/dresser, Norman (Tom Courtnay), who has been with him for many years. Sir is most abusive toward Norman and never acknowledges his devotion and loyal service. He barely acknowledges his aging wife who is also a member of the company. Sir dies of natural causes after a magnificent performance of *King Lear*, murmuring, "Never, never, never, never."

The film is based on a play by Ronald Harwood. Sir is modeled on Sir Donald Wolfit, an actor with a commanding presence and a mellifluous voice who had been on stage from the 1920s until his death in 1968. The film has some moving and memorable scenes. Sir commands a train that is pulling out of the station with a shout that must have been heard miles away, "Stop thaaat train!" On a small-town street Sir momentarily loses control and, thinking he is Lear, takes off all his clothes and shouts about the ingratitude of children and fate. After his master's death, Norman gets drunk, cries inconsolably and talks of Sir's shabby treatment of him, complaining, "He never took me out for a meal." It is the acting that raises the film above the commonplace. Seldom have there been in a movie two performances of the caliber of Albert

Finney's and Tom Courtnay's. The film also benefits from a moving performance by Eileen Atkins as the long-suffering stage
manageress who has been in love with the old man for many
years. *The Dresser* is the first film of any consequence that Yates
made after *Bullitt* (1968).

The Exterminating Angel

Angel Exterminador. 1962. 95 min. Mexico. **Prod.** Gustavo Alatriste; **Dir.** Luis Buñuel;
Scr. Luis Buñuel, Luis Alcoriza (based on a play by Jose Bergamin); **Cin.** Gabriel Figueroa;
Ed. Carlos Savage; **Art D.** Jesus Bracho; **Mus.** Alessandro Scarlatti, Pietro Domenico Para-
disi; **Cast:** Silvia Pinal, Enrique Rambal, Jacqueline Andere, Jose Baviera, Augusto
Benedico, Antonio Bravo, Ofelia Montesco.

A wealthy couple invite some twenty friends, fellow aristocrats,
to have supper at their luxurious mansion in Mexico City after
the opera. All servants except the butler leave. The guests arrive
and enjoy themselves. Dawn approaches and no one wants to
depart. They sleep in the salon, hallways, closets and bathrooms.
Days pass and, although there is nothing to stop them from leaving, they choose to remain. They are without water and food. One
guest dies and he is placed in the cupboard. A pair of lovers hide in
the closet, then commit suicide. A flock of sheep is let loose and
enters the mansion. Some guests make solemn vows to go to
Lourdes and throw themselves at the feet of the Virgin Mary. They
finally leave and go to a nearby church. The movie ends without
our knowing whether they will ever leave the church.

One of Buñuel's more bizarre films. He has himself explained,
"Basically I see a group of people who couldn't do what they
wanted—leave a room." The film's theme somewhat resembles
Jean Paul Sartre's play *No Exit*: hell is what we make of it.

A Face in the Crowd

1957. 125 min. b.w. U.S. **Prod.** Elia Kazan; **Dir.** Elia Kazan; **Scr.** Budd Schulberg (based on his short story "The Arkansas Traveler"); **Cin.** Harry Stradling, Gayne Rescher; **Ed.** Gene Milford; **Art D.** Richard Sylbert; **Mus.** Tom Glazer; **Cast:** Andy Griffith, Patricia Neal, Anthony Franciosa, Walter Matthau, Lee Remick.

A radio and TV reporter (Patricia Neal) interviews a hillbilly guitarist (Andy Griffith) with a passable voice in an Arkansas prison. She discovers he has a talent for down-home philosophy and puts him on TV. He becomes a favorite and attracts a large following. Soon the networks take an interest and he is given a weekly one-hour show. His fame and influence spread and he becomes a political kingmaker courted by politicians and captains of industry. It is soon apparent that he has much higher ambitions and that he is a vicious, amoral animal who will stop at nothing. His career ends accidentally when he is heard berating his faithful audience, unaware that the microphone had not been turned off. Griffith gives too grand a performance. Even Kazan, probably the best actor's director, could not entirely control him. Patricia Neal is well cast. The first two-thirds of the film are excellent Kazan and Schulberg, but it becomes overheated, melodramatic and preachy regarding the growing influence of television.

The Fallen Idol

1948. 94 min. b.w. British. **Prod.** David O. Selznick; **Dir.** Carol Reed; **Scr.** Graham Greene, Lesley Storm, William Templeton (based on the story "The Basement Room" by Graham Greene); **Cin.** Georges Perinal; **Ed.** Oswald Hafenrichter; **Prod. D.** Vincent Korda; **Mus.** William Alwyn; **Cast:** Ralph Richardson, Michele Morgan, Bobby Henry, Jack Hawkins, Sonia Dresdel, Bernard Lee, Denis O'Dea.

The story is set in a foreign embassy in London. The ambassador must leave for a few days on official business and leaves his eight-year-old son Felipe (Bobby Henry) in the charge of Baines the butler (Ralph Richardson) and Mrs. Baines (Sonia Dresdel).

Felipe is neglected by his parents. He idolizes the kindly Baines and with equal passion dislikes the shrewish, authoritarian Mrs. Baines. Baines has been having an affair with the embassy typist, Julie (Michele Morgan). Felipe overhears Baines and Julie agree that they will end their relationship as Mrs. Baines will never agree to a divorce. Later that evening Felipe hears a loud argument between Baines and his wife. What Felipe does not see is that Mrs. Baines in her rage accidentally falls down the staircase to her death. The police are called and Felipe, in order to protect his idol whom he believes is guilty of murder, withholds evidence that actually could exonerate and prove the innocence of Baines.

The film is a variation of Graham Greene's short story "The Basement Room" about a boy who unintentionally betrays to the authorities his adult friend who is guilty of murder. Greene, who worked on the script, changed the plot. Under the superb direction of Carol Reed there are an impressive variety of camera angles and stylized lighting of the vast embassy halls and the rain-swept London streets. The film has one of the very best acting efforts of Ralph Richardson. Bobby Henry in his screen debut as the jittery, intelligent child is the only actor who ever upstaged Richardson. One of the best scenes in the film, which is not in Greene's story, is when Felipe, running out of the embassy in his pajamas, is taken to a police station. There is a hooker at the station. Felipe puts his head on her lap and tells the police "My father is the ambassador." The tart brightens and says, "Oh, I know your daddy." Reed is not known as an actor's director, but very few directors could have extracted such an accomplished performance from an eight-year-old child.

Fargo

1996. 97 min. color. U.S. **Prod.** Ethan Coen; **Dir.** Joel Coen; **Scr.** Ethan Coen, Joel Coen; **Cin.** Roger Deakins; **Ed.** Roderick Jaynes; **Art D.** Thomas P. Wilkins; **Mus.** Carter Burwell; **Cast:** Frances McDormand, William H. Macy, Steve Buscemi, Harve Presnell, Peter Stormare, John Carroll Lynch, Kristin Rudrud.

A scatterbrained, heavily indebted car salesman in Minnesota (William H. Macy) has come up with a foolproof scheme to repay all his debts. He hires two hoodlums from North Dakota (Steve Buscemi and Peter Stormare) to kidnap his wife (Kristin Rudrud) and demand a ransom for her release. His wealthy father-in-law (Harve Presnell) will be forced to pay the ransom that Macy will share with the two crooks, ending all his troubles. But, of course, everything goes wrong and there is mayhem and murder.

Fargo is an original film that borders on black comedy, well directed and with an excellent script. What elevates the film, however, is the casting, especially Macy as the dumb car salesman and Frances McDormand as the very pregnant local sheriff, Marge, who steals the film in one of the great performances of recent years. She is portrayed as a mother figure, a dutiful wife and straight cop. A short scene of her with a former admirer in a bar is a good example of her fine acting. McDormand has also mastered a very broad Minnesota accent, with her most common phrase being, "You betcha. Yah." She won a well-deserved Oscar as best actress and William Macy was a nominee for best supporting actor.

Five Easy Pieces

1970. 98 min. color. U.S. **Prod.** Bob Rafelson, Richard Wechsler; **Dir.** Bob Rafelson; **Scr.** Adrien Joyce; **Cin.** Laszlo Kovacs; **Ed.** Gerald Shepard, Christopher Holmes; **Art D.** Tobe Rafelson; **Mus.** Bach, Mozart, Chopin; **Cast:** Jack Nicholson, Karen Black, Lois Smith, Ralph Waite, Susan Anspach, Billy Green Bush, Fannie Flag.

Robert "Bobby" Eroica DuPea (Jack Nicholson) comes from a well-to-do family of musicians who live in a large mansion on Puget Sound. He had shown early promise as a concert pianist but had become impatient with the routine of incessant practicing and his nonconformist instincts took over. When the film begins we see him in Texas as an oil rigger. He has become a redneck and lives with a not too-bright-girl, Rayette (Karen Black), in a trailer. Their passions are bowling and consuming vast quantities of beer. When he hears that his father has had two strokes and is paralyzed, he drives with Rayette north to Washington state. His brother, also a musician, is engaged to a sensitive cultured girl (Susan Anspach). Bobby is immediately attracted to her and wastes no time in seducing her. After a brief tearful visit with his dying father, he and Rayette leave and head south. In a very effective last scene, they stop at a gas station. When she goes for coffee, he leaves his car with the key and even his jacket, and gets a ride on a truck going to Alaska. He has shed himself of all attachments and responsibility. His alienation is complete and he has become a total outsider.

The film is worthwhile for the acting. There is a memorable scene at a diner as Bobby's pent up anger explodes. Nicholson had reached the height of his acting talents and is ideal as the nonconformist Bobby. But even greater roles such as Gittes in *Chinatown* (1974), and McMurphy in *One Flew Over the Cuckoo's Nest* (1975) were yet to come. The cinematography of Laszlo Kovacs contrasts the garish atmosphere of Texas with the natural beauty of the Pacific northwest.

---

5 Fingers

1952. 108 min. b.w. U.S. **Prod.** Otto Lang; **Dir.** Joseph Mankiewicz; **Scr.** Michael Wilson (based on the book *Operation Cicero* by L. C. Moyzisch); **Cin.** Norbert Brodine; **Ed.** James B. Clark; **Art D.** Lyle Wheeler; **Mus.** Bernard Herrmann; **Cast:** James Mason, Danielle Darrieux, Michael Rennie, Walter Hampden, Oscar Karlweis, Herbert Berghof, John Wengraf.

This is the story of a gentleman's gentleman, Cicero (James Mason), who is the valet to Sir Frederic (Walter Hampden), the British ambassador to neutral Turkey during World War II. The story is set sometime in the early months of 1944 before the

Normandy landings by the Allies. Cicero has much higher ambitions. He wants to join the ranks of the idle rich and take as his lover a former employer, a beautiful refugee Polish countess (Danielle Darrieux). He begins by photographing top secret documents from the embassy safe and selling them to the German military attaché at Ankara. His task is made easier by Sir Frederic's strict adherence to a fixed schedule. Cicero has unfettered access to the embassy safe during the ambassador's daily bath and afternoon nap. The story, however, takes many twists as there are double and triple crosses.

The film is more than an espionage thriller. Under Mankiewicz's direction and the excellent script by Michael Wilson, it is witty with a telling commentary on the aristocracy and the leisure class. The entire cast is very good. The film is mostly based on fact. The British ambassador at the time, Sir Knachbull Huggesson, a seasoned diplomat who had previously served as minister to Tehran, was known for his rigid adherence to his daily routine. Cicero, the Albanian-born valet, sold more than thirty-five secret documents to the Germans, who did not believe in their authenticity and failed to act upon them. Among them were plans for "Operation Overlord," the Allied invasion of mainland Europe.

Five Graves to Cairo

1943. 96 min. b.w. U.S. **Prod.** Charles Brackett; **Dir.** Billy Wilder; **Scr.** Charles Brackett, Billy Wilder (based on the play *Hotel Imperial* by Lajos Biro); **Cin.** John Seitz; **Ed.** Doane Harrison; **Art D.** Hans Dreier; **Mus.** Miklos Rosza; **Cast:** Franchot Tone, Ann Baxter, Akim Tamiroff, Erich Von Stroheim, Peter Van Eyck, Fortunio Bonanova, Miles Mander.

The film is set in the early summer of 1942 in North Africa, somewhere in the desert between Libya and Egypt. A British corporal (Franchot Tone) cut off from his unit comes to a hotel in an oasis that soon becomes the temporary headquarters of Field Marshal Rommel. He impersonates a German spy who had been employed at the hotel but recently was killed by a British aerial bombardment. He is able to alert the British High Command of an impending attack by German forces at El Alamein and, more

important, the location of hundreds of thousands of barrels of oil
that had been hidden by a German Egyptologist some five years
earlier for future German use in war. It is a nonsense plot that
defies credulity. The Egyptologist must have been a seer and a
prophet who foresaw a crucial battle in North Africa and the
German need for fuel.

It is a suspenseful and well-directed film with an extremely
witty script. It is not really either a war movie or an espionage
story. The Italians, Germany's allies, are ridiculed throughout as
music lovers, not soldiers. Rommel says, "No one counts in or on
the Italians." Later an Italian general says of the Germans, "Can a
nation that belches understand singing?" The movie is memorable for the performance of Stroheim as Rommel, almost
replicating his role in *La Grande Illusion* (1937). Akim Tamiroff
and Fortunio Bonanova bring comedy, and Peter Van Eyck, who
played Germans for thirty years, is his usual nasty Nazi. Franchot
Tone is fine. The photography of John Seitz is excellent.

The Flight of the Phoenix

1965. 149 min. color. U.S. **Prod.** Robert Aldrich; **Dir.** Robert Aldrich; **Scr.** Lukas Heller
(based on a novel by Elleston Trevor); **Cin.** Joseph Biroc; **Ed.** Michael Luciano; **Art D.**
William Glasgow; **Mus.** Frank DeVol; **Cast:** James Stewart, Richard Attenborough, Peter
Finch, Hardy Kruger, Ernest Borgnine, Ian Bannen, Ronald Fraser, Christian Marquand,
Dan Duryea, George Kennedy.

A cargo plane carrying oil-drilling equipment and some ten
passengers is forced to crash-land in the North African desert. The
pilot (James Stewart), an old timer, assumes responsibility for the
crash though it is the fault of his boozy navigator (Richard Attenborough). The survivors wait in vain for a rescue plane. A British
army captain leaves on foot to find an oasis and get help but meets
with dire consequences. When all seems lost, a young German
passenger (Hardy Kruger) who is visiting his brother announces
he is a plane designer and can build a single engine plane from the
salvaged wreckage of the cargo plane. The survivors work feverishly, but it is revealed that the German is merely a designer for a

model plane manufacturer. What begins as an ordinary disaster movie assumes other dimensions. Robert Aldrich, an old pro who had worked as an assistant with some of the best in Hollywood, including Chaplin, Milestone, Renoir, and Wellman, is at his best. Nearly every character is well developed and the tension between the brash model plane designer and the old weather-beaten pilot is emphasized. There is fine acting by the entire cast.

Foreign Correspondent

1940. 119 min. b.w. U.S. **Prod.** Walter Wanger; **Dir.** Alfred Hitchcock; **Scr.** Charles Bennett, Joan Harrison, James Hilton, Robert Benchley; **Cin.** Rudolph Maté; **Ed.** Otho Lovering, Dorothy Spencer; **Art D.** Alexander Golitzen; **Mus.** Alfred Newman; **Cast:** Joel McCrea, Laraine Day, Herbert Marshall, George Sanders, Albert Basserman, Robert Benchley, Edmund Gwenn, Eduardo Ciannelli, Harry Davenport.

The film is set in Amsterdam in 1939 before the start of World War II. An experienced crime reporter, Johnny Jones (Joel McCrea), expects to be fired by his newspaper after having punched a policeman in an altercation. Instead the managing editor decides to send Jones to Europe, which is on the brink of war, "since he knows nothing of Europe, he will view events with a fresh, unused mind." His first assignment is in Amsterdam to interview an internationally known Dutch pacifist, Van Meer (Albert Basserman), who is leading a campaign to stop the impending outbreak of war. There is a peace rally that Van Meer has just addressed. As he is descending the stairs he is shot by an unknown assailant and declared dead. Jones who has witnessed the scene finds it strange that both the assassin and the victim's body have disappeared. He is convinced that the person killed was not Van Meer, who must have been abducted. The balance of the film covers Jones's search for Van Meer and his uncovering a vast German spy network fronted by a respectable Englishman.

Foreign Correspondent is not one of Hitchcock's best films. It has a weak and very thin plot. It will be remembered more for its set pieces that compare favorably to Hitchcock's best. The attempted assassination of Van Meer on the steps of a large building in pouring rain is magnificently staged. The search for Van Meer in a wind-mill and the unsuccessful attempt to assassinate Jones in a cathedral tower stand out. The art director Alexander Golitzen re-created an authentic looking Amsterdam replete with a windmill on the studio lot. The cinematography of Rudolph Maté is also very good. The cast is excellent. Joel McCrea, whom Hitchcock used only in this film, was a much better actor than Robert Cummings, whom Hitchcock cast both in *Saboteur* (1942) and *Dial M For Murder* (1954). The off-type casting of the kindly Edmund Gwenn as a paid assassin was an excellent idea. The film is about ten minutes too long, the scenes of McCrea and Laraine Day as the innocent daughter of Herbert Marshall the master spy don't work and the triumphant radio broadcast of McCrea is too contrived.

The French Connection

1971. 104 min. color. U.S. **Prod.** Philip D'Antoni; **Dir.** William Friedkin; **Scr.** Ernest Tidyman (based on the book by Robin Moore); **Cin.** Owen Roizman; **Ed.** Jerry Greenberg; **Art D.** Ben Kazaskow; **Mus.** Don Ellis; **Cast:** Gene Hackman, Fernando Rey, Roy Scheider, Tony LoBianco, Marcel Bozzuffi, Bill Hickman, Frederic de Pasquale.

A heroin cartel based in Marseilles ships 120 pounds of pure heroin to New York City in a French actor's car. An undisciplined cop who hates drug pushers, Jimmy "Popeye" Doyle (Gene Hackman), and his partner, Buddy Russo (Roy Scheider), stumble onto one of the key contacts of the ring in New York. There follows a massive surveillance, and with the help of the federal authorities all members of the U.S. operation are either captured or killed. The kingpin from Marseilles, Alain Charneir (Fernando Rey), eludes the police and gets away.

The movie is based on the true New York case, which was the largest confiscation of heroin in the U.S. The movie is well put together and the scenes of the city streets and inhabitants are realistic. The very opening scene of a gangster shooting a French "flic" in Marseilles is very effective and sets the tone for what follows. The scene of Doyle chasing an elevated train by car is harrowing and a feat of great cinematography. The casting of Fernando Rey adds character to the film. The acting of the rest of the cast, especially Hackman, Scheider and Tony LoBianco as the main middleman is excellent. The movie is too tense and hectic, however, with no respite. There is an excess of cross-cutting, and Friedkin doesn't give the viewer a chance to take a deep breath. The film won Academy Awards for best picture, best actor (Gene Hackman), best director, best adapted screenplay, and best editing, and received nominations in several other categories.

From Here to Eternity

1953. 118 min. b.w. U.S. **Prod.** Buddy Adler; **Dir.** Fred Zinnemann; **Scr.** Daniel Taradash (based on the novel by James Jones); **Cin.** Burnett Guffey; **Ed.** William Lyon; **Art D.** Cary Odell; **Mus.** George Duning; **Cast:** Burt Lancaster, Montgomery Clift, Deborah Kerr, Donna Reed, Frank Sinatra, Ernest Borgnine, Mickey Shaughnessy, Philip Ober, Jack Warden, Claude Akins.

The film begins in the summer of 1941 at Schofield Barracks, Pearl Harbor. Robert E. Lee Prewitt (Montgomery Clift) has transferred to Schofield and reports for duty. Prewitt had been the first bugler at his former camp but asked for a transfer, giving up his rank of corporal when someone else had been named first bugler. Schofield is commanded by Captain Holmes (Philip Ober), a philanderer who spends no more than fifteen minutes a day at his office. Sergeant Milton Warden (Burt Lancaster) in effect runs the base. Prewitt's reputation as a fine boxer has preceded him, and Captain Holmes, who hopes to be promoted to major by having the Schofield boxing team win the inter-service competition, decides to personally interview Prewitt. Holmes promises Prewitt the first bugler position if he will join the boxing team. Prewitt, who had blinded a soldier in the ring, refuses. Holmes orders Sergeant Warden to assign Prewitt to the dirtiest and most backbreaking chores until he comes around and agrees to box. There are several interwoven stories. Sergeant Warden begins a heated affair with Captain Holmes' neglected and abused wife, Karen (Deborah Kerr). Prewitt, on the rare occasions he can get leave, visits a hostess club and starts a relationship with one of the girls, Alma Lorene (Donna Reed). Prewitt's only friend is Maggio (Frank Sinatra), an undisciplined soldier from Little Italy in New York. By 7 December 1941 Maggio is dead from injuries sustained by severe beatings in the stockade. Prewitt is killed by friendly fire while returning to the base during the high alert on December 7. Captain Holmes is cashiered out of the army for his inhuman treatment of men under his command. Sergeant Warden is the only survivor.

The film is based on James Jones' nearly 850-page novel. It is not elegantly written, but it is one of the best novels of World War II. The bawdy scenes and rough language have been deleted from the film script. The parts dealing with the brutal beatings of Maggio in the stockade have been deleted, the brothel where Prewitt begins a romance with Alma is now a social club, and Captain Holmes who is promoted to major in the book is dismissed from the army in the film. But the film is true to the core story of the leading protagonists. Zinnemann directed an intelligent film. The story of each character is told in a lean and coherent manner. The film also stands out for excellent acting. Montgomery Clift gives his best performance. The scenes with Prewitt in a bar blowing the blues on his bugle and later when he plays taps for the murdered Maggio with tears running down his face and the camera moving to the faces of the soldiers across the barracks are extremely well acted and controlled by Zinnemann. Burt Lancaster has a role in which he excels. Although the film is dominated by males, both Deborah Kerr and especially Donna Reed are very good. The film swept the Oscars, winning in all major categories except best actor and actress.

The Front Page

1931. 103 min. b.w. U.S. **Prod.** Howard Hughes; **Dir.** Lewis Milestone; **Scr.** Bartlett Cormack, Ben Hecht (uncredited), Charles Lederer (based on the play by Ben Hecht, Charles MacArthur); **Cin.** Glen MacWilliams, Hal Mohr, Tony Gaudio; **Ed.** Duncan Mansfield, **Art D.** Richard Day; **Cast:** Adolph Menjou, Pat O'Brien, Mary Brian, Edward Everett Horton, Walter Catlett, Mae Clarke, George E. Stone, Slim Summerville, Frank McHugh.

Adolph Menjou plays Walter Burns, the ruthless editor of a Chicago tabloid, and Pat O'Brien plays his star reporter, Hildy Johnson. The film is set in the pressroom of a courthouse where reporters have gathered for the execution of an anarchist who shot a policeman. The cynicism of the reporters is established early when one of them begs the sheriff to advance the hour of the execution to five in the morning so the story can make the first edition of his paper. It is Hildy's last day on the job, as he is determined to marry his girl Peggy (Mary Brian) and go to New York to work for an advertising firm. For the rest of the film, Burns uses every ploy to keep Hildy on the paper.

This is the first film version of the 1925 play by Ben Hecht and Charles MacArthur, followed by the very enjoyable *His Girl Friday* (1940) and the disastrous 1974 Billy Wilder version. The direction is a bit stagy and the pace is much slower than the machine-gun pace of *His Girl Friday*. It is Adolph Menjou's film with an excellent supporting cast, especially Edward Everett Horton and Walter Catlett. The chief merit of *The Front Page* is its authenticity. The sleaziness of the tabloids and city hall corruption that was at the heart of the Hecht/MacArthur play comes over very well. The film was made at the very beginning of the sound era and it creaks in parts.

Gaslight

1940. 84 min. b.w. British. **Prod.** John Corfield; **Dir.** Thorold Dickinson; **Scr.** A. R. Rawlinson, Bridget Boland (based on the play by Patrick Hamilton); **Cin.** Bernard Knowles; **Ed.** Sidney Cole; **Mus.** Richard Addinsell; **Cast:** Anton Walbrook, Diana Wynyard, Frank Pettingell, Robert Newton, Cathleen Cordell.

The story takes place in London toward the end of the nineteenth century and opens with a soundless scene at No. 12 Pimlico Square. An old lady is doing needlework. An unseen man approaches and strangles her. The murderer feverishly goes through each room. He tears up bedding and upholstery and opens every chest and drawer but can't find what he is looking for. There is a long dissolve to some years later. No. 12 has been renovated and is now occupied by newlyweds, Paul Mallen (Anton Walbrook) and Bella Mallen (Diana Wynyard). Bella is the niece of the murdered woman and has inherited No. 12 as well as the adjacent, unoccupied house at No. 14. Nearby lives Rough (Frank Pettingell) who, as a young policeman, was assigned to the unsolved murder. He is now semiretired and is in the business of renting carriages. He remembers Bella as a very young girl at the time of the murder and attempts to see her but is prevented by her husband. Rough becomes suspicious and begins keeping tabs on Paul Mallen. Soon a pattern emerges: Mallen leaves No. 12 every evening, sneaks into the adjoining No. 14 and comes out always dishevelled. We find out he has a subtle plan to drive his wife mad and ultimately commit her to an insane asylum. He begins hiding her personal effects. He places his own watch in her purse and then accuses her of loss of memory and theft. There are two maids in the house whom he makes sure witness his wife's erratic behavior. We soon discover that the prime suspect of the murder had been one Louis Bauer who had disappeared. The murdered woman had owned some priceless rubies that the murderer had been after.

The film derives its title from the gaslights in No. 12 that flicker down whenever Mallen turns the lights on in No. 14 to search for the rubies. *Gaslight* is very well crafted. The ominous atmosphere and the lurking menace is generated as much by Dickinson's excellent direction as by the fluid camera work of Bernard Knowles. Dickinson made very few films. His other notable contribution is Pushkin's *Queen of Spades* (1949). Anton Walbrook, a very fine actor, is superb as the villain with his hissing and menacing voice. Diana Wynyard and Frank Pettingell are outstanding too. Columbia purchased the rights to the movie in 1941, but never remade the film. They opted instead to sell the property to MGM, which produced a remake in 1944 with Ingrid Bergman and Charles Boyer. Louis B. Mayer had ordered the prints and negative of the 1940 original destroyed so it would not compete with MGM's production. Fortunately several prints escaped destruction. The MGM film is well done and has the virtuoso acting of Ingrid Bergman, but this original version is superior.

General Della Rovere

1959. 129 min. b.w. Italian. **Prod.** Moris Ergas; **Dir.** Roberto Rossellini; **Scr.** Roberto Rossellini, Sergio Amedei, Diego Fabbri, Indro Montanelli; **Cin.** Carlo Carlini; **Ed.** Anna Maria Montanari, Cesare Cavagna; **Art D.** Piero Zuffi; **Mus.** Renzo Rossellini; **Cast:** Vittorio De Sica, Hannes Messemer, Sandra Milo, Giovanna Ralli, Vittorio Caprioli, Giuseppe Rossetti, Ivo Garrani, Baronessa Barzani, Anne Vernon.

The film is set in the winter of 1943–44 during the German occupation of northern Italy. Mussolini has been overthrown, but the Germans are offering fierce resistance. Italian partisan fighters are harassing the German forces. The story begins in Genoa. The leader of the southern partisans, General Della Rovere, is killed in an ambush by German troops, but the local German commander, Colonel Mueller (Hannes Messemer), keeps Della Rovere's death a secret. Victorio Emanuele Bardone (Vittorio De Sica) is a swindler and con man who sports good manners and preys on desperate old men, and women whose husbands and sons are in German prisons. He promises to have them released through his contacts and influence with German officers, even in some cases after they already have been executed. He is caught attempting to bribe a German sergeant, a crime for which he could be executed. Colonel Mueller forces Bardone to impersonate General Della Rovere in exchange for his subsequent freedom. He is sent to a large prison in Milan to identify the northern partisan leader Fabrizio (Ivo Garrani) whom the Germans believe is among the prisoners. General Della Rovere was to have met Fabrizio to consolidate their plans when he was killed. Once in jail Bardone witnesses horrible tortures and summary executions. Gradually he begins to identify with his fellow prisoners. He also becomes aware of the respect and admiration extended toward him as Della Rovere. His assumption of the persona of the famed resistance fighter is now nearly complete. Della Rovere was the scion of an old family. His wife Contessa Della Rovere (Baronessa Barzani) comes to see her husband but is not allowed. She writes him a letter and encloses a photograph of their son. Bardone reads the letter and is moved to tears. He begins to feel disgust with himself and the life he has led. He decides he will not betray Fabrizio whose identity he has learned. When the local Fascist leader in Milan is assassinated by partisans, Field Marshal Kesselring, the commander of German forces in Italy, orders the execution of some prisoners. Bardone forces himself into the group to be executed. Colonel Mueller cannot stop him without disclosing to the other prisoners that there are informers planted among them.

The film is made unforgettable by De Sica's portrayal of Bardone/Della Rovere. It is one of the virtuoso pieces of acting in film. We see the transformation of a petty swindler into a heroic figure. De Sica had been an actor in Italian cinema long before he became a noted director. Rossellini, who had wasted some key years of his productive life in making some awful films, revived his career with this film. *General Della Rovere* was shot in six weeks on a shoestring budget. He could not raise funds to have sets replicating war-ravaged Italy. The war had been over for fourteen years and there were no war ruins left to film, so the authenticity and documentary look of his early films are absent here. The film has other drawbacks. There are some unnecessary scenes. The entire scene at the bordello is superfluous. At 130 minutes, the film is at least fifteen minutes too long. Despite these flaws, a great film emerges.

Genevieve

1953. 86 min. color. British. **Prod.** Henry Cornelius; **Dir.** Henry Cornelius; **Scr.** William Rose; **Cin.** Christopher Challis; **Ed.** Clive Donner; **Mus.** Larry Adler; **Cast:** Dinah Sheridan, John Gregson, Kay Kendall, Kenneth More, Joyce Grenfell.

Two friends, classic car enthusiasts, take part in the annual London to Brighton vintage car rally. A 1904 Darraqe, nicknamed Genevieve, is owned by John Gregson and his wife Dinah Sheridan. A 1904 Spyker is owned by bachelor Kenneth More who brings along a beautiful model, Kay Kendall. More's ambition has been to have the ultimate emotional experience: to finish the race and bed a beautiful woman. He is disappointed in both. The highlight of the film is a trumpet solo by Kay Kendall at a Brighton nightclub. *Genevieve* is one of the most charming comedies. The entire cast is very good and we even get the incomparable Joyce Grenfell in a short scene. The score by Larry Adler on his harmonica suits the film perfectly. Cornelius had been an assistant to René Clair in the two films Clair directed in England. *Genevieve's* leisurely pace bears his influence.

Gigi

1958. 116 min. color. U.S. **Prod.** Arthur Freed; **Dir.** Vincente Minnelli; **Scr.** Alan Jay Lerner (based on the play by Anita Loos from the novel by Colette); **Cin.** Joseph Ruttenberg, Ray June; **Ed.** Adrienne Fazan; **Art D.** William A. Horning; **Prod. D.** Cecil Beaton; **Mus.** Frederick Loewe; **Cast:** Leslie Caron, Maurice Chevalier, Louis Jordan, Hermione Gingold, Eva Gabor, Isabel Jeans, Jacques Bergerac, John Abbott.

Based on the Colette novel, the story is set in Paris at the end of the nineteenth century. It is another variation on the mythical tale of Pygmalion, the remolding of a young girl. Gigi (Leslie Caron) is raised by her grandmother (Hermione Gingold) and great aunt (Isabel Jeans) to become a courtesan, which is a family tradition. They are horrified when the most eligible bachelor in Paris, Gaston (Louis Jordan), falls in love with her and proposes marriage.

Gigi is one of the best musicals, although it is often overlooked mainly because most of the songs are of the sing/recite variety. No one in the cast qualified as a tenor or soprano (Leslie Caron was dubbed by Betty Ward). Chevalier's songs were tailor-made for him, and his immense charm, as always, more than compensates for lack of a musically outstanding voice. The three songs he sings are the highlights of the film: "Thank Heaven for Little Girls," "I Remember It Well" and "I'm Glad I'm Not Young Anymore." The film is greatly enhanced by Cecil Beaton's wonderful costumes and set designs, Vincent Minnelli's smooth and professional direction and the presence of two charming veterans, Hermione Gingold and Isabel Jeans. Alan Jay Lerner had insisted on the signing of Chevalier and Beaton. The film swept the Academy Awards in almost all non-acting categories.

Glory

1989. 122 min. color. U.S. **Prod.** Freddie Fields; **Dir.** Edward Zwick; **Scr.** Kevin Jarre (based on the books *Lay This Laurel* by Lincoln Kirstein, *One Gallant Rush* by Peter Burchard and the letters of Robert Gould Shaw); **Cin.** Freddie Francis; **Ed.** Steven Rosenblum; **Prod. D.** Norman Garwood; **Art D.** Keith Pain, Dan Webster; **Mus.** James Horner; **Cast:** Matthew Broderick, Denzel Washington, Cary Elwes, Morgan Freeman, Jihmi Kennedy, Andre Braugher, John Finn.

Abolitionists had argued from the onset of the American Civil War that blacks should be allowed to enlist in the Union army. On 7 January 1863 the Emancipation Proclamation became law. At the urging of Frederick Douglass, the most prominent black in America, the 54th Regiment of the Massachusetts Volunteer Infantry was formed by the governor of the state. About one thousand freed or escaped slaves enlisted, including Frederick Douglass' two sons. The officers, all white, came from prominent Massachusetts families. Twenty-five-year-old Colonel Robert Gould Shaw (Matthew Broderick) who came from a family of abolitionists was chosen as the commander of the regiment. He had left Harvard to enlist in the Union army and had been wounded at the battle of Antietam Creek. At the outset the army had no intention to use the volunteer blacks in combat. They were to do manual labor and menial tasks behind the front lines.

The film is based on two books and Shaw's letters to his mother read by the unbilled Jane Alexander in a voice-over narration. The screenplay introduced the other principals who are fictitious. The focus is on four soldiers who have been quartered in one tent. There is Trip (Denzel Washington), a runaway slave from Tennessee and an embittered young man who is seething with hostility. John Rawlins (Morgan Freeman), a former gravedigger who, having seen enough people die, has a calming influence on everyone and is the voice of moderation. Searles (Andre Braugher) is an educated young man who has known Colonel Shaw since childhood. Trip calls him "a nigger who talks like a white man." The fourth is Sharts (Jihmi Kennedy), a deeply religious boy with a stammer. Despite a threat by the Confederates of summary execution of any black wearing a Union uniform, no one deserts. The black volunteers undergo extensive training, but they are not given shoes, uniforms or rifles, and their monthly salary is well below that of white soldiers. Trip incites others to refuse to draw their wages and with Colonel Shaw's support the entire regiment sides with Trip. They are finally accepted as equals by the War Department. In a minor skirmish the 54th gives a good account of itself. They are then ordered to assault an impregnable harbor fortification, South Carolina's Fort Wagner. The regiment loses two-thirds of its men in a brave but futile and suicidal charge. Colonel Shaw who led the assault is one of those lost. Fort Wagner was never taken during the entire war.

Glory is an impressive and important film. Among a dozen or so films on the Civil War, none has dealt with the role of blacks in that struggle. By the end of the war blacks constituted nearly ten percent of the Union army though only a mere one percent of the population of the northern states. More than thirty thousand black soldiers died in the Civil War. The film captures the look and feel of the period and the battle scenes are extremely well done. The scene on the night before the climactic battle where the soldiers are gathered around a fire is very moving. The excellent cast makes one aware of the untapped wealth of black actors in Hollywood. Morgan Freeman and Denzel Washington, who won an Academy Award for best supporting actor, are excellent. The film also received an Academy Award for best cinematography, but as a war film it probably would have been even more effective if shot in black and white.

The Go-Between

1971. 116 min. color. British. **Prod.** John Heyman, Norman Priggen; **Dir.** Joseph Losey; **Scr.** Harold Pinter (based on the novel by L. P. Hartley); **Cin.** Gerry Fisher; **Ed.** Reginald Beck; **Art D.** Carmen Dillon; **Mus.** Michel Legrand; **Cast:** Julie Christie, Alan Bates, Dominic Guard, Margaret Leighton, Michael Gough, Edward Fox, Michael Redgrave, Richard Gibson.

A twelve-year-old boy, Leo Colston (Dominic Guard) who comes from a respectable but impoverished family, is invited by a school friend, Marcus Maudsley (Richard Gibson), to spend his summer holiday at Marcus' parents large estate. Marcus comes from a wealthy upper-class family. A few days after Leo's arrival Marcus comes down with measles and Leo is left to roam the vast grounds alone. Marian (Julie Christie), Marcus' beautiful older sister, takes a liking to Leo and takes him to town and buys him a light jacket more suitable for the exceptionally hot summer. One day as Leo explores the grounds he injures his knee. The young tenant farmer, Ted Burgess (Alan Bates), bandages the wound and a friendship begins. Ted asks him to take a letter to Marian, which he explains as a "business letter," and swears Leo to secrecy. Leo soon becomes the messenger between the two lovers. He becomes confused, however, when he finds that Marian is engaged to the decent but stuffy Boer War veteran Viscount Trimingham (Edward Fox) and refuses to carry any further letters. On Leo's thirteenth birthday, Marian, who has bought a bicycle for him, does not show up. Mrs. Maudsley (Margaret Leighton) becomes suspicious and, having once seen Marian give a letter to Leo, forces him to divulge where Marian has gone. She drags Leo with her to Ted Burgess' farm and finds Marian and Burgess making passionate love. Burgess commits suicide and some time later Marian is married to Viscount Trimingham.

The film begins with the elderly Leo Colston (Michael Redgrave) making a journey to Norfolk where he spent the summer fifty years earlier. He has been asked to come by Lady Trimingham, now a widow. Leo has never recovered from the traumatic experience of that summer and has remained a bachelor. The aged Marian, totally oblivious to the harm done to the sensitive young Leo, asks for another favor. She wants him once again to act as a go-between to make peace with her grandson. She mentions in passing that her grandson bears a striking resemblance to Ted Burgess whom Leo always had liked.

The Go-Between is Joseph Losey's best film by far. It is based on a fine novel by L. P. Hartley that portrays the British class system and its attendant hypocrisy. It is leisurely paced, and there is lovely photography of the grounds of the estate and the Norfolk countryside. It is beautifully acted by the young Dominic Guard, Alan Bates, Edward Fox and Michael Gough. The film, however, belongs to the elegant and sensitive performance of Margaret Leighton. The horror in her face as she sees her orderly world begin to disintegrate before her eyes is riveting. She is prepared to go to any length to maintain class status and have her daughter married to a suitable person. Her efforts were recognized by an Academy nomination as best supporting actress.

The Godfather, Part II

1974. 200 mins. color. U.S. **Prod.** Francis Ford Coppola, Gray Frederickson, Fred Roos; **Dir.** Francis Ford Coppola; **Scr.** Francis Ford Coppola, Mario Puzo (based on the characters from his novel); **Cin.** Gordon Willis; **Ed.** Peter Zinner, Barry Malkin, Richard Marks; **Prod. D.** Dean Tavoularis; **Art D.** Angelo Graham; **Mus.** Nino Rota; **Cast:** Al Pacino, Robert Duvall, Diane Keaton, Robert De Niro, John Cazale, Talia Shire, Lee Strasberg, Michael V. Gazzo.

Part one ended with the death of Don Vito Corleone and Michael (Al Pacino) anointed as the Godfather, assuring Kay, his wife, that he did not order the killing of Carlo, his sister's husband. Part two begins some ten years later, around 1955. Michael is an established Mafia don. The family has moved from New York to Nevada and he lives in a large compound on Lake Tahoe. He is now after respectability and status and is hosting a sumptuous First Communion party for his son. Coppola intercuts with lengthy flashbacks that begin in Sicily in the village of Corleon circa 1901 and with the murder of Vito's father and later his brother, sister and mother by the local Mafia head. To save Vito's life, relatives send him to America. We follow him as a young man (Robert De Niro); his joining the Sicilian Black Hand and the beginning of his life in crime, his marriage and the birth of his children. The flashback ends and there is a return to events following the First Communion party. Soon afterward there is an unsuccessful attempt on Michael's life. He learns that Hyman Roth (Lee Strasberg), a racketeer friend of his father, was behind the attempt with inside help from his brother Fredo (John Cazale). He has Roth killed but waits until his mother's death before having Fredo done away with. The don now has been reduced to fratricide. We see him at the end, his wife and children have left him, and Tom Hagen his trusted advisor has been dismissed. He is alone in ruling over his criminal empire.

Part two reeks with moral decay. Fredo informs on his brother, the straight Hagen now has a mistress and Connie, the only sister, keeps changing husbands. It is a more ambitious film than its predecessor and technically better. The scenes of Don Corleone's early years in New York are particularly well designed, directed and photographed. But some parts lag or are artificial. The opening scene of the communion party does not compare with the wedding in part one. The scenes in Cuba are too staged. The attempt to show the corruption and sleaze in Batista's Cuba is self-conscious. The Senate hearing scenes are mechanical and the brothel scene with the sado-masochistic Senator Geary is purely to titillate the audience. The absence of Brando leaves a large gap and the absence of Richard Castellano is also felt. The excellent acting of Pacino, De Niro, Duvall, Cazale and Shire are not enough to make the film equal to the first *Godfather*, but it is still a very fine film. It won Academy Awards for best picture, supporting actor (De Niro), director, adapted screenplay, musical score and art direction; and also received nominations for best actor (Pacino), supporting actor (Michael V. Gazzo, Lee Strasberg), supporting actress (Shire) and costume design.

Gone with the Wind

1939. 220 min. color. U.S. **Prod.** David O. Selznick; **Dir.** Victor Fleming; George Cukor, Sam Wood; **Scr.** Sidney Howard, Jo Swerling, Charles MacArthur, Ben Hecht, John Lee Mahin, John Van Druten, Oliver H. P. Garrett, Winston Miller, John Balderston, Michael Foster, Edwin Justus Mayer, F. Scott Fitzgerald, David O. Selznick (based on the novel by Margaret Mitchell); **Cin.** Ernest Haller, Ray Rennahan, Lee Garmes; **Ed.** Hal C. Kern, James E. Newcom; **Prod. D.** William Cameron Menzies; **Art D.** Lyle Wheeler, Hobe Erwin; **Mus.** Max Steiner; **Cast:** Clark Gable, Vivien Leigh, Leslie Howard, Olivia De Havilland, Thomas Mitchell, Victor Jory, Hattie McDaniel, Harry Davenport, Butterfly McQueen, Ona Munson.

Gerald O'Hara (Thomas Mitchell), an Irish immigrant, settles in Georgia. He becomes the prosperous owner of a large plantation, Tara. He marries the daughter of a prominent family and they have three daughters. The eldest, Scarlett (Vivien Leigh), has been in love with the honorable but reticent Ashley Wilkes (Leslie Howard) of a nearby estate. At a party Ashley unexpectedly announces his engagement to the gentle Melanie Hamilton (Olivia De Havilland). The self-centered Scarlett pleads with Ashley to marry her instead. To spite Ashley, Scarlett marries Melanie's brother, Charles Hamilton. Soon there is war and both Ashley and Charles join the Confederate army. Charles is killed and Scarlett moves to Atlanta. At a charity ball for the Confederacy, Rhett Butler (Clark Gable), who had made a fortune as a blockade runner, flirts with Scarlett. Although still in mourning, she dances with him, shocking the good ladies of Atlanta. Subsequently, the city is besieged under heavy artillery fire. Rhett rescues Melanie, her baby and Scarlett from burning Atlanta. The South is devastated and the war has taken its toll on Scarlett. Her mother is dead, her father blind, and Tara has been badly damaged. In need of money, Scarlett marries a tradesman who soon thereafter dies. She now accepts Rhett's offer of marriage. They have a daughter who dies in a riding accident. Rhett finds that Scarlett is still in love with Ashley and leaves.

Scripted by an array of established Hollywood writers and based on Margaret Mitchell's best-selling novel, the film presents a biased and misleading account of the American Civil War. There is no reference whatsoever to the underlying causes of the North-South conflict. The South of Margaret Mitchell is populated by debonair gentlemen, refined and beautiful ladies, and happy slaves. The film works because of the collaborative efforts of some of the outstanding Hollywood technicians and artisans of the time. The result is a number of great visual scenes. Among them are the flight of Scarlett, Melanie and her newborn child in a carriage driven by Rhett Butler through an engulfing fire; the shooting of a Union soldier who has come to Tara to loot and rape; and the railroad yard where Scarlett must make her way through what appears to be thousands of wounded and dying soldiers. The acting, on the whole, is good. Clark Gable is perfect as Rhett. Vivien Leigh is equally good. Thomas Mitchell, Hattie McDaniel and Butterfly McQueen steal every scene they are in. Leslie Howard, a competent actor, does not seem comfortable in his role. The best segments of the film are in the middle. From there on the pace slows considerably.

The Great Dictator

1940. 128 min. b.w. U.S. **Prod.** Charles Chaplin; **Dir.** Charles Chaplin; **Scr.** Charles Chaplin; **Cin.** Roland Totheroh, Karl Struss; **Ed.** Willard Nico; **Art D.** Russell Spencer; **Mus.** Meredith Wilson; **Cast:** Charles Chaplin, Paulette Goddard, Jack Oakie, Reginald Gardiner, Maurice Moscovich, Billy Gilbert, Henry Daniell.

The film revolves around a series of episodes more than a structured plot. It is about two look-alikes: Adenoid Hynkel, the dictator of Tomania who rules the country under the sign of the Double Cross, and a simple nameless Jewish barber who has a shop in the ghetto (both parts played by Chaplin). The barber had served in World War I and was injured. When he awakes from a state of amnesia some years after the war he finds he cannot pursue his career as a barber as Hynkel has adopted a policy of harassing and repressing Jews. Through a series of events the barber is mistaken for Hynkel and he delivers an impassioned speech asking the citizens of Tomania for tolerance and peace amongst nations.

The film has several short scenes as well as longer set pieces that compare with the best of Chaplin. There is a ballet to the music of Wagner's *Lohengrin* with Hynkel bouncing a large air filled globe of the world and caressing it so lovingly that it bursts. And there is the barber rhythmically shaving a customer to the music of Brahms' Hungarian Dance No. 5. There are very funny scenes of Hynkel greeting Benzino Napaloni (Jack Oakie) the dictator of Bacteria at the train station and later their joint visit to an air show. In their constant one-upmanship Napaloni gets the better of Hynkel. In a brief scene of Hynkel whipping up the crowd on radio in German and English gibberish, with grotesque facial contortions he declares, "Democratia Shtunk! Liberstad Shtunk!" There are also revealing scenes of Hynkel's fits of insane rage and his love of flattery. Chaplin selected an excellent cast. Henry Daniell as Garbitsch and Billy Gilbert as Herring are outstanding. The casting of Jack Oakie as Napaloni was inspired. In the scenes where he appears with Chaplin, he more than holds his own. What is mystifying is what Chaplin was trying to say in the film. After *Modern Times* (1936), Chaplin began work on a film about Napoleon in which the British send Napoleon's double to St. Helena and the real Napoleon becomes a bookseller in Paris. Chaplin abandoned the idea because he considered Napoleon as a superior intellect not to be trifled with. He then began work on a parody on Hitler. By the time the film was released World War II had started. Hitler had invaded Poland and defeated and occupied France and the Low Countries. Although the world was still unaware of the extent of the Nazi atrocities, Hitler was no laughing matter. Chaplin would later argue that, "ridicule is a powerful weapon." *The Great Dictator* is not one of Chaplin's best films, but it has enough great scenes to make it very enjoyable.

The Great McGinty

1940. 81 min. b.w. U.S. **Prod.** Paul Jones; **Dir.** Preston Sturges; **Scr.** Preston Sturges; **Cin.** William Mellor; **Ed.** Hugh Bennett; **Art D.** Hans Dreier, Earl Hedrick; **Mus.** Frederick Hollander; **Cast:** Brian Donlevy, Muriel Angelus, Akim Tamiroff, Allyn Joslyn, William Demarest, Louis Jean Heydt, Thurston Hall.

The film opens in an unnamed city in a banana republic. Dan McGinty (Brian Donlevy) is the bartender in a café frequented by expatriate Americans. He thwarts the suicide of Thompson (Louis Jean Heydt), a fellow American. Thompson tells him he had been the chief cashier of a bank in the U.S. and one day he impulsively embezzled a large sum of money and has been on the run ever since. To soothe him McGinty admits he too has been on the run and begins to tell his story, which unravels in a lengthy flashback. McGinty, a hungry hobo, comes to a large city on an election day. He is approached by a city alderman (William Demarest) and promised two dollars for every vote he can cast, giving him the names of dead citizens. By the time the polls close he has voted thirty-seven times. To get paid he is taken by the alderman to a function hosted by the city political "Boss" (Akim Tamiroff) who is celebrating the election of his candidate as mayor. The Boss, impressed by anyone who could vote thirty-seven times, pays him off and appoints him as the "collection agent" for the protection racket he is running. McGinty is successful in his new job in which he uses charm and guile and if necessary a strong arm. Having passed his test, the Boss has him elected as alderman, later mayor and ultimately governor. While running for public office the Boss convinces him to get married as "women voters don't like bachelors." He marries his secretary Catherine (Muriel Angelus), a widow with two children. Under the influence of a good woman McGinty becomes an honest governor. He attempts to rid the state of graft and bribery. He tries to expose the Boss but his own background catches up with him and together with the Boss he escapes from the U.S. and settles in the Central American republic.

The movie is the directorial debut of Preston Sturges. He had been at Paramount for several years working on scripts and screenplays. The studio finally allowed him to direct his own original story and script. He was given a three-week shooting schedule with a $350,000 budget. Sturges was limited in his casting to secondary and character actors. Although lacking in star power, the cast gives a very good account of itself. Brian Donlevy and Akim Tamiroff make an excellent comedy team. William Demarest became a fixture in later Sturges films. *The Great McGinty* is in many ways among the first Hollywood films that dissect corruption in the American political system. Additionally very few movies have such engaging dialogue: the alderman to McGinty, "You gotta pay somebody to protect you from human greed." McGinty to the madam of a brothel, "You gotta pay protection. You don't want to be at the mercy of any guy in uniform." And finally the best, "If you didn't have graft, you'd have a lower class of people in politics."

The Gunfighter

1950. 84 min. b.w. U.S. **Prod.** Nunnally Johnson; **Dir.** Henry King; **Scr.** William Bowers, William Sellers, Nunnally Johnson, Andre De Toth (based on a story by Bowers); **Cin.** Arthur Miller; **Ed.** Barbara McLean; **Art D.** Lyle Wheeler; **Mus.** Alfred Newman; **Cast:** Gregory Peck, Helen Westcott, Millard Mitchell, Jean Parker, Karl Malden, Skip Homeier, Ellen Corby, Richard Jaeckel, Anthony Ross.

Jimmy Ringo (Gregory Peck), an aging former outlaw and one of the fastest guns, rides from town to town trying to find his wife and young son whom he had left years ago. The trouble is that his reputation has made him a target for every punk who wants to make a name for himself. The film begins in a small-town saloon. Eddie (Richard Jaeckel), the town's fastest gun, wants to test him: "He doesn't look that fast to me." Ringo tries to talk him out of it, but Eddie draws and is killed. The dead man's three brothers are now after Ringo, not caring who drew first. At the next town, with the help of the local sheriff (Millard Mitchell), a reformed outlaw and a former comrade, he finds his wife Peggy (Helen Westcott) and his son who have since changed their names. She is the local school teacher. He tells Peggy he has changed and wants to settle down. It is agreed he will come back in a year when he has made arrangements to support them. Before he can leave town he has to face another punk, Hunt Bromley (Skip Homeier).

A film ahead of Westerns of the time, showing the gunfighter's unglamorous life and the end that awaited him. Ringo with his handlebar mustache and ill-fitting clothes says at one point, "I'm thirty-five years old and ain't even got a good watch." It is well directed by the experienced Henry King, whose career spanned half a century. His two best films are *Twelve O'Clock High* (1949) and *The Gunfighter*. They also happen to have two of Peck's very best performances. The shots of a clock to heighten the tension was used in this film two years before *High Noon* (1952). The high contrast cinematography of Arthur Miller gave the film added realism. The supporting cast of Helen Westcott, Millard Mitchell, Karl Malden and Jean Parker add a great deal. Skip Homeier, however, is slightly too modern for the part. There is a memorable catharsis at the end when the vicious Hunt Bromley is given an ominous warning by the dying Ringo then dragged off and beaten by the sheriff.

Henry V

1989. 137 min. color. British. **Prod.** Bruce Sharman; **Dir.** Kenneth Branagh; **Scr.** Kenneth Branagh (based on the play by William Shakespeare); **Cin.** Kenneth MacMillan; **Ed.** Michael Bradsell; **Prod. D.** Tim Harvey; **Art D.** Norman Dorme; **Mus.** Pat Doyle; **Cast:** Kenneth Branagh, Derek Jacobi, Ian Holm, Robert Stephens, Judi Dench, Paul Scofield, Emma Thompson, Simon Shepherd, Charles Kay, Robbie Coltrane.

An original and powerful production of *Henry V* by Kenneth Branagh in his first directorial effort at age twenty-eight. Branagh had been a stage actor who had appeared only in one film and the medium was relatively unknown to him. As Olivier's 1944 *Henry V* was also a first directorial effort, the two films are inevitably compared although they are vastly different. Both are based on a jingoistic play and are perforce themselves jingoistic. Olivier's film was made during one of England's most difficult periods and it is an ode to England. Branagh's film, forty-five years later, is not as poetic and less passionate. In this film Henry clearly wants to be the king of France and wants to go to war to secure his ambition. His tenuous claim to the French throne runs through Isabella, daughter of Philip IV of France, who married Edward II of England, Henry's great-great-grandfather. Like many other rulers before and since, when they want war they create the justification. In this instance the Archbishop of Canterbury sanctioned the war. Branagh also has included the role of the plotters who conspire with the French king to overthrow Henry. Olivier depicts the battle of Agincourt almost as a pageant. Branagh attempts realism and depicts the horrors of war more graphically. In Olivier's film the opposing combatants are clearly separated and the longbow plays the crucial part. In Branagh's film, the emphasis is on hand-to-hand combat with swords, daggers and clubs. The field of battle is tangled and the two sides are indistinguishable. Most of the action takes place on rain-soaked muddy fields and not the green pastures of Olivier's film. Branagh's cinematographer's emphasis is on close-ups.

Although Olivier is the better actor, Branagh is a better director, and his film has a better cast. It hosts some of England's finest actors: Derek Jacobi as the chorus, Paul Scofield as the senile king of France, Judi Dench as mistress Quickly, Emma Thompson as the future Queen Katherine, and the great Ian Holm as Fluellen. Branagh uses flashbacks and even Falstaff makes a brief appearance. A great feat for a first-time director who also plays the lead role.

Hiroshima Mon Amour

1959. 91 min. b.w. French/Japanese. **Prod.** Samy Halfon; **Dir.** Alain Resnais; **Scr.** Marguerite Duras; **Cin.** Sacha Vierny, Michio Takahashi; **Ed.** Henri Colpi, Jasmine Chasney, Anne Sarraute; **Prod. D.** Esaka, Mayo, Petri; **Mus.** Georges Delerue, Giovanni Fusco; **Cast:** Emmanuelle Riva, Eiji Okada, Stella Dassas, Bernard Fresson, Pierre Barbaud.

A French actress (Emmanuelle Riva) has come to Hiroshima to make a film about peace against the backdrop of the most horrific event of World War II. She meets a Japanese architect (Eiji Okada). She is attracted to him and invites him to her hotel. Neither is identified by name. The actress is referred to as "She" and the architect as "He." The film covers twenty-four hours of their lives. We are first introduced to them after they have made love and are talking. It appears they are both happily married although each has had a troubled past. Her merely being in Hiroshima makes her remember a long-repressed incident in her life. She had been in love with a German soldier in her hometown of Nevers during the German occupation of France. When France was liberated, the German soldier had been shot and her head was shaved for consorting with the enemy. She had been hidden by her shamed parents in the cellar of their house. At one point in recounting her lost love and the shame she had brought on herself and her family she becomes hysterical. Her Japanese lover must slap her to quiet her and she continues her story. She had left Nevers for Paris when the war in Europe was over. The architect is also emotionally scarred over the bombing of his home city, Hiroshima. The next morning she realizes she is not psychologically capable of handling the love affair and asks him to leave. They meet later in the afternoon and he begs her to stay longer, but she declines. The film ends with their farewells of one word. She says, "Hiroshima," and he says, "Nevers."

This was Resnais' first feature film. He cinematically introduced several imaginative approaches to showing how one's long-repressed memories come to the foreground involuntarily. He uses the flashback without any dissolve or fade and leaves us in doubt as to whether we are in the past or present. The story she tells of her experience in Nevers is not in sequence but as the memories come forward in her mind. The theme was meant to be the senselessness of war, but the film is less about the horrors of Hiroshima than how the mind works in retrieving pieces from the memory.

Resnais had only made documentaries and short films when he was asked by a Japanese group to make a film about Hiroshima fourteen years after the first atomic bomb was dropped. He chose to make *Hiroshima Mon Amour* based on a script by the noted French writer Marguerite Duras. He selected Emmanuelle Riva, a French stage actress, and Eiji Okada, a Japanese stage and film actor. The exteriors were all shot in Hiroshima and the interiors in Tokyo. The footage of the burnt-out Hiroshima is from a documentary film by the Japanese director Hideo Sekibawa, made in 1953.

His Girl Friday

1940. 92 min. b.w. U.S. **Prod.** Howard Hawks; **Dir.** Howard Hawks; **Scr.** Charles Lederer (based on the play by Ben Hecht, Charles MacArthur); **Cin.** Joseph Walker; **Ed.** Gene Havlick; **Art D.** Lionel Banks; **Mus.** M. W. Stoloff; **Cast:** Cary Grant, Rosalind Russell, Ralph Bellamy, Gene Lockhart, Porter Hall, Roscoe Karns, John Qualen, Billy Gilbert, Helen Mack, Ernest Truex.

Hildy Johnson (Rosalind Russell) was the star reporter on a newspaper in a large Midwestern city. She had been married to the editor, Walter Burns (Cary Grant), but divorced him and resigned from the paper. She has a new beau, Bruce Baldwin (Ralph Bellamy), an insurance salesman. They drop by the newspaper office to say goodbye to her coworkers and her ex-husband. She tells Walter about her impending marriage to Bruce and their leaving for the East the next day. But now, more than ever, Walter needs his brilliant reporter. Earl Williams (John Qualen), an anarchist who had shot and killed a black policeman, is to hang the next day. He has asked for a reprieve from the governor who has gone fishing. The corrupt mayor and sheriff's reelections are dependent on their hanging Williams. Additionally, Walter is still in love with Hildy and wants her back. He does everything possible to ingratiate himself with her, including buying a life insurance policy from the slow, plodding and boring Bruce, although he immediately has a pickpocket retrieve his check. Hildy is persuaded to accept one last assignment.

From this point, the film becomes a whirlwind. Characters move and speak at a frantic pace with overlapping dialogue. *His Girl Friday* is a reworking of *The Front Page* (1931), an excellent comedy about newspapers and reporters. The Ben Hecht and Charles MacArthur play was changed by Howard Hawks and rescripted by Charles Lederer to make reporter Hildy Johnson a woman. It is a finely crafted film, but it does not altogether match the authenticity of *The Front Page*. Furthermore, the earlier film dealt with city hall corruption more explicitly. But *His Girl Friday* still shows the sleazy tabloids where anything goes and the only goal is increased circulation, and machine politicians who are willing to sacrifice anybody to enhance their reelection prospects. Cary Grant as the unprincipled editor who intimidates and lies to get his way has one of his choice roles and is at his best. This is probably also true of Rosalind Russell. Ralph Bellamy, the quintessential second lead who always loses the girl, does his part as the innocent bloke. The supporting cast boasts some of the best actors in Hollywood. There are some inside jokes in the film: Walter tells Hildy that Bruce Baldwin "looks like that actor...Ralph Bellamy." Another is when Cary Grant says, "The last man who said that was Archie Leach just before he cut his own throat." Cary Grant was born Archibald Leach.

The Horse's Mouth

1958. 93 min. color. British. **Prod.** John Bryan; **Dir.** Ronald Neame; **Scr.** Alec Guinness (based on the novel by Joyce Carey); **Cin.** Arthur Ibbetson; **Ed.** Anne V. Coates; **Mus.** Ken Jones; **Cast:** Alec Guinness, Kay Walsh, Renee Houston, Mike Morgan, Michael Gough, Ernest Thesiger, Robert Coote, Arthur Macrae.

The film begins with Gulley Jimson (Alec Guinness), a scruffy misfit released from prison after serving time for vagrancy. Gulley is a painter who had moderate success and recognition in his early years. He has of late begun to consider himself a failure as he has never been able to put his true vision on canvas. He lives on a dilapidated tugboat and the only people who care for him are a local barmaid, Coker (Kay Walsh), and a young boy, Nosey (Mike Morgan), who wants to be an artist. Gulley is a rogue who is not above swindling or extorting money from anyone he can. He had abandoned his wife (Renee Houston) years ago and now tries to retrieve some of his early paintings that she has kept. He attempts to extract additional money from people who had previously bought his paintings. A wealthy collector, Sir William Beeder (Robert Coote), has shown an interest in his work. He learns Sir William and his family will be away in Jamaica for some six weeks. In their absence he moves into their home and begins painting a large mural on the vast walls, titling the work "The Raising of Lazarus," almost destroying the apartment in the process. As always he is disappointed by his inability to capture his vision: "Not what I meant…not the vision I had in my mind." On the family's return Gulley is chucked out of the house, but at the end of the film he appears to have found a larger and more unorthodox place for his murals.

Alec Guinness wrote the screenplay from the novel by Joyce Carey, which is in part based on the early life of his friend Dylan Thomas. The novel is about the artist as a nonconformist but the film dwells more on the eccentricities of artists. It is still a rare and beautiful movie with many touching aspects. The unspoken love of Coker for Gulley, and Gulley's account of how he became a painter. "One day I saw a painting by Matisse…it gave me the shock of my life. It skinned my eyes…and I became a different man…like a conversion." Alec Guinness is magnificent as the tragicomic figure with a rough, grating voice, always a little tipsy. Kay Walsh has one of her best roles as the barmaid who has many a tale to tell. The only drawback of the film is the uninspired direction and especially the cinematography that shows too few of Gulley's paintings. Neame directed several other enjoyable films: *The Man Who Never Was* (1957), *The Prime of Miss Brodie* (1970), and *Hopscotch* (1981).

Hud

1963. 112 min. b.w. U.S. **Prod.** Martin Ritt, Irving Ravetch; **Dir.** Martin Ritt; **Scr.** Irving Ravetch, Harriet Frank, Jr., (based on the novel *Horseman, Pass* By by Larry McMurtry); **Cin.** James Wong Howe; **Ed.** Frank Bracht; **Art D.** Hal Pereira, Tambi Larsen; **Mus.** Elmer Bernstein; **Cast:** Paul Newman, Patricia Neal, Melvyn Douglas, Brandon de Wilde, Whit Bissell.

Set in the Texas panhandle, it is the story of a conflict between a father and son and their widely different values. It is also a commentary on the changing of the American West. The father, Homer Bannon (Melvyn Douglas), is a cattle rancher who represents the pioneering spirit of the Old West and is content to remain a rancher. He refuses oil lease offers because he doesn't want the land to be disfigured. When his cattle are infected with hoof-and-mouth disease he does not hesitate to slaughter the entire herd. His only surviving son, Hud (Paul Newman), wants to sell the infected herd to unsuspecting buyers. He also attempts to have his father declared incompetent so he can then lease the land to oil prospectors. Some years back Hud's older brother died in a car accident driven by a drunken Hud. When the film opens Hud is the role model for his dead brother's sixteen-year-old son, Lon (Brandon de Wilde). By the end of the film Hud is revealed as an amoral, greedy heel with no redeeming features. When Homer dies, Lon realizes that he doesn't want to stay with his uncle and leaves.

Hud could have been a far better film were it not too ambitious. It goes beyond the father and son conflict and attempts to show the decline of values and the emergence of a culture that is rooted in greed. The film is handsomely designed by Hal Pereira and photographed by the great veteran James Wong Howe. It is also one of the very best films of director Martin Ritt. Its chief merit is the uniformly great acting by the entire cast of Paul Newman, Melvyn Douglas, Brandon de Wilde and Patricia Neal in her best role as the housekeeper. Whit Bissell is also excellent as the representative of the Department of Agriculture. Patricia Neal and Melvyn Douglas won Academy Awards for best actress and supporting actor and Paul Newman and Martin Ritt were nominated for best actor and director.

The Hunchback of Notre Dame

1939. 115 min. b.w. U.S. **Prod.** Pandro S. Berman; **Dir.** William Dieterle; **Scr.** Sonya Levien, Bruno Frank (based on the novel by Victor Hugo); **Cin.** Joseph August; **Ed.** William Hamilton, Robert Wise; **Art D.** Van Nest Polglase; **Mus.** Alfred Newman; **Cast:** Charles Laughton, Cedric Hardwicke, Thomas Mitchell, Maureen O'Hara, Edmond O'Brien, Alan Marshal, Walter Hampden, Harry Davenport, George Zucco.

The focus of the film is the story of a grotesquely deformed hunchback, Quasimodo (Charles Laughton), who lives in the cathedral and whose sole function is to ring the huge bells that have made him deaf. He is a childlike creature who enjoys his task as the bells are the only sounds he can hear. In a lovely scene he is shown lying on his back ringing the bells rhythmically with his feet. He sacrifices himself for the love of a beautiful gypsy, Esmeralda (Maureen O'Hara), wrongly accused of murder. She had given him a cup of water after he was whipped mercilessly and pilloried in the public square.

The film, based on the Victor Hugo novel, is set during the reign of Louis XI toward the end of the fifteenth century as the Renaissance was beginning to have an impact on France. The king is depicted as having an open mind. In a very early scene we see him arguing, to the dismay of his ministers, that the earth could possibly be round. The film is successful in depicting the contrast between medievalism and the dawn of enlightenment. It also deals with the prejudices remaining from the dark ages, the machinations of the church and the abject poverty of the masses. It is this realism that distinguishes the film. It is also an exceptionally directed, photographed and acted film. Joseph August's expressionist lighting and tracking shots of the dark alleys and catacombs of Paris give added dimension to the direction of William Dieterle. The acting is faultless. One can't take one's eyes away from Charles Laughton. Edmond O'Brien as Gringoire, a poet/actor fashioned on the contemporary French poet François

Villon, and Maureen O'Hara, both in their first film, are very good. Cedric Hardwicke as the sadistic, repressed ecclesiastic and Harry Davenport as King Louis stand out. The film is a remake of Lon Chaney's excellent silent film of 1923.

The Hustler

1961. 135 min. b.w. U.S. **Prod.** Robert Rossen; **Dir.** Robert Rossen; **Scr.** Sidney Carroll, Robert Rossen (based on the novel by Walter Tevis); **Cin.** Eugene Schuftan; **Ed.** Dede Allen; **Prod. D.** Harry Horner; **Art D.** Albert Brenner, Harry Horner; **Mus.** Kenyon Hopkins; **Cast:** Paul Newman, Jackie Gleason, Piper Laurie, George C. Scott, Myron McCormick, Murray Hamilton, Jake LaMotta, Vincent Gardenia.

"Fast Eddie" Felson (Paul Newman), an exceptionally talented pool player, has been waiting for his chance to play Minnesota Fats (Jackie Gleason), acknowledged as the best. In order to raise money for the challenge, Felson and his backer, Charlie Bums (Myron McCormick), have been traveling across the country hustling unsuspecting pool players. They now have enough money to tempt Fats. They arrive at Ames Billiard Parlor in New York City, the mecca of pool players, and let the word out that they are there to challenge Minnesota Fats. As always, the punctual, dapper and classy Fats arrives at 6:00 p.m. sharp and he and Eddie play an epic twenty-five-hour match. Fats is bankrolled by Bert Gordon (George C. Scott), a professional gambler. Eddie wins the early rounds and a substantial amount of money. Fats feels he is beaten and is about to retire, but Bert, who detects a weakness of character in Eddie, tells Fats, "Stick with this kid, he's a loser." Eddie's downfall comes about from his arrogance and the large quantity of bourbon that he drinks vying with Fats who handles his alcohol much better. Eddie loses everything and even forces Charlie to hand over his share of winnings from other matches. Eddie and Charlie dissolve their partnership. Eddie is broke. He becomes involved with a crippled, alcoholic girl, Sarah (Piper Laurie), whose love restores his confidence. One night at a bar he hustles a young pool player and wins a close game. When taunted by his opponent and the young player's friends, his arrogance forces him to show how good he really is and he trounces the young player handily. They beat him up and break his thumbs. Sarah nurses him back to health. He joins Bert Gordon, an almost satanic figure, and they go on the road accompanied by Sarah to play in games arranged by Bert. Sarah feels she is losing Eddie who is completely under Bert's influence. Sensing her uselessness to Eddie she goes to bed with Bert, and then the tortured girl commits suicide. Eddie with his road winnings is ready for Fats and returns to Ames pool hall. Eddie beats Fats and is acknowledged as the best. He walks out on Bert and refuses to give him his share of the winnings, even knowing that with Bert's connections he will never be allowed to play the game again.

The Hustler is a very well-made film, but it is too ambitious. It is about overweening pride, a hopeless love affair, betrayal and redemption. For a film that is shot almost entirely indoors, Rossen and his photographer, Schuftan, somehow make the interiors much larger and the pool hall cavernous. The acting by the entire cast is of a very high order. Gleason with his charm and detached air moves effortlessly around the pool table despite his great weight. There is also one of the best performances by Newman matching his later great performances in *Hud* (1963) and *The Verdict* (1982). It is certainly Piper Laurie's best. George C. Scott's role is not well fleshed out, but he does his best. The only shortcoming of the film is the often unnecessary and affected dialogue that has a ring of self-conscious lyricism. *The Hustler* won Academy Awards for cinematography and art direction, and received nominations for all top seven categories.

If

1968. 111 min. color. b.w. British. **Prod.** Michael Medwin, Lindsay Anderson; **Dir.** Lindsay Anderson; **Scr.** David Sherwin; **Cin.** Miroslav Ondricek; **Ed.** David Gladwell; **Art D.** Brian Eatwell; **Mus.** Marc Wilkinson; **Cast:** Malcolm McDowell, David Wood, Richard Warwick, Robert Swann, Christine Noonan, Rupert Webster.

The film is set at an English boys' public school (the equivalent of private school in the U.S.). In a series of eight scenes the story unfolds. Boys come back from their holidays for the winter term. They go to their rooms and unpack, then gather in the dining hall for a series of speeches from faculty and headmaster. Next is the medical examination by the matron who fondles each boy's penis. Then classes begin. The focus of the film is on three boys: Mick Travers (Malcolm McDowell), Johnny (David Wood) and Wallace (Richard Warwick), all seniors and close friends. Their leader is implicitly Mick. The three skip a rugger match and go into town. They meet a local girl (Christine Noonan) and together "borrow" a motorcycle to have some fun. School authority, as in all English public schools, rests with the prefects. The senior prefect, Rountree (Robert Swann), is more powerful than either the headmaster or the housemasters. A typical command is given early in the film when Rountree orders a scum (a lower classman) to warm the lavatory seat for him. Another of the prefects has his eyes on a young boy, a gymnast, and he is waiting for the right time to corner him. The three truant boys' escapade is reported to the senior prefect and they are subjected to a brutal caning. Mick, as the leader, is beaten to the point of unconsciousness. The three take a blood oath to strike back. They select Founder's Day, when most parents will be present. Also attending is a high-ranking general, a bishop, and a member of the royal family. The three boys, joined by the girl from town and the young gymnast, break into the armory, take automatic weapons and grenades, and go to the roof. They begin shooting at everyone. The headmaster who tries to reason with them is shot by the girl. There is a counterattack by the establishment and a bloodbath ensues. The last scene of the film is that of the defiant boys continuing their fire. The film does not conclude with the traditional "The End" but with the word "If."

The title derives from Kipling's poem of the same name. *If* is a very ambitious film, but it works as a powerful allegory on the use of arbitrary and irrational power. The Vietnam War was certainly present in the minds of the makers of the film. The Tet offensive of January 1968 had been launched about the time production got underway. An atmosphere of repressed sexuality is also present. We have the matron feeling the boys' penises, and the housemaster's wife running naked through the corridors when the boys are on the playing fields. The sexual exploitation of younger boys by their elders is explicit. The film is influenced by, and is a homage to, Jean Vigo's *Zero De Conduite* (1933). In Vigo's film the school is run by weird people. In *If* the figures of authority are establishment types. More important, in Vigo's film there is still hope and some light. In *If* the time has passed for any reform. The ending is all darkness.

In a Lonely Place

1950. 91 min. b.w. U.S. **Prod.** Robert Lord, Henry S. Kesler; **Dir.** Nicholas Ray; **Scr.** Andrew Solt (based on a story by Edmund H. North from the novel by Dorothy B. Hughes); **Cin.** Burnett Guffey; **Ed.** Viola Lawrence; **Art D.** Robert Peterson; **Mus.** George Antheil, **Cast:** Humphrey Bogart, Gloria Grahame, Frank Lovejoy, Robert Warwick, Jeff Donnell, Martha Stewart, Art Smith, Morris Ankrum, William Ching.

Dixon Steele (Humphrey Bogart) is an experienced and talented screenwriter. He has been unemployed lately because of his combative nature, volatile temper and heavy drinking. His devoted agent and friend, Mel Lippman (Art Smith), manages to get him work writing the screenplay of a best-selling novel. Dixon is to meet Mel and the proposed director of the film in a Hollywood restaurant. Dixon has harsh words for the director and accuses him of making the same film over and over again. Later he punches an arrogant producer who had insulted his friend, a broken-down actor. Mel somehow soothes all the anger and hurt feelings and urges Dixon to go home and read the novel, and take a crack at writing the script. Dixon knows the novel is a commonplace potboiler and doesn't want to waste his time. When the hatcheck girl, Mildred Atkinson (Martha Stewart), tells Dixon she has read the novel and loved it, Dixon asks her to his bungalow. He listens to the girl, but soon becomes bored. He gives her cab fare and sends her off. Across the courtyard a neighbor, Laurel Gray (Gloria Grahame), sees Dixon and Mildred enter and, later, the girl leave. The next day Mildred's disfigured body is found and it is established that Dixon was the last person to have seen her alive. Suspicion falls on him and he is brought in by the police for several rounds of questioning. Laurel, however, tells them that she saw Mildred leave and the pressure on Dixon is somewhat relieved. Laurel had been a starlet who had not made it. She had been kept by several men but had decided to leave Hollywood. Now that she has started a relationship with Dixon she hopes for a fresh start. Dixon's violent temper erupts again under the pressure of unceasing police attention. He beats up a youngster who was driving recklessly. Later, he nearly strangles Laurel when he finds a plane ticket in her purse and thinks she is leaving him for another man. Before matters go any further, the police extract a murder confession from Mildred's boyfriend. Dixon is absolved, but the relationship with Laurel is over.

This is Nicholas Ray's best film and is masterfully directed. He maintains the suspense and we are never sure whether Dixon is the murderer or whether Laurel is truthful and actually saw the murdered girl leave. A number of scenes persuade us that even if Dixon did not kill the girl, he is certainly capable of murder. We are given bits of information that Dixon abused his former girlfriends and that he is a man on the edge of a breakdown and needs psychiatric help. Even the setting of the film in the enclosed bungalow complex, the now demolished Garden of Allah on Sunset Boulevard, contributes to the tension. For Humphrey Bogart, his role is not very different from Fred C. Dobbs in *The Treasure of the Sierra Madre* (1948) or Captain Queeg in *The Caine Mutiny*

(1954). In all three films the character carries the seeds of his own downfall. Gloria Grahame was married to Nicholas Ray at the time of this film. She is mostly remembered as a dumb blonde or a gangster's moll but showed her versatility with this portrayal. The supporting cast is especially good. The film was read by some critics as representing the paranoia in Hollywood regarding the red scare and witch hunts of the late forties and early fifties. It may have been in Nicholas Ray's mind, but the film comes off more as a story about a mentally disturbed individual.

Intruder in the Dust

1949. 87 min. b.w. U.S. **Prod.** Clarence Brown; **Dir.** Clarence Brown; **Scr.** Ben Maddow (based on the novel by William Faulkner); **Cin.** Robert Surtees; **Ed.** Robert J. Kern; **Art D.** Cedric Gibbons; **Mus.** Adolph Deutsch; **Cast:** David Brian, Claude Jarman, Jr., Juano Hernandez, Porter Hall, Elizabeth Patterson, Charles Kemper, Will Geer.

Based on the William Faulkner novel the story is set in a small Southern town. One Sunday morning the townspeople learn that one of the Gowrie boys has been murdered in the nearby woods and Lucas Beauchamp (Juano Hernandez) has been arrested and brought to town for trial. Lucas, an elderly man, is the only black farmer in the area who owns property. The town resents him for his haughty ways and carrying himself as an equal of the white folks. As Lucas is being led to jail he spots a sixteen-year-old white boy, Chick Mallison (Claude Jarman, Jr.), who comes from a prominent family. Lucas had once saved Chick from drowning, given him food and dry clothes, putting young Chick in his debt. Lucas asks Chick to get his lawyer uncle, John Gavin Stevens (David Brian), to represent him. Stevens at first is reluctant, knowing he will be shunned by everyone, but later accepts. After speaking with Lucas he becomes convinced of his innocence. Meanwhile the murdered man's brother, Crawford Gowrie (Charles Kemper), incites the crowd to lynch Lucas. That night Chick together with elderly Miss Habersham (Elizabeth Patterson) dig up the dead man's grave to prove the gun that killed Gowrie could not have been Lucas' gun. To their surprise the grave is empty. The body is later found in a shallow swamp. The sheriff tricks the killer into giving himself away while Miss Habersham guards the prison door and holds the lynch mob at bay. It is the murdered man's brother, Crawford, who is guilty of fratricide. Lucas is released. The following Saturday Lucas comes to town in his frock coat and high hat as arrogant as ever. He crosses the town's main square to John Stevens' office and insists on paying two silver dollars for services rendered.

It was only after World War II that Hollywood began to pay attention to race relations in the U.S. In 1949 two other films, *Home of the Brave* and *Pinky*, were released, exploring the same themes. *Intruder in the Dust* is by far the best of the three. It has some fine acting and memorable scenes. There are the chilling scenes of the townspeople assembled near the jail looking forward to the spectacle of a lynching. Loud music is coming from a record shop and radios. A group of men are playing cards. Robert Surtees' camera gives an almost surrealistic touch to the hideous plan. Juano Hernandez as the insufferably proud Lucas and Elizabeth Patterson as the courageous old lady are magnificent. Porter Hall as the father of the murdered man, Will Geer as the sheriff and Claude Jarman, Jr. are excellent. David Brian is a bit stiff. What weakens the film is David Brian's unnecessary lecture to Chick at the end stating the obvious: "Lucas wasn't in trouble. We were in trouble." *Intruder in the Dust* is Clarence Brown's best film, and the best realized film of a William Faulkner story. It was shot entirely in Oxford, Mississippi, Faulkner's hometown.

Invasion of the Body Snatchers

1956. 80 min. b.w. U.S. **Prod.** Walter Wanger; **Dir.** Don Siegel; **Scr.** Geoffrey Homes (based on the novel *The Body Snatchers* by Jack Finney); **Cin.** Ellsworth Fredricks; **Ed.** Robert S. Eisen; **Prod. D.** Joseph Kish; **Art D.** Ted Haworth; **Mus.** Carmen Dragon; **Cast:** Kevin McCarthy, Dana Wynter, Larry Gates, King Donovan, Carolyn Jones, Ralph Dumke.

Dr. Miles Bennel (Kevin McCarthy) has just returned from a medical convention to his small-town practice in Santa Mira, Cal-

ifornia. He has a long waiting list of patients. A ten-year-old boy
claims his mother is not his mother. A woman says her Uncle Ira is
not her Uncle Ira. Another women says her sister is not her sister.
There is not much he can do to calm his patients. He consults
with the local psychiatrist and they agree it is some kind of mass
neurosis or hysteria perhaps due to anxiety about what is going on
in the world. After a few days the people who had complained
cancel their appointments and Dr. Bennel is relieved. Becky
Driscoll (Dana Wynter), an old flame of Miles, has come back to
town and they begin to see each other regularly. One night his
friend Jack (King Donovan) and his wife Theodora (Carolyn
Jones) call and must see him urgently. In their greenhouse they
had discovered enormous pods containing bodies with mask-like
faces. Two are exact replicas of Jack and his wife. With pitchforks
they deface and destroy as many of the pods as they can and call
the police. It soon becomes apparent that almost everyone in the
town including the police has been replaced by emotionless look-
alike pod creatures. In a memorable scene a man at a gas station
holding a small pod asks his wife, "Shall I put this pod with the
baby?" She replies, "Yes. Then there will be no crying." Soon
everyone is replaced except Miles and Becky. They are told that all
they have to do is go to sleep and they will wake up as one of
them. They will then never know pain or worry. Miles and Becky
escape and hide in a cave, but exhaustion overcomes Becky. She
closes her eyes and falls asleep for only a few seconds during
which time she is transformed. Miles makes it to the highway
leading to San Francisco. He shouts frantically at all passing cars,
"You are next!" He is hit by a car and taken to a hospital.

The film starts with Miles in the hospital. No one believes his
account of the pods. There is then a long flashback and the story
unfolds. Now, just as they are to take him to the psychiatric ward,
a truck driver whose truck has overturned on the highway bury-
ing him under a load of pods is brought to the hospital. The truck
was coming from Santa Mira. The doctor in charge is now convinced. He calls the FBI and the president of the United States.

One of the very best science-fiction films ever made. It is
deceiving as it begins at a leisurely pace and the viewer is pre-

pared for the usual absurdist plot of other sci-fi films. However, in the hands of one of the most professional directors in Hollywood, it becomes a realistic and suspenseful film. Siegel began his career as a special effects director but here avoids all special-effects to give the film an authentic small-town feel that makes it more menacing. Kevin McCarthy, an underrated actor, and the secondary cast are excellent. *Invasion of the Body Snatchers* was made at the height of the Cold War when moviegoers were told that communists were automatons, and that communist governments would sacrifice millions to achieve their aims. There was some controversy as to whether the body snatchers were the McCarthyites or the communists. A cursory review of Siegel's work such as *Coogan's Bluff* (1965) and *Dirty Harry* (1971) would indicate that the body snatchers likely were the reds. The film was remade in 1978 by Philip Kaufman but it comes nowhere near the original.

It Happened One Night

1934. 105 min. b.w. U.S. **Prod.** Harry Cohn; **Dir.** Frank Capra; **Scr.** Robert Riskin (based on the story "Night Bus" by Samuel Hopkins Adams); **Cin.** Joseph Walker; **Ed.** Gene Havlick; **Art D.** Stephen Gooson; **Mus.** Louis Silvers; **Cast:** Clark Gable, Claudette Colbert, Walter Connolly, Roscoe Karns, Alan Hale, Ward Bond, Henry Wadsworth, Claire McDowell.

An heiress, Ellie Andrews (Claudette Colbert), is to marry a playboy aviator. Her father is opposed to the marriage and she is virtually imprisoned on the family yacht. She dives off, swims to shore and takes a bus from Miami to New York. Her picture is in all the papers and she is recognized by a fellow passenger, Peter Warne (Clark Gable), a newspaper man. She has no money and is hungry. He agrees to help her if he could have the exclusive story of her escape and intended marriage. In the course of the next few days they fall in love.

One of the very first madcap heiress movies, it was made during the Great Depression and has little of the sentimentality associated with later Capra films. However, like many films of the period it aims to show how happy the poor are, and how miserable the rich. There are several very charming scenes: Gable teaching Colbert how to dunk a donut; Colbert lifting her skirt to hitch a ride; Gable scaring off a lecherous fellow passenger; and the final scene when the "walls of Jerico" fall down. The acting of the leads is superb and the supporting cast is excellent. *It Happened One Night* was the first film to win the top five Oscars.

It's a Wonderful Life

1946. 129 min. b.w. U.S. **Prod.** Frank Capra; **Dir.** Frank Capra; **Scr.** Frances Goodrich, Albert Hackett, Frank Capra, Jo Swerling (based on the story "The Greatest Gift" by Philip Van Doren Stern); **Cin.** Joseph Walker, Joseph Biroc; **Ed.** William Hornbeck; **Art D.** Jack Okey. **Mus.** Dimitri Tiomkin; **Cast:** James Stewart, Donna Reed, Lionel Barrymore, Thomas Mitchell, Henry Travers, Beulah Bondi, Frank Faylen, Ward Bond, Gloria Grahame, H. B. Warner, Samuel S. Hinds, Sheldon Leonard.

George Bailey (James Stewart) is about to commit suicide by jumping off a bridge into an icy river. He faces imprisonment, financial ruin, and subjecting his wife and small children to a life of poverty. He has a life insurance policy that makes him worth more dead than alive. Before jumping, he mutters to himself that everyone would have been better off had he never been born. Clarence Oddbody (Henry Travers), a gentle elderly angel, is sent to stop George. In flashbacks, we learn George was born in Bedford Falls and has never left. His father (Samuel S. Hinds) was the founder of the small Bailey Building and Loan Association. He had refused to sell it to the greedy and unprincipled Mr. Potter (Lionel Barrymore), who owned everything else in Bedford Falls. As a boy George had saved his brother Harry from drowning. Working in the local drugstore, he had also come to the rescue of the owner, Mr. Gower (H. B. Warner), when he was about to sell a wrongly filled prescription that contained poison. George had wanted to go to college to get out of Bedford Falls, but with his father's death he had to stay and run the business. He gave his college money to his brother and married his high school sweet-heart, Mary (Donna Reed). Some time later, drunken Uncle Billy (Thomas Mitchell) was to take a large sum of money to the bank for deposit in the firm's account, but he misplaced it. The mean old Mr. Potter found the money and kept it. Potter then told the police and the bank examiner that the Bailey Building and Loan had cheated its customers. Bankrupt and despondent, George feels his life is so worthless that the only answer is suicide. Clarence, his guardian angel, however, takes George through his life, demonstrating what would have happened had he not been born. Mr. Gower, the druggist, would have died in prison. In the best shots of the movie, we see a prematurely aged Mary, an old maid working in the public library. George's mother is all alone with her only son having drowned. His jovial and warm friends (Ward Bond, Frank Faylen and Sheldon Leonard) are embittered, humorless men.

It is a dark and somber film, but there is a happy ending as in almost all Capra films. Though usually well received when first introduced, Capra's films have been denigrated over the years by film critics and even by the public. *It's a Wonderful Life* together with *It Happened One Night* (1934) and *Mr. Smith Goes to Washington* (1939) are exceptions. It was too somber for the immediate postwar audience, but has now become accepted as a Christmas classic. In many ways, it is his best and most controlled film and it has not dated. It was James Stewart's first movie after serving in the military, and he clearly dominates it. This was Donna Reed's first starring role and she, and the rest of the cast, are very good. What gives an added dimension to the film is the fact that it is not merely a fairy tale about guardian angels and miracles. It is disguised realism, the story of a man who is having a nervous breakdown and conjures up miracles.

Jaws

1975. 124 min. color. U.S. **Prod.** Richard D. Zanuck, David Brown; **Dir.** Steven Spielberg; **Scr.** Peter Benchley, Carl Gotlieb, Howard Sackler (based on the novel by Peter Benchley); **Cin.** Bill Butler; **Ed.** Verna Fields; **Prod. D.** Joe Alves; **Mus.** John Williams; **Cast:** Roy Scheider, Robert Shaw, Richard Dreyfuss, Lorraine Gary, Murray Hamilton.

Amity Island off the New England coast is terrorized by a monstrously large shark that has already killed two people. The town hires Quint (Robert Shaw), a former sailor who has hunted sharks for many years, to kill the shark. He is accompanied in his boat by the head of the local police, Martin Brody (Roy Scheider) who feels it is his duty to help, and a young ichthyologist, Matt Hooper (Richard Dreyfuss), who volunteers. The characters are only barely sketched and not developed. The unnecessary scenes about the sheriff's family life are not enlightening. There is no story other than the pursuit of the shark. Despite these basic shortcomings *Jaws* is a great suspense film. The masterful opening scene has a young woman, on holiday with a group of people, deciding to swim naked in the ocean and being torn apart by an unseen beast. Spielberg uses every cinematic trick to mount the tension and sustain suspense. The shark is not even seen for the first half of the film, which makes it even more terrifying. When we finally see it, its sheer size spells doom and we almost give up on the three people pursuing it in a small boat. What helps heighten the suspense is the great score by John Williams that has a special percussive theme for the shark. The editing of the film is masterful. The acting of the three leads and Murray Hamilton as the town mayor is very good, but it is Robert Shaw who stands out. His recounting of the fate of the sinking of the S. S. Indianapolis in the waning days of World War II is chilling.

Judgement at Nuremberg

1961. 178 min. b.w. U.S. **Prod.** Stanley Kramer; **Dir.** Stanley Kramer; **Scr.** Abby Mann; **Cin.** Ernest Laszlo; **Ed.** Frederic Knudtson; **Prod. D.** Rudolph Sternad; **Mus.** Ernest Gold; **Cast:** Spencer Tracy, Burt Lancaster, Richard Widmark, Marlene Dietrich, Judy Garland, Maximilian Schell, Montgomery Clift, William Shatner, Edward Binns, Ray Teal.

The film at 190 minutes is long by any standard, yet it holds one's interest to the very end. The acting is uneven. Burt Lancaster as a legal scholar and a judge under the Nazi regime is colorless. Judy Garland as a victim of Nazi social laws is totally miscast. But Spencer Tracy as the chief Allied judge, Marlene Dietrich as the widow of a German general executed for the slaughter of American prisoners at Malmédy, and Maximilian Schell as the attorney for the German defendants are at their very best and more than carry the film. It is a powerful film, the first on war crimes, a subject avoided until then by filmmakers. The producer/director Stanley Kramer has been much maligned for some of his films, but this one cannot be held against him.

Julius Caesar

1953. 120 min. b.w. U.S. **Prod.** John Houseman; **Dir.** Joseph Mankiewicz; **Scr.** Joseph Mankiewicz (based on the play by William Shakespeare); **Cin.** Joseph Ruttenberg; **Ed.** John Dunning; **Art D.** Cedric Gibbons, Edward Carfagno; **Mus.** Miklos Rosza; **Cast:** Marlon Brando, James Mason, John Gielgud, Louis Calhern, Edmond O'Brien, Greer Garson, Deborah Kerr, George Macready, Alan Napier, Edmund Purdom, John Hay.

There is a prologue from Plutarch: "Upon Caesar's return to Rome after defeating Pompey in the civil war he was chosen for a fourth time consul and dictator for life. Then he became odious to the moderate men through the extravagance of his titles and the powers that were heaped upon him." The film begins in Rome in 44 B.C. and we see statues of Caesar (Louis Calhern) everywhere. Caesar and his legions have returned from the wars. As Caesar is about to enter a coliseum, a blind man warns him of

the ides of March. Brutus (James Mason) and Cassius (John Gielgud) remain behind. Caesar is offered the crown three times and
each time he refuses with decreasing reluctance. Cassius vents his
anger. He refers to Caesar's recurring fits of epilepsy, his assumption of absolute power and the current talk of his becoming a
king. Rome has lost its freedom and all have become underlings.
The film moves along to the gathering of the conspirators and
the assassination of Caesar in the Senate. There is the oration by
Brutus, followed by Marc Antony (Marlon Brando) who turns
the populace around. The conspirators flee Rome. A triumvirate
of Octavius, Marc Antony and Lepidus rule Rome and Brutus
and Cassius die at Filippi. As in all of Shakespeare's plays there is
an end to anarchy and mob rule, and order is restored.

The film was the brainchild of John Houseman, an intelligent,
imaginative producer and actor, who had collaborated with Orson
Welles in the 1937 stage production of *Julius Caesar* in modern
dress where the supporters of Caesar wore the Fascist black shirts.
Houseman brought the project to Dore Schary, the new head of
MGM, who approved the film but granted only a limited budget.
Houseman chose Joseph Mankiewicz, one of the most literate
directors, and insisted on Brando, Gielgud and Mason. The secondary cast of Louis Calhern and Edmond O'Brien as Casca were
also excellent choices. The Romans of rank, with the exception of
Brando, O'Brien, John Hoyt and George Macready, were British,
while the Roman mob was comprised of American actors. As in
all of Mankiewicz's films there are no fancy camera shots. The film
relies on the strength of the script and the performances.
Mankiewicz was intent on avoiding a replication of the MGM
Roman spectacles and decided to shoot in black and white. Marlon Brando is magnificent as Antony. His oration is a masterpiece
of passion and anger. Gielgud, who had never before appeared in
an American film, is great as the lean and hungry Cassius. Louis
Calhern, a professional of the first rank, has the regal bearing of a
caesar. The only disappointment is James Mason as Brutus. Shakespeare's play is more about Brutus than Caesar or Antony.
According to Plutarch, Brutus was the illegitimate son of Caesar,
which makes his part in the assassination of Caesar more painful.

Mason somehow was not able to endow the character with any intensity. Greer Garson as Calpurnia and Deborah Kerr as Brutus' wife Portia have limited roles. *Julius Caesar* still ranks among the very best of Shakespeare on film.

Key Largo

1948. 101 min. color. U.S. **Prod.** Jerry Wald; **Dir.** John Huston; **Scr.** Richard Brooks (based on the play by Maxwell Anderson); **Cin.** Karl Freund; **Ed.** Rudi Fehr; **Art D.** Leo K. Kuter; **Mus.** Max Steiner; **Cast:** Humphrey Bogart, Edward G. Robinson, Lauren Bacall, Lionel Barrymore, Claire Trevor, Thomas Gomez, Harry Lewis, Marc Lawrence, Dan Seymour.

Major Frank McCloud (Humphrey Bogart), an alienated World War II veteran, travels to Key Largo, Florida, to pay his respects to the family of a fellow officer who was killed in the war. He arrives at a run-down hotel owned and operated by John Temple (Lionel Barrymore), his dead friend's father, and Nora Temple (Lauren Bacall), his widow. Unknown to McCloud, the hotel has been taken over by gangsters headed by Johnny Rocco (Edward G. Robinson), a notorious mobster who had been deported and settled in Cuba. The gangsters are waiting for a gang from the north to exchange a large amount of counterfeit dollars made in Cuba for real currency. McCloud along with John Temple and Nora are imprisoned at the hotel for the duration of the gangsters' stay. Rocco's men have already killed a sheriff's deputy and two Seminole Indians seeking shelter from an oncoming hurricane. When the transaction is completed Rocco orders Frank, who has experience with boats, to take him and his gang back to Cuba. In a bloody shootout on the boat Frank ambushes and kills the four gangsters and brings the boat back to Key Largo.

The film is based on an undistinguished play in blank verse by Maxwell Anderson about a disillusioned soldier returning from World War I. Huston turned it into an excellent fast-moving gangster film with most of the pretensions and preachy lines about good and evil left out. Karl Freund's sharp-focus photography contributes to the gradually built-up suspense in the claustropho-bic setting of a decaying hotel. The scenes of an approaching hurricane are also well shot. There is excellent acting by Edward G. Robinson who dominates all his scenes. Robinson, who had made his name playing gangsters, had not played a gangster for about ten years. His effective first appearance has him in a bathtub with a large cigar in his mouth. He has some memorable lines: "I was deported from the U.S. like I was a red or something." He also has prophetic lines about Florida politics and counting and recounting of votes "until they turn out right." Bogart is overshad-owed by Robinson, but gives a competent, subdued performance. Claire Trevor as Gay Dawn, an alcoholic ex-singer who had been Rocco's moll but is dumped and not taken along to Cuba, won an Academy Award as best supporting actress. Lionel Barrymore, Thomas Gomez and Marc Lawrence stand out.

The Killing

1956. 83 min. b.w. U.S. **Prod.** James B. Harris; **Dir.** Stanley Kubrick; **Scr.** Stanley Kubrick, Jim Thompson (based on the novel *Clean Break* by Lionel White); **Cin.** Lucien Ballard; **Ed.** Betty Steinberg; **Art D.** Ruth Sobotka Kubrick; **Mus.** Gerald Fried; **Cast:** Sterling Hayden, Coleen Gray, Vince Edwards, Jay C. Flippen, Ted de Corsia, Marie Windsor, Joe Sawyer, Elisha Cook, Jr., Timothy Carey, Maurice Obokhoff.

Johnny Clay (Sterling Hayden) has just been released from prison after serving a five-year sentence. While in prison he mapped out a plan to rob a racetrack's payroll, estimated at $2 million. He also put together a list of accomplices for the job, none of whom has a police record. He is being bankrolled by Marvin Unger (Jay C. Flippen), a father figure who has regarded Johnny as a son. The first person Johnny sees is his childhood sweetheart, Fay (Coleen Gray), and tells her of his plan. She is worried, but Johnny assures her the risks are worth taking. Later that night he has his first meeting with his collaborators and goes over the plans. There is a policeman, Randy Kennan (Ted de Corsia), who owes some gambling debts to the mob and has been warned to pay up. Next is Mike O'Reilly (Joe Sawyer), a bartender at the track who needs money to provide nursing care for his seriously ill wife. And there is George Peatty (Elisha Cook, Jr.) who is servile to his nagging wife, Sherry (Marie Windsor), and her expensive tastes. George is unaware that his wife is having an affair with a petty hoodlum, Val Cannon (Vince Edwards). When Sherry learns that her husband is involved in a big robbery she tells Val hoping the two can somehow get all the money. Johnny also hires two other men for flat fees: part-time wrestler and chess player Kola (Maurice Obokhoff) to start a brawl and pull away the security guards, and Nikki (Timothy Carey) to shoot Red Lightning, the favorite horse in the seventh race, causing another diversion. The robbery is executed perfectly. The stolen money is placed in a laundry bag and tossed out of the window of the payroll office to a waiting Randy who picks it up and puts it in his police patrol car. What no one had foreseen is Val's attempt to rob the gang of the $2 million. There is a bloody end with only Fay and Johnny remaining alive but facing an uncertain future.

The Killing is really Kubrick's debut as the filmmaker we came to know later. A former photographer he had made a short documentary in 1950, *Day of the Fight,* and another in 1951, *Flying Padre.* He also made two features, *Fear and Desire* (1953) and *Killer's Kiss* (1955) on a minuscule budget of $40,000 that he produced, wrote, photographed and edited himself. *The Killing* had a budget of only $320,000, but Kubrick at least managed to get a professional cast. The limited budget is evident. The sets are very small: a one-bedroom apartment, the racetrack offices, the tiny cashier cages and the little locker room. Kubrick compensates for the small sets by shooting from different angels. He got excellent performances from the entire cast, especially Sterling Hayden, Marie Windsor, Elisha Cook, Jr. and Coleen Gray, all underrated actors. What makes the film extraordinary is the decision by Kubrick to tell his story in a nonchronological order. The film starts with the announcement at the racetrack that the seventh race is about to begin, followed by a flashback to a week earlier when the robbers held their first meeting. Thereafter, in a series of complex yet thoroughly coherent flashbacks, we see the role of each of the participants separately, and then the robbery is reshown as it was carried out by the entire gang. *The Killing* established Kubrick as an important young director and, in many ways, is even better than some of his later films.

Kiss Me Kate

1953. 109 min. color. U.S. **Prod.** Jack Cummings; **Dir.** George Sidney; **Scr.** Dorothy Kingsley (based on the play by Cole Porter, Sam Spewack, Bella Spewack from the play *The Taming of the Shrew* by William Shakespeare); **Cin.** Charles Rosher; **Ed.** Ralph E. Winters; **Art D.** Cedric Gibbons, Urie McCleary; **Mus.** Cole Porter; **Mus. Dir.** Andre Previn, Saul Chaplin; **Chor.** Hermes Pan; **Cast:** Kathryn Grayson, Howard Keel, Ann Miller, Tommy Rall, Bobby Van, Keenan Wynn, James Whitmore, Bob Fosse, Ron Randell.

An underrated film, the musical numbers have the wit and charm of a Cole Porter work. The story revolves around the staging of a musical version of *The Taming of the Shrew* and the backstage goings-on in the lives of members of the cast. The dance numbers are beautifully choreographed by Hermes Pan and danced with gusto by Bob Fosse, Tommy Rall, Bobby Van and Ann Miller. The weakness of the film is in the casting of the leads. Kathryn Grayson and Howard Keel are not as good as the stars of the original Broadway production of 1948, Patricia Morison and Alfred Drake. Also, George Sidney's direction is indifferent; Vincent Minnelli would have turned out a better film. But any musical that has songs like "I've Come to Wive It Wealthily in Padua," "Where Is the Life that Late I Led?" (both titles taken from Shakespeare's text) and Ann Miller's rendition of "It's Too Darn Hot" is perforce elevated. The film also has a number, "Brush Up Your Shakespeare," by a couple of gangsters (Keenan Wynn and James Whitmore) that is a showstopper, with lines such as "If you quote a few lines from *Othello*, she will think you're a hell of a fellow"; or, "With the wife of the British ambassador, try a crack out of *Troilus and Cressida*. If she says your behavior is heinous, kick her right in the *Coriolanus*." Shakespeare probably would have approved.

Kiss of Death

1947. 98 min. b.w. U.S. **Prod.** Fred Kohlmar; **Dir.** Henry Hathaway; **Scr.** Ben Hecht, Charles Lederer (based on a story by Eleazar Lipsky); **Cin.** Norbert Brodine; **Ed.** J. Watson Webb; **Art D.** Lyle Wheeler, Leland Fuller; **Mus.** David Buttolph; **Cast:** Victor Mature, Brian Donlevy, Coleen Gray, Richard Widmark, Karl Malden, Taylor Holmes, Mildred Dunnock, Anthony Ross, Millard Mitchell.

Nick Bianco (Victor Mature) comes from a family of criminals. His father had been killed during an attempted robbery, and Nick has grown up like him—a petty hoodlum and thief. He is unemployed and desperately needs money to feed his wife and two little girls. On Christmas Eve, together with two gang members, he robs a jewelry store. He is the only one caught, and sentenced to twenty years. Assistant District Attorney D'Angelo (Brian Donlevy) finds Nick is married with two youngsters and takes pity on him. He offers him parole if he were to name his accomplices. Nick refuses. While in prison he learns that his wife has committed suicide and his two daughters have been placed in an orphanage. Now he is willing to squeal in exchange for parole. D'Angelo has become interested in the higher-ups in the gang, especially Tommy Udo (Richard Widmark), a psychopathic murderer. Nick is told to ingratiate himself with Udo and comes back with a great deal of incriminating information. Udo is indicted, but D'Angelo says the only way to convict him is for Nick to testify at the trial. Nick agrees but the jury acquits Udo and Nick's cover is now blown. In the meanwhile Nick has married Nettie (Coleen Gray) who had been a babysitter employed by his deceased wife and had been in love with him for years. D'Angelo has arranged for Nick to move with Nettie and the children to a house outside the city. Nick is certain Tommy Udo will seek revenge and sooner or later attempt to kill him and his children. The police can't give him protection day and night. In desperation Nick decides to force Udo's hand. Nick is badly wounded but recovers. Udo is caught and this time he will be convicted.

Kiss of Death was one of the great sleepers of the late forties. It is a noirish film that examines the world of petty criminals and is

directed by the underrated Henry Hathaway, who was a forerunner of shooting on actual locations. He had directed *The House on
92nd Street* (1945) in New York City, the locale of the events. He
was able to convince Fox to shoot *Kiss of Death* entirely in New
York, which gave it added realism.

The film introduced a newcomer, Richard Widmark, as
Tommy Udo. He electrified the audience with his high-pitched
voice and hyena laugh. One of the most unsettling scenes in the
evolution of movie violence is when he pushes the elderly
wheelchair-bound mother of an alleged squealer down a long
flight of stairs. Victor Mature had given a fine performance for
Hathaway's friend John Ford in *My Darling Clementine*. Hathaway
chose him for the lead as the petty hoodlum and reluctant
squealer gone straight, and he gives a very moving performance.
Brian Donlevy as the Assistant D.A. and the veteran Taylor
Holmes as the aged shyster are very good. Coleen Gray gives a
beguiling performance, but her sentimental narration at the end
of the film is unnecessary. The film constituted a break with the
gangster movies of the thirties. The gangsters then were megalo-
maniacs after power and money. In *Kiss of Death* they resort to
crime to make a living.

Knife in the Water

Noz w Wodzie. 1962. 94 min. b.w. Polish. **Prod.** Stanislaw Zylewicz; **Dir.** Roman Polan-
ski; **Scr.** Roman Polansky, Jerzy Skolimowski, Jakub Goldberg; **Cin.** Jerzy Lipman; **Ed.**
Halina Prugar; **Mus.** Krzysztof Komeda; **Cast:** Leon Niemczyk, Jolanta Umecka, Zygmunt
Malanowicz.

Andrzej (Leon Niemczyk), a thirty-six-year-old sports writer
and his younger wife Christine (Jolanta Umecka) are traveling by
car to the lake district in Poland to spend the weekend on their
yacht. Out of nowhere a hitchhiker appears on the road. Andrzej
brakes just in time and roundly curses the young man (Zygmunt
Malanowicz) who is nameless throughout the film. The hitchhiker
calmly asks if he can have a ride. Taken aback by the youngster's

self-assured manner, Andrzej impulsively asks him to join them on the boat. Once on board Andrzej attempts to impress the young man with his skills and sailing prowess. He also wants to impress him with his possessions and his social status. The boy reacts blandly, but soon he joins in the game of one-upmanship. His only possession is a switchblade knife and shows his agility and dexterity in its use. He repeatedly plunges the knife into the spaces between his fingers without the knife touching any part of his hand. Christine is an amused onlooker in this battle of egos. She is aware, however, that the exhibition by the two is also intended to impress her. Andrzej, in a fit of annoyance, throws the boy's knife into the lake. The boy attempts to punch Andrzej but is thrown overboard. The boy had said he couldn't swim and the husband and wife are now worried as they see no trace of him. Andrzej leaves the boat to go to the police station and report a possible drowning. The boy who could in fact swim had hidden behind a buoy and comes back on board. Christine dries him and then willingly submits to him. The boy leaves before Andrzej's return. She tells him the boy had not drowned and had come back on the boat. She also tells him she has been unfaithful. The film ends as they drive to a junction, one road leading to the police station and the other to their home. Andrzej is faced with a dilemma. As he is unwilling to believe his wife he must decide whether to confirm a possible drowning to the police or admit sexual humiliation to himself. The last scene shows the couple sitting in the car as Andrzej has not made a choice.

Knife In the Water was Polanski's first film and showed great promise. He has made a lean mystery where very little takes place. The characters are developed and our interest is sustained. As in almost all of Polanski's films the characters are not likeable or sympathetic, whether it be *Repulsion* (1965), *Rosemary's Baby* (1968) or *Chinatown* (1974). The film was nominated for the best foreign language film award.

La Belle Noiseuse

The Beautiful Troublemaker. 1991. 240 min. color. French. **Prod.** Pierre Grise; **Dir.** Jacques Rivette; **Scr.** Jacques Rivette, Christine Laurent, Pascal Bonitzer; **Cin.** William Lubtchansky; **Ed.** Nicole Lubtchansky; **Mus.** Stravinsky; **Cast:** Michel Piccoli, Jane Birkin, Emmanuelle Béart, Marianne Denicourt, David Bursztein.

An unusual and engrossing film on the theme of the artist and the model, it tells the story of a well-known artist (Michel Piccoli) who, for reasons not entirely explained, has not painted in ten years. A beautiful girl (Emmanuelle Béart) who is traveling in the region with her boyfriend inspires him and he begins to work feverishly. It is a long and deliberately slow film that gives an insight into the artist at work. The details of drawing sketch after sketch, the light in the studio, the model's pose and even the configuration of the drawing pens on the table must be in a certain way before he can capture on canvas what he is after. It is one of the very rare films that successfully explores the artistic process, much sharper than *Lust for Life* (1956) or *The Moon and Sixpence* (1942). There are simple repeated scenes of the painter sketching with the only sound being the scratching of the metal-tipped pen against the paper. Both the artist and his muse change during the course of time. The painter's dormant sexual desires for his wife (Jane Birkin) are aroused. The film is well acted by the leads. Rivette, less known than other New Wave directors, was one of the most independent and innovative of the young directors who had worked for *Cahiers du Cinema*, but his films did not find favor with the moviegoing audience.

Lacombe Lucien

1974. 137 min. color. French. **Prod.** Louis Malle; **Dir.** Louis Malle; **Scr.** Louis Malle, Patrick Modiani; **Cin.** Tonino Delli Colli; **Ed.** Suzanne Baron; **Art D.** Ghislain Uhry; **Mus.** performed by Django Reinhardt, André Claveau, Iréne De Trebert; **Cast:** Pierre Blaise, Aurore Clement, Holger Lowenadler, Therese Gieshe, Stephane Bouy.

Set in a city in western France not far from the Spanish border, the film takes place in early spring of 1944, before the Allied landing in Normandy. Seventeen-year-old French peasant boy Lucien (Pierre Blaise) works as a floor mopper in an infirmary. There is nothing remarkable about the boy except his cruelty. Early in the film he is shown killing pigeons with his slingshot, and randomly shooting rabbits. He is aimless and bored and calls on a former teacher whom he knows is active in the Resistance. He offers to join but is told he is too young. His next stop is the headquarters of the French Gestapo where he is welcomed when he reveals the names of Resistance fighters. He is wined and introduced to women who work there. When he takes part in the torture of prisoners, he becomes a trusted agent. Once the Allies land on French soil, the Resistance steps up its raids on German installations, and even the Gestapo headquarters is attacked. Lucien, meanwhile, has fallen in love with France (Aurore Clement), the daughter of a Jewish tailor from Paris who has been hiding under an assumed name. He attempts to save the girl. He kills a German soldier, takes his car and heads to the Spanish border with the girl and her grandmother. Lucien is caught by the Resistance and executed pursuant to a verdict by a tribunal.

This was the first film to deal in depth with the distasteful subject of French collaboration. It gives several portraits of collaborators: a former cycling champion, a third-rate actress, assorted upper-class Frenchmen, and rabid anti-Semites. The film is dispassionate and neutral. There are some vivid characterizations. The Jewish tailor, Albert Horn (Holger Lowenadler), tired of hiding, wants a moment of dignity and goes to the most prominent restaurant in town, knowing that it is frequented by German officers and French Gestapo, and that he will be recognized. In another scene we learn that the Gestapo receives more than two hundred letters a day from people denouncing or informing on each other. The film is a fictionalized account of collaborators that Marcel Ophuls depicted in his great documentary *The Sorrow and the Pity* (1970). Both Pierre Blaise and Aurore Clement were nonprofessionals, but they give very credible performances.

L.A. Confidential

1997. 136 min. color. U.S. **Prod.** Arnon Milchan, Curtis Hanson, Michael Nathanson; **Dir.** Curtis Hanson; **Scr.** Brian Helgeland, Curtis Hanson (based on the novel by James Ellroy); **Cin.** Dante Spinotti; **Ed.** Peter Honess; **Prod. D.** Jeannine Oppewall; **Mus.** Jerry Goldsmith; **Cast:** Kevin Spacey, Russell Crowe, Guy Pearce, James Cromwell, David Strathairn, Kim Basinger, Danny De Vito.

Set in the early fifties, *L.A. Confidential* is the story of corruption and racism in the Los Angeles police department until a few honest cops take a stand. Micky Cohen, a small-time racketeer and former protégé of the slain mobster Bugsy Siegel is now the kingpin of crime in Los Angeles. He and nearly all of his subordinates are put out of the way. A small secret faction in the L.A.P.D. led by the chief of homicide, Captain Dudley Smith (James Cromwell), plots to take over the leaderless crime syndicate. It all begins with a massacre of six people, including a former cop and a call girl in a coffee shop, The Nite Owl. By pure coincidence an honest and dedicated cop, Ed Exley (Guy Pearce), is the first detective to reach the scene of the crime and later becomes the lead investigating officer of the murders. Three black men with criminal records are arrested and it is generally believed that the case has been resolved. As Exley and fellow cops Bud White (Russell Crowe) and Jack Vincennes (Kevin Spacey) pursue the matter, it becomes apparent there is a conspiracy by senior members of the L.A.P.D. to silence them.

There are a number of subplots. There is the operator of an upmarket call girl operation whose girls are look-alikes of movie stars of the day, some helped by plastic surgery. There is the publisher of a scandal magazine *Hush, Hush*, with close connections to the police department. There is also a passionate love affair between Bud White and one of the call girls, a Veronica Lake look-alike, Lyn Bracken (Kim Basinger).

Curtis Hanson, the director who also cowrote the script did a magnificent job of bringing the complicated and convoluted novel of James Ellroy to the screen. *L.A. Confidential* is one of the best mystery/thriller movies of the last two decades. Not since

Chinatown (1974) has there been as well crafted and enjoyable a mystery film. Some eight or nine characters are developed and despite the complicated plot we get all the answers at the end. The excellent photography and set designs capture the color, tone and mood of Los Angeles of the immediate post–World War II years. The acting is most convincing. James Cromwell is as good as any of the movie villains of the thirties and forties. Kevin Spacey, a gifted actor, brings his usual self-confidence and easy charm to his part. Kim Basinger has one of her best roles.

La Dolce Vita

The Sweet Life. 1960. 175 min. b.w. Italian. **Prod.** Giuseppe Amato, Angelo Rizzoli; **Dir.** Federico Fellini; **Scr.** Federico Fellini, Ennio Flaiano, Tullio Pinelli, Brunello Rondi; **Cin.** Otello Martelli; **Ed.** Leo Catozzo; **Art D.** Piero Gherardi; **Mus.** Nino Rota; **Cast:** Marcello Mastroianni, Anita Ekberg, Anouk Aimée, Yvonne Furneaux, Lex Barker, Nadia Gray.

The opening shot is of a helicopter carrying away a statue of Christ suspended by cable. With Christ having abandoned Rome, Fellini shows the moral and spiritual decay of the city through a journey by a young journalist, Marcello Rubini (Marcello Mastroianni). Marcello is a hack who writes for the tabloids—mostly sensational stories, the comings and goings of the upper classes and the escapades of showbiz people. He hopes to be a serious writer, but he is too drawn to and submerged in his current work. In some ten episodes we see Marcello and a wealthy socialite (Anouk Aimée) picking up a prostitute; his obsession with and following a voluptuous Hollywood movie star (Anita Ekberg) until the early hours of the morning with his passions still ungratified; the media hysteria about two children who claim to have seen the Virgin Mary in a field; Marcello arranging for his father to spend a night with a nightclub hostess; and finally Marcello coming across the one and only innocent girl in Rome, with whom he cannot even communicate. This last, incongruous scene runs counter to anything that has passed, and we are led to believe that the amoral tabloid reporter will reform.

The movie has not dated because of some fine cinematography and the eroticism running through the film. The irony is that what Fellini condemns about hedonistic Rome he presents in the most sensual way. At 175 minutes it could have been shortened and one or two episodes and some peripheral characters eliminated. The film belongs to Mastroianni whose career took off after this. He was the everyman who could play diverse roles.

The Lady Eve

1941. 94 min. b.w. U.S. **Prod.** Paul Jones; **Dir.** Preston Sturges; **Scr.** Preston Sturges (based on the story "The Faithful Heart" by Monckton Hoffe); **Cin.** Victor Milner; **Ed.** Stuart Gilmore; **Art D.** Hans Dreier; Ernst Fegte; **Mus.** Sigmund Krumgold; **Cast:** Barbara Stanwick, Henry Fonda, Charles Coburn, Eugene Pallette, William Demarest, Eric Blore, Melville Cooper.

Charles Pike (Henry Fonda) is the scion of a wealthy family that owns a large number of breweries. He is a shy, awkward young man who has spent a year in the jungles of South America looking for unknown species of snakes. He is accompanied by his gruff bodyguard Muggsy (William Demarest). A holiday cruise ship makes an unscheduled stop to pick them up from an island. Every woman on board ship is after Charles, including Jean Harrington (Barbara Stanwick) who professes interest in snakes. Jean soon captivates him and he proposes marriage. Jean, her father "Colonel" Harry Harrington (Charles Coburn) and their supposed butler, Gerald (Melville Cooper), are a team of cardsharps who look for easy prey on cruise ships. They entice Charles who considers himself a good poker player and allow him to win a few hands, then take him to the cleaners. Once he discovers Jean is a con artist and cardsharp, he calls everything off. Jean who has fallen in love with him devises another plan to get him back.

A witty and charming movie. Whereas most of the thirties screwball comedies had dealt with runaway or eccentric heiresses, Sturges fashioned a bright comedy around an eccentric male heir to a fortune. Henry Fonda and the entire supporting cast are excellent. Although *The Lady Eve* is one of the best roles for Barbara Stanwick she falls flat when she tries to put on an English accent over her natural Brooklynese. This was Preston Sturges' third directorial effort and it established him as a rare talent.

The Ladykillers

1955. 90 min. color. British. **Prod.** Michael Balcon; **Dir.** Alexander Mackendrick; **Scr.** William Rose; **Cin.** Otto Heller; **Ed.** Jack Harris; **Art D.** Jim Morahan; **Mus.** Tristam Cary; **Cast:** Alec Guinness, Katie Johnson, Cecil Parker, Herbert Lom, Peter Sellers, Danny Green, Frankie Howerd, Jack Warner, Philip Stainton.

Mrs. Wilberforce (Katie Johnson), a sweet eighty-year-old lady, lives alone with her parrot, General Gordon, in an old house near St. Pancras station. She remembers Queen Victoria's death as it coincided with her twenty-first birthday and she still wears high-neck Victorian garments. Her husband was a sea captain who went down with his ship some thirty years ago. She entertains a few old ladies for a weekly tea party and regularly calls at the local police station for a friendly chat. Her memory isn't what it used to be and she sometimes gets her facts mixed up but she is treated very kindly and the police superintendent listens to all her complaints and tall tales that she has borrowed from popular detective stories. A weird-looking man who calls himself Professor Marcus (Alec Guinness), a music teacher, rents a room that she had advertised. He tells her that four friends will call on him from time to time to practice. They are part of a string quintet. We soon find out they are crooks and would-be bank robbers. The professor's four colleagues are a phony major (Cecil Parker); Louis (Herbert Lom), a more seasoned crook; Harry (Peter Sellers), a plump Teddy boy; and a punch-drunk ex-boxer, One Round (Danny Green). They all come with musical instruments and while plotting their robbery they play a phonograph record of a Boccherini quintet over and over again, which delights Mrs. Wilberforce greatly. The robbery goes smoothly and they place the loot in a trunk which they check at the railroad station and ask the unsuspecting Mrs. Wilberforce to pick up for them. As they are about to leave the house, a cello case full of money falls open. It finally dawns on Mrs. Wilberforce that her tenants are bank robbers. The quintet decides to do away with the old lady but no one has the heart to do the job. While they are deciding each of the robbers meets his death in the most unusual and unforeseen way. Mrs. Wilberforce, who has been left with the loot, goes to the police station. No one believes her story and the superintendent advises her to keep the money.

The Ladykillers was the last of the Ealing Studios comedies, the studio that had introduced a new brand of comedy in the late forties. It is perfectly directed by Alexander Mackendrick who left England for the U.S. to direct his most memorable film Sweet *Smell of Success* (1957). The star of *The Ladykillers* is the eighty-two-year-old Katie Johnson who steals every scene. In the best scene of the film the five robbers have no choice but to accept Mrs. Wilberforce's invitation and attend her weekly tea party with her little old lady friends. Alec Guinness as the mad professor wears grotesque makeup with protruding fang-like teeth. Cecil Parker is good as always and Peter Sellers as an incompetent Teddy boy in one of his early films is fine. Herbert Lom and Danny Green are also perfect in their parts. Despite the unforeseen deaths of the gang there is no violence.

The Lady Vanishes

1938. 97 min. b.w. British. **Prod.** Edward Black; **Dir.** Alfred Hitchcock; **Scr.** Alma Reville, Sidney Gilliat, Frank Launder (based on the novel *The Wheel Spins* by Ethel Lina White); **Cin.** Jack Cox; **Ed.** Alfred Roome, R. E. Dearing; **Art D.** Alex Vetchinsky; **Mus.** Louis Levy; **Cast:** Margaret Lockwood, Michael Redgrave, Paul Lucas, Dame May Whitty, Googie Withers, Cecil Parker, Naunton Wayne, Basil Radford, Linden Travers, Emile Boreo, Mary Clare.

A train going from Eastern Europe westward is stopped by an avalanche. The passengers are stranded and have to spend the night in an overcrowded "third-rate hotel in a third-rate country." The focus of the film is on the six British nationals. There is Iris Henderson (Margaret Lockwood), an heiress on holiday with some young women, returning to England to marry her upper-class fiancé. Gilbert Redman (Michael Redgrave) is a Cambridge musicologist collecting Tyrolean folk songs. Two bachelors on holiday, Caldicott (Naunton Wayne) and Charters (Basil Radford), who by the time they choose to dress formally for dinner find nothing is left for them to eat. Their only concern in the troubled world, when Germany has annexed Austria and Czechoslovakia has been dismembered, is that they will miss a cricket test match in Manchester. There is also a pompous barrister, Eric Todhunter (Cecil Parker) and his mistress, Margaret (Linden Travers). Todhunter is a pacifist who has traveled to Eastern Europe to attend a peace conference. The last and the key character is Miss Froy (Dame May Whitty), a plump matronly spinster who presumably is a governess and interested in the local music. However we later learn she is a spy collecting information on Eastern Europe for the Foreign Office.

Iris befriends Miss Froy and as they are about to reboard the train, a flowerpot intended for Miss Froy lands on her head. At the suggestion of Miss Froy, Iris takes a nap in their crowded compartment. On waking up she finds Miss Froy is gone. Everyone in the compartment denies ever seeing Miss Froy and the woman seated next to her is now a baroness (Mary Clare). Even the two zealous cricket fans who don't want the train to be delayed again deny ever having seen her. The barrister, fearing a scandal, instructs his mistress to deny ever having seen Miss Froy on the train. The only person who assists Iris is Gilbert, the young musicologist, and after a series of unusual twists they find Miss Froy, whose life is in danger. Before she escapes from the train she imparts her secret to Gilbert encoded in a melody that he is to remember and give to the Foreign Office if she does not survive.

Hitchcock teases us and gives only small clues. The first half hour of the film is light comedy, but then the sinister intrigues take over. Most of the film takes place on the train, but Hitchcock opens it up toward the end and as usual introduces several ingenious twists. The performances are uniformly good. This was Redgrave's first film appearance. The comic pair of Naunton Wayne and Basil Radford were utilized in several subsequent

British films. Cecil Parker and Linden Travers appeared together in the best segment of the film *Quartet* (1948). Hitchcock made just one more film in Britain before entering into a contract with Selznick and leaving for the U.S. Only two of his later films were shot in Britain, *Stage Fright* (1950) and *Frenzy* (1972). *The Lady Vanishes* is technically superior to any of his previous films, and with *The 39 Steps* (1935) the most charming and enjoyable of Hitchcock's pre-war films in Britain, both with witty scripts.

Last Holiday

1950. 89 min. b.w. British. **Prod.** Stephen Mitchell, A. D. Peters, J. B. Priestly; **Dir.** Henry Cass. **Scr.** J. B. Priestley; **Cin.** Ray Elton; **Mus.** Francis Chagrin; **Cast:** Alec Guinness, Beatrice Campbell, Kay Walsh, Bernard Lee, Wilfrid Hyde-White, Sidney James, Ernest Thesiger.

A nondescript clerk is told he has no more than six weeks to live. He decides to go out in style. He buys a couple of Saville Row suits and checks in at a posh resort hotel. With no need to put on a front and not bothered by the concerns of ordinary people, he finds happiness, success and even love. Equally important he has a liberating effect on other guests. An underrated film, it has a lovely performance by Alec Guinness and a great cast of British professionals. Much of the melancholy is ameliorated by some humorous scenes. What slightly mars the film is a maudlin musical theme played throughout by a blind street violinist.

The Last Hurrah

1958. 121 min. b.w. U.S. **Prod.** John Ford; **Dir.** John Ford; **Scr.** Frank S. Nugent (based on the novel by Edwin O'Connor); **Cin.** Charles Lawton, Jr.; **Ed.** Jack Murray; **Art D.** Robert Peterson; **Cast:** Spencer Tracy, Jeffrey Hunter, Dianne Foster, Basil Rathbone, Pat O'Brien, Donald Crisp, James Gleason, Ed Brophy, John Carradine, Frank McHugh, Jane Darwell, Arthur Walsh, O. Z. Whitehead, Basil Ruysdael, Ricardo Cortez, Anna Lee.

The Last Hurrah is the story of the last campaign of Frank Skeffington (Spencer Tracy), a four-term mayor of an unidentified city which is unmistakably Boston. He is now seeking an unprecedented fifth term. Skeffington owes his success to taking care of the base of his support, largely Irish Americans. This base, however, has dwindled over the years as many have become afflu-ent and their political loyalties have shifted. His opponent is a nincompoop who has almost nothing to say. He is relying only on TV advertising, which has become a major factor in political cam-paigns. Skeffington wages an old-fashioned personal campaign. He loses the election and shortly thereafter dies of a heart attack.

The novel by Edwin O'Connor, on which the film is based, took its inspiration from the last mayoral campaign of James M. Curley of Boston. Spencer Tracy is ideal for the lead role and gives one of his very best performances. The novel is rich in local charac-ters as well. John Ford's decision to keep most of these characters brings a great deal of charm and humor to the film. He chose some of the finest character actors in Hollywood. The film is also distin-guished by the work of the experienced cinematographer, Charles Lawton, Jr.. *The Last Hurrah* is a commentary on old-style politi-cians who held office in most of the large cities of the northeast. Some were rogues, but they ran an efficient city hall and tended well to the needs of their constituents. The Anglican bishop, played by Basil Ruysdael, comments, "I prefer an engaging rogue to a complete fool." Ford's sympathies are clearly with Skeffington and his crowd. They are shown in a much better light than the privi-leged WASPs of Boston. The film's only blemish lies in the excess of sentimentality common to much of John Ford's work.

The Last Picture Show

1971. 118 min. b.w. U.S. **Prod.** Stephen Friedman; **Dir.** Peter Bogdanovich; **Scr.** Peter Bogdanovich, Larry McMurtry (based on the novel by Larry McMurtry); **Cin.** Robert Sur-tees; **Ed.** Donn Cambern; **Prod. D.** Polly Platt; **Art D.** Walter Scott Herndon; **Mus.** contemporary recordings; **Cast:** Timothy Bottoms, Jeff Bridges, Ben Johnson, Cloris Leach-man, Ellen Burstyn, Cybill Shepherd, Eileen Brennan, Sam Bottoms, Sharon Taggart.

The Last Picture Show is set in a small town in north Texas. It is the story of two boys, Sonny Crawford (Timothy Bottoms) and Duane

Johnson (Jeff Bridges); an aging man, Sam "the Lion" (Ben Johnson); and the three women in their lives. The boys are seniors at the local high school and stars of the football team. They are best friends, though with totally different personalities. Sonny is introspective and withdrawn. Duane is outgoing and aggressive. Sonny is going steady with Jacy Farrow (Cybill Shepherd), a spoiled girl who is eager to lose her virginity and be different from other girls of her age. Her mother, Lois Farrow (Ellen Burstyn), is married to the richest man in town and wants her daughter also to find someone of means. Lois had been in love with Sam, but chose to marry wealth. Sam is both a father figure and role model for the two boys. He owns the only fun places in town: the movie house, the pool hall and the all-night diner. As the story unfolds, Sonny and Jacy separate and Duane takes up with Jacy. Sonny becomes involved with the sex-starved wife of his high-school football coach. By the end of the film, Sam dies of a stroke, and the two boys are called for military service and sent to Korea.

The film is far from a soap opera. It bears no resemblance to the usual Hollywood exploitation movies that expose the dark secrets of a town. It is set in a bleak town with a flat landscape and only a small brook on its outskirts. Although it is a nostalgic look at the late forties and early fifties, it is free of sentimentality. The problems of adolescence and growing up are honestly presented. A difficult movie for the sheer number of people in the story, and Bogdanovich ably develops some seven diverse characters. The acting is uniformly good. Ben Johnson, Cloris Leachman, Ellen Burstyn and Eileen Brennan stand out. *The Last Picture Show* is Bogdanovich's second and finest film, and has not dated. Bogdanovich pays homage to Howard Hawks by having *Red River* as the final "show" at the local movie house, which is scheduled to close down.

L'Atalante

1934. 89 min. b.w. French. **Prod.** Jacques-Louis Nounez; **Dir.** Jean Vigo; **Scr.** Jean Vigo, Albert Riera (based on a scenario by R. de Guichen); **Cin.** Boris Kaufman, Louis Berger; **Ed.** Louis Chavance; **Mus.** Maurice Jaubert; **Cast:** Michel Simon, Dita Parlo, Jean Daste, Gilles Margaritis, Louis Lefebvre.

Jean (Jean Daste) is the captain of the barge *L'Atalante* which travels the river Seine carrying goods and raw materials. The film begins with his wedding. He marries a beautiful village girl, Juliette (Dita Parlo), who has never left her home. Immediately after the ceremony bride and groom board the barge. He takes her to his quarters and wants to make love. She runs away frightened and embarrassed but comes back and yields. She washes his clothes which haven't been washed for several months. She also washes the clothes of the sailor Pere Jules (Michel Simon) and the cabin boy (Louis Lefebvre). Next morning Pere Jules and the cabin boy sing for Jean and Juliette's wake-up call. She is now radiant and makes herself useful by cleaning the decks and the kitchen. Juliette longs to see Paris and is glued to the Paris radio station. Once they reach the city, Jean takes her sightseeing and to a café. A peddler makes a play for her and dances with her. Jean is upset and takes her back to the barge. She is hurt, refuses to talk and feigns sleep. He is now more upset and leaves the boat. Later she sneaks away and is mesmerized by the lights and shops. A thief steals her purse and by the time she comes back Jean has ordered the barge to sail away. Jean then realizes what he has done. He searches for her and finally Pere Jules finds her in Le Havre at a phonograph record shop working as a clerk. Jean and Juliette are reunited.

L'Atalante is a very simple story. It is a tale of love lost and love found. Jean Vigo, the son of a well-known French anarchist, died of leukemia before he could complete the editing of the film. He was twenty-nine years old and had suffered from tuberculosis most of his life. He made four films but *L'Atalante* is his only feature length film. In his short career he showed a mastery of the art. In *L'Atalante* his blending of lyricism with surrealism leaves one with a glimpse of what he could have accomplished had he lived. There are some scenes of stunning beauty. Michel Simon, whose career stretched over fifty years in French cinema, takes acting honors. His portrayal of Pere Jules, the good-hearted, well-traveled sailor whose body is a mass of tattoos and who has collected the oddest souvenirs, is masterful. Dita Parlo as Juliette is also excellent. The film is beautifully photographed by Vigo's friend Boris Kaufman who worked with Vigo in all of his four films and years later worked with directors of the caliber of Kazan in *On the Waterfront* (1954) and Sidney Lumet in *12 Angry Men* (1957). The film has a beautiful score by Maurice Jaubert that is leisurely while on the barge with the tempo picking up when they reach Paris.

Laura

1944. 85 min. b.w. U.S. **Prod.** Otto Preminger. **Dir.** Otto Preminger; **Scr.** Jay Dratler, Betty Reinhardt, Samuel Hoffenstein (based on the novel by Vera Caspary); **Cin.** Joseph La Shelle; **Ed.** Louis Loeffler; **Prod. D.** Thomas Little, Paul S. Fox. **Art D.** Lyle Wheeler, Leland Fuller; **Mus.** David Raksin; **Cast:** Gene Tierney, Dana Andrews, Clifton Webb, Vincent Price, Judith Anderson.

On a Friday night Laura Hunt (Gene Tierney), a beautiful advertising executive, is found murdered in her apartment, shot in the face with a shotgun. She is identified only by the robe she is wearing. Homicide detective Mark McPherson (Dana Andrews) has been assigned to investigate the case. The murder weapon cannot be found, but there are three prime suspects. One is Waldo Lydecker (Clifton Webb), a widely read influential society columnist who had discovered Laura when she was a draftswoman in a fashion house. Lydecker had praised her in his columns and by the time of her murder she had become an important voice in the fashion world. She had also become a constant companion of Lydecker, who liked to be seen with beautiful women. Lydecker is impotent, which makes him resentful of any man who even tries to befriend his companions. The second suspect is Shelby Carpenter (Vincent Price), a money-hungry gigolo whose engagement to Laura had been broken off just prior to her murder. He is also carrying on with Laura's aunt, Ann Treadwell (Judith Anderson), a wealthy middle-aged woman who has been supporting him for some time. Ann Treadwell herself is a suspect and may have killed Laura out of jealousy. After a round of questioning, McPherson returns to Laura's apartment to further check for clues. He becomes infatuated with Laura's portrait and while sitting and studying it dozes off. He is awakened by Laura entering the room. She appears to him to be an apparition. She had been away for the weekend and the woman killed was a model, Dianah Redfern, another woman with whom Carpenter had been having an affair. He had given her the key to Laura's apartment knowing Laura would be away. In time McPherson finds the murder weapon and knows the identity of the murderer.

A well-crafted film that moves at a deliberately slow pace that adds to the mounting suspense throughout. It is shot entirely indoors, hence there is great regard for lighting and detail. The camera examines every room, the carpets, the curtains and the furniture, which indicate the status of the owner. Characters are also developed slowly. McPherson, an ordinary policeman who classifies all females as dames or dolls, is awkward with them. He falls in love with the portrait of a woman who is dead. He is envious of men who have a way with women and punches Shelby Carpenter in the stomach for no apparent reason. The more complex character, Lydecker, could have been explored further. In the novel by Vera Caspary he is described as impotent and a crypto-homosexual which the film only hints at. Acting honors go to Clifton Webb, Dana Andrews and Judith Anderson. Gene Tierney's beauty and presence is enough to carry her role. Vincent Price is miscast. The theme music for *Laura* is a beautiful and haunting melody by David Raksin. The film was to be directed by Rouben Mamoulian who was fired by Fox head Daryl Zanuck. Preminger took over, reshot Mamoulian's footage and replaced the cinematographer Lucian Ballard with Joseph La Shelle who won an Academy Award.

The Lavender Hill Mob

1951. 82 min. b.w. British. **Prod.** Michael Balcon, Michael Truman; **Dir.** Charles Crichton; **Scr.** T. E. B. Clarke; **Cin.** Douglas Slocombe; **Ed.** Seth Holt; **Art D.** William Kellner; **Mus.** Georges Auric; **Cast:** Alec Guinness, Stanley Holloway, Sidney James, Alfie Bass, John Gregson, Marjorie Fielding, Edie Martin.

Henry Holland (Alec Guinness) is a timid and withdrawn man who has worked for a bank in a lowly position for a number of years. His primary duty is to escort gold bullion, in an armored car with two armed guards from the refineries, to the vaults of the Bank of England. When he is offered a promotion he refuses, prompting the bank manager to tell him, "The trouble with you, Holland, is that you haven't enough ambition." What no one could have imagined is that Henry Holland been considering for years of how easy it would be to hijack the armored car. What has stopped him is the difficulty of disposing the gold bars. When he meets a new neighbor, Mr. Pendlebury (Stanley Holloway), a friendly and cheerful sort who makes paperweights, Holland knows his solution is at hand. In one of the best scenes of the movie, he slowly and indirectly proposes a scheme to get the gold out of the country. Pendlebury will melt down the gold and make paperweights in the shape of Eiffel Towers to be exported to France. The plan is set in motion. They recruit two inept burglars (Sidney James and Alfie Bass), and the Lavender Hill mob is formed. Everything goes wrong in the robbery, but they are nevertheless successful. Holland is deliberately roughed up by his cohorts and he emerges as a hero. When they go to Paris to get possession of the Eiffel Towers they discover a few of the paperweights have been sold to visiting English schoolgirls, and trouble begins.

The first three-quarters of the movie is one of the most original and funniest of comedies. The last segment, which consists of attempts to retrieve the sold pieces, becomes cops and robbers and slightly falls off. The entire cast is magnificent and Alec Guinness was firmly established after making two superb comedies in 1951, the other being *The Man in the White Suit*. Charles Crichton, the director, gave us another highly enjoyable film, *The Titfield Thunderbolt* (1953), a classic Ealing Studios comedy.

L'Avventura

1960. 145 min. b.w. Italian. **Prod.** Amato Pennasilico; **Dir.** Michelangelo Antonioni; **Scr.** Michelangelo Antonioni, Elio Bartolini, Tonino Guerra; **Cin.** Aldo Scavarda; **Ed.** Eraldo da Roma; **Art D.** Piero Poletto; **Mus.** Giovanni Fusco; **Cast:** Monica Vitti, Gabriele Ferzetti, Lea Massari, Dominique Blanchar.

A group of well-to-do Italians have planned a yachting trip to a small island off the coast of Sicily. In the group are Anna (Lea Massari), her best friend Claudia (Monica Vitti) and Anna's lover Sandro (Gabriele Ferzetti), an architect. Anna has refused to marry Sandro for unexplained reasons. We later learn that Sandro is a philanderer incapable of loyalty toward any woman. They reach a desolate volcanic island and go sightseeing. When they are about to leave, Anna cannot be found. They begin a search for her. Sandro and Claudia together look in every corner of the island, but there is no trace of her. Police rescue squads from Sicily join in the futile search. The police conclude that she may have fallen accidentally to her death, the waves carrying her far from the island. They don't rule out suicide or kidnapping by a band of smugglers who had been seen around the island. While searching for Anna, Sandro begins to pursue Claudia and they soon become lovers. In Sicily they continue meaningless enquiries. They stay at a large cavernous hotel. Claudia falls asleep exhausted. She awakens in the early hours of the morning and realizes Sandro has been away all night. She frantically comes down to the lobby and searches for him. She finds him making love with a prostitute in the isolated lobby. Claudia runs hysterically through the streets. Sandro pays the pickup and pursues Claudia finally catching up in a park. He sits on a bench and cries inconsolably. Claudia gently puts her hands on his head and the film ends with a close-up of her hands comforting him. Claudia has understood and accepted him as he is.

L'Avventura is the best of the trilogy of films made by Antonioni in the early sixties, which includes *La Notte* (1961) and *L'Eclisse* (1962). Most of his films are virtually plotless. His cynical and alienated characters are unable to communicate with each other and there is a prevailing sense of despair. They are revealed more by sustained close-ups than through dialogue. Antonioni's films appear deliberately slow and *L'Avventura* at 145 minutes is no exception, but the suspense and mystery is sustained. There is good use of natural sound and the breaking of the waves is used to great effect.

Les Diaboliques

The Fiends. 1955. 114 min. b.w. French. **Prod.** Henri-Georges Clouzot; **Dir.** Henri-Georges Clouzot; **Scr.** Henri-Georges Clouzot, Jerome Geronimi, Frederic Grendel, Rene Masson (based on the novel *Celle Qui N'etait Pas* by Pierre Boileau, Thomas Narcejac); **Cin.** Armand Thirard; **Ed.** Madeleine Gug; **Art D.** Leon Barsacq; **Mus.** Georges Van Parys; **Cast:** Simone Signoret, Vera Clouzot, Paul Meurisse, Charles Vanel.

Michel Delasalle (Paul Meurisse) is the sadistic headmaster of a provincial French boarding school for boys. He operates the run-down school as his personal fiefdom. The school is owned and financed by his well-to-do wife, Christina (Vera Clouzot), who has a history of heart problems. She is treated as an abused servant by her husband. Nicole Horner (Simone Signoret) is a teacher at the school and Michel's mistress. When the film opens, Michel has broken off the relationship. The two women devise a plan to poison and drown him, and dump the corpse in the school swimming pool. A few days later, when the pool is drained for cleaning, no corpse is found. To add to the mystery, one of the students swears he has seen the headmaster. The tension becomes too much for the women, especially Christina and her weak heart.

The setting establishes the ominous story: a run-down school and a dirty swimming pool. The last twenty minutes of the film are a masterpiece of suspense that has seldom been equaled. The acting of Simone Signoret, Vera Clouzot and Charles Vanel, playing a retired police detective, is uniformly good. The film is based on a mediocre novel by Pierre Boileau and Thomas Narcejac, who later wrote the story that became the basis of Hitchcock's *Vertigo* (1958). A similar earlier film, *Conflict* (1945) with Humphrey Bogart, is too contrived to be of any note.

Les Enfants du Paradis

Children of Paradise. 1945. 145 min. b.w. French **Prod.** Fred Orain, Raymond Borderie; **Dir.** Marcel Carne; **Scr.** Jacques Prévert; **Cin.** Roger Hubert; **Art D.** Alexander Trauner, Leon Barsacq, Raymond Gabutti; **Mus.** Joseph Kosma, Maurice Thiriet; **Cast:** Jean-Louis Barrault, Arletty, Pierre Brasseur, Marcel Herrand, Pierre Renoir, Etienne Decroux, Louis Salou, Albert Remy, Maria Casares.

The film begins in the 1820s. Garrance (Arletty), a beautiful and elegant woman, had been raised in poverty but through a succession of lovers has made her life comfortable while intensely guarding her independence. She is taking a walk with her lover, Lacenaire (Marcel Herrand), a petty thief, along Boulevard du Temple, and they stop to watch Baptiste (Jean-Louis Barrault), a mime, performing outside the theater Funambules. In one of the best scenes there is a disturbance in the crowd of spectators. Lacenaire has picked the pocket of a corpulent gentleman and Garrance is suspected. Baptiste mimes a reenactment of the crime and suspicion is lifted from Garrance. A strange brooding love begins between the two, which is the main thread of the story. Baptiste is poor and lives in an attic. Garrance goes there and offers herself to him, but Baptiste, wanting to preserve his image of a "perfect" woman, does not take her. Several years pass. Baptiste is the most famous mime in France. He has married Natalie (Maria Casares), an actress, and they have a young son. Garrance has had a love affair with Frederick Lemaitre (Pierre Brasseur) who had lived in the same tenement as Baptiste and has become a great tragedian and the first actor of France. She is now the mistress of an icy cold, passionless count (Louis Salou), but still yearns for Baptiste. Lacenaire has also risen in the world. He is no longer a petty thief but a high-class swindler and blackmailer. He is jealous of Garrance's relationship with the count and murders him in a memorable scene in a Turkish bath. Garrance offers herself once more to Baptiste, but it is a doomed relationship.

The film is basically a homage to nineteenth-century French theater and the actors of the period. It has a complex structure with several subplots and a play within a play. The character of

Baptiste is based on Debureau, the greatest mime of the nine-teenth century. Shooting began in late summer of 1943 and completed when Paris was still under German occupation. The release was timed so that it would be the first film to premiere when Paris was liberated. It was also the most expensive French film to that date, the cost being FF 60 million ($1.2 million). The art director, Alexander Trauner, added much to the film with his set designs and re-creation of nineteenth-century Paris. The cast includes the cream of French theater and film: Pierre Brasseur, one of the great French actors seldom seen in films, Arletty, Marcel Herrand and Jean-Louis Barrault, the greatest mime of the twentieth century. The term "children of paradise" refers to the poor people who sat in the uppermost balcony of theaters along Boulevard du Temple and hence were closer to heaven. Marcel Carne, a well-known French director in the thirties and forties, is now mostly remembered for only two films: *Le Jour se Leve* (1939) and *Les Enfants du Paradis.*

A Letter to Three Wives

1948. 103 min. b.w. U.S. **Prod.** Sol C. Siegel; **Dir.** Joseph L. Mankiewicz; **Scr.** Joseph L. Mankiewicz, Vera Caspary; **Cin.** Arthur Miller; **Ed.** J. Watson Webb; **Art D.** Lyle Wheeler; **Mus.** Alfred Newman; **Cast:** Jeanne Crain, Linda Darnell, Ann Sothern, Kirk Douglas, Paul Douglas, Jeffrey Lynn, Barbara Lawrence, Florence Bates, Thelma Ritter, Connie Gilchrist, Hobart Cavanaugh, Celeste Holm as the voice of the letter writer (Addie Ross).

The film begins with an effective shot as the camera pans an affluent suburb of New York City along the Hudson River with its stately homes. We hear the off-screen voice of Addie Ross (Celeste Holm) telling us she has written a letter to three wives whom she had known well, saying that by the end of that day one of their husbands will not be home as he has run away with her. The three wives are about to board a steamer on a river trip as chaperons for a group of youngsters when the letters are delivered by messenger. They board the steamer, each believing that it is her husband who has left. We then get flashbacks that examine the state of the marriage of each wife.

Deborah Bishop (Jeanne Crain) is married to Brad Bishop (Jeffrey Lynn), the scion of a prominent and wealthy family in the valley. They met when she was a navy Wave and Brad an officer. Deborah comes from an average family and felt uncomfortable marrying someone above her class. Her insecurity had been heightened when they came to Brad's hometown and she had to mix with the country club set. Lora May Finney (Linda Darnell) comes from a poor family. A very attractive girl, she lived with her mother near the railroad tracks. She worked as a salesgirl at the Hollingsway department store and was dated by Porter Hollingsway (Paul Douglas), the wealthy owner of a chain of stores. She refused to sleep with him unless they were married. Porter relented and married her. Porter is still suspicious that Lora May married him for his money and may one day leave him. Rita (Ann Sothern), a radio scriptwriter, is married to George Phipps (Kirk Douglas) who is a high-school English teacher. She is a self-assured girl who makes much more money than her husband. She has pushed him to leave teaching and write soap operas. He resents her aggressiveness and has no intention to abandon teaching. Each wife has reason to believe it is her husband who has left with Addie. The flashbacks end and it is only in the final scene that we learn who has left and whether any of the three wives has been a loser.

The film is a well-written examination of three marriages, with a great deal of humor. Joseph Mankiewicz has fashioned a witty and absorbing script. Although Addie never appears, we form a well-rounded opinion of her charm and character. The acting of the two Douglases stand out. Darnell's mother, played by Connie Gilchrist, and her best friend, the great Thelma Ritter, make an excellent comedy team. The film won Academy Awards for best director and screenplay, and a nomination for best picture.

The Life and Death of Colonel Blimp

1943. 163 min. color. British. **Prod.** Michael Powell, Emeric Pressburger; **Dir.** Michael Powell; **Scr.** Michael Powell, Emeric Pressburger; **Cin.** Jack Cardiff, Georges Perinal; **Ed.** John Seabourne, **Art D.** Alfred Junge; **Mus.** Allan Gray; **Cast:** Roger Livesey, Deborah Kerr, Anton Walbrook, Roland Carver, James McKechnie, Albert Lieven.

The film covers the life and career of Clive Candy (Roger Livesey), a decent, good-hearted but stodgy British officer, from his youth in 1902 to old age in 1943. We first see him in the Boer War where he won a Victoria Cross for exceptional bravery. There are segments dealing with his career in World War I and now in World War II he is in the Home Guard. During the inter-war years he had met and befriended Theo Kretschmar-Schuldorff (Anton Walbrook). They dueled on a point of honor and Candy had lost the girl he loved to Kretschmar-Schuldorff. However, their friendship endured. Kretschmar-Schuldorff had been against the Nazis and in 1939 on the eve of World War II had sought asylum in England. They meet again and their friendship is renewed. Kretschmar-Schuldorff warns Candy that the coming war will be different from past wars. The Nazis will use any means to further their goals and England must be ready to answer accordingly. Candy argues with his friend and can't condone a fight using the enemy's methods. He has to hold on to his belief that one must fight honorably and it is better to lose the war than descend to the level of the barbaric Nazis.

A very generous and exceedingly low-key wartime propaganda film which made it even more effective. It is a nostalgic look at Britain and the honor of Englishmen. It is also saying in 1943 when the war was far from over that the German people are decent. It is the Hitlers who have corrupted them. There is excellent acting by the three leads. Deborah Kerr plays three women in Candy's life, each from a different period. Powell and Pressburger are known for their original and unconventional films. From the forties onward they produced, directed and wrote screenplays for a series of remarkable films: *I Know Where I'm Going* (1945), *Stairway to Heaven* (1946) and *Black Narcissus*

(1947). Colonel Blimp is a sympathetic character created by the cartoonist David Lowe in the *London Evening Standard*. He typified the good-hearted but bumbling and blundering British officer. Powell and Pressburger made the Blimp/Candy character so believable and amusing that Winston Churchill ordered the film withdrawn from exhibition. Later, the Ministry of Information lifted the ban and the film was shown in Great Britain; however, it was not allowed to be exported to the U.S. for the duration of the war. When it finally reached the U.S. it was butchered by distributors and cut from 163 minutes to 93 minutes. A 1986 restored version is now available.

Lifeboat

1944. 96 min. b.w. U.S. **Prod.** Kenneth MacGowen; **Dir.** Alfred Hitchcock; **Scr.** Jo Swerling (based on the story by John Steinbeck); **Cin.** Glen MacWilliams; **Ed.** Dorothy Spencer; **Art D.** James Basevi, Maurice Ransford; **Mus.** Hugo Friedhofer; **Cast:** Tallulah Bankhead, William Bendix, Walter Slezak, John Hodiak, Henry Hull, Hume Cronyn, Mary Anderson, Heather Angel, Canada Lee.

A U-boat has sunk a freighter in the Atlantic and the survivors are on a small, crowded lifeboat. They are Connie Porter (Tallulah Bankhead), a chic and sophisticated journalist; Rittenhouse (Henry Hull), an industrial tycoon; Gus (William Bendix), a wounded stoker whose gangrenous leg poses a serious threat to his life; Kovak (John Hodiak), an articulate and socially conscious seaman; Stanley Garrett (Hume Cronyn), the radio operator on the ill-fated freighter; Alice (Mary Anderson), a nurse; Joe (Canada Lee), a black steward; and Mrs. Higgins (Heather Angel), a mother in shock who is clutching her dead infant. The U-boat that had torpedoed the freighter is in turn sunk by an Allied ship and a lone survivor (Walter Slezak) is taken aboard the lifeboat. The devious German pretends he cannot speak English and does not tell the rest he was the captain of the U-boat or that he has a compass. An experienced seaman and a surgeon in civilian life he soon becomes the dominating person and the navigator of the lifeboat. Instead of heading for land he steers to a location where a German supply ship has anchored. He saves Gus's life by amputating his gangrenous leg. But later in the journey when Gus sees him stealing some of the rationed food and water in the middle of the night, the German throws him overboard and explains that Gus had committed suicide. Through several incidents the survivors learn the truth and in a very ugly scene beat him senseless and throw him overboard. The industrial tycoon who had been the most sympathetic to the German is one of the leaders of the attack. He continues beating him with his shoe when the German is in the water. The only person who does not take part is Joe who has seen enough violence and lynching.

The inhabitants of the lifeboat are a microcosm of the Allies who are torn by differences while the German is single-minded. A very strange film that is not just anti-Nazi but also runs down democracy and argues for one united front in wartime with no dissension. Hitchcock's reputation in 1944 was in decline. He was offered to do *Lifeboat* which was difficult both for its theme and confined setting. It is amazing how he overcame the technical difficulties of a film entirely confined to a lifeboat. He did a credible job and even infused the film with action and suspense. The acting is fine all around, but it is Tallulah Bankhead's film. She essentially plays two roles: the fashionable superior journalist and, by the end of the film, a woman stripped of all arrogance and fake persona who may even become involved with the common sailor Kovak.

The Life of Emile Zola

1937. 116 min. b.w. U.S. **Prod.** Henry Blanke; **Dir.** William Dieterle; **Scr.** Norman Reilly Raine, Heinz Herald, Geza Herczeg; **Cin.** Tony Gaudio; **Ed.** Warren Low; **Art D.** Anton Grot; **Mus.** Max Steiner; **Cast:** Paul Muni, Gale Sondergaard, Joseph Schildkraut, Donald Crisp, Morris Carnovsky, Louis Calhern, Harry Davenport, Gloria Holden, Erin O'Brien-Moore, Henry O'Neill, Vladimir Sokoloff.

The film begins with Zola (Paul Muni) as a struggling young writer living in an unheated attic with Paul Cezanne (Vladimir Sokoloff). Zola's last published book had not been well received by the establishment as it deals with issues of social injustice and the plight of workers. His first success is *Nana*, about the sordid life of a prostitute (Erin O'Brien-Moore) and the conditions that forced her to choose such a life. He is visited by Lucie Dreyfus (Gale Sondergaard), wife of Captain Alfred Dreyfus (Joseph Schildkraut) who has been wrongly convicted of treason and sentenced to life imprisonment on Devil's Island. Dreyfus had been chosen by a cabal of military officers as a scapegoat when, in fact, it had been a Captain Esterhazi who had sold military secrets to Germany. With the help of fellow writers, most notably Anatole France (Morris Carnovsky), Zola begins a campaign for judicial review of the case. In 1898 he publishes "J'accuse," an open letter to the president of the Republic, setting forth the facts, the miscarriage of justice, and demanding the release and rehabilitation of the wrongly imprisoned Dreyfus. Dreyfus is freed and cleared of all charges. Zola, fearing for his life, flees to England. When he is given assurances of safety, he returns to Paris where he dies of carbon monoxide poisoning from a blocked chimney. The film ends with Anatole France giving his famous oration at the bier, "A Moment in the Consciousness of Man."

The Warner studio was known for producing biographies of notables, mostly played by Paul Muni: *The Story of Louis Pasteur* (1936) and *Juarez* (1939). *The Life of Emile Zola* is the best of the three. It has Muni's best acting and an accurate and literate screenplay, devoid of effusive praise, leaving it to the viewer to measure the stature of the writer, Emile Zola. The film is too cautious, however. There is no reference to Dreyfus being a Jew, and ignores the political climate of France and the rabid anti-Semitism in the military and the establishment that led to the selection of Dreyfus as the scapegoat. The film received Academy Awards for best picture (the first for a Warner Bros. film), best supporting actor (Joseph Schildkraut), and best screenplay and nominations for best actor, director, score and art direction, among others. These biopictures, in addition to being intelligent and very well made, performed an important function: they introduced the isolationist American audiences of the thirties to European history.

The Lion in Winter

1968. 135 min. color. British. **Prod.** Martin Poll; **Dir.** Anthony Harvey; **Scr.** James Gold-man (based on his play); **Cin.** Douglas Slocombe; **Ed.** John Bloom; **Art D.** Peter Murton, Gilbert Margerie; **Mus.** John Barry; **Cast:** Peter O'Toole, Katharine Hepburn, Jane Merrow, Anthony Hopkins, Timothy Dalton, John Castle, Nigel Stock, Nigel Terry.

This English historical drama is about King Henry II (Peter O'Toole), his three sons (John Castle, Nigel Terry, Anthony Hopkins) and his queen (Katharine Hepburn), all jockeying for power. It is enjoyable for the sharp characterizations of the manipulative queen, the shrewd king and the ungrateful, ambitious sons. Anthony Hopkins as the future King Richard the Lion-heart in an excellent portrayal shows him to be dull-witted. Nigel Terry is devious as the future King John. The acting of Hepburn and O'Toole is outstanding, and Katharine Hepburn was the first actress to win a third best actress award.

Local Hero

1983. 111 min. color. British. **Prod.** David Puttnam; **Dir.** Bill Forsyth; **Scr.** Bill Forsyth; **Cin.** Chris Menges; **Ed.** Michael Bradsell; **Prod. D.** Roger Murray-Leach; **Art D.** Richard James, Adrienne Atkinson, Frank Walsh, Ian Watson; **Mus.** Mark Knopfler; **Cast:** Burt Lancaster, Peter Riegert, Fulton Mackay, Denis Lawson, Norman Chancer, Peter Capaldi, Jenny Seagrove.

This is a film that reminds one of the golden age of British comedies. It has its share of eccentric characters as in *The Lavender Hill Mob* (1951) and a lyrical beauty in the mold of *I Know Where I'm Going* (1945). It tells the story of an ambitious Texas-based oil executive, MacIntyre (Peter Riegert), who is sent by the chairman of the board, Felix Happer (Burt Lancaster), to Ferness, a village in Scotland. He is to buy the entire village and the surrounding area for an oil refinery site. The twist is that all the residents are more than happy to sell their land and homes if the price is right and couldn't care less if their beautiful surroundings are ruined. Mac has been sent to Scotland because of his name, but his ancestry is not Scottish. He is the son of Hungarian immigrants who chose the name MacIntyre as it sounded more "American." Mr. Happer, the all-powerful chairman of the board, has to make a visit to the idyllic village and there is an unexpected ending to the film.

The film is more about Mac, whose life is turned around by the discovery of his Shangri-la. Peter Riegert, a fine, intelligent actor, has his best role. Burt Lancaster's role is limited, but his presence is felt in his few scenes, although there is too much dwelling on his psychological problems. The British cast is uniformly excellent, and there is beautiful photography of Scotland.

The Long Voyage Home

1940. 105 min. b.w. U.S. **Prod.** Walter Wanger; **Dir.** John Ford; **Scr.** Dudley Nichols (based on the plays *The Moon of the Caribbees, In the Zone, Bound East for Cardiff, The Long Voyage Home* by Eugene O'Neill); **Cin.** Gregg Toland; **Ed.** Sherman Todd; **Art D.** James Basevi; **Mus.** Richard Hageman; **Cast:** John Wayne, Thomas Mitchell, Ian Hunter, Ward Bond, Barry Fitzgerald, Wilfrid Lawson, Mildred Natwick, John Qualen, Arthur Shields.

This is the story of merchant seamen aboard the British freighter *Glencairn* during the early days of World War II. The film in essence is in two parts, but John Ford has given it a thematic unity. It begins when the *Glencairn* is about to leave an island in the West Indies after its crew has enjoyed a night of shore leave. The ship then heads for Baltimore to pick up a shipment of high explosives for delivery to a port in Britain. After a hazardous journey during which they are attacked by a German plane and lose two of their mates, the vessel reaches its destination and delivers the cargo. The second part of the film concerns Ole Olsen (John Wayne), a hard-working, good-natured Swede who had signed on to make enough money to buy a small farm in Sweden and raise a family. He is drugged and carried to another ship, the *Amindra*. His shipmates find out and rescue him at the cost of losing their leader, Driscoll (Thomas Mitchell), to the *Amindra*.

The film is based on four one-act plays by Eugene O'Neill, which were very ably adapted for the screen by scriptwriter Dudley Nichols. It is a study of seamen, the life they have chosen and their hopes and dreams. They appear to long to return home, but most of them know they will sail again and again until they die. The only weak segment is the brief sentimental episode of Smitty (Ian Hunter), a former British naval officer dismissed from the service for alcoholism, who has joined the crew of the Glencairn as an ordinary seaman. *The Long Voyage Home* is one of the most beautifully photographed films. Gregg Toland's high-contrast lighting, camera movement and deep-focus shots are masterpieces. The last scene, no more than fifteen seconds long, is truly striking: a newspaper floating in the water has the headline "*Amindra* torpedoed." Ford chose an excellent cast. Most of the players were from Dublin's Abbey Theatre whom Ford had brought over for his 1936 film, *The Plough and the Stars*. Some had settled in the U.S., including Barry Fitzgerald, his brother Arthur Shields, and Mildred Natwick. Thomas Mitchell has one of his best roles as a brawling, combative seaman. John Wayne puts on a passable Swedish accent. Although the film is a story of men, Mildred Natwick gets acting honors for her brief role as a devious barmaid.

Los Olvidados

The Young and the Damned. 1950. 88 min. b.w. Mexican. **Prod.** Oscar Dancigers; **Dir.** Luis Buñuel; **Scr.** Luis Buñuel, Luis Alcoriza; **Cin.** Gabriel Figueroa; **Ed.** Carlos Savage; **Mus.** Gustavo Pittaluga; **Cast:** Alfonso Mejia, Roberto Cobo, Estella Inda, Miguel Inclan.

This is the story of two boys who live in one of Mexico City's worst slums. The elder, Jaibo (Roberto Cobo), has just been released from a youth prison and soon becomes the leader of a local gang of boys in their mid-teens. There is not an ounce of decency in him. He is cruel, vicious and sadistic. Jaibo kills one of his own gang members in the presence of Pedro (Alfonso Mejia) and a strange bond is formed between the two boys. Pedro appears to possess a spark of decency although he follows Jaibo blindly. While afraid of Jaibo, he is fascinated by his strong leader-ship. The gang beats up, robs and tortures anyone that comes their way as long as they can get away with it. They drag a legless man through the street and torture a blind beggar. They don't steal out of need but only for the excitement. Jaibo, sensing that Pedro somehow considers himself better and is not totally submissive, kills Pedro in a fit of repressed jealousy. At the end of the film Jaibo is himself killed by his own gang and his body is dumped on a pile of garbage.

Buñuel had not directed a worthwhile film since 1930. He had left Spain for Mexico where he made a series of commercial and mediocre films. According to his own account he was impressed by DeSica's *Shoeshine* (1946) and other Italian neorealist directors, and made *Los Olvidados* in a mere twenty-one days. However, unlike the Italian neo-realists, he does not dwell on socio-eco-nomic causes of poverty and does not condemn society for the state of affairs. The juveniles in this film are solely responsible for their actions. The victims are not treated with any sympathy either. The blind man is shown to be a pedophile and he is just as hateful a figure as the youths. It is a horrifying portrait of how the poor prey on the poor. What Buñuel has fashioned is a powerful bleak tale with no light. With this film he came out of the critical wilderness, was voted best director at Cannes in 1951 and began his series of great films. The camera work of Gabriel Figueroa presents the surrealistic dream scenes perfectly. The actors are all unknown but give satisfactory performances. The film was released in the U.S. in 1951 as *The Young and the Damned*.

The Lost Weekend

1945. 101 min. b.w. U.S. **Prod.** Charles Brackett; **Dir.** Billy Wilder; **Scr.** Charles Brackett, Billy Wilder (based on the novel by Charles R. Jackson); **Cin.** John Seitz; **Ed.** Doane Harrison; **Art D.** Hans Dreier, Earl Hedrick; **Mus.** Miklos Rozsa, **Cast:** Ray Milland, Jane Wyman, Phillip Terry, Howard Da Silva, Doris Dowling, Frank Faylen.

Don Birnam (Ray Milland) is an alcoholic who has been on the wagon for ten days. He is an aspiring writer working on his first novel that he is having difficulty finishing. He is engaged to Helen (Jane Wyman) who works for *Time* magazine. He lives with his sensible brother Nick (Phillip Terry) who has to go away for three or four days and is worried about leaving Don alone. Don assures him he will remain dry and concentrate on his writing. The film is a chronicle of the next five days. Once his brother is gone, Don begins a descent into hell. He steals the money his brother had left for the maid and buys two bottles of rye that he hides in a most unlikely place. He goes to a nightclub and steals $10 from the purse of a women sitting close by. He is found out and forced to leave. He is humiliated and starts to drink more heavily. He can't find the two bottles he had hidden and tries to pawn his typewriter, but the pawnshops are closed. He is picked up and thrown into the alcoholic ward of Bellvue Hospital where he is taunted and mentally tortured by a sadistic male nurse (Frank Faylen). He escapes from the hospital and comes home. He has the DTs and hallucinates, seeing crawling rodents and bats coming out of cracks in the wall and devouring a mouse. He is found by his brother and girlfriend. The film ends on an unconvincing upbeat note forced by the production code. We are led to believe that there will be an immediate end to his misery.

The Lost Weekend was deemed so controversial that Paramount executives briefly considered withholding its release. The liquor industry offered to buy and destroy the negatives. Alcoholics generally had been shown in films as comic figures. They were amusing and should be left alone to have their fun. *The Lost Weekend* is an intense and cruel film and graphically shows the torment of alcoholics. There is first-rate cinematography. John Seitz's camera work in the celebrated rodent attack scene and his depiction of a lonely and impersonal New York are masterpieces. Ray Milland, a very competent actor who had been cast mostly in light comedies and romances like Billy Wilder's *The Major and The Minor* (1942), gives an intelligent and well-nuanced performance—by far his best work. Howard Da Silva as Nat the bartender and Frank Faylen as Bim the sadistic nurse are excellent. Jane Wyman's role is limited. The only weak acting is

Phillip Terry's. Wilder was recognized with an Academy Award. The film also got awards for best picture, actor and screenplay.

Love in the Afternoon

1957. 130 min. b.w. U.S. **Prod.** Billy Wilder; **Dir.** Billy Wilder; **Scr.** Billy Wilder, I. A. L. Diamond (based on the novel *Ariane* by Claude Anet); **Cin.** William Mellor; **Ed.** Leonid Azar; **Art D.** Alexander Trauner; **Mus.** Franz Waxman; **Cast:** Gary Cooper, Audrey Hepburn, Maurice Chevalier, John McGiver.

A very wealthy American playboy (Gary Cooper), a notorious womanizer, is being followed by a private detective (Maurice Chevalier) hired by a cuckolded husband (John McGiver). When told who his wife's paramour is, the husband goes to shoot the playboy. The private detective's young daughter (Audrey Hepburn), a cello student, decides to warn the playboy and that is the beginning of the story. The film may be a few minutes too long, but with its Paris locations it has a special charm. The scenes of a trio of gypsy violinists who serenade the playboy on every conceivable occasion and the running theme of "Fascination" give the film a distinctly Wilder flavor. Audrey Hepburn and John McGiver complement their parts very well, and even the aging Gary Cooper brings his appeal. The mere presence of Maurice Chevalier enhances and enlivens the film greatly.

Major Barbara

1941. 135 min. b.w. British. **Prod.** Gabriel Pascal; **Dir.** Gabriel Pascal, Harold French, David Lean; **Scr.** Anatole de Grunwald, George Bernard Shaw (based on his play); **Cin.** Ronald Neame; **Ed.** Charles Frend; **Prod. D.** Vincent Korda; **Mus.** William Walton; **Cast:** Wendy Hiller, Rex Harrison, Robert Morley, Robert Newton, Emlyn Williams, Sybil Thorndike, Deborah Kerr, Marie Lohr.

Barbara Undershaft (Wendy Hiller) is a major in the Salvation Army. She is an idealist who wants to save souls and help the poor. Adolphus Cusins (Rex Harrison) is a professor of Greek who is madly in love with Major Barbara. Although he shares her ideals he is more pragmatic and believes there must be other ways to eradicate poverty. However, in order to be near her he joins the Salvation Army band. Major Barbara becomes disillusioned with the Army when it accepts a large donation from her father, Andrew Undershaft (Robert Morley), a munitions manufacturer and one of the richest men in Great Britain. Andrew Undershaft believes poverty is a disease that cannot be cured by prayer and can only be eradicated by creating jobs. He takes his daughter and Cusins on a tour of his factories and shows them the housing and other facilities he has built for his workers. He proudly says he too wants to save souls, and creating more jobs is his only religion. Undershaft is impressed by Cusins, his future son-in-law, and offers him the job of running his empire. Barbara has a change of heart and agrees that eradication of poverty is a better way to save souls.

Major Barbara is a literate and enjoyable film. Shaw himself collaborated in preparing the script from his 1905 play, hence all his socialist beliefs have been retained. What the film suffers from is the pedestrian direction of Pascal who had sole production rights to Shaw's plays. He began to take himself seriously and decided to direct this film as well. Although assisted by young David Lean, the result is a static film. Equally unfortunate was the casting of thirty-two-year-old Robert Morley as the aging tycoon. Morley was much better in lighter comedy and was not up to the demands of Shaw. Wendy Hiller is just as good and convincing as she was in Shaw's *Pygmalion* (1938). Emlyn Williams and Sybil Thorndike are excellent. Robert Newton again overacts. A much better role for him was Shaw's *Androcles and the Lion* (1952) where his style of acting was more suitable. The rest of the cast is good, including Deborah Kerr in her screen debut.

A Man Escaped

Un Condamné a Mort S'est Echappé, ou Le Vent Souffle où Il Veut. 1956. 102 min. b.w. French. **Prod.** Jean Thuillier, Alain Poire; **Dir.** Robert Bresson; **Scr.** Robert Bresson (based on a book by André Devigny); **Cin.** L. H. Burel; **Ed.** Raymond Lamy; **Art D.** Pierre Charbonnier; **Mus.** Mozart; **Cast:** Francois Leterrier, Charles Le Clainche, Roland Monot, Maurice Beerblock, Roger Tréherne.

The film is set during the German occupation of France. A young former lieutenant Fontaine (Francois Leterrier) is arrested by the Gestapo. While being driven to prison he tries to escape. He is caught and badly beaten. He is thrown into a cell in the largest prison in Lyon, a former fortress from which escape is impossible. He recovers and establishes contact with some of the inmates, most of whom had been in the Resistance. He decides to escape and works out a methodical plan. With a flattened spoon as his only tool it takes him several weeks to loosen the panels of the cell's wooden door. He removes his bedsprings and wraps all the bedclothes around the straightened wires which gives him a sturdy rope of some thirty-five meters. He then makes hooks from his window frames. His ingenuity in making the implements of escape is shown in minute detail. He learns he has been found guilty of having been a member of the underground and is to be executed soon. He is now under pressure and just as he is about to attempt his escape a sixteen-year-year-old French boy, Francois (Charles Le Clainche), a volunteer who had deserted from the German army, is thrown into his cell. Fontaine wonders if the boy is a planted informer. He does not have much time. He either has to kill the boy or include him in his plan. He decides to take him along. The last quarter of the film is devoted to their escape. The arrival of Francois proves to have been a blessing. Without him Fontaine could not have made it.

The film is based on an autobiography by André Devigny, a Resistance hero, which in part recounts his escape from the German prison in Lyon. Bresson, one of the great directors, wrote the script. The plans for the escape as well as its execution are meticulously dealt with. The film is about faith. The music is Mozart's Mass in C Minor and at key moments it reaches a crescendo of exaltation indicating a transcendental force at work. The alternate title of the film, *The Wind Bloweth Where It Listeth,* makes Bresson's intent fairly obvious. As in Bresson's first major film, *Diary of a Country Priest* (1951), this film is lean and austere and the cast is nonprofessional. Most of it was shot in the Lyon prison. The sound track is used functionally and is very effective: the sound of a distant train or streetcar; the ominous sound of the guard's key; the opening and closing of the doors of the cells; and especially the sound of a spoon scraping the cell door.

Manhattan

1979. 96 min. b.w. U.S. **Prod.** Charles H. Joffe; **Dir.** Woody Allen; **Scr.** Woody Allen, Marshall Brickman; **Cin.** Gordon Willis; **Ed.** Susan E. Morse; **Prod. D.** Mel Bourne; **Mus.** George Gershwin; **Cast:** Woody Allen, Diane Keaton, Michael Murphy, Mariel Hemingway, Meryl Streep, Anne Byrne.

Forty-two-year-old Isaac Davis (Woody Allen) is a TV writer who is tired of the medium and wants to be a serious author. He is having an affair with seventeen-year-old Tracy (Mariel Hemingway), a drama student. Isaac loves Tracy, but feeling guilty over their age difference he decides to end the relationship. Tracy goes to London for six months to enroll at the Royal Academy of Dramatic Arts. He now seeks the advice of his best friend, Yale (Michael Murphy), who is cheating on his wife and having an affair with Mary Wilke (Diane Keaton). Yale is tiring of Mary and introduces her to Isaac who at first finds her pretentious and opinionated, but soon comes to admire her. Meanwhile, Isaac's ex-wife, Jill (Meryl Streep), who left him for a lesbian relationship, is about to publish a book about their marriage that will ridicule and highlight Isaac's eccentricities. By the end of the film Isaac realizes his one true love is Tracy and longs for her return.

The film is about relationships in Manhattan and has the usual dose of Allen's wit and sarcasm. However, it is the cinematography and music that distinguish it. The film opens with a shot of Central Park against the Westside skyline accompanied by

"Rhapsody in Blue." From then on it is a feast for the eyes and ears. We see Manhattan landmarks and hear "Someone to Watch Over Me," "Love Is Sweeping the Country," "Embraceable You" and, at the end when Tracy returns, "Strike Up the Band." No one has portrayed Manhattan as lovingly as Woody Allen and Gordon Willis, the cinematographer. Although not as funny, it is a better film than *Annie Hall* (1977).

Man Hunt

1941. 105 min. b.w. U.S. **Prod.** Kenneth MacGowan; **Dir.** Fritz Lang; **Scr.** Dudley Nichols; **Cin.** Arthur Miller; **Ed.** Allen McNeill; **Art D.** Richard Day, Wiard Ihnen; **Mus.** Alfred Newman; **Cast:** Walter Pidgeon, Joan Bennett, George Sanders, John Carradine, Roddy McDowall.

The film begins in Germany in 1939, a few months before World War II. An English big-game hunter, Captain Thorndike (Walter Pidgeon), is in Germany on a holiday somewhere very close to Hitler's retreat in Berchtesgaden. Quite accidentally he discovers he has a chance to assassinate Hitler. He has him in his gun sight and ponders for a few seconds but doesn't pull the trigger. He is knocked unconscious by a guard and charged with the attempted assassination of the Führer. He is interrogated by a Gestapo officer, Quive-Smith (George Sanders). He argues that he had no intention of assassinating Hitler. He just wanted to prove that it could be done. When he refuses to sign a confession, the Nazis arrange an accidental death and throw him off a cliff. Miraculously he survives the fall and makes his way back to England as a stowaway on a Danish steamer. In London he is pursued by a paid assassin, Mr. Jones (John Carradine), and the Gestapo officer Quive-Smith. With the help of a cockney street-walker, Jerry (Joan Bennett), he overcomes Mr. Jones in a memorable showdown in a subway tunnel. He has to rely on all his hunting skills when he is trapped by Quive-Smith in a cave in the countryside outside London.

Man Hunt is not among the best works of Fritz Lang but is still a very superior movie. The scenes in the London underground, however, do stand with the best of Lang and cinematographer Arthur Miller. The showdown with Quive-Smith at the end is measured and deliberately slow to make it effective. The three leads are all very good, but Joan Bennett's cockney accent does not quite work. There is an epilogue with an off screen narration that is unnecessary and weakens the impact of the film. *Man Hunt* was very low budgeted and it is apparent throughout.

————

Marty

1955. 91 min. b.w. U.S. **Prod.** Harold Hecht; **Dir.** Delbert Mann; **Scr.** Paddy Chayefsky; **Cin.** Joseph La Shelle; **Ed.** Alan Crosland, Jr.; **Art D.** Ted Haworth, Walter M. Simonds; **Mus.** Roy Webb; **Cast:** Ernest Borgnine, Betsy Blair, Joe Mantell, Joe De Santis, Esther Minciotti, Karen Steele, Jerry Paris, Frank Sutton, Augusta Ciolli.

Marty is a story of two lonely people who meet at the Stardust Ballroom, which is frequented by singles. Neither is handsome or pretty. Clara (Betsy Blair) had a blind date who has left her. Marty Pilletti (Ernest Borgnine) is there with his sidekick, Angie (Joe Mantell). Marty takes pity on the stranded girl and they talk and dance. Marty is a Bronx butcher whose brother and sisters are married. His customers chide him constantly why at thirty-four he is still unmarried. Clara has a bachelor's degree from NYU and teaches chemistry at a high school. Marty soon realizes how much they enjoy one another's company and they begin to see each other regularly, which irritates his friends who feel neglected. They describe Clara as a "dog" and tell him he could do better. His mother (Esther Minciotti) is also displeased because she is not Italian-American and she also fears she will be left alone if he marries. Despite the taunts and objections, Marty and Clara will marry.

With the advent of television in the early fifties, Hollywood decided to answer the challenge by making epics and big-budget pictures, which audiences soon tired of. Television produced a large number of plays, some of which Hollywood realized could be made into movies. *Marty*, written for TV by Paddy Chayefsky, was made into a movie on a budget of around $300,000. What makes *Marty* work is primarily the acting. The two leads are perfect. Borgnine plays the moon-faced butcher with great sensitivity and Betsy Blair, who was too pretty to be called a "dog" gives an equally compelling performance. The supporting cast of Joe Mantell, Esther Minciotti as Marty's mother and Augusta Ciolli as Marty's aunt are excellent. There is also some very good humor in the film. Angie believes Mickey Spillane is the greatest writer in the world: "Boy, he sure can write." And Marty, to soothe Clara's feelings, tells her, "You're not really as much of a dog as you think." The film's constantly repeated question between Marty and Angie, "Whadda ya wanna do tonight?" became a common byword. *Marty* was the first American film to win the Golden Palm at Cannes. It also won Academy Awards for best picture, actor and screenplay, and received nominations for best actress, supporting actor (Mantell), cinematography and art direction.

Mean Streets

1973. 110 min. color. U.S. **Prod.** Jonathan T. Taplin; **Dir.** Martin Scorsese; **Scr.** Martin Scorsese, Mardik Martin; **Cin.** Kent Wakeford; **Ed.** Sidney Levin; **Cast:** Robert De Niro, Harvey Keitel, David Proval, Amy Robinson, Richard Romanus, Cesare Danova.

The film is set in New York City's Little Italy around 1956. It is the story of four hoodlums in their mid to late twenties, all second-generation Americans. Tony (David Proval) runs a topless bar; Mike (Richard Romanus) is a hustler who cheats visitors to Little Italy; and Johnny Boy (Robert De Niro) is an aimless compulsive gambler who in his spare time blows up mailboxes. He makes the mistake of borrowing money from loan sharks thinking he can get away with not paying back. The last of the four on whom more of the film is focused is Charlie (Harvey Keitel), the nephew of Giovanni (Cesare Danova), a middle-ranking Mafia don. Charlie has been promised by his uncle that soon he will run and own a restaurant. Charlie is a devout Catholic and feels guilty about his actions on the streets and running around with hoodlums. He is also afraid of the hereafter. His closest friend is Johnny Boy, and Charlie has fallen in love with Johnny's epileptic sister, Teresa (Amy Robinson). His uncle does not like Johnny Boy and is firmly opposed to any involvement with Teresa. Charlie can't make any decisions on his own and is totally under his uncle's thumb. He foresees a gloomy future for himself but can't get away.

Mean Streets is Scorsese's third film and established him as a young director of promise. He himself had grown up in Little Italy and the film is partly autobiographical, modelled on Fellini's *I Vitelloni* (1953). In many ways it is Scorsese's best film. It is well controlled with some very well-done set pieces. The acting of the entire cast is good, but Keitel and De Niro stand out. Rock music is very effectively used.

Missing

1982. 122 min. color. U.S. **Prod.** Edward Lewis, Mildred Lewis; **Dir.** Constantin Costa-Gavras; **Scr.** Donald Stewart, Constantin Costa-Gavras (based on *The Execution of Charles Horman* by Thomas Hauser); **Cin.** Ricardo Aronovich; **Ed.** Francoise Bonnot; **Prod. D.** Peter Jamison; **Art D.** Agustin Ytuarte; **Mus.** Vangelis; **Cast:** Jack Lemmon, Sissy Spacek, Melanie Mayron, John Shea, Charles Cioffi, David Clennon, Richard Venture.

The film portrays the aftermath of the 1973 military coup in Chile that led to the overthrow and death of its elected president, Salvador Allende, and the installation of General Pinochet. Although the name of the country and leaders are not mentioned, various references make it clear it is Chile. It tells the story of the disappearance and murder of Charles Horman (John Shea), a young Harvard-educated American counter-culture journalist, by the Chilean military with the probable knowledge of some U.S. officials on the scene. Horman had been executed by the Chileans because he had gained knowledge of U.S. involvement in the coup. The focus of the film is the visit of the victim's father, Ed Horman (Jack Lemmon), to Santiago to help his daughter-in-law, Beth (Sissy Spacek), find the whereabouts of Charles, whom they hope and believe to be alive. Ed Horman is a political conservative and a deeply religious man, a Christian Scientist. He had faith in his government and always accepted what the government said without question. The visit to Santiago is the beginning of his disillusionment. Ed had not approved of his son's politics but had never imagined that he would be murdered for his political beliefs. The most touching parts of the film are his growing attachment to his daughter-in-law and how they become dependant upon each other.

Missing is an extremely powerful film that prompted sharp denials by U.S. officials. It is Constantin Costa-Gavras' best film since *Z* (1969). Though not as good, it's as emotionally involving, with fine performances by Lemmon and Spacek. Costa-Gavras wisely chose to make the film a mystery/thriller without sacrificing the political content. It is also beautifully photographed by Ricardo Aronovich, especially the scenes of a city under martial law, where even the brightly lit streets at night look ominous and frightening.

Modern Times

1936. 89 min. b.w. Silent. U.S. **Prod.** Charles Chaplin; **Dir.** Charles Chaplin; **Scr.** Charles Chaplin; **Cin.** Roland Tetheroh, Ira Morgan; **Art D.** Charles D. Hall, J. Russell Spencer. **Mus.** Charles Chaplin; **Cast:** Charles Chaplin, Paulette Goddard, Henry Bergman, Chester Conklin, Tiny Sandford.

Chaplin is a factory worker who loses his job during the Great Depression. He is thrown in jail when he accidentally becomes part of a march by a group of striking workers. After his release he meets a young girl (Paulette Goddard) who has run away from an orphanage. Together they set up home in a shack. He gets a job as a night watchman in a department store but he is soon fired. He then becomes a singing waiter. But the authorities catch up with the young girl and the couple run away together.

This is one of Chaplin's best films, but it ranks below *The Gold Rush* (1925) and *City Lights* (1931). Chaplin was never good when he philosophized or made pronouncements about "humanity in pursuit of happiness." The scenes of the factory assembly line, mostly borrowed from René Clair's *A Nous La Liberte* (1931), are very funny. Chaplin uses the assembly line as his vision of people being dehumanized and becoming robots. There are also some marvelous original scenes. The factory he works for has purchased a feeding machine to cut the lunchtime of the workers. Chaplin who works on the assembly line is selected as the guinea pig. After the machine has fed him his soup, a corncob is placed in his mouth, and the machine breaks down and goes haywire. There is also a scene of the graceful Chaplin on roller skates. His talents as a skater had been shown much earlier in *The Rink* (1916). Here, in order to impress the girl, he skates blindfolded on the second floor of the department store, unaware that he is close to the edge of a big drop. There are also very funny scenes when, as a singing waiter, he sings incomprehensible gibberish, and this was the first time one heard Chaplin's voice. This was Chaplin's first film in five years and again he decided against using the spoken word. *Modern Times* is also the last time we see the tramp. Beginning with *The Great Dictator* (1940) Chaplin began to adopt other personae.

Mr. Deeds Goes to Town

1936. 115 min. b.w. U.S. **Prod.** Frank Capra; **Dir.** Frank Capra; **Scr.** Robert Riskin (based on the story "Opera Hat" by Clarence Budington Kelland) **Cin.** Joseph Walker; **Ed.** Gene Havlick; **Art D.** Stephen Goosson; **Mus.** Howard Jackson; **Cast:** Gary Cooper, Jean Arthur, George Bancroft, Lionel Stander, Douglas Dumbrille, Raymond Walburn, Walter Catlett, H. B. Warner.

Longfellow Deeds (Gary Cooper) lives in Mandrake Falls, Vermont. He writes greeting card verses and plays the tuba to relax. He is informed by his uncle's lawyer that he has inherited $20 million. His first reaction is "I didn't need it." He has to travel to

New York City to sign the necessary papers and becomes head-line news in the tabloids. Without his knowledge he has already been appointed by the board of the opera company as its chair-man. He is approached by parasites with all kinds of schemes. Soon he becomes disillusioned and seeing the hardship and abject poverty caused by the Great Depression he decides to establish a communal farm for dispossessed farmers. Greedy rela-tives led by his late uncle's lawyer (Douglas Dumbrille) begin a court action to declare him insane. Deeds is so emotionally wounded that he refuses to defend himself. When he learns that the girl he has fallen in love with (Jean Arthur) cares for him he comes to life. The principal witnesses against him are two elderly spinster sisters from Mandrake Falls who have testified that Deeds is "pixilated" (i.e. pixies have gotten to his brain). He soon estab-lishes that the sisters believe everyone including the judge is pixilated. Deeds is declared sane and can now go ahead with his plan to help the destitute.

The movie is not much different from other glowingly opti-mistic fantasy films Capra made in the thirties. It has great humor, especially the testimony of the spinster sisters, but what elevates the film is the fine acting of Cooper and Arthur and an excellent supporting cast. Cooper had been in mostly mediocre films for nearly ten years. He had been an expressionless wooden actor with a shy smile and hesitant delivery. Beginning with this film he brought an endearing sincerity to his parts, as long as he didn't have too many lines. Jean Arthur had been a minor actress. She was now recognized as a major comedienne. Most of Capra's films have dated somewhat. *Mr. Deeds Goes to Town* is one of the few exceptions. It received an Academy Award for best director and nominations for best picture, actor, screenplay and sound.

Murder My Sweet

(a.k.a. *Farewell My Lovely*) 1944. 95 min. b.w. U.S. **Prod.** Adrian Scott; **Dir.** Edward Dmytryk; **Scr.** John Paxton (based on the novel *Farewell, My Lovely* by Raymond Chandler); **Cin.** Harry Wild; **Ed.** Joseph Noriega; **Art D.** Albert S. D'Agostino; **Mus.** Roy Webb; **Cast:** Dick Powell, Claire Trevor, Anne Shirley, Otto Kruger, Mike Mazurki, Miles Mander.

The film begins with Raymond Chandler's legendary private detective, Philip Marlowe (Dick Powell), being interrogated by a team of detectives about a series of unsolved murders. There is then a lengthy flashback. Marlowe relates how one night Moose Malloy (Mike Mazurki), a giant of a man, just released from prison after serving eight years, calls on him. He asks if Marlowe could locate the love of his life, Velma (Claire Trevor), who had been a taxi dancer. Marlowe is next hired by a man who is involved in the return of a stolen jade necklace and seeks a bodyguard. The plot becomes more complicated when Marlowe is knocked out and the man who hired him is murdered. Slowly the two assignments merge and become interconnected. Velma, it turns out, has married a high-society millionaire under an assumed name and she is involved in blackmail and murder. At the end some five people are murdered, but Marlowe is absolved.

The film shifts effortlessly from the seediest parts of Los Angeles to luxurious gambling boats in the harbor. From high society con men to a world of sadistic violence, organized prostitution, white slavery and drugs. Director Dmytryk was at the height of his directorial powers and together with the excellent camera work of Harry Wild captures the lurid atmosphere. The screenplay by John Paxton is one of the best film adaptations of a Chandler novel. Dick Powell, a very average musical comedy actor, was cast in the film by chance and plays the down-and-out $25-a-day detective to perfection. Powell is as good as any of the other actors who have played Marlowe, including Bogart, Mitchum and George Sanders. The rest of the cast is also fine.

My Favorite Year

1982. 92 min. color. U.S. **Prod.** Michael Gruskoff; **Dir.** Richard Benjamin; **Scr.** Norman Steinberg, Dennis Palumbo; **Cin.** Gerald Hirschfeld; **Ed.** Richard Chew; **Prod. D.** Charles Rosen; **Mus.** Ralph Burns, **Cast:** Peter O'Toole, Mark Linn-Baker, Jessica Harper, Joseph Bologna, Bill Macy, Lou Jacobi, Adolph Green, Lainie Kazan, Cameron Mitchell.

Benji Stone (Mark Linn-Baker) is a junior writer for "Comedy Cavalcade," a popular weekly TV show hosted by King Kaiser (Joseph Bologna), a Sid Caesar-type comedian. It is 1954, the early days of TV, when most shows were broadcast live. Benji is assigned to be the minder for the next special guest star, the aging Alan Swann (Peter O'Toole). Swann is a very popular Hollywood star who gained his fame in swashbucklers. He is an alcoholic given to rowdy behavior and starting fights. Benji is to keep him away from booze, women and fights until his appearance in the next "Comedy Cavalcade" program. Kaiser's last few shows have parodied a corrupt powerful labor union boss (Cameron Mitchell) who has objected and wants the skit discontinued. Kaiser has ignored his threats and plans to go on. The union boss intends to storm the set with his goons and disrupt the program. Swann, who has taken a liking to Benji, behaves as well as he is able during the first two days of his stay in New York. But just before going on the air he learns that the show is being televised live. He panics and in a memorable line says, "I'm not an actor. I'm a movie star." He then falls off the wagon. The last scene of the movie has Kaiser and a drunken swashbuckling Swann beating off the goons to the delight of the audience who believe it is all part of the show.

My Favorite Year was a delightful sleeper. It is partly based on the experience of Mel Brooks as a young writer on the Sid Caesar show. Brooks had been charged with chaperoning the rowdy Errol Flynn and keeping him out of trouble until his appearance on the show. The film paints a nostalgic portrait of early television. There is an unnecessary sentimental scene when Swann travels to see his daughter. O'Toole has one of his best roles. Joseph Bologna as the host of the show and Cameron Mitchell as the crooked union boss are perfect. Equally good are Mark Linn-Baker, his mother (Lainie Kazan) who is married to a Filipino ex–bantam-weight boxer, and the late Adolph Green, the well-known comedy writer of stage and screen, playing one of the writers of the show.

The Naked City

1948. 96 min. b.w. U.S. **Prod.** Mark Hellinger; **Dir.** Jules Dassin; **Scr.** Albert Maltz, Malvin Wald; **Cin.** William Daniels; **Ed.** Paul Weatherwax; **Art D.** John DeCuir; **Mus.** Miklos Rozsa, Frank Skinner; **Cast:** Barry Fitzgerald, Howard Duff, Don Taylor, Dorothy Hart, Ted de Corsia, House Jameson.

A beautiful ex-model with a shady background has been murdered and the police have very few clues. Detective Dan Muldoon (Barry Fitzgerald) who has been on the force for over thirty-five years is assigned to the case with rookie detective Jimmy Halloran (Don Taylor) on his first case. As the investigation proceeds, we learn that the murdered girl's lover, a well-known society doctor, has been blackmailed into giving the names of patients who have expensive jewelry. The patients are later robbed by a gang of burglars with whom the girl was working. The detectives doggedly run down every lead.

Barry Fitzgerald brings a great deal of charm to his role. Don Taylor as the rookie and Howard Duff as a congenital liar are both excellent. The film is flawlessly directed by Jules Dassin and photographed by William Daniels. This highly influential film that still looks fresh and authentic was shot in over one hundred locations in New York City with the aid of a mobile camera. Although the depiction of the routine work of police is tedious, Dassin maintains the suspense and also has one great scene of emotional intensity. When the murdered girl's parents are brought to identify the body, the mother keeps repeating, "I hate her" But the minute she sees the body she breaks down in uncontrollable sobs and cries, "O my baby! Dear God, why wasn't she born ugly?" This same lament is uttered in L.A. Confidential (1997).

The Narrow Margin

1952. 70 min. b.w. U.S. **Prod.** Stanley Rubin; **Dir.** Richard Fleischer; **Scr.** Earl Fenton (based on a story by Martin Goldsmith and Jack Leonard); **Cin.** George E. Diskant; **Ed.** Robert Swink; **Art D.** Albert S. D'Agostino, Jack Okey; **Cast:** Charles McGraw, Marie Windsor, Jacqueline White, Don Beddoe, Paul Maxey, Gordon Gebert, David Clarke, Peter Virgo.

Two Los Angeles policemen—Walter Brown (Charles McGraw) and his partner Gus Forbes (Don Beddoe), an elderly cop near retirement—arrive by train in Chicago. They are to escort and guard Mrs. Neall (Marie Windsor), the widow of an important racketeer, to Los Angeles to testify before a grand jury investigating organized crime. They know the gangsters will do anything to stop her from testifying. They are to pick her up at an apartment the Chicago police have provided for her. A hit man has followed them, and on their way out of the apartment he fatally shoots Forbes in his attempt to kill Mrs Neall. Brown, a hardened detective who had instinctively disliked Mrs. Neall, now hates her with greater passion. They board the train for Los Angeles and he hides her in an adjoining compartment. There are two gangsters on the train who are assigned to kill Mrs. Neall and a third comes on board at the next stop. The only advantage Brown has is that they don't know what Mrs. Neall looks like. They try to bribe Brown, but he can't be bought. There is a woman on the train with her young son, Mrs. Ann Sinclair (Jacqueline White), who is the exact opposite of the hard and brassy Mrs. Neall. The gangsters soon learn that the compartment next to Brown is occupied by Mrs. Neall who is, in fact, a police-woman with the Internal Division of the LA Police. She was assigned as a decoy to throw off the gangsters but also to test the honesty of Brown and Forbes. Once the gangsters discover she is a policewoman, they kill her and go after Mrs. Sinclair.

The film has no stars and was shot on a shoestring budget entirely in confined spaces: a small run-down apartment, a short scene in a taxi, and the rest on a train with narrow corridors and small compartments. The very claustrophobic sets add to the tension. The relationship between Brown and Mrs. Neall is established at the very outset and gives an added theme to the film. While in the cab to pick up Mrs. Neall, Brown makes a bet with his partner that he knows exactly what the gangster's wife would look like: "A dish, a sixty cent special, cheap, flashy, strictly poison under the gravy." Brown wins the bet. Mrs. Neall is contrasted with Ann Sinclair who is reserved, soft spoken and a good mother. The irony of stereotypes is underscored when we find that Mrs. Neall is a policewoman merely playing a part and Ann Sinclair is the real gangster's wife. Marie Windsor pretending to be the sleazy wife has the best lines and gets acting honors. McGraw usually had roles of mean, coldhearted men—*T-Men* (1947) and *Spartacus* (1960)—and he is very good here as the hard-boiled detective. *The Narrow Margin* is directed by an intelligent old Hollywood hand, Richard Fleischer, and is one of the best crime mystery films, marred only by the gimmicky final shootout. The film was made for $230,000. A remake in 1990 with a very fine actor, Gene Hackman, was made for $25 million and it is vastly inferior.

Nashville

1975. 159 min. color. U.S. **Prod.** Robert Altman; **Dir.** Robert Altman; **Scr.** Joan Tewkesbury; **Cin.** Paul Lohmann; **Ed.** Sidney Levin, Dennis M. Hill; **Mus.** Richard Baskin; **Cast:** David Arkin, Ned Beatty, Henry Gibson, Michael Murphy, Karen Black, Barbara Baxley, Ronee Blakley, Keith Carradine, Geraldine Chaplin, Lily Tomlin, Alan Garfield, Shelley Duvall, Keenan Wynn, Timothy Brown, Barbara Harris, Jeff Goldblum.

The events take place in Nashville during the last five days of a country music festival. Either by design or otherwise, the event coincides with the launching of the campaign of Hal Phillip Walker, the candidate of the Replacement Party, for the presidency of the United States. Walker's top aides, Delbert Reese (Ned Beatty) and John Triplette (Michael Murphy), are planning to stage a star-studded television extravaganza prior to Walker's official announcement. The candidate himself never appears in the film, but from his two aides we get a clear sense of his brand of politics.

He is much like George Wallace, who ran as a third-party candidate in 1968 and 1972 on a state's rights and end to desegregation platform. *Nashville* is an ambitious film that attempts to develop some twenty-four characters, and succeeds for the most part. There is Barbara Jean (Ronee Blakley), a former festival queen who is recovering from a nervous breakdown. She is hoping that her performance at the current festival will regain her earlier popularity. Her appearance does not go well. She gets a second chance when her manager arranges a prominent slot for her at the Walker event. Tom Frank (Keith Carradine) is a singer in a trio who is there also to bed down as many women as he can. Opal (Geraldine Chaplin) is an annoying and pretentious correspondent who is covering the festival for the BBC. There are Connie White (Karen Black), a scheming and manipulative singer who will do anything to be the next queen of the festival; and Haven Hamilton (Henry Gibson), a veteran performer who despite his amiability is unprincipled and calculating. Then there is Reese's lonely wife, Linnea (Lily Tomlin), who will be easy prey for Tom Frank. At the Walker gala, Barbara Jean reestablishes herself. As she is taking her bows, she is shot by a disturbed man (echoes of George Wallace shot by a drifter). As she is being taken to an ambulance, a girl jumps on the stage, grabs the microphone and begins belting out a song. This ambitious unknown will win recognition and a new career is launched.

Nashville is an inventive and original film. It is an expertly structured and directed film with some fine performances. However, some of the more than twenty-four characters are not sufficiently developed. Altman's intention to portray the festival as a microcosm of U.S. society is probably where the film does not live up to expectations.

Nightmare Alley

1947. 111 min. b.w. U.S. **Prod.** George Jessel; **Dir.** Edmund Goulding; **Scr.** Jules Furthman (based on the novel by William Lindsay Gresham); **Cin.** Lee Garmes; **Ed.** Barbara McLean; **Art D.** Lyle Wheeler, J. Russell Spencer; **Mus.** Cyril J. Mockridge; **Cast:** Tyrone Power, Joan Blondell, Coleen Gray, Helen Walker, Taylor Holmes, Mike Mazurki, Ian Keith, Roy Roberts, James Burke.

The film begins with Stanton Carlisle (Tyrone Power), a clever farm boy who lands a job as a barker in a small carnival. Of the carnival's two biggest draws one is a mind-reading act with Zeena (Joan Blondell) and her husband, Pete (Ian Keith). The other is an illegal act that features a geek, a dipsomaniac who works in a pit and eats a live chicken for a bottle of booze. Stanton, seeing the act, says, "How could someone sink so low?" Pete dies by drinking wood alcohol accidentally given to him by Stanton who by now had become Zeena's lover and had learned their code. Stanton replaces Pete, but soon he discards Zeena for a younger girl, Molly (Coleen Gray). They become a major act in a supper club in Chicago. He meets an unprincipled psychiatrist, Dr. Lilith Ritter (Helen Walker), and makes a financial arrangement to get confidential information about her patients, giving her a substantial cut of what he extorts from them. He meets an elderly industrialist, Ezra Grindle (Taylor Holmes), whose sole desire is to contact his youthful sweetheart who died fifty years earlier. In return he will give $150,000 to build a spiritual tabernacle. Grindle is killed accidentally and Dr. Ritter threatens Stanton with blackmail and exposure. He escapes, but Ritter keeps all the money he gave her for safekeeping. While on the run he starts drinking. After a few odd jobs he is asked by a carnival operator if he would accept a job as a geek and Stanton replies, "I was made for it."

A most unusual dark film made by a major studio barely two years after WWII. For people having gone through four years of a wartime climate, the usual fare offered was light comedies, stories of returning veterans and escapist love stories. At the urging of Tyrone Power, Fox's most important contract player who was becoming restless in his career, Fox purchased the novel *Night-mare Alley* as his next film. The studio added a scene to soften the ending. Power insisted on hiring Edmund Goulding, a director who had a reputation for extracting good performances from his actors: Joan Crawford in *Grand Hotel*, (1932), Bette Davis in *Dark Victory* (1939) and Tyrone Power himself in *The Razor's Edge* (1946). However, Power could not achieve the level of acting he aspired to and only performed competently. The best acting is by Helen Walker, Joan Blondell and Coleen Gray.

Nights of Cabiria

Le Notti Di Cabiria. 1957. 110 min. b.w. Italian. **Prod.** Dino De Laurentis; **Dir.** Federico Fellini; **Scr.** Federico Fellini, Ennio Flaiano, Tullio Pinelli, Pier Paolo Pasolini; **Cin.** Aldo Tonti, Otello Martelli; **Ed.** Leo Catozzo; **Art D.** Piero Gherardi; **Mus.** Nino Rota; **Cast:** Giulietta Masina, Francois Perier, Amedeo Nazzari, Franca Marzi, Dorian Gray, Aldo Silvani.

Cabiria (Giulietta Masina) is a prostitute who works on the streets of Rome and lives in a shack on the outskirts of the city. She is hopeful she will meet a loving man and live with him for the rest of her life. Nothing deters her from this dream. We first meet her being thrown out of a rowboat into a lake by a man trying to steal her money. Fortunately she can swim to shore and emerges without complaint. That evening she is picked up by a famous movie star whose girlfriend has left him. After spending hours in the actor's sumptuous villa she is unceremoniously dumped and told to leave without being paid. Cabiria is still hopeful and a few days later she goes to a shrine and prays that something good will come to her. Afterward, a fortune-teller predicts someone she will soon meet will offer her real love. When she meets Oscar (Francois Perier), a shy, hard-working man, she is certain that he is the one the fortune teller has predicted. They see each other regularly and he proposes marriage. In anticipation she abandons her shack and gives it to her best friend. She also withdraws all her savings from the bank. Oscar it turns out has been after her meager savings. He beats and robs her and is about to throw her over a cliff when he takes pity on her and lets her go. She is destitute and cries inconsolably. As she walks in the woods she sees a group of young people laughing and singing. She stops crying, her big smile returns and she becomes her ever-hopeful self.

The film is all Giulietta Masina and one of Fellini's very best. Although the subject was ripe for sentimentality, Fellini avoided it and on the strength of Massina's characterization made it a bittersweet comedy. The film was mutilated by various distributors a few years after its release. It was not until 1997 that film archivists returned it to its original 110 minutes.

Odd Man Out

1947. 115 min. b.w. British. **Prod.** Carol Reed; **Dir.** Carol Reed; **Scr.** F. L. Green, R. C. Sherriff (based on the novel by F. L.Green); **Cin.** Robert Krasker; **Ed.** Fergus McDonell; **Prod. D.** Roger Furse; **Art D.** Ralph Brinton; **Mus.** William Alwyn; **Cast:** James Mason, Robert Newton, Kathleen Ryan, Robert Beatty, Cyril Cusack, William Hartnell, Denis O'Dea, Dan O'Herlihy, F. J. McCormick, Fay Compton, W. G. Fay, Beryl Measor.

The film is set in Belfast, Northern Ireland shortly after World War II and the story takes place between four in the afternoon and midnight on a cold winter day. Johnny McQueen (James Mason), an IRA leader convicted of gunrunning, has broken out of jail and is hiding with his devoted sweetheart, Kathleen (Kathleen Ryan), at her grandmother's house. While in prison Johnny had planned to rob a mill's payroll to fund his IRA cell. During the robbery he accidentally kills a guard and is himself critically wounded. The driver of the getaway car panics and Johnny, who is standing on the running board, is thrown off. He hides in deserted buildings and then moves to a junkyard. He stumbles out nearly delirious and is helped to his feet by two kind spinsters, Rosie (Fay Compton) and Mandie (Beryl Measor), and taken to their home. They serve him tea, but when they realize he has been shot and is probably a fugitive, they bandage him and let him go. He staggers in dark alleys until spotted by Shell (F. J.

McCormick), a derelict and an informer. Then he falls into the hands of a half-mad painter, Lukey (Robert Newton), who has been waiting to paint the look of a dying man and capture his pain and suffering. Johnny gets away and drags himself to a church. Kathleen, who had been frantically searching for him and had made arrangements for Johnny to get away on a ship, finds him and takes him to the docks. The police close in and Kathleen fires at them. Both Kathleen and Johnny are shot dead.

Odd Man Out is the first collaboration of Carol Reed and cinematographer Robert Krasker. It was followed by *The Fallen Idol* and *The Third Man* (both 1948). The stylized lighting and shadows first used in this film were further refined in *The Third Man*. The film captures the seediness of Belfast at the time and the characters represent a cross section of the working class. The cast is first rate. James Mason, who appeared in films for over forty years, considered this performance as his best. Fay Compton, Beryl Measor, Cyril Cusack, Kathleen Ryan and F. J. McCormick are very good, and Robert Newton's customary overacting suits the character he portrays, the mad Lukey. The film is much more than the chase of a fugitive. It is the last moments on earth of a disillusioned dying man and James Mason does indeed give his finest performance.

The Ox-Bow Incident

1943. 75 min. b.w. U.S. **Prod.** Lamar Trotti; **Dir.** William Wellman; **Scr.** Lamar Trotti (based on the novel by Walter Van Tilburg Clark); **Cin.** Arthur Miller; **Ed.** Allen McNeil; **Art D.** Richard Day, James Basevi; **Mus.** Cyril J. Mockridge; **Cast:** Henry Fonda, Dana Andrews, Mary Beth Hughes, Anthony Quinn, William Eythe, Henry (Harry) Morgan, Jane Darwell, Frank Conroy, Harry Davenport, Matt Briggs, Francis Ford, Paul Hurst, Leigh Whipper.

The film opens in the small town of Bridger's Wells, Nevada in 1885. Two cowboys, Gil Carter (Henry Fonda) and Art Croft (Henry Morgan), have completed their jobs at a nearby ranch and are leaving to find other work. They head to the local saloon. Before they have finished their first drink, an excited cowboy

comes in with the news that rustlers have killed a rancher, Larry
Kinkaid, and stolen his cattle. Immediately someone begins to
excite the crowd in the saloon and shouts for a posse to go after
the rustlers. Tetley (Frank Conroy), a prominent town citizen and
former major in the Confederate army, shows up in his uniform
to lead the posse. Despite the protests of the local storekeeper, old
man Arthur Davies (Harry Davenport), the deputy sheriff depu-
tizes the mob. A hearty elderly woman, Ma Grier (Jane Darwell),
who runs a boarding house joins the posse. Sparky (Leigh Whipper), an old black handyman who had witnessed the lynching of
his own brothers some years back, decides to go along to pray for
the men who will die. Carter and Croft, being strangers and having already had an argument with one of the rabble-rousers,
decide to go lest they be suspects themselves. A short time later,
the posse runs into three men sleeping by their campfire in Ox-
Bow Valley. They have fifty head of cattle with Kinkaid's brand and
no bill of sale. Donald Martin (Dana Andrews), a young home-
steader, says he bought the cattle for cash and Kinkaid promised to
mail the receipt. Martin has two helpers: a senile old man (Francis
Ford) and a young Mexican, Juan Martines (Anthony Quinn),
who is wearing a gun that someone in the posse identifies as
belonging to Kinkaid. Martines says he found the gun on the trail,
but no one believes him, especially when someone else recognizes
him as a former outlaw. The three suspects are tied up and the
posse is to decide their fate by sunrise. Some in the posse get
drunk and others fondle old Ma Grier who is enjoying herself and
laughing raucously. At sunrise, Major Tetley calls for a vote.
Twenty-one vote for hanging and seven, including Carter, Croft,
Davies and Sparky, vote to wait until the sheriff arrives. A surprise
vote against hanging comes from the major's son Gerald (William
Eythe), who was forced to join the posse by his father to "make a
man of him." The condemned Martin asks to write a letter to his
wife after which the three are hanged. On the way back to town,
the posse runs into the sheriff who tells them Larry Kinkaid is not
dead and the rustlers who shot him have been caught. He says,
"May the Lord have mercy on you, you won't have it from me."

When the posse gets to town, the major goes to his home and shoots himself. The rest go to the bar where Carter reads Martin's letter aloud and all fall silent.

The film, scripted by Lamar Trotti, is based on the novel by Walter Van Tilburg Clark. The letter read by Gil Carter at the end of the film does not appear in the book but was added by Trotti. Given the difficulty of trying to amplify the philosophical thrust of the book in a film, the brotherhood of man and individual responsibility, Trotti decided to distill it in the letter. Although the film is set in Nevada and has cowboys, homesteaders and rustlers, neither the book nor the film is a Western. It is contemporary social drama. In a true Western, the hero would have stopped the lynching. The film stands out for its cinematography. The dimly lit sets, the victims and the posse near the campfire, the actual hanging and especially the reading of the letter by Henry Fonda, photographed from a side angle lit only by a kerosene lamp, are all beautifully shot. The film is also notable for the number of vivid characters it develops. Wellman gets good performances from the entire cast, but Dana Andrews is a cut above the rest. Henry Fonda brings sincerity and decency to his role. Henry Morgan (also known as Harry Morgan), Darwell, Davenport and Conroy make up an exceedingly good supporting cast.

Point Blank

1967. 92 min. color. U.S. **Prod.** Judd Bernard, Robert Chartoff; **Dir.** John Boorman; **Scr.** Alexander Jacobs, David Newhouse, Rafe Newhouse (based on the novel *The Hunter* by Richard Stark); **Cin.** Philip Lathrop; **Ed.** Henry Berman; **Art D.** George W. Davis, Albert Brenner; **Mus.** Johnny Mandel; **Cast:** Lee Marvin, Angie Dickinson, Keenan Wynn, Carroll O'Connor, Lloyd Bochner, Michael Strong, John Vernon, Sharon Acker.

Mal Reese (John Vernon), Walker (Lee Marvin) and Walker's wife, Lynne (Sharon Acker), pull a daring job robbing the payroll of a crime syndicate as it is being delivered at the empty and abandoned prison on Alcatraz Island. Walker is double crossed by Reese and his own wife and is shot and left for dead. He drags himself to the bay and the currents carry him to shore. After the passage of several years he is approached by someone named Fairfax (Keenan Wynn) who methodically guides him toward the recovery of his share of the heist and in getting revenge on those who double crossed him. Walker is unaware that Fairfax is a member of the syndicate who is using him to eliminate those senior to him and become its head. Walker's wife abandoned by Reese and overcome with guilt and shame committed suicide. Walker is helped by her sister Chris (Angie Dickinson) and gains access to Reese who after the robbery made an arrangement with the syndicate and has become a member. Reese falls to his death from a building, but Walker still cannot get his hands on the $93,000 that was his share of the robbery. The syndicate has changed over the years. It has become a corporation with legitimate enterprises as a front. It is run by officers and directors and Walker can't understand why they don't have cash. With Fairfax's help he gets to the highest corporate officers and eliminates them all. Walker gets his $93,000 and Fairfax is ready to reach the top.

Point Blank is well directed and is one of the most stylish movies of the late sixties. It begins with a flashback of Walker being shot by Reese. Thereafter there are staccato flashbacks throughout the movie. This was John Boorman's second film and his first in Hollywood. He was influenced heavily by the French New Wave directors, most notably Alain Resnais' themes of memory and remembrance. What also makes the film interesting is how out of place Walker has become. He feels alien in a society where crime is run by corporations whose officers have no cash. Walker just wants his $93,000, nothing more or less. Although there is good acting by the entire cast the real star is Boorman. The only weakness is the sparsity of the script. There could have been a line or two here and there to round out the characters, most of whom are stereotypes and only a few are fully developed.

Pretty Poison

1968. 89 min. b.w. U.S. **Prod.** Marshal Backlar, Noel Black; **Dir.** Noel Black; **Scr.** Lorenzo Semple, Jr. (based on the novel *She Let Him Continue* by Stephen Geller); **Cin.** David Quaid; **Ed.** William Ziegler; **Art D.** Jack Martin Smith, Harold Michelson; **Mus.** Johnny Mandel; **Cast:** Anthony Perkins, Tuesday Weld, Beverly Garland, John Randolph, Dick O'Neill, Don Fellows.

A mentally disturbed young man, Dennis Pitt (Anthony Perkins), lives in a paranoiac dream world. He thinks that he works for the CIA and the company that has recently employed him is poisoning the nearby river. He has just been released on parole after serving part of a sentence for killing his aunt by burning down her house. He had claimed he didn't know she was at home. He meets a pretty eighteen-year-old high-school senior, Sue Ann (Tuesday Weld), and falls in love with her. He appears to be influencing her, but through a series of incidents we realize she is more disturbed than he, and he is cleverly being manipulated by her. She kills a night watchman at the lumber company where Dennis works and later kills her own mother in cold blood. She accuses Dennis of the murders and he refuses to defend himself. He is taken back to prison where he will serve a life term. In the last scene of the film we see her picking up a young man and making up a series of stories about her background.

This was director Noel Black's first feature film. He never approached the professionalism of the suspense-filled *Pretty Poison* in his later films. The key element is the acting. Anthony Perkins excels in roles of emotionally scarred individuals as in *Fear Strikes Out* (1956), or the totally deranged as in *Psycho* (1960). But it is the acting of the sweet young Tuesday Weld as the improbable pathological killer that is the most chilling and dominates the film.

The Prime of Miss Jean Brodie

1969. 116 min. color. British. **Prod.** Robert Fryer; **Dir.** Ronald Neame; **Scr.** Jay Presson Allen (based on the novel by Muriel Spark); **Cin.** Ted Moore; **Ed.** Norman Savage; **Prod. D.** John Howell; **Art D.** Brian Herbert; **Mus.** Rod McKuen; **Cast:** Maggie Smith, Robert Stephens, Pamela Franklin, Gordon Jackson, Celia Johnson, Diane Grayson, Jane Carr.

Not entirely a successful film but, *The Prime of Miss Jean Brodie* stands out for the great performance of Maggie Smith as Jean Brodie. It is set in the 1930s in Edinburgh. She teaches history and art at the exclusive Marcia Blaine school for girls. She is an eccentric teacher who daydreams about the glories of Rome and Italy's Renaissance art. She is in love with everything Italian, including Mussolini's Fascist regime. She dotes on her best students whom she refers to as the "crème de la crème." They are equally devoted to her, and she takes them on long walks and picnics in the country. She is courted by a shy fellow teacher (Gordon Jackson), but she is not interested. She is attracted to an art teacher (Robert Stephens) who is married with children. When it is found that her political preachings have led to the death of one of her favorite students in the Spanish Civil War, she is dismissed. This is Maggie Smith's best film for which she won an Academy Award. The darkened classroom scene in which she shows slides and talks of Renaissance artists with tears in her eyes is one of the great movie scenes. Celia Johnson as the repressed head mistress is also very good. The concluding segment of the film becomes unnecessarily melodramatic.

The Producers

1967. 88 min. color. U.S. **Prod.** Sidney Glazier; **Dir.** Mel Brooks; **Scr.** Mel Brooks; **Cin.** Joseph Coffey; **Ed.** Ralph Rosenblum; **Art D.** Charles Rosen; **Mus.** John Morris; **Cast:** Zero Mostel, Gene Wilder, Kenneth Mars, Dick Shawn, Lee Meredith, Estelle Winwood, Christopher Hewett.

An unsuccessful Broadway producer, Max Bialystock (Zero Mostel), on the advice of his accountant, Leo Bloom (Gene

Wilder), decides to produce a show that is bound to fail. He sells 25,000 percent of the play to unsuspecting subscribers. When the play flops he need not pay the backers and can pocket all the money. After an exhaustive search for a bad play he selects *Springtime for Hitler* written by an avid Nazi, Franz Liebkind (Kenneth Mars), who wants the world to see the real Hitler that he loved—the Hitler who was a better dancer than Churchill; the Hitler who was a great painter. "He could finish an apartment in one afternoon, two coats." For director they select Roger De Bris (Christopher Hewett), a transvestite whose plays have never lasted beyond opening night. De Bris turns it into a musical, "A gay romp with Adolf and Eva in Berchtesgaden." Max advertises the play as "The Hitler with a song in his heart." For the lead actor they select a hippie, Larenzo St. Du Bois (Dick Shawn), who is so stoned he can't remember his own name. The play is a tremendous hit.

The film is about how bad taste succeeds. *The Producers* is Mel Brooks' first film and by far his most original. The humor is strained in the last fifteen minutes. There is no direction, as such, and it is overacted, especially by the supporting cast. But it is an original, funny and highly enjoyable movie.

Psycho

1960. 109 min. b.w. U.S. **Prod.** Alfred Hitchcock; **Dir.** Alfred Hitchcock; **Scr.** Joseph Stefano (based on the novel by Robert Bloch); **Cin.** John L. Russell, Jr.; **Ed.** George Tomasini; **Prod.** D. Joseph Hurley, Robert Clatworthy; **Mus.** Bernard Herrmann; **Cast:** Anthony Perkins, Janet Leigh, Vera Miles, John Gavin, Martin Balsam, John McIntire, Simon Oakland, Frank Albertson.

The film opens with two lovers, Marion Crane (Janet Leigh) and Sam Loomis (John Gavin), discussing their future in the bedroom of an apartment. Sam can't marry Marion because of financial difficulties. He owns a hardware store but has to pay his late father's debts and alimony to his ex-wife. The next scene has Marion as a secretary in a real estate office. A coarse loud-mouthed man has closed a deal for the purchase of a house for his daughter and leaves a cash deposit of $40,000. As it is late and banks are near closing, Marion is entrusted with its safe keeping until the next day. Marion gets into her car to head home but impulsively decides to leave town with the $40,000. She drives for several hours, but as it gets dark she becomes aware of the futility of her action and realizes Sam would be horrified if he found out. Exhausted, she stops at a small, deserted motel next to an old house off the main road. She has a brief chat with the motel manager, Norman Bates (Anthony Perkins). Norman lives in the old house taking care of his elderly, infirm mother. He is shy and withdrawn and devoted to his mother. Marion retires to her room and begins to take a shower. We see the relief on her face as she has decided to go back and return the money. In one of the most startling scenes for which we are totally unprepared, we see an old woman with white hair pull back the shower curtain and stab Marion a half dozen times. The scene is back lit and we don't get a clear picture of the face of the murderer. We next see Norman cleaning up what his mother has done. He throws Marion, her suitcase and her clothing into her car. The $40,000 had been hidden inside some newspapers that Norman unknowingly throws into the car as well. He then pushes the vehicle into a swamp. Some months later Sam and Marion's sister, Lila (Vera Miles), having traced Marion's route, stop to question Norman who denies ever meeting Marion. Later an insurance investigator, Milton Arbogast (Martin Balsam), questions Norman. While searching the house he is stabbed to death by the old lady in another virtuoso scene in which the camera follows the stabbed investigator tumbling from the top of the stairs to where he finally lands. Sam and Lila seek the help of the local sheriff who tells them that Norman's mother had died about eight years earlier. The plot now takes another turn.

Hitchcock has played with the viewer from the very outset. He begins the film as if it were about an investigation of a crime. The very opening scenes give us the place, date and time of the events to follow, reminiscent of the semi-documentary Fox films of Henry Hathaway like *Call Northside 777* (1948), and Elia Kazan's *Boomerang* (1947). Hitchcock sets a deliberately slow pace for the first third of the movie and leads us to believe that it is about the theft of the $40,000 and whether or how Marion will be caught. The most prominent name in the film, Janet Leigh, is then murdered and we wonder where the plot will go now. The revelation by the sheriff almost in passing that Mrs. Bates is dead is the first direct clue Hitchcock gives the viewer. The entire cast, save John Gavin, is good and Anthony Perkins gives an especially fine performance. The film is marred by the psychiatrist's facile explanation at the end. Norman is described as a "schizophrenic with a multiple personality with homicidal rages." Hitchcock could have done better or left it alone. *Psycho* is a fine film, despite a mediocre script.

The Quiet Man

1952. 129 min. color. U.S. **Prod.** Merian C. Cooper, John Ford, Michael Killanin; **Dir.** John Ford; **Scr.** Frank S. Nugent, Richard Llewellyn (based on the story by Maurice Walsh); **Cin.** Winton C. Hoch, Archie Stout, **Ed.** Jack Murray; **Art D.** Frank Hotaling; **Mus.** Victor Young; **Cast:** John Wayne, Maureen O'Hara, Barry Fitzgerald, Victor McLaglen, Mildred Natwick, Arthur Shields, Ward Bond, Ken Curtis, Francis Ford.

A "quiet man," Sean Thornton (John Wayne), has bought a little cottage in Innisfree, Ireland, where he was born, from the widow Mrs. Tillane (Mildred Natwick). He had been a prize fighter in America, but had retired after accidentally killing his opponent in the ring. Sean has decided to settle in his native land with his boxing earnings. In buying the cottage he has made an enemy of the wealthiest and meanest man in Innisfree, Red Will Danaher (Victor McLaglen), who has coveted the small plot of land. On his way to the cottage with the village cabby Sean sees what appears to be an apparition of a goddess, the beautiful red-haired Mary Kate (Maureen O'Hara), and is immediately smitten. She is the sister of the greedy Red Will and lives with her brother in a nearby cottage. They soon marry, but Red Will, out of sheer spite, refuses to give his sister her belongings and her dowry. Mary Kate asserts her right. "Whoever I wed, what's my own goes with me."

She is deeply hurt that Sean won't fight for her rights. She isn't aware that he fears he may kill again. Kate refuses to consummate the marriage. The film ends with what is probably its best sequence, when Sean is forced to fight Red Will with everyone from the village and neighboring areas as excited spectators.

The film is a good mix of several themes. Foremost is John Ford's nostalgic look at his ancestral land with his favorite actor playing a young Ford. It is the story of a man in search of peace and quiet, and a woman who wants and gets what is her due. The film is probably fifteen minutes too long, but it is made memorable by the introduction of some wonderful characters. There is Michaeleen Flynn, well played by Barry Fitzgerald, a pixy-like figure who is not above fomenting discord among his neighbors for a good fight; the local Catholic priest, Father Lonergan (Ward Bond), who is more interested in fishing or watching a donnybrook than in tending to his flock; the Anglican pastor, Reverend Cyril Playfair (Arthur Shields), who is accepted by the Catholic community as one of their own. The film is beautifully photographed by Winton Hoch and captures the pastoral beauty of Ireland. In this Ireland of John Ford, unlike in *The Informer* (1935), there is no strife, but peace and harmony. The film won Academy Awards for best direction and best cinematography, and received nominations for best picture, best supporting actor (Victor McLaglen), among several others.

Raise the Red Lantern

Da Hong Denglong Gao Gao Gua. 1991. 125 min. color. Chinese. **Prod.** Chiu Fu-Sheng; **Dir.** Zhang Yimou; **Scr.** Ni Zhen (based on the novel *Wives and Concubines* by Su Tong); **Cin.** Zhao Fei; **Ed.** Du Yuan; **Art D.** Cao Jiuping, Dong Huamiao; **Mus.** Zhao Jiping; **Cast:** Gong Li, Ma Jingwu, He Caifei, Cao Cuifeng, Jin Shuyuan, Ma Jingwu.

Set in China in the 1920's, Songlian (Gong Li), an educated nineteen-year-old beauty, in order to get away from her uncaring and harsh stepmother, agrees to become the fourth wife of an aging, wealthy and powerful man. Each wife has her own house and servant in a large compound. The wives have a communal lunch, but at night a red lantern is placed at the door of the wife the master has chosen for that night. The favored wife has the privilege of choosing the lunch menu for the next day and additional foot massages. There is intense jealousy and intrigue amongst the wives, each not only trying to gain the master's favor, but to demean her rivals. Although Songlian is the most beautiful and the most intelligent of the wives, she is unable to compete in this atmosphere of paranoia and hatred and meets a tragic end.

Zhang Yimou burst on the motion picture world with *Red Sorghum* (1987) and *Ju Dou* (1989). *Raise the Red Lantern* is his most mature and complex film. Not only are there more and better defined characters, but lyricism, dazzling cinematography, and imaginative use of sound, which are an integral part of all of Yimou's films, combine with a well maintained element of mystery and suspense. This is Gong Li's third film for Yimou and her best acting. This collaboration, that had been so fruitful for both ended after *Shanghai Triad* (1955)

Ran

1985. 161 min. color. Japanese. **Prod.** Masato Hara, Serge Silberman; **Dir.** Akira Kurosawa; **Scr.** Akira Kurosawa, Hideo Oguni, Masato Ide (based on the play *King Lear* by William Shakespeare); **Cin.** Takao Saito, Masaharu Ueda, Asa Kazu Nakai; **Ed.** Akira Kurosawa; **Prod.** D. Yoshiro Muraki, Shinobu Muraki; **Art D.** Yoshiro Muraki; **Mus.** Toru Takemitsu; **Cast:** Tatsuya Nakadai, Akira Terao, Jinpachi Nezu, Daisuke Ryu, Mieko Harada, Yoshiko Miyazaki, Herald Ace.

Set in sixteenth-century Japan, Hidetora Ichimonji (Tatsuya Nakadai), an aging warlord just turned seventy, cedes his authority to his eldest son and divides his fiefdom among his three sons. The principal castle goes to the eldest, Tarotakatora Ichimonji (Akira Terao), and the outlying castles are given to the other sons. The two eldest thank their father profusely. The youngest, Saburonaotora Ichimonji (Daisuke Ryu), however, questions the wisdom of the decision, calls his father an old fool and is banished. As the film

unfolds we learn that Hidetora had come from humble beginnings but, over fifty years of bloodshed and cruelty, had eliminated
all other warlords and now rules over a vast territory. The
youngest son genuinely loves his father and knows greed and
ambition will prevail. His fears are realized. The father is humiliated by the two elder sons, driven out of his castle and stripped of
his escort guards. The two brothers wage war against each other
for control of the entire domain, egged on by the eldest son's wife,
Lady Kaede (Mieko Harada). Destitute, their father takes to the
hills and a tragic end awaits all as "*ran*" (chaos) ensues.

The film is based on *King Lear*. Kurosawa has kept the main
structure of the Shakespeare play, but to cater to his Japanese
audience, he changed Lear's three daughters into three sons. The
medieval setting of Shakespeare has been transposed to sixteenth-
century Japan and the figure of King Lear is now a Japanese
warlord. Kent, Lear's trusted advisor, is the faithful Tango. The role
of the Fool is intact. Lady Kaede is an amalgam of Goneril,
Regan and Edmund, the bastard son of Gloucester; but Kurosawa
has also imbued her with some of the attributes of Lady Macbeth. The youngest son is Cordelia, although Cordelia would not
have spoken as harshly to her father. As in *Throne of Blood* (1957),
Kurosawa's adaptation of *Macbeth, Ran* is a visual feast, but it is
not Shakespeare's *King Lear.* Once the language of Shakespeare is
relinquished, the tragedy of *Lear* loses most of its depth and
power and it becomes merely a depiction of the ingratitude of
monstrous children and the warlord's arrogance and cruelty in
attaining power.

Ran is Kurosawa's twenty-seventh film, and he was at the
height of his creative power. The staging and photography of the
battle scenes are much better than *Kagemusha* (1980). The musical
score by Toru Takemitsu blends better with the film than some of
the early Kurosawa films. Denied the narrative and poetry of
Shakespeare, Kurosawa has added scenes early in the film that
establish the character of the three sons. Hidetora's suffering is the
beginning of wisdom and Kurosawa succeeds in depicting that
transformation before Hidetora dies. The acting, especially by
Nakadai as Hidetora and Harada as Lady Kaede, is very effective.

Rebecca

1940. 130 min. b.w. U.S. **Prod.** David O. Selznick; **Dir.** Alfred Hitchcock; **Scr.** Robert E. Sherwood, Joan Harrison (based on the novel by Daphne du Maurier); **Cin.** George Barnes; **Ed.** James Newcom, Hal C. Kern; **Art D.** Lyle Wheeler; **Mus.** Franz Waxman; **Cast:** Laurence Olivier, Joan Fontaine, George Sanders, Judith Anderson, Nigel Bruce, Reginald Denny, C. Aubrey Smith, Gladys Cooper, Florence Bates, Leo G. Carroll, Melville Cooper.

A brooding, wealthy Maxim de Winter (Laurence Olivier) has come to Monte Carlo to forget the tragic death of his beautiful wife Rebecca in a drowning accident. He meets a young, shy girl (Joan Fontaine) who is there as a paid companion to a vain and demanding matron. After three or four days of casual encounters he asks her to marry him. She is in love with him and agrees. They return to Maxim's ancestral home, Manderley, a vast estate in Cornwall. She is confronted by a large staff of servants and the housekeeper, Mrs. Danvers (Judith Anderson), who appears hostile to the young tongue-tied bride. Mrs. Danvers had adored Rebecca and does everything to make the new Mrs.. de Winter uncomfortable. She reminds her of how beautiful and elegant the first Mrs.. de Winter had been. Rebecca's death is shrouded in mystery and no one, including Maxim, is willing to discuss it. Finally, Rebecca's character is revealed culminating in a tale of infidelity and blackmail.

Hitchcock, in this his first American film, brings suspense to the popular novel of Daphne du Maurier. He turns a routine romantic novel into a superb Gothic tale. The film has an excellent secondary cast with Judith Anderson giving a truly unforgettable performance as the deranged Mrs. Danvers. Gladys Cooper as Maxim's thoughtful and sensible sister and George Sanders as the cousin and lover of Rebecca are both superb. Joan Fontaine gives one of her best performances as well. She is also the off-screen narrator of the film. Laurence Olivier is slightly stiff and not at his best. *Rebecca* is the only Hitchcock film to have won an Academy Award for best picture. The moody cinematography of George Barnes also won an Academy Award. The film received nine other nominations.

The Red Badge of Courage

1951. 69 min. b.w. U.S. **Prod.** Gottfried Reinhardt; **Dir.** John Huston; **Scr.** John Huston, Albert Band (based on the novel by Stephen Crane); **Cin.** Harold Rosson; **Ed.** Ben Lewis; **Art D.** Cedric Gibbons, Hans Peters; **Mus.** Bronislau Kaper; **Cast:** Audie Murphy, Bill Mauldin, Douglas Dick, Royal Dano, Arthur Hunnicutt, Andy Devine, John Dierkes.

The film is set during the American Civil War. A young man of twenty-two, Henry Fleming (Audie Murphy), has his baptism of fire against a Confederate regiment near Chancellorville, Virginia, in May 1863. The Union soldiers have established a defensive position, facing an impending attack by the Confederates. Most of the Union soldiers are green and untried. As they talk amongst themselves we find some have never been in battle nor seen a man killed before. Fleming has just completed a letter to his mother, "I hope my conduct on the battlefield will make you proud of your loving son." Fleming and his two closest friends, Tom Wilson (Bill Mauldin) and Jim Conlin (John Dierkes), the Tall Soldier, talk about what they would do if the Confederates were about to overrun their positions. The Tall Soldier says, "If I see others running, I would run, but if they stand, I will stand." Fleming says he won't ever run and Tom agrees. At the first charge, the Confederates are driven back and the line is held, but the Confederates regroup and charge the Union line again. Fleming runs away, abandons his rifle and gear and hides in the nearby woods. He had hoped he would sustain a bloody wound, his "red badge of courage." He is deeply ashamed and decides to go back. He comes upon some Union soldiers running away and tries to stop them, but he is hit by a rifle butt and knocked unconscious. Fleming is found and revived by the Fat Soldier (Andy Devine). Fleming rejoins his regiment which is sent to the woods to dislodge the Confederates. He charges the enemy position and even carries the flag. He is now a hero in the eyes of his comrades. When the fighting abates he confides to Tom that he had run away after the first encounter. Tom who had been a braggart now confesses that he too had tried to run away but had been stopped by the lieutenant (Douglas Dick).

Harold Rosson has photographed some of the best staged battle scenes on film. Several other scenes stand out. The Tall Soldier has been shot in the stomach and climbs a hill where he wants to die. In another scene a Union soldier is shot and loses his eyeglasses. He bends down, picks them up, then collapses and dies. The film is also rich in characterization. John Huston went against convention and incurred the enmity of MGM bosses when he did not cast any of their stars. For the lead he selected Audie Murphy, the most highly decorated American soldier in World War II. For the second lead he chose Bill Mauldin, another veteran of WWII who had introduced the scathing cartoons of high brass and depicted the plight of the ordinary soldier in the G.I. newspaper *Stars and Stripes.* Murphy had limited acting experience and a more seasoned actor probably would have been more effective. Bill Mauldin had never appeared in a film but he is credible. The other speaking parts went to actors who most resembled the characters in Stephen Crane's fine novel. When shooting was completed Huston left for Africa where he was to direct his next film, *The African Queen* (1951). In his absence, MGM executives butchered the film. Entire scenes were eliminated or decimated and the film was cut to a mere sixty-nine minutes. The basic themes of the novel and the film about the fine line between bravery and cowardice, the tragedy of Americans fighting Americans and the antiwar message were blurred. L. B. Mayer had been opposed to the making of the film from the outset. The tension and disagreements between Mayer and Dore Schary, the studio production head, again erupted and Mayer subsequently was forced to resign under pressure from the MGM New York office. Unfortunately no print of Huston's final cut has survived. He always believed his final cut was the best film he had directed. *The Red Badge of Courage* is still a near masterpiece.

Red River

1948. 133 min. b.w. U.S. **Prod.** Howard Hawks; **Dir.** Howard Hawks; **Scr.** Borden Chase, Charles Schnee (based on the novel *The Chisholm Trail* by Borden Chase); **Cin.** Russell Harlan; **Ed.** Christian Nyby; **Art D.** John Datu Arensma; **Mus.** Dimitri Tiomkin; **Cast:** John Wayne, Montgomery Clift, Walter Brennan, Joanne Dru, John Ireland, Noah Beery, Jr., Paul Fix, Coleen Gray, Harry Carey, Harry Carey, Jr.

The film begins in the late 1840s. A wagon train of men, women and children are heading west. A young man, Tom Dunson (John Wayne), and his sidekick, Groot Nadine (Walter Brennan), take their wagon out of the line, bid farewell and head south toward the Texas panhandle and the Red River. Tom leaves his sweetheart, Fen (Coleen Gray), behind hoping to bring her to Texas once he is settled. When they are a good distance away they notice black smoke behind them on the horizon and know Indians have attacked and burned the wagons. The next day they find a dazed and incoherent boy, Matthew Garth, the sole survivor of the wagon train massacre, and they take him with them. Once in Texas, Dunson lays claim to a large stretch of land, killing the agent of the claimant who had based his right on a deed from the king of Spain. As years go by Dunson builds a cattle empire and defends his ownership by killing seven other claimants and "reads over ´em from the Bible." The grown Matthew, "Matt" (Montgomery Clift) now returns from the Civil War and runs the operation for Dunson, his surrogate father. Dunson has become financially strapped and needs money. The Civil War has bankrupted the South and the largest cattle market is now in the North. There is talk that the railroad has reached Abeline, Kansas, but no one can confirm it. Dunson therefore decides to drive his cattle north by the Chisholm Trail to Missouri, which is by all accounts more difficult and hazardous. As conditions worsen and a few cowhands lose their lives, there is strife in the ranks and some even desert. Matt and most of the cowboys, including a hired gun, Cherry Valance (John Ireland), argue to change the route, but Dunson refuses. The last straw is when Dunson is about to hang three cowhands who had deserted. Matt forcibly stops him and he is made to leave the drive with a few of his loyalists. Dunson threatens to be back and kill Matt. The herd is taken to Abeline and sold for a good price and Matt waits for a showdown with Dunson.

The first three-quarters of the movie is flawless. Although it was shot on the studio ranch, there are magnificent scenes of vast spaces, valleys and rivers. The start of the drive is beautifully photographed. The scenes of crossing the river, the storm and the stampede preceded by eerie silence and the restless movement of the cattle are amongst the best on film. Unfortunately the last quarter becomes commonplace Hollywood. With the introduction of Tess Millay (Joanne Dru) who is rescued by Matt from an Indian attack, it becomes contrived. She stops the climactic fistfight between Dunson and Matt simply by lecturing them about what they mean to each other. Hawks has attempted to make the fight realistic by having Dunson shot in the arm by the gunman Cherry Valance. We are now supposed to think it is an even match between the six-foot-three-inch one-armed John Wayne and the slightly built Montgomery Clift. *Red River* is still a magnificent film and there is a certain grandeur to it. The reliable Howard Hawks was an excellent storyteller and never made a bad film in his long career. He directed every type of film—gangster, screwball comedy, adventure, Western and even musical comedy. He is assisted here by the fine photography of Russell Harlan. There is a good script by Borden Chase, although Hawks changed the ending and the character of Cherry Valance is not fully developed. John Wayne, an orthodox Hollywood actor, and Clift, a "method" actor, are both very good. Walter Brennan, John Ireland and the rest of the supporting cast are excellent. Joanne Dru, one of the most beautiful actresses in Hollywood, is radiant but superfluous to the film.

Repulsion

1965. 104 min. b.w. British. **Prod.** Gene Gutowski; **Dir.** Roman Polanski; **Scr.** Roman Polanski, Gerard Brach, David Stone; **Cin.** Gilbert Taylor; **Ed.** Alistair McIntyre; **Art D.** Seamus Flannery; **Mus.** Chico Hamilton; **Cast:** Catherine Deneuve, Ian Hendry, John Fraser, Patrick Wymark, Yvonne Furneaux, Renee Houston, Helen Fraser.

A beautiful young Belgian girl, Carol Ledoux (Catherine Deneuve), is a manicurist in a London beauty salon and lives with her sister, Helen (Yvonne Furneaux), who is employed in the same salon. We first see Carol at work, totally withdrawn, shy and barely saying a word. During her lunch hour at a local pub she does not touch her food. She is being courted by a proper, young Englishman, John (John Fraser). Despite his pleas for a lunch or dinner date, she does not respond. At the end of the day she goes home, compulsively washes her hands and feet, and goes to bed. Her sister comes home with her lover, Michael (Ian Hendry). Carol is awakened by the sighs and moans of the lovers in the next room and can't sleep. The following night she hears the same ecstatic sighs and has another restless night. Her sister and lover leave for a short holiday to Italy and once alone her condition worsens. At work she deliberately injures the finger of a customer she is manicuring. The manager, believing Carol is disturbed by personal problems, lets her go home. John, who had tried to reach her several times, calls on her but she won't open the door. He forces it open and comes in. When he turns to close the door she clubs him to death with a heavy instrument. She later stabs and kills the lecherous landlord who has come to collect back rent. The film closes with her sister and Michael returning and, to their horror, finding the bodies. An effective close-up of a photograph of the two sisters as children ends the film.

Repulsion is one of Polanski's best films. It is a portrait of the disintegration of a woman repulsed by, and yet obsessed with, sex. Her surroundings, accentuated by the active sex life of her sister, finally unhinge her and she descends into a world of destructive nightmares. She cannot cleanse herself by merely washing her hands and feet. She must destroy anyone who poses a sexual threat. Polanski, in his first feature film in English, has done a masterful job. Instead of giving us a verbal explanation of Carol's madness, he lets us enter her nightmares by the ingenious use of images and sounds within the confines of the apartment, especially her bedroom, which also prepare us for the Grand Guignol ending. The film relies so much on sight and sound that the acting is only supplementary.

Ride the High Country

1962. 94 min. color. U.S. **Prod.** Richard E. Lyons; **Dir.** Sam Peckinpah; **Scr.** N. B. Stone, Jr.; **Cin.** Lucien Ballard; **Ed.** Frank Santillo; **Art D.** George W. Davis, Leroy Coleman; **Mus.** George Bassman; **Cast:** Randolph Scott, Joel McCrea, Mariette Hartley, Ronald Starr, Edgar Buchanan, R. G. Armstrong, Warren Oates, L. Q. Jones, James Drury.

The film is set at the turn of the twentieth century. It opens with Steve Judd (Joel McCrea), a retired lawman, riding down the street of the northern California town of Hornitos. He is down on his luck and has learned that a bank needs a security guard to escort a shipment of gold worth $250,000 from the mining town of Coarse Gold to the bank in Hornitos. His shirt cuffs are frayed and he tucks them under his sleeve and walks into the bank. The banker and his son are taken aback by his age. They explain it is a hazardous job and it pays $20 a day. Judd says he will need two helpers at $10 a day. The bankers agree to offer him a contract. In another telling scene, Judd goes to the bathroom and puts on his glasses to read the contract. He does not want his employers to know his eyesight is wanting. Judd accepts the job and leaves the bank. He runs into a former lawman and friend, Gil Westrum (Randolph Scott), who has also fallen on hard times as he has aged. He has been reduced to putting on a Wild West show as the Oregon Kid with feats of marksmanship. Judd hires Westrum and his young sidekick Heck Longtree (Ronald Starr). What Judd is unaware of is that Westrum is no longer the straight lawman he had known. He has become corrupt and would do anything to lay his hands on some money. Westrum accepts the job but plans to steal the gold at his first opportunity. On their

trip to Coarse Gold they stop at the house of a farmer, Joshua
Knudsen (R. G. Armstrong), a religious zealot who can't stop
preaching and treats his neglected and repressed daughter Elsa
(Mariette Hartley) harshly. To escape her father's grip Elsa runs
away and begs Judd to let her accompany them to Coarse Gold.
Elsa has accepted the offer of marriage of Billy Hammond (James
Drury), one of four brothers who work in the mining town. The
Hammonds are a primitive lot. The minute they eye Elsa it is
understood amongst them that when she is married to Billy they
all will share her. Elsa is married in the local brothel. The madam
is the bridesmaid and the other whores are the flower girls.
Drunken judge Tolliver (Edgar Buchanan) performs the ceremony. Judd takes delivery of the gold, but having witnessed the
plight of Elsa, who is beaten and nearly raped by the brothers, he
rescues her and they take her with them. Once out of town,
Westrum makes his move to steal the gold, but young Heck
refuses to go along with him. Judd stops Westrum and ties his
hands. Next the Hammonds attack. The final sequence has Judd,
Heck and Elsa trapped in a ditch. Judd has been shot and his
movements are restricted. Westrum who had escaped now
returns. Judd and Westrum have a showdown with the Hammonds in true Western style.

   Ride the High Country is in many ways an equal of *The Wild
Bunch* (1969). It does not have the same broad scope, but it is
equally well directed and controlled by Peckinpah who has great
empathy and understanding of the Old West. The film is beautifully photographed by Lucien Ballard against a background of
the California/Nevada Sierra Mountains. Almost all of Peckinpah's films deal with people who have survived long past their
time, whether in *The Wild Bunch* (1969) or *The Ballad of Cable
Hogue* (1970). The very first scene in *Ride the High Country* has
Judd riding his horse into the streets of Hornitos, which is in the
midst of some celebration with parades, bands and cheering people lining the street. Judd acknowledges their cheers, believing
the crowd has recognized him as a prominent former lawman.
Then he is nearly run over and driven off the street by a contraption called an automobile that the public has come to see. We

then see Judd's fraying cuffs and his need for eyeglasses, and we know that he is poor and time has passed him by. The end of the film is well done with no sentimentality. The wounded Judd, is thankful for Westrum's return to help against the three surviving Hammond brothers. The five men face each other. The Hammonds are killed. Westrum promises the dying Judd that he will deliver the gold. Judd says, "Hell, I know that. I always did. You just forgot for a while, that's all." Judd also asks Westrum not to let Elsa or Heck see him die and adds, "I'll go it alone." Westrum says, "See you later." Peckinpah picked two aging, almost forgotten actors who had been in movies for thirty years. Randolph Scott appeared mostly in B Westerns. McCrea had a wider range and had worked with prominent directors such as Wyler, Hitchcock, George Stevens and Sturges, in some fine films. Warren Oates and L. Q. Jones who play two of the Hammond brothers became favorites of Peckinpah and he cast them in his later films.

Rififi

Du Rififi Chez Les Hommes. 1954. 115 min. b.w. French. **Prod.** Rene G. Vauttoux; **Dir.** Jules Dassin; **Scr.** Jules Dassin, Rene Wheeler, Auguste Le Breton (based on the novel by Auguste Le Breton); **Cin.** Philippe Agostini; **Ed.** Roger Dwyer; **Art D.** Auguste Capelier; **Mus.** Georges Auric; **Cast:** Jean Servais, Carl Mohner, Magali Noel, Robert Manuel, Jules Dassin, Marie Sabouret, Janine Darcy, Robert Hossein, Marcel Lupovici.

Tony (Jean Servais) has just been released from prison. He had turned himself in on a robbery charge to protect Joe (Carl Mohner), his godson, who is married and has a little boy. Tony finds his wife living with a rival gangster, Pierre (Marcel Lupovici). He has planned a heist at the very upscale, well-protected English jewelry shop on the Rue de Rivoli. He recruits Joe and two others: Mario (Robert Manuel), an expert on alarms, and Cesar (Jules Dassin), an artist at safe-cracking. The robbery goes well but Cesar, a confirmed womanizer, gives a stolen jewel to one of his pickups. Soon the rival gang is alerted. They kidnap Joe's son and there is a bloody end for both gangs.

The robbery itself is the centerpiece of the film. It starts at midnight and ends at six in the morning. The robbers meticulously drill through the store's ceiling, descend to the floor below, disconnect the alarm and crack the safe. Throughout the operation not a word is spoken and the only sounds are those of the thieves at work. It is this sequence that takes the film to a level that matches the best of Hollywood's caper films and is far superior to any other French gangster film. *Rififi*, which essentially means "trouble," becomes almost a documentary on how to commit the perfect heist. It has some excellent scenes of deserted Paris streets in the early morning hours and also captures the atmosphere of the seedy nightclubs. There is no memorable acting. The film comes close to *The Asphalt Jungle* (1950) directed by John Huston, but the Huston film has much better acting and crisper dialogue. Dassin was unofficially blacklisted and could not find work in Hollywood. He went into self-exile in Paris and made *Rififi*, his first film in five years. None of his European films, including *Topkapi* (1964), stand up to *Rififi*. Dassin shared best director prize at the 1955 Cannes Film Festival.

Rocky

1976. 119 min. color. U.S. **Prod.** Irwin Winkler, Robert Chartoff; **Dir.** John G. Avildsen; **Scr.** Sylvester Stallone; **Cin.** James Crabe; **Ed.** Richard Halsey, Scott Conrad; **Prod.** D. William J. Cassidy; **Art D.** James S. Spencer; **Mus.** Bill Conti; **Cast:** Sylvester Stallone, Talia Shire, Burt Young, Carl Weathers, Burgess Meredith, Thayer David, Joe Spinel.

Rocky Balboa (Sylvester Stallone) is a thirty-year-old club boxer from Philadelphia who is past his prime. Between fights he works as a collector for a loan shark. The undefeated heavyweight champion of the world, Apollo Creed (Carl Weathers), is running out of challengers. No one has ever gone the distance with the champion. As a publicity stunt, Apollo offers to fight an unknown boxer on the Fourth of July to demonstrate that the American dream is alive and every American has a chance at greatness. Rocky is selected. He is from Philadelphia, the birthplace of the nation. He is of Italian descent, has won his last fight and has a catchy fight name, "The Italian Stallion." Rocky chooses as his manager/trainer a seventy-six-year-old ex-boxer, Mickey (Burgess Meredith), who had fought on the same bill as the Dempsey/Firpo title fight. Rocky's ambition is to go the distance with the champ to prove to his girl, Adrian (Talia Shire), his manager and himself that he is not just another bum. He begins training each day at dawn. He runs for miles through the streets of Philadelphia and up the steps of the Art Museum. For a punching bag he pounds the frozen carcasses in a slaughterhouse freezer, and he does hundreds of one-arm push-ups every day. The months of merciless training pays off, and he goes the distance.

This Cinderella fairy tale is immensely enjoyable. The script, written by Stallone, has humor and was inspired by Terry Malloy's memorable line in *On the Waterfront* (1954), "I coulda been a contender…instead of a bum, which I am." The scenes of Rocky training to the accompaniment of the theme song "Gonna Fly Now" are the best parts of the movie—much better than the artificial choreography of the fight scenes. The pacing of the direction is flawless and the cast gives uniformly excellent performances. Stallone, Burt Young and Talia Shire are very good, but best of all is Burgess Meredith who, having appeared in more than forty films, gives the performance of a lifetime. The film won Academy Awards for best picture, best director and editing; and received nominations for best actor, supporting actors (Meredith and Young) and best song.

Roman Holiday

1953. 119 min. b.w. U.S. **Prod.** William Wyler; **Dir.** William Wyler; **Scr.** Ian McLellan Hunter, John Dighton (based on a story by Dalton Trumbo); **Cin.** Franz Planer, Henri Alekan; **Ed.** Robert Swink; **Art D.** Hal Pereira, Walter Tyler; **Mus.** Georges Auric; **Cast:** Gregory Peck, Audrey Hepburn, Eddie Albert, Tullio Carminati, Hartley Power, Paolo Carlini, Harcourt Williams, Margaret Rawlings, Alberto Rizzo, Claudio Ermolli.

A reverse Cinderella story. Princess Anne, the young heir to the throne of an unnamed European country, is in Rome as part of a goodwill tour. After a particularly strenuous day of making the same speeches, visiting factories and schools, and attending receptions, she is somewhat agitated and given a sedative to make her sleep. She has lived a sheltered life, and now wants to see Rome on her own and find out how ordinary people live. She sneaks out unnoticed but soon falls asleep on a park bench. She is barely awakened by a young wire service reporter, Joe Bradley (Gregory Peck), who, thinking it unsafe for a girl alone, takes her to his small apartment. Next day Bradley recognizes her but pretends he doesn't know who she is. Every reporter in Rome has been trying to interview the princess and Bradley knows he has a scoop. He arranges with a news photographer friend, Irving Radovich (Eddie Albert), to secretly snap pictures as he takes her around Rome. They all go sightseeing and have great fun. An unspoken romance develops, but late that night he takes her back to her embassy.

William Wyler had never made a comedy, but in his first attempt he fashioned a charming and highly enjoyable film. There are some funny and endearing scenes: the princess getting a modern haircut by a flirtatious hairdresser; her first introduction in a café to the gregarious news photographer; a dance on a crowded pier that ends up in a free-for-all brawl; the dispatch of some twenty secret service men by her country to find the princess; and the princess' last press conference before leaving Rome. Wyler usually extracted first-rate performances from women and smoothly guided Hepburn in her first major film role. Peck is his dependable self, but better still is Eddie Albert who dominates all of his scenes. A contingent of minor Italian actors contribute greatly to the enjoyment of the film: Alberto Rizzo as the cabbie; Paolo Carlini as the amorous hairdresser; and Claudio Ermolli as the janitor of Peck's apartment building. There has been a great deal of speculation as to how the film would have been improved had it been directed by Lubitsch or Wilder. It's an enticing question, but Wyler turned in an excellent job.

Rome, Open City

(a.k.a. *Open City*) *Roma, Città Aperta*. 1945. 105 min. b.w. Italian. **Dir.** Roberto Rossellini; **Scr.** Sergio Amidei, Federico Fellini, Roberto Rossellini; **Cin.** Ubaldo Arata; **Ed.** Eraldo Da Roma; **Mus.** Renzo Rossellini; **Cast:** Aldo Fabrizi, Anna Magnani, Marcello Pagliero, Maria Michi, Harry Feist, Francesco Grandjacquet.

The film is set some time after 10 September, 1943, when Italy had withdrawn from the war and German tr oops occupied Rome. A Resistance leader, Manfredi (Marcello Pagliero), must deliver money to the underground. He hides at the apartment of his friend, Francesco (Francesco Grandjacquet),who lives there with his pregnant fiancée, Pina (Anna Magnani). The building is raided by the Gestapo and Francesco is taken away. In the most memorable scene in the movie, Pina runs screaming after the truck and is shot down on the street by German troops. Manfredi escapes and contacts Don Pietro (Aldo Fabrizi), a priest, to make the delivery. They are both arrested. Manfredi is killed under torture without revealing any names and Don Pietro is shot.

Open City holds up well today, but it had a much greater impact at the time of its release. It depicts Rome shortly before its liberation by the Allies, and has the look of newsreel authenticity. No lighting was used and no sets were erected. It was shot on the streets of Rome. Almost all the actors were nonprofessionals. If there is any drawback to the film it is the script, which does not give much depth to the characters. Together with *Shoeshine* (1946), *Open City* constitutes the beginning of Italian neorealist cinema. The movement greatly influenced the French new wave of the late fifties, and the semi-documentary style in the U.S. shortly after the war.

Rules of the Game

La Regle du Jeu. 1939. 113 min. b.w. French. **Prod.** Jean Renoir; **Dir.** Jean Renoir; **Scr.** Jean Renoir with Carl Koch, Camille Francois, the cast; **Cin.** Jean Bachelet, Jacques Lemare, Jean-Paul Alphen, Alan Renior; **Ed.** Marguerite Renior, Marthe Huguet; **Art D.** Eugene Lourie, Max Douy; **Mus.** Roger Desormieres, Saint-Saens, Mozart, Johann Strauss, Chopin, et al; **Cast:** Marcel Dalio, Nora Gregor, Mila Parely, Jean Renoir, Gaston Modot, Roland Toutain, Paulette Dubost, Julien Carette, Odette Talazac, Pierre Magnier.

Andre Jurieu (Roland Toutain), an aviator, has landed at Le Bourget airport having completed a record-breaking transatlantic flight. He is met by his friend Octave (Jean Renoir), and an ecstatic crowd. In a radio interview at the airport he announces that he undertook the flight for the love of a woman and is disappointed she is not at the airport. The object of his love is Christine de la Chesnaye (Nora Gregor) who is married to Robert de la Chesnaye (Marcel Dalio), a wealthy aristocrat with a house in Paris and a château in the country. Robert knows of his wife's affair with Andre but does not want to do anything that may result in losing her. Robert himself has a mistress in Paris, Genevieve (Mila Parely). Robert has organized a weekend party at his château for a rabbit shoot and Octave (Jean Renoir), a close friend of Robert and Christine, arranges for Andre to be invited. Genevieve who is also invited brings her maid, Lisette (Paulette Dubost), the wife of Schumacker (Gaston Modot), the game-keeper at the château. Lisette is flirtatious and prefers to be in Paris away from her husband. Schumacker, an intensely jealous man, is very pleased to have his wife with him at least for the weekend. In preparing for the shoot the next day, Robert finds a poacher, Marceau (Julien Carette). He is amused by him and instead of ejecting him from the grounds offers him a job as a servant at the château. The guests all arrive and trouble begins. Marceau, now a servant, begins to chase the maid Lisette who seems to be enjoying his attentions, which increasingly angers Schumacker. Christine, who had decided to break with Andre, catches her husband kissing his mistress during the hunt. She changes her mind and decides to go away with Andre. Schumacker now goes after Marceau with a vengeance. Robert dismisses both the gamekeeper and the poacher, but it is too late. The farce turns to tragedy. Somehow the gamekeeper believes Octave is having an affair with his wife and goes after him with a rifle but mistakenly shoots and kills Andre.

Rules of the Game is one of the most imitated films. It could have been set in England or Scotland. The Shooting Party (1984) is a prime example. It is the story of infidelity and the decadence of the aristocracy on the eve of World War II. In this comedy of manners there are rules society has set for how husbands, wives and mistresses should behave. You don't broadcast your affair with a married woman on radio. You don't passionately kiss your mistress where you can be seen. These rules must be adhered to by the people "upstairs" as well as by servants and gamekeepers "downstairs." Octave at the end admits it is not easy for everyone to adhere to these rules as "everyone has his own reasons." The irony in the film is that Octave who observes these rules is himself an unfulfilled character. It is the best photographed of Renoir's films of the thirties. There are also some fine performances. Marcel Dalio has the role of a lifetime. During the war years he was in the U.S. and appeared in several Hollywood films in small roles. Renoir shows himself to be a fine actor. Julien Carette as the poacher is also excellent. Mila Parely is the best of the women. This unusual blend of farce and tragedy, like Grand Illusion (1937), is a very personal film for Renoir. It is a cry from the heart.

Sansho the Bailiff

Sansho Dayu. 1954. 125 min. b.w. Japanese. **Prod.** Masaichi Nagata; **Dir.** Kenji Mizoguchi; **Scr.** Yahiro Fuji, Yoshikata Yoda (based on the novel Sansho Dayu by Ogai Mori); **Cin.** Kazuo Miyagawa; **Ed.** Mitsuji Miyata; **Art D.** Kisaku Ito; **Mus.** Fumio Hayasaka, Kanahichi Odera, Tamekichi Mochizuki; **Cast:** Yoshiaki Hanayagi, Kinuyo Tanaka, Kyoko Kagawa, Eitaro Shindo.

Set in eleventh-century Japan, Tamaki (Kinuyo Tanaka), the wife of a former official who has been exiled by his enemies, has been searching for her husband. She is with her young daughter, Anju (Kyoko Kagawa), and son, Zushio (Yoshiaki Hanayagi). The film begins as they travel through the woods. They come across a priestess in the employ of river pirates. She misleads them into taking the wrong road where they are set upon by kidnappers. The wife is sold into prostitution and sent to a remote island. The children are sold as slaves to a powerful bailiff, Sansho (Eitaro Shindo), who runs a large slave compound. After the passing of some ten years Zushio has become the administrator of Sansho's vast holdings. He has acquired the confidence of Sansho by his cruel and harsh treatment of the slaves. He is still haunted, however, by the fate of his father and mother. He has also become aware that slavery itself promotes cruelty and there must be an end to it. He decides to escape the compound with Anju. At the last minute Anju, who feels she will be a burden as she will not be able to keep pace and if arrested she may reveal his whereabouts under torture, drowns herself. Alone Zushio reaches Kyoto, his ancestral home. Much to his surprise he discovers his father is now remembered as a hero and songs have been written about his good deeds. The ruler of Kyoto, in order to correct the wrong done to his father, appoints Zushio governor of the province where Sansho operates his farm. Zushio's first edict is to outlaw slavery and banish Sansho. Zushio institutes reforms for the humane treatment of workers. When his work is done he resigns from the governorship and begins his search for his mother. He finally finds her on Sado Island, near death. In a beautiful recognition scene mother and son are reunited.

Mizoguchi was the first important Japanese director. The main theme in most of his films is the status of women and in *Ugetsu Monogatari* (1953) the conflict arising from the role of women in a transitional Japanese society was explored. In *Sansho the Bailiff* there is also the theme of human suffering and redemption. Mizoguchi's films are distinguished by great care for detail. In the outdoor scenes the elements of nature are captured with realism and his use of deep-focus shots underline the emotional suffering of his protagonists.

Scarface

1932. 90 min. b.w. U.S. **Prod.** Howard Hughes; **Dir.** Howard Hawks; **Scr.** Ben Hecht, Seton I. Miller, John Lee Mahin, W. R. Burnett, Fred Pasley (based on the novel by Armitage Trail); **Cin.** Lee Garmes, L. W. O'Connell; **Ed.** Edward Curtiss; **Prod.** D. Harry Olivier; **Mus.** Adolf Tandler, Gus Arnheim; **Cast:** Paul Muni, Ann Dvorak, George Raft, Boris Karloff, Karen Morley, Osgood Perkins, Henry Gordon, Vince Barnett, Henry Vejar.

Scarface is the violent story of a brutal killer who eliminates all his rivals and becomes the crime boss of an unidentified Midwestern city. Tony Camonte (Paul Muni) is the scarred hoodlum. He works for gangster Johnny Lovo (Osgood Perkins) who is in charge of the south-side operations of the city. Lovo himself takes his orders from the crime boss, Big Louis (Henry Vejar). We first see Tony as he murders a rival mobster on the orders of Lovo. He is arrested, but the mob lawyer has him released. Tony has his own triggerman, Guino Rinaldo (George Raft), who takes orders only from him. He has an attractive sister, Cesca (Ann Dvorak) who is carrying on a romance with Guino without Tony's knowledge. Tony talks Lovo into assassinating Big Louis and becoming the boss. With Big Louis eliminated Lovo realizes that Tony has ambitions of his own and arranges for his murder, which fails. In retaliation Tony kills Lovo and the north-side boss Gaffney (Boris Karloff) becoming the undisputed crime boss. When he finds his sister in Guino's apartment he shoots him dead, not knowing that the two were married that very day. This is the beginning of the end for Tony Camonte. The police corner him and both he and his sister are killed in the shootout.

Scarface is one of Hawks' best and probably the best of the thirties gangster films. It gives an excellent portrait of a gangster who has no redeeming features. He kills his boss and acquires his moll not for emotional but for acquisitive reasons. He kills his one trusted henchman without giving him a chance to explain. He cannot communicate with anyone, in fact he can barely speak English. He loves gaudy clothes and jewelry, and prides himself on wearing a new shirt every day. The film is well directed with numerous imaginative scenes. In the very opening scene, when

Camonte murders a mobster, he is shown in shadows. The murder of Gaffney is also not shown in its entirety. We have Gaffney in a bowling alley picking up a ball. The camera then follows the ball, which knocks down all the pins except one. This pin finally falls signifying Gaffney's death. The film is well acted, particularly by Muni, Perkins (an accomplished stage and screen actor and father of Anthony Perkins) and Karen Morley as Lovo's moll. Raft has very few lines and is stiff; however, he left his imprint on films with his trademark flipping of a coin. The characters are loosely modeled on the Chicago gangsters of the twenties and thirties: Camonte, after Al Capone; Big Louis after Big Jim Colisimo; and Gaffney after Bugs Moran. The film had a censorship problem both for its violence and implied theme of incest. A subtitle was added by the Hays office: *Shame of a Nation*.

Scarlet Street

1945. 103 min. b.w. U.S. **Prod.** Fritz Lang; **Dir.** Fritz Lang; **Scr.** Dudley Nichols (based on the novel and play *La Chienne* by Georges de la Fouchardiere, Mouezy-Eon); **Cin.** Milton Krasner; **Ed.** Arthur Hilton; **Art D.** Alexander Golitzen, John B. Goodman; **Mus.** H. J. Salter; **Cast:** Edward G. Robinson, Joan Bennett, Dan Duryea, Margaret Lindsay, Rosalind Ivan, Samuel S. Hinds, Vladimir Sokolof, Jess Barker.

Christopher Cross (Edward G. Robinson) is a middle-aged cashier for a New York City retailer. He is a withdrawn and private person, married to a shrewish unattractive woman. He spends most of his spare time painting, despite the loud objections of his wife who accuses him of wasting money on paint and canvases. The film opens at a banquet honoring his twenty-five years of service to the company. On his way home he sees a man beating a woman and goes to her rescue. He knocks down the assailant with his umbrella. The woman, Kitty March (Joan Bennett), dissuades him from calling the police. He asks her to have a drink with him and, to make an impression, tells her he is a successful artist. Before long his infatuation becomes serious and she leads him on. Cross is not aware that Kitty lives with the hoodlum Johnny Prince (Dan

Duryea), who was beating her. Kitty talks him into renting a studio in Greenwich Village that can be used both for his painting and as a place for them to meet. Cross is so touched that he has at last found someone who is interested in his work that he brings some paintings to the newly rented place. Soon the expenses of entertaining Kitty and the rental of the studio are too much and he is forced to embezzle from his employer. Kitty and Johnny, impressed with Cross' outlay of cash, begin to think that perhaps his paintings are worth something. They remove Cross' signature from the paintings and substitute Kitty's. They bring experts from nearby art galleries who find the works original and estimate that each could be sold for several thousand dollars. While Kitty and her lover are selling his paintings, Cross learns that his wife's first husband, who had disappeared a long time ago and was presumed dead, is alive. Now that he is no longer married, Cross rushes to Kitty to propose marriage. Kitty, basking in the unexpected income from the paintings, is unusually cruel. She tells him about her lover, Johnny, how they have used him for his money and that he would be the last person she would marry. An enraged Cross stabs her to death. Johnny Prince is arrested for the murder, tried and executed. Cross has been dismissed by his employers for embezzlement. He is destitute and has taken to walking the streets, looking for handouts. The last scene has him passing a gallery window where he sees one of his paintings, signed by Kitty, selling for thousands of dollars.

Scarlet Street is one of the ugliest films ever made. But it is Lang's territory and he handles it well. The deceiving couple are so hateful that the audience can take no pity on their demise. Christopher Cross evokes little sympathy. Anyone so gullible and foolish deserves his descent. It is one of the few films to pass censorship in which a murderer gets away with his crime. The film is a remake of Jean Renoir's first sound film, *La Chienne* (1931), which is set in Montmartre and is more explicit in identifying Kitty as a prostitute and Johnny as her pimp. Lang got a first-rate script from Dudley Nichols and excellent camera work from Milton Krasner who had photographed *Woman in the Window* (1944) starring the same three leads. Edward G. Robinson convincingly portrays a man in mid-life crisis. Dan Duryea was a method actor before its time and his specialty was villains. It is Joan Bennett who stands out, however. Her third husband, producer Walter Wanger, guided her later career and arranged for her to appear in films by master directors. She made four films for Fritz Lang between 1941 and 1948, *The Reckless Moment* (1949) for Max Ophuls, and *Father of the Bride* (1950) for Vincent Minnelli.

Schindler's List

1993. 195 min. b.w./color. U.S. **Prod.** Steven Spielberg, Gerald R. Molen, Branko Lustig; **Dir.** Steven Spielberg; **Scr.** Steve Zaillian (based on the novel *Schindler's Ark* by Thomas Keneally); **Cin.** Janusz Kaminski; **Ed.** Michael Kahn, Bill Kimberlin; **Prod.** D. Allan Starski; **Art D.** Maciej Walczak; **Mus.** John Williams; **Cast:** Liam Neeson, Ben Kingsley, Ralph Fiennes, Caroline Goodall, Jonathan Sagalle, Embeth Davidtz, Malgoscha Gebel.

Schindler's List begins very effectively. The holocaust is symbolized by a few candles burning down until there is only vapor. The film is set after the German invasion and occupation of Poland, and the establishment of a ghetto for the Jews of Krakow, in the latter stages of World War II. It tells the true story of a small-time businessman, Oscar Schindler (Liam Neeson), a German Catholic from the Sudetenland, who comes to Krakow hoping to make money with cheap labor. Through the ingenuity of a Jewish accountant, Itzhak Stern (Ben Kingsley), and Schindler's own conscience and daring they save the lives of at least 1,100 Jews.

Producer/director Spielberg attempted to make an impossible film. No one book or film can tell the history of the holocaust, the origin of which goes back two thousand years to the birth of Christianity. You can't make a film about Einsatzgruppen, Auschwitz-Birkenau or other extermination camps where six million Jews disappeared. Spielberg has succeeded in making a moving and intelligent film about the bravery of one man. It wisely does not attempt to simplify Schindler's motives. It is a well-controlled film with excellent editing and cinematography. The use of hand-held cameras for some scenes lends a documentary look. Despite its length of three hours and fifteen minutes the film never drags. There is also excellent acting by the three principals, especially Ben Kingsley as the trusted Jewish accountant and Liam Neeson as the sympathetic and complicated German entrepreneur. Schindler's breakdown at the end of the movie when he cries inconsolably for not having saved more Jews is very powerful. Ralph Fiennes as the personification of evil does a very convincing job. However, the film is not free from faults. A brief scene at the end of the movie shot in color is unnecessary. It is the only time in the film that Spielberg makes an obvious effort to gain our sympathies, even though he had already involved the viewer with powerful scenes. Spielberg has made an important film, far better than anything he had done since *Jaws* (1975). *Schindler's List* swept the Academy Awards in every major category except for the nominated best actor, Neeson, and supporting actor, Fiennes.

Séance on a Wet Afternoon

1964. 115 min. b.w. British. **Prod.** Richard Attenborough, Bryan Forbes; **Dir.** Bryan Forbes; **Scr.** Bryan Forbes (based on the novel by Mark McShane); **Cin.** Gerry Turpin; **Ed.** Derek York; **Art D.** Ray Simm; **Mus.** John Barry; **Cast:** Kim Stanley, Richard Attenborough, Mark Eden, Patrick Magee, Nanette Newman, Judith Donner, Gerald Sim, Maria Kazan.

Myra Savage (Kim Stanley) is a professional medium with a small clientele. She believes she is in touch with the other world through her stillborn son, Arthur, whose death she cannot accept. She is married to Billy Savage (Richard Attenborough), a weak and gentle person who knows the slightest shock or mishap could totally imbalance his wife. In his love for her he will do anything she asks of him. Myra feels she is not recognized as a medium and conceives a plan whereby she would gain fame. Billy will kidnap the child of an industrialist. After the ransom has been paid she will volunteer as a clairvoyant and the child and the ransom money will be found. Myra would then be celebrated. She tells Billy what they are really doing is "borrowing a child for a day or two." The weak husband does exactly as he is told and abducts the child. They take the little girl to their house and place her in a room Myra had designed for Arthur, telling her she is in a hospital and can't see anybody. The ransom is paid. Myra then contacts the parents and offers her services, but things don't work out as Myra had envisaged. The child contracts a fever and Myra's mental condition takes a turn for the worse.

The film is very well made. There is suspense throughout and there are scenes of great technical skill. The delivery of the ransom money takes place in Leicester Square during the rush hour using hidden cameras. It is edited so well that it ranks as one of the great movie scenes. The acting of the two principals is superb. Kim Stanley, one of the most intense method actors, was renowned for her work on stage. Her health often interfered with her work and she appeared in only five films between 1958 and 1983. Her acting in this film is mesmerizing as she depicts Myra slowly going mad. Stanley was nominated for an Academy Award as best actress but in an ironic twist lost to Julie Andrews in *Mary Poppins.* Richard Attenborough also has one of his finest roles. The film's story of kidnapping and mental illness is distasteful. The realism of the film and the intense acting of Stanley make it even more unnerving.

The Search

1948. 105 min. b.w. U.S. **Prod.** Lazar Wechsler; **Dir.** Fred Zinnemann; **Scr.** Richard Schweizer, David Wechsler, Paul Jerrico; **Cin.** Emil Berna; **Ed.** Hermann Haller; **Mus.** Robert Blum; **Cast:** Montgomery Clift, Aline MacMahon, Jarmila Novotna, Wendell Corey, Ivan Jandl.

The Search is a simple story about orphaned and displaced children in the aftermath of World War II who are being cared for by the United Nations in special camps in Europe. It takes place in southeastern Germany and the focus is on Karel Malik (Ivan Jandl), a nine-year-old traumatized Czech boy whose last contact with his mother was some four years earlier. The children are being transferred by the United Nations Relief and Rehabilitation Agency (UNRRA) to a better-equipped camp. They are being moved in a Red Cross ambulance. Some of the children, knowing of German trucks equipped for gassing, run away. Karel and another child decide to cross a river. Karel reaches the far bank, but the other child drowns. Karel hides in bombed-out buildings for a few days, but sheer hunger drives him into the open. He is seen by a young American officer, Ralph Stevenson (Montgomery Clift), who offers him food and takes him to his apartment that he shares with another officer, Jerry Fischer (Wendell Corey). Ralph becomes a surrogate older brother and together with Fischer, who has children of his own back in the States, they gain Karel's trust and patiently teach him some English. They attempt to tell him that his mother may be dead. The mother (Jarmila Novotna) is, in fact, alive and has gone to numerous camps in search of her son. She has been told that Karel is believed to be dead. They had found a cap by the riverbank and assumed Karel had also drowned. Ralph by now has contacted several officers of UNRRA and by the end of the film mother and son are reunited.

This was one of the great sleepers of the late forties. Fred Zinnemann, an underrated director, did not get his chance to direct a decently budgeted film until *The Seventh Cross* (1944). Although well acclaimed, it was four years later with *The Search* that Zinnemann became established. It is the first film to be shot in postwar Germany, with the background of Nuremberg adding to the film's authenticity. The acting is uniformly good. The entire cast, other than Clift, Corey and Aline MacMahon as a UNRRA officer, were nonprofessional actors, though Novotna was a well known opera singer. Ivan Jandl was discovered in Prague singing in a boy's choir. He received a special Oscar as a juvenile, but his parents were against his continuing as an actor. Clift had just finished *Red River* (1948) for Howard Hawks when Zinnemann offered him the lead in this modest film. *The Search* was released before *Red River,* hence it became known as his first film. The role was very becoming to Clift's persona. Clift improvised a line that gave poignancy to a scene. He tells Karel his mother may be dead but adds, "She will be with you in all ways," instead of "always." The film received Oscar nominations for best actor, director, story and screenplay, as well as the special award to Ivan Jandl.

Shadow of a Doubt

1943. 108 min. b.w. U.S. **Prod.** Jack H. Skirball; **Dir.** Alfred Hitchcock; **Scr.** Thornton Wilder, Sally Benson, Alma Reville; **Cin.** Joseph Valentine; **Ed.** Milton Carrith; **Art D.** John B. Goodman, Robert Boyle; **Mus.** Dimitri Tiomkin; **Cast:** Teresa Wright, Joseph Cotton, Macdonald Carey, Patricia Collinge, Henry Travers, Wallace Ford, Hume Cronyn, Edna May Wonacott.

Charles Cockley (Joseph Cotton), known to his family as Uncle Charlie, is a psychopathic murderer. His victims are wealthy elderly women whom he courts and then murders for their money and jewelry. The police have been after him for some while and the press refers to him as "the merry widow murderer." When we first see him he barely gets away from the police and boards a train heading west to Santa Rosa, a quiet town in California. He has wired his sister, Emma Newton (Patricia Collinge), her husband Joseph (Henry Travers), and their three children, informing them of his visit. The Newton's elder child (Teresa Wright) is a young girl named Charlie after her uncle. She adores him for his wit, worldliness and charm, and is most excited since she has not seen him for several years. In fact, the entire family is excited. They meet his train and they are saddened to see him walk with a cane. Uncle Charlie claims he is ill and does not want to see strangers. The next day he deposits the large sum of $40,000 in the local bank. The president of the bank asks him to make Santa Rosa his permanent home. Before long two police detectives who had been assigned to the "merry widow" case come to Santa Rosa. On the basis of profiles and other clues they suspect Cockley to be the killer. Through a series of events Charlie begins to suspect her favorite uncle and one of the detectives, Jack Graham (Macdonald Carey), reinforces Charlie's suspicions. Soon Uncle Charlie becomes aware that his niece suspects him and attempts to have her killed in a series of staged accidents. When another suspect in the case is inadvertently killed by the police in the East, the search for the "merry widow" killer comes to an end and Uncle Charlie decides to go back East to more fertile grounds. He makes one last attempt to get rid of young Charlie. He asks her at least to come to the train station to bid him farewell. He prevents her from getting off the train and as it begins to move attempts to throw her overboard. He loses his footing, falls off and is crushed to death by a passing train. The film ends with a large elaborate funeral in Santa Rosa. The detective and Charlie, the only ones who know who uncle Charlie really was, say nothing.

Shadow of a Doubt, often forgotten, is one of Hitchcock's best films and his own favorite. It is a fine portrayal of a demented killer in a respectable Middle America setting. Some six or seven believable characters are fully developed. It is one of the few Hitchcock mystery movies without comedy and the suspense is sustained from beginning to end. There is, however, a touch of sardonic irony in the relationship and nonending conversations between Joseph Newton and his neighbor Herbie Hawkins (Hume Cronyn). Herbie drops by every evening after dinner and has long conversations with Newton about perfect murders. It is a game they play while Uncle Charlie sits disinterested and indifferent to the chattering of two hopeless amateurs. The script is principally by Thornton Wilder and it is crisp and economical. The film hosts a perfect cast.

Shame

Skammen. 1968. 103min. b.w. Swedish. **Dir.** Ingmar Bergman; **Scr.** Ingmar Bergman; **Cin.** Sven Nykvist; **Ed.** Ulla Ryghe; **Art D.** P. A. Lundgren, Lennart Blomkvist. **Cast:** Liv Ullmann, Max Von Sydow, Gunnar Bjornstrand, Sigge Furst, Brigitta Valberg, Hans Alfredson, Ingvar Kjellson.

A childless couple, Jan and Eva Rosenberg (Max Von Sydow and Liv Ullmann), former violinists in a symphony orchestra live on a small island off an unnamed country. They own a small farm raising fruits and vegetables, which they sell on the mainland. There is a civil war raging in the country and the couple, although totally apolitical, become engulfed in the turmoil. The island is attacked and retaken several times by opposing forces. Jan and Eva are taken prisoner and humiliated. To save themselves Jan becomes a vicious killer and the sensitive and loyal Eva gives away her favors to an opportunistic and amoral Colonel Jacobi (Gunnar Bjornstrand). They both have changed from apolitical pacifists into calculating survivors. They now look at each other with shame and contempt. Even after having paid the price of selling their souls they face an uncertain future.

Shame is one of the great films of Ingmar Bergman. It depicts the dehumanizing effects of war on a man and woman of artistic sensibilities. In one of his simplest films, he rages against the world of tomorrow. It is shot in black and white with an economy of camera movement by the master cinematographer Sven Nykvist. There is no musical score though the story is about musicians. Ullmann has the more difficult role but all three of the leads are superb. The film had an added impact having been released in 1968 at the very height of the Vietnam war.

Shenandoah

1965. 105 min. color. U.S. **Prod.** Robert Arthur; **Dir.** Andrew V. McLaglen; **Scr.** James Lee Barrett; **Cin.** William Clothier; **Ed.** Otho Lovering; **Art D.** Alexander Golitzen, Alfred Sweeney; **Mus.** Frank Skinner; **Cast:** James Stewart, Doug McClure, Glenn Corbett, Patrick Wayne, Rosemary Forsyth, Phillip Alford, Katharine Ross, Charles Robinson, James McMullan, Tim McIntire, Harry Carey, Jr., Warren Oates, Strother Martin, Denver Pyle, George Kennedy.

A Virginia widower (James Stewart) with six sons and one daughter works his farm ignoring the war raging between the North and the South. He doesn't believe in slavery but wants no part in a war that doesn't concern him or his family. This changes when his youngest son of sixteen is captured by Union soldiers as a Rebel; his son-in-law is called up by the Confederate army; a son and his wife are murdered by looting Confederates; and another son is killed by a Confederate guardsman. *Shenandoah* is by far the best film of director Andrew McLaglen, the son of actor Victor McLaglen. The battle scenes are particularly well done. A mature James Stewart is his usual warm low-keyed self until his wrath is aroused. He is supported by an excellent cast of stalwarts like Harry Carey, Jr., Warren Oates, Strother Martin and George Kennedy.

The Shop Around the Corner

1940. 97 min. b.w. U.S. **Prod.** Ernst Lubitsch; **Dir.** Ernst Lubitsch; **Scr.** Samson Raphaelson (based on the play *Parfumerie* by Nikolaus Laszlo); **Cin.** William Daniels; **Ed.** Gene Ruggiero; **Art D.** Cedric Gibbons; **Mus.** Werner R. Heymann; **Cast:** Margaret Sullavan, James Stewart, Frank Morgan, Joseph Schildkraut, Sara Hadden, William Tracy, Felix Bressart.

The film is set in Budapest in the thirties, before World War II. Alfred Kralik (James Stewart) is the senior clerk in Matuschek and Company, owned by Hugo Matuschek (Frank Morgan). Alfred is the loyal and trusted friend of the owner and has had the rare privilege of being invited to Mr. and Mrs.. Matuschek's home. Alfred runs a very efficient store. His team of coworkers include Pirovitch (Felix Bressart), an aging man near retirement; Vadas (Joseph Schildkraut), a vain and boasting Lothario; and a confused young clerk, Katona (William Tracy), who is ordered around by everybody. One day an attractive young woman, Klara Novak (Margaret Sullavan), comes to the shop seeking employment. She begs Matuschek to hire her as help for the coming Christmas holidays. She is turned down but before leaving demonstrates her usefulness. She sells a lady a musical cigar box to be used as a candy box. Matuschek is impressed and gives her a job, much to Alfred's dismay. Klara and Alfred, who had disliked each other from their first encounter, develop an even deeper antipathy. Alfred is also concerned about a more pressing personal matter. He had responded to a lonely hearts club ad and had been matched with a girl listed as postbox 237. After an exchange of a number of letters each is convinced they are right for each other and they arrange to meet at a café. Both Alfred and Klara are there, but as each expects someone else, they ignore one another. Meanwhile Mr. Matuschek has found that his wife is having an affair with one of the shop employees. Since Alfred is the only one of them who has ever met her, he is dismissed. Matuschek soon learns it is Vadas who has been his wife's lover and apologizes and rehires Alfred. Klara and Alfred finally reveal themselves as the correspondents of postbox 237.

The film is charming with the delicate Lubitsch touch apparent in every scene. The love-hate relationship between two lonely people, Stewart and Sullavan, is handled very well and both give beautiful performances. Frank Morgan gives the best performance of his career. The three had appeared together successfully in *The Mortal Storm*, released some six months earlier.

The Silence

Tystnaden. 1963. 95 min. b.w. Swedish. **Dir.** Ingmar Bergman; **Scr.** Ingmar Bergman; **Cin.** Sven Nykvist; **Ed.** Ulla Ryghe; **Art D.** P. A. Lundgren; **Mus.** Bo Nilsson, Bach. **Cast:** Ingrid Thulin, Gunnel Lindblom, Jorgen Lindstrom, Haken Jahnberg, Birger Malmsten, Eduardo Futierrez

The film covers twenty-four hours. Two women, Ester (Ingrid Thulin) and Anna (Gunnel Lindblom), and Anna's ten-year-old son are returning by train to their country. Ester, the elder of the two, is gravely ill and they are forced to stop before reaching their destination. Ester is a linguist and translator. Other than these bare facts, Bergman does not give us any further information. The name of the country they stop in is not mentioned. We see tanks being carried by rail cars. The country is either at war or occupied by a neighboring country, or there may be serious civil unrest. The inhabitants speak no language but their own and neither woman knows the language. The two women and the boy stop at an almost uninhabited large hotel and get a two-bedroom suite. Anna asks Ester whether she should call a doctor but Ester is satisfied with ordering a large bottle of brandy, brought by an old waiter who appears to be the only employee in the hotel. Anna and her son take a bath and a short nap. Ester continues drinking. The boy goes out to the cavernous hallways and runs around. He meets a troupe of dwarfs staying at the hotel who entertain him, but their manager sends him away. The boy now has only the old waiter to amuse him. Anna pretties herself and, despite an hysterical outburst by Ester, goes out. Anna goes to a café, has a drink and gives a large bill to the waiter who is obviously attracted to her. Anna then goes to a club that features an erotic show. She also watches a couple copulating in a dark corner. The same afternoon she goes back to the café and brings the waiter to her room. Later that evening because of her compulsive sexuality she has sex with the waiter again. Ester who has not seen Anna for a while comes into Anna's room and watches with horror. Whatever bond there was between the two women is now broken. Anna and her son leave the next day, leaving the sick Ester to die alone.

Bergman purposely leaves us in the dark. The women may or may not be sisters. We are led to believe there is a familial relationship between the little boy and Ester and she could be his aunt, although neither woman is especially concerned about his safety. There may be a lesbian relationship between them. When Ester sees Anna giving herself to a strange man and copulating emotionlessly, there is horror and disgust in her face. Her solace is in alcohol. The only indirect cue we have is that *The Silence* is the third and last film of Bergman's "crisis of faith" trilogy after *Through a Glass Darkly* (1961) and *Winter Light* (1962). But *The Silence* is not about crisis of faith or abandonment by God. It is more an allegory of non-communication between human beings, set again in a loveless and godless world. It is a Chekhovian world where communication is nonexistent. *The Silence* is superior to the two earlier films in the trilogy and one of the best photographed films of Sven Nykvist. The scenes of Ester's suffering and unbearable pain are most effectively photographed at odd angles. The close-ups of the boy's face showing innocence and lack of awareness are equally effective. Thulin and Lindblom give matchless performances.

Smiles of a Summer Night

Sommarnattens Leende. 1955. 108 min. b.w. Swedish. **Prod.** Allan Ekelund; **Dir.** Ingmar Bergman; **Scr.** Ingmar Bergman; **Cin.** Gunnar Fischer; **Ed.** Oscar Rosander; **Art D.** P. A. Lundgren; **Mus.** Erik Nordgren; **Cast:** Ulla Jacobsson, Eva Dahlbeck, Margit Carlqvist, Harriet Andersson, Gunnar Bjornstrand, Bjorn Bjelvenstam, Jarl Kulle.

This minor film by the master Ingmar Bergman is set at the turn of the twentieth century in a country mansion near Stockholm. A beautiful and accomplished actress, Desiree Armfeldt (Eva Dahlbeck), invites her former lover, Fredrik Egerman (Gunnar Bjornstrand), a successful lawyer who had left her and married twenty-year-old Anne (Ulla Jacobsson), to her mother's country mansion for a weekend. For reasons unknown, Fredrik has chosen not to consummate his two-year marriage to Anne. Also invited is Fredrik's son by a previous marriage, Henrik (Bjorn Bjelvenstam), a nineteen-year-old seminary student. The other guests are Desiree's present lover, the vain Count Malcolm (Jarl Kulle), and his wife, Charlotte (Margit Carlqvist). Desiree knows she is beginning to age and has devised a plan whereby she would get her "rewards in this world" and not wait for promises of paradise in the next. Things turn out as she had hoped. Anne runs off with her stepson. Fredrik renews his liaison with Desiree and Count Malcolm goes back to his wife. As a side event, the maid Petra (Harriet Andersson) and the coachman, who are not restrained by conventions, do what their hearts desire.

As in most of his films Bergman is decidedly on the side of women and admires their strength and sophistication. Women are shown to be resilient while men are pompous hypocrites. The exteriors and the countryside are beautifully photographed. The interior sets of the mansion and the costumes are among the best in Bergman's films. This elegant comedy is also one of Bergman's most erotic and the performances are uniformly good. The film won an award at the 1956 Cannes Festival as best comedy and served as inspiration for Stephen Sondheim's stage musical *A Little Night Music* (1958) and Woody Allen's *A Mid Summer Night's Sex Comedy* (1982).

The Spider's Stratagem

La Strategia de Regno. 1970. 100 min. color. Italian. **Prod.** Giovanni Bertolucci; **Dir.** Bernardo Bertolucci; **Scr.** Bernardo Bertolucci, Eduardo de Gregorio, Marilu Parolini (based on the story "The Theme of the Traitor and the Hero" by Jorge Luis Borges); **Cin.** Vittorio Storaro, Franco di Giacomo; **Mus.** Verdi, Schoenberg; **Cast:** Giulio Brogi, Alida Valli, Tino Scotti, Pippo Campanini.

A young man, Athos Magnani (Giulio Brogi), comes to the town of his birth in the Po Valley in Italy for the first time in thirty years to investigate the murder of his father by the Fascists in 1936. Athos was born after his father's death and his mother took him away to another town. His father is now considered a hero. A street is named after him and there is a statue of him in the town square. By talking to his father's mistress (Alida Valli) and some of his surviving comrades he finds his father had, in fact, betrayed his anti-Fascist comrades and informed on them. When found out, he willingly accepted his own death sentence. As a way to salvage his reputation, he asked to be killed at the opera during a performance of *Rigoletto*. The people would blame the Fascists who would then be hated even more.

The film is an adaptation of a Jorge Luis Borges' short story—a minor and incomplete piece by a great director. Its central weakness is that neither the son nor the father (shown in flashbacks and also played by Brogi) are even barely sketched. But it is a visual feast with stunning cinematography and heightened color. The background music of *Rigoletto* is perfect for a story about duplicity, perfidy and betrayal.

The Spiral Staircase

1946. 83 min. b.w. U.S. **Prod.** Dore Schary, **Dir.** Robert Siodmak; **Scr.** Mel Dinelli (based on the novel *Some Must Watch* by Ethel Lina White); **Cin.** Nicholas Musuraca; **Ed.** Harry Marker, Harry Gerstad; **Art D.** Albert S. D'Agostino, Jack Okey; **Mus.** Roy Webb; **Cast:** Dorothy McGuire, George Brent, Ethel Barrymore, Kent Smith, Rhonda Fleming, Elsa Lanchester, Rhys Williams, Sara Algood, Gordon Oliver, Ellen Corby.

The film is set in a New England town in 1906 where some townspeople are watching a silent movie. The camera gradually moves to a room upstairs in the same building where we see a frightened girl about to be murdered by an unseen man. The camera now moves to a grand Gothic mansion belonging to a widowed invalid, Mrs. Warren (Ethel Barrymore), and her two sons. The elder son is the gentle, soft-spoken Professor Warren (George Brent) and the younger, the irresponsible and irresolute Steve (Gordon Oliver). A young girl, Helen Capel (Dorothy McGuire), is employed as a maid, principally to take care of the demanding bedridden Mrs.. Warren. Helen is mute as a result of a childhood trauma. She instinctively likes the kind professor and is wary of young Steve. Soon two more girls are murdered. What links the victims is that they all were young and physically handicapped and Helen becomes terrified. The police believe the murderer is a psychotic who is bent to rid the world of any woman who does not meet his idea of physical perfection. Through a series of incidents Helen discovers that the murderer lives in the mansion and she manages to lock him into a room. But it is the wrong man and the murderer now has a free hand to kill her. She is saved unexpectedly by Mrs. Warren.

The Spiral Staircase is directed by the ingenious Robert Siodmak who made several other good films in the mid-forties, notably *The Phantom Lady* (1944), *The Suspect* (1944) and *The Killers* (1946). In most of his films he employs expressionist lighting and here he extracts maximum suspense from the dimly lit Gothic mansion where most of the action takes place. The use of sound—be it creaking doors, windblown curtains or a fierce storm—gives the film a nightmare quality. The film has two beautiful performances by Dorothy McGuire and Ethel Barrymore. The only shortcoming is George Brent who was probably one of the most expressionless and unconvincing leading men to appear in a host of Warner Bros. melodramas of the thirties and forties.

Stairway to Heaven

(a.k.a. *A Matter of Life and Death*). 1946. 104 min. b.w. British. **Prod.** Michael Powell, Emeric Pressburger; **Dir.** Michael Powell, Emeric Pressburger; **Scr.** Michael Powell, Emeric Pressburger; **Cin.** Jack Cardiff; **Ed.** Reginald Mills; **Prod.** D. Alfred Junge; **Art D.** Arthur Lawson; **Mus.** Allan Gray; **Cast:** David Niven, Kim Hunter, Raymond Massey, Roger Livesey, Robert Coote, Marius Goring, Richard Attenborough, Kathleen Byron.

Squadron Leader Peter Carter (David Niven) is a bomber pilot returning from a mission and is approaching the southern coast of Britain. His plane aflame, his entire crew dead or having parachuted out and himself left with a torn parachute, he makes radio contact with an American WAC, June (Kim Hunter), at a nearby coastal station. In the few minutes before his plane plunges toward the sea he establishes a tender relationship with her, bids farewell and jumps out of the plane. He miraculously escapes death and is washed ashore. In the strangest coincidence he sees June on the beach and they embrace emotionally. Carter has suffered a serious head injury and June's friend Dr. Reeves (Roger Livesey), a brain surgeon, decides to operate immediately. While the operation is underway an emissary arrives in the person of Heavenly Conductor Number 71 (Marius Goring), an effete French aristocrat who had been guillotined by the Jacobeans during the French Revolution. The emissary says that a serious mistake had been made in Carter's case. He should have died and must now leave this world. Carter argues that because of the error made in heaven, he has now fallen in love and he is entitled to an appeal at the very least. Heaven agrees, and although given the choice of an advocate from a gallery of the greatest minds in history, Carter selects Dr. Reeves. The case for his death is made by Abraham Farlan (Raymond Massey), a Bostonian who was the first American killed by the British at the outset of the American War of Independence. Carter wins his case and is entitled to live out his natural life. Meanwhile the brain operation has been successful.

The film was made at the recommendation of the British Ministry of Information to foster and maintain the goodwill created between Britain and the U.S. during World War II. The great team of Powell and Pressburger had previously made *49th Parallel* (1941), a fine straightforward propaganda film also at the urging of the Ministry of Information. Why the team came up with the somewhat strange *Stairway to Heaven* is hard to say. The film could be read as the hallucination of a pilot suffering over the loss of his crew and feeling guilty that he survived, but it has great charm and wit. In almost all of Powell and Pressbrger's films there are anti-realist and fantasy elements. It is beautifully photographed by Jack Cardiff with fantasy sequences in black and white and the scenes on earth in color. The film also has some imaginative sets by Alfred Junge and is complimented by a very good cast.

State Secret

(a.k.a. *The Great Manhunt*). 1950. 104 min. b.w. British. **Prod.** Frank Launder, Sidney Gilliat; **Dir.** Sidney Gilliat; **Scr.** Sidney Gilliat (based on the novel *Appointment with Fear* by Roy Huggins); **Cin.** Robert Krasker; **Ed.** Thelma Myers; **Mus.** William Alwyn; **Cast:** Douglas Fairbanks, Jr., Glynis Johns, Herbert Lom, Jack Hawkins, Walter Rilla.

An American neurosurgeon, Dr. Marlow (Douglas Fairbanks, Jr.), is in London giving a series of lectures and demonstrating an operation he has perfected. He is invited to visit Vosnia, an Eastern European country with an authoritarian regime. He is to be honored at a ceremony. Unknown to him, the real purpose of the invitation is for Marlow to operate on the aging dictator of Vosnia who has been diagnosed with a brain tumor. Although the operation is successful, the patient dies a few days later. The regime decides to keep the death a secret for a few months until his successor is chosen. In the meantime, the interim rulers will present a look-alike to the public. Dr. Marlow now realizes his life is in danger and escapes to the border with the help of a showgirl (Glynis

Johns) and a smuggler (Herbert Lom). He is captured and about to be shot, when a new twist is introduced at the end of the film.

An intelligent and well-improvised film with a good deal of suspense and a witty script. The photography of the veteran Robert Krasker creates a realistic atmosphere and depicts the drabness of life in a communist country. The acting is uniformly good. The film has Douglas Fairbanks, Jr.'s best acting since *The Prisoner of Zenda* (1937). Jack Hawkins, as one of the key operatives of the Vosnian government, holding the posts of Minister for Internal Security, Minister of Interior and Minister of Health simultaneously, has one of his good roles. Glynis Johns and Herbert Lom also do well. An ingenious feature of the film is the invention of a language by a Cambridge don, partly Slavic and partly Latinate. It is spoken from time to time by everyone in the cast except Dr. Marlow without need for subtitles or translation, moving the film along faster. An example is "natalni," meaning "naturally." A minor film that holds up well for the ingenuity of the plot and elements of suspense. In a very rare coincidence *Crisis,* a film also released in 1950 with Cary Grant and José Ferrer, about a Latin American dictator, has essentially the same story. *State Secret* is far superior.

The Straight Story

1999. 111 min. color. U.S. **Dir.** David Lynch; **Scr.** Mary Sweeny, John Roach; **Cast:** Richard Farnsworth, Sissy Spacek, Everett McGill, Harry Dean Stanton, Jane Galloway Heitz, Jennifer Edwards, Barbara Robertson, John Farley.

Alvin Straight (Richard Farnsworth), a seventy-three-year-old World War II veteran, lives in Iowa. When he hears that Lyle, his brother from whom he has been estranged for ten years, has had a stroke he decides to visit him. The problem is Lyle lives some two hundred miles away in Wisconsin, and Alvin can barely walk, his eyesight has deteriorated and he has been denied renewal of his driving license. He buys a motorized mower that requires no license to drive, hitches a small wooden trailer to it and starts out.

He meets people along his slow ride, including a fellow veteran with whom he talks of the horrors of war, a young girl who has run away from home, and some people who help fix his mower and allow him to sleep on their property. He finally gets to Lyle's place. They talk quietly without either mentioning their argument of ten years ago. Then they just sit side by side gazing at the sky. One of the most beautifully conceived and photographed films of recent years. The journey is one long scenic feast for the eyes. Seldom has farmland and rural America looked so entrancing. David Lynch's leisurely, almost poetic direction is unlike anything he had done before. He is much better known for his near-surrealist films, most notably *Blue Velvet* (1986). *The Straight Story* is a low-keyed film with scenes of special poignancy. Farnsworth unfortunately came late to acting. He received an Academy Award nomination for best actor for this film.

Strangers on a Train

1951. 101 min. b.w. U.S. **Prod.** Alfred Hitchcock; **Dir.** Alfred Hitchcock; **Scr.** Raymond Chandler, Czenzi Ormonde, Whitfield Cook (based on the novel by Patricia Highsmith); **Cin.** Robert Burks; **Ed.** William Ziegler; **Art D.** Ted Haworth; **Mus.** Dimitri Tiomkin; **Cast:** Farley Granger, Robert Walker, Ruth Roman, Leo G. Carroll, Patricia Hitchcock, Laura Elliot, Marion Lorne, Howard St. John.

Purely by chance two strangers with completely differing personalities meet in the club car of a train from New York to Washington, D.C. Guy Haines (Farley Granger) comes from a modest background but has risen to become a prominent tennis player. He is in the midst of a nasty divorce and has made a financial settlement with his wife, Miriam (Laura Elliot), expecting she will sign the final papers. He hopes to marry Anne Morton (Ruth Roman), a senator's daughter, and intends to go into politics once his tennis career is over. Bruno Anthony (Robert Walker) is a mentally disturbed young man who has been expelled from three colleges for drinking and gambling. He comes from a wealthy family and has been spoiled by his mother who is also mentally troubled. He hates his father with a passion. He boasts of having been in a car going 150 miles an hour while blindfolded. "You should do everything before you die." Bruno has read in the newspapers about Guy's difficult divorce proceeding and his romantic link with the daughter of a senator. Bruno discusses his own problems and proposes that they each murder the person who is an obstacle to the other's happiness. Bruno would murder Guy's wife and in exchange Guy would murder Bruno's father. Bruno believes these would then be regarded as motiveless crimes with no chance of linking them to either Guy or himself. Guy is shocked by the proposal and ignores Bruno, but Bruno believes a bargain has been struck. Guy stops at the town where his wife lives. Miriam is coarse and common. Having read about Guy's romance with Anne, she now says she won't give him a divorce nor would she return the money she received as a settlement. They have a loud row witnessed by several people nearby. Much to his horror Guy later learns that Bruno has strangled Miriam. Bruno contacts Guy and warns him that he expects him to carry out his part of the bargain. Guy has mishandled everything. He has not told the police nor Anne about Bruno. Now he is a suspect himself. Equally troubling to Guy is that he subconsciously knew that he would be better off with his wife out of the way.

Strangers on a Train is not one of Hitchcock's best films, but as always Hitchcock through his mastery of the medium elevates it and engrosses the viewer. In the very opening scene, the personalities of Guy and Bruno are established without our seeing their faces or hearing any dialogue. We first see a man, Bruno, shown from the waist down walking hurriedly with nervous steps toward a train. He is wearing two-tone, black and white shoes. Guy is shown wearing conservative black shoes walking with a self-assured, measured gait. Bruno is seen mostly at night or in shadow while Guy is usually shown during the day in full light. The film is well edited with effective cross-cutting. It has its weaknesses, however. None of the characters is fully developed and Farley Granger and Ruth Roman are not much help. Hitchcock's previous two films, *Under Capricorn* (1949) and *Stage Fright* (1950), both inferior films, had been failures at the box office. Warners insisted on Granger and Roman, two contract players, to play the leads and Hitchcock had little choice. The film is carried by Robert Walker's fine performance along with Patricia Hitchcock, Marion Lorne playing Bruno's dotty mother and the reliable Leo G. Carroll. The tennis match is badly photographed. Both the pro and the double for Granger are too obvious and we are asked to believe that the first three hotly contested sets took a mere one hour. The last scene on the merry-go-round is too theatrical and beneath the talents of Hitchcock.

A Streetcar Named Desire

1951. 122 min. b.w. U.S. **Prod.** Charles K. Feldman; **Dir.** Elia Kazan; **Scr.** Tennessee Williams, Oscar Saul (based on the play by Tennessee Williams); **Cin.** Harry Stradling; **Ed.** David Weisbart; **Art D.** Richard Day; **Mus.** Alex North; **Cast:** Marlon Brando, Vivien Leigh, Kim Hunter, Karl Malden, Rudy Bond, Nick Dennis, Peg Hillias, Richard Garrick.

Blanche Dubois (Vivien Leigh), a former school teacher in Mississippi who was dismissed for a sexual indiscretion, comes to New Orleans' Latin Quarter to stay with her pregnant sister, Stella (Kim Hunter). Stella is married to Stanley Kowalski (Marlon Brando), a blue-collar worker. She is madly in love with her brutish and overtly sexual husband and proudly presents him to her older sister. Blanche is a sensitive, fragile, aging woman who had been married to a young poet who committed suicide shortly after their marriage. She has never been the same since, and her mannerism and attire indicate her attachment to the past. Stanley is unimpressed with her aristocratic airs as a Southern belle. Blanche foolishly tries to charm the ignorant Stanley who mistakes her actions for sexual advances. Stanley also believes Blanche is financially well off and his wife may have been cheated out of the family inheritance. He attempts to get more information about Blanche in Mississippi and discovers the reasons for her dismissal. Tensions rise, and one night when Stella is away he rapes Blanche.

In the aftermath of the traumatic incident Blanche loses all touch with reality and is to be committed to an asylum. The film ends with Blanche being taken away by a doctor and nurse and Blanche's memorable line as she takes the doctor's proffered arm, "I have always depended upon the kindness of strangers."

Streetcar has the beautiful but highly stylized prose of Tennessee Williams. In many ways it is a filmed play. The entire film takes place in the seedy, dilapidated Kowalski apartment and courtyard. The camera has no room to move and stays close to the actors. The film will be remembered for two magnificent performances. Brando had made his name in the Broadway production of *Streetcar* and his first film, *The Men* (1950), but audiences still were not prepared for the sheer force of Brando's acting. He is almost a savage beast let loose. Vivien Leigh was ideal as the doomed heroine who does not want "realism," but "magic." The contrast in acting styles between Leigh, a British-trained actress, and Brando, the epitome of method acting, is both interesting and effective. Kim Hunter, Karl Malden as Mitch (a suitor for Blanche), and Rudy Bond and Nick Dennis (Stanley's coworkers and poker-playing buddies), had all been part of the original Broadway cast and give seasoned performances. For fear of censorship the references to Blanche's homosexual husband were eliminated. In an unnecessary ending, not in the play, we are led to believe Stella may leave Stanley because of the rape of her sister.

Suspicion

1941. 99 min. b.w. U.S. **Prod.** Alfred Hitchcock; **Dir.** Alfred Hitchcock; **Scr.** Samson Raphaelson, Joan Harrison, Alma Reville (based on the novel *Before the Fact* by Frances Iles); **Cin.** Harry Stradling; **Ed.** William Hamilton; **Art. D.** Van Nest Polglase, Caroll Clark; **Mus.** Franz Waxman; **Cast:** Cary Grant, Joan Fontaine, Cedric Hardwicke, Nigel Bruce, Dame May Whitty, Isabel Jeans, Leo G. Caroll.

Lina McLaidlaw (Joan Fontaine), a shy and withdrawn girl, desperately wants to get away from her straight-laced and stuffy mother (Dame May Whitty) and father (Cedric Hardwicke) a retired general. She falls in love with a philanderer and ladies' man, Johnnie Aysgarth (Cary Grant), who begins to court her. His character is established early when we see him in a first-class railroad car carrying a third-class ticket. Despite rumors about Johnnie's reckless and dishonest past, and the cold reception by her disapproving parents, she marries him. All past warnings slowly begin to materialize. Johnnie is a gambler and totally irresponsible. Without her knowledge he sells her family heirlooms. Unable to borrow any more money, he gets a job with a real estate company from which he is soon dismissed for embezzlement. Lina begins to suspect him of the murder of his closest friend, Beaky Thwaite (Nigel Bruce), who had been his principal backer in a property scheme. Beaky had been found dead in a Paris hotel at a time when Johnnie had been absent from home. Soon she begins to suspect him of planning to murder her.

Except for an unsatisfactory ending, *Suspicion* is one of the best examples of Hitchcock's craftsmanship. In a fairly leisurely paced film, Hitchcock teases the audience and leaves us guessing whether Johnnie is a murderer. In one celebrated scene, the exhausted and emotionally drained Lina has retired to her bed. Johnnie brings a glass of milk, which Hitchcock had eerily illuminated by a bulb concealed in the glass. Lina and the audience are convinced the milk is poisoned. Earlier, in an equally effective scene, the two are playing Scrabble with Beaky. As the men are talking, Lina arranges the letters on the table and, without being aware, the word formed is "murder." There is fine acting by the entire cast. Cary Grant had the talent to be as charming as ever, even when suspected of being a potential murderer. Joan Fontaine gives one of her best performances and Nigel Bruce is his affable bumbling self. It is not until the final scene that we find out whether Johnnie is guilty as suspected. The RKO executives forced a false ending on the film.

Sweet Smell of Success

1957. 96 min. b.w. U.S. **Prod.** James Hill; **Dir.** Alexander Mackendrick; **Scr.** Clifford Odets, Ernest Lehman (based on the story "Tell Me About It Tomorrow" by Ernest Lehman); **Cin.** James Wong Howe; **Ed.** Alan Crosland, Jr.; **Art D.** Edward Carrere; **Mus.** Elmer Bernstein; **Cast:** Burt Lancaster, Tony Curtis, Martin Milner, Sam Levene, Barbara Nichols, Susan Harrison, Emile Meyer.

This story is about a New York gossip columnist, J. J. Hunsacker (Burt Lancaster), who has a nationwide readership. He is required reading for anyone connected with show business, but his influence extends much further. He could ruin the career of any national figure. Hunsacker is modeled after the late Walter Winchell, and spends his nights sipping coffee at a night spot fashioned after the fabled Stork Club. A very select number of people have the privilege of exchanging words with him. He is a recluse and lives with his young sister Susan (Susan Harrison). Hunsacker finds his sister has been going out with a jazz musician, Steve Dallas (Martin Milner). The overprotective brother orders Susan to terminate the relationship, but she ignores his demand. He asks Sidney Falco (Tony Curtis), a brash Broadway press agent whose income depends on getting his clients' names in the media, to break up the relationship any way he can. Since ultimate success is a complimentary mention in Hunsacker's column, Falco, who has not been in Hunsacker's good graces recently, gladly obeys. He arranges for another columnist to run an item that Dallas is a pot-smoking communist. Dallas is fired from his job, but Susan continues to see him. Falco then plants a reefer in Dallas' overcoat and Hunsacker orders a sadistic police detective, Harry Kello (Emile Meyer), to rough up Dallas. Susan, sounding suicidal, calls Falco who rushes over to her apartment. Hunsacker unexpectedly comes home and finds Falco in his sister's bedroom. Susan, who has learned of Falco's involvement in Dallas losing his job, tells her brother that Falco had been making advances. The film ends with Hunsacker ordering Kello to beat up Falco, and Susan packing her bags and leaving her brother.

A more damning film about the fourth estate than even Wilder's *Ace in the Hole* (1951). The film's success is primarily due to the imaginative direction of Alexander Mackendrick in his first American film. Elmer Bernstein's score and the magnificent cinematography of James Wong Howe contribute greatly to its excellence. Seldom has the look of New York at night and the sleaze been captured this well. The acting of the principals is merely adequate. There is a tense script by Clifford Odets and Ernest Lehman, but it has some weaknesses. Falco's character is well rounded and his motivations are clear. He hopes to become another Hunsacker. The character of Hunsacker, however, is not fully developed. His cruelty and viciousness is left unexplained. His near incestuous relationship with his sister is also glossed over.

Taxi Driver

1976. 113 min. color. U.S. **Prod.** Michael Phillips, Julia Phillips; **Dir.** Martin Scorsese; **Scr.** Paul Schrader; **Cin.** Michael Chapman; **Ed.** Marcia Lucas, Tom Rolf, Melvin Shapiro; **Art D.** Charles Rosen; **Mus.** Bernard Herrmann; **Cast:** Robert De Niro, Cybill Shepherd, Harvey Keitel, Peter Boyle, Jodie Foster, Albert Brooks, Leonard Harris, Martin Scorsese.

Travis Bickle (Robert De Niro), a Vietnam war veteran, is a cab driver in New York City. He works from six in the evening to six in the morning, sometimes seven nights a week. He has recurrent headaches and takes masses of pills. He is lonely, angry and alienated. He has difficulty sleeping and goes to porn movie houses to assuage both his solitude and his sexual frustrations. He befriends a passenger, Betsy (Cybill Shepherd), who is a young volunteer in the campaign headquarters of a presidential candidate. He asks for a date. He is awkward and takes her to the porn movie house, the only place he feels comfortable. She storms out and, despite all his apologies, won't talk to him. His depression deepens and he buys a large number of handguns from an underground dealer. His first target is the political candidate but he is spotted by the guards and runs away. To placate his mounting tension he decides to have sex. A neighborhood pimp, Sport (Harvey Keitel), arranges for him to meet a thirteen-year-old prostitute, Iris (Jodie Foster) who has run away from home. On seeing the girl Travis becomes deeply affected by her plight. He does not have sex with her but tells her to stop working as a hooker and even offers to pay for her trip back home. The pimp later talks her into staying and she is again on the streets. Travis arms himself to the teeth and goes to the pimp's place to rescue the girl. He shoots the pimp and his two bodyguards. In the fight he is wounded and tries to shoot himself, but the gun is empty so he just waits for the police. When his story is told, he becomes an overnight hero, championed by a media that colors his exploits. Even Betsy now wants to see him again. At film's end Travis remains a deeply troubled person. We are left to wonder what he might do next in his hated New York City.

No one has depicted New York as well as Scorsese. And few films have captured the stark, frightening reality of urban alienation as brilliantly as *Taxi Driver*. The Times Square area of the time is shown in all its ugliness, squalor and neon sleaze. It is the best photographed and edited of Scorsese's films. Bernard Herrmann's score, his last as he died shortly thereafter, makes the area more ominous. Robert De Niro has one of his best roles as the near psychotic who hates the city with a passion.

3:10 to Yuma

1957. 92 min. b.w. U.S. **Prod.** David Heilweil; **Dir.** Delmer Daves; **Scr.** Halstead Welles (based on the story by Elmore Leonard); **Cin.** Charles Lawton, Jr.; **Ed.** Al Clark; **Art D.** Frank Hotaling; **Mus.** George Duning; **Cast:** Van Heflin, Glenn Ford, Felicia Farr, Leora Dana, Richard Jaeckel, Henry Jones, Robert Emhardt.

Dan Evans (Van Heflin), a peaceful rancher, married with two sons, is facing hard times. His ranch is suffering from a long drought that has dwindled his herd. To save the rest of his cattle he must dig a well, but he doesn't have the necessary $200. A notorious outlaw, Ben Wade (Glenn Ford), has been captured after robbing a stagecoach and killing the driver. In order to whisk him away without his gang becoming aware, just one man is needed to take him to the state prison in Yuma, Arizona. In the meantime, Wade must be taken to the nearest town and hidden in a hotel to wait for the train. The reward is $200. Although there is danger involved, Dan accepts the offer knowing what the money can do for his family. They make it safely to the next town and hole up in the hotel. The train is still a day away and Wade cleverly begins to tempt Dan. He offers $10,000 if he would just look the other way while he escapes. Dan is sorely tempted but refuses. He saves Wade from being killed when the brothers of the murdered stagecoach driver burst into the room and Evans manages to disarm them. By now Wade's gang has found out where their boss is and wait for Dan and Wade to come out. The town officials, who had promised Dan to help, run away. Even the owner of the stagecoach company, Mr. Butterfield (Robert Emhardt), who had put up the reward money, abandons him. The only one who remains with him is the town drunk, but he is killed by the outlaws. The train is arriving. Dan and the handcuffed Wade begin their perilous crossing to the railroad station. In an unusual twist, Wade, in return for Dan having saved his life, helps him evade the gang saying, "I owed you that," and both board the train. The film ends with Wade delivered to the state prison and Dan returning to the ranch and his family. The skies open up with a torrent of rain and the drought ends.

The film is thematically similar to *High Noon* (1952). Dan is abandoned by everyone save for the hopeless town drunk, and has to face the gang alone. Delmer Daves was a very competent and literate director of Westerns, including: *Broken Arrow* (1950) which dealt with racial issues; *Jubal* (1956), a reworking of *Othello* and the green-eyed monster theme; and *The Last Wagon* (1956), again with racial themes. *3:10 to Yuma* comes from a short story by the prolific and engaging writer Elmore Leonard. Although by necessity somewhat too talky, Daves gets maximum tension from the confines of a small hotel room. There is very convincing acting by Van Heflin, who plays a simple man weighed down by problems, as in *Shane* (1953). Glenn Ford oozes with snakelike charm. Although Felicia Farr has a brief role as Dan's wife, she carries it well with her beauty and bearing.

Throne of Blood

Kumonosu-Jo. 1957. 108 min. b.w. Japanese. **Prod.** Akira Kurosawa, Sojiro Motoki; **Dir.** Akira Kurosawa; **Scr.** Hideo Oguni, Shinobu Hashimoto, Ryuzo Kikushima, Akira Kurosawa (based on the play *Macbeth* by William Shakespeare); **Cin.** Asaichi Nakai; **Ed.** Akira Kurosawa; **Art D.** Yoshiro Muraki, Kohei Ezaki; **Mus.** Masaru Sato; **Cast:** Toshiro Mifune, Isuzu Yamada, Takashi Shimura, Minoru Chiaki, Akira Kubo.

The film is set in sixteenth-century medieval Japan. Taketoki Washizu (Toshiro Mifune), a brave warrior, and his warrior friend Yoshaki Miki (Minoru Chiaki) have put down a revolt against their warlord master Noriyasu Odagura (Takashi Shimura) and have been ordered to come to their lord's castle for an audience. As they ride through a dense forest they encounter a ghostlike old woman who prophecizes that Washizu will soon be in command of the castle and replace his master as the warlord. She also foretells that his rule will be brief. Washizu is well received by his lord but goaded by his wife, Asaji (Isuzu Yamada); remembering the prophecy of the old woman and spurred by his own ambition, he murders his comrade and lord. As foretold Washizu's rule is brief and he comes to a bloody end as his own warriors turn against him.

Kurosawa had wanted to make films of Shakespeare's plays for many years. *Throne of Blood,* based on *Macbeth,* was his first. It would be twenty-eight years until he made his even more ambitious, *Ran* (1985) based on the tragedy of *King Lear. Throne of Blood* loosely follows Shakespeare's plot. The central characters of *Macbeth*—Lady Macbeth, Duncan and Banquo—are intact although most of the minor characters have been eliminated. *Throne of Blood* is one of Kurosawa's most imaginative films. The mist-shrouded forests, the galloping horses, the rain and the last scene when Washizu is pierced by tens of arrows are all visually stunning. But as in *Ran,* without Shakespeare's words it is not *Macbeth.*

Tristana

1970. 98 min. b.w. French/Spanish/Italian. **Prod.** Juan Estelrich; **Dir.** Luis Buñuel ; **Scr.** Luis Buñuel , Julio Alejandro (based on the novel by Benito Perez Galdos); **Cin.** Jose F. Aguayo; **Ed.** Pedro del Rey; **Art D.** Enrique Alarcon; **Cast:** Catherine Deneuve, Fernando Rey, Franco Nero, Jesus Fernandez, Lola Gaos, Antonio Casas.

The story is set in the mid 1920's in Toledo, Spain. A young girl, Tristana (Catherine Deneuve), becomes the ward of an agnostic, vain gentleman, Don Lope (Fernando Rey), who has gone through his inherited wealth and is now impoverished. He imparts his confused hedonistic principles to the impressionable girl and soon asks her to share his bed. Having accepted his teachings, she accepts the offer. She becomes bored with the aging lover who is a creature of habit with no imagination. The dissatisfied Tristana falls in love with a young painter, Horacio (Franco Nero), and leaves Don Lope. The painter leaves Toledo, and she follows him. She asks him to marry her. When he refuses she returns to Toledo. Don Lope, who has inherited a small fortune from a sister, welcomes her back. Tristana, however, conditions her return to him upon their formal marriage in a church, to which he agrees. She later is stricken with illness and when a tumor is found, her leg is amputated. He tells her, "Some men would find you more attractive than ever now." During the following winter Don Lope becomes ill and asks Tristana to call a doctor. She leaves the room and feigns a call. Don Lope dies. The last scene of the film has Tristana opening wide the windows of the house despite the coldness of winter and the snow falling outside. She is ridding the house of the spirit of Don Lope.

The film is based on a minor novella of some eighty pages, written by an obscure Spanish writer, Benito Perez Galdos, at the end of the nineteenth century. Buñuel moved the story to 1920s Toledo. *Tristana* is not one of Buñuel 's greatest works, but it is still an interesting film by the master. There is, as always, the savage Buñuel wit and his obsessive attack on the Catholic church. He had been educated by Jesuit priests and the Spain of Buñuel was dominated by the church. In 1935, just before the start of the civil war, there were more than 110,000 monks, nuns and priests and over 5,000 convents and monasteries. In addition to Buñuel's usual irreverence, the film also attacks the establishment and its hypocrisy. Fernando Rey as the lustful Don Lope dominates the film. Catherine Deneuve and Franco Nero, although dubbed, do a credible job.

Trouble in Paradise

1932. 83 min. b.w. U.S. **Prod.** Ernst Lubitsch; **Dir.** Ernst Lubitsch; **Scr.** Grover Jones, Samson Raphaelson (based on the play *The Honest Finder* by Laszlo Aladar); **Cin.** Victor Milner; **Art D.** Hans Dreier; **Mus.** W. Franke Harling; **Cast:** Miriam Hopkins, Kay Francis, Herbert Marshall, Charlie Ruggles, Edward Everett Horton, C. Aubrey Smith, Leonid Kinsky, Robert Greig.

The film is set at the beginning of the Great Depression. It opens in Venice as two jewel thieves posing as aristocrats, Gaston Monescu (Herbert Marshall) and Lily Vautier (Miriam Hopkins), having robbed several people, travel to Paris for their next prey. They decide on a wealthy beautiful widow, Mariette Colet (Kay Francis), the proprietor of a successful perfumery, managed since her husband's death by the apparently reputable elderly businessman Adolph Giron (C. Aubrey Smith). We discover later Giron is an even bigger crook and is stealing from Mariette and the company. Mariette has two suitors but is not interested in either. When she loses her diamond-studded handbag at the opera and offers a large reward for its return, tens of people bring her a variety of handbags claiming the reward. Gaston, who stole the handbag, shows up with it but refuses to accept the reward. He tells her he is one of the countless victims of the stock market crash. Mariette taken by his honesty and sincerity offers him a job as her secretary. Soon Lily, on Gaston's recommendation, is appointed as Mariette's social secretary. Plans are made to steal Mariette's entire cash holdings, but trouble begins in their paradise when Gaston starts falling in love with Mariette.

The dialogue is sophisticated and contains much sexual innu-
endo. The film has the famed Lubitsch touch and oozes with
charm. The very opening scene has a gondolier singing "O Sole
Mio" as he rows his gondola to the banks of the canal. We soon
realize he is a garbage collector doing his rounds and is serenad-
ing his boatful of garbage. Lubitsch depicts the idle rich during
the Depression. The two suitors of Mariette played by Charlie
Ruggles and Edward Everett Horton are in a privileged world of
their own, totally oblivious to everything beyond. The entire cast
is among the best of Hollywood of the thirties. Although it has
dated somewhat, it is still a charming and delightful film.

2001: A Space Odyssey

1968. 130 min. color. British/U.S. **Prod.** Stanley Kubrick; **Dir.** Stanley Kubrick; **Scr.**
Stanley Kubrick, Arthur C. Clarke (based on the story "The Sentinel" by Arthur C. Clarke);
Cin. Geoffrey Unsworth, John Alcott; **Ed.** Ray Lovejoy; **Prod. D.** Tony Masters, Harry
Lange, Ernest Archer; **Art D.** John Hoesli; **Mus.** classical excerpts; **Cast:** Keir Dullea, Gary
Lockwood, William Sylvester, Daniel Richter, Douglas Rain (as voice of Hal).

The film begins with the title "The Dawn of Man." Some four
million years ago, a monolithic slab is discovered by a family of
apes and their lives are forever changed. Once they touch the slab
they are transformed from vegetarians to carnivores, and learn to
use bones as tools and weapons to hunt for food and defend
themselves against hostile apes. Cut to 2001, a distant celestial
body where U.S. scientists have discovered a monolithic slab that
sends signals in the direction of Jupiter. They keep the discovery
secret and send a spaceship to travel five hundred million miles to
Jupiter. The ship is manned by two astronauts, David Bowman
(Keir Dullea) and Frank Poole (Gary Lockwood). Neither knows
the purpose of the mission. Several other astronauts are on board,
but to save oxygen they have been put into hibernation to be
awakened months hence when they are near Jupiter. A super
computer, Hal 4000, with a mellifluous voice and human quali-
ties has been programmed to handle the ship and every

contingency that might arise. For reasons not entirely explained Hal kills the sleeping astronauts as well as Poole. Hal also attempts unsuccessfully to eliminate Bowman, who disconnects Hal and renders it inoperative. Bowman reaches Jupiter and we see him in an eighteenth-century bedroom suite. He has aged, dies and is reborn in a cosmic burst. The plot narrative becomes more confused. Instead of explanations, we are shown a light and sound fantasy and the viewer's bewilderment is deepened further.

There is a minimum of dialogue in the film. We are left with our own wits trying to understand what Kubrick is saying. There is little acting in the film and Hal takes acting honors. But Kubrick has entertained us with a major achievement in cinematography and special effects. An ape throws a bone into the sky, and the bone is transformed into a graceful spaceship floating to the strains of the "Blue Danube Waltz"—a much-copied depiction of technology in waltz time. The wonderment of the apes is accompanied by the sonorous music of Richard Strauss' "Thus Spake Zarathustra." All Kubrick's films from this point onward are flawed and not well thought out. In *Lolita* (1962) he let Peter Sellers ham up the picture. *Barry Lyndon* (1975) could have been a great film, but he cast a weak actor, and in *The Shining* (1980), one of his worst films, he allowed a wild Jack Nicholson to do as he pleased.

Umberto D

1952. 89 min. b.w. Italian. **Prod.** Vittorio De Sica; **Dir.** Vittorio De Sica; **Scr.** Cesare Zavattini, Vittorio De Sica; **Cin.** Aldo Graziati; **Ed.** Eraldo di Roma; **Prod.** D. Virgilio Marchi; **Mus.** Alessandro Cicognini; **Cast:** Carlo Battisti, Maria Pia Casilio, Lina Gennari, Alberto Albani Barbieri.

The film opens in post-World War II Rome with a sizable demonstration in front of a government building by old men demanding an increase in their pensions. Umberto Domenico Ferrari (Carlo Battisti) is one of the demonstrators. Police disperse the crowd and Umberto with his dog Flike return to his rooming house. He is briefly locked out by the proprietor who has rented it for a few hours to a couple for an assignation. Umberto is a retired civil servant living on a pitifully small pension. He is several months behind in his rent and it is only a matter of time before he is thrown out. His only friends are his dog and the kind young maid, Maria (Maria Pia Casilio), who has problems of her own as she has become pregnant by one of her soldier boyfriends. Umberto is ignored by his better-off colleagues. He even attempts to become a beggar but is too shy to attract attention. He becomes ill and spends a few days at the government hospital, leaving early because he misses his dog. He becomes frantic when he can't find him, but soon Flike shows up. After a few weeks he is dispossessed and his meager belongings sold. He contemplates suicide and stands on the railroad tracks with Flike waiting for a train. The dog runs away and he discards the idea because he doesn't want his small dog fighting for food on the streets after he is gone. The film ends with a fade out of Umberto and the dog walking along a wooded street.

Umberto D. is a pure and simple film. It was filmed on the streets of Rome. Umberto is played by a retired professor of philology. De Sica based the central character on his own father who had been a pensioner.

Under Fire

1983. 128 min. color. U.S. **Prod.** Jonathan T. Taplin; **Dir.** Roger Spottiswoode; **Scr.** Ron Shelton, Clayton Frohman; **Cin.** John Alcott; **Ed.** John Bloom; **Art D.** Agustin Ytuarte, Toby Rafelson; **Mus.** Jerry Goldsmith; **Cast:** Nick Nolte, Gene Hackman, Joanna Cassidy, Ed Harris, Jean-Louis Trintignant, Alma Martinez, Holly Palance.

The film is set in Nicaragua in late 1979, during the uprising led by the Sandinista National Liberation Front (FSLN) against the forty-year rule of the Somoza family. It tells the story of three journalists: Russell Price (Nick Nolte), a photojournalist with *Time* magazine; Claire (Joanna Cassidy), a reporter for National Public Radio who had recently broken a lengthy relationship with Alex Grazier (Gene Hackman), a network news anchor. They are staying at the posh Intercontinental Hotel in Managua with no contact with the revolutionaries nor any exposure to the abject poverty of Nicaraguans and the brutality of the Somoza National Guard. The U.S. had installed the elder Somoza as the president in 1937 and since his assassination in 1956 his son has ruled the country. The Somoza family owns more than half of the impoverished country. Through Claire and her contacts, Russell establishes communication with the Sandinistas. Their leader is Rafael who is killed in a raid. Russell touches up an old photograph of the leader to make it appear he is still alive and the photo is distributed amongst the masses. The key incident that gives momentum to the uprising is the cold-blooded murder of Grazier by the National Guard, which Russell captures on film. With the release of the film, U.S. backing for Somoza collapses.

Under Fire is perhaps too ambitious a film with too small a budget and limited shooting time. Both Hackman and Nolte appeared for much less than their usual fee. The film is a little too long and it has two peripheral characters who are not sufficiently developed: Jean-Louis Trintignant playing a Frenchman working for the CIA, and Ed Harris as a mercenary soldier. The main strength of the film lies in the superb performances by the three leads: Nick Nolte with his bulk and husky voice and the beautiful Joanne Cassidy as lovers in time of war, and Hackman who is effective as always. It is an intelligent and well-made film.

The Verdict

1982. 129 min. color. U.S. **Prod.** Richard D. Zanuck, David Brown; **Dir.** Sidney Lumet; **Scr.** David Mamet (based on the novel by Barry Reed); **Cin.** Andrzej Bartkowiak; **Ed.** Peter C. Frank; **Prod. D.** Edward Pisoni; **Art D.** John Kasarda; **Mus.** Johnny Mandel; **Cast:** Paul Newman, Charlotte Rampling, Jack Warden, James Mason, Milo O'Shea, Edward Binns, Julie Bovasso, Lindsay Crouse, Roxanne Hart, James Hand.

Frank Galvin (Paul Newman), a burned-out lawyer who has come close to disbarment for jury tampering, has been without a client for a good while. By pure chance, he is given a malpractice suit instituted by a patient's sister against a doctor and a large hospital in Boston. The patient, a young woman in perfect health, had gone to the hospital to deliver a baby, but due to the gross negligence of the doctor, she was given a wrong dosage of anesthesia, turning her into a vegetable. Galvin had not realized that the hospital is owned by the Catholic church, and represented by a large, prestigious law firm. There is a cover-up conspiracy and no witnesses are forthcoming. Galvin is offered a settlement that he refuses and the case goes to trial. The film now becomes the story of a washed-up man given one more chance.

Sidney Lumet, who had directed what is probably the best courtroom drama on film, *12 Angry Men* (1957), handles this assignment with equal facility. The opening scene visually establishes the depths to which Galvin has fallen. We first see him drinking and playing a pinball machine in a bar during the daytime. Next, we see him as an ambulance chaser at a funeral parlor, bribing the manager to let him hand his cards to the bereaved. The film is also well acted. Paul Newman gives one of his best performances. Jack Warden as Galvin's friend; James Mason, the lead lawyer for the law firm representing the hospital; Milo O'Shea as the judge; and Lindsay Crouse as a nurse are excellent. The film is marred by a few sentimental scenes and the undefined character of Charlotte Rampling playing a planted informer for the law firm.

Vertigo

1958. 128 min. color. U.S. **Prod.** Alfred Hitchcock; **Dir.** Alfred Hitchcock; **Scr.** Alec Coppel, Samuel Taylor (based on the novel *D'Entre les Morts* by Pierre Boileau, Thomas Narcejac); **Cin.** Robert Burks; **Ed.** George Tomasini; **Art D.** Hal Pereira, Henry Bumstead; **Mus.** Bernard Herrmann; **Cast:** James Stewart, Kim Novak, Barbara Bel Geddes, Tom Helmore, Henry Jones, Raymond Bailey, Ellen Corby, Konstantin Shayne.

John "Scottie" Ferguson (James Stewart), a police detective, resigns from the force when he realizes he suffers from acrophobia and was responsible for the death of a fellow officer while they were chasing a criminal. He later is asked by an acquaintance, Gavin Elster (Tom Helmore), to watch over his wife, Madeleine (Kim Novak), who has shown suicidal tendencies. In following her, Scottie discovers Madeleine is suffering from a delusion that she is the reincarnation of Carlotta, a prominent Spanish woman in northern California who had committed suicide some fifty years before. Scottie rescues Madeleine when she throws herself into the San Francisco Bay. Soon an intimacy develops and Scottie falls in love with her. Madeleine also has a vision of an old Spanish mission church that Carlotta had often visited. Scottie agrees to take her there hoping her delusions will be done away with. Once at the mission she runs away from him and climbs the stairs to the top of the church tower. He can't follow her for his fear of heights. He watches hopelessly as she throws herself to her death. There is an inquest and her death is ruled a suicide. Scottie suffers a nervous breakdown. Some time later he runs into a girl, Judy Barton (also Kim Novak), who resembles Madeleine in an uncanny way. He again falls in love, but still obsessed with the memory of Madeleine he attempts to remake her in Madeleine's image with the same makeup, hair and clothes. Since he had initially set eyes on Madeleine at Ernie's, a fashionable restaurant in San Francisco, he decides to take Judy there for their first outing. Judy has also fallen in love and in order to please him puts on the beautiful necklace Carlotta had worn in her portrait. Scottie had seen it before and realizes Judy and Madeleine are the same person. He knows now that Judy had been Elster's mistress, portraying his wife Madeleine. Elster had planned to murder his wife and in order to have a fool-proof alibi had chosen Scottie to follow her, knowing his fear of heights would prevent him from climbing the church tower and witnessing the murder. Scottie is overwrought at having been used in a murder plot. He takes Judy to the church tower to re-create the events of Elster's wife's murder. In the end Scottie's fear of heights is cured at the cost of losing his love for the second time. Whether he can bring Elster to justice is now irrelevant. He has destroyed himself.

Vertigo is one of Hitchcock's most imaginative and well-crafted films, but the narrative is based on so many improbabilities that ultimately it damages the movie. It is foremost a story about obsessive love, not an espionage story where things need not necessarily be accounted for. Hitchcock could get away with the improbable uranium in *Notorious* (1946) or the unexplained microfilms in *North by Northwest* (1959). In *Vertigo* the viewer does need answers. How could a well-trained police officer not bother to examine Madeleine's body in the hope that she may still be alive, especially since he was insanely in love with her? Less likely is that Elster should have counted on Scottie not viewing Madeleine's body after her fall. Judy, who had beautifully deceived Scottie when posing as Madeleine, is then foolish enough to wear a piece of jewelry that she must have known Scottie had seen before. James Stewart has one of the most difficult roles of his career and he is superb as the vulnerable, tragic figure. Kim Novak is passable as the refined Madeleine when she has the bare minimum of lines. But when she is transformed into an ordinary classless shop girl, the demands on her are obviously too much. Hitchcock had planned to star Vera Miles who had given a good performance in his film *The Wrong Man* (1956), but Miles was expecting a child and Hitchcock had to consider casting another icy, remote blonde. Barbara Bel Geddes, a talented actress, is very competent as Midge whose love and devotion to Scottie is unreturned.

Viridiana

1961. 90 min. b.w. Spanish. **Prod.** Ricardo Munoz Suay; **Dir.** Luis Buñuel ; **Scr.** Luis Buñuel, Julio Alejandro; **Cin.** José F. Agayo; **Ed.** Pedro del Rey; **Art D.** Francisco Canet; **Mus.** Mozart, Handel; **Cast:** Francisco Rabal, Silvia Pinal, Fernando Rey, Margarita Lozano, Victoria Zinny, Teresa Rabal.

Just before taking her final vows as a nun, an innocent girl, Viridiana (Silvia Pinal), visits her elderly uncle, Don Jaime (Fernando Rey), who has been her benefactor. Don Jaime is a wealthy man. His wife had died some thirty years ago on their wedding night just as he was to consummate their marriage. He has saved her wedding dress, which he caresses often and occasionally wears. He is taken by Viridiana who bears a resemblance to his late wife. He tells her he is lonely and offers her marriage. She is shocked and refuses. He next asks her to gratify one last desire and wear his wife's wedding dress. He drugs her tea and once she is unconscious attempts to rape her but can't bring himself to do it. The next day he falsely tells her he had in fact seduced her. Viridiana is about to leave when she is told her uncle has strangled himself. Don Jaime's illegitimate son, Jorge (Francisco Rabal), inherits the large estate. He asks Viridiana to stay and help him run a religious charity. She feels that, since she never can take her vows now, she should devote her life to the advancement of her religion. They open the house to the destitute to feed them and teach them the ways of the Lord. Their enterprise ends with one disaster after another. Viridiana is assaulted and almost raped by the beggars. Jorge, the more pragmatic of the two, convinces Viridiana to abandon the project, give up her aspirations to sainthood and establish a conjugal relationship with him as his mistress.

Buñuel 's films are fiercely anti-religion. In most of them he accomplishes his purpose with ridicule, mockery and irony. Here Buñuel goes for the jugular. It is a rage against the church and false piety told in memorable imagery by the master of surrealism. The centerpiece of the film is a long sequence in which Buñuel re-creates da Vinci's painting of the Last Supper with a blind beggar seated in Christ's place. The beggars are a drunken, degenerate, lecherous lot who dance lewdly to a background of jazz mixed with strains of Handel's *Messiah*. Buñuel had been invited by the government of Spain to return after a self-imposed exile of twenty-three years and make a film of his choosing. When he finished *Viridiana,* he left for France where it won the Golden Palm Award at the Cannes Film Festival. It was banned in Spain. The film established Fernando Rey's reputation as a fine actor.

Wild River

1960. 110 min. color. U.S. **Prod.** Elia Kazan; **Dir.** Elia Kazan; **Scr.** Paul Osborn (based on the novels *Mud on the Stars* by William Bradford Huie and *Dunbar's Cove* by Borden Deal); **Cin.** Ellsworth Fredricks; **Ed.** William Reynolds; **Art D.** Lyle Wheeler, Herman A. Blumenthal; **Mus.** Kenyon Hopkins; **Cast:** Montgomery Clift, Lee Remick, Jo Van Fleet, Albert Salmi, Jay C. Flippen, James Westerfield, Robert Earl Jones, Frank Overton.

The Tennessee Valley Authority (TVA) was established by an act of Congress in 1933 to build a series of dams to control the floods that devastated Tennessee; to generate hydroelectric power to rural and backward areas; and equally important to create jobs in the midst of a deep economic depression. *Wild River* begins with footage from a documentary film showing how the floods wreak havoc on the region. The story focuses on Chuck Glover (Montgomery Clift), an agent of TVA which is in the process of clearing land for a proposed dam. Most of the land on the banks of the Mississippi River had been sequestered by TVA and compensation was paid to the owners, or they were resettled nearby at government expense. There is, however, one holdout, Ella Garth (Jo Van Fleet), an eighty-year-old woman who has lived in the same house for fifty years. She lives with her widowed granddaughter, Carol (Lee Remick), and a servant. Glover has several sessions with her, but she won't yield. She is a matriarchal figure who rules over her entire family and is set in her ways. Glover is also beset by other problems. The locals regard him as an interloper from the north and resent his presence. When he hires some blacks, their hostility increases. The racist roughnecks attempt to beat him up and drive him away. In time, Ella gives up the battle and she is moved to another house. She dies shortly afterward. Meanwhile, Glover and Carol have fallen in love and marry.

An important film for its subject matter, which is often overlooked. It depicts the inherent conflict of progress pitted against local traditions, customs and entrenched prejudices. It was too serious, and was a commercial failure. It is a nearly forgotten Kazan film. As always, Kazan extracts excellent performances from his actors. Jo Van Fleet dominates the film. Lee Remick, a much underrated, talented actress, seldom got good parts. Frank Overton and Jay C. Flippen, two experienced actors, are very good. The only disappointment is Montgomery Clift, who was not the actor he had been eight or nine years earlier.

The Window

1949. 73 min. b.w. U.S. **Prod.** Frederic Ullman, Jr.; **Dir.** Ted Tetzlaff; **Scr.** Mel Dinelli (based on the novelette *The Boy Cried Murder* by Cornell Woolrich); **Cin.** William Steiner; **Ed.** Frederic Knudtson; **Art D.** Walter E. Keller, Sam Corso; **Mus.** Roy Webb; **Cast:** Bobby Driscoll, Barbara Hale, Arthur Kennedy, Paul Stewart, Ruth Roman, Anthony Ross.

The film is about a ten-year-old boy, Tommy Woodry (Bobby Driscoll), who cried wolf once too often. He lives with his parents (Arthur Kennedy and Barbara Hale) in a run-down New York City tenement. He has a lively imagination and, without meaning any harm, makes up far-fetched stories. His parents have repeatedly warned him to stop, but to no avail. One hot night he sleeps outside on the fire escape. Through the open window opposite he witnesses the Kellertons (Paul Stewart and Ruth Roman) trying to rob a drunk they have lured to their apartment. In the ensuing struggle, they stab and kill the stranger. The next day, Tommy tells his parents, but they don't believe him and warn him not to make up any more tales. Tommy goes to the local police station and a detective (Anthony Ross) is sent to the Kellertons' apartment. The detective sees no sign of a struggle nor anything unusual. Tommy's mother forces him to apologize to the Kellertons. They humor him, but it is only a matter of time before they move to do away with Tommy.

The Window is a little gem— another sleeper from RKO made on a budget of just over $200,000. Ted Tetzlaff, a former director of photography, had been promoted to director and had made a few very low-budget thrillers. He got his chance with *The Window* and it is by far his best film. He had been director of photography on Hitchcock's *Notorious* (1946) and had learned a great deal about suspense and its construction and pacing. The film benefits from the sets of dilapidated and claustrophobic tenements designed by Walter E. Keller and Sam Corso. *The Window* is based on a story by Cornell Woolrich who had also written the story on which *Rear Window* (1954) would later be modelled. Bobby Driscoll, who was a juvenile actor in Disney films, was an excellent choice. The supporting cast comprised seasoned professionals: Arthur Kennedy, Barbara Hale, Paul Stewart and Anthony Ross.

Witness for the Prosecution

1957. 114 min. b.w. U.S. **Prod.** Arthur Hornblow, Jr.; **Dir.** Billy Wilder; **Scr.** Billy Wilder, Harry Kurnitz, Larry Marcus (based on the novel and the play by Agatha Christie); **Cin.** Russell Harlan; **Ed.** Daniel Mandell; **Art D.** Alexander Trauner; **Mus.** Matty Malneck; **Cast:** Marlene Dietrich, Tyrone Power, Charles Laughton, Elsa Lanchester, John Williams, Henry Daniell, Una O'Connor, Torin Thatcher, Francis Compton.

Famous barrister Sir Wilfrid Robarts (Charles Laughton) has recovered from a heart attack and returns home from the hospital. He is accompanied by a private nurse, Miss Plimsol (Elsa Lanchester), who is to enforce his strict diet and limit his activity. Because of his high blood pressure he is specifically warned not to accept any legal work. Barely home, a solicitor friend, Mayhew (Henry Daniell), brings a client, Leonard Stephen Vole (Tyrone Power). Vole is a Canadian who had done military service in Germany and now lives in England. The police want him for the murder of a well-to-do widow. Vole pleads complete innocence and categorically states that he was with his wife at the time of the murder. He claims he visited the widow's house merely as a helpful friend. Sir Wilfrid has devised a test to determine whether his clients are telling the truth. Vole passes his test easily. Vole is soon arrested and charged with the murder when it is learned that, according to a recently drawn will, Vole is the sole beneficiary of the widow's estate. Sir Wilfrid also has a short but distasteful interview with Christine Vole (Marlene Dietrich), the German-born wife of Vole. She professes to love her husband but says he was not with her the night of the murder. Christine miserably fails Sir Wilfrid's test. Despite the objections of Miss Plimsol, Sir Wilfrid accepts the case. There is one twist after another during the course of the trial and a surprise ending.

Based on the play by Agatha Christie, Wilder and his coscriptwriters added a great deal of humor to the tortuous plot. With the exception of a short flashback, the scene at Sir Wilfrid's house and a short scene in a pub, the film takes place at the Old Bailey for which Alexander Trauner built an exact replica. Cinematographer Russell Harlan masterfully moves the camera to break up the static court scenes. What makes this film the most enjoyable of Agatha Christie's filmed plays is the cast. The supporting players—Elsa Lanchester, John Williams and Henry Daniell is superb. Tyrone Power became a better actor over the years and does a credible job here. Marlene Dietrich as the woman who sacrifices everything to save the man she loves has one of her best roles. She even sings in one of the flashbacks, "I Never Go There Anymore." In her scene as a cockney hussy she shows her hitherto unknown talent for imitating accents. But the film belongs to Charles Laughton. He was up against great scene stealers of the caliber of his wife, Elsa Lanchester, and John Williams, but he still dominates every scene. Laughton modeled his role on Winston Churchill and there was talk of his playing Churchill in a film. He died before a project could bear fruition.

The Wizard of Oz

1939. 101 min. b.w./color. U.S. **Prod.** Mervin LeRoy; **Dir.** Victor Fleming, King Vidor; **Scr.** Noel Langley, Florence Ryerson, Edgar Allan Woolf (based on the novel by L. Frank Baum); **Cin.** Harold Rosson; **Ed.** Daniel Mandell; **Art D.** Cedric Gibbons; **Mus.** Herbert Stothart; **Cast:** Judy Garland, Ray Bolger, Bert Lahr, Jack Haley, Frank Morgan, Billie Burke, Margaret Hamilton, Charley Grapewin, Clara Blandick.

Young Dorothy (Judy Garland), lives with Aunt Em (Clara Blandick) on a Kansas farm. She is lonely and bored. Her only companion is her mischievous dog Toto, who is a bother to a neighbor, Miss Gulch (Margaret Hamilton). Dorothy longs for exotic and faraway places. A severe tornado strikes the area and everyone hurries to the cellar. Dorothy can't make it and she is struck by a flying chair. When she wakes up she is somewhere beyond the rainbow in Munchkinland with Toto. On the advice of Glinda, the Good Witch of the East (Billie Burke), she takes the yellow brick road to Emerald City to ask the all-knowing Wizard of Oz (Frank Morgan) how she can get back to her home in Kansas. Along the way she picks up three friends who also want to see the wizard: a Tin Man (Jack Haley) who wants a heart, a Cowardly Lion (Bert Lahr) who wants courage and a Scarecrow (Ray Bolger) who wants a brain. The Wicked Witch of the West (also Margaret Hamilton) tries to prevent them from getting to Emerald City, but they make it. The Wizard is revealed to be a charlatan with no powers. But now Dorothy recovers from her blow and wakes up in the farmhouse surrounded by her aunt, three farmhands—Hunk, Zeke and Hickory, the spitting images of the three odd friends she had met on the road to Emerald City—and Professor Marvel, the snake oil salesman who looks exactly like the Wizard.

The Wizard of Oz, one of the loveliest fairy tales, is about the feeling of a child wanting to belong and teaches that "there's no place like home." L. Frank Baum's novel is a quintessential American story. It tells us not to accept politicians and hucksters on blind faith. The Wizard turns out to be a hollow man who cannot perform miracles. The film begins and ends in black and white, resembling old sepia photographs. The dream part, far from Kansas, is in color. Sixteen-year-old Judy Garland was selected over Shirley Temple and Deanna Durbin, and it was a fortuitous choice. Garland had a look of vulnerability that made her so good for the part. She made "Somewhere Over the Rainbow" her signature song. The rest of the cast is the cream of MGM. There is a good deal of humor in the film and the songs by Bolger, Lahr and Haley, each wishing for a human organ or emotion, are fetching, but Lahr outshines the other two. The film has dated a little and some scenes are wanting, but it is still charming its third generation of viewers.

THE NEAR-GREAT

A Nous La Liberté

Freedom for Us. 1931. 97 min. b.w. French. **Dir.** René Clair; **Scr.** René Clair; **Cin.** Georges Périnel; **Ed.** René Clair; **Mus.** Georges Aurie; **Cast:** Raymond Cordy, Henri Marchand, Rolla France, Paul Olivier, Jacques Shelly.

Two vagrants, Emile (Henri Marchand) and Louis (Raymond Cordy), are in prison. They share the same cell and plan an escape. Only Louis succeeds. He knocks down a racing cyclist who is far in front of the other cyclists and rides off. The judges mistakenly declare Louis the winner and give him the prize money. Louis begins selling phonograph records, then builds a manufacturing plant, and soon he is the king of the record industry. Emile, a gentle soul, escapes on his next attempt. By chance he gets a job on the long assembly line at Louis' factory. He is seen by Louis but ignored. Some gangsters discover Louis' true identity and blackmail him. When Louis sees policemen in the factory yard, he decides to run and Emile goes along with him. In the last scene they have become friends again, and without a care in the world they take to the road singing and walking toward the horizon.

This sweet film has dated. It is a musical comedy with a social message on the dehumanization of the worker on mass production assembly lines. The workers are regarded as robots and are treated in the same way as convicts in prisons. Chaplin borrowed heavily from this film for his *Modern Times* (1936). It led to a lawsuit that was resolved when Clair and Chaplin tacitly admitted borrowing from each other. In later years René Clair acknowledged Chaplin as the father of all screen comedies.

Ace in the Hole

(a.k.a. *The Big Carnival*) 1951. 112 min. b.w. U.S. **Prod.** Billy Wilder; **Dir.** Billy Wilder; **Scr.** Billy Wilder, Lesser Samuels, Walter Newman; **Cin.** Charles Long; **Ed.** Arthur Schmidt; **Art D.** Hal Pereira, Earl Hedrick; **Mus.** Hugo Friedhofer; **Cast:** Kirk Douglas, Jan Sterling, Bob Arthur, Porter Hall, Richard Benedict, Ray Teal.

A hard-drinking, womanizing, unprincipled reporter, Charles Tatum (Kirk Douglas), fired from several jobs in the East lands a job with a small paper in Albuquerque, New Mexico. On an assignment to cover a rattlesnake hunt he accidentally stumbles across a man who while searching for Indian relics had become buried in a collapsed cave. Instead of seeking immediate help, he persuades the local sheriff that if the story could be played out for a few days, both he and the sheriff, who is running for reelection, would benefit from the publicity, and the trapped man would be rescued in time. The sheriff agrees to keep other reporters away and Tatum becomes the only contact with the trapped man. Tatum is offered up to $1,000 for every story he files and several large circulation papers offer him jobs. The delay is too long and the trapped man dies.

Ace in the Hole is the most cynical of Wilder's films and there is not the slightest respite. It depicts the worst elements in human nature. What mars a finely acted film is a contrived ending where Tatum is also killed. It has powerful acting by Kirk Douglas. Ray Teal as the hard-bitten sheriff, Porter Hall as the owner of the local paper, Richard Benedict as the doomed man and Jan Sterling as his sluttish wife are excellent. The film captures people's morbid fascination with impending tragedy or disaster, and the carnival atmosphere of the thousands who have gathered to witness the event.

Adam's Rib

1949. 101 min. b.w. U.S. **Prod.** Lawrence Weingarten; **Dir.** George Cukor; **Scr.** Ruth Gordon, Garson Kanin; **Cin.** George Folsey; **Ed.** George Boemler; **Art D.** Cedric Gibbons, William Ferrari; **Mus.** Miklos Rosza; **Cast:** Spencer Tracy, Katharine Hepburn, Judy Holliday, Tom Ewell, David Wayne, Jean Hagen.

This witty, well-scripted and well-directed battle of the sexes between lawyers, Spencer Tracy and Katharine Hepburn, will be remembered more for Judy Holliday who steals the show in her film debut. There are good cameo performances by Tom Ewell, David Wayne and Jean Hagen. Tracy and Hepburn are, of course, magic. *Adam's Rib* is the most enjoyable of the Tracy/Hepburn films. There is also a lovely song "Farewell Amanda" that Cole Porter wrote for the film.

Alexander Nevsky

Aleksandr Nyevski. 1938. 108 min. b.w. Russia. **Dir.** Sergei Eisenstein; **Scr.** Sergei Eisenstein, Piotr Pavienko; **Cin.** Edouard Tissé; **Mus.** Sergei Prokofiev; **Cast:** Nikolai Cherkassov, Nikolai Okhlopkov, Alexander Abrikossov, Dimitri Orlov, Andrei Abrikosov.

The story takes place in mid-thirteenth-century Russia when the country is invaded from the east by the Tartars and from the west by the Germanic Teutonic Knights. The country is leaderless and turns to Prince Alexander (Nikolai Cherkassov) who had recently defeated the Swedes on the Neva River. After that victory, the honorary name Nevsky was bestowed on him. Now in retirement, spending his time as a fisherman, the people turn to him once again and implore him to lead them. Nevsky organizes a people's army including peasants and women. The invading Teutonic knights belong to a fanatical religious order and show no mercy. They destroy villages, kill women and burn children. The decisive battle takes place in 1242 on frozen Lake Peipus. The Huns are in heavy armor and ride large horses that are themselves heavily protected. Their combined weight is too much for the ice. It breaks and they are swallowed by the freezing waters of the lake. Russia is saved!

This is Eisenstein's most spectacular film and resembles American films in composition. He used his favorite cinematographer, Edouard Tissé, who shot a magnificently staged battle on the lake. Eisenstein's editing is more conventional than in *Potemkin* (1925). *Alexander Nevsky* was his first film in ten years. He had been in disfavor since the late twenties. He received authorization for this film at a time when Stalin was becoming increasingly apprehensive about German intentions toward the Soviet Union. In addition, the project had a semidivine figure as its hero with whom Stalin wanted to be identified. The full resources of the Soviet army were put at Eisenstein's disposal, and he used thousands of extras in his battle scenes. The film was great propaganda but ironically it had no Communist content. It was more an appeal to Russian nationalism. The message of Alexander Nevsky is, "Go home and tell all in foreign lands that Russia lives. Let them come as guests…[he] who comes by the sword will perish by the sword." The battle on the frozen lake and the sinking of the Huns is almost biblical in scope. The Huns are devoured by the lake as pharaoh's army was drowned in the Red Sea. When the film was completed, the Soviet Union and Germany were beginning a dialogue that culminated in the Soviet-German pact of 1939 and the film was withdrawn from circulation. With the German attack on the Soviet Union in June 1941, it was re-released to a rapturous reception by the Soviet public. Eisenstein regained favor and was allowed to begin work on *Ivan the Terrible* Part I (1943) and Part II (1946) which is an uninteresting film and has been referred to as "no more than a collection of still shots."

As eminent as the film itself is the score by Prokofiev, which dominates the film. It has become a popular concert piece, often performed as a cantata.

All Through the Night

1942. 107 min. b.w. U.S. **Prod.** Jerry Wald; **Dir.** Vincent Sherman; **Scr.** Leonard Spigelgass, Edwin Gilbert (based on a story by Leonard Spigelgass and Leonard Ross); **Cin.** Sid Hickox; **Ed.** Rudi Fehr; **Art D.** Max Parker; **Mus.** Adolph Deutsch; **Cast:** Humphrey Bogart, Conrad Veidt, Peter Lorre, Judith Anderson, Jane Darwell, William Demarest, Jackie Gleason, Phil Silvers, Barton MacLane, Frank McHugh, Karen Verne.

A minor comedy that Humphrey Bogart made immediately after *The Maltese Falcon* (1941). Bogart plays Gloves Donahue, a former mobster turned big-time gambler and man about Broadway. With the help of his underworld friends, he exposes and captures a gang of Nazi fifth columnists who plan to sabotage a battleship in New York harbor. The film is enjoyable for its cast of Runyonesque characters; William Demarest as fast double-talking Sunshine, Jackie Gleason as Starchie and Phil Silvers. To balance the score the Nazi spies are played by certified film heavies: Conrad Veidt, Peter Lorre and Judith Anderson. An auction scene in this movie is similar to Hitchcock's *North by Northwest* (1959).

An American in Paris

1951. 115 min. color. U.S. **Prod.** Arthur Freed; **Dir.** Vincente Minnelli; **Scr.** Alan J. Lerner; **Cin.** Alfred Gilks, John Alton; **Ed.** Adrienne Fazan; **Art D.** Cedric Gibbons, Preston Ames; **Mus.** George Gershwin; **Cast:** Gene Kelly, Leslie Caron, Oscar Levant, Georges Guetary, Nina Foch.

An overblown and pretentious film with a mundane plot. What redeems it are the Gershwin songs: Gene Kelly's smiling face in "I Got Rhythm," "Embraceable You" and "'S Wonderful"; and the show stopper, the Georges Guetary number, "I'll Build a Stairway to Paradise." The film won a host of Academy Awards, including best picture.

Anastasia.

1956. 105 min. color. U.S. **Prod.** Buddy Adler; **Dir.** Anatole Litvak; **Scr.** Arthur Laurents (based on Guy Bolton's adaption of a play by Marcelle Maurette). **Cin.** Jack Hildyard; **Ed.** Bert Bates; **Art D.** Andre Andrejew, Bill Andrews; **Mus.** Alfred Newman; **Cast:** Ingrid Bergman, Yul Brynner, Helen Hayes, Akim Tamiroff, Martita Hunt, Felix Aylmer.

This is the story of a destitute woman (Ingrid Bergman) who appears in Paris in 1928 claiming to be the Grand Duchess Anastasia, the youngest daughter of Czar Nicholas and Empress Alexandra and the sole survivor of the mass murder of her family a decade earlier. A well-directed film, and it stands out for the superb acting of Ingrid Bergman, especially the "recognition" scene between Bergman and Helen Hayes. The film is also blessed with great scenes by the superb veteran actors Akim Tamiroff, Felix Aylmer, and Martita Hunt. The movie is, however, too glossy with a sugar-coated false ending.

Andrei Rublev

1966. 185 min. b.w. color. Russian. **Dir.** Andrei Tarkovsky; **Scr.** Andrei Tarkovsky, Andrei Mikhalkov-Konchalovsky; **Cin.** Vadim Yusof; **Mus.** Viacheslav Tcherniaiev; **Cast:** Anatoli Solonitzine, Ivan Lapikov, Nikolai Grinko.

This lyrical film chronicles the life and work of Andrei Rublev, a fifteenth-century Russian monk. He is an icon painter—and a Christ-like figure himself. Russia is under the rule of the Tartar invaders and Rublev, having witnessed untold horrors, abandons his art and even refuses to talk. He resumes painting after the Tartars have been driven out. The film has eight segments. What makes this often slow-moving film in black and white worthwhile is the last segment in color, when the viewer finally gets to see the brilliance of the painter's work.

Tarovksy's last film *The Sacrifice* (1986), released after his death, is powerful and visually stunning. In it World War III has begun and most of Europe is devastated. A prominent man of letters renounces all his family and belongings for the world to return to pre-war status

Androcles and the Lion

1952. 98 min. b.w. U.S. **Prod.** Gabriel Pascal; **Dir.** Chester Erskine. **Scr.** Chester Erskine, Ken Englund (based on the play by George Bernard Shaw); **Cin.** Harrry Stradling; **Ed.** Roland Cross; **Art D.** Victor Kempster; **Mus.** Frederick Hollander; **Cast:** Jean Simmons, Victor Mature, Alan Young, Maurice Evans, Robert Newton, Elsa Lanchester.

This is the classic tale of the Christian Androcles, whose kind heart surmounts his fear as he removes a painful thorn from a lion's paw. Later, when masses of Christians are sent into the arena to fight hungry lions, Androcles is pitted against his old friend who remembers and submits to him. Despite miscasting in the lead roles and shifting the focus of the tale to an inane love story, Shaw's wit still shines through with some excellent acting by Maurice Evans as the Roman emperor and Robert Newton as a burly, brawling plebian recently converted to Christianity but still unable to control his aggressive instincts. At the end, Shaw, with tongue in cheek, has the emperor say he wants all his Praetorian Guards to be Christians because they are fierce fighters.

Angels in the Outfield

1951. 99 min. color. U.S. **Prod.** Clarence Brown; **Dir.** Clarence Brown; **Scr.** Dorothy Kingsley, George Wells (based on a story by Richard Conlin); **Cin.** Paul C. Vogel; **Ed.** Robert J. Kern; **Mus.** Daniele Amfitheatrof; **Cast:** Paul Douglas, Janet Leigh, Keenan Wynn, Donna Corcoran, Lewis Stone, Spring Byington, Bruce Bennett, Marvin Kaplan.

Guffy McGovern (Paul Douglas) is the manager of the lowly Pittsburgh Pirates baseball team, currently in last place in the National League. Guffy is a foul-mouthed, irreverent soul. He is in constant trouble with the umpires and his own players who are not willing to extend themselves. The team's most loyal fan is a little orphan girl in a convent who prays for the team every night. Her prayers are finally answered when one night the angel Gabriel descends from the heavens and tells Guffy that if he were to stop cussing and treat his players humanely the team may do better. Guffy reforms and the team slowly comes out of the cellar and even wins the pennant. A very charming film that owes its success mostly to the acting of Paul Douglas, a fine actor who excelled in light comedy roles in his brief career.

Animal Crackers

1930. 98 min. b.w. U.S. **Dir.** Victor Heerman; **Scr.** Morrie Ryskind (based on the musical play by Morrie Ryskind and George S. Kaufman); **Cin.** George Foley; **Mus.** Bert Kalmar, Harry Ruby; **Cast:** Groucho, Harpo, Chico and Zeppo Marx, Margaret Dumont, Lillian Roth.

This creaking and stagy second film of the Marx Brothers is still more enjoyable than the film that followed (*A Night at the Opera* 1935). Groucho is Captain Spaulding, the noted African hunter and explorer. Margaret Dumont is Mrs. Rittenhouse, a wealthy hostess who introduces him to society. The highlight of the film is the song "Hooray for Captain Spaulding" sung by Groucho.

Anna and the King of Siam

1946. 128 min. b.w. U.S. **Prod.** Louis D. Lighton; **Dir.** John Cromwell; **Scr.** Talbot Jennings, Sally Benson (based on the book by Margaret Landon); **Cin.** Arthur Miller; **Ed.** Harmon Jones; **Art D.** Lyle Wheeler, William Darling; **Mus.** Bernard Herrmann; **Cast:** Irene Dunne, Rex Harrison, Lee J. Cobb, Linda Darnell, Gale Sondergaard, Mikhail Rasumny.

Anna and the King of Siam is based on the true story of a British tutor (Irene Dunne) who travels to Siam (Thailand) in 1862 to educate the many wives and children of the king (Rex Harrison). He is interested in Western ideas and culture but wishes to maintain many outdated customs and repressive traditions. The willful tutor and the autocratic king clash at first, but mutual respect and compromise ultimately develop. The film brings drama, history and comedy into play. Irene Dunne handles her role well. Rex

Harrison in his Hollywood debut gives one of his best screen performances. But it is Lee J. Cobb as the king's loyal chief minister who renders the best portrayal. It is an engaging story and is well directed. John Cromwell was a reliable, competent director who seldom made a bad movie. He is remembered for some superior films: *The Prisoner of Zenda* (1937), *Algiers* (1938), and *Abe Lincoln in Illinois* (1940). The film was made into an entertaining musical, *The King and I* (1956)

Annie Hall

1977. 94 min. color. U.S. **Prod.** Jack Rollins, Charles H. Joffe; **Dir.** Woody Allen; **Scr.** Woody Allen, Marshall Brickman; **Cin.** Gordon Willis; **Ed.** Ralph Rosenbloom, Wendy Greene Bricmont; **Art D.** Mel Bourne; **Cast:** Woody Allen, Diane Keaton, Tony Roberts, Paul Simon, Shelley Duvall, Colleen Dewhurst, Christopher Walken.

This film takes a humorous look at relationships in the 1970s, and is probably based on a real life love affair. Made at the height of the psychotherapy boom, it is self-conscious. A transitional film in Woody Allen's career as it is more personal and revealing than his previous movies. An enjoyable film that has dated.

Apocalypse Now

1979. 150 min. color. U.S. **Prod.** Francis Ford Coppola; **Dir.** Francis Ford Coppola; **Scr.** Michael Herr, John Milius, Francis Ford Coppola; **Cin.** Vittorio Storaro; **Ed.** Richard Marks; **Art D.** Angelo Graham; **Mus.** Carmine Coppola, Francis Ford Coppola; **Cast:** Marlon Brando, Robert Duvall, Martin Sheen, Frederic Forest, Albert Hall, Sam Bottoms, Dennis Hopper.

Captain Willard (Martin Sheen), an experienced and cynical army captain stationed in South Vietnam, is ordered to assemble a crew and journey by gunboat upriver to Cambodia. He is to find and "terminate with extreme prejudice" Colonel Kurtz (Marlon Brando), a former Green Beret officer who has deserted and established himself as a godlike figure among a tribe of primitive Montagnard warriors. He uses the tribe to wage personal wars.

The film is a record of Willard and his crew's journey, the horrific events he witnesses, and his confrontation with Kurtz.

A too ambitious and grand film with grand flaws. It is an intellectually honest film that aims to depict the folly of the U.S. involvement in a far-off country. The movie becomes pretentious when it begins to meditate on the nature of evil and on *The Heart of Darkness*, the Conrad novel upon which it is loosely based. The surrealistic ending makes it even more confusing. Marlon Brando gives an unexpectedly mediocre performance. The redeeming features of the film, in addition to its honesty, are the superb cinematography of Vittorio Storaro and some extraordinary powerful scenes. The historically inaccurate and dishonest *The Deer Hunter* (1978) was better put together and executed.

Atlantic City

1980. 104 min. color. U.S./Canadian/French. **Prod.** Denis Heroux; **Dir.** Louis Malle; **Scr.** John Guare; **Cin.** Richard Ciupka; **Ed.** Suzanne Baron; **Prod. D.** Anne Pritchard; **Mus.** Michel Legrand; **Cast:** Burt Lancaster, Susan Sarandon, Kate Reid, Michel Piccoli, Hollis McLaren.

Small-time aging hood Lou (Burt Lancaster), who had been only an errand boy for a big-time gangster, now takes care of the late gangster's bed-ridden moll (Kate Reid). He exaggerates his role in the old days and claims he was a hit man for the mob. Across the courtyard lives Sally (Susan Sarandon) who works in a hotel's clam bar and occasionally in the casino, hoping to be a croupier in Monte Carlo. Lou gets his chance to put into practice his idle boasts and helps Sally to pursue her dream. Lancaster gives what is probably his best performance. Sarandon, Reid and Piccoli in a cameo role as the casino manager are very good. Louis Malle's direction is smooth and flowing.

Au Hasard Balthazar

(a.k.a. *Balthazar*). 1966. 95 min. b.w. French. **Prod.** Mag Bodard; **Dir.** Robert Bresson; **Scr.** Robert Bresson; **Cin.** Ghislain Cloquet; **Art D.** Pierre Charbonnier; **Mus.** Jean Wiener, Franz Schubert; **Cast:** Anne Wiazemsky, Francois Lafarge, Philippe Asselin, Nathalie Joyaut, Walter Green.

Bresson depicts the life of a donkey from birth to death as a parable on the story of mankind. The donkey is named Balthazar, one of the Magi, by a little girl who is the first owner of the animal. It has a blissful existence and is the object of the attention and love of children. The next owner is an insensitive farmer who beats and abuses the donkey, overloading it beyond endurance. Balthazar has several other owners and is witness to wanton cruelty, including the gang rape of the now grown first owner. The last owners are a group of smugglers who use the animal to transport contraband. Balthazar is shot by a customs agent attempting to stop the smugglers. The final scene has the dead donkey in a field surrounded by grazing sheep.

Bresson used mostly nonprofessional actors, as in the majority of his films, and there is great attention to detail. The film has a lyricism that is enhanced by a Schubert piano sonata score. Bresson's world is the same in all of his films and he comes closest to the definition of an "auteur."

Avanti!

1972. 144 min. color. U.S. **Prod.** Billy Wilder; **Dir.** Billy Wilder; **Scr.** Billy Wilder, I. A. L. Diamond (based on the play by Samuel Taylor); **Cin.** Luigi Kuveiller; **Mus.** Carlo Rustichelli; **Cast:** Jack Lemmon, Juliet Mills, Clive Revill, Edward Andrews.

An arrogant, prudish American businessman from Baltimore (Jack Lemmon) has come to the scenic island of Ischia, a tourist haven in Italy, to claim and take back the body of his father who died in a car accident. An English girl (Juliet Mills) has come from London to claim the body of her mother who died in the same car. Unknown to Lemmon's character, the deceased had been lovers for some time and spent one month each summer together in Ischia. The bureaucratic hassle to claim the bodies draws the two together and history repeats itself. Not one of Wilder's best comedies, it drags a bit in parts, but the Wilder touch is there and the movie has a charm of its own. There is competent acting by the two leads but Clive Revill as the hotel manager has the best lines and steals the movie. Wilder has cast some of the most unusual and memorable faces in minor roles.

The Awful Truth

1937. 90 min. b.w. U.S. **Prod.** Leo McCarey; **Dir.** Leo McCarey; **Scr.** Vina Delmar (based on the play by Arthur Richman); **Cin.** Joseph Walker; **Ed.** Al Clark; **Art D.** Stephen Goosson, Lionel Banks; **Mus.** Morris Stoloff; **Cast:** Irene Dunne, Cary Grant, Ralph Bellamy, Cecil Cunningham, Mary Forbes, Molly Lamont, Joyce Compton.

Husband and wife (Cary Grant and Irene Dunne) get a ninety-day interlocutory divorce. Each wrongly believes the other has been unfaithful. After the decree Grant goes after an attractive nightclub singer and then becomes engaged to marry a socialite. Dunne meets and agrees to marry an oil tycoon from Texas (Ralph Bellamy). Each now tries to ruin the marriage plans of the other. Both succeed and they get back together. One of the popular Hollywood plots of the thirties was about divorced couples who reunite. *The Awful Truth* is one of the more successful attempts. The film has some funny scenes, especially Irene Dunne barging into the socialite's mansion, acting drunk and talking incessantly in an attempt to foil Grant's plans. Leo McCarey had directed several of the early Laurel and Hardy films and acquired a knack for creating funny scenes.

The Bad and the Beautiful

1952. 116 min. b.w. U.S. **Prod.** John Houseman; **Dir.** Vincente Minnelli; **Scr.** Charles Schnee (based on a story by George Bradshaw); **Cin.** Robert Sertees; **Ed.** Conrad A. Nervig; **Art D.** Cedric Gibbons, Edward Carfagno; **Mus.** David Raksin; **Cast:** Kirk Douglas, Lana Turner, Dick Powell, Gloria Grahame, Barry Sullivan, Walter Pidgeon, Gilbert Roland.

This story follows the rise and fall of a ruthless, driven man, Jonathan Shields (Kirk Douglas), who becomes the most important producer in Hollywood. The film is told in three long flashbacks and we see how Shields affected the lives of three people: a director (Barry Sullivan), a southern academic turned novelist then screenwriter (Dick Powell), and a pretty former alcoholic extra, now a star (Lana Turner). Although he cheated and lied to the three, they readily admit that Shields was responsible for their success. However, when he is attempting a comeback they refuse to have anything to do with him. The acting is uniformly good with the single exception of Lana Turner's below-par performance. The film lacks the power or the bite of Billy Wilder's story of Hollywood, *Sunset Boulevard* (1950), but it is very well made with the imprint of producer John Houseman and director Vincente Minnelli, and an excellent screenplay. Gloria Grahame won the best supporting actress award as a Zelda-type wife of Dick Powell. The film won awards for best screenplay, cinematography and art direction. It is made more interesting by several oblique references to past film people and the question of whether the Shields character is based on a real person.

The Baker's Wife

La Femme Du Boulanger. 1938. 124 min. b.w. French. **Prod.** Robert Hakim, Raymond Hakim; **Dir.** Marcel Pagnol; **Scr.** Marcel Pagnol; **Cin.** G. Benoit, R. Lendruz, N. Daries; **Ed.** Suzanne de Troeye; **Mus.** Vincent Scotto; **Cast:** Raimu, Ginette Leclerc, Charles Moulin, Robert Vattier, Fernand Charpin, Robert Bassa.

Everyone in a village in Provence is excited about the arrival of the new baker, Aimable (Raimu). The former baker had commit-

ted suicide and the people have been left breadless for several
months. The new baker who has recently married an attractive
young wife, Aurelie (Ginette Leclerc), is greeted very warmly.
Soon he demonstrates that he is a master of his profession and the
townspeople turn cheerful once again and old animosities are
forgotten. But Aurelie is serenaded and courted by a young,
handsome shepherd, Dominique (Charles Moulin), and the two
run off together. Aimable refuses to bake and takes to alcohol. He
even attempts to hang himself. The wealthiest man in the village,
the Marquis (Robert Vattier), is very upset. Not only is he denied
his brioche, but it appears the shepherd has taken his best horse.
He organizes search parties that resemble a military expedition.
After some days the local agnostic teacher and the priest, who
always argue amongst themselves, find the lovers on a nearby
small island. The shepherd, seeing the priest, runs away abandoning Aurelie. She loses all respect for him as he has shown himself
to be a coward and returns to the baker after dark. She is forgiven
and the baker promises to bake even tastier bread.

One of the most popular films in its day, *The Baker's Wife* is now
forgotten. It may have dated somewhat but is still one of the most
charming films of the thirties and is a showcase for Raimu, one of
the great clowns. Marcel Pagnol was a better writer than a director.
Here his direction is flat, but his script is witty and very amusing.

Ball of Fire

1941. 111 min. b.w. U.S. **Prod.** Samuel Goldwyn; **Dir.** Howard Hawks; **Scr.** Charles
Brackett, Billy Wilder (based on the story "From A to Z" by Thomas Monroe, Billy
Wilder); **Cin.** Greg Toland; **Ed.** Daniel Mandell; **Art D.** Perry Ferguson; **Mus.** Alfred New-
man; **Cast:** Gary Cooper, Barbara Stanwyck, Oscar Homolka, Dana Andrews, Dan
Duryea, S. Z. Sakall, Richard Haydn, Henry Travers.

A group of unworldly cloistered experts in various fields live in
a large mansion preparing an updated encyclopedia. Bertram
Potts (Gary Cooper), the youngest of the group, is a linguist and
is most eager to include new words, especially slang, that have

come into the language since the last edition. He goes to a night-club to hear the new jargon and meets a stripper, Sugarpuss O'Shea (Barbara Stanwyck), whose every other word is slang. Her gangster boyfriend is up for trial and in order to avoid testifying she seeks refuge with the innocent academicians, creating a Snow White and seven dwarfs scenario. Things get complicated when the gangster wants his girl back. The film is too cute, but under the able direction of Howard Hawks it all works.

Barry Lyndon

1975. 183 min. color. British. **Prod.** Stanley Kubrick; **Dir.** Stanley Kubrick; **Scr.** Stanley Kubrick (based on the novel by William Makepeace Thackeray); **Cin.** John Alcott; **Ed.** Tony Lawson; **Prod. D.** Ken Adam; **Art D.** Roy Walker; **Mus.** Leonard Rosenman; **Cast:** Ryan O'Neal, Marisa Berenson, Patrick Magee, Hardy Kruger, Gay Hamilton, Leonard Rossiter, Arthur O'Sullivan, Michael Hordem (narration).

Based on William Makepeace Thackeray's novel set in the eighteenth-century, the film recounts the adventures of Barry Lyndon (Ryan O'Neal), a poor Irish boy who is forced to leave his home. Fortune smiles on him and he is helped and befriended first by a highwayman, later in Europe by a Prussian officer and then by an English spy who is a card cheat in his leisure time. Lyndon becomes wealthy and, in his eagerness to raise his status in the well ordered society of the time, marries a widowed aristocrat (Marisa Berenson) that proves to be the beginning of his downfall. A beautiful film with the most subdued colors and a faultless re-creation of the eighteenth-century world. The story is told at a deliberate pace in 183 minutes, but the viewer's interest is sustained. Where the film suffers is in the overly subdued and emotionless acting of Ryan O'Neal.

Beau Geste

1939. 114 min. b.w. U.S. **Prod.** William Wellman; **Dir.** William Wellman; **Scr.** Robert Carson (based on the novel by Percival Christopher Wren); **Cin.** Theodor Sparkuhl, Archie Stout; **Ed.** Thomas Scott; **Art D.** Hans Dreier, Robert Odell; **Mus.** Alfred Newman; **Cast:** Gary Cooper, Ray Milland, Robert Preston, Brian Donlevy, J. Carrol Naish, Albert Dekker, Susan Hayward, Donald O'Connor, Broderick Crawford.

The film is based on one of the best "boy's own story" novels. This version of the well-known Percival Christopher Wren novel begins with a virtuoso opening scene of a deserted French Foreign Legion fort in North Africa with all defenders lying dead at their posts. Then there is a long flashback about three orphan boys and "Blue Water," one of the world's rarest gems. The rest of the film explains the link between the two. There is ingenious direction by William Wellman, good acting by the leads and even better acting by the supporting cast of J. Carrol Naish, Albert Dekker and Brian Donlevy as the sadistic sergeant who steals the movie.

Beauty and the Beast

La Belle et la Bete. 1946. 95 min. b.w. French. **Prod.** Andre Paulve; **Dir.** Jean Cocteau; **Scr.** Jean Cocteau (based on the fairy tale by Madame Leprince de Beaumont); **Cin.** Henri Alekan; **Ed.** Claude Iberia; **Art D.** Christian Berard; **Mus.** George Auric; **Cast:** Jean Marais, Josette Day, Marcel Andre, Mila Parély, Michel Auclair, Nane Germon.

Jean Cocteau's second and most fully realized film is an adaptation of an eighteenth-century fairy tale set by Cocteau in seventeenth-century Holland. The film is enjoyable for its introduction of the "fantastic" and the sets and costumes designed by Christian Berard. But the segments outside "the enchanted castle" drag and have dated badly. *Beauty and the Beast* and Cocteau's first film, *Blood of a Poet* (1930), remain his best and most influential works. Cocteau's contribution to film also includes the highly original Orpheus (1950). Although all his films are very personal, he had a great influence on French cinema, most particularly on decor and set design.

Being There

1979. 130 min. color. U.S. **Prod.** Andrew Braunsberg; **Dir.** Hal Ashby; **Scr.** Jerzy Kosinski (based on his novel); **Cin.** Caleb Deschanel; **Ed.** Don Zimmerman; **Art D.** James Schoppe; **Mus.** Johnny Mandel; **Cast:** Peter Sellers, Shirley MacLaine, Melvyn Douglas, Jack Warden.

A highly enjoyable and original film that tells the story of an illiterate, mentally retarded man who, by a quirk of fate, becomes the trusted advisor to a dying industrial tycoon and later to the president of the United States. There are superb performances by Peter Sellers, Melvyn Douglas and Jack Warden in difficult roles. What mars the film is its length, repetitive scenes and touches of sentimentality. Hal Ashby's other superior films are *The Last Detail* (1973) and *Bound for Glory* (1976)

Beverly Hills Cop

1984. 105 min. color. U.S. **Prod.** Don Simpson, Jerry Bruckheimer; **Dir.** Martin Brest; **Scr.** Daniel Petrie, Jr; **Cin.** Bruce Surtees; **Ed.** Billy Weber, Arthur Coburn; **Prod. D.** Angelo Graham; **Art D.** James J. Murakami; **Mus.** Harold Faltermeyer; **Cast:** Eddie Murphy, Judge Reinhold, John Ashton, Lisa Eilbacher, Ronny Cox, Steven Berkoff, James Russo.

A very entertaining movie about a sassy, street-smart black detective who goes to Beverly Hills to find the murderer of his policeman friend. He outsmarts local cops and captures the crooks and murderers. Eddie Murphy is in top form with an excellent supporting cast including Judge Reinhold and John Ashton.

The Big Clock

1948. 95 min. b.w. U.S. **Prod.** Richard Maibaum; **Dir.** John Farrow; **Scr.** Jonathan Latimer (based on the novel by Kenneth Fearing); **Cin.** John Seitz; **Ed.** Gene Ruggiero; **Art D.** Hans Dreier; **Mus.** Victor Young; **Cast:** Ray Milland, Charles Laughton, Maureen O'Sullivan, George Macready, Henry Morgan, Elsa Lanchester, William Corrigan.

A megalomaniacal publishing tycoon, Earl Janoth (Charles Laughton), murders his mistress with a phallic object when she

mocks his sexual potency. As he believes no one has seen him, he
assigns George Stroud (Ray Milland), the editor of *Crimeways*
magazine, one of his vast number of publications, to investigate
the case. The trouble is that Stroud had met the murdered woman
purely by chance a few hours before the murder and accompanied her home. Ironically, the evidence points to Stroud as the
murderer. The movie begins and ends with Stroud being trapped
in the publisher's huge office building with all the doors locked at
Janoth's order. He is nearly killed by Janoth's bodyguard, a deaf-
mute killer. Stroud is able to clear himself, which spells doom for
the publisher.

The film is well directed by John Farrow and, although we
know from the outset who the murderer is, suspense is maintained. The high-contrast photography of veteran John Seitz, and
the set designs, particularly the enormous clock tower, give added
power to the film. Laughton, a great actor, appears uncomfortable
in his role and does not give one of his legendary performances.
Milland and George Macready as the senior deputy in the publishing empire are both very good. Henry Morgan as the
deaf-mute gives a chilling performance. As always, Elsa Lanchester as an eccentric artist steals all her scenes.

The Big Parade

1925. 115 min. b.w. Silent. U.S. **Prod.** King Vidor; **Dir.** King Vidor; **Scr.** Laurence
Stallings, Harry Behn, Joseph W. Farnham; **Cin.** John Arnold; **Ed.** Hugh Wynn; **Art D.**
Cedric Gibbons, James Basevi; **Cast:** John Gilbert, Renee Adoree, Hobart Bosworth, Claire
McDowell, Claire Adams, Karl Dane.

One of the best and probably the only pacifist film of the silent
era with realistic battle scenes of World War I and fluid camera
work. The film has dated somewhat and there are many mawk-
ishly sentimental scenes, but it shows the maligned John Gilbert
as a good silent screen actor. King Vidor, one of the pioneer
directors made several other good films. Most impressive are, *The
Citadel* (1938) and *Northwest Passage* (1940).

Billy Budd

1962. 119 min. b.w. U.S./British. **Prod.** Peter Ustinov; **Dir.** Peter Ustinov; **Scr.** Peter Ustinov, Robert Rossen (based on the novel by Herman Melville); **Cin.** Robert Krasker; **Ed.** Jack Harris; **Art D.** Don Ashton; **Mus.** Anthony Hopkins; **Cast:** Robert Ryan, Peter Ustinov, Melvyn Douglas, Terence Stamp, David McCallum.

The last work of Herman Melville is an allegory on good and evil. This film follows an innocent, pure young seaman, Billy Budd (Terence Stamp), aboard an English warship in 1797. Billy is abused and tormented by the tyrannical and sadistic first mate, Claggart (Robert Ryan). Billy is court-martialed and hanged for the unintended killing of Claggart. A powerful, well-acted film dominated by the forceful performance of Robert Ryan. It is a noble effort by producer/director/screenwriter/actor Peter Ustinov, but Melville's confrontation between good and evil has been shifted more to the issue of the administration of justice in wartime.

The Birds

1963. 120 min. color. U.S. **Prod.** Alfred Hitchcock; **Dir.** Alfred Hitchcock; **Scr.** Evan Hunter (based on the story by Daphne du Maurier); **Cin.** Robert Burks; **Ed.** George Tomasini; **Prod. D.** Norman Deming; **Mus.** Bernard Herrmann; **Cast:** Rod Taylor, Tippi Hedren, Jessica Tandy, Suzanne Pleshette, Charles McGraw.

Another yarn from Daphne du Maurier about one of nature's innocent and least harmful creatures. Hundreds and thousands of birds begin to attack men, women and children. Are they seeking revenge for being caged and shot at? The film is too long at 120 minutes and it takes almost a half hour before we realize it is about aggressive birds. We are led to believe it is about a domineering but insecure mother and her son who has become interested in a beautiful though spoiled woman. The color is bad and the acting is artificial. But from the moment the birds gather in large numbers as a prelude to their attack there is great suspense. It was a difficult film to have made at the time. Special effects were not advanced, but the attack and regrouping of birds are well simulated. Despite all the drawbacks, Hitchcock was able to make yet another suspenseful and highly enjoyable film.

The Birth of a Nation

1915. 159 min. b.w. Silent. U.S. **Prod. D.** W. Griffith, Harry E. Aitken; **Dir.** D. W. Griffith; **Scr.** D. W. Griffith, Frank E. Woods (based on the novel *The Clansman* by Reverend Thomas Dixon, Jr.); **Cin.** Billy Bitzer; **Mus.** Joseph Carl Breil, written to accompany the film; **Cast:** Lillian Gish, Mae Marsh, Henry B. Walthall, Miriam Cooper, Spottiswood Aitken, Ralph Lewis, George Siegmann, Donald Crisp, Raoul Walsh, Eugene Pallette, Erich von Stoheim, Wallace Reid.

One of the most important films before the advent of sound and selected by some critics as the single most influential film ever made. Its importance is limited, however, to its quantum advance in cinematography and its ability to hold the viewers of the day for 160 minutes. Most films up to 1915 had almost no plot and usually ran about forty to forty-five minutes. D. W. Griffith, a former stage actor, had been making films since 1908. His photographer, Billy Bitzer, had perfected techniques to move the camera and shoot a scene from multiple angles. The two had also found ways to shoot a close-up in such a way as to add to the emotional impact on the viewer. The cross-cutting in the last fifteen minutes is still a marvel.

The Birth of a Nation is based on *The Clansman*, a popular pulp novel about the American Civil War and its aftermath; how the South had been wronged and how it had been saved by the Ku Klux Klan. Griffith had a pronounced bias toward the South as his father had been a colonel in the Confederate army. This bias is clearly evident. The viewer is never told that the war was about slavery and the fragmentation of the United States. Despite its merits in cinematography and its historical importance in filmmaking, it remains an embarrassing record of racism, but is imperative watching.

The Bishop's Wife

1947. 105 min. b.w. U.S. **Prod.** Samuel Goldwyn; **Dir.** Henry Koster; **Scr.** Robert E. Sherwood, Leonardo Bercovici (based on a novel by Robert Nathan); **Cin.** Gregg Tolan; **Ed.** Monica Collingwood; **Art D.** Charles Henderson; **Mus.** Hugo Friedhofer; **Cast:** Cary Grant, Loretta Young, David Niven, Monty Woolley, James Gleason, Gladys Cooper, Elsa Lanchester.

An Episcopalian bishop (David Niven) begins to question his faith. An angel (Cary Grant) is sent to support him. Once on earth, the angel also sorts out the problems of the bishop's wife (Loretta Young), a selfish wealthy widow (Gladys Cooper), a disgruntled cab driver (James Gleason), and a classics scholar (Monty Woolley) who has lost his inspiration. A finely acted and charming film.

The Black Stallion

1979. 118 min. color. U.S. **Prod.** Fred Roos, Tom Sternberg; **Dir.** Carroll Ballard; **Scr.** Melissa Mathison, Jeanne Rosenberg, William D. Wittliff (based on the novel by Walter Farley); **Cin.** Caleb Deschanel; **Ed.** Robert Dalva; **Art D.** Aurelio Crugnola, Earl Preston; **Mus.** Carmine Coppola; **Cast:** Kelly Reno, Mickey Rooney, Teri Garr.

A beautifully photographed, mythical story of a bond between a boy and a horse. The exhilarating scenes of a boy riding the stallion along an island beach constitute the best part of the movie. Mickey Rooney as a retired horse trainer gives a well-modulated performance and was nominated for best supporting actor. There is also a rousing score by Carmine Coppola. It is unfortunate that director Carroll Ballard made very few films after *The Black Stallion*, a little gem, and none were nearly as good.

Blowup

1966. 111 min. color. British. **Prod.** Pierre Rouve, Carlo Ponti; **Dir.** Michelangelo Antonioni; **Scr.** Michelangelo Antonioni, Tonino Guerra, Edward Bond (based on a story by Julio Cortazar); **Cin.** Carlo di Palma; **Ed.** Frank Clarke; **Art D.** Assherton Gorton; **Mus.** Herbie Hancock; **Cast:** Vanessa Redgrave, David Hemmings, Sarah Miles, Peter Bowles.

Michelangelo Antonioni's first film in English is much better at initial viewing. In subsequent viewings it appears confused and does not fare as well. It is neither a mystery story nor a Pirandello-type rumination on sanity and insanity, or illusion versus reality. The dialogue is pretentious and scenes of swinging London appear forced. As in almost all Antonioni films there is minimal communication between the characters. But there are some masterfully done scenes: the photography in the park and the "blowup" sequences.

The Body Snatcher

1945. 77 min. b.w. U.S. **Prod.** Val Lewton; **Dir.** Robert Wise; **Scr.** Philip MacDonald, Carlos Keith; **Cin.** Robert de Grasse; **Ed.** J. R. Whittredge; **Art D.** Albert S. D'Agostino, Walter E. Keller; **Mus.** Roy Webb; **Cast:** Boris Karloff, Bela Lugosi, Henry Daniell, Edith Atwater, Russell Wade.

This film is one of producer Val Lewton's best, masterfully directed by Robert Wise. Set in nineteenth-century Edinburgh, an eminent doctor (Henry Daniell) makes the mistake of dealing with a murderous hansom cabbie (Boris Karloff) to get cadavers for medical experiments. The film stands out for the acting of Boris Karloff and the presence of the dour Henry Daniell, who never smiled in his more than forty films. Bela Lugosi has a short part as a handyman. The atmosphere of the dimly lit cobblestone streets, the street singers and period taverns is ideal for the tale.

Bonnie and Clyde

1967. 111 min. color. U.S. **Prod.** Warren Beatty; **Dir.** Arthur Penn; **Scr.** David Newman, Robert Benton; **Cin.** Burnett Guffey; **Ed.** Dede Allen; **Art D.** Dean Tavoularis; **Mus.** Charles Strouse; **Cast:** Warren Beatty, Faye Dunaway, Michael J. Pollard, Gene Hackman, Estelle Parsons, Gene Wilder, Dub Taylor.

The film follows the exploits of a pair of amoral vicious killers, but it is told as a fairy tale in an idyllic setting. The Great Depression is merely a backdrop in time with barely a mention. An important film for its time, but on subsequent viewings one sees that it has been overrated. It is not a particularly well-directed film, although it is magnificently photographed and expertly edited. The death scene of Bonnie and Clyde is masterful, perhaps the best scene in the film. Acting honors go to Faye Dunaway, as Bonnie and the excellent supporting cast of Estelle Parsons, Dub Taylor and Michael J. Pollard. The star, Warren Beatty, is uneven and Gene Hackman is not at his best. The film won Academy Awards for best supporting actress (Estelle Parsons) and best cinematography, and received some eight nominations, including best picture.

Boudu Saved from Drowning

Boudu Sauvé Dex Eaux. 1932. 87 min. b.w. French. **Prod.** Michel Simon, Jean Gehret; **Dir.** Jean Renoir; **Scr.** Jean Renoir (based on a play by Rene Fauchois); **Cin.** Marcel Lucien; **Ed.** Suzanne de Troeye, Marguerite Renoir; **Art D.** Hugues Laurent, Jean Castanier; **Mus.** Leo Daniderff, Rafael; **Cast:** Michel Simon, Charles Granval, Marcelle Hainia.

A tramp, Boudu (Michel Simon), grief-stricken over the loss of his dog, attempts suicide by throwing himself in the Seine. He is saved from drowning by a respectable antiquarian bookseller (Charles Granval). The kindly bookseller invites him to stay with his family until he overcomes his sorrow. The ungrateful tramp wreaks havoc on the household. He damages some rare books, and seduces the bookseller's wife and maid. He wins a large sum in a lottery and marries the attractive maid. He must now decide whether he wants a respectable bourgeois life or to remain a free nonconformist. After only one day he abandons his wife and, having wrecked the life of the bookseller, takes to the road and freedom. Michel Simon as the unkempt, long-haired, heavily bearded tramp is perfect. This Renoir satire on the bourgeoisie is in many ways similar to the later work of Buñuel . The little gem, lost for over thirty years, was found and released in 1967.

Boyz N the Hood

1991. 107 min. color. U.S. **Prod.** Steve Nicolaides; **Dir.** John Singleton; **Scr.** John Singleton; **Cin.** Charles Mills; **Ed.** Bruce Cannon; **Art D.** Bruce Bellamy; **Mus.** Stanley Clarke; **Cast:** Larry Fishburne, Ice Cube, Cuba Gooding, Jr., Nia Long, Morris Chestnut, Tyra Ferrell, Angela Bassett, Meta King, Whitman Mayo, Hudhail Al-Amir.

The story of the trials and hopelessness of living in the depressed ghetto of South Central Los Angeles, the film focuses on a divorced father (Larry Fishburne) trying to raise his son (Cuba Gooding, Jr.) with ethical values. Ultimately the poverty, drugs, violence and bitterness of his surroundings keep the boy from fulfilling his aspirations for an education. This bleak film is the first effort of the twenty-three-year-old director and screenwriter John Singleton. He manages to bring in references to black history, and social and cultural biases.

Breathless

À Bout De Souffle. 1959. 89 min. b.w. French. **Prod.** Georges de Beauregard; **Dir.** Jean-Luc Godard; **Scr.** Jean-Luc Godard (based on a story by Francois Truffaut); **Cin.** Raoul Coutard; **Ed.** Cecile Decugis, Lila Herman; **Art D.** Claude Chabrol; **Mus.** Martial Solal; **Cast:** Jean-Paul Belmondo, Jean Seberg, Daniel Boulanger, Henri-Jacques Huet, Jean-Pierre Melville, Jean-Luc Godard.

The plot is as banal as most Hollywood gangster films of the thirties on which it is based. Michel Poiccard, alias Laszlo Kovaks (Jean-Paul Belmondo), is a petty criminal who has modeled himself after the gangster roles of Humphrey Bogart. En route to Marseilles in a stolen car he shoots and kills a traffic cop trying to arrest him for speeding. After the murder he is on the run with his American girlfriend, Patricia Franchini (Jean Seberg), and he lays low in her apartment. For reasons not satisfactorily explained, Patricia calls the police and tells them where to find Michel. She also tells Michel that she has betrayed him. The police are on the lookout and shoot him in the street. His dying words are "It is disgusting."

Michel is established at the outset as an amoral hoodlum. Patricia's character is more puzzling. She is shown to love Michel but informs on him knowing it will mean his death. Her character is not developed in the script, and Seberg's limited acting talents add no substance to the role. In Godard's later films the women are generally a nasty lot. Belmondo, an ex-boxer and bit player, went on to become a French movie idol. This least pretentious of the New Wave films became the most influential. It was important for its editing and for its daring use of the camera. The film was mostly shot on the streets of Paris, sometimes with handheld cameras. Directors of the sixties and seventies were greatly influenced by it and many even copied some of Godard's innovative devices. He used the jump cut to great affect, even at times to the point of sacrificing the logical continuity of the plot. Godard finished the film in thirty days for $90,000 and dedicated it to Monogram Pictures, known for its cheap B movies. Despite its initial influence, the film has dated somewhat now. Godard's body of work is uneven and as he became more political, his films became less comprehensible. *Weekend* (1967) is the only one of his later political films that still holds up.

The Bride of Frankenstein

1935. 75 min. b.w. U.S. **Prod.** Carl Laemmle, Jr.; **Dir.** James Whale; **Scr.** William Hurl-but, John Balderston (based on the novel by Mary Shelley); **Cin.** John Mescall; **Ed.** Ted J. Kent; **Art. D.** Charles D. Hall; **Mus.** Franz Waxman; **Cast:** Boris Karloff, Colin Clive, Valerie Hobson, Elsa Lanchester, O.P. Heggie, Una O'Connor, Ernest Thesiger, Gavin Gordon, Douglas Walton.

The 1931 movie *Frankenstein* ended with injured Dr. Frankenstein being taken to his castle to recover and the monster engulfed in flames in an old mill. This film begins with the same scene but continues with the monster finding a subterranean stream and saving himself. He makes his way to the countryside, injures and kills more villagers, then takes refuge with a blind hermit. The evil alchemist Dr. Septimus Pretorius (Ernest Thesiger) finds the monster and together they kidnap Dr. Frankenstein's wife (Valerie Hobson) to blackmail Dr. Frankenstein into creating a woman who will be the monster's bride (Elsa Lanchester). She comes to life with the last spark of lightning. She takes one look at her husband-to-be and she is repulsed. The monster realizes how ugly and loathsome he is. He frees Dr. Frankenstein and his wife, and destroys the castle killing himself, his bride and the evil Dr. Pretorius.

The Bride of Frankenstein is superior to *Frankenstein*. There are very original sets and the special effects and camera work had progressed considerably. There is an imaginative score by Franz Waxman. There is even acting by the monster; however, Ernest Thesiger steals the movie. In a very clever prologue, the film has Lord Byron and his friend Percy Shelley talking Mary Shelley (also played by Elsa Lanchester) into writing a sequel to her novel Frankenstein. *The Bride of Frankenstein* is not the horror film that scared the daylights out of every youngster who saw the first *Frankenstein*, it is more of a black comedy.

Bringing Up Baby

1936. 102 min. b.w. U.S. **Prod.** Howard Hawks; **Dir.** Howard Hawks; **Scr.** Dudley Nichols, Hagar Wilde (based on a story by Hagar Wilde); **Cin.** Russell Metty; **Ed.** George Hively; **Art. D.** Van Nest Polglase; **Mus.** Roy Webb; **Cast:** Cary Grant, Katharine Hepburn, Charlie Ruggles, May Robson, Barry Fitzgerald, Walter Catlett, Ward Bond, Virginia Walker.

In a story that borders on the absurd, Cary Grant plays David Huxley, an absent-minded paleontologist who is working in a museum reconstructing a huge dinosaur skeleton bone by bone. An eccentric heiress, Susan Vance (Katharine Hepburn), comes accidentally into his life and nearly ruins it. Her dog, Asta of *The Thin Man* series, steals the last bone needed to complete his reconstruction. He follows Susan and her dog to her Connecticut country house to retrieve the bone. The madcap plot thickens. Susan has a tame pet leopard, Baby, which is mistaken for a vicious leopard that has escaped from the zoo. Susan has an aunt (May Robson) who was on the verge of giving $1 million to Huxley's museum but begins to have doubts when she first meets Huxley wearing Susan's negligee.

The movie is well controlled and moves along at a very good pace. The second half has some extremely funny scenes. The two leads and the entire supporting cast, especially Charlie Ruggles as a cowardly big-game hunter, May Robson, Walter Catlett, and Barry Fitzgerald, are excellent. Katharine Hepburn's character is not merely spoiled and eccentric, she is really mad. The film is similar to other escapist Depression era movies when the public for unexplained reasons was obsessed with scatterbrained heiresses.

The Browning Version

1951. 97 min. b.w. British. **Prod.** Teddy Baird; **Dir.** Anthony Asquith; **Scr.** Terence Rattigan (based on his play); **Cin.** Desmond Dickinson; **Ed.** John D. Guthridge; **Art D.** Carmen Dillon; **Mus.** Mark Isham; **Cast:** Michael Redgrave, Jean Kent, Nigel Patrick, Wilfred Hyde-White, Bill Travers.

This film focuses on a middle-aged classics teacher at a British public school who is retiring early due to ill health and is denied his pension. He had once been a great teacher but having married a shrewish and deceitful woman his life began to change. She is presently carrying on with a science teacher which is common knowledge among most faculty members. She belittles him in front of other teachers and even students. Over the years he has become a tyrant in class and is no longer interested in teaching. In his retirement address to the students he admits to having failed them and asks forgiveness. It all becomes worthwhile when one of his students gives him a parting gift of Robert Browning's incomplete translation of Aeschylus' *Agamemnon*. He tells the boy he will try to complete it. It is not a particularly well-directed film and, being based on a play, it is somewhat theatrical. Anthony Asquith (the son of British prime minister Lord Asquith) made better directed films, including *Pygmalion* (1938) and the *Winslow Boy* (1948). *The Browning Version* is redeemed, however, by one of the greatest screen performances by Michael Redgrave in the lead role.

Brute Force

1947. 98 min. b.w. U.S. **Prod.** Mark Hellinger; **Dir.** Jules Dassin; **Scr.** Richard Brooks (based on a story by Robert Patterson); **Cin.** William Daniels; **Ed.** Edward Curtiss; **Art D.** Bernard Herzbrun, John DeCuir; **Mus.** Miklos Rozsa; **Cast:** Burt Lancaster, Hume Cronyn, Charles Bickford, Yvonne De Carlo, Ann Blyth, Ella Raines, Howard Duff, Whit Bissell, Jeff Corey, Sam Levine, Roman Bohnen Art Smith, Ryan Teal.

Brute Force is the story of an attempted prison break with the focus on four cellmates. When the humane warden (Roman Bohnen) is forced to resign by the Prison Board and replaced by a gestapo-type sadistic chief of guards, Captain Munsey (Hume Cronyn), the inmates led by Joe Collins (Burt Lancaster) plan a breakout. In a series of flashbacks we learn how the four landed in prison. There are several uncompromising violent scenes that were too graphic for their day; the brutal lashing of an inmate (Sam Levine) by Munsey against the background music of Wagner's *Tannhauser;* and the last scene of the movie with Collins throwing Munsey from a guard tower into a mob of inmates.

An extremely well-made film but with a few blemishes. Some of the dialogue between the prison doctor (Art Smith) and Munsey about prison reform and the use of brute force is gratuitous. The flashback to the role of women in the lives of the four inmates slows the film and only brings touches of sentimentality. Burt Lancaster is slightly wooden but the entire supporting cast is fine, especially Charles Bickford as the inmate editor of the prison paper, Sam Levine as his reporter, the ever evil Ray Teal as one of the guards and the reliable Whit Bissell. The film belongs to Hume Cronyn who has his most memorable role as an American Himmler. *Brute Force* is one of the best of Jules Dassin's films, along with *The Naked City* (1948) and *Rififi* (1954). Richard Brooks wrote a tense script.

Cabaret

1972. 128 min. color. U.S. **Prod.** Cy Feuer; **Dir.** Bob Fosse; **Scr.** Jay Presson Allen (based on the play by Joe Masteroff, the play *I Am a Camera* by John Van Druten and the writings of Christopher Isherwood); **Cin.** Geoffrey Unsworth; **Ed.** David Bretherton; **Art. D.** Jurgen Kiebach; **Mus.** Ralph Burns; **Cast:** Liza Minnelli, Michael York, Helmut Griem, Joel Grey, Marissa Berenson.

The film is set in 1931, two years before Hitler is appointed chancellor. The National Socialist Party sad already begun suppressing all opposition and Nazi thugs are roaming the streets. A young English would-be writer, Brian Roberts (Michael York), comes to Berlin to give private English lessons. He takes a small apartment and meets his neighbor, the American Sally Bowles (Liza Minnelli), who sings at the sleazy Kit Kat club. Brian, a bisexual, becomes involved with Sally and her lover, a wealthy German young man (Helmut Griem) who becomes his first student. The film takes us through the ominous rise of the Nazis, the suppression of all opposition and the enactment of the early anti-Semitic legislation. The growing influence of the Nazis is intercut with the garish scenes at the Kit Kat club.

The film is uneven but has some original musical numbers. The opening song "Willkommen," sung by the master of ceremonies, Joel Grey, who is the star of the movie, is a prelude to "Money" and "Mein Herr." Probably the most chilling song, "Tomorrow Belongs to Me," is sung by a Hitler youth in a country beer garden. The setting and faces at the Kit Kat club are influenced by the paintings of George Grosz and Egon Schiele. Bob Fosse was a very good choreographer, but as a director he falls short. The middle part of the movie drags. The casting of Liza Minnelli as Sally does not work. She is not quite sexy enough and her acting is not much help. Michael York as the young Englishman who is meant to be Christopher Isherwood is adequate. Neither Helmut Griem nor Marisa Berenson contribute very much. It is Joel Grey who remains in your mind.

The Caine Mutiny

1954. 123 min. color. U.S. **Prod.** Stanley Kramer; **Dir.** Edward Dmytryk; **Scr.** Stanley Roberts, Michael Blankfort (based on the play and novel by Herman Wouk); **Cin.** Franz Planer; **Ed.** William Lyon, Henry Batista; **Prod. D.** Rudolph Sternad; **Art D.** Carey Odell; **Mus.** Max Steiner; **Cast:** Humphrey Bogart, Jose Ferrer, Van Johnson, Robert Francis, May Wynn, Fred MacMurray, E. G. Marshall, Lee Marvin, Tom Tully.

This is the story of the mutiny aboard the *Caine*, a destroyer and minesweeper in the Pacific during the latter stages of World War II. Captain Queeg (Humphrey Bogart) has just assumed command. From the outset his erratic behavior disturbs the officers and crew. There is even an incident of loss of nerve when Queeg orders the destroyer to turn around before it has fulfilled its mission. It soon becomes evident that Queeg is paranoid, suffering from delusions. Later during a raging storm Queeg panics and gives contradictory orders inviting the breakup of the ship. Lieutenant Maryk (Van Johnson), the executive officer, relieves Queeg from command and navigates the ship to safety. Maryk is charged with mutiny and at his court-martial he is defended by Lieutenant Greenwald (Jose Ferrer). Under cross-examination, Queeg comes apart, evidencing his delusions, and Maryk is absolved. There is a gratuitous love story that slows the film, but what mars the film emanates from the Wouk novel. The book focuses on Lieutenant Keefer (Fred MacMurrray) who is made the villain because as a writer and intellectual he looks down on Queeg from the outset and induces Maryk to mutiny. To Wouk the real heroes of World War II were the Captain Queegs, the pre-Pearl Harbor regular army and navy professionals and not the subsequent draftees and volunteers. Bogart gives an astounding performance.

The Candidate

1972. 109 min. color. U.S. **Prod.** Walter Coblenz; **Dir.** Michael Ritchie; **Scr.** Jeremy Larner; **Cin.** Victor J. Kemper, John Korty; **Ed.** Richard A. Harris, Robert Estrin; **Mus.** John Rubinstein; **Cast:** Robert Redford, Peter Boyle, Don Porter, Allen Garfield, Melvyn Douglas, Kenneth Tobey.

A young idealistic California lawyer, Bill McKay (Robert Redford), has a practice consisting of only legal aid and pro bono cases. His father (Melvyn Douglas) had been governor of the state and young McKay had witnessed the deals and compromises politicians make to get elected. McKay is approached by two seasoned political operatives (Peter Boyle and Allen Garfield) to make a run against the incumbent senator (Don Porter) who appears unbeatable. McKay is reluctant at first but finally agrees provided his father is kept out of the campaign and he can say what he believes in with no interference from any source. As he gains in the polls he begins to compromise on his platform of sound environmental regulations and consumer interests and wins the election. In a most telling line at the end of the film, he asks his handlers, "What do I do now?" The film is a near documentary on American politics with a first-rate screenplay. This is one of Robert Redford's better films with excellent acting from Boyle and Garfield.

Captains Courageous

1937. 116 min. b.w. U.S. **Prod.** Louis D. Lighton; **Dir.** Victor Fleming; **Scr.** John Lee Mahin, Marc Connelly, Dale Van Every (based on the novel by Rudyard Kipling); **Cin.** Harold Rosson; **Ed.** Elmo Veron; **Art D.** Cedric Gibbons; **Mus.** Franz Waxman; **Cast:** Freddie Bartholomew, Spencer Tracy, Lionel Barrymore, Melvyn Douglas, Charles Grapewin, John Carradine, Mickey Rooney.

An updated Kipling story about a very spoiled twelve-year-old (Freddie Bartholomew) who thinks he can cheat, lie and buy his way through everything. His father, a business tycoon (Melvyn Douglas) who has had no time to devote to his son, withdraws him from school to take an ocean voyage to Europe together. The boy falls off the ship's railing and is rescued by a Gloucester-based fishing schooner. He is befriended by a warm-hearted Portuguese fisherman (Spencer Tracy) who becomes the boy's idol. The fisherman patiently sets him straight. The film has an impeccable supporting cast that includes Lionel Barrymore, John Carradine and Mickey Rooney, and is well directed by the reliable Victor Fleming. Spencer Tracy, who didn't particularly care for the part, brought his usual magic and won an Academy Award as best actor.

Casque D'Or

Golden Marie. 1952. 96 min. b.w. French. **Dir.** Jacques Becker; **Scr.** Jacques Becker, Jacques Companeez; **Cin.** Robert Le Febvre; **Ed.** Marguerite Renoir; **Art D.** Jean D'Eaubonne; **Mus.** Georges Van Parys; **Cast:** Simone Signoret, Serge Reggiani, Claude Dauphin, Raymond Bussières, Gaston Modot.

The film is set toward the beginning of the twentieth century when a group of gangsters who came to be known as "Apache" held sway in the Paris underworld. It tells the story of a carpenter (Serge Reggiani) and a gangster's moll, Golden Marie (Simone Signoret), who fall in love. The machinations of the head of the gang spell doom for the carpenter. The film evokes the Paris of pre-World War I and has one of Signoret's best portrayals. It is the best work of Jacques Becker, now a forgotten director, who had been assistant director to Jean Renoir.

The Chaplin Revue

1958. 119 min. b.w. Silent. U.S. **Dir.** Charles Chaplin; **Scr.** Charles Chaplin; **Cin.** R. H. Totheroh.

A package of three-and four-reel Chaplin films have been grouped together for redistribution. In *A Dog's Life* (1918) poor Charlie shares his misfortune with a stray dog he calls Scraps, and also shares his subsequent good fortune. In *Shoulder Arms* (1918) Charlie is an army trainee in World War I who has a dream that he captures the kaiser. *The Pilgrim* (1923) has Charlie as an escaped convict disguised as a minister—and he actually serves his congregation.

Chariots of Fire

1981. 123 min. color. British. **Prod.** David Puttnam; **Dir.** Hugh Hudson; **Scr.** Colin Welland; **Cin.** David Watkin; **Ed.** Terry Rawlings; **Art D.** Roger Hall; **Mus.** Vangelis; **Cast:** Ben Cross, Ian Charleson, Nigel Havers, Cheryl Campbell, Ian Holm, John Gielgud, Lindsay Anderson, Nigel Davenport, Nicholas Farrell.

Set around the 1924 Olympics, *Chariots of Fire* is the story of two athletes. One is Eric Liddel (Ian Charleson), a 400-meter runner. He is a divinity student who is slated to go to China as a missionary. He runs to promote Christianity: "When I run, I feel His [God's] pleasure." The other is Harold Abraham, a 100-meter runner. He is a Cambridge University student. As a Jew, he desperately wants to prove himself and be accepted by others. The film is well directed and beautifully photographed. It has a few memorable scenes, the most notable being the athletes relaxing in the ship's saloon and singing Gilbert and Sullivan songs as they cross the channel to the Games in Paris; and the scenes of the team running along a sandy beach accompanied by the rousing

Vangelis score. The film also boasts good acting by the entire cast and a memorable performance by Ian Holm as Abraham's coach. The movie, however, suffers from excessive sentimentality and repeated slow-motion sequences during the races. It is a very good film that director Hugh Hudson never matched.

Charlie Chaplin Festival

1938. 75 min. b.w. Silent. U.S. **Dir.** Charles Chaplin; **Scr.** Charles Chaplin; **Cin.** R. H. Totheroh.

A package of four Chaplin two-reel films grouped together for distribution. *The Immigrant* (1917) is the story of Charlie's storm-tossed crossing to America where he finds romance. *The Adventurer* (1917) tells of an escaped convict who is ultimately caught. The best are the last two, *The Cure* (1917) and *Easy Street* (1917). *The Cure* has the drunken Charlie at a spa taking the water cure. The bottles of liquor he has smuggled in his luggage are discovered and accidentally poured into the curative water well resulting in a raucous party by all the guests. In *Easy Street* Charlie goes into a mission and is reformed by the minister. He becomes a policeman and clears Easy Street of roughnecks. This collection equals any of Chaplin's full-length features.

The Chess Players

Shatranj Ke Khilari. 1977. 135 min. color. Indian (in Hindi and English). **Prod.** Suresh Jindal; **Dir.** Satyajit Ray; **Scr.** Satyajit Ray (based on a story by Prem Chand); **Cin.** Soumendou Roy; **Ed.** Dulal Dutta; **Mus.** Satyajit Ray; **Cast:** Sanjeev Kumar, Saeed Jaffrey, Richard Attenborough, Amjad Khan.

The Chess Player is set in Lucknow in 1856 when Victorian England was gobbling up the last of the semi-independent principalities in India. It is the story of two wealthy Indian noblemen who are obsessed with chess, which they play every single day. This allegory of the war game played by the indolent nobility in

India who put up no resistance in a real war could have been one of Ray's best films. But Ray loses purpose and control and the film becomes a comedy and costume drama.

The Circus

1928 72 min. b.w. Silent. U.S. **Prod.** Charles Chaplin; **Dir.** Charles Chaplin; **Scr.** Charles Chaplin; **Cin.** Rollie Totheroh, Jack Wilson, Mark Marklatt; **Art D.** Charles Hall; **Mus.** Charles Chaplin; **Cast:** Charles Chaplin, Merna Kennedy, Allan Garcia, Harry Crocker.

Chaplin is on the run from the police. He is so masterful in evading capture that the circus managers offer him a job as a clown. He falls in love with a bareback rider, but he cannot compete with the high-wire performer with whom the girl is in love. When the circus moves to another town he is left behind. *The Circus* is not in the same league as Chaplin's masterpieces, *The Gold Rush* (1925) or *City Lights* (1931), but it shows his genius for creating very funny scenes from ordinary events.

The Citadel

1938. 112 min. b.w. British. **Prod.** Victor Saville; **Dir.** King Vidor; **Scr.** Ian Dalrymple, Frank Wead, Elizabeth Hill, Emlyn Williams (based on the novel by A. J. Cronin); **Cin.** Harry Stradling; **Ed.** Charles Frend; **Art D.** Lazare Meerson, Alfred Junge; **Mus.** Louis Levy; **Cast:** Robert Donat, Rosalind Russell, Ralph Richardson, Rex Harrison, Emlyn Williams, Francis L. Sullivan, Cecil Parker, Penelope Dudley-Ward.

The story of a dedicated idealistic doctor who treats T.B.-infected workers in a mining town in Wales. He is lured to come to Harley Street in London, the mecca of overpaid physicians, with promises that he can do research. His work is soon reduced to treating wealthy, spoiled patients, some with imaginary illnesses. He is convinced by his wife to return to Wales. An intelligent but dated film about the British medical profession before World War II with fine acting by the entire cast.

Claire's Knee

Le Genou De Claire. 1970. 103 min. color. French. **Prod.** Pierre Cottrell; **Dir.** Eric Rohmer; **Scr.** Eric Rohmer; **Cin.** Nestor Almendros; **Ed.** Cecile Decuqis; **Cast:** Jean-Claude Brialy, Aurora Cornu, Beatrice Romand, Laurence de Monaghan.

A thirtyish French diplomat, Jerome (Jean-Claude Brialy), is about to marry a Swedish woman whom he believes he loves but for whom he feels no special passion. Before the intended marriage he travels to Annecy a small resort town, to sell the family vacation house. There, he meets two teenage sisters. He is especially taken by Claire (Laurence de Monaghan), a seventeen-year-old, and becomes obsessed with her knees. Claire is totally involved with her slightly older boyfriend. She is oblivious to Jerome's attention and his desire to touch or kiss her knee. A story made of almost nothing, this tale of passion and fetishism is beautifully realized by Rohmer in the fifth of his "moral tales." It is witty and even has an element of suspense.

Cluny Brown

1946. 100 min. b.w. U.S. **Prod.** Ernst Lubitsch; **Dir.** Ernst Lubitsch; **Scr.** Samuel Hoffenstein, Elizabeth Reinhardt (based on the novel by Margery Sharp); **Cin.** Joseph La Shelle; **Ed.** Dorothy Spencer; **Art D.** Lyle Wheeler, J. Russell Spencer; **Mus.** Cyril J. Mockridge; **Cast:** Charles Boyer, Jennifer Jones, Peter Lawford, Helen Walker, Reginald Gardiner, C. Aubrey Smith, Reginald Owen, Richard Haydn, Sara Algood.

In the late thirties just before World War II, Charles Boyer, a penniless Czech refugee, is staying with an upper-class British family in the country. The hosts and their British guests don't have the foggiest idea of what is happening on the continent. They have heard a former Austrian corporal has written a book (*Mein Kampf*) that has stirred some people unnecessarily. Their life is a succession of garden parties and afternoon teas. Jennifer Jones plays the daughter of a plumber, who is the maid at the country manor. Together with Boyer she stirs things up. This charming film was the last one from the master Ernst Lubitsch. A lyrical comedy of manners, it pokes fun at the British class system. Boyer is good, supported by an excellent cast of British actors in Hollywood. This was one of the very few films where Jennifer Jones is fairly relaxed and does not bite her lips.

Compulsion

1959. 103 min. b.w. U.S. **Prod.** Richard D. Zanuck; **Dir.** Richard Fleischer; **Scr.** Richard Murphy (based on the novel by Meyer Levin); **Cin.** William Mellor; **Ed.** William Reynolds; **Mus.** Lionel Newman; **Cast:** Orson Welles, Diane Varsi, Dean Stockwell, Bradford Dillman, E. G. Marshall, Martin Milner, Richard Anderson.

Compulsion is a dramatization of the notorious 1924 Leopold-Leob case in Chicago. Two highly intelligent students from wealthy families (Bradford Dillman and Dean Stockwell) murder a boy simply for the experience and to demonstrate that their intellectual superiority enables them to commit an unsolvable crime. They were defended by Clarence Darrow (Orson Welles), the great trial lawyer of the time, who argued against capital punishment and made the spurious claim that the rich are also entitled to a fair trial. Their lives were spared and they were sentenced to terms of life imprisonment. Though slightly pretentious, it is Fleischer's next best film after *The Narrow Margin* (1952), with fine acting by Dillman and Stockwell, and a virtuoso fifteen minutes by Orson Welles.

Cool Hand Luke

1967. 126 min. color. U.S. **Prod.** Gordon Carroll; **Dir.** Stuart Rosenberg; **Scr.** Donn Pearce, Frank Pierson (based on a novel by Pearce); **Cin.** Conrad Hall; **Ed.** Sam O'Steen; **Art D.** Cary Odell; **Mus.** Lalo Schifrin; **Cast:** Paul Newman, George Kennedy, Strother Martin, Jo Van Fleet, Anthony Zerbe, Harry Dean Stanton, J. D. Cannon, Lou Antonio, Robert Drivas.

The story of a nonconformist who is put in a chain gang for breaking parking meters while drunk. The film works very well until the end when Luke is depicted as a saintly figure. There is inspired acting by Paul Newman and George Kennedy, and an even greater performance by Jo Van Fleet in a cameo role. At 126 minutes, the film is slow in parts.

Cornered

1945. 102 min. b.w. U.S. **Prod.** Adrian Scott; **Dir.** Edward Dmytryk; **Scr.** John Paxton (based on a story by John Wexley); **Cin.** Harry Wild; **Ed.** Joseph Noriega; **Art D.** Albert S. D'Agostino, Carroll Clark; **Mus.** Roy Webb; **Cast:** Dick Powell, Walter Slezak, Micheline Cheirel, Morris Carnovsky, Luther Adler, Nina Vale, Edgar Barrier, Steven Geray, Jack LaRue.

Gerard (Dick Powell), a Canadian air force flyer, is released from a German prison at war's end. His sole aim is to find and kill a high-ranking Vichy official, Jarmac (Luther Adler), who murdered his French war bride. Most people believe Jarmac is dead, but others give Gerard tips that he may be in Belgium or Switzerland. Gerard is finally convinced that Jarmac is in Buenos Aires and travels there. He is assisted by a group of Nazi hunters headed by Santana (Morris Carnovsky), and in an unexpected ending finds his wife's killer. One of Edward Dmytryk's best films. Dick Powell had been able to free himself from his usual song and dance roles, and gives a good performance in his second film in a straight part.

Cyrano de Bergerac

1990. 138 min. color. French. **Prod.** Rene Cleitman, Michel Seydoux; **Dir.** Jean-Paul Rappeneau; **Scr.** Jean-Claude Carriere, Jean-Paul Rappeneau (based on the play by Edmond Rostand); **Cin.** Pierre Lhomme; **Ed.** Noelle Boisson; **Art D.** Ezio Frigerio; **Mus.** Jean-Claude Petit; **Cast:** Gerard Depardieu, Anne Brochet, Vincent Perez, Jacque Weber, Roland Bertin, Philippe Morier-Genoud.

Edmond Rostand's well-known play is about a seventeenth-century swordsman and poet whose ungainly large nose could have sunk a thousand ships. This screen version is much better than the 1950 Jose Ferrer film—more cinematic with first-rate camera work. Director Jean-Paul Rappeneau has made it a near epic. Finely acted by Gerard Depardieu, the best French actor of his generation, who gives the definitive portrayal of the awkward hero and his unfulfilled love.

The Damned

La Caduta Degli Dei. 1969. 155 min. color. Italian. **Prod.** Alfred Levy, Ever Haggiag; **Dir.** Luchino Visconti; **Scr.** Luchino Visconti, Nicola Badalucco, Enrico Medioli; **Cin.** Armando Nannuzzi, Pasquale De Santis; **Ed.** Ruggero Mastroianni; **Mus.** Maurice Jarre; **Cast:** Dirk Bogarde, Ingrid Thulin, Helmut Griem, Helmut Berger, Charlotte Rampling, Renaud Verley, Umberto Orsini, Rene Kolldehoff, Albrecht Schoenhals.

The film is set in 1933–34 and follows the fortunes of the Essenbeck family, the owners of a steel empire, modeled after the Krupp family. On a parallel line it also covers the coming to power of the Nazi's, the Reichstag fire, the assassination of Ernst Rohm and the total ascendancy of Hitler. It is too ambitious a film, resembling a grand opera tragedy. There are, however, several outstanding scenes, most notably the "Night of the Long Knives" when the entire top hierarchy of Rohm's Brown Shirts was wiped out on Hitler's orders.

With the exception of three or four films, most of Visconti's works have been over-praised. His reputation rests on the decorative aspect of his films, heavily influenced by his having been a director of plays and grand operas.

Danton

1982. 136 min. color. French/Polish. **Prod.** Margaret Menegoz; **Dir.** Andrzej Wajda; **Scr.** Jean-Claude Carriere, Andrzej Wajda, Agnieszka Holland, Boleslaw Michalek, Jacek Gasiorowski (based on the play *The Danton Affair* by Stanislawa Przybyszewska); **Cin.** Igor Luther; **Ed.** Halina Prugar-Ketling; **Art D.** Allan Starski, Gilles Vaster; **Mus.** Jean Prodromides; **Cast:** Gerard Depardieu, Wojciech Pszoniak, Patrice Chereau, Angela Winkler, Boguslaw Linda, Roland Blanche, Serge Merlin.

The film is set in early 1794, the second year of the French Republic following the beheading of King Louis XVI and Marie Antoinette. The Committee of Public Safety led by Robespierre and Saint Just is devouring the children of the Revolution. Danton, a more moderate leader of the Revolution who has temporarily left Paris for the country, decides to return and curb the excesses of Robespierre. Danton loses the struggle and he and those close to him are led to the guillotine, but not before shouting to Robespierre, "You will follow me in three months." This was director Andrzej Wajda's first film outside Poland. It falters in the second half and becomes somewhat theatrical but is still a fine ambitious film. It created a great deal of excitement when released. Wajda is first and foremost a Polish nationalist and there were analogies to contemporary Poland with Robespierre as General Jaruzelski and Danton as Leck Walesa. Gerard Depardieu as the humanist Danton is fine but acting honors go to the Polish actor Pszoniak as the ascetic Robespierre.

Das Boot

The Boat. 1981. 150 min. color. German. **Prod.** Gunter Rohrbach; **Dir.** Wolfgang Peterson; **Scr.** Wolfgang Petersen (based on the novel by Lothar-Gunther Buchheim); **Cin.** Jost Vacano; **Ed.** Hannes Nikel; **Art D.** Rolf Zehetbauer, Gotz Weidner; **Mus.** Klaus Doldinger; **Cast:** Jurgen Prochnow, Herbert Gronemeyer, Klaus Wennemann, Hubertus Bengsch, Martin Semmelrogge.

The film chronicles a 1941 mission by a U-boat in the Atlantic. It is an anti-Nazi and generally an anti-war film. Where it distinguishes itself is the excellent camera work that brings to life the claustrophobic atmosphere of a submarine.

David Copperfield

1935. 130 min. b.w. U.S. **Prod.** David O. Selznick; **Dir.** George Cukor; **Scr.** Howard Estabrook, Hugh Walpole (based on the novel by Charles Dickens); **Cin.** Oliver T. Marsh; **Ed.** Robert J. Kern; **Art D.** Cedric Gibbons; **Mus.** Herbert Stothart; **Cast:** Freddie Bartholomew, Frank Lawton, W. C. Fields, Lionel Barrymore, Roland Young, Basil Rathbone, Edna May Oliver, Maureen O'Sullivan, Elsa Lanchester, Lewis Stone, Elizabeth Allen.

It is the wonderful Dickens characters that are the most enjoyable elements in any of his novels. Although the film is faithful to the story, it has cut at least four or five characters. In a very strong cast, Edna May Oliver as Aunt Betsy and W. C. Fields as Micawber stand out. Fields treats the role as any other of his comedies. He insisted on keeping his American accent and his own inimitable delivery. This is not the best of Dickens on film; *Great Expectations* (1946) and *Oliver Twist* (1948) are superior.

A Day in the Country

Une Partie De Campagne. 1946. 40 min. b.w. French. **Prod.** Pierre Braunberger; **Dir.** Jean Renoir; **Scr.** Jean Renoir; **Cin.** Claude Renoir, Jean Bourgoin; **Mus.** Joseph Kosma; **Cast:** Sylvia Bataille, Georges Darnoux, Jacques Brunius, Jane Marken, Jean Renoir, Andre Gabriello, Jacques Borel.

On a summer's day in the 1890s, a merchant, Monsieur Dufour, his wife (Jane Marken), their young daughter, Henriette (Sylvia Bataille), and future son-in-law travel to the country. They stop at an inn on the banks of the Marne for lunch. Monsieur Dufour and the prospective son-in-law go fishing. Two young men who are also having lunch invite Madame Dufour and Henriette to row on the river. Rodolph (Jacques Borel), the more playful of the two ends up with Madame Dufour on one bank, and Henriette with the serious yet tender Henri (Georges

Darnoux) on the opposite bank. Henriette is seduced. Years later she and her boring husband stop at the same inn. She again meets her lover of many years ago. Both reveal how their encounter had been the most precious experience of their lives.

The film runs a mere forty minutes. It is a segment of what was intended as a three-part film of short stories of De Maupassant that was never completed. Jean Renoir's film of abandoned love in many ways appears to be a tribute to his father, Auguste Renoir. The sun shines brightly casting light on the trees, the river and the faces of the lovers. Though the film is in black and white it captures the spirit of his father's impressionist paintings. It is a minor film, but anyone who admires Renoir's films will be captivated.

Day of Wrath

Vredens Dag. 1943. 95 min. b.w. Danish. **Prod.** Carl-Theodor Dreyer; **Dir.** Carl-Theodor Dreyer; **Scr.** Carl-Theodor Dreyer, Poul Knudsen, Mogens Skot-Hansen (based on the novel by Wiers Jenssens); **Cin.** Carl Anderson; **Ed.** Edith Schlussel, Anne Marie Petersen; **Art D.** Erik Aaes; **Mus.** Poul Scheirbeck; **Cast:** Thirkild Roose, Lisbeth Movin, Sigrid Nei-iendam, Preben Lerdorff-Rye.

Set in early-seventeenth-century Flanders, a young girl, Anne (Lisbeth Movin), who is married to an elderly, stern pastor (Thirkild Roose), falls in love with the pastor's young son from a previous marriage. The pastor is told of his wife's liaison and he dies shortly thereafter of a heart attack. The pastor's mother accuses Anne of being a witch and having willed her husband's death. Anne is interrogated by ecclesiastical authorities. Soon even her lover turns against her and confirms she is a witch. After repeated rounds of questioning and mental torture, Anne begins to accept the accusations. She is overwhelmed by the ceaseless interrogation and goes willingly to the stake. Dreyer presents the guilt-ridden girl as having no choice but to concede to her accusers. It is an intense film on bigotry and ignorance. Although slow in parts, it bears an emotional impact. *Day of Wrath* was made during the Nazi occupation of Denmark and it has been suggested that it is an allegory on the German occupation. No such thing appears intimated or implied.

The Dead Poets Society

1989. 128 min. color. U.S. **Prod.** Steven M. Haft, Paul Junger Witt, Tony Thomas; **Dir.** Peter Weir; **Scr.** Tom Schulman; **Cin.** John Seale; **Ed.** William Anderson; **Prod. D.** Wendy Stites; **Art D.** Sandy Veneziano; **Mus.** Maurice Jarre; **Cast:** Robin Willams, Robert Sean Leonard, Ethan Hawke, Josh Charles, Gale Hansen, Dylan Kussman, Kurtwood Smith, Norman Lloyd.

John Keating (Robin Williams) is a recently employed teacher of English in a traditional New England prep school. He ignores the conventional methods of teaching literature and the dry text books. Instead he elicits from his students emotional involvement with great works of literature. Some of them are deeply affected, form a secret society and recite poetry. Their lives are changed leading both to tragedy and liberation. The film is well acted and Robin Williams, a superb comedian, plays it straight to great effect. Director Peter Weir made several other good films: *Gallipoli* (1980), *The Year of Living Dangerously* (1982), and *Witness* (1985).

Deadline U.S.A.

1952. 87 min. b.w. U.S. **Prod.** Sol C. Siegel; **Dir.** Richard Brooks; **Scr.** Richard Brooks; **Cin.** Milton Krasner; **Ed.** William B. Murphy; **Art D.** Lyle Wheeler, George Patrick; **Mus.** Cyril J. Mockridge; **Cast:** Humphrey Bogart, Ethel Barrymore, Kim Hunter, Ed Begley, Paul Stewart, Martin Gabel.

Bogart is the crusading editor of a daily newspaper that is exposing a crime syndicate in the city. Despite threats he continues. A much tougher task is to convince the owner of the newspaper, Ethel Barrymore, not to sell. One of the minor sleepers, this film is well directed with a superb cast. Ethel Barrymore once again gives a fine performance and dominates all her scenes.

Richard Brooks was a seasoned director and made some interesting films: *Blackboard Jungle* (1955) and *Elmer Gantry* (1960).

The Deadly Affair

1967. 107 min. color. British. **Prod.** Sidney Lumet; **Dir.** Sidney Lumet; **Scr.** Paul Dehn (based on the novel *Call for the Dead* by John Le Carré); **Cin.** Freddie Young; **Ed.** Thelma Connell; **Art D.** Jean Howell; **Mus.** Quincy Jones; **Cast:** James Mason, Simone Signoret, Maximilian Schell, Harriet Andersson, Harry Andrews, Lynn Redgrave.

The Deadly Affair has the same themes of betrayal and treachery as all of Le Carré's earlier novels. It has an excellent cast in which Simone Signoret and Harry Andrews stand out. But despite the quality of the cast, and the solid story and direction by Lumet, the movie falls short. With the exception of *The Spy Who Came in from the Cold* (1965), none of John Le Carré's novels have been presented well on screen, even by capable directors.

Death and the Maiden

1994. 103 min. color. U.S./French/British. **Prod.** Thom Mount, Josh Kramer; **Dir.** Roman Polanski; **Scr.** Ariel Dorfman, Rafael Yglesias (based on the play by Ariel Dorfman); **Cin.** Tonino Delli Colli; **Ed.** Herve De Luze; **Prod. D.** Pierre Guffroy; **Art D.** Claude Moesching; **Mus.** Wojciech Kilar; **Cast:** Sigourney Weaver, Ben Kingsley, Stuart Wilson.

The film takes place in an unnamed South American country, most probably Argentina or Chile. Pauline (Sigourney Weaver), a political activist, had been a victim of torture and sexual abuse by the former regime. She is now married to Gerardo (Stuart Wilson), a distinguished lawyer soon to be the head of a commission investigating human rights abuses of the former regime. After a blown-tire incident, Gerardo is given a ride home by a stranger, Dr. Miranda (Ben Kingsley). Once Pauline hears Dr. Miranda's voice, she is certain he was the chief investigating officer who humiliated and tortured her. She imprisons and subjects him to ceaseless questioning to get a confession. As in most of his films,

Polanski is a master of atmosphere and *Death and the Maiden* has the claustrophobic sets that enhance the suspense. The only weakness of the film rests with the acting. Despite three seasoned performers, the film suffers from both overacting and underacting. It is nevertheless an engrossing and serious film that explores themes of justice, revenge and forgiveness.

Death in Venice

1971. 130 min. color. Italian (in English). **Prod.** Luchino Visconti; **Dir.** Luchino Visconti; **Scr.** Luchino Visconti, Nicola Badalucco (based on the novel by Thomas Mann); **Cin.** Pasqualino De Santis; **Ed.** Ruggero Mastroianni; **Art D.** Ferdinando Scarfiotti; **Mus.** Gustav Mahler; **Cast:** Dirk Bogarde, Mark Burns, Marisa Berenson, Silvana Mangano, Bjorn Andersen, Romolo Vali.

This is the story of a burned-out composer who travels to Venice for a holiday and his fatal encounter with a handsome young boy. Visconti took too many liberties with Thomas Mann's novella, not merely his turning the writer into a composer. The result is a visually stunning film that nonetheless fails for excessive sentimentality.

Decision before Dawn

1952. 119 min. b.w. U.S. **Prod.** Anatole Litvak, Frank McCarthy; **Dir.** Anatole Litvak; **Scr.** Peter Viertel (based on the novel *Call It Treason* by George Howe); **Cin.** Franz Planer; **Ed.** Dorothy Spencer; **Art D.** Ludwig Reiber; **Mus.** Franz Waxman; **Cast:** Richard Basehart, Gary Merrill, Oskar Werner, Hildegarde Neff, Dominique Blanchar, O. E. Hasse, Wilfried Seyferth, Hans Christian Blech.

The story is set in early 1945, the waning days of the war in Europe. The American army is on German soil and it is only a matter of time before the Germans surrender. In order to avoid unnecessary casualties, the U.S. army attempts to recruit Germans as spies to identify pockets of German resistance and concentrations of troops. The film deals with the story of a German medic (Oskar Werner), nicknamed "Happy" by his captors for his sad face. Happy volunteers to spy for the Americans. Happy does not believe it is a betrayal of his country; it is saving lives. A most unusual film both for its subject matter and its semidocumentary look with first-rate cinematography by Franz Planer. The best acting is by Oskar Werner in one of his earlier roles and Richard Basehart as the American recruiting officer.

Deliverance

1972. 109 min. color. U.S. **Prod.** John Boorman; **Dir.** John Boorman; **Scr.** James Dickey (based on his novel); **Cin.** Vilmos Zsigmond; **Ed.** Tom Priestley; **Art D.** Fred Harpman; **Mus.** Eric Weissberg; **Cast:** John Voight, Burt Reynolds, Ned Beatty, Ronny Cox, James Dickey, Bill McKinney, Herbert Coward.

Four Atlanta businessmen decide to spend a canoeing weekend on a river in Appalachia before the area is flooded by a new dam. Their adventure turns into a nightmare. One is drowned, another is raped by a wild mountain man and they are hunted by the relatives of the rapist whom they were forced to kill. The film has glaring weaknesses. The four men are too different from each other to be close friends and, more important, the film never establishes what it wants to say. Is it saying city people have become too indolent to cope with the challenges of nature in the raw or is it a commentary on man's inherent beastly nature. But it is a well made film and there are extraordinary scenes of the wilds, and the backwardness and poverty of the inhabitants.

Desperate Hours

1955. 112 min. b.w. U.S. **Prod.** William Wyler; **Dir.** William Wyler; **Scr.** Joseph Hayes (based on his novel and play); **Cin.** Lee Garmes; **Ed.** Robert Swink; **Art D.** Hal Pereira, Joseph MacMillan Johnson; **Mus.** Gail Kubik; **Cast:** Humphrey Bogart, Fredric March, Arthur Kennedy, Martha Scott, Dewey Martin, Gig Young, Mary Murphy, Robert Middleton, Alan Reed, Richard Eyer.

Three prison escapees led by Glenn (Humphrey Bogart) take over the upper-middle-class home of Dan Hilliard (Fredric March) and terrorize his wife, daughter and young son. Glenn's former girlfriend is supposed to come with the money he had hidden, at which point the three will leave. Hilliard knows they will take members of his family with them as hostages and it becomes a battle of wits to thwart the fugitives. The film's power rests with the excellent acting of two accomplished actors, Bogart and March. This was Bogart's next-to-last film. Twenty years earlier Bogart had come to the attention of the public and the studios in *The Petrified Forest* (1936), playing the same type of character, an escaped convict terrorizing a roadside café.

Destry Rides Again

1939. 94 min. b.w. U.S. **Prod.** Joe Pasternak; **Dir.** George Marshall; **Scr.** Felix Jackson, Henry Myers, Gertrude Purcell (based on the novel by Max Brand); **Cin.** Hal Mohr; **Ed.** Milton Caruth; **Art D.** Jack Otterson; **Mus.** Frank Skinner; **Cast:** James Stewart, Marlene Dietrich, Charles Winninger, Brian Donlevy, Una Merkel, Mischa Auer, Allen Jenkins, Jack Carson, Billy Gilbert, Samuel S. Hinds.

A delightful comedy/Western, *Destry Rides Again* is beautifully acted with a witty script. The film revived the sagging career of Marlene Dietrich who belts out in her inimitable way "See What the Boys in the Back Room Will Have." The lawless town of Bottleneck is run by a ruthless thief and gambler (Brian Donlevy). The deputy sheriff, Tom Destry (James Stewart), who is to clean up the town, is a mild-mannered shy man who wears no gun but manages to get rid of the gambler and his henchmen.

Devil in the Flesh

Le Diable au Corps. 1946. 110 min. b.w. French. **Prod.** Paul Graetz; **Dir.** Claude Autant-Lara; **Scr.** Jean Aurenche, Pierre Bost (based on the novel by Raymond Radiguet); **Cin.** Michel Kelber; **Ed.** Madelaine Gug; **Mus.** Rene Cloerec; **Cast:** Gérard Philipe, Micheline Presle, Denise Grey, Pierre Palau, Jean Varas, Jacques Tati, Jeanne Perez.

The story is set in 1918 during the final phase of World War I. Told in a flashback, a seventeen-year-old schoolboy (Gérard Philipe) recounts his passionate love affair with an unhappy older married woman (Micheline Presle) whose husband is at the front. The woman dies, her husband returns from the war and the boy is barred from attending her funeral. The novel, which may have been autobiographical, was written by Raymond Radiguet at age eighteen, two years before his death. The film is carried principally by the acting of the two leads, primarily Gérard Philipe as the petulant and selfish schoolboy. On the strength of this film and *L'Idiot* (1946), Philipe became France's leading young actor. He too died young at age thirty-seven. The film had grave censorship problems in many countries, including the U.S. The director, Claude Autant-Lara, has been unfairly criticized by New Wave directors, especially Truffaut, as one whose traditionalism impeded the progress of French cinema.

The Devil's General

Des Teufels General. 1956. 124 min. color. German. **Dir.** Helmut Kautner; **Scr.** Georg Hurdalek, Helmut Kautner; **Cin.** Albert Benitz; **Mus.** Archive music; **Cast:** Curt Jurgens, Marrianne Koch, Victor de Kowa, Karl John, Werner Fuetterer.

The film opens in December 1941 with war raging on the Russian front and in North Africa. It is the story of General Harras (Curt Jurgens), an ace World War I pilot who hates Hitler and the Nazi regime. His only alternative is to sabotage the German war effort. When several new model bombers crash, the SS begins an investigation and Harras comes under suspicion. He decides to make the ultimate sacrifice and crashes his newly developed bomber. To maintain appearances, the Nazi regime accords a hero's funeral to General Harras. The film is based on the life of the most famous ace of World War I, Ernst Udet, who committed suicide just prior to the outset of World War II. It is made effective mainly by the acting of Curt Jurgens who came to international attention. With his dignified bearing he was perfect in his role as a man of conscience. Victor de Kowa as the SS officer also gives an impressive performance. *The Devil's General* marked the postwar renaissance of German cinema.

Diary of a Chambermaid

Le Journal D'Une Femme De Chambre. 1964. 97 min. b.w. French. **Prod.** Serge Silberman, Michel Safra; **Dir.** Luis Buñuel ; **Scr.** Luis Buñuel , Jean-Claude Carriere (based on the novel by Octave Mirbeau); **Cin.** Roger Fellous; **Ed.** Louisette Hautecoeur; **Art D.** George Wakhevitch; **Cast:** Jeanne Moreau, George Géret, Michel Piccoli, Françoise Lugagne, Jean Ozenne, Daniel Ivernel, Jean-Claude Carriere.

Set in the late 1920s with the rise of right wing and Fascist parties in France, the film tells the story of an ambitious girl, Celestine (Jeanne Moreau), who becomes the chambermaid to a well-to-do provincial bourgeois family. The nominal head is Monsieur Monteil (Michel Piccoli), an incorrigible womanizer married to a frigid wife (Françoise Lugagne) with whom he maintains a distant relationship. His wife's father (Jean Ozenne) is a harmless old man who has a shoe fetish. The household is really run by the long time servant, Joseph (George Géret). Joseph is an active member of the newly formed Fascist Party. Celestine with her native intelligence becomes almost a coequal of Joseph. She keeps everyone in the family content. She models shoes for the old man, is most deferential toward Madame Monteil and flirtatious with Monsieur. Monteil.

Buñuel and his coscriptwriter updated Octave Mirbeau's turn-of-the-twentieth-century novel and made it more political. The focus of the film is on bourgeois institutions and the emergence of Fascist leagues. Joseph is shown to be not only an amoral opportunist but also a rapist and murderer. The famous rape and murder scene is shown without violence and is notable for its brevity and horror. Celestine, even being aware of what Joseph is capable of, joins him at the end of the film sharing his political beliefs. Jean Renoir had made a film of Mirbeau's novel in 1946. It is totally eclipsed by Buñuel 's work eighteen years later.

The Diary of a Country Priest

Le Journal D'Un Curé De Campagne. 1950. 120 min. b.w. French. **Prod.** Léon Carré; **Dir.** Robert Bresson; **Scr.** Robert Bresson (based on the novel by Georges Bernanos); **Cin.** L. H. Burel; **Ed.** Paulette Robert; **Art. D.** Pierre Charbonnier; **Mus.** Jean-Jacques Grunenwald; **Cast:** Claude Laydu, Nicole Ladmiral, Jean Riveyre, André Guibert, Nicole Maurey, Marie Monique Arkell, Antoine Balpetré.

A young priest (Claude Laydu) has been assigned to the village of Ambricourt near Pas de Calais. He suffers from severe stomach pains and his sole sustenance is a diet of stale bread dipped in wine. This is his first parish and his natural timidity and incessant pain have made him inarticulate and a disappointment to all who call on him. Despite the encouragement of an old priest (André Guibert) in a nearby town he feels incapable of being of any help to his parishioners. He has kept a diary that records his anguish and despair. The most prominent family in the village is that of a wealthy count (Jean Riveyre) who has taken his daughter's governess as his mistress. The countess (Marie Monique Arkell) has been embittered by the death of her baby son many years ago and has no love for her husband, troubled daughter or a son who has enlisted in the Foreign Legion. The countess dies and her daughter, Chantal (Nicole Ladmiral), accuses the priest of having caused her mother's death because he failed her. The priest is soon diagnosed as having stomach cancer. He is cared for by a friend from his seminary days who has abandoned his studies and lives with his mistress who has refused to marry him in case he once again decides to become a priest. The young priest dies in terrible pain. His last words are, "All is grace."

The film is based on the celebrated 1936 novel of Georges Bernanos dealing with guilt, self doubt and redemption, which are difficult subjects for any film. Bresson, a devout Catholic, has made a beautiful film about the spiritual journey of a tormented soul. After an absence from the screen of five years, with this his third film, he began using mostly unknown and nonprofessional actors. Bresson has been called a "minimalist." He reduces scenes to their bare essentials, very similar to Carl Dreyer. Often times in this film he avoids a dramatic scene by resorting to the reading of the diaries off-screen while the camera focuses on the facial reaction of the young priest. Claude Laydu, a nonprofessional with an expressive face, was an excellent choice for the lead.

Dinner at Eight

1933. 113 min. b.w. U.S. **Prod.** David O. Selznick; **Dir.** George Cukor; **Scr.** Frances Marion, Herman J. Mankiewicz, Donald Ogden Stewart (based on the play by George S. Kaufman and Edna Ferber); **Cin.** William Daniels; **Ed.** Ben Lewis; **Art D.** Cedric Gibbons, Hobe Erwin, Fredric Hope; **Mus.** William Axt; **Cast:** Marie Dressler, John Barrymore, Wallace Beery, Jean Harlow, Lionel Barrymore, Billie Burke, Lee Tracy, Edmund Lowe, Madge Evans, Jean Hersholt.

A comedy/drama built around a group of people of varying social stations who are invited to a posh dinner party. Beneath the glossy surfaces the lives of the guests and host are revealed as unhappy, even tragic. Among the star-studded cast, Jean Harlow more than holds her own. Cukor gets very good performances from Jean Harlow and Billie Burke. The script is by some of the best Hollywood writers of the time and the stylish sets started the art deco trend.

Doctor Zhivago

1965. 197 min. color. U.S. **Prod.** Carlo Ponti; **Dir.** David Lean; **Scr.** Robert Bolt (based on the novel by Boris Pasternak); **Cin.** Freddie Young; **Ed.** Norman Savage; **Prod. D.** John Box; **Art D.** Terence Marsh; **Mus.** Maurice Jarre; **Cast:** Omar Sharif, Julie Christie, Geraldine Chaplin, Tom Courtenay, Alec Guinness, Siobhan McKenna, Ralph Richardson, Rod Steiger, Rita Tushingham, Adrienne Corri.

Cinematically one of the best films, but it is mushy Hollywood. The scenes of Zhivago (Omar Sharif) with tears in his eyes writing the Lara poems are embarrassing. But then the scenes of the Bolshevik revolution and the fierce Russian winters are extremely well done. The cinematography of Freddie Young and David Lean's editing of the trans-Siberian train journey, the sound of ball bearings in a laboratory becoming the sound of a streetcar starting its journey, and winter turning to spring are outstanding. The film also suffers somewhat from uneven acting—the great acting of Ralph Richardson, the non-acting of Geraldine Chaplin and the overacting of Rod Steiger.

Dr. Ehrlich's Magic Bullet

1940. 103 min. b.w. U.S. **Prod.** Wolfgang Reinhardt; **Dir.** William Dieterle; **Scr.** John Huston, Heinz Herald, Norman Burnstein (based on a story by Burnstein from letters and notes of the Ehrlich family); **Cin.** James Wong Howe; **Ed.** Warren Low; **Art D.** Carl Jules Weyl; **Mus.** Max Steiner; **Cast:** Edward G. Robinson, Ruth Gordon, Otto Kruger, Donald Crisp, Maria Ouspenskaya, Montagu Love, Sig Rumann, Donald Meek, Henry O'Neill, Albert Basserman.

Another of Warner Studios' well-made intelligent biographies covering the life and contribution of Paul Ehrlich (Edward G. Robinson) who shared the Nobel Prize for physiology and medicine in 1908. What elevates the film is the attention to minute details of Ehrlich's thirty years of research in discovering the first vaccine for diphtheria and later an effective cure for syphilis. Biographies played an important part in educating movie audiences. They began with superficial, amusing pictures such as *Disraeli* (1929) and *Voltaire* (1933) and matured with *The Story of Louis Pasteur* (1936), *The Life of Emile Zola* (1937) and *Madam Curie* (1943). *Dr. Ehrlich's Magic Bullet* has an excellent screenplay and is extremely well acted by Robinson and Otto Kruger. Robinson was finally able to shed the hard gangster image which had begun with *Little Caesar* (1930). It would be eight years until he again played the role of a gangster in John Huston's *Key Largo* (1948).

A Double Life

1947. 104 min. b.w. U.S. **Prod.** Michael Kanin; **Dir.** George Cukor; **Scr.** Ruth Gordon, Garson Kanin (with scenes from *Othello* by William Shakespeare); **Cin.** Milton Krasner; **Ed.** Robert Parrish; **Prod. D.** Harry Horner; **Art D.** Bernard Herzbrun; **Mus.** Miklos Rozsa; **Cast:** Ronald Colman, Signe Hasso, Edmond O'Brien, Shelley Winters, Ray Collins, Millard Mitchell, Whit Bissell.

A gifted stage actor, Anthony John (Ronald Colman), has a history of identifying with the role he is currently playing. When the film opens he is playing in a comedy and he is kind and light-hearted. He often teams up with his former wife, Brita (Signe Hasso), and despite their divorce they still have a very amiable relationship. Producers suggest his next role be Othello with Brita playing Desdemona. Despite misgivings by both, Anthony accepts the challenge. Once in the role, his personality changes and "the green–eyed monster" consumes him. He begins to believe Brita is carrying on with a press agent, Bill Friend (Edmond O'Brien). Gradually he assumes the Moor's persona and a murderous mood takes over.

The film is really a thriller, set largely within the confines of the theater, which are the best parts. The scenes outside the theater do not easily jell and seem forced. Signe Hasso does not bring much to the film. Edmond O'Brien and Whit Bissell as the coroner give their usual reliable performances. Ronald Colman is at his best and won the Academy Award for best actor. Miklos Rozsa also won an Oscar for his score.

Dreams

(a.k.a. *Akira Kurosawa's Dreams*). 1990. 120 min. color. Japanese. **Prod.** Hisao Kuro-sawa, Mike Y. Inoue; **Dir.** Akira Kurosawa; **Scr.** Akira Kurosawa; **Cin.** Takao Saito, Masahuro Ueda; **Ed.** Tome Minami; **Art D.** Yoshiro Muraki, Akira Sakuragi; **Mus.** Shinichiro Ikebe; **Cast:** Akira Terao, Mitsuko Baisho, Mieko Harada, Toshihico Nakano, Mitsunori Isaki, Masayuki Yui, Shu Nakajima, Sakae Kimura, Yoshitaka Zushi.

Kurosawa at age eighty distills his hopes, fears and vision of the future in eight segments. The central common theme is man's relationship with nature and his fellow man. Some segments are better expressed than others. But the film is more important for Kurosawa's mastery of a new style, different from anything he had done before.

Drums Along the Mohawk

1939. 103 min. b.w. U.S. **Prod.** Darryl Zanuck; **Dir.** John Ford; **Scr.** Lamar Trotti, Sonya Levien (based on the novel by Walter D. Edmonds); **Cin.** Bert Glennon, Ray Rennahan; **Ed.** Robert Simpson; **Art D.** Richard Day, Mark-Lee Kirk; **Mus.** Alfred Newman; **Cast:** Claudette Colbert, Henry Fonda, Edna May Oliver, John Carradine, Arthur Shields, Ward Bond, Eddie Collins, Doris Bowdon.

The film is set near the beginning of the American Revolu-tion. Newlyweds (Henry Fonda and Claudette Colbert) have moved to a farming community in the Mohawk Valley in upstate New York. The restless native Indians, prodded and incited by British forces, begin to attack the settlement. By far the most exciting part of the film is when Fonda volunteers to go to the nearby fort to seek help to repel the Indians. It becomes a cross-country race as he is pursued by two Indians. John Ford's first color film is distinguished for its fine photography and vivid and lush colors. The film drags a little in places. Despite the drama and excitement, Fonda is rather bland and Claudette Colbert's cos-tumes are too fresh and stylish for an eighteenth-century farmer's wife. The best acting is by Edna May Oliver as an indomitable old lady confronting the marauding Indians.

Duel

1971. 90 min. color. U.S. **Prod.** George Eckstein; **Dir.** Steven Spielberg; **Scr.** Richard Matheson; **Cin.** Jack A. Marta; **Ed.** Frack Morriss; **Art D.** Robert S. Smith; **Mus.** Billy Goldenberg; **Cast:** Dennis Weaver, Eddie Firestone, Tim Herbert, Charles Seel.

A 1971 TV movie by the twenty-seven-year-old Steven Spielberg that was not exhibited in movie houses in the U.S. until 1983. The story has a salesman (Dennis Weaver) driving in a rented car toward Bakersfield, California, on a seldom traveled two-lane road. A huge tanker truck is annoyed at being passed. When it is passed a second time it starts a murderous game in which the truck tries to run over the small passenger car. After several near-death situations, the passenger car gets the upper hand and tricks the truck into going over a cliff where it bursts into flames. As the fire engulfs the truck we hear what sounds like the death throes of a wild beast. It is an extremely well-made film and Spielberg has the viewer in the palm of his hand. We never see the driver of the truck, and it often appears there is no driver. The scenes of the deadly duel are interspersed and contrasted with the down-to-earth scenes of Dennis Weaver making phone calls to his wife and desperately attempting to contact the police.

E.T. The Extra-Terrestrial

1982. 115 min. color. U.S. **Prod.** Steven Spielberg, Kathleen Kennedy; **Dir.** Steven Spielberg; **Scr.** Melissa Mathison; **Cin.** Allen Daviau; **Ed.** Carol Littleton; **Prod. D.** James Bissell; **Mus.** John Williams; **Cast:** Dee Wallace, Henry Thomas, Peter Coyote, Robert MacNaughton, Drew Barrymore, K. C. Martel, Sean Frye, Tom Howell.

A well-made modern fairy tale of an alien visitor to earth who is left behind by his spaceship. He gains a rapport and understanding with children. It is the rational and suspicious adults who are the villains.

East of Eden

1955. 115 min. color. U.S. **Prod.** Elia Kazan; **Dir.** Elia Kazan; **Scr.** Paul Osborn (based on the novel by John Steinbeck); **Cin.** Ted McCord; **Ed.** Owen Marks; **Art D.** James Basevi; **Mus.** Leonard Rosenman; **Cast:** Julie Harris, James Dean, Raymond Massey, Jo Van Fleet, Burl Ives, Richard Davalos, Albert Dekker, Timothy Carey.

This shortened version of the Steinbeck novel is an allegory on the Cain and Abel story. Two sons of a stern religious father (Raymond Massey) compete for his love and attention. It is set in the Salinas Valley of California, the lettuce basket of the U.S., just prior to America's entry into World War I. The story is too unrelenting and heavy, but it is redeemed by the fine direction of Elia Kazan, the panoramic cinematography and the excellent cast. Acting honors go to Raymond Massey and Jo Van Fleet who won an Academy Award for best supporting actress, and newcomer James Dean in his first film. The contrast of the acting styles of Dean and Massey is very effective.

Easy Rider

1969. 94 min. color. U.S. **Prod.** Peter Fonda; **Dir.** Dennis Hopper; **Scr.** Peter Fonda, Dennis Hopper, Terry Southern; **Cin.** Laszlo Kovacs; **Ed.** Donn Cambern; **Art D.** Jerry Kay; **Cast:** Peter Fonda, Dennis Hopper, Jack Nicholson, Karen Black.

A tale of two hippie motorcyclists who set out to find the "real America." They become disillusioned and in a powerful ending both are mindlessly killed. This story of alienated youths touched a chord with most viewers. The film has dated badly, but the totally unexpected ending is still effective. Jack Nicholson made his mark as the cynical boozy civil rights lawyer and became recognized as the fine actor he is.

Edge of the City

1957. 85 min. b.w. U.S. **Prod.** David Susskind; **Dir.** Martin Ritt; **Scr.** Robert Alan Aurthur; **Cin.** Joseph Brun; **Ed.** Sidney Meyers; **Art D.** Richard Sylbert; **Mus.** Leonard Rosenman; **Cast:** John Cassavetes, Sidney Poitier, Jack Warden, Ruby Dee, Kathleen Maguire.

Edge of the City is an underrated film about loyalty and friendship. An army deserter (John Cassavetes) gets a job as a dock worker. He is befriended by an honest hard–working black worker (Sidney Poitier). They are harassed by the corrupt, bigoted foreman (Jack Warden) who is only interested in kickbacks. Poitier comes to Cassavetes' defense at the cost of his own life. Very well acted and well directed by Martin Ritt in his first feature, filmed in actual locales.

The Emigrants

Utvandrarna. 1971. 151 min. color. Swedish. **Prod.** Bengt Forslund; **Dir.** Jan Troell; **Scr.** Jan Troell, Bengt Forslund (based on the novels by Vilhelm Moberg); **Cin.** Jan Troell; **Ed.** Jan Troell; **Art D.** P .A. Lundgren, Berndt Fritiof; **Mus.** Erik Nordgren; **Cast:** Max von Sydow, Liv Ullmann, Eddie Axberg, Allan Edwall, Monica Zetterlund, Pierre Lindstedt, Hans Alfredson, Sveenolof Bern, Alina Alfredsson.

Set in the mid–nineteenth century, a group of Swedish peasants who have undergone unbearable suffering decide to immigrate to America. The film is divided into three segments: their lonely life in Sweden; the harrowing transatlantic voyage in a cramped boat more suited for cattle; their arrival on America's shore and then the long journey to Minnesota. It is a well–directed film with an excellent cast headed by two veteran performers, Max von Sydow and Liv Ullmann. The film is an ode to human perseverance and determination. A sequel was made by the same director and cast, *The New Land* (1972), which covers their settling in Minnesota and the hardships they endure there.

Enchanted April

1991. 101 min. color. British. **Prod.** Ann Scott; **Dir.** Mike Newell; **Scr.** Peter Barnes, Elizabeth Von Amim (based on her novel); **Cin.** Rex Maidment; **Ed.** Dick Allen; **Prod. D.** Malcolm Thornton; **Mus.** Richard Rodney Bennet; **Cast:** Josie Lawrence, Miranda Richardson, Joan Plowright, Polly Walker, Alfred Molina, Michael Kitchen, Jim Broadbent.

Four women rent an old Italian villa to get away from their troubled existences. Josie Lawrence is the dominated and submissive wife of a rigid husband. Miranda Richardson is the neglected wife of a philanderer. Through an ad in the newspaper they are joined by Polly Walker who is tired of her reputation as only a renowned beauty and Joan Plowright, a pompous, lonely aging widow. The villa and the setting is indeed beautiful and the problems of the four women vanish. The film is predictable, but it is a charming romance. The London rain is contrasted with the bright Italian sun. Romance in marriage blossoms when out of its usual humdrum environment. The entire cast is competent, but it is Josie Lawrence and Alfred Molina, as her husband, who sustain the comedy. Joan Plowright, the widow of Laurence Olivier, is an imperious presence in all her scenes. The film shows the wealth of talent on the London stage and in cinema.

The Enforcer

1951. 87 min. b.w. U.S. **Prod.** Milton Sperling; **Dir.** Bretaigne Windust; **Scr.** Martin Rackin; **Cin.** Robert Burks; **Ed.** Fred Allen; **Art D.** Charles H. Clarke; **Mus.** David Buttolph; **Cast:** Humphrey Bogart, Zero Mostel, Ted de Corsia, Everett Sloane, Roy Roberts, Lawrence Tolan, Bob Steele, Adelaide Klein, Don Beddoe, Jack Lambert.

Senator Estes Kefauver's 1950 committee investigating organized crime in the U.S. revealed the existence of a shadowy group called Murder Inc. headed by Alberto Anastasia. Gang members or any ordinary person could enter into an arrangement with Murder Inc. to have a rival or foe murdered. Murder Inc. even had its own cemetery. The film deals with the efforts of an assistant D.A. (Humphrey Bogart) to dismantle the group and bring to trial all the people involved. The film influenced crime films from the fifties through the seventies. It introduced terms such as "contracts" and "hits." A suspenseful noirish film, made very documentary-like. It is not among Bogart's best-acted films but the members of the secondary cast give good performances, notably Ted de Corsia, Zero Mostel, Everett Sloane and Jack Lambert.

Europa, Europa

1991. 115 min. color. French/German. **Prod.** Margaret Menegoz, Artur Brauner; **Dir.** Agnieszka Holland; **Scr.** Agnieszka Holland, Paul Hengge (based on the book *Mémoires* by Solomon Perel); **Cin.** Jacek Petrycki; **Ed.** Ewa Smal, Isabelle Lorente; **Prod. D.** Allan Starski; **Mus.** Zbigniew Preisner; **Cast:** Marco Hofschneider, Rene Hofschneider, Julie Delpy, Andre Wilms, Solomon Perel, Aschley Wanninger.

The film is based on the true life story of Solomon Perel (Marco Hofschneider) who was born in Germany to German-speaking Polish Jews. During a pogrom his sister is killed by Nazi thugs, but he escapes and, with his parents, moves to Poland. When Germany invades Poland Solomon is separated from his parents. He adopts the name Joseph Peters and poses as an "Aryan." He comes to the attention of the German invaders and because he is handsome, speaks perfect German and shares Hitler's birthday, April 25, he is sent to an elite Nazi youth camp and hailed as a perfect "Aryan." He is later enlisted in an elite corps of the German army. The film follows Solomon's adventures and survival. Director/screenwriter Agnieszka Holland has done a masterful job. She had made several other films about stateless people, but this is her best. The script is witty and the humorous scenes are juxtaposed with the horrors the Jews were subjected to. There is also credible acting by Hofschneider. The film is marred, however, by some unnecessary dream sequences.

Fail Safe.

1964. 111 min. b.w. U.S. **Prod.** Max E. Youngstein; **Dir.** Sidney Lumet; **Scr.** Walter Bernstein (based on the novel by Eugene Burdick and Harvey Wheeler); **Cin.** Gerald Herschfeld; **Ed.** Ralph Rosenblum; **Art D.** Albert Brenner; **Cast:** Henry Fonda, Walter Matthau, Fritz Weaver, Dan O'Herlihy, Larry Hagman, Frank Overton, Dom De Luise, Edward Binns, William Hanson, Russell Hardie, Russell Collins.

A well-made somber nuclear disaster film that was overshadowed by the brilliant macabre humor of *Dr. Strangelove,* released by the same studio (Columbia) some eight months earlier. Henry Fonda, Dan O'Herlihy, Frank Overton and Edward Binns are excellent. Walter Matthau as the hawkish overzealous scientist is miscast.

Fantasia

1940. 120 min. color. Animated. U.S. **Prod.** Walt Disney; **Supervisor** Ben Sharpsteen; **Mus. Dir.** Edward H. Plumb; **Mus.** Played by Leopold Stokowski and the Philadelphia Symphony Orchestra; **Narrator** Deems Taylor.

Of the eight segments in this uneven film, two are most imaginative: Mickey Mouse being taught a lesson in humility in Dukas' "Sorcerer's Apprentice," and the dawn of creation in Stravinsky's "Rite of Spring." An impressive Leopold Stokowski conducts the Philadelphia Symphony Orchestra with his expressive hands without baton.

The Farmer's Daughter

1947. 97 min. b.w. U.S. **Prod.** Dore Schary; **Dir.** H. C. Potter; **Scr.** Allen Rivkin, Laura Kerr (based on the play *Hulda, Daughter of Parliament* by Juhni Tervataa); **Cin.** Milton Krasner; **Ed.** Harry Marker; **Art D.** Albert S. D'Agostino; **Mus.** Leigh Harline; **Cast:** Loretta Young, Joseph Cotton, Ethel Barrymore, Charles Bickford, Harry Davenport, Rhys Williams.

The film is set in an unnamed Midwestern state. Katrin (Loretta Young), a Swedish farmer's daughter, becomes a housekeeper in the mansion of a prominent political family. Glenn Morley (Joseph Cotton) is a member of the U.S. Congress and his mother (Ethel Barrymore) is a political force in the state. Katrin learns a great deal about politics from the long-serving butler (Charles Bickford). When the Morleys attempt to promote a mediocre local politician to fill a vacant congressional seat, Katrin, despite her loyalty to the family, revolts, becomes a candidate herself and wins the election. We are led to believe there will be a romantic union between Congressman Morley and the former housekeeper. This fairy tale is well directed by H. C. Potter who had made several good comedies, most notably *Mr. Blandings Builds His Dream House* (1948). It is well acted overall. Loretta Young won the Academy Award for best actress and Charles Bickford was nominated for best supporting actor. Ethel Barrymore also should have been honored for her performance.

Fat City

1972. 100 min. color. U.S. **Dir.** John Huston; **Scr.** Leonard Gardner (based on his novel); **Cin.** Conrad Hall; **Ed.** Margaret Booth; **Prod. D.** Richard Sylbert; **Mus.** Marvin Hamlisch; **Cast:** Stacy Keach, Jeff Bridges, Susan Tyrrell, Candy Clark, Nicholas Colasanto, Art Aragon.

For a brief period, 1966 to 1972, Huston made several inferior films. He then chose to make *Fat City*, a low-budget film without any major stars. It is a downbeat story of the lower echelon of professional boxers—losers who pursue unattainable dreams, a theme Huston had dealt with before. In *Fat City* a twenty-nine-year old boxer, Billy Tully (Stacy Keach), has become a drifter and an alcoholic, brought about by the death of his wife and losing the single most important fight of his career. He meets an eighteen-year-old promising boxer, Ernie Munger (Jeff Bridges). Billy introduces Ernie to his former trainer and he himself decides to make a comeback. But Billy resumes his drinking. Ernie wins a couple of preliminaries; however, his ascent in ranking is uncertain.

Huston's film is neither about the brutality nor corruption of boxing. It is about two losers. Huston himself had been a good amateur boxer and always retained his passion for the sport. He is not condescending toward his characters; in fact, he treats them with affection and respect. It is a well-acted film with the realistic background of Stockton, California. It begins with a very effective rendition of "Help Me Make It Through the Night," sung by Kris Kristofferson.

Father of the Bride

1950. 93 min. b.w. U.S. **Prod.** Pandro S. Berman; **Dir.** Vincente Minnelli; **Scr.** Frances Goodrich, Albert Hackett (based on the novel by Edward Streeter); **Cin.** John Alton; **Ed.** Ferris Webster; **Art D.** Cedric Gibbons, Leonid Vasian; **Mus.** Adolph Deutsch; **Cast:** Spencer Tracy, Joan Bennett, Elizabeth Taylor, Billie Burke, Leo G. Carroll, Don Taylor, Moroni Olsen, Melville Cooper, Taylor Holmes, Paul Harvey.

In this flawlessly directed charming comedy, Spencer Tracy plays a well-to-do father whose daughter (Elizabeth Taylor), the apple of his eye, is being married. Wedding arrangements turn the household topsy-turvy, but the hosting of the reception falls mainly on his shoulders. The film will be remembered for the versatility of Spencer Tracy and some wonderful character actors: Leo G. Carroll as the caterer, Melville Cooper as the church usher, Paul Harvey as the minister and Billie Burke as the groom's mother.

The Firemen's Ball

Hori Ma Panenko. 1967. 73 min. color. Czech. **Prod.** Barrandov, Carlo Ponti; **Dir.** Milos Forman; **Scr.** Milos Forman, Ivan Passer, Jaroslav Papousek; **Cin.** Miroslav Ondricek; **Ed.** Miroslav Hajek; **Mus.** Karel Mares; **Cast:** Vaclav Stockel, Josef Svet, Josef Kolb, Jan Vostrcil, Frantisek Debelka, Josef Sebanek, Karel Valnoha, Marie Jezkova, Anina Lipoldova.

A ball is being held by the firemen of a small Czech town honoring an eighty-six-year-old former commander of the fire brigade. He is to be given a silver-plated hatchet. There will also be a beauty contest selecting the prettiest girl in town. Everything begins to go wrong. The hatchet is stolen during the festivities.

The old honoree, who has to go to the bathroom, is kept standing at the podium while a search is carried out. There are arguments amongst the mothers of the beauty contestants and attempts to sway the jury. To round out the unsatisfactory evening, a fire breaks out and by the time the firemen get their equipment and reach the site, an old man's house is burned to the ground.

This warm and humorous film was made possible during the brief "liberal spring" in Czechoslovakia. Forman pokes fun at the communist regime. Soon after the release of the film, the authorities cracked down on films that demeaned the government. Forman left the country and settled briefly in Paris and later the United States where he made several notable films: *One Flew Over the Cuckoo's Nest* (1975) and *Amadeus* (1984).

Foolish Wives

1922. 180 min. b.w. Silent. U.S. **Dir.** Erich von Stroheim; **Scr.** Erich von Stoheim; **Cin.** Ben Reynolds, William Daniels; **Art D.** E. E. Sheeley, Richard Day; **Mus.** Sigmund Romberg; **Cast:** Erich von Stroheim, Rudolph Christians, Miss Du Pont, Maude George, Mae Busch, Louis K. Webb.

Foolish Wives is the third film directed by Erich von Stroheim. As in the previous two it is a tale of adultery. A German military officer posing as a member of the nobility begins flirting with the wife of an American diplomat in Monte Carlo. It soon leads to seduction, blackmail and murder. As in all of Stroheim's films there is a pervasive air of eroticism. It is also characteristically rich in realistic detail. Great attention is given to the sets and décor. Stroheim had a perfect replica of the Monte Carlo Casino built at a cost of over a million dollars, nearly bankrupting Universal Studios. The film is all Stroheim and it reinforced his reputation as "the man you love to hate."

For Whom the Bell Tolls

1943. 130 min. color. U.S. **Prod.** Sam Wood; **Dir.** Sam Wood; **Scr.** Dudley Nichols (based on the novel by Ernest Hemingway); **Cin.** Ray Rennahan; **Ed.** Sherman Todd, John F. Link; **Prod. D.** William Cameron Menzies; **Art D.** Hans Dreier, Haldane Douglas; **Mus.** Victor Young; **Cast:** Gary Cooper, Ingrid Bergman, Akim Tamiroff, Arturo de Cordova, Joseph Calleia, Katina Paxinou, Vladimir Sokoloff, Mikhail Rasumny, Fortunio Bonanova.

The last chapter of the novel is among the best of Hemingway. In the hands of director Sam Wood the film is too laid back and staid. Its original running time of 170 minutes was too long and the subsequent cutting to 130 minutes made it even weaker. The movie still is enjoyable for its use of the wealth of European talent that had come to Hollywood during World War II. There are great performances from Akim Tamiroff, Joseph Calleia, Mikhail Rasumny and Katina Paxinou, who won the Academy Award for best supporting actress for her role as Pilar.

Forbidden Planet

1956. 98 min. color. U.S. **Prod.** Nicholas Nayfack; **Dir.** Fred M. Wilcox; **Scr.** Cyril Hume (based on a story by Irving Block, Allen Adler); **Cin.** George Folsey; **Ed.** Ferris Webster; **Art D.** Cedric Gibbons, Arthur Lonergan; **Mus.** Louis Barron, Bebe Barron; **Cast:** Walter Pidgeon, Anne Francis, Leslie Nielsen, Warren Stevens, Jack Kelly, Richard Anderson, Earl Holliman.

This film is a science fiction version of Shakespeare's *The Tempest*. An American spaceship is sent in the year 2000 to find survivors of a previous flight to the remote planet Altair-4 where the sky is green and the sand is pink. The only survivors of the earlier trip are Dr. Morbius/Prospero (Walter Pidgeon), his daughter, Altaira/Miranda (Anne Francis), and a very obedient robot, Robby/Ariel. Dr. Morbius has led a hermit-like existence devoted to learning and is not happy to see the new arrivals. But there is an idyllic romance between his daughter and the new ship's captain (Leslie Nielsen). There is also an evil monster/Caliban who harasses and is intent on killing the crew. *Forbidden Planet* is an imaginative film, well conceived and highly entertaining. The main drawbacks are that it is slow at times and, with the exception of Walter Pidgeon, it is burdened with a mediocre cast. The film could have incorporated in the dialogue some of Shakespeare's great poetry from *The Tempest:* "We are such stuff as dreams are made on, and our little life is rounded with a sleep."

Force of Evil

1948. 78 min. b.w. U.S. **Prod.** Bob Roberts; **Dir.** Abraham Polonsky; **Scr.** Abraham Polonsky, Ira Wolfert (based on his novel *Tucker's People*); **Cin.** George Barnes; **Ed.** Walter Thompson, Arthur Seid; **Art D.** Richard Day; **Mus.** David Raksin; **Cast:** John Garfield, Beatrice Pearson, Thomas Gomez, Roy Roberts, Marie Windsor, Paul McVey, Howland Chamberlin, Sheldon Leonard.

Force of Evil is the story of a lower eastside kid, Joe Morse (John Garfield), who has made it as a prominent Wall Street lawyer. He is indebted to his older brother, Leo (Thomas Gomez), who has helped him throughout his life and paid for his education. Leo owns a small numbers bank. He sees himself as a small business-man and runs his shop as if it were a family business. He knows he makes his money by exploiting the poor but believes that is the system. Joe has his sights on bigger things. He ties up with one of his clients, Ben Tucker (Roy Roberts), a shady gangster-type busi-nessman who has come up with a scheme where he can make millions. On July 4, most people bet on the number combination 776. Tucker has arranged with the syndicate to have that number come up. The result would be that most of the betting shops will be bankrupted. Tucker will then take over their operations and will become the kingpin of the numbers racket. Warned by Tucker not to inform Leo about the fix, Joe attempts to talk his brother into closing his operation on July 4, but Leo refuses explaining his customers expect him to stay open. The number combination 776 comes up and Tucker takes over. Meanwhile other gangsters move in for a piece of the action and they all come to a bloody end. Joe decides to go to the authorities to expose the social and moral evils of the numbers racket.

Abraham Polonsky called his film "an autopsy of capitalism." Tucker is more a business tycoon than a gangster. Leo is depicted as a simple crook who inevitably ends up in a racket where the rich exploit the poor. Polonsky portrays his heroes, Joe and Leo, as having no choice under the capitalist system. *Force of Evil* is one of the very few overtly anticapitalist films. Polonsky was black-listed for being an uncooperative witness before the House Un-American Activities Committee. His next venture in movies was twenty years later when he wrote the script for Don Siegel's *Madigan* (1968) and then directed *Tell Them Willie Boy Is Here* (1969). Polonsky was known for his terse scripts. The best examples are his earlier *Body and Soul* (1947) and the present film, both starring John Garfield. There is excellent acting by Garfield, a fine actor. There is also excellent cinematography by George Barnes, an Oscar winner for Hitchcock's *Rebecca* (1940), and the score by David Raksin of *Laura* (1944) fame is very good. What mars the film is the overly complicated plot, too many peripheral characters and the doctrinaire anticapitalist line.

A Foreign Affair

1948. 113 min. b.w. U.S. **Prod.** Charles Brackett; **Dir.** Billy Wilder; **Scr.** Charles Brackett, Billy Wilder, Richard Breen, Robert Harari; **Cin.** Charles B. Lang, Jr.; **Ed.** Doane Harrison; **Art D.** Hans Dreier, Walter Tyler; **Mus.** Frederick Hollander; **Cast:** Jean Arthur, Marlene Dietrich, John Lund, Millard Mitchell.

Set in 1948 Berlin, the United States Congress is concerned that American soldiers in Germany are being corrupted by consorting with German women and are trading on the black market. A congressional committee is empowered to investigate. A prim and proper congresswoman, Phoebe Frost (Jean Arthur) from Iowa, is a member of the delegation. Miss Frost fails in her assignment, and worse, she falls in love with a U.S. army captain (John Lund) who is keeping the former mistress of a Nazi general, Erica Von Schluetow (Marlene Dietrich). Not one of Wilder's best, but it is very witty and touches on contemporary political events.

The film belongs to Marlene Dietrich as a singer in a subterranean nightclub. Her three songs are topical and rendered in Dietrich's inimitable style. Millard Mitchell as a broad-minded army colonel is also excellent. Jean Arthur is not entirely comfortable in her role except in a scene when she lets out with the song "Iowa," John Lund is colorless. The newsreel footage of a devastated Berlin punctuates the humor.

Fort Apache

1948. 127 min. b.w. U.S. **Prod.** John Ford, Merian C. Cooper; **Dir.** John Ford; **Scr.** Frank S. Nugent (based on the story "Massacre" by James Warner Bellah); **Cin.** Archie Stout; **Ed.** Jack Murray; **Art D.** James Basevi; **Mus.** Richard Hageman; **Cast:** Henry Fonda, John Wayne, Shirley Temple, Pedro Armendariz, John Agar, Ward Bond, Victor McLaglen, George O'Brien, Irene Rich, Anna Lee.

Embittered cavalry officer Lieutenant Colonel Owen Thursday (Henry Fonda) is sent to Arizona territory to keep the peace with restless Indians led by Cochise. Thursday had been promoted to the rank of general during the Civil War. Now in peacetime his rank has reverted to Lieutenant Colonel. He has no knowledge of Indians and their customs and looks down on them as savages. He ignores the advice of his experienced Indian fighter, Captain Kerby York (John Wayne), and humiliates the Indians. In order to make a name for himself and come to the attention of the War Department, and perhaps regain his wartime rank, he leads an ill-planned suicidal charge into the Indian stronghold. His troops are wiped out and he himself is killed. To boost troop morale, Captain York who has now taken command creates the legend that Thursday was a brave officer and should be accorded the status of hero.

Fort Apache is a variation on the legend of George Custer and is the first of John Ford's cavalry trilogy followed by *She Wore a Yellow Ribbon* (1949) and *Rio Grande* (1950), both inferior to *Fort Apache*. Ford dismisses Indians whom he believes impede progress in the West. The film is marred by a silly love story by two weak actors, Shirley Temple and John Agar, and the usual

Ford sentimentality. There is, however, the beautiful and awesome scenes of Monument Valley and some great action sequences. Henry Fonda is excellent as the wrong-headed Lieutenant Colonel Thursday. John Wayne and the stable of Ford's favorites—Victor McLaglen, Ward Bond and Pedro Armendariz—are also very good.

The Four Feathers

1939. 115 min. color. British. **Prod.** Alexander Korda; **Dir.** Zoltan Korda; **Scr.** R. C. Sherriff, Lajos Biro, Arthur Wimperis (based on the novel by A. E. W. Mason); **Cin.** Georges Perinal, Osmond Borradaile, Jack Cardiff; **Ed.** William Hornbeck, Henry Cornelius; **Prod. D.** Vincent Korda; **Mus.** Miklos Rozsa; **Cast:** John Clements, Ralph Richardson, C. Aubrey Smith, June Duprez, Allan Jeayes, Jack Allen, Donald Grey.

The Four Feathers is a perfect "boy's own" story about honor and courage. Unfortunately, British imperialism fighting "Fuzzie Wuzzies" in the Sudan dates the film badly.

Alexander Korda, producer/director, Zoltan Korda, director, and Vincent Korda, art director and designer, were a remarkable family. They did a great deal for the British film industry, making many good films, beginning with *The Private Life of Henry VIII* (1933), *The Scarlet Pimpernel* (1934) and *The Thief of Baghdad* (1940).

Frankenstein

1931. 70 min. b.w. U.S. **Prod.** Carl Laemmle, Jr.; **Dir.** James Whale; **Scr.** Garrett Fort, Francis Edwards Faragoh, John Balderston, Robert Florey (based on the novel by Mary Shelley and the play by Peggy Webling); **Cin.** Arthur Edeson; **Ed.** Maurice Pivar, Clarence Kolster; **Art D.** Charles D. Hall; **Mus.** David Boekman; **Cast:** Colin Clive, Mae Clarke, Boris Karloff, John Boles, Edward Van Sloan, Frederick Kerr, Lionel Belmore, Dwight Frye.

Dr. Henry Frankenstein (Colin Clive) has decided to play God and create a human being. Despite the opposition of his colleagues, friends and his fiancée (Mae Clarke), he continues his work. With the help of his servant, the deformed hunchback Fritz (Dwight

Frye), he steals a newly buried corpse from the graveyard. They then cut loose from the gallows a recently hanged criminal. Fritz mistakenly steals an abnormal brain from a laboratory. Dr. Franken-stein then assembles the organs and features of the corpses into one body. In a well-done scene for its day, the wired body is hoisted to the top of the castle during a fierce electric storm. After receiving charges from the lightning, the body is lowered and we see signs of life as the creature's hand moves. The creature (Boris Karloff) looks so hideously ugly and threatening that he is chained and put in a cellar. He is tortured by the sadistic Fritz and one day breaks his chains, kills Fritz and runs away. The monster injures Dr. Franken-stein and kills several more people including a little girl. The people in the village are aroused and begin to hunt for him. He is cor-nered at a mill which is set on fire. The monster apparently is consumed by the flames.

Frankenstein was a turning point in horror films and surpassed all those preceding. James Whale brought great craftsmanship to the picture and great attention to details. Dr. Frankenstein's labo-ratory is meticulously conceived. Boris Karloff's makeup with his black motionless eyes, heavy eyelids and huge seven-foot stature made him more menacing than anything before on the screen. Karloff's performance is one of the best of any actor in a horror film. Clive as the nervous and frenzied doctor is fine. The film has a scene that is one of the most horrifying in any movie, the drowning of the peasant girl by the monster. It is a delicately slow scene that begins as a game as the two throw petals into a pond. When they have run out of petals the monster throws the girl in the pond, that is not shown on screen. There is then a touch of remorse in the monster who has lost a playmate. Most critics believe *Bride of Frankenstein* (1935) is a better film, but *Franken-stein* is a far more frightening one.

French Can-Can

1955. 93 min. color. French. **Prod.** Louis Wipf; **Dir.** Jean Renoir; **Scr.** Jean Renoir; **Cin.** Michel Kelber; **Ed.** Borys Lewin; **Art D.** Max Douy; **Mus.** Georges Van Parys; **Cast:** Jean Gabin, Francoise Arnoul, Maria Felix, Jean-Roger Caussimon, Gianni Esposito, Philippe Clay, Michel Piccoli, Edith Piaf, Patachou.

Jean Gabin plays Dangland, a theater impresario who has fallen on hard times. He puts all the money he has into starting a new cabaret that he names Moulin Rouge. He searches for talent and even convinces a Montmartre laundress (Francoise Arnoul) to become a dancer. The film shows the rigorous training the girls undergo to become high kickers with acrobatic skills. Moulin Rouge opens in 1888 and becomes the rage of Paris. This was Jean Renoir's first film in France in over fifteen years. He is reunited with Jean Gabin who had appeared in two previous Renoir films. Francoise Arnoul as the laundress who becomes the star of the cabaret and with whom Dangland has an extended affair, and Maria Felix as his mistress were perfect for their parts. Two legendary French singers, Edith Piaf and Patachou, also have brief scenes. In beautiful color the film evokes the era of the French impressionists, including Renoir's father. The exuberance of the concluding dance number is still one of the greatest scenes, unmatched by subsequent films on the same era.

The Front

1976. 94 min. color. U.S. **Prod.** Martin Ritt; **Dir.** Martin Ritt; **Scr.** Walter Bernstein; **Cin.** Michael Chapman; **Ed.** Sidney Levin; **Art D.** Charles Bailey; **Mus.** Dave Grusin; **Cast:** Woody Allen, Zero Mostel, Herschel Bernardi, Michael Murphy, Andrea Marcovicci, Remak Ramsay, Lloyd Gough, David Margulies, Danny Aiello.

Set during the anti–communist preoccupation of the 1950s, a nondescript restaurant cashier and petty bookie (Woody Allen) with no particular political convictions agrees to his name being used by several blacklisted television writers and receives ten per-cent of their fee. He eventually arouses the attention of the network "clearance consultant." He begins to take himself seriously and to criticize and question the material he is fed. His identification with the blacklisted writers becomes complete when he is called before a congressional committee to name names. He refuses and scolds the committee. An altogether original and well-done film that belongs to Woody Allen. It is his role and his acting that lends humor to a somber subject.

The Fugitive

1947. 104 min. b.w. U.S. **Prod.** John Ford, Merian C. Cooper; **Dir.** John Ford; **Scr.** Dudley Nichols (based on the novels *The Labyrinthine Ways* and *The Power and the Glory* by Graham Greene); **Cin.** Gabriel Figueroa; **Ed.** Jack Murray; **Art D.** Alfred Ybarra; **Mus.** Richard Hageman; **Cast:** Henry Fonda, Dolores Del Rio, Pedro Armendariz, J. Carrol Naish, Leo Carrillo, Ward Bond, Robert Armstrong, John Qualen, Fortunio Bonanova.

The film is set in a Latin American country where the regime has banned the church and intends to silence the priests. A young priest (Henry Fonda) cannot fathom the government edict and wants to remain a priest and tend to people's needs. He hides in a small village and secretly resumes his work. He baptizes a child born out of wedlock and comforts an escaped American gangster (Ward Bond). A Judas-type character (J. Carrol Naish) sells out the priest to the brutal police captain (Pedro Armendariz). The film has simplified Graham Greene's novel *The Power and the Glory* which deals with the power of faith. It is well acted by Fonda, Armandariz and Naish, and the presence of the legendary beauty Dolores Del Rio as a Mary Magdalene figure enhances the movie. What truly elevates it, however, is the great cinematography of Gabriel Figueroa who has brought a painter's eye to his work. It is not one of John Ford's greatest films, although he considered it as his favorite.

Fury

1936. 90 min. b.w. U.S. **Prod.** Joseph L. Mankiewicz; **Dir.** Fritz Lang; **Scr.** Bartlett Cormack, Fritz Lang (based on the story by Norman Krasna); **Cin.** Joseph Ruttenberg; **Ed.** Frank Sullivan; **Art D.** Cedric Gibbons, William Horning, Edwin B. Willis; **Mus.** Franz Waxman; **Cast:** Spencer Tracy, Sylvia Sidney, Walter Abel, Edward Ellis, Walter Brennan, Bruce Cabot, George Walcott, Frank Albertson.

Fury was one of the first films that dealt with mob mentality. An innocent man, Joe Wilson (Spencer Tracy), is falsely charged with kidnapping and is imprisoned pending trial. Incited by the local roughneck, a mob sets the jail on fire. Wilson miraculously escapes unseen and is presumed dead. A brave district attorney charges twenty-four citizens with murder and they are put on trial. Wilson, bent on revenge, remains in hiding, listening on the radio to the proceedings. A powerful study of mob rule, the film has some potent images: a hysterical woman hurling a torch on the cans of kerosene piled up at the jailhouse door; and a woman holding her child up to get a better view of the raging fire. The film also shows how mob violence can change an innocent man into a vengeful animal. *Fury* was Fritz Lang's first Hollywood film and he introduced his expressionistic lighting and shadows. It was also Spencer Tracy's first leading role and he dominates the film. There is good acting by Walter Abel as the D.A. and Sylvia Sidney as Wilson's fiancée. What weakens the film is the studio's insistence on a contrived ending.

The Garden of the Finzi-Continis

Il Giardino Dei Finzi-Contini. 1971. 95 min. color. Italian. **Prod.** Arthur Cohn, Gianni Hecht Lucari; **Dir.** Vittorio De Sica; **Scr.** Cesare Zavattini, Vittorio Bonicelli, Ugo Pirro (based on the novel by Giorgio Bassani); **Cin.** Ennio Guarnieri; **Ed.** Adriana Novelli; **Art D.** Giancarlo Bartolini, Salimbeni; **Mus.** Manuel De Sica; **Cast:** Dominique Sanda, Lino Capolicchio, Helmut Berger, Fabio Testi, Romolo Valli, Raffaele Curi.

Set in Ferrara during Mussolini's Fascist dictatorship, the film begins in 1938 and ends in 1943. It tells the story of a prosperous

Jewish family who have chosen to remain in Italy as they cannot imagine being harmed. They live on a large estate, totally oblivious to the world outside. Even when Mussolini begins to fashion his country on the model of Nazi Germany they refuse to flee. They soon are rounded up and sent to an extermination camp. The film has a lyrical beauty and serenity despite its horrifying end. Beautifully photographed, it was the best of Vittorio De Sica in almost fifteen years. There is a haunting score by De Sica's son, Manuel De Sica. Where the film falls short is in a weak cast.

Gaslight

1944. 114 min. b.w. U.S. **Prod.** Arthur Hornblow, Jr.; **Dir.** George Cukor; **Scr.** John Van Druten, Walter Reisch, John Balderston (based on the play *Angel Street* by Patrick Hamilton); **Cin.** Joseph Ruttenberg; **Ed.** Ralph E. Winters; **Art D.** Cedric Gibbons, William Ferrari; **Mus.** Broneslau Kaper; **Cast:** Ingrid Bergman, Charles Boyer, Joseph Cotton, Dame May Whitty, Angela Lansbury.

This is the story of a man attempting to torment his wife to madness. The British-made 1940 version of *Gaslight* is superior to this MGM movie, which is too glossy and some half hour longer. There are several unnecessary additions: the honeymoon of Charles Boyer and Ingrid Bergman in Italy; the wasteful casting of Joseph Cotton, a very fine actor, solely to intimate a budding romance with Bergman once her husband has been found out. But there are redeeming features in the American film. Charles Boyer's portrayal is almost comparable to Anton Walbrook's, and Ingrid Bergman, in her Academy Award-winning role, gives one of her best performances. Angela Lansbury, in her first Hollywood film, is excellent as the devious maid. George Cukor was a very good actor's director and elicited fine performances over the years.

Gate of Hell

Jigokumen. 1953. 89 min. color. Japanese. **Prod.** Masaichi Nagata; **Dir.** Teinosuke Kinugasa; **Scr.** Teinosuke Kinugasa (based on a play by Kan Kikuchi); **Cin.** Kohei Sugiyama; **Mus.** Yasushi Akutagawa; **Cast:** Machiko Kyo, Kazuo Hasegawa, Isao Yamagata, Koreya Senda, Yataro Kurokawa, Kikue Mohri.

Set in twelfth-century Japan, a proud and victorious warrior, Moritoh (Kazuo Hasegawa), is offered by his grateful ruler anything his heart desires. Moritoh asks for the hand of a beautiful woman, Lady Kesa (Machiko Kyo), whose life he had saved during a palace revolt. He is told she is already married, but Moritoh insists and remains adamant. Attempts are made by the ruler and his court to persuade Lady Kesa to leave her husband, but she is devoted to him and refuses. Moritoh pursues his demand, ultimately driving Lady Kesa to suicide. In his sorrow Moritoh becomes a monk. The director, Teinosuke Kinugasa, has made a number of films beginning in the silent era, but it appears *Gate of Hell* is the only one that is available in the U.S. and the U.K. Its greatest asset is its stunning color. The film won the Academy Award for best foreign film in 1954 and the Grand Prize at Cannes.

The Ghost and Mrs. Muir

1947. 104 min. b.w. U.S. **Prod.** Fred Kolmar; **Dir.** Joseph Mankiewicz; **Scr.** Philip Dunne (based on the novel by R. A. Dick); **Cin.** Charles Lang; **Ed.** Dorothy Spencer; **Art D.** Richard Day, George W. Davis; **Mus.** Bernard Herrmann; **Cast:** Gene Tierney, Rex Harrison, George Sanders, Vanessa Brown, Robert Coote, Natalie Wood, Edna Best.

A widow (Gene Tierney) buys a coastal cottage that is haunted by the ghost of a previous owner, a dashing sea captain (Rex Harrison). He unsuccessfully tries to frighten the widow away and the two stubborn characters grow to respect one another. He saves her from a married suitor (George Sanders) and when her money runs out he dictates his life story to her, which she sells as a novel. They fall in love, but it is an impossible relationship. He returns to his own world and leaves the widow to rejoin the living. This charming romance is made more enchanting by the chemistry between the two leads. Gene Tierney, one of the most beautiful women to appear in films, has one of her best roles. It is an imaginative story with a fine musical score that enhances the mood.

Gold Diggers of 1933

1933. 96 min. b.w. U.S. **Prod.** Robert Lord; **Dir.** Mervyn LeRoy; **Scr.** Erwin Gelsey, James Seymour, David Boehm, Ben Markson (based on the play *Gold Diggers of Broadway* by Avery Hopwood); **Cin.** Sol Polito; **Ed.** George Amy; **Art D.** Anton Grot; **Mus.** songs by Harry Warren and Al Dubin; **Chor.** Busby Berkeley; **Cast:** Warren William, Joan Blondell, Ruby Keeler, Aline MacMahon, Dick Powell, Ginger Rogers, Guy Kibbee, Sterling Holloway, Ned Sparks.

In this thinly plotted film, a rich, wellborn young man who is an aspiring composer in love with a showgirl of whom his family disapproves. He writes a musical show starring his sweetheart that becomes a huge success. What makes this movie different is that it is the only musical about the Great Depression of 1929 and pleads the cause of the common man. The opening number has Ginger Rogers dressed from head to toe in silver dollars, singing, "We're in the Money." When she finishes her song the cast is told the show can't go on because the producer is bankrupt. Concluding the film is a very original number, "Forgotten Man," about World War I veterans now unemployed and destitute, with hundreds of extras marching as returning veterans, their rows being transformed into a shuffling bread line. Warner Bros. Studios infused many of its movies with social issues. The film opened in Washington, D.C., on the day of Roosevelt's inauguration in March 1933 and was advertised as "a new deal in entertainment," echoing F.D.R.'s "New Deal" promise. This minor film is also remembered for Busby Berkeley's over-the-top choreography.

534 MY FAVORITE FILMS

The Golden Coach

Le Carrosse D'Or. 1952. 105 min. color. French/Italian; **Prod.** Francesco Alliata; **Dir.** Jean Renoir; **Scr.** Jean Renoir, Renzo Avanzo, Jack Kirkland, Ginette Doynel, Giulio Macchi (based on the play *La Carrosse du Saint-Sacrement* by Prosper Merimee); **Cin.** Claude Renoir, Ronald Hill; **Ed.** Mario Serandrei, David Hawkins; **Mus.** Antonio Vivaldi; **Cast:** Anna Magnani, Odoardo Spadaro, Nada Fiorelli, Dante, Duncan Lamont, George Higgins, Ralph Truman, Paul Campbell, Ricardo Rioli.

Set in eighteenth-century Peru, *The Golden Coach* tells the story of a troupe of Comedia dell'Arte actors touring South America. The mainstay of the troupe is its leading actress, Camilla (Anna Magnani). She captivates the hearts of the Spanish viceroy, a romantic officer and a vain bullfighter. When the viceroy presents her with his prized golden coach, made for kings and used only on royal occasions, it appears he will win her. But Camilla's heart is with the theatre and she makes a gift of the coach to the church. The film represents Jean Renoir's third and last phase of filmmaking, following the French and American periods, and his return to Europe after making *The River* (1951) in India. *The Golden Coach* is somewhat stagy, but this is compensated for by beautiful cinematography by Claude Renoir, dazzling color and décor, and the best acting of Anna Magnani's career. The film also shows Jean Renoir's fascination with theater and his love of actors.

The Good Earth

1937. 138 min. b.w. U.S. **Prod.** Irving Thalberg, Albert Lewin; **Dir.** Sidney Franklin; **Scr.** Talbot Jennings, Tess Slesinger, Frances Marion (uncredited), Claudine West (based on the novel by Pearl S. Buck); **Cin.** Karl Freund; **Ed.** Basil Wrangell; **Art D.** Cedric Gibbons, Harry Oliver, Arnold Gillespie; **Mus.** Herbert Stothart; **Cast:** Paul Muni, Luise Rainer, Walter Connolly, Charley Grapewin, Key Luke, Tilly Losch, Jessie Ralph.

A typical grand MGM melodrama, *The Good Earth* tells the story of the hardships and ultimate success of a poor Chinese rice farmer and his wife. What makes the film still good to watch is the great feats of cinematography that capture some extraordinary scenes: the invasion of locusts and the mob scenes in the midst of a revolution. The film also has one of the most subtle and moving performances by Luise Rainer, which won her an Academy Award as best actress.

Grand Hotel

1932. 113 min. b.w. U.S. **Prod.** Irving Thalberg; **Dir.** Edmund Goulding; **Scr.** William A. Drake (based on the novel *Menschen im Hotel* by Vicki Baum); **Cin.** William Daniels; **Ed.** Blanche Sewell; **Art D.** Cedric Gibbons; **Cast:** Greta Garbo, John Barrymore, Joan Crawford, Wallace Beery, Lionel Barrymore, Lewis Stone, Jean Hersholt.

This star-studded film looks at the entangled lives of five people staying at Berlin's Grand Hotel during the Weimar Republic. Greta Garbo is a tired and disillusioned prima ballerina. John Barrymore is a nobleman who has become a thief and intends to rob Garbo, but they fall in love. Wallace Beery is an unprincipled textile tycoon facing bankruptcy. He is accompanied by Joan Crawford, an attractive, ambitious stenographer. Lionel Barrymore is a simple bookkeeper who is dying of an incurable disease and is spending all his savings enjoying a brief stay at the Grand Hotel. Lewis Stone, as a doctor and Jean Hersholt as the head porter serve as a Greek chorus, observing the goings-on. What makes this dated film still enjoyable is the interaction among the leading actors of the day.

Green for Danger

1946. 93 min. b.w. British. **Prod.** Frank Launder, Sidney Gilliat; **Dir.** Sidney Gilliat; **Scr.** Sidney Gilliat, Claude Guerney (based on a novel by Christianna Brand); **Cin.** Wilkie Cooper; **Ed.** Thelma Myers; **Prod. D.** Peter Proud. **Mus.** William Alwyn; **Cast:** Alistair Sim, Sally Gray, Trevor Howard, Leo Genn, Rosamund John, Judy Campbell, Megs Jenkins, Marc Marriott.

It is 14 August 1944 in wartime Britain. The Germans are attacking with their new weapon, the V-1 buzz bomb. A postman,

Joe Higgins (Marc Marriott), has been slightly injured. We are introduced to the team of doctors and nurses in a makeshift hospital. There is Mr. Eden (Leo Genn), a highly regarded surgeon. Mr. Eden attracts women wherever he is and has left many broken hearts. He is currently involved with Sister Marion Bates (Judy Campbell). (In England surgeons are addressed as "Mr." and senior nurses are addressed as "sister"). The anesthesiologist, Dr. Barney Barnes (Trevor Howard), has a volatile temper and Nurse Linley (Sally Gray) has just broken off her engagement to him. The last character is Nurse Esther Sanson (Rosamund John) who is on the verge of a nervous breakdown following her mother's death in an air raid. The postman dies on the operating table under anesthesia and the death is written off as an accident. A preplanned hospital staff dance goes on and they all are enjoying themselves. Sister Bates who is slightly drunk announces that the postman was murdered and she has the evidence to prove it. She leaves the dance hall and goes to the operating room to retrieve the evidence where she is stabbed to death by someone in a white robe. It is now time for Scotland Yard in the person of Inspector Cockrill (Alistair Sim) to enter the scene. Cockrill brings skill and humor to the investigation. By persistence and clever deduction the murderer is found. The modest Cockrill admits at the end, "Not one of my most successful cases."

The title of the film refers to the murderer's repainting of a carbon dioxide cylinder green so as to be mistaken for oxygen. It is the witty script of Sidney Gilliat who was one of the writers for the skillful *The Lady Vanishes* (1938) that makes this film a small gem.

The Grey Fox

1982. 92 min. color. Canadian. **Prod.** Peter O'Brian; **Dir.** Philip Borsos; **Scr.** John Hunter; **Cin.** Frank Tidy; **Ed.** Frank Irvine; **Art D.** William Brodie; **Mus.** Michael Conway Baker, The Chieftains; **Cast:** Richard Farnsworth, Jackie Burroughs, Wayne Robson, Ken Pogue, Timothy Webber, Gary Reineke.

In 1863 sixteen-year-old Bill Miner (Richard Farnsworth) holds up the Arizona Pony Express netting $200. He continues robbing stagecoaches in the far West. He is finally captured and spends thirty-three years in San Quentin. He is released in 1901, into the twentieth century, and receives the biggest shock of his life. His first years are spent with his sister and her husband helping with chores on their farm. One day he ventures into town and goes to a nickelodeon. He watches the first American narrative film, *The Great Train Robbery*. He enjoys the film immensely, especially when the robbers make their escape attempt. He later spends a great deal of time studying trains, forms a gang of three and commits his first train robbery. He escapes to western Canada where he pulls off another robbery netting him several thousands of dollars. He moves east to a Canadian frontier town and meets a cultured middle-aged suffragette, Kate Flynn (Jackie Burroughs). She is a trade union organizer, who is also interested in nature and photography. Soon a strong bond is formed between Flynn and Miner, but Pinkerton detectives are closing in on the fugitive. Kate Flynn moves to Chicago and opens a successful photography shop. Miner pulls one last job and we later learn the two have traveled and settled in Europe.

The Grey Fox is a low-budget minor gem starring a sixty-two-year-old former stuntman in his first leading role. The film successfully depicts a country in transition, a delicate love story and some beautiful landscape scenery. The story is based on a real-life train robber, Bill Miner, very well played by Farnsworth. Jackie Burroughs and the rest of the cast are equally convincing. The pace of the film is measured and lyrical.

Gunga Din

1939. 117 min. b.w. U.S. **Prod.** George Stevens; **Dir.** George Stevens; **Scr.** Fred Guiol (based on the story by Ben Hecht, Charles MacArthur, William Faulkner from the poem by Rudyard Kipling); **Cin.** Joseph August; **Ed.** Henry Berman, John Lockert; **Art D.** Van Nest Polglase, Perry Ferguson; **Mus.** Alfred Newman; **Cast:** Cary Grant, Victor McLaglen, Douglas Fairbanks, Jr., Joan Fontaine, Sam Jaffe, Eduardo Ciannelli, Montagu Love, Robert Coote, Cecil Kellaway.

Gunga Din is another film of the British Raj that Hollywood studios turned out in the thirties along with *Lives of a Bengal Lancer* (Paramount 1935) and *The Rains Came* (Fox 1939), among others. Not to be outdone, RKO spent some $2 million and made *Gunga Din*, an expansion of a short Kipling poem. The film is about three army sergeants who kill Indians with abandon. It is a well-made film with excellent cinematography and a rousing score. The acting also stands out, particularly Cary Grant and Victor McLaglen. But the person who stays in one's mind is the unforgettably menacing, blood-thirsty Eduardo Ciannelli as the leader of the Indian rebels. No viewer can resist this "fun" picture although one cringes at its racial content.

Hail the Conquering Hero

1944. 101 min. b.w. U.S. **Prod.** Preston Sturges; **Dir.** Preston Sturges; **Scr.** Preston Sturges; **Cin.** John Seitz; **Ed.** Stuart Gilmore; **Art D.** Hans Dreier, Haldane Douglas; **Mus.** Werner R. Heymann; **Cast:** Eddie Bracken, Ella Raines, Raymond Walburn, William Demarest, Elizabeth Patterson, Franklin Pangborn, Bill Edwards, Jimmie Dundee, Freddie Steele, Georgia Caine.

Woodrow Lafayette Pershing Truesmith (Eddie Bracken), the son of a deceased World War I hero, enlists in the Marines but is discharged for severe hay fever. He is ashamed to go home and writes his mother that he has been sent overseas. He also writes his girl (Ella Raines) that he doesn't love her anymore and she is free to marry someone else. In the meantime he gets a job as a shipyard worker in another town. At a bar he runs into a group of

Marines, real heroes just back from Guadalcanal, who take pity on Truesmith drowning in his beer. They talk him into going home, because it is not fair to his mother. They make him wear a uniform and without his knowing send a letter to his mom and fiancée, indicating that Truesmith is a combat hero. He is welcomed at the train station by the whole town, two brass bands and the mayor. Things begin to get complicated when he is nominated to run against the incumbent mayor.

Hail the Conquering Hero is an original film from one of the most original writer/directors in filmmaking. It pokes fun at several American sacred cows—heroism and momism. The film has a witty script with sharp dialogue and some great acting by seasoned pros William Demarest, Raymond Walburn and Franklin Pangborn. Preston Sturges also made *The Miracle of Morgan's Creek* in the same year and received Academy Award nominations for best original screenplay for both films.

Hamlet

1948. 155 min. b.w. British. **Prod.** Laurence Olivier; **Dir.** Laurence Olivier; **Scr.** Alan Dent (based on the play by William Shakespeare); **Cin.** Desmond Dickinson; **Ed.** Helga Cranston; **Art D.** Carmen Dillon; **Mus.** William Walton; **Cast:** Laurence Olivier, Eileen Herlie, Basil Sidney, Felix Aylmer, Jean Simmons, Stanley Holloway, Peter Cushing, Terrence Morgan, Norman Wooland.

Heavily influenced by the Shakespearean critic J. Dover Wilson and a noted psychoanalyst Ernest Jones, it is the most Oedipal *Hamlet* on stage or screen. Never an exceptional film director, Laurence Olivier appears to be at a loss as to where the camera should be. The scenes are full of shadows and his camera often ineffectively wanders along badly lit empty corridors or to the top of Elsinore Castle. It is nevertheless a noble effort, and is still a superior *Hamlet* to the 1969 Tony Richardson, the 1996 Kenneth Branagh and the Russian 1964 Kozintsev productions. Olivier has been criticized for eliminating the parts of Rosencrantz and Guildenstern and two soliloquys. *Hamlet* is Shakespeare's longest play. Olivier had little choice as the film, presently at 155 minutes, would have run 240 minutes. The cuts were intelligently made. Olivier is fine in the role of Hamlet but the more interesting performances are by Stanley Holloway as the gravedigger, Eileen Herlie as Queen Gertrude, Felix Aylmer as Polonius and Jean Simmons as Ophelia. The film received a host of Academy Awards including best picture, best actor best art direction, and several nominations.

Hamlet

1964. 150 min. b.w. Russian. **Dir.** Grigori Kozintsev; **Scr.** Grigori Kozintsev (based on Boris Pasternak's translation of the play by William Shakespeare); **Cin.** Jonas Gritsyus; **Mus.** Shostakovich; **Cast:** Innokenti Smoktunovsky, Michail Nazvanov, Elza Radzin-Szolkonis, Yuri Tolubeyev, Anastasia Vertinskaya, S. Oleksenko.

Although this Hamlet (Innokenti Smoktunovsky) takes his time to avenge his father's murder, he is not detained by any psychological inhibitions. He is bold, quick tempered and not given much to rumination. He is closer to Nicol Williamson's 1969 Hamlet than Laurence Olivier's 1948 portrayal. The very first scene differentiates him from Olivier. We see him riding furiously toward Elsinore. This *Hamlet* is about power politics and territorial expansion, and at the end Fortinbras not only restores order, he annexes a country. In addition to being well acted and photographed, it is translated into Russian by the great Russian poet, Boris Pasternak, and there is a very good score by Shostakovich. The production, however, is as stagy as Olivier's and some of the soliloquys have been shortened. "To be or not to be" is a mere six lines. The film was made in celebration of the four hundredth anniversary of Shakespeare's birth.

Harvey

1950. 104 min. b.w. U.S. **Prod.** John Beck; **Dir.** Henry Koster; **Scr.** Mary Chase, Oscar Brodney (based on the play by Chase); **Cin.** William Daniels; **Ed.** Ralph Dawson; **Art D.** Nathan Juran, Bernard Herzbrun; **Mus.** Frank Skinner; **Cast:** James Stewart, Josephine Hull, Peggy Dow, Charles Drake, Cecil Kellaway, Victoria Horne, Jesse White, Wallace Ford.

Affable Elwood P. Dowd (James Stewart), having been hurt by reality, lives in a dream world with his friend, Harvey, a six-foot rabbit who is invisible to everyone but Elwood. He is an embarrassment to his family, and his somewhat dizzy sister, Veta (Josephine Hull), tries to have him committed to an institution. Even the attempted commitment is handled with gentle humor and Veta changes her mind. There is a fine cast of professionals. James Stewart's special brand of charm was perfect for his role.

He Walked by Night

1948. 79 min. b.w. U.S. **Prod.** Robert T. Kane; **Dir.** Alfred L. Werker; **Scr.** John C. Higgins, Crane Wilbur, Harry Essex (uncredited), Beck Murray (based on a story by Wilbur); **Cin.** John Alton; **Ed.** Al De Gaetano; **Art D.** Edward L. Ilou; **Mus.** Leonid Raab; **Cast:** Richard Basehart, Scott Brady, Roy Roberts, Whit Bissell, Jack Webb, James Cardwell.

A low-budget minor film, *He Walked by Night* is as well made as any of the better-known and better-praised thrillers. The final chase scene in L.A. sewers with the thief/cop killer stands out. The underrated Richard Basehart does a fine job.

Heaven Can Wait

1943. 112 min. color. U.S. **Prod.** Ernst Lubitsch; **Dir.** Ernst Lubitsch; **Scr.** Samson Raphaelson (based on the play *Birthdays* by Ladislaus Bus-Fekete); **Cin.** Edward Cronjager; **Ed.** Dorothy Spencer; **Art D.** James Basevi, Leland Fuller; **Mus.** Alfred Newman; **Cast:** Gene Tierney, Don Ameche, Charles Coburn, Marjory Main, Laird Kregar, Spring Byington, Allyn Joslyn, Eugene Pallette, Signe Hasso, Louis Calhern.

Don Ameche has died and stands before the Devil requesting admission to hell, feeling that he has been a terrible sinner. His life is reviewed in an infancy to death flashback. Despite Ameche's lifetime of peccadillos his one true love is Gene Tierney. He is shown to be not as wicked as he had supposed. An appealing romantic comedy by Ernst Lubitsch, the master of the form. It also has Ameche's charming portrayal, Tierney's beauty and a witty script by Samson Raphaelson.

Hobson's Choice

1954. 107 min. b.w. British. **Prod.** David Lean; **Dir.** David Lean; **Scr.** David Lean, Norman Spencer, Wynyard Browne (based on the play by Harold Brighouse); **Cin.** Jack Hildyard; **Ed.** Peter Taylor; **Prod. D.** Wilfred Shingleton; **Mus.** Malcolm Arnold; **Cast:** Charles Laughton, John Mills, Brenda de Banzie, Prunella Scales, Richard Wattis, Daphne Anderson, Helen Haye.

This rare David Lean comedy is set in the 1890s in the English Midlands. Charles Laughton, a boozing widower, owns the best boot shop in town. He has three unmarried daughters who help. He is a tyrant who rules over his daughters and has no intention of letting them marry because if they left he would have to pay wages to their replacements. The eldest daughter, Brenda de Banzie, is thirty and "on the shelf." She runs the business and puts her drunken father to bed every night. She eventually revolts and marries John Mills, an illiterate, simpleminded worker who is the best boot maker they have. When her father refuses to give her a dowry, she opens a rival shop with the help of a well-to-do former customer. Soon she becomes a successful competitor to her father and under favorable terms they merge. With her help, her two sisters are also married off. There is fine acting by Laughton and de Banzie. This excellent comedy is somewhat slow and creaks a bit toward the end.

Hold Back the Dawn

1941. 115 min. b.w. U.S. **Prod.** Arthur Hornblow, Jr.; **Dir.** Mitchell Leisen; **Scr.** Charles Brackett, Billy Wilder (based on a story by Ketti Frings); **Cin.** Leo Tover; **Ed.** Doane Harrison; **Art D.** Hans Dreier, Robert Usher; **Mus.** Victor Young; **Cast:** Charles Boyer, Olivia de Havilland, Paulette Goddard, Victor Francen, Walter Abel, Rosemary De Camp.

Charles Boyer is a Romanian émigré living in a run-down hotel in a Mexican town near the U.S. border that houses refugees fleeing the Nazi occupation of Europe. He had been a gigolo and ladies' escort. His only chance of gaining entry to the U.S. is if he marries an American citizen. He finds an easy prey, a spinster schoolmarm (Olivia de Havilland) who has brought a busload of schoolgirls to Mexico for the Fourth of July weekend. He courts and marries her. But he becomes conscience stricken when his past is exposed by a former mistress (Paulette Goddard). The story continues with several unexpected twists. There is a most unusual opening scene when Boyer, who has gained entry to the U.S., approaches the film's director, Mitchell Leisen, who is on a set directing another film and tries to sell him his story. The film then goes to a long flashback. This sort of enticing reverse opening was later used by scriptwriters Wilder and Bracket in *Double Indemnity* (1944) and with greater effect in *Sunset Boulevard* (1950). *Hold Back the Dawn* is a well-directed film. The scenes at the dilapidated hotel with desperate refugees are realistically done. Boyer and de Havilland handle their roles sensitively, and the acting of Victor Francen, the great Belgian actor, as a Dutch refugee professor who is a father figure to the others stands out.

Leisen had a long career as a director and made several highly entertaining and well-made movies, the most notable being *Midnight* (1939) and *Golden Earrings* (1947).

Hombre

1967. 111 min. color. U.S. **Prod.** Martin Ritt, Irving Ravetch; **Dir.** Martin Ritt; **Scr.** Irving Ravetch, Harriet Frank, Jr., (based on the novel by Elmore Leonard); **Cin.** James Wong Howe; **Ed.** Frank Bracht; **Art D.** Jack Martin Smith, Robert E. Smith; **Mus.** David Rose; **Cast:** Paul Newman, Fredric March, Richard Boone, Diane Cilento, Cameron Mitchell, Barbara Rush, Martin Balsam.

An offbeat western set in the 1880s in Arizona; *Hombre* has similarities to *Stagecoach*, but is not nearly as good. It deals with some of the same issues, mainly duplicity and hypocrisy. A white boy (Paul Newman) raised by Indians is shunned by fellow passengers on a stagecoach, but when their lives are at stake he is begged to be their leader. Finely acted by Newman and Richard Boone who is perfect as a mean bandit.

Hope and Glory

1987. 113 min. color. British. **Prod.** John Boorman, Michael Dryhurst; **Dir.** John Boorman; **Scr.** John Boorman; **Cin.** Philippe Rousselot, John Harris; **Ed.** Ian Crafford; **Prod. D.** Anthony Pratt; **Art D.** Don Dossett; **Mus.** Peter Martin; **Cast:** Sarah Miles, David Hayman, Derrick O'Connor, Ian Bannen, Sebastian Rice Edwards, Geraldine Muir, Sammi Davis, Sara Langton.

Hope and Glory is the story of an English family during the Second World War at the height of the Blitz. It is told in a series of episodes as seen through the eyes of a nine-year-old boy, Bill Rohan. To young Bill the day and night bombardments by the Luftwaffe are just one exciting, nonending display of fireworks. When their modest house is burned down, the mother, Grace (Sarah Miles), takes her son and older daughter to a London suburb near the Thames to live with their grandparents. The film shows how wartime sorrows can become commonplace and how values shift during war; the games the boys play in the destruction and rubble that surrounds them, and Bill's older sister with her "overfed and oversexed" GI boyfriends. It is partially an autobiographical account by John Boorman—who produced and directed the film, and wrote the screenplay—of what it was like to grow up in wartime England.

Hopscotch

1980. 104 min. color. U.S. **Prod.** Edie Landau, Ely Landau; **Dir.** Ronald Neame; **Scr.** Brian Garfield, Bryan Forbes (based on the novel by Garfield); **Cin.** Arthur Ibbetson; **Ed.** Carl Kress; **Prod. D.** William J. Creber; **Mus.** Ian Fraser; **Cast:** Walter Matthau, Glenda Jackson, Sam Waterston, Ned Beatty, Herbert Lom.

Experienced CIA agent Miles Kendig (Walter Matthau), deliberately lets a Soviet spy (Herbert Lom) get away in Germany because he could be of use to him later. His shortsighted superior in Washington (Ned Beatty) is upset and demotes him to a desk job. Kendig thoroughly disillusioned destroys all his personnel files and takes off for Salzburg to see an old flame and former agent (Glenda Jackson). He begins to write his memoirs to embarrass the entire international espionage community and mails each completed chapter to intelligence agencies in the world's major capitals. He is now the target of Washington, Moscow, London and Paris and a concerted effort is made to stop Kendig. The movie bears a resemblance to *Charley Varick* (1973) where Matthau made fools of the Mafia. Here he ridicules the great spy organizations. *Hopscotch* could have been much better. The script is too thin and the best parts of the movie are in the first hour. It is still very funny and provides a perfect role for the talents of Matthau.

Horse Feathers

1932. 68 min. b.w. U.S. **Prod.** Herman J. Mankiewicz; **Dir.** Norman Z. McLeod; **Scr.** Bert Kalmar, Harry Ruby, S. J. Perelman; **Cin.** Ray June, **Mus.** Bert Kalmar, Harry Ruby; **Cast:** Groucho, Harpo, Chico and Zeppo Marx, Thelma Todd, David Landua, Robert Greig, Nat Pendleton, Florine McKinney.

Horse Feathers is one of the better Marx brothers films during their tenure at Paramount but by no means their best. This time

Groucho is Professor Quincy Adams Wagstaff recently named president of Huxley College, which hasn't won a single football game since its founding in 1888. The film is about Groucho trying to recruit a football team—academic excellence and pursuit of learning be damned. As always there are the great one-liners. Groucho to his son Zeppo, who has not graduated after ten years in college: "I'd horsewhip you if I had a horse." The password to get into a speakeasy is "fish." Groucho to Chico, the doorman, "Sturgeon." Chico; "You're crazy. Sturgeon is a doctor who cuts you up."

The House on 92nd St.

1945. 88 min. b.w. U.S. **Prod.** Louis de Rochemont; **Dir.** Henry Hathaway; **Scr.** Barre Lyndon, Charles G. Booth, John Monks, Jr. (based on the story by Booth); **Cin.** Norbert Brodine; **Ed.** Harmon Jones; **Art D.** Lyle Wheeler, Lewis Creber; **Mus.** David Buttolph; **Cast:** William Eythe, Lloyd Nolan, Signe Hasso, Gene Lockhart, Leo G. Caroll.

The film, set in 1941–2, is based on an actual case. A brilliant German–American university student (William Eythe) in a Midwestern college is approached by German agents. He reports it to the FBI. At their recommendation he accepts the offer of a training course in Germany and on his return becomes a double agent and helps to expose the Nazi espionage ring. The film may have dated a little but it is very well made by Henry Hathaway, one of the pioneers of docudrama: *13 Rue Madeleine* (1947) and the very effective *Call Northside 777* (1948). Shot on location in New York City, some actual FBI surveillance footage has been woven into the film that gives it further authenticity.

Howard's End

1992. 140 min. color. British. **Prod.** Ismail Merchant; **Dir.** James Ivory; **Scr.** Ruth Prawer Jhabvala (based on the novel by E. M. Forster); **Cin.** Tony Pierce Roberts; **Ed.** Andrew Marcus; **Prod. D.** Luciana Arrighi; **Art D.** John Ralph; **Mus.** Richard Robbins; **Cast:** Anthony Hopkins, Vanessa Redgrave, Helena Bonham Carter, Emma Thompson, James Wilby, Jemma Redgrave, Sam West, Prunella Scales, Joseph Bennett, Simon Callow.

Based on a 1910 E. M. Forster novel, this film is largely about the British class system. Upper-class Vanessa Redgrave who is in failing health befriends an intelligent, cultured, middle-class young woman (Emma Thompson) with whom she feels a strong rapport. As she is dying she writes a note bequeathing Howard's End, the estate where she was born and which she dearly loves, to her new young friend. Her class-conscious, ill-intentioned husband (Anthony Hopkins) and their daughter destroy the note. In a strange unexpected way Redgrave's wish is finally fulfilled. Not Merchant/Ivory's best film, but the superb acting of Vanessa Redgrave, Anthony Hopkins and Emma Thompson makes it noteworthy.

I Am a Fugitive from a Chain Gang

1932. 93 min. b.w. U.S. **Prod.** Hal B. Wallis; **Dir.** Mervin LeRoy; **Scr.** Howard J. Green, Brown Holmes, Sheridan Gibney (based on the autobiography *I Am a Fugitive from a Georgia Chain Gang* by Robert Elliot Burns); **Cin.** Sol Polito; **Ed.** William Holmes; **Art D.** Jock Okey; **Mus.** Leo Forbstein; **Cast:** Paul Muni, Glenda Farrell, Helen Vinson, Preston Foster, Allen Jenkins.

A World War I veteran is out of work and takes to the road. While in a Georgia town, he involuntarily becomes involved in a $15 holdup at a diner. He is arrested and sentenced to ten years of hard labor. He escapes, and over the course of time becomes the head of a construction company. His duplicitous wife informs on him. The northern state where he is living refuses extradition, so the state of Georgia offers that if he voluntarily returns he will be pardoned after serving only ninety days. The state reneges on its promise and he is put back on the chain gang and worked sixteen hours a day. He escapes again but is now forced to live the life of a vagrant, sleeping by day, traveling at night, and pilfering food. A true story, based on the life of Robert Elliot Burns. Paul Muni does him justice. It is a typical Warner Brothers socially conscious Depression-era film of the thirties. Though it is somewhat melodramatic and dated, it is still absorbing. It was banned in the state of Georgia and prompted a lawsuit against Warner Brothers that was resolved out of court.

I Never Sang for My Father

1970. 93 min. color. U.S. **Prod.** Gilbert Cates; **Dir.** Gilbert Cates; **Scr.** Robert W. Anderson (based on his play); **Cin.** Morris Hartzband, George Stoetzel; **Ed.** Angelo Ross; **Art D.** Hank Aldrich; **Mus.** Barry Mann, Al Gorgoni; **Cast:** Melvyn Douglas, Gene Hackman, Dorothy Stickney, Estelle Parsons.

Gene Hackman plays a middle-aged repressed college professor. In an uncharacteristic bold move he tells his mother he intends to marry a widowed doctor, leave New York and move to California. Just before the wedding his mother dies of a heart attack and he is left to care for his demanding father who had never reciprocated his love. His plans are altered and now he will never be able to sever the paternal chain. This depressing film has one of the finest pieces of ensemble acting. Melvyn Douglas, in the twilight of a distinguished career as the aged father, and Gene Hackman give what are among the great performances in film history. Douglas was nominated for best actor and Hackman for best supporting actor.

I Remember Mama

1948. 134 min. b.w. U.S. **Prod.** Harriet Parsons; **Dir.** George Stevens; **Scr.** De Witt Bodeen (based on the play by John Van Druten and the novel *Mama's Bank Account* by Kathryn Forbes); **Cin.** Nicholas Musuraca; **Ed.** Robert Swink, Tholen Gladden; **Art D.** Albert S. D'Agostino, Carroll Clark; **Mus.** Roy Webb; **Cast:** Irene Dunne, Barbara Bel Geddes, Oscar Homolka, Philip Dorn, Cedric Hardwicke, Edgar Bergen, Rudy Vallee, Florence Bates, Ellen Corby, Barbara O'Neil.

This is the story of a Norwegian immigrant family in San Francisco at the turn of the twentieth century. It is beautifully told and well acted by a cast headed by Irene Dunne as Mama, Barbara Bel Geddes as the eldest daughter, Katrin, and Oscar Homolka as Uncle Chris. Edgar Bergen, the famous ventriloquist/comedian handles his straight role well. *I Remember Mama* is a charming film but too long at 134 minutes.

In the Heat of the Night.

1967. 109 min. color. U.S. **Prod.** Walter Mirisch; **Dir.** Norman Jewison; **Scr.** Stirling Silliphant (based on the novel by John Ball); **Cin.** Haskell Wexler; **Ed.** Al Ashby; **Art D.** Paul Groesse; **Mus.** Quincy Jones; **Cast:** Sidney Poitier, Rod Steiger, Warren Oates, Lee Grant, Larry Gates, Quentin Dean, James Patterson.

Set in Mississippi, a wealthy Northerner who had intended to bring industry and jobs to the small town of Sparta is murdered on the streets at night. A black homicide detective (Sidney Poitier) from Philadelphia who is traveling to Mississippi to see his mother is arrested at the railroad station as a suspect. When his identity is ascertained, he is released and about to leave. But at the urging of the murdered man's widow (Lee Grant) and the Philadelphia Police Department, the bigoted local sheriff (Rod Steiger) is forced to seek his help. There are two strands running through the film. One is Poitier's expertise and methodical approach to finding the killer and the other is the bond of friendship and respect that develops between the two very different cops. A well-paced movie that moves briskly and is finely acted by the entire cast. Where it is not entirely satisfying is in failing to show how Poitier is finally able to identify the murderer. The film won Academy Awards for best picture, best actor (Rod Steiger), adapted screenplay, editing and sound. Norman Jewison also directed some light, entertaining movies: *The Russians Are Coming, The Russians Are Coming* (1967) and *Moonstruck* (1981).

The Informer

1935. 91 min. b.w. U.S. **Prod.** Cliff Reid; **Dir.** John Ford; **Scr.** Dudley Nichols (based on the novel by Liam O'Flaherty); **Cin.** Joseph August; **Ed.** George Hively; **Art D.** Van Nest Polglase, Charles Kirk; **Mus.** Max Steiner; **Cast:** Victor McLaglen, Heather Angel, Preson Foster, Joe Sawyer, Wallace Ford, Donald Meek, Margot Grahame, J. M. Kerrigan, Una O'Conner.

Set in Dublin in 1921 during the occupation of Ireland by British forces and the Sinn Fein (We Ourselves) rebellion. It is the story of the betrayal of a friend and one's own ideals. Gypo Nolan (Victor McLaglen) is an ignorant and not very bright loafer who betrays his fugitive friend Frankie McPhillip (Wallace Ford) to the British for a reward of £20. Gypo had been a member of Sinn Fein but had been court-martialed and expelled for incompetence and unreliability. He is attracted to Katie (Margot Grahame), a shabby street prostitute, with whom he hopes to marry and immigrate with her to America. A boat ticket is £10. When Katie taunts him and says neither of them will ever see £20, Gypo's vanity is pierced. He goes to the British and informs them of Frankie's whereabouts. Frankie is hunted down and killed. Gypo squanders the £20 reward in an orgy of drinking and whoring. The Sinn Fein leadership is alerted and he is brought in for questioning. He denies informing and blames a tailor. He is wounded as he tries to escape and takes refuge in a church where he dies.

The film has a mawkish ending and even at 91 minutes it drags. It shows its age, but it is still a very worthwhile film. John Ford's *The Lost Patrol*, made a year earlier, had gone largely unnoticed. This film established him. The photography of Joseph August is superb and Victor McLaglen gives a performance that he never equaled in the 150 or more films in which he appeared. *The Informer* was nominated for best picture and received Academy Awards for McLaglen as best actor, John Ford as director, Dudley Nichols as screenwriter and best score by Max Steiner.

Inherit the Wind

1960. 127 min. b.w. U.S. **Prod.** Stanley Kramer; **Dir.** Stanley Kramer; **Scr.** Nathan E. Douglas, Harold Jacob Smith (based on the play by Jerome Lawrence, Robert E. Lee); **Cin.** Ernest Laszlo; **Ed.** Frederic Knudtson; **Prod. D.** Rudolph Sternad; **Mus.** Ernest Gold; **Cast:** Spencer Tracy, Fredric March, Gene Kelly, Florence Eldridge, Dick York, Harry (Henry) Morgan, Claude Akins, Noah Beery, Jr.

The film is about the 1925 historic Scopes "monkey trial" in which a Tennessee high-school teacher, John T. Scopes (Dick York), is prosecuted for teaching Darwin's theory of evolution, violating its prohibition by state law. All the names are changed, but the story is true to history. The prosecution is handled by a character portraying the famed fundamentalist and three-time presidential candidate William Jennings Bryan (Fredric March), and the defense by the rationalist and most famed lawyer of the time, Clarence Darrow (Spencer Tracy). It is an explosive court-room duel between the two and is powerfully acted. Only Gene Kelly representing the acerbic journalist H. L. Mencken falls short.

Investigation of a Citizen Above Suspicion

1970. 115 min. color. Italian. **Prod.** Daniele Senatore; **Dir.** Elio Petri; **Scr.** Ugo Pirro, Elio Petri; **Cin.** Luigi Kuveiller; **Ed.** Ruggero Mastroianni; **Prod. D.** Romano Cardarelli; **Mus.** Ennio Morricone; **Cast:** Gian Maria Volonte, Florinda Bolkan, Salvo Randone, Gianni Santuccio, Arturo Dominici.

A member of the Fascist party is promoted to become the head of the homicide department of a large Italian city. He is an arrogant man whose previous job had been to track down political opponents of the regime. In order to test the power of his recently elevated status, he brutally murders his mistress, plants evidence to incriminate himself and anonymously telephones the police to report the murder. The police ignore the evidence and he remains free. Some time later, he writes a confession and sends it to the police. He knows he is above the law and will not be arrested. This Kafkaesque story, which resembles "In a Penal Colony," is an ambitious film by the politically-oriented director Elio Petrie that examines guilt and the masochistic urge to be found out. Somewhat over-directed, the film has a too self-conscious visual style.

The Invisible Man

1933. 71 min. b.w. U.S. **Prod.** Carl Laemmle, Jr.; **Dir.** James Whale; **Scr.** R. C. Sherriff (based on the novel by H. G. Wells); **Cin.** Arthur Edeson; **Ed.** Ted Kent; **Art D.** Charles D. Hall; **Mus.** W. Franke Harling; **Cast:** Claude Rains, Gloria Stuart, William Harrigan, Henry Travers, Una O'Connor, Forrester Harvey, Dudley Digges.

The film begins as a comedy. A scientist (Claude Rains) experiments with a drug that makes one invisible. He plays games on the villagers. However, the drug is mind-altering and his pranks turn into murderous games. This well-made film was imaginatively constructed by James Whale who directed *Frankenstein* (1931) two years earlier. Special effects play an essential part in the film. When the invisible man removes his covering bandages, we don't see anyone. Doors open by themselves; there are footprints in the snow with no one walking; someone is punched in the jaw and we just see the victim. Claude Rain's dramatic voice and a good script play a great part in making the film work.

Isadora

1968. 131 min. color. British. **Prod.** Robert Hakim, Raymond Hakim; **Dir.** Karel Reisz; **Scr.** Melvyn Bragg, Clive Exton, Margaret Drabble (based on *My Life* by Isadora Duncan, and *Isadora Duncan — An Intimate Portrait* by Sewell Stokes); **Cin.** Larry Pizer; **Ed.** Tom Priestley; **Art D.** Jocelyn Herbert; **Mus.** Maurice Jarre; **Cast:** Vanessa Redgrave, James Fox, Jason Robards, Ivan Tchenko, John Fraser, Bessie Love.

The story of the tragic life of Isadora Duncan (Vanessa Redgrave), the founder of the modern dance movement. Duncan was also known for her political idealism and her uninhibited and hedonistic lifestyle. She scandalized European and American society by her marriages and numerous lovers. An ambitious film that had the potential of being a great film, but it is too episodic and lacks logical continuity. It is also too venturesome in attempting to portray ancient Greek dance. The film is dominated by the great actress Vanessa Redgrave, who, though not a dancer, gives an excellent portrayal.

It Happens Every Spring

1949. 87 min. b.w. U.S. **Prod.** William Perlberg; **Dir.** Lloyd Bacon; **Scr.** Valentine Davies; **Cin.** Joseph MacDonald; **Ed.** Bruce B. Pierce; **Art D.** Lyle Wheeler, J. Russell Spencer; **Mus.** Leigh Harline; **Cast:** Ray Milland, Jean Peters, Paul Douglas, Ed Begley, Ted de Corsia, Ray Collins, Jessie Royce Landis, Alan Hale, Jr., Debra Paget.

An unpretentious film with a witty script and excellent cast, it tells the story of a chemistry professor (Ray Milland) who by accident discovers a formula that repels wood. As an ardent baseball fan, the first thing he thinks of is baseball bats. He leaves the university, becomes a major league pitcher, has a twenty-game season and wins the last game of the World Series. Ray Milland brings an unassuming charm to his role. Paul Douglas as his catcher is excellent as always in light comedy roles. Some old pros—Ed Begley, Ray Collins and Jesse Royce Landis—contribute greatly to this winsome film.

Johnny Belinda

1948. 103 min. b.w. U.S. **Prod.** Jerry Wald; **Dir.** Jean Negulesco; **Scr.** Irmgard Von Cube, Allen Vincent (based on the play by Elmer Harris); **Cin.** Ted McCord; **Ed.** David Weisbart; **Art D.** Robert Haas; **Mus.** Max Steiner; **Cast:** Jane Wyman, Lew Ayres, Charles Bickford, Jan Sterling, Agnes Morehead, Stephen McNally, Alan Napier, Dan Seymour.

Set in a small New England coastal town, it is the story of a deaf and mute girl (Jane Wyman) whose mother died in childbirth. She learns sign language from the local doctor (Lew Ayres) and begins to communicate. She is raped by a local fisherman (Stephen McNally) and gives birth to a child. The community believes it is the doctor who fathered the child. A well-crafted film with Jane Wyman giving a moving portrayal of innocence. Wyman had mostly appeared in light comedy roles and few expected her excellent performance. This was also the best directorial effort of Jean Negulesco who began as a painter and came into films as a set designer. Wyman received an Academy Award as best actress.

Johnny Guitar

1954. 110 min. color. U.S. **Prod.** Herbert J. Yates; **Dir.** Nicholas Ray; **Scr.** Philip Yordan (based on the novel by Roy Chanslor); **Cin.** Harry Stradling; **Ed.** Richard L. Van Enger; **Art D.** James Sullivan; **Mus.** Victor Young; **Cast:** Joan Crawford, Sterling Hayden, Scott Brady, Mercedes McCambridge, Ward Bond, Ben Cooper, Ernest Borgnine, Royal Dano, John Carradine, Paul Fix, Frank Ferguson.

Johnny Guitar is the oddest cowboy film. All the roles are reversed. The saloon girl now owns the place. She wears cowboy clothes, all in black, and packs a gun in a studded holster. The male protagonists are a dancer and a guitar player who vie for her affection. Her enemy is a sexually starved woman who wants to drive her out of town. Yet this confusing film has its moments.

Jour de Fête.

1949. 70 min. b.w. French. **Prod.** Fred Orain; **Dir.** Jacques Tati; **Scr.** Jacques Tati, Rene Wheeler, Henri Marquet; **Cin.** Jacques Mercanton; **Ed.** Marcel Morreau; **Art D.** Rene Moullaert; **Mus.** Jean Yatove; **Cast:** Jacques Tati, Guy Decombie, Paul Frankeur, Santa Relli, Maine Vallee.

A bicycle-riding postman in a French village is very impressed with the rapid mail delivery in the U.S. His experiments to update the local system result in chaos. As with all of Jacques Tati's later films, *Jour de Fête* is plotless, but the episodes have great originality. A simple scene of the postman's fight with a fly that has followed his bicycle is worth tens of gags. This was the first feature film by Tati and it established him as a unique comedian.

Ju Dou

1989. 95 min. color. Chinese. **Prod.** Zhang Wenze, Hu Jian, Yasuyoshi Tokuma; **Dir.** Zhang Yimou; **Scr.** Lui Heng; **Cin.** Gu Changwei, Lang Lun; **Ed.** Du Yuan; **Art D.** Fei Jiupeng; **Mus.** Xia Ru-Jin; **Cast:** Gong Li, Li Wei, Li Bao-Tian, Zhang Yi, Zheng Ji-An.

Set in China in the 1920s, Ju Dou (Gong Li), a beautiful peasant girl, is purchased by an old man who owns a textile dyeing plant to be his bride. The old man proves to be impotent and she can't bear him the children he desperately wants. In his rage he abuses and beats his wife to near death. In her despair and loneliness she strikes a friendship with a young man who is the sole worker at the plant and a distant relative of her husband. He too is abused by the old man. They become lovers and she becomes pregnant. The old man is crippled in an accident and the lovers now take their revenge, unaware that a tragic end awaits them all. Visually the film is extraordinary. The brightly colored fabrics hung row upon row is stunning. *Ju Dou*, Zhang Yimou's second feature, firmly established him as a director of note. The story has echoes of *The Postman Always Rings Twice* (1946). His best film, *Raise the Red Lantern* (1991), was yet to come.

Jules et Jim

1961. 104 min. b.w. French. **Prod.** Marcel Berbert; **Dir.** Francois Truffaut; **Scr.** Francois Truffaut, Jean Gruault (based on the novel by Henri-Pierre Roch); **Cin.** Raoul Coutard; **Ed.** Claudine Bouche; **Mus.** Georges Delerue; **Cast:** Jeanne Moreau, Oskar Werner, Henri Serre, Marie Dubois, Vanna Urbino, Sabine Haudepin.

The film begins in Paris in 1912 and ends with the worldwide Depression of the early thirties and the rise of Hitler in Germany. It is the story of two young aspiring writers, the Austrian Jules (Oskar Werner) and the Frenchman Jim (Henri Serre), and their relationship with Catherine (Jeanne Moreau), a headstrong obsessively willful French girl. Jules is captivated by Catherine and they marry and have a daughter. Jules and Jim remain close friends although they fight in opposing armies during World War I. After the war Jules invites Jim to stay with them at their home in the Rhineland. Jim senses the tension and discord between Jules and Catherine and learns that Catherine is ready to desert Jules for another of their friends. Jules has accepted Catherine's affairs but cannot bear to have her leave him. He encourages Jim to become involved with Catherine and they begin an intense and passionate affair. Jim unlike Jules cannot be subjugated by Catherine and leaves her to marry his long-time lover. Catherine resumes a former affair, but no one had gauged the intensity of the feelings and psychological makeup of Catherine. She is the liberated woman who wants to be free to leave any man, but no one can leave her. Her psychotic tendencies assert themselves in the end.

Jules et Jim had a tremendous impact on first viewing, but on subsequent viewings it has dated somewhat. It is the most ambitious work of Francois Truffaut and the film has two superb pieces of acting by Jeanne Moreau and Oskar Werner.

The Jungle Book

1967. 78 min. color. Animated. U.S. **Prod.** Walt Disney; **Dir.** Wolfgang Reitherman; **Scr.** Larry Clemmons, Ralph Wright, Ken Anderson, Vance Gerry (based on the Mowgli stories in *The Jungle Book* by Rudyard Kipling); **Ed.** Tom Acosta, Norman Carlisle; **Mus.** George Bruns; Voices: Phil Harris, Sebastian Cabot, Louis Prima, George Sanders, Sterling Holloway, J. Pat O'Malley, Bruce Reitherman, Verna Felton, Clint Howard.

This is the story of Mowgli, a boy raised by wolves. With the voices of Phil Harris as Baloo the bear singing "The Bare Necessities"; George Sanders as Shere Khan the tiger; Sterling Holloway as Kaa the snake; J. Pat O'Malley as Colonel Hathi the elephant; and Louis Prima as the king of the monkeys. *The Jungle Book* is one of the very best of Disney's full-length films and the last to be supervised by him.

Kagemusha

1980. 159 min. color. Japanese. **Prod.** Akira Kurosawa; **Dir.** Akira Kurosawa; **Scr.** Akira Kurosawa, Mosato Ida; **Cin.** Takao Saito, Shoji Ueda, Kazuo Miyagawa, Asaichi Nikai; **Art D.** Yoshiro Muraki; **Mus.** Shinichiro Ikebe, **Cast:** Tatsuya Nakadai, Tsutomu Yamazaki, Kenichi Hagiwara, Kota Yui, Hideji Otaki.

Not one of Akira Kurosawa's best; *Kagemusha* has some well-done scenes in brilliant color, but it is too long and at times confusing. Set in sixteenth-century Japan, it tells the story of a powerful head of a warrior clan who is slain in battle. In order to make the enemy believe he is alive and commanding his army, a common thief who bears an uncanny resemblance to the slain chief is selected to pose as the commander. The thief gains self-esteem and dignity in the process. *Kagemusha* is somewhat similar in theme to, but not as good as, Rossellini's *General Della Rovere* (1959).

Kansas City Confidential

1952. 98 min. b.w. U.S. **Prod.** Edward Small; **Dir.** Phil Karlson; **Scr.** George Bruce, Harry Essex; **Cin.** George Diskant; **Ed.** Buddy Small, Edward L. Ilon; **Mus.** Paul Sawtell; **Cast:** John Payne, Coleen Gray, Preston Foster, Lee Van Cleef, Neville Brand, Jack Elam.

A retired police captain (Preston Foster), wearing a mask to conceal his identity, engineers a daring armored car robbery with three hired hoods. They are to meet later in the year in Guatemala to divide the loot. An innocent ex-convict, a flower delivery man (John Payne), is arrested and grilled mercilessly by the police. When he finally is released he goes after the men who had framed him. A well-acted film with credible performances by romantic actor John Payne; old pro Preston Foster, who had been in films since the very early thirties; and a trio of established heavies, Lee Van Cleef, Neville Brand and Jack Elam as the gangsters. It is also well directed by Phil Karlson, a talented and proficient maker of good B movies including, *The Phenix City Story, Tight Spot,* and *5 Against the House*, an effective film that is also about a robbery, all in 1955.

Khane-ye Doust Kodjast?

Where Is the Friend's House? 1988. 90 min. color. Iranian. **Prod.** Alireza Zarin—Institute for the Intellectual Development of Children and Young Adults; **Dir.** Abbas Kiarostami; **Scr.** Abbas Kiarostami; **Cin.** Farhad Saba; **Ed.** Abbas Kiarostami; **Prod. D.** Nasser Zerati; **Mus.** Aminollah Amin; **Cast:** Ahmad Ahmadpour, Babak Ahmadpour, Khodabakhsh Defa'i.

A young boy of nine or ten (Ahmad Ahmadpour) lives in a farming area. When he comes home from school he realizes that mistakenly he has taken the notebook of the boy seated next to him. His classmate already has been reprimanded twice for failing to complete his homework and if he fails once again he will be expelled. In order to prevent his classmate's expulsion he walks some distance to a neighboring village to return the notebook, even though he barely knows the boy. The film becomes Ahmadpour's fruitless odyssey to find his "friend." He finally returns home, stays up late to do both his own homework and his class-mate's, and the next day delivers them both to the teacher. A simple and touching film about moral obligations. Its strength lies in the director's attention to details. The people the boy runs into are developed by broad strokes or a telling commentary. The actors are mostly nonprofessional, which gives the film greater realism. Kiarostami's films have minimum dialogue but he devel-ops the story in a way that we become aware of the subtleties of motivation and interrelationships. He showed promise from his very first professional, commercial film, *The Report* (*Gozaresh*, 1977). He has now made some twenty-five films. *Khane-ye Doust Kodjast?* established him as probably the best of the post-revolu-tion Iranian directors. A later film, *A Taste of Cherry* (*Ta'm-e Guilass,* 1997) won the Golden Palm award at Cannes.

Khane-ye Doust Kodjast (*Where Is the Friend's House?*) restates the bond of humanity, echoing John Donne's "…never send to know for whom the bell tolls; it tolls for thee."

The Killers

1946. 105 min. b.w. U.S. **Prod.** Mark Hellinger; **Dir.** Robert Siodmak; **Scr.** Anthony Veiller, John Huston (based on the story by Ernest Hemingway); **Cin.** Elwood Bredell; **Ed.** Arthur Hilton; **Art D.** Jack Otterson; **Mus.** Miklos Rozsa; **Cast:** Burt Lancaster, Ava Gardner, Edmond O'Brien, Albert Dekker, Sam Levene, William Conrad, Charles McGraw, Phil Brown.

The film opens with its best scene as two hired killers (William Conrad and Charles McGraw) walk toward Henry's diner. They enter from opposite ends and we know they are professionals. In the diner are Nick Adams, a young man having coffee, Sam the cook and George the owner/waiter. "We are here to kill the Swede…we're doing a favor for a friend." When they realize Swede isn't coming, the gangsters tie up the three and head for Swede's rooming house. Nick frees himself and takes a shortcut to warn the Swede, Ole Anderson (Burt Lancaster), that two men are coming to kill him. The Swede just lays in bed and says lacon-ically, "I'm through with all the running around…. I did something wrong once." Nick leaves and a few minutes later the killers enter. Swede lies motionless and they empty their guns. Nick comes back to the diner very disturbed and says, "I'm going to get out of this town." George says, "Well, you better not think about it." So ends Ernest Hemingway's great short story of some three thousand words. Screenwriters Anthony Veiller and an uncredited John Huston expanded the story to show why and how the Swede had become involved in crime and why he now accepts his death as something inevitable. The film covers the Swede's background as a washed-up boxer who becomes involved in a payroll robbery through the clever manipulation of a beautiful, deceitful girl, Kitty Collins (Ava Gardner). An insurance detective, Jim Reardon (Edmond O'Brien), is assigned to find out what happened to the insured stolen money.

This is one of those rare instances where the expansion of a well-known short story has been done imaginatively and intelligently, although it doesn't come close to having the impact of Hemingway's lean story. In the expansion we lose the thrust of the original, which is more about Nick than the Swede. As in many of Hemingway's early short stories he is concerned with a young man's initiation into the real world and his discovery of evil. The Hemingway story does not end with Swede's resignation to death but goes on for more than a page dealing with Nick's reaction to the murder and his decision to leave town. The film is well directed. The veteran Robert Siodmak's use of shadows, especially in the opening scenes, is very effective. It has an excellent score by Miklos Rozsa. Edmond O'Brien, Albert Dekker and Sam Levene are very good, as is the supporting cast. Ava Gardner is her most alluring and Burt Lancaster in his debut, before he became too mannered, is convincing.

King and Country

1964. 90 min. b.w. British. **Prod.** Joseph Losey; **Dir.** Joseph Losey; **Scr.** Evan Jones (based on the play *Hamp* by John Wilson from an episode in the novel *Return to the Wood* by James Lonsdale Hodson); **Cin.** Denys Coop; **Ed.** Reginald Mills; **Art D.** Peter Mullins; **Mus.** Larry Adler; **Cast:** Dirk Bogarde, Tom Courtenay, Leo McKern, Barry Foster, James Villiers.

The film is set in late 1917 after the battles of Ypres and Passchendaele in World War I where close to four hundred thousand British men and officers were slaughtered. An arrogant and class-conscious captain Hargreaves (Dirk Bogarde) is assigned to defend a poorly educated, inarticulate, shell-shocked soldier, Arthur Hamp (Tom Courtenay), accused of desertion. The captain is dismayed by his task and plans to spend as little time as possible at the court-martial. His superiors also want a quick conviction. In preparing a nominal defense Hargreaves learns that Hamp is the sole battle survivor of his entire company. One day he had decided "to go for a walk," and after twenty-four hours on the road he was arrested. The captain also slowly learns that Hamp had been dared and goaded by friends into enlisting at the very beginning of the war. After three years of witnessing the carnage at the front and recently having learned of his wife's infidelity, he had decided to go home. Hargreaves begins to have sympathy for the fellow and puts up a vigorous defense, but Hamp is convicted and awaits execution. A powerful antiwar film with excellent performances by the entire cast, especially Courtenay. More than two-thirds of the movie takes place in dark, rat-infested cells that heighten an atmosphere of futility. It also has a moving score by Larry Adler on the harmonica.

562 MY FAVORITE FILMS

King Kong

1933. 103 min. b.w. U.S. **Prod.** Merian C. Cooper, Ernest B. Schoedsack; **Dir.** Merian C. Cooper, Ernest B. Schoedsack; **Scr.** James Ashmore Creelman, Ruth Rose (based on a story by Cooper and Edgar Wallace); **Cin.** Eddie Linden, Vernon Walker, J. O. Taylor; **Ed.** Ted Cheesman; **Art D.** Carroll Clark, Al Herman, Van Nest Polglase; **Mus.** Max Steiner; **Cast:** Fay Wray, Robert Armstrong, Bruce Cabot, Frank Reicher, Sam Hardy.

King Kong is the story of a fifty-foot ape who falls in love with a five-foot-two screaming blonde. The ape is the only actor in the film who gives a credible performance. His death scene is theatrical and he dies a victim not a villain. The film's semi-realism is the work of Willis O'Brien who made an eighteen-inch model, and the camera took over from there. Max Steiner's score makes the beast even more ominous. The film has dated, but it is still enjoyable. *King Kong* was produced and directed by Merian C. Cooper, a world traveler who wrote *Grass* (1925), about the annual migration of the Bakhtiari tribe of Iran, which he later made into a documentary film. After having served in both world wars, Cooper formed Argosy Pictures with John Ford and coproduced several of Ford's films.

King's Row

1942. 127 min. b.w. U.S. **Prod.** David Lewis; **Dir.** Sam Wood; **Scr.** Casey Robinson (based on the novel by Henry Bellamann); **Cin.** James Wong Howe; **Ed.** Ralph Dawson; **Prod. D.** William Cameron Menzies; **Art D.** Carl Jules Weyl; **Mus.** Erich Wolfgang Korngold; **Cast:** Ann Sheridan, Robert Cummings, Ronald Reagan, Betty Field, Charles Coburn, Claude Rains, Judith Anderson, Maria Ouspenskaya, Nancy Coleman.

The story is set in the first decade of the twentieth century in King's Row, a small town in the U.S., but most unlike the town where MGM's Andy Hardy and his family lived. The film begins with the sign as you enter town: "A good place to live in. A good place to raise your children." The sign gives you every indication it will be a soap opera. But it is not soap territory. There is a sadistic doctor who performs surgery without anesthesia. He unnecessarily amputates the leg of a young man of whom he does not approve. Besides sadism there is inherited insanity, incest, suicide and murder.

Though uneven and at least ten minutes too long, the film still holds up. Producer David Lewis assembled some of the best craftsmen in Hollywood. It is director Sam Wood's best film. It has detailed sets by William Cameron Menzies, the impressive deep-focus cinematography of James Wong Howe and a very haunting score by Erich Wolfang Korngold. There is also a literate script by Casey Robinson who mildly sanitized the novel. The weakness of the film is the cast. Robert Cummings was a limited actor. Nancy Coleman and Betty Field add nothing to the film either. Even the reliable Claude Rains and Judith Anderson are not at their best. The film has the best acting of Ronald Reagan's career and Ann Sheridan handles her part well.

Klute

1971. 114 min. color. U.S. **Prod.** Alan J. Pakula, David Lang, **Dir.** Alan J. Pakula; **Scr.** Andy Lewis, Dave Lewis; **Cin.** Gordon Willis; **Ed.** Carl Lerner; **Art D.** George Jenkins; **Mus.** Michael Small; **Cast:** Jane Fonda, Donald Sutherland, Charles Cioffi, Roy Sheider, Rita Gam, Dorothy Tristan.

A businessman from upstate New York has disappeared and the police can't help. His close friend, local police detective John Klute (Donald Sutherland), is prevailed upon to look into the matter. His only lead is Bree Daniels (Jane Fonda), a hooker in New York City with ambitions to become an actress, to whom the missing man is supposed to have written obscene letters. It is soon revealed that there is a psychopathic killer loose in the city who has killed a call girl. Klute becomes Bree's protector. A flawed movie, overdirected with too many scenes shot at odd angels. Even the plot narrative is confusing. We never find out how Klute identifies the murderer. But the film is an interesting character study of an intelligent, emotionally troubled, vulnerable girl, with Jane Fonda giving an excellent performance for which she won an Oscar. Alan J. Pakula was a master at creating an atmosphere of paranoia, which he used to even greater effect in *The Parallax View* (1976) and *All the President's Men* (1976).

Knock on Wood

1954. 103 min. color. U.S. **Prod.** Norman Panama, Melvin Frank; **Dir.** Norman Panama, Melvin Frank; **Scr.** Norman Panama, Melvin Frank; **Cin.** Daniel Fapp; **Ed.** Alma Macrorie; **Mus.** Leith Stevens; **Cast:** Danny Kaye, Mai Zetterling, Torin Thatcher, David Burns, Leon Askin, Abner Biberman, Steven Geray.

Jerry (Danny Kaye) is a ventriloquist working in nightclubs in Europe. His professional and personal life are being ruined by his dummy who talks back and insults audiences and friends. In his frustration he breaks the dummy, then gives it to a restorer to put back together. When, unbeknown to him, foreign spies stuff blueprints for an ultra-secret weapon in the dummy, Jerry's life is put in danger. To escape the spies and assassins he impersonates an Irish tenor, a ballet dancer in a Russian troupe and a car salesman. An ideal film for Danny Kaye to showcase his myriad talents. The witty script also has him impersonating an upper-class Englishman just returned from India who when asked how he liked the Himalayas replies in impeccable King's English, "Loved her, hated him."

La Guerre Est Finie

The War Is Over. 1966. 121 min. b.w. French. **Prod.** Catherine Winter, Gisele Rebillon; **Dir.** Alain Resnais; **Scr.** Jorge Semprun; **Cin.** Sacha Vierny; **Ed.** Eric Pluet; **Mus.** Giovanni Fusco; **Cast:** Yves Montand, Ingrid Thulin, Genevieve Bujold, Michel Piccoli, Jean Dasté, Dominique Rozan, Jorge Semprun (narrator).

Three days in the life of an aging Spanish revolutionary (Yves Montand) are depicted. He is a refugee who has lived in exile in France for nearly thirty years. He is working for the overthrow of Franco by smuggling pamphlets and handbills into Spain and maintaining contact with fellow aging former revolutionaries. He is considered irrelevant by the younger exile opposition elements who advocate greater activism, even assassination, paving the way for a revolution. But what the film is saying is embodied in its title: *The War Is Over.* Any change must come from the Spanish people within Spain. Both the older and younger exiles are irrelevant. The film also has moving segments of Montand's relationship with his mistress, beautifully acted by Ingrid Thulin, and a brief dalliance with a younger girl (Genevieve Bujold). Resnais also introduces his perennial themes of memory and remembrance throughout the film as Montand goes back over his own life.

La Nuit de Varennes

The Night of Varennes. 1982. 135 min. color. French. **Prod.** Renzo Rossellini; **Dir.** Ettore Scola; **Scr.** Ettore Scola, Sergio Amidei; **Cin.** Armando Nannuzzi; **Ed.** Raimondo Crociani; **Art D.** Dante Ferretti; **Mus.** Armando Travajoi; **Cast:** Marcello Mastroianni, Jean-Louis Barrault, Hanna Schygulla, Harvey Keitel, Jean-Claude Brialy, Daniel Gelin, Jean-Louis Trintignant, Michel Piccoli, Eleonore Hirt.

This fictional story is built around an historic incident. In 1791, Louis XVI and Queen Marie Antoinette with a very small entourage fled from Paris, which had been taken over by the revolutionaries. They stopped overnight at an inn in Varennes. They were captured the next day and sent back to Paris. This much is historic fact. The screenplay places the following also at the inn that night: an aging and decrepit Casanova (Marcello Mastroianni); Thomas Paine (Harvey Keitel), the great pamphleteer of the American Revolution; Restif de la Bretonne (Jean-Louis Barrault), a popular writer of the time; plus an Italian opera singer, a countess and a wealthy landowner. A brilliant concept that does not entirely work. It is slightly too long and there is little interaction among the characters, but it is original and well acted.

The Lady from Shanghai

1948. 87 min. b.w. U.S. **Prod.** Orson Welles; **Dir.** Orson Welles; **Scr.** Orson Welles; **Cin.** Charles Lawton, Jr.; **Ed.** Viola Lawrence; **Art D.** Stephen Goosson, Sturges Carne; **Mus.** Heinz Roemheld; **Cast:** Rita Hayworth, Orson Welles, Everett Sloane, Ted de Corsia, Erskine Sanford, Glen Anders.

Michael O'Hara (Orson Welles), a good-natured but gullible itinerant seaman, is tricked by an alluring woman, Elsa (Rita Hayworth), and her calculating lawyer husband, Arthur Bannister (Everett Sloane), into signing a confession to a murder that never occurred, in return for a fee of $5,000. Later, when Bannister's associate is murdered, O'Hara is put on trial. He is defended by Bannister who deliberately mishandles the defense to have O'Hara convicted and executed. O'Hara escapes and has a showdown with Elsa and her husband. One of the most convoluted and confusing plots, not helped by Orson Welles' heavy Irish brogue. Both men were fine actors, but poor Rita Hayworth (then married to Welles) was beyond her depth. The film, however, has touches of Welles' brilliance, and the surrealistic shoot-out in a hall of mirrors is one of the more imaginative movie scenes.

L'Age D'Or

1930. 60 min. b.w. French. **Prod.** Charles Vicomte de Noailles; **Dir.** Luis Buñuel ; **Scr.** Luis Buñuel , Salvador Dali; **Cin.** Albert Dubergen; **Ed.** Luis Buñuel ; **Art D.** Schilzneck; **Mus.** Georges Van Parys; **Cast:** Lya Lys, Gaston Modot, Max Ernst, Pierre Prevert, Caridad de Laberdesque, Lionel Salem, Madame Noizet, Jose Artigas, Jacques Brunius.

In anticipation of making love, a man and a woman attempt to rid themselves of all their inhibitions whether they be the suffocating influence of the church or bourgeois social conventions. This is shown through a series of startling images: a priest turns into a skeleton; a cow wanders into their bedroom. This very strange film is much more Buñuel than Dali whose contribution is minimal. There are nearly all the themes that became more explicit in Buñuel 's later films; his enmity toward conventional morality, the bourgeois establishment and foremost the Catholic Church. *L'Age D'Or* has not dated and can still shock the viewer.

L'Argent

Money. 1983. 90 min. color. French/Swiss. **Prod.** Jean-Marc Henchoz; **Dir.** Robert Bresson; **Scr.** Robert Bresson (based on the story "The False Note" by Leo Tolstoy); **Cin.** Emmanuel Machuel, Pasqualino De Santis; **Ed.** Jean Francois Naudon; **Art D.** Pierre Guffroy; **Mus.** Bach; **Cast:** Christain Patey, Sylvie van den Elsen, Michel Briguet, Caroline Lang, Vincent Risterucci, Marc Ernest Fourneau.

L'Argent was the last film of one of the most original directors, Robert Bresson. It is a commentary on greed and the consequences of thoughtless acts. The simple story concerns the passing of counterfeit bills by a young schoolboy that ruins the life of an innocent working-class recipient.

The Last Bridge

Die Letzte Brücke. 1954. 104 mins. b.w. Austrian. **Dir.** Helmut Käutner; **Scr.** Helmut Käutner, Norbert Kunze; **Cin.** Fred Kollhanek; **Mus.** Carl De Groof; **Cast:** Maria Schell, Bernhard Wicki, Barbara Rutting, Carl Mohner, Horst Haechler.

Maria Schell in her finest performance plays a German doctor captured by Yugoslav partisans in World War II. She is reluctant at first to help wounded partisans but soon realizes her oath as a physician obligates her to tend to the wounded in whatever uniform. An intelligent antiwar film that won first prize at the Cannes Film Festival.

The Last Emperor

1987. 160 min. color. British. **Prod.** Jeremy Thomas; **Dir.** Bernardo Bertolucci; **Scr.** Mark Peplo, Bernardo Bertolucci, Enzo Ungari (based on *From Emperor to Citizen,* autobiography of Pu Yi); **Cin.** Vittorio Storaro; **Ed.** Gabriella Cristiani; **Prod. D.** Ferdinando Scarfiotti; **Art D.** Gianni Giovagnoni, Gianni Silvestri; **Mus.** Ryuichi Sakamoto, David Byrne, Cong Su; **Cast:** John Lone, Joan Chen, Peter O'Toole, Victor Wong, Ying Ruocheng, Ryuichi Sakamoto.

The life of Pu Yi (1906–1967) who in 1908, at the age of two, ascends the throne and becomes emperor of China. He is forced to abdicate at age six when China becomes a republic but is allowed to remain in the Forbidden City. Beginning with the Japanese invasion of China and Manchuria, Pu Yi became the puppet of the Japanese with the title of Emperor of Manchuria. After World War II he became a prisoner of the Soviet Union. He was released in 1950 and sent to Communist China for indoctrination and rehabilitation. The film is told in a series of flashbacks and flash-forwards and ends with Pu Yi's release from detention and living out his years as a gardener at Beijing's Botanical Gardens. The film remains remote and soulless and there can be little empathy with Pu Yi who is shown to be a cruel, arrogant mediocrity elevated to the position of "Little God" by the vagaries of birth. But *The Last Emperor* is one of the most beautiful feats of cinematography created by the collaborative efforts of director Bernardo Bertolucci and cinematographer Vittorio Storaro. Other than for acting, *The Last Emperor* won almost all other Academy Awards.

Last Tango in Paris

1973. 129 min. color. French/Italian (in English). **Prod.** Alberto Grimaldi; **Dir.** Bernardo Bertolucci; **Scr.** Bernardo Bertolucci, Franco Arcalli, Agnes Varda; **Cin.** Vittorio Storaro; **Ed.** Franco Arcalli; **Prod. D.** Ferdinando Scarfiotti; **Mus.** Gato Barbieri; **Cast:** Marlon Brando, Maria Schneider, Jean-Pierre Leaud, Massimo Girotti.

Paul (Marlon Brando), a middle-aged American, has lived in Paris for the past seven years in a run-down hotel owned by his wife. The film opens on the day his wife has committed suicide for no apparent reason. He finds out she had an extended affair with someone he never suspected. He is confused and shattered and to rid himself of his guilt he wanders into the streets and ends up looking for apartments for rent. In an empty apartment he runs into a twenty-year-old girl, Jeanne (Maria Schneider), who is searching for an apartment. She is soon to be married to a young, aspiring film director (Jean-Pierre Leaud). With barely a few words exchanged Paul and Jeanne are making passionate love. They agree to see each other regularly at the same place but Paul establishes rules. They are not to ask questions of each other or reveal any personal matter about themselves. The film ends with a totally unexpected twist. *Last Tango in Paris* is an imaginative and original work and filmed beautifully by Vittorio Storaro. But it is a confusing movie and difficult to fathom what Bertolucci is saying. What gives the film great power is the virtuoso acting of Marlon Brando. But he is allowed to go too far. In the scene at the end, moments before his death, Brando takes chewing gum out of his mouth. The subplot involving Schneider and Jean-Pierre Leaud is not sufficiently developed and slows the movie.

The Late George Apley

1947. 98 min. b.w. U.S. **Prod.** Fred Kohlmar; **Dir.** Joseph L. Mankiewicz; **Scr.** Philip Dunne (based on the novel by John P. Marquand); **Cin.** Joseph LaShelle; **Ed.** James B. Clark; **Art D.** James Basevi; **Mus.** Cyril Mockridge; **Cast:** Ronald Colman, Peggy Cummins, Vanessa Brown, Richard Haydn, Richard Ney, Mildred Natwick.

The WASP Yankee, George Apley, impeccably played by Ronald Colman, believes Boston is the center of the universe, Harvard is the only seat of learning, and other colleges are for "others." He doesn't want his daughter to marry a Yalie. He objects to Ralph Waldo Emerson being labeled a "radical." The film, based on John P. Marquand's novel (and later play), is a loving satire on the Boston Brahmins. Eleven years later in *The Last*

Hurrah (1958) John Ford introduced us to the other side of Boston, the Irish side.

Laughter in Paradise

1951. 95 min. b.w. British. **Prod.** Mario Zampi; **Dir.** Mario Zampi; **Scr.** Michael Pertwee, Jack Davies; **Cin.** William McLeod; **Ed.** Giulio Zampi; **Art D.** Ivan King; **Mus.** Stanley Black; **Cast:** Alistair Sim, Joyce Grenfell, Hugh Griffith, Fay Compton, Guy Middleton, George Cole, Beatrice Campbell, Audrey Hepburn.

A wealthy man dies leaving his fortune to several family members with the stipulation that they each perform certain tasks that are directly connected to their character flaws. Fay Compton as a sister who abuses her servants must become a maid for a designated period to learn humility. Guy Middleton as a Lothario who has jilted many women must marry the first woman he flirts with. Alistair Sim as a respectable stuffy man who secretly writes detective pulp has to get himself thrown in jail. There is a marvelous surprise ending.

Le Boucher

The Butcher. 1969. 93 min. color. French/Italian. **Prod.** Andre Genoves; **Dir.** Claude Chabrol; **Scr.** Claude Chabrol; **Cin.** Jean Rabier; **Ed.** Jacques Gaillard; **Mus.** Pierre Jansen; **Cast:** Stephane Audran, Jean Yanne, Antonio Passalia, Mario Beccaria, Pasquale Ferone, Roger Rudel.

An attractive school teacher, Helene (Stephane Audran), meets the pleasant local butcher, Popaul (Jean Yanne), at a wedding party in a small French town. Popaul had been away for fifteen years. Early on, he had learned his trade from his father but had left to join the army. It had been a traumatic experience as he had witnessed carnage and atrocities. Helene had been headmistress of a school in another town but had asked for a transfer after an unhappy episode with a former boyfriend. Helene and Popaul begin to see each other regularly. Soon the town is stricken with a series of unsolved murders of women. On a picnic with her students, the girls find the body of a victim. Helene finds a cigarette lighter nearby and the evidence points to Popaul. Several unexpected twists now dominate the film.

Le Boucher is director Claude Chabrol's second-best film, La Femme Infidèle (1969) being the best, both released in the same year. Le Boucher is more overtly influenced by Hitchcock, one of Chabrol's idols. It becomes a study of the psychological makeup of a serial killer. The best part is how the relationship between the schoolteacher and the butcher is established, especially the scene of their walk from a wedding party with brief exchanges of their backgrounds. It is an uneven film and slows down in parts. The acting of the two leads is adequate, although Audran, Chabrol's wife, may be too attractive and elegant for the role of a country schoolteacher.

Le Million

1931. 85 min. b.w. French. **Dir.** René Clair; **Scr.** René Clair; **Cin.** Georges Perinal; **Mus.** Georges Van Parys; **Cast:** Annabella, Rene Lefevre, Paul Olivier, Louis Allibert, Vanda Gréville, Raymond Cordy.

A musician who owes money to all the tradesmen in his neighborhood is informed he has won a lottery. In his excitement he invites all his creditors to celebrate. But the tattered coat with the ticket in its pocket has been sold to a second-hand shop and purchased for a nominal sum by a tenor to wear for his role as an impoverished student in La Boheme. The film becomes a chase for the coat all over Paris ending on the stage of the opera house during the performance, followed by creditors, the police and thieves. The film ends happily. This enjoyable work was made shortly after the advent of sound and there are some innovative devices such as the actors singing some of their lines. Like most films of that very early sound era, it has dated somewhat. What are memorable are the last scenes on the opera stage that may have influenced the Marx Brothers in A Night at the Opera (1935).

Le Plaisir

House of Pleasure. 1952. 97 min. b.w. French. **Dir.** Max Ophuls; **Scr.** Jacques Natanson, Max Ophuls (based on three stories by Guy de Maupassant); **Cin.** Christian Matras, Philippe Agostini; **Mus.** Joe Hajos; **Cast:** Jean Gabin, Danielle Darrieux, Simone Simon, Claude Dauphin, Gaby Morlay, Pierre Brasseur, Madeleine Renaud, Daniel Gelin.

The film is based on three short stories by Guy de Maupassant in three separate and unconnected segments. The first and third segments are well made, but it is better remembered for the second segment, which tells the story of the proprietress of a brothel (Madeleine Renaud) who closes her establishment to attend her niece's first communion in a village a distance away. She takes her five girls with her and they stay at a farmhouse owned by her brother (Jean Gabin). The film dwells on the effect of fresh air on the girls, primarily on Danielle Darrieux, and the deprivation of the townspeople by their temporary absence.

The Leopard

Il Gattopardo. 1963. 205 min. color. Italian. **Prod.** Goffredo Lombardo; **Dir.** Luchino Visconti; **Scr.** Luchino Visconti, Suso Cecchi D'Amico, Pasquale Festa Campanile, Enrico Medioli, Massimo Franciosa (based on the novel by Giuseppe Lampedusa); **Cin.** Giuseppe Rotunno; **Ed.** Mario Serandrei; **Art D.** Mario Garbuglia; **Mus.** Nino Rota, Verdi; **Cast:** Burt Lancaster, Alain Delon, Claudia Cardinale, Rina Morelli, Paolo Stoppa, Romolo Valli, Serge Reggiani.

The story is set in Sicily when Garibaldi and his Red Shirts were driving the Austrians and the French out of Italy, and the movement for unification of the country was gaining momentum. Prince Don Fabrizio Salina (Burt Lancaster) is the head of the house of Salina, which had ruled Sicily for several generations. He realizes that the first victims of unification will be the aristocracy and their rule over certain enclaves. Don Fabrizio has seven unmarried sheltered daughters and a penniless nephew, Tancredi (Alain Delon). Tancredi joins the Garibaldi forces and Don Fabrizio silently approves. As the fortunes of Garibaldi's republican movement wane, Tancredi joins the monarchists. Don Fabrizio is again quietly pleased and does not consider Tancredi's moves as a betrayal of his class. Soon thereafter Don Fabrizio arranges the marriage of Tancredi to Angelica (Claudia Cardinale), a daughter of the richest merchant in the area. With Tancredi's future secure, Don Fabrizio will now marry off his daughters. He is offered a seat in the soon to be formed senate, under the rule of Victor Emanuel, the new king of a unified Italy. He knows he will have no substantive role in the governing of Italy and declines the offer.

The film's distinction lies in the last hour which includes a forty-minute scene of Tancredi's wedding banquet. It is one of the greatest set pieces in movie history. Staged like a scene from grand opera, the huge ballroom followed by room after room filled with guests in colorful costumes is a visual feast. Don Fabrizio, as the senior member of Tancredi's family, goes from one room to the other exchanging a few words with the guests. He sees matronly ladies who had been his mistresses in the past. The last scene is his quiet departure and walk home in the early-morning silence. *The Leopard* was released in 1963 to critical acclaim in Europe. Twentieth Century Fox, which had financed the film, mutilated it on its U.S. release. In 1983, the director's cut was released—a 205-minute version that is also far from perfect. *The Leopard* is not a well-acted film, but it will survive for the artistry of the wedding banquet. Francis Ford Coppola's *The Godfather* (1972) and Michael Cimino's *The Deer Hunter* (1978), show the heavy influence of *The Leopard* in their elaborate opening wedding scenes. A film that could have been Visconti's masterpiece has been ruined by the casting, indiscriminate cutting and difficulties with the dubbing. But the last hour shines.

Les Miserables

1935. 108 min. b.w. U.S. **Prod.** Darryl F. Zanuck; **Dir.** Richard Boleslawski; **Scr.** W. P. Lipscomb (based on the novel by Victor Hugo); **Cin.** Greg Toland; **Ed.** Barbara McLean; **Art D.** Richard Day; **Mus.** Alfred Newman; **Cast:** Fredric March, Charles Laughton, Cedric Hardwicke, Rochelle Hudson, Frances Drake, John Beal, Florence Eldridge.

This is the most imposing and best of the numerous films of Victor Hugo's 1862 novel, a tale of the hunter and the hunted. The script by W. P. Lipscomb pared down the novel to a manageable 108 minutes while maintaining all the basic and major incidents: Jean Valjean (Fredric March) committing his first theft; his release from prison; the kindness shown to him by a bishop Cedric Hardwicke; becoming the mayor of a town; his encounters with Inspector Javert (Charles Laughton); and scenes of the 1848 Paris uprising. The film is beautifully photographed by a young Greg Toland and there is superlative acting by Fredric March, Charles Laughton, Florence Eldridge and Cedric Hardwicke in his first Hollywood film. There have been at least six filmed versions of the novel and the only other one deserving of mention is the 1934, three-hour-plus French production that starred the great actor Harry Baur.

Letter from an Unknown Woman

1948. 90 min. b.w. U.S. **Prod.** John Houseman; **Dir.** Max Ophuls; **Scr.** Howard Koch (based on the novel *Brief Einer Unbekannten* by Stefan Zweig); **Cin.** Franz Planer; **Ed.** Ted J. Kent; **Art D.** Alexander Golitzen; **Mus.** Daniele Amfitheatrof; **Cast:** Joan Fontaine, Louis Jourdan, Art Smith, Mady Christians, Marcel Journet.

Lisa Brendle (Joan Fontaine), a teenager, lives with her widowed mother in turn-of-the-twentieth-century Vienna. After a time a young handsome concert pianist, Stefan Brand (Louis Jourdan), moves into a neighboring house. She spends hours listening to him practice and adores him from afar. They finally meet and she is convinced he loves her even though she has seen other women coming to spend the night with him. He seduces her, leaves her pregnant and totally forgets her. She resigns herself to having been one of his many conquests. In order to protect the unborn child, she enters into a loveless marriage with an older man who takes care of her and her son. Some years later she meets the amoral pianist again. He does not recognize her. His years of living a dissolute life to the neglect of his music has caught up with him. He no longer has the adoring concert crowds and his fame is in decline. She is convinced that now he truly loves her. He seduces her and once again forgets her. A year or two pass and mother and young son become seriously ill in the aftermath of a typhus epidemic and her son dies. In her own last hours she writes a long letter telling Stefan of their relation-ship and the son he has lost. Meanwhile the pianist has been challenged to a duel by the husband of one of his paramours. He has decided to leave town as he knows he will not have a chance against his challenger. After reading Lisa's letter, he goes with his seconds to the dueling ground and certain death.

Fontaine cries and suffers during the entire film. In the hands of a lesser director it would have been just another tear jerker. Max Ophuls makes it a masterful work. Franz Planer's camera moves effortlessly. It circles the players while focusing mainly on the suffering of Joan Fontaine. Sets and backgrounds always play an important part in Ophuls' films. The art director, Alexander Golitzen, re-creates a Vienna of houses, restaurants and shops. This was the best film Ophuls made while in self-exile in the U.S. dur-ing the war years. It is also one of Joan Fontaine's best performances. She ages from fourteen to twenty-nine years old. Art Smith as Stefan's mute butler is excellent. The handsome Louis Jourdan fits his part.

The Letter

1940. 95 min. b.w. U.S. **Prod.** Robert Lord; **Dir.** William Wyler; **Scr.** Howard Koch (based on the story by Somerset Maugham); **Cin.** Tony Gaudio; **Ed.** George Amy; **Art D.** Carl Jules Weyl; **Mus.** Max Steiner; **Cast:** Bette Davis, Herbert Marshall, James Stephenson, Gale Sondergaard, Bruce Lester, Elizabeth Inglis, Cecil Kellaway.

Bette Davis, the wife of a rubber plantation manager in Singapore, shoots her lover dead. It is an extremely effective opening, far superior to the rest of the film. The ending imposed by the Hays Office, that there must be retribution for a murder, is forced and mechanical. A flawed film but still one of William Wyler's better works.

Limelight

1952. 145 min. b.w. U.S. **Prod.** Charles Chaplin; **Dir.** Charles Chaplin; **Scr.** Charles Chaplin; **Cin.** Karl Struss; **Ed.** Joe Inge; **Art D.** Eugene Laurie; **Mus.** Charles Chaplin; **Cast:** Charles Chaplin, Claire Bloom, Nigel Bruce, Buster Keaton, Sydney Chaplin, Norman Lloyd, Charles Chaplin, Jr., Andre Eglevsky (dancer), Melissa Hayden (danseuse).

Set in 1914 London before the outbreak of the war, *Limelight* is the story of Calvero (Charles Chaplin), an aging, out-of-work comedian who had been a headliner a few years earlier. He lives in a dilapidated tenement and has taken to alcohol. He nurses back to health a neighboring young talented dancer, Terry (Claire Bloom), who had attempted suicide. With his encouragement Terry gets the leading part in a new ballet written by a young composer, Neville (Sydney Chaplin). Terry now gets Calvero a job as a clown and pleads with him to marry her. Calvero, realizing what an incongruous couple they are, leaves but is found by Terry. The ballet impresario (Nigel Bruce) recognizes him and arranges for him to perform at a large benefit. He is appreciated and acclaimed but has a heart attack on stage and dies. Terry and Neville are destined to get together.

Charlie Chaplin's script is maudlin and self-glorifying. Chaplin does too much philosophizing in search of "truth." It is a semi-autobiography of one who, according to George Bernard Shaw, was "the only genius developed in motion pictures." Ironically for a silent star, there is excessive talking as Chaplin bares his ego. In several scenes the camera is almost glued to his face. Chaplin was not a good director of full-length films. Even with the presence of Robert Aldrich as assistant director, the film is slow and drags. Despite the drawbacks, it has several very good scenes; some solo songs by Chaplin and a wonderful scene with Buster Keaton. Claire Bloom was an excellent choice and is most charming in her second film. Chaplin's musical score won an Academy Award, not in 1952, the year of the film's release, but in 1972, because it was not shown in Los Angeles until that year. Chaplin, while traveling to England for the premier of the film, had his re-entry visa revoked as he was perceived as being immoral and a communist sympathizer. Chaplin made only two films after *Limelight*: *A King in New York* (1957) and *Countess from Hong Kong* (1967). Both films are vastly inferior to his earlier output.

Little Big Man

1970. 150 min. color. U.S. **Prod.** Stuart Millar; **Dir.** Arthur Penn; **Scr.** Calder Willingham (based on the novel by Thomas Berger); **Cin.** Harry Stradling, Jr.; **Ed.** Dede Allen; **Prod. D.** Tavoularis; **Art D.** Angelo Graham; **Mus.** John Hammond; **Cast:** Dustin Hoffman, Faye Dunaway, Martin Balsam, Chief Dan George, Jeff Corey, Richard Mulligan.

A 121-year-old man, Jack Crabb (Dustin Hoffman), is recounting his life. At age ten he had been captured and raised among the Cheyenne Indians by Chief Old Lodge Skins (Chief Dan George) as an Indian brave. When the cavalry attacks the Indian settlement, he is revealed to be white and is spared. For the next twenty years he passes back and forth between white and Indian cultures. He becomes a scout for Custer at Little Bighorn and is the only survivor of Custer's last stand. The movie's first hour is broad comedy. It is only in the last segments that it becomes a story of genocide with the indiscriminate slaughter of Indians. Throughout the film, the Indians refer to themselves as "Human Beings" and the rest are just called white men. The film, at one hundred and fifty minutes, is at least twenty-five minutes too long. Tens of characters come and go with only cameo performances, some totally unrelated to what has already transpired as well as what follows. But there are scenes of immense power and some touching moments. It was made during the height of the Vietnam war and there are allusions to the My Lai massacre. Among the very large and able cast, it is Chief Dan George who carries the film along and steals every scene he is in. He received an Academy Award nomination for best supporting actor. The film resembles *Bonnie and Clyde* (1967), also directed by Arthur Penn, in that it has some unnecessary scenes of comedy amidst carnage and mayhem. Penn made some important films in the sixties and seventies but unfortunately has since stopped working.

Little Caesar

1930. 80 min. b.w. U.S. **Prod.** Hal B. Wallis; **Dir.** Mervyn LeRoy; **Scr.** Robert N. Lee, Francis Edwards Farago, Robert Lord (based on the novel by W. R. Burnett); **Cin.** Tony Gaudio; **Ed.** Ray Curtiss; **Art D.** Anton Grot; **Mus.** Erno Rapee; **Cast:** Edward G. Robinson, Douglas Fairbanks, Jr., Glenda Farrell, Sidney Blackmer, William Collier, Jr., Ralph Ince.

Little Caesar was one of the first sound films that dealt with the rise and fall of a gangster. Although it is somewhat primitive, as the actors were not entirely relaxed speaking to off-screen microphones, the personality and acting of Edward G. Robinson as Rico Bandello assured the success of the film. Robinson had been trained as a stage actor and had made a few appearances in silent movies. He was of slight build and not handsome, but during the Depression era the audience identified with the little guy and Robinson became a star. Here, as in all gangster films, the hero/villain is tempted by money and power. He rises to the top but makes the fatal mistake of shooting the crime commissioner during an assault on a nightclub owned by a rival gang. He goes into hiding but is lured out and killed. His effective last lines are "Mother of God, is this the end of Rico?" The film is all Edward G. Robinson and established the persona with which he long was identified.

Little Women

1933. 115 min. b.w. U.S. **Prod.** Kenneth MacGowan; **Dir.** George Cukor; **Scr.** Sarah Y. Mason, Victor Heerman (based on the novel by Louisa May Alcott); **Cin.** Henry Gerrard; **Ed.** Jack Kitchin; **Art D.** Van Nest Polglase; **Mus.** Max Steiner; **Cast:** Katharine Hepburn, Joan Bennett, Paul Lukas, Frances Dee, Jean Parker, Edna May Oliver, Spring Byington, Henry Stevenson, John Lodge, Douglas Montgomery.

A lovely, well-directed film about a New England family of Concord, Massachusetts, during the Civil War. The March family has four daughters. They face a difficult time with the country at war and their father away at the front. Their loving mother, Marmee (Spring Byington), has the hard task of raising the family alone. The four girls are very attached to each other. Jo (Katharine Hepburn) wants to be a writer and decides to go to New York to further her career. She meets a kind professor (Paul Lukas) who proposes marriage. But Jo can't break away from her sisters and returns home. By the end of the film, their father has come home from the war; two of the sisters have married; a younger sister has died after a prolonged illness; and Jo's suitor, the professor, has come to Concord and Jo will now agree to marry him. The film is perfectly cast, but it is really Katharine Hepburn's film. Though the story is ripe for sentimentality, George Cukor controls the film well. It begins in winter and there is excellent photography of the New England setting and the changing of the seasons. It is a period film that has not dated. It received Academy Award nominations for best picture and director, and won an award for best adapted screenplay.

Lola Montez

1955. 110 min. color. French/German. **Dir.** Max Ophuls; **Scr.** Max Ophuls, Jacques Natanson, Franz Geiger, Annette Wademant (based on the unpublished novel by Cecil Saint-Laurent); **Cin.** Christian Matras; **Ed.** Madeleine Gug; **Art D.** Jean d'Eaubonne, Willy Schatz; **Mus.** Georges Auric; **Cast:** Martine Carol, Peter Ustinov, Anton Walbrook, Oscar Werner, Ivan Desny, Will Quadflieg.

This is the story of the legendary nineteenth-century beauty who had numerous lovers and had been the mistress of many, including Franz Liszt and Ludwig I of Bavaria, now reduced to a circus performer touring America. This, the last film of the master Max Ophuls, is his only film in color. Ophuls was seriously ill during the filming and, as he lay dying, producers and distributors in the U.S. cut the 140-minute film to 100 and later to 90 minutes. The mutilated film is still a feast for the eyes with Ophuls' fluid camera work, but it was too ambitious and it does not entirely work. Martine Carol is totally inadequate and no ships would be launched or wars fought for her. Peter Ustinov, the ringmaster, is no Anton Walbrook of *La Ronde*, and even Walbrook as King Ludwig is not at his best. Another fine actor, Oscar Werner, has only a few passing scenes. Despite all this, the film still has many touches of the master.

The Loneliness of the Long Distance Runner

1962. 103 min. b.w. British. **Prod.** Tony Richardson; **Dir.** Tony Richardson; **Scr.** Alan Sillitoe (based on his story); **Cin.** Walter Lassally; **Ed.** Anthony Gibbs; **Prod. D.** Ralph Brinton; **Art D.** Ted Marshall; **Mus.** John Addison; **Cast:** Michael Redgrave, Tom Courtenay, Avis Bunnage, Peter Madden, James Bolam, Alec McCowen, James Fox.

One of the best socially-conscious films of the sixties and the film debut of a fine actor, Tom Courtenay. The film is set in the Midlands and tells the story of an alienated youth from the slums who is involved in petty crime. After an unsuccessful theft he is sent to a Borstal. The governor of the Borstal (Michael Redgrave) believes that truant youths can be rehabilitated through sports. The boy is a born long distance runner but when his chance comes to ingratiate himself with the authorities he deliberately throws the race. The film questions the class system and what constitutes success.

Lonely Are the Brave

1962. 107 min. b.w. U.S. **Prod.** Edward Lewis; **Dir.** David Miller; **Scr.** Dalton Trumbo (based on the novel *Brave Cowboy* by Edward Abbey); **Cin.** Philip Lathrop; **Ed.** Leon Barsha, Edward Mann; **Art D.** Alexander Golitzen, Robert E. Smith; **Mus.** Jerry Goldsmith; **Cast:** Kirk Douglas, Gena Rowlands, Walter Matthau, Carroll O'Connor, George Kennedy, William Schallert, Michael Kane, Karl Swenson.

Set in the modern West, the film tells the story of an aging cowboy, Jack Burns (Kirk Douglas), trying to live by his own code. He has no home and sleeps on the prairie by a campfire, next to his horse. He travels to a small town to see a friend and finds him in jail on charges of aiding the illegal entry of Mexicans into the U.S. To help his friend escape he gets himself thrown in jail by inciting a brawl. But his friend does not want to escape, preferring to serve out his sentence. Burns escapes alone and finds his horse. Soon there is a posse after him headed by the sheriff (Walter Matthau). He is pursued by jeeps and helicopters but eludes them all and makes it to the foot of the mountains. He can now get away, but the horse can't make it across the mountains. He does not want to be separated from his horse and takes the highway where both are killed by a truck carrying a shipment of toilets.

The film takes a nostalgic but unsentimental look at the disappearing old West and an individual's confrontation with the mechanized world. Douglas and Matthau give beautiful well-nuanced performances. The rest of the cast is as good. *Lonely are the Brave* is, by far, director David Miller's best work. It has one of the most effective opening scenes: Kirk Douglas resting on the open prairie with his horse nearby, when we see and hear a roaring jet passing overhead that highlights the anachronism of a cowboy in the jet age.

Long Day's Journey into Night

1962. 174 min. b.w. U.S. **Prod.** Ely Landau, Jack J. Dreyfus, Jr.; **Dir.** Sidney Lumet; **Scr.** Based on the play by Eugene O'Neill; **Cin.** Boris Kaufman; **Ed.** Ralph Rosenbaum; **Prod. D.** Richard Sylbert; **Art D.** Richard Sylbert; **Mus.** Andre Previn; **Cast:** Katharine Hepburn, Ralph Richardson, Jason Robards, Jr.; Dean Stockwell, Jeanne Barr.

Set in the early 1900s, it is a day and night in the lives of the Tyrones, a dysfunctional and tragic family, in which the members reveal themselves and their relationships. Katharine Hepburn is the wellborn mother who has become a morphine addict. Ralph Richardson is the successful actor father whose early poverty has made him a miser to the extent that he neglects the needs of his family. Jason Robards is the oldest son who tried to follow in his father's footsteps as an actor but failed and took to drink. Dean Stockwell is the tubercular younger son, an aspiring writer. The film is a precise adaptation of Eugene O'Neill's great autobiographical play with only a few minor cuts. Hepburn, Richardson and Robards were among the very best stage and screen actors of the last century. Their acting holds you despite the film's length of almost three hours.

The Longest Day

1962. 180 min. b.w. U.S. **Prod.** Darryl F. Zanuck; **Dir.** Ken Annakin, Andrew Marton, Bernard Wicki, Gerd Oswald; **Scr.** Cornelius Ryan, Romain Gary, James Jones, David Pursall, Jack Seddon (based on the novel by Cornelius Ryan); **Cin.** Jean Bourgoin, Walter Wottitz, Henri Persin, Guy Tabary; **Ed.** Samuel E. Beetley; **Art D.** Ted Haworth, Leon Barsacq, Vincent Korda; **Mus.** Maurice Jarre; **Cast:** John Wayne, Rod Steiger, Robert Ryan, Peter Lawford, Henry Fonda, Robert Mitchum, Richard Burton, Richard Beymer, Robert Wagner, Curt Jurgens, Red Buttons, Bourvil, Jean-Louis Barrault, Arletty, Eddie Albert, Edmond O'Brien, Gerd Froebe, Rod Steiger, Leo Genn, Kenneth More.

The Longest Day is the story of the first day of Operation Overlord, the invasion of Europe by the Allies and opening of a second front, with an international cast of over thirty well-known actors and four separate directors. It is disjointed in places and the huge cast is uneven. However, against all odds it works and has scenes of immense power. It is by far the most impressive epic of World War II.

The Lost Patrol

1934. 73 min. b.w. U.S. **Prod.** Cliff Reid; **Dir.** John Ford; **Scr.** Dudley Nichols, Garrett Fort (based on the novel *Patrol* by Philip MacDonald); **Cin.** Harold Wenstrom; **Ed.** Paul Weatherwax; **Art D.** Van Nest Polglase, Sidney Ullman; **Mus.** Max Steiner; **Cast:** Victor McLaglen, Boris Karloff, Wallace Ford, Reginald Denny, Alan Hale, J. M. Kerrigan, Billy Bevan.

The Lost Patrol was the first important John Ford film. It is set in the Mesopotamian desert during World War I. The officer leading a cavalry patrol is killed by a sniper. The rest of the patrol has no idea of their mission or destination. The sergeant (Victor McLaglen) takes over. Slowly every one of them is picked off by unseen snipers. It is a great visual film, shot in the Arizona desert. Suspense is maintained throughout and there is uniformly good acting. Boris Karloff as a British soldier and Christian zealot gives one of his fine performances.

M.A.S.H

1970. 116 min. color. U.S. **Prod.** Ingo Preminger; **Dir.** Robert Altman; **Scr.** Ring Lardner, Jr. (based on the novel by Richard Hooker); **Cin.** Harold Stein; **Ed.** Danford B. Greene; **Art D.** Jack Martin Smith, Arthur Lonergan; **Mus.** Johnny Mandel; **Cast:** Donald Sutherland, Elliott Gould, Tom Skeritt, Sally Kellerman, Robert Duvall, Gary Burghoff, Joe Ann Pflug.

Made in 1970 at the height of the Vietnam War, the film is set during the Korean War, 1950 to 1953. It tells the story of the surgeons and nurses of a M.A.S.H. (Mobile Army Surgical Hospital) unit and how they cope with the horrors of war and their antics in trying to remain sane. The realism on the operating table and the pools of blood, never so graphically shown in movies, was enough to send its message. War is depicted as a machine that grinds the bones and flesh of combatants. There is no structured plot and the story is told in unrelated comic episodes. Donald Sutherland as Hawkeye Pierce dominates the acting. It is an uneven film. The humiliation of Sally Kellerman and Robert Duvall goes on too long. There is an unnecessary trip to Japan by Pierce and Trapper John McIntyre (Elliott Gould). The final football game is over the top. They are more than compensated for, however, by many exceedingly funny incidents, most notably the frequent Radio Tokyo broadcasts of American popular songs sung in Japanese. Made during the height of the Vietnam war, M.A.S.H. is one of the best black comedies with a serious antiwar stance and witty and original dialogue.

The Magic Box

1951. 118 min. color. British. **Prod.** Ronald Neame; **Dir.** John Boulting; **Scr.** Eric Ambler (based on the book *Friese-Greene, Close-up of an Inventor* by Ray Allister); **Cin.** Jack Cardiff; **Ed.** Richard Best; **Prod. D.** John Bryan; **Art D.** T. Hopewell Ash; **Mus.** William Alwyn; **Cast:** Robert Donat, Maria Schell, Margaret Johnston, Robert Beatty, James Kenney, Bernard Miles, Laurence Olivier, Michael Redgrave, Eric Portman, Glynis Johns, Emlyn Williams.

The life of William Friese-Greene (Robert Donat) who invented and patented the first motion picture camera is explored. Almost every well-known British cinema actor of the day appears, if only briefly, in the movie. The film's memorable moment comes when Friese-Greene, after years of setbacks, perfects his apparatus and wants someone to share his elation. He runs to the street and brings in a policeman (Laurence Olivier) doing his rounds and shows him the moving picture. The scene is pure magic.

The Magician

(a.k.a *The Face) Ansiktet.* 1958. 102 min. b.w. Swedish. **Prod.** Allan Ekelund; **Dir.** Ingmar Bergman; **Scr.** Ingmar Bergman; **Cin.** Gunnar Fischer, Rolf Halmquist; **Ed.** Oscar Rosander; **Art D.** P. A. Lundgren; **Mus.** Erik Nordgren; **Cast:** Max von Sydow, Ingrid Thulin, Gunnar Bjornstrand, Bibi Andersson, Erland Josephson.

A nineteenth-century magician and mesmerist, Albert Emanuel Vogler (Max von Sydow), and his troupe are on the run from creditors. Vogler has also been accused of blasphemy. On their way to Stockholm, they are stopped at a small town by the magistrate. They can proceed only if Vogler can show to the local physician (Gunnar Bjornstrand) that he is not a charlatan. The physician is a rationalist and does not believe in magic or any such nonsense. The magician is forced to demonstrate his art, bringing horror and chaos to the doctor's household. He is now free to proceed to Stockholm where he will probably give a royal performance. Bergman himself considered the film as a comedy. It is, however, more Grand Guignol than comedy. The film embodies some of Bergman's favorite themes: illusion versus reality and skepticism versus faith.

The Magnificent Yankee

1950. 89 min. b.w. U.S. **Prod.** Armand Deutsch; **Dir.** John Sturges; **Scr.** Emmett Lavery (based on the book *Mr. Justice Holmes* by Francis Biddle and the play by Emmett Lavery); **Cin.** Joseph Ruttenberg; **Ed.** Ferris Webster; **Art D.** Cedric Gibbons, Arthur Lonergan; **Mus.** David Raksin; **Cast:** Louis Calhern, Ann Harding, Eduard Franz, James Lydon, Philip Ober, Ian Wolfe, Richard Anderson.

The film looks at the life of Oliver Wendell Holmes (Louis Calhern) during his years as a justice of the U.S. Supreme Court, 1902–1932. Holmes had fought in the American Civil War and was wounded three times. A man of great erudition, he had written an influential treatise on the common law. He became known as the "great dissenter," with many of his dissenting opinions later becoming law. An intelligent film with excellent performances that chronicles contemporary history and explores Holmes' relationship with his wife (Ann Harding) and his close friendship with fellow justice Louis Brandeis (Eduard Franz).

The Major and the Minor

1942. 100 min. b.w. U.S. **Prod.** Arthur Hornblow, Jr.; **Dir.** Billy Wilder; **Scr.** Billy Wilder, Charles Brackett (based on the play *Connie Goes Home* by Edward Childs Carpenter and the story "Sunny Goes Home" by Fannie Kilbourne); **Cin.** Leo Tover; **Ed.** Doane Harrison; **Art D.** Hans Dreier, Roland Anderson; **Mus.** Robert Emmett Dolan; **Cast:** Ginger Rogers, Ray Miland, Rita Johnson, Robert Benchley, Diana Lynn, Edward Fielding.

A young Iowa girl (Ginger Rogers) is in New York City starting a career as a facial and scalp masseuse. She is already disillusioned by the big city and when, in one of the funniest scenes of the movie, a lecherous client makes seductive proposals she decides to go home. She does not have the full train fare and is forced to become a pigtailed twelve-year-old bobby-soxer to qualify for the "minor" fare. On the train an army major (Ray Miland) who teaches at a boys' military school takes pity on the lonely youngster and becomes her protector. Complications arise when she reaches the school. The major's fiancée (Rita Johnson) begins to have doubts about the "minor's" age, considering her developed body that the "youngster" passes off as "some sort of gland trouble." She is also faced with fending off the amorous young cadets. A well acted film, especially by Ginger Rogers. Among the supporting cast, Diana Lynn as the fiancée's precocious young sister and Robert Benchley in a very brief role stand out. Wilder's first directorial effort was an auspicious beginning.

A Man and a Woman

Un Homme et Une Femme. 1966. 102 min. French. **Prod.** Claude Lelouch; **Dir.** Claude Lelouch; **Scr.** Claude Lelouch, Pierre Uytterhoeven; **Cin.** Claude Lelouch; **Ed.** Claude Lelouch, G. Boisser, Claude Barrois; **Art D.** Robert Luchaire; **Mus.** Francis Lai; **Cast:** Anouk Aimee, Jean-Lous Trintignant, Pierre Barouh, Valerie Lagrange.

This charming love story is from a lesser-known French director. It was *A Man and a Woman* that introduced a new generation to French films and was much acclaimed and copied. But technique wins over substance. The characters are cardboard "beautiful people" with glamorous jobs. Claude Lelouch was not able to replicate this success or equal the charm of *A Man and a Woman* in his later films.

A Man for All Seasons

1966. 120 min. color. British. **Prod.** Fred Zinnemann; **Dir.** Fred Zinnemann; **Scr.** Robert Bolt, Constance Willis (based on the play by Robert Bolt); **Cin.** Ted Moore; **Ed.** Ralph Kemplen; **Prod. D.** John Box; **Art D.** Terence Marsh; **Mus.** Georges Delerue; **Cast:** Paul Scofield, Wendy Hiller, Leo McKern, Robert Shaw, Orson Welles, Susannah York, John Hurt, Vanessa Redgrave, Corin Redgrave.

Henry VIII (Robert Shaw) needs male heirs and wants to annul his marriage to his barren wife. The Pope, for religious and political reasons, refuses to grant an annulment. Henry breaks with Rome and appoints himself as head of the new Church of England. He turns to Sir Thomas More (Paul Scofield), a companion from his youth, recently elevated as Lord Chancellor, to sanction the divorce and the break with the Catholic church. Sir Thomas has divided loyalties—to his king and "to his immortal soul"—and after soul-searching refuses to sanction the divorce. The king orders his death.

The film is too somber and More is depicted from the very outset as a saintly figure headed toward martyrdom. It is only More's philosophy of life and his ruminations we hear. Robert Bolt's script allows no debate on the matter. It is, however, a well-crafted film with great acting. Paul Scofield gives a remarkable performance. Wendy Hiller as More's sympathetic wife and Robert Shaw, both great actors, give equally fine performances. Orson Welles as Cardinal Wolsey delivers one of his finest pieces of acting in a five-minute scene that stays in the viewer's mind. The power of the film lies with the depiction of an individual who is able to remain true to his principles and say no in the most difficult and dire circumstances. The film won Academy Awards for best picture, best actor for Scofield, best director, best adapted screenplay and cinematography; and received nominations for best supporting actor and actress for Robert Shaw and Wendy Hiller.

Man of the West

1958. 100 min. color. U.S. **Prod.** Walter M. Mirisch; **Dir.** Anthony Mann; **Scr.** Reginald Rose (based on the novel *The Border Jumpers* by Will C. Brown); **Cin.** Ernest Haller; **Ed.** Richard Heermance; **Art D.** Hilyard Brown; **Mus.** Leigh Harline; **Cast:** Gary Cooper, Julie London, Lee J. Cobb, Arthur O'Connell, Jack Lord, John Dehner, Royal Dano.

Link Jones (Gary Cooper), a mild-mannered, middle-aged married man, is traveling by train to Fort Worth, Texas. He is to employ a schoolteacher for his hometown, and is carrying the money raised by the townspeople. The train is held up by the notorious Tobin gang and everyone, including Link, is robbed. The train begins to pull away and he is stranded in the wilderness along with Sam Beasley (Arthur O'Connell), a con man, and Billie (Julie London), a former saloon girl. As they begin their long walk, the area begins to look familiar to Link and he comes to a cabin he remembers from his youth. It is the hideout of Dock Tobin (Lee J. Cobb), his uncle who had raised him as a son. The rest of the gang, mostly his cousins, a vicious and sadistic lot, are also there. Dock Tobin is pleased to see Link and embraces him warmly. Dock is convinced Link, after an absence of some years, has come back to join the gang. Link introduces Billie as his girl and Beasley as a harmless fellow passenger on the train. Soon, in

order to test him, Dock sends Link on a robbery. Witnessing wanton cruelty and murder of bystanders, Link kills most of the gang
members. On returning he finds Billie has been beaten and raped
by Dock. In the showdown he kills Dock. Link gets his money
back and tells Billie, who had fallen in love with him, that he will
be returning to his wife and children.

   Man of the West is more than an ordinary Western. It is the story
of a gunfighter and robber who just decided one day to leave the
gang and begin a new life. Midway in the film Link confesses: "I
never had a family, just that man there. He took care of me. He
taught me killing and cheating. I didn't know any better. Then
one day I grew up so I busted away." What is also interesting is the
theme of patricide and the commentary on the inevitability of
man's baser instincts surfacing in hostile circumstances. There is
excellent acting by Cooper and Cobb. Cooper played Cobb's
nephew while in fact he was ten years older. In almost all of
Anthony Mann's Westerns, beginning with *Winchester '73* (1950),
his heroes have inner conflicts and suffer from guilt and alienation that Mann brings out well.

The Man Who Would Be King

1975. 129 min. color. British. **Prod.** John Foreman; **Dir.** John Huston; **Scr.** John Huston,
Gladys Hill (based on the story by Rudyard Kipling); **Cin.** Oswald Morris; **Ed.** Russell
Lloyd; **Prod. D.** Alexander Trauner; **Art D.** Tony Inglis; **Mus.** Maurice Jarre; **Cast:** Sean
Connery, Michael Caine, Christopher Plummer, Saeed Jaffrey, Jack May, Shakira Caine.

   This is the story of two unruly English soldiers in colonial India
who have wasted their wages and savings on whoring and vice.
They resign their commissions and head for Kafiristan, high in the
mountains of eastern Afghanistan, where they hope to rule the
primitive people and make their fortune. Daniel Dravot (Sean
Connery) and Peachy Carnahan (Michael Caine), with their rifles
and army training, convince the natives of their invulnerability and
become rulers. But they overreach and meet tragic ends.

The Kipling short story had always attracted John Huston. It had a theme that was relevant to many of his films—people who are consumed by greed and overreach: *The Maltese Falcon* (1941), *The Treasure of the Sierra Madre* (1948), and *The Asphalt Jungle* (1950). In the late forties Huston had in mind Clark Gable and Humphrey Bogart; in the sixties, Richard Burton and Peter O'Toole. Both projects fell through as he could not get financial backing. On paper Sean Connery and Michael Caine seemed good choices, but they fail to live up to the demands of their roles. Connery became the straight man and Caine the comic and the film, in parts, approaches broad comedy. There is, however, good acting by Christopher Plummer as Kipling, Saeed Jaffrey as Billy Fish, and Shakira Caine as Roxanne. Despite shortcomings in the acting, the film is well constructed with a very effective ending. Huston considered it as one of his personal best.

The Manchurian Candidate

1962. 126 min. b.w. U.S. **Prod.** George Axelrod, John Frankenheimer; **Dir.** John Frankenheimer; **Scr.** George Axelrod (based on the novel by Richard Condon); **Cin.** Lionel Lindon; **Ed.** Ferris Webster; **Prod. D.** Richard Sylbert; **Art D.** Richard Sylbert, Philip Jefferies; **Mus.** David Amram; **Cast:** Frank Sinatra, Laurence Harvey, Janet Leigh, Angela Lansbury, Henry Silva, James Gregory, John McGiver, James Edwards, Khigh Dhiegh.

The film is set during the Korean War. A platoon of U.S. infantrymen led by Captain Marco (Frank Sinatra) is betrayed by their Korean guide and is captured. They are taken to a P.O.W. camp somewhere on the Chinese-North Korean border. We next see them in a large hall where the captured soldiers are seated on a stage and are introduced to a group of Soviet, Chinese and North Korean officers and functionaries. The chief interrogator is Yen Lo (Khigh Dhiegh), a specialist on brainwashing from the Peking Institute. He mildly asks one of the captured Americans, Sergeant Raymond Shaw (Laurence Harvey), to shoot the platoon's youngest soldier. Shaw obeys and emotionlessly shoots the soldier in the head. The captives are released subsequently but are told they have escaped through the efforts of Sergeant Shaw.

Back in the United States several of those discharged soldiers start having recurring nightmares reliving the cold-blooded killing by Sergeant Shaw. Yet whenever asked about Shaw they all say that Shaw "was the best and bravest individual I had ever met." Captain Marco, who detests Sergeant Shaw, can't understand why he praises him. Shaw is to receive the Congressional Medal of Honor for having arranged the daring mass escape of his platoon. As the story unfolds we learn that Shaw was programmed into an assassin to do the work of the Chinese and the Soviets when ordered by prearranged signal. The triggering device is a phone call asking him to play solitaire. We also learn that Shaw's mother (Angela Lansbury) is a communist agent who has married Senator Iselin (James Gregory), a nitwit demagogue who has risen to prominence by alleging there are 207 communists in the U.S. government. Shaw assassinates several people at the order of his mother without being conscious of it. His final task is to assassinate the presidential candidate whereby his stepfather, under his mother's control, would become the nominee and the next president of the U.S.

The basic story revolves around an international communist plot to take over the U.S. government. It mocks professional anti-communists in the U.S. whose reckless behavior greatly helped the Soviets. The film established John Frankenheimer, who had mostly worked in TV, as an important newcomer. It is directed with self-confidence and frantic energy. Frankenheimer uses every means at his disposal. There are abrupt cuts used to great effect and awkward camera angels to heighten the paranoia. However, the film has several drawbacks. The romance between Sinatra and Janet Leigh is unnecessary and slows the action. The film is easily ten minutes too long. There is nothing remarkable about the acting of Sinatra or Laurence Harvey. The supporting cast, however, is very good and Angela Lansbury, James Gregory as a Joseph McCarthy type, and John McGiver are excellent.

The Mask of Dimitrios

1944. 95 min. b.w. U.S. **Prod.** Henry Blanke; **Dir.** Jean Negulesco; **Scr.** Frank Gruber (based on the novel *A Coffin for Dimitrios* by Eric Ambler); **Cin.** Arthur Edeson; **Ed.** Frederick Richards; **Art D.** Ted Smith; **Mus.** Adolph Deutsch; **Cast:** Peter Lorre, Sydney Greenstreet, Zachary Scott, Faye Emerson, Victor Francen, Steven Geray, George Tobias, Florence Bates, Eduardo Ciannelli, Kurt Katch.

A Dutch mystery writer (Peter Lorre) becomes interested in the life and career of Dimitrios (Zachary Scott), an amoral international swindler, spy and murderer who has eluded the police of several Balkan countries. The film is set in the inter-war years and told in flashbacks as Dimitrios' cohorts, lovers and victims tell of their encounters. It is one of the best works of director Jean Negulesco who made some worthwhile films while at Warners: *Three Strangers* (1946) and *Johnny Belinda* (1948). He then moved to Fox where he made sentimental nonsense. *The Mask of Dimitrios* is distinguished by a literate script and a very good cast, especially Victor Francen as the master spy and Steven Geray as one of Dimitrios' victims. Ironically the two most reliable actors, Sydney Greenstreet and Peter Lorre, do not seem comfortable in their roles.

Mayerling

1936. 89 min. b.w. French. **Prod.** B. Robert Dorfmann; **Dir.** Anatole Litvak; **Scr.** Joseph Kessel, Irma Von Cube (based on the novel *Idyl's End* by Claude Anet); **Cin.** Armand Thirard; **Ed.** Henri Rust; **Mus.** Arthur Honegger; **Cast:** Charles Boyer, Danielle Darrieux, Suzy Prim, Vladimir Sokoloff, Jean Dax, Gabrielle Dorziat, Jean Debucourt.

Set in 1889 Vienna Archduke Rudolph of Austria (Charles Boyer), heir to the throne, had been forced by the emperor Franz Joseph into a loveless marriage. He has become a dissolute drunkard and spends his nights with dance hall girls. At a ballet performance he meets the innocent seventeen-year-old Marie Vetsera (Danielle Darrieux) and they fall in love. When the Pope refuses to annul his marriage, he and Marie go to Mayerling, a hunting lodge in the woods. In a suicide pact, he shoots her and himself.

A very skillful film. When the lovers' eyes first meet at the ballet the camera captures their love in dreamlike beauty. There are other fluid scenes throughout the film. Both Boyer and Darrieux are perfect. Anatole Litvak was never able to replicate the mastery he showed in this film. Only two of his subsequent films came close: *The Snake Pit* (1948) and *Anastasia* (1956).

The McKenzie Break

1970. 106 min. color. British. **Prod.** Jules Levy, Arthur Gardner, Arnold Laven; **Dir.** Lamont Johnson; **Scr.** William Norton (based on the novel *The Bowmanville Break* by Sidney Shelley); **Cin.** Michael Reed; **Ed.** Tom Rolph; **Prod. D.** Frank White; **Mus.** Riz Ortolani; **Cast:** Brian Keith, Helmut Griem, Ian Hendry, Jack Watson, Patrick O'Connell, Horst Janson, Alexander Allerson, John Abineri.

A reversal of movies we had been accustomed to—it is not about allied prisoners. This film is about German prisoners of war at Camp McKenzie in the Scottish highlands. The prisoners are mostly U-boat officers and only have escape on their minds. It becomes mainly a battle of wits between a British intelligence officer (Brian Keith) sent to prevent a mass escape and the leader of the P.O.W.s, a young, fanatic Nazi U-boat captain (Helmut Griem). An intelligent script with unusual twists complements the fine acting of the entire cast, especially Brian Keith, a highly underrated actor.

Meeting Venus

1991. 117 min. color. British. **Prod.** David Puttnam; **Dir.** Istvan Szabo; **Scr.** Istvan Szabo, Michael Hirst; **Cin.** Lajos Koltai; **Ed.** Jim Clark; **Art D.** Attila Kovacs; **Mus.** Daisy Boschan; **Cast:** Glenn Close, Niels Arestrup, Erland Josephson, Johanna Ter Steege, Moscu Alcalay, Macha Meril.

A multinational production of Wagner's *Tannhauser* at the Paris opera is to be conducted by a relatively unknown Hungarian conductor (Niels Arestrup). The singers are from six different countries and there is near chaos from the beginning. The diva is a Swedish singer (Glenn Close) who takes an immediate dislike to the conductor. A chapter of a local union is threatening a walkout. The opera administrators are as egotistical and temperamental as the artists and the artists are as commercially-minded as the administrators. To complicate matters, an affair develops between the married conductor and the mercurial diva. Despite all, the improvised opening night is beautifully staged. Glenn Close (whose voice was dubbed by Kiri Te Kanewa) is very good and the unknown supporting cast carries its weight. Where the film really succeeds is in the comedy. It weakens in its attempt to convey a sort of metaphor on the European union. The film's highlight is the "Pilgrim's Chorus" from *Tannhauser* where the singers carrying flashlights enter from the rear of the dark auditorium onto an undecorated and barren stage.

Meet Me in St. Louis

1944. 113 min. color. U.S. **Prod.** Arthur Freed; **Dir.** Vincente Minnelli; **Scr.** Irving Brecher, Fred Finklehoffe (based on stories by Sally Benson); **Cin.** George Folsey; **Ed.** Albert Akst; **Art D.** Cedric Gibbons, Lemuel Ayers, Martin Smith; **Mus.** Songs by Ralph Blane, Hugh Martin; **Cast:** Judy Garland, Margaret O'Brien, Mary Astor, Lucille Bremer, June Lockhart, Tom Drake, Marjorie Main, Harry Davenport, Leon Ames.

Pure Americana, this film is set in 1903 St. Louis site of the World's Fair. It tells the story of a businessman who is offered a better job in New York and the reaction of his family to leaving their dear St. Louis. An expertly made nostalgic film with some very good musical numbers, especially "The Trolley Song." Although one of Judy Garland's best, it is seven-year-old Margaret O'Brien who steals every scene she is in.

Melvin and Howard

1980. 95 min. color. U.S. **Prod.** Art Linson, Don Phillips; **Dir.** Jonathan Demme; **Scr.** Bo Goldman; **Cin.** Tak Fujimoto; **Ed.** Craig McKay; **Prod. D.** Toby Rafelson; **Art D.** Richard Sawyer; **Mus.** Bruce Langhorne; **Cast:** Paul LeMat, Jason Robards, Jr., Mary Steenburgen, Michael J. Pollard, Gloria Grahame, Dabney Coleman.

Melvin Dummar (Paul LeMat), is an ordinary fellow who has had odd jobs in a magnesium plant, a gas station and as a milkman. He claims he once picked up an old hobo in the Nevada desert, took him to Las Vegas, and gave him a quarter. Eight years later, after his divorce and remarriage, he produced a will where the hobo, presumably Howard Hughes (Jason Robards, Jr.), had left him $156 million. The so-called "Mormon will" was dismissed by the courts, but Dummar received national publicity. The film is more than a story of a born loser. It is the story of the average guy, most likely in debt up to his ears, who believes in lotteries, TV game shows, and that his ship will one day come in. The best scene in the movie comes early. An unshaven, dishevelled man, supposedly Howard Hughes, is given a lift by Melvin. To cheer him up, Melvin sings a silly song he has written. He then insists that Hughes sing. In a very poignant, beautifully acted scene, Hughes quietly sings "Bye Bye Blackbird." We see in Robards' eyes that the character has been given a new lease on life, and he feels revived.

Melvin and Howard has a very thin plot, but the screenplay by Bo Goldman develops the characters well, and Jonathan Demme's low-keyed direction moves the film at the right pace. In addition to Robards' amazing characterization of Hughes, the entire cast is very good. It has been aptly said of this lyrical comedy, it is "what might have happened if Jean Renoir had directed a comedy script by Preston Sturges."

Mephisto

1981. 144 min. color. Hungarian/West German. **Prod.** Manfred Durniok; **Dir.** Istvan Szabo; **Scr.** Istvan Szabo, Peter Dobai (based on the novel by Klaus Mann); **Cin.** Lajos Koltai; **Ed.** Zsuzsa Csakany; **Art D.** Jozsef Romvari; **Mus.** Zdenko Tamassy; **Cast:** Klaus Maria Brandauer, Krystyna Janda, Ildiko Bansagi, Karin Boyd, Rolf Hoppe, Christine Harbort.

The story begins circa 1933 with the rise of Hitler and his appointment as Chancellor of Germany. Its focus is on an ambitious left-leaning provincial Hamburg actor, Hendrik Hofgen (Klaus Maria Brandauer), who had hoped to establish a workers' theater. His ambition overrides his principles and he leaves Hamburg for Berlin. He soon comes to the attention of the Nazi hierarchy and joins the Nazi party. He betrays friends, lovers and family, and ultimately sells his soul. The Minister for Prussia (Rolf Hoppe) takes an interest in him and his rise thereafter is meteoric. The characters he is ordered to play range from Faust to Hamlet, both depicted as men of action with a Nordic heritage and imbued with Nazi ideology. The film ends with his total enslavement.

A most original film, but what is most memorable is the towering, almost hypnotic performance of Klaus Maria Brandauer in one of the most bravura and energetic performances in movie history. The supporting cast is very good, especially Rolf Hoppe, a Goebbels-like character as the Minister for Prussia, and Karin Boyd as the dancer/mistress whom Brandauer betrays. The direction by Istvan Szabo who also wrote the screenplay is almost perfect, but the film drags a bit and at 144 minutes is some ten to fifteen minutes too long.

The Merry Widow

1934. 99 min. b.w. U.S. **Prod.** Irving Thalberg; **Dir.** Ernst Lubitsch; **Scr.** Samson Raphaelson, Ernest Vajda (based on the operetta by Franz Lehár, Victor Leon, Leo Stein); **Cin.** Oliver T. Marsh; **Ed.** Frances Marsh; **Art D.** Cedric Gibbons, Frederic Hope; **Mus.** Franz Lehár adapted by Herbert Stothart; **Cast:** Maurice Chevalier, Jeanette MacDonald, Una Merkel, Edward Everett Horton, George Barbier, Minna Gombell, Ruth Channing, Sterling Holloway.

Jeanette MacDonald is a widow whose wealth sustains the country of Marshovia. When she moves to Paris to find a husband, the king, fearing the country will become bankrupt, sends Maurice Chevalier to woo her back. They fall in love, but MacDonald learns of his mission and rejects him. The story ends happily, of course. Lubitsch's version is the best and most lavish of several screen adaptations of the Franz Lehár operetta which also enjoys new lyrics by Lorenz Hart, Gus Kahn and Richard Rogers. The famed "Merry Widow Waltz" performed in a large hall of mirrors is still among the best musical sequences on film.

Midnight Run

1988. 122 min. color. U.S. **Prod.** Martin Brest; **Dir.** Martin Brest; **Scr.** George Gallo; **Cin.** Donald Thorin; **Ed.** Billy Weber, Chris Lebenzon, Michael Tronick; **Prod. D.** Angelo Graham; **Mus.** Danny Elfman; **Cast:** Robert De Niro, Charles Grodin, Yaphet Kotto, John Ashton, Dennis Farina, Joe Pantoliano.

An ex-cop turned bounty hunter (Robert De Niro) is hired by a bail bondsman to take a former Los Angeles Mafia accountant (Charles Grodin) from New York to Los Angeles. The mob also want Grodin who has embezzled $15 million, given it away to charity and skipped bail. During an eventful and sometimes hilarious cross-country chase much is revealed about the two men and a relationship develops. The comedy and sentiment far supersede the violence. The dialogue is sharp and the two leads are very good.

The Ministry of Fear

1944. 85 min. b.w. U.S. **Prod.** Seton I. Miller; **Dir.** Fritz Lang; **Scr.** Seton I. Miller (based on the novel by Graham Greene); **Cin.** Henry Sharp; **Ed.** Archie Marshek; **Art D.** Hans Dreier, Hal Pereira; **Mus.** Victor Young; **Cast:** Ray Milland, Marjorie Reynolds, Carl Esmond, Dan Duryea, Alan Napier, Hillary Brooke, Erskine Sanford.

The Ministry of Fear is an espionage film noir by the master Fritz Lang. The film is based on a Graham Greene novel, but there is nothing of the ever-present Greene theme of guilt and redemption. The first half of the movie is Lang at his best with atmospheric sets, low-key lighting, dark alleys, rooms, train stations and shadows. Ray Milland is excellent as a tortured ex-convict, but the rest of the cast is mediocre at best. In the second half the movie wavers and does not match Lang's best work.

Miracle in Milan

Miracolo a Milano. 1951. 95 min. b.w. Italian. **Prod.** Vittorio De Sica; **Dir.** Vittorio De Sica; **Scr.** Cesare Zavattini, Vittorio De Sica, Suso Cecchi D'Amico, Mario Chiari, Adolf Franci (based on the story "Toto Il Buono" by Cesare Zavattini); **Cin.** Aldo Graziati; **Ed.** Eraldo Da Roma; **Art D.** Guido Fiorini; **Mus.** Alessandro Cicognini; **Cast:** Branduani Gianni, Francesco Golisano, Paolo Stoppa, Emma Gramatica.

This neorealist fairy tale by Vittorio De Sica which followed *Bicycle Thief* (1947), but is totally different. What they share is only the social commentary on the condition of the poor in post-World War II Italy. There is expert casting of mostly nonprofessionals.

The Miracle of Morgan's Creek

1944. 99 min. b.w. U.S. **Prod.** Preston Sturges; **Dir.** Preston Sturges; **Scr.** Preston Sturges; **Cin.** John Seitz; **Ed.** Stuart Gilmore; **Art D.** Hans Dreier; Ernst Fegte; **Mus.** Leo Shuken; **Cast:** Eddie Bracken, Betty Hutton, William Demarest, Diana Lynn, Brian Donlevy, Akim Tamiroff, Porter Hall.

A small town (Morgan's Creek) bank clerk, Norvall Jones (Eddie Bracken), desperately wants to join the armed forces but is rejected by the army on medical grounds. He has been in love with Trudy Kockenlocker (Betty Hutton) since kindergarten, but she is not interested in him romantically. Trudy is man crazy and loves dancing. She wants to go to a farewell party for the soldiers of a nearby camp, but her father (William Demarest), the equivalent of a town sheriff, doesn't allow her. She prevails on Norvall to take her to a movie and her father, feeling safe with Norvall, gives his permission. Once out of the house she begs Norvall to drop her off at the party. He goes to the movies alone and waits for her until the early hours of the morning to bring her home. The fruit punch had been spiked and Trudy had gotten drunk. All she remembers is that she had spent most of the night with six soldiers and married one of them. His name had been something like Ratsky or Watsky or Ratziwasi. The soldiers had left the camp that morning. Soon she finds she is pregnant. She seeks the advice of her youngest sister, Emmy (Diana Lynn), who tells her she must marry someone immediately. Norvall needs no inducement. But soon he is charged with some ten criminal counts, including bigamy, impersonating a soldier, forgery and corrupting the morals of a minor. The only thing that can save him is a miracle. A miracle does happen. She gives birth to sextuplets, which puts Morgan's Creek on the map. Governor McGinty (Brian Donlevy of the 1940 movie *The Great McGinty* fame) pardons Norvall.

A very funny movie, *The Miracle of Morgan Creek* has dated somewhat and has other drawbacks. The casting of Betty Hutton was a mistake. She was all right in musical comedies, but she was incapable of a straight performance. She moved and mugged too much. The rest of the cast is very good. It was an irreverent and daring film for its day as it made fun of some sacred American values, marriage and motherhood, and reflected badly on soldiers, especially in wartime. The film was held up for close to eight months as it was reviewed by the Hays office for censorship problems.

The Miracle Worker

1962. 106 min.. b.w. U.S. **Prod.** Fred Coe; **Dir.** Arthur Penn; **Scr.** William Gibson (based on his play and the book *The Story of My Life* by Helen Keller); **Cin.** Ernesto Caparros; **Ed.** Aram Avakian; **Art D.** George Jenkins, Mel Bourne; **Mus.** Laurence Rosenthal; **Cast:** Anne Bancroft, Patty Duke, Victor Jory, Inga Swenson, Andrew Prine, Kathleen Comegys.

This is the best work of director Arthur Penn who also directed the stage play. Seldom has a film had two performances of this caliber. It is an unrelenting film, without a touch of sentimentality or optimism, about the early years of the remarkable deaf mute Helen Keller. Anne Bancroft as Annie Sullivan and Patty Duke as the young Helen Keller received Oscars for best actress and best supporting actress respectively.

Mister Roberts

1955. 123 min. color. U.S. **Prod.** Leland Hayward; **Dir.** John Ford, Mervin Le Roy; **Scr.** Joshua Logan, Frank S. Nugent (based on the play by Joshua Logan and Thomas Heggen and the novel by Thomas Heggen); **Cin.** Winton C. Hoch; **Ed.** Jack Murray; **Art D.** Art Loel; **Mus.** Franz Waxman; **Cast:** Henry Fonda, James Cagney, William Powell, Jack Lemmon, Betsy Palmer, Ward Bond, Nick Adams.

Mister Roberts is a seriocomic story of the officers of a World War II navy cargo ship. It is a disjointed film with too many directors. John Ford began the film but had an acrimonious relationship with Henry Fonda who had played his role on Broadway for several years and was unwilling to change his approach. Ford left the film and Mervin Le Roy took over. Le Roy was well past his prime and needed help from Joshua Logan who had directed the Broadway play. Henry Fonda and William Powell are first rate. Jack Lemmon established himself as a great comedian. But James Cagney does not seem comfortable in his part. Fonda's portrayal of Lieutenant Roberts is enough to carry the film and make it thoroughly enjoyable.

Moby Dick

1956. 116 min. color. U.S. **Prod.** John Huston, Vaughan N. Dean; **Dir.** John Huston; **Scr.** John Huston, Ray Bradbury (based on the novel by Herman Melville); **Cin.** Oswald Morris; **Ed.** Russell Lloyd; **Art D.** Ralph Brinton; **Mus.** Philip Stainton; **Cast:** Gregory Peck, Richard Basehart, Leo Genn, Harry Andrews, Bernard Miles, Orson Welles, Mervyn Jones, Noel Purcell, Frederick Ledebur, James Roberson Justice.

Captain Ahab has spent four years on his whaling ship in obsessive pursuit of the great whale, Moby Dick, seeking revenge for the loss of his leg. A very difficult film for the 1950s, since you couldn't build a realistic whale as with *Jaws'* shark (1975), and the technology for filming ocean scenes was not advanced. Huston filmed in Ireland, Portugal, the Canary Islands, the Azores and Wales, on real oceans, not in studio tanks. He wisely directed the film as an adventure story without the multiple and complicated layers of symbolism in Melville's masterpiece. Moby Dick had taken more than Ahab's leg, he had taken his soul. The obvious drawback to the film was the choice of Gregory Peck as Ahab. He looks more Lincolnesque than a fierce tormented sea captain. Huston had planned for his father, Walter Huston, to play Ahab, but he died in 1950. The rest of the cast, however, is magnificent. Orson Welles as Father Maple gives one of his great performances. Richard Basehart as Ishmael, Harry Andrews as Stubb, Bernard Miles as Manxman and Frederick Ledebur as Queequeg give superlative performances. Only Leo Genn, a fine actor, is below par.

This was the third and by far the best filming of *Moby Dick*. The first was a 1926 silent version, the other a sound film in 1930, both with John Barrymore. It is an ambitious and honest effort by Huston that does not entirely work. In addition to several literary classics, Huston also brought to the screen works of such notable contemporary authors as Flannery O'Connor and Tennessee Williams.

Moonstruck

1987. 102 min. color. U.S. **Prod.** Patrick Palmer, Norman Jewison; **Dir.** Norman Jewison; **Scr.** John Patrick Stanley; **Cin.** David Watkin; **Ed.** Lou Lombardo; **Prod. D.** Philip Rosenberg; **Mus.** Dick Hyman; **Cast:** Cher, Nicolas Cage, Vincent Gardenia, Olympia Dukakis, Danny Aiello, Feodor Chaliapin, Jr.

Moonstruck is an enchanting comedy, well directed and beautifully photographed. The one scene of the full moon over the Brooklyn Bridge and the Manhattan skyline with Dean Martin crooning "That's Amore" is worth its weight in gold. The duet from "La Boheme," another musical theme, adds to the charm of the movie. There is some overacting by Nicolas Cage, but well deserved Oscars for Cher and Olympia Dukakis.

Mother

1926. 90 min. b.w. Silent. Russian. **Dir.** Vsevolod Pudovkin; **Scr.** Nathan Zarkhi, Vsevolod Pudovkin (based on the novel by Maxim Gorky); **Cin.** Anatoli Golovnya; **Cast:** Vera Baranovskaya, A. P. Khristiakov, Nicolai Batalov, Ivan Koval-Samborsky, Anna Zemtsova, Vsevolod Pudovkin.

The film is set during the 1905 uprising in Russia. A young revolutionary has organized a strike and gathered a cache of arms. His mother is tricked by the police into inadvertently tipping off his whereabouts. Learning of her son's dire fate, the mother becomes a revolutionary. The film has dated, but it is carried by a good cast. In contrast to Eisenstein whose heroes were the masses, Vsevolod Pudovkin considered the individual as the hero and the choice of actors crucial. Pudovkin himself plays a police interrogator and the rest of the cast were experienced actors from the Moscow Art Theatre.

Movie Movie

1978. 107 min. b.w. color. U.S. **Prod.** Stanley Donen; **Dir.** Stanley Donen; **Scr.** Larry Gelbart, Sheldon Keller; **Cin.** Charles Rosher, Jr., Bruce Surtees; **Ed.** George Hively; **Art D.** Jack Fisk; **Mus.** Ralph Burns; **Cast:** George C. Scott, Trish Van Devere, Eli Wallach, Red Buttons, Barbara Harris, Art Carney, Ann Reinking, Jocelyn Brando, Michael Kidd, Barry Bostwick, Harry Hamlin.

Movie Movie is an irreverent spoof of films of the thirties. It is a double feature. The first feature is "Dynamite Hands," a black and white boxing story of a law student from the slums who becomes a boxer to make money for his sister's desperately needed eye operation. He not only attains riches and fame but finishes law school and goes after the crooked boxing promoters. The dialogue is rampant with distorted clichés. The next is a color musical, "Baxter's Beauties of 1933," an amalgam of *Gold Diggers of 1933* (1933) and *42nd Street* (1933). This is an overnight chorus girl to star tale. Michael Kidd carries off the Busby Berkeley-type choreography well. There is even a "Coming Attractions" trailer for a movie about World War I pilots, "Zero Hour." Today's trailers actually have no less hyperbole and drama. The entire film is satirical nostalgia for movie buffs.

Mr. Smith Goes to Washington

1939. 129 min. b.w. U.S. **Prod.** Frank Capra; **Dir.** Frank Capra; **Scr.** Sidney Buchman (based on the novel *The Gentleman from Montana* by Lewis R. Foster); **Cin.** Joseph Walker; **Ed.** Gene Havlick, Al Clark; **Art D.** Lionel Banks; **Mus.** Dimitri Tiomkin; **Cast:** James Stewart, Jean Arthur, Claude Rains, Edward Arnold, Guy Kibbe, Thomas Mitchell, Eugene Pallette, Beulah Bondi, Harry Carey, H. B. Warner, Porter Hall, Jack Carson.

This very enjoyable, improbable story of a naive idealistic freshman senator who wins out over corruption has Capra's usual sugarcoating. It was more enjoyable when viewers were more innocent and knew even less about their government. Though it has dated considerably, one can still appreciate the very fine cast and well told story.

Mutiny on the Bounty

1935. 132 min. b.w. U.S. **Prod.** Irving Thalberg; **Dir.** Frank Lloyd; **Scr.** Talbot Jennings, Jules Furthman, Carey Wilson (based on the novels *Mutiny on the Bounty* and *Men against the Sea* by Charles Nordhoff and James Norman Hall); **Cin.** Arthur Edeson; **Ed.** Margaret Booth; **Art D.** Cedric Gibbons, Arnold Gillespie; **Mus.** Herbert Stothart; **Cast:** Charles Laughton, Clark Gable, Franchot Tone, Herbert Mundin, Dudley Digges, Edie Quillan, Donald Crisp, Movita, Spring Byington, Henry Stephenson.

In 1787, *HMS Bounty* sails from Portsmouth, England, to Tahiti to bring back breadfruit trees destined for the West Indies as cheap food for plantation slaves. Captain Bligh (Charles Laughton) is sadistic and abuses the crew leading to a mutiny headed by First Mate Fletcher Christian (Clark Gable). Bligh is put on a small boat with eighteen of his loyalists with meager provisions. Christian and the mutineers, with the reluctant midshipman Roger Byam (Franchot Tone), take the ship back to Tahiti and evade capture. Some of the mutineers are caught and the film ends with their court-martial trial.

MGM put all its resources and usual gloss into this technically impressive film with some fine cinematography. There is excellent acting by the three leads—Charles Laughton, Clark Gable and Franchot Tone—who all received Academy Award nominations. Never before or since have three actors from the same film been nominated for best actor.

My Fair Lady

1964. 170 min. color. U.S. **Prod.** Jack L. Warner; **Dir.** George Cukor; **Scr.** Alan Jay Lerner (based on the musical play by Alan Jay Lerner and Frederick Loewe from the play *Pygmalion* by George Bernard Shaw); **Cin.** Harry Stradling; **Ed.** William Ziegler; **Prod. D.** Cecil Beaton; **Art D.** Gene Allen; **Mus.** Frederick Loewe; **Chor.** Hermes Pan; **Cast:** Rex Harrison, Audrey Hepburn, Stanley Holloway, Wilfrid Hyde-White, Gladys Cooper, Jeremy Brett, Theodore Bikel, Henry Daniel, Mona Washburn.

This is one of the weaker adaptations of a great musical from stage to screen. Audrey Hepburn's singing voice was dubbed, and she looked too haute couture even as a "squashed cabbage." But the film has the great choreography of Hermes Pan, the beautiful sets and costumes of Cecil Beaton and many of the words of George Bernard Shaw, particularly in the songs. The excellent supporting cast of Stanley Holloway, Wilfrid Hyde-White, Gladys Cooper and Mona Washburn help to make the film enjoyable.

My Man Godfrey

1936. 95 min. b.w. U.S. **Prod.** Gregory La Cava; **Dir.** Gregory La Cava; **Scr.** Morrie Ryskind, Eric Hatch, Gregory La Cava (based on the story "1101 Park Avenue" by Eric Hatch); **Cin.** Ted Tetzlaff; **Ed.** Ted J. Kent; **Art D.** Charles D. Hall; **Mus.** Charles Previn; **Cast:** William Powell, Carole Lombard, Gail Patrick, Alice Brady, Eugene Pallette, Alan Mowbray, Mischa Auer, Franklin Pangborn.

A screwball comedy set during the Great Depression, *My Man Godfrey* tells the story of a dysfunctional family and how Godfrey Parke (William Powell), a Harvard-educated proper Bostonian gentleman, turned by circumstance into a hobo, saves a wealthy family. The Bullocks, headed by Alexander Bullock (Eugene Pallette), a successful businessman, live in a sumptuous house on Park Avenue. He is the only sane person in the family. His dim-witted wife (Alice Brady) keeps Carlo (Mischa Auer), a no-good loafer, as a pet. Their eldest daughter is the mean, calculating Cornelia (Gail Patrick) and their younger daughter, the spontaneous, slightly scatterbrained, beautiful Irene (Carole Lombard). The family is hosting a large charity event with a scavenger hunt as its main theme. One of the items on the scavenger list is a "forgotten man." Irene finds Godfrey, a destitute hobo, takes him to the party and wins first prize. Godfrey becomes the household butler. He saves the family from bankruptcy, kicks Carlo the loafer out, teaches Cornelia a lesson in humility and will probably win Irene's hand. A finely acted film with William Powell and Carole Lombard at their best. Eugene Pallette, Alice Brady and Mischa Auer are equally winning. The promised social message of this Depression-era film is sacrificed for budding romance, and there is a somewhat mechanical ending when the Bullock family decides to open a nightclub. But it is a very entertaining, fast-moving film with a witty script.

My Night at Maud's

Ma Nuit Chez Maud. 1969. 105 min. b.w. French. **Prod.** Pierre Cottrell, Barbet Schroeder; **Dir.** Eric Rohmer; **Scr.** Eric Rohmer; **Cin.** Nestor Almendros; **Ed.** Cecile Decugis; **Art D.** Nicole Rachline; **Cast:** Jean-Louis Trintignant, Francoise Fabian, Marie-Christine Barrault, Antoine Vitez, Anne Dubot.

The film is set in Clermont Ferrand, a city southeast of Paris. Jean-Louis (Jean-Louis Trintignant), a young engineer and devout Catholic, is a good friend of Vidal (Antoine Vitez), a Marxist professor. Jean-Louis has fallen in love at first sight with blonde Francoise (Marie-Christine Barrault) whom he had seen at church. He was too shy to approach her but has made up his mind to marry her. On a cold winter evening Vidal invites him to dinner at the home of his lover, Maud (Francoise Fabian), an agnostic divorcée. The evening is one long discussion about the French philosopher and mathematician, Pascal, and free choice. Jean-Louis argues that he firmly believes in Pascal's "Pensées", that it is less risky to believe in God; if you win, you win eternity, and if you lose, you lose nothing. Maud and Vidal reject the proposition. Vidal leaves but Jean-Louis stays and continues the discussion. As it is snowing heavily he is offered to stay the night. He leaves the next morning, his chastity intact despite advances by Maud. The film jumps several years forward. Jean-Louis has married the girl of his dreams, but he has found she had been the mistress of Maud's former husband.

As in all of Eric Rohmer's films very little happens on the surface, but the characters explain their feelings and lay bare their souls in conversation: Jean-Louis' dream of marrying a chaste Catholic girl, and Maud revealing that she had a lover who died and her husband had a lovely, young devout Catholic mistress. This was the fourth of Rohmer's six morality tales, and established him as one of the foremost filmmakers of his day, both literate and original. Rohmer also showed that meaningful discussions, even lengthy ones, could also be cinematic. The film is by no means static. Nestor Almendros' camera moves constantly and often closely focuses on the speaker for added effect. Blaise Pascal was born in 1623 in Clermont Ferrand, hence the setting.

Mysteries of the Treasure of Phantom Valley

Asrar-e Ganj-e Darre-ye Jenni. 1974. color. Iranian. **Prod.** Ebrahim Golestan; **Dir.** Ebrahim Golestan; **Scr.** Ebrahim Golestan (based on his novel); **Cin.** Ebrahim Golestan and Amir Karari; **Ed.** Ebrahim Golestan; **Prod. D.** Rahman Asadi with paintings and statues by Bahman Dadkhah, Kave Golestan; **Mus.** Farhad Meshkat; **Cast:** Parviz Sayad, Mary Apik, Shahnaz Tehrani, Sadeq Bahram, Loretta, Mani Haqiqi.

A poor farmer, Samad (Parviz Sayad), while working to remove a large stone from his land has the earth collapse from under him revealing a large cave filled with untold treasures of precious stones and ancient artifacts. He secretly removes some objects and sells them. Although he had been perfectly content with his home and dutiful wife, he now marries a "city girl" and builds a huge ostentatious mansion. He imports furniture from abroad and wears the most fashionable apparel. Soon others begin to vie for his treasure. He loses it all when, in the course of road building, an explosion buries the cave once again.

The celebrated writer and filmmaker Ebrahim Golestan chose to make a veiled political parody on Iran's most precious natural resource. The film is more notable for its message than for its craftsmanship. It can be read as an allegory on oil, the proceeds of which were wasted by the government on foolish projects; or an allegory on unnecessary conspicuous consumption, and the import of incongruous Western values. It was daring for its time. Golestan was a pioneer of cinema in Iran and much of today's fine films by young, internationally recognized directors owe a great deal to him. Another early Iranian director, a contemporary of Golestan, is Farrokh Ghaffari. In 1958 he made *Jonoub-e Shahr* (*The South of the City*), an important film for its social themes, inspired by the neorealist films of Vittorio De Sica.

Network

1976. 120 min. color. U.S. **Prod.** Howard Gottfried; **Dir.** Sidney Lumet; **Scr.** Paddy Chayefsky; **Cin.** Owen Roizman; **Ed.** Alan Hein; **Prod. D.** Philip Rosenberg; **Mus.** Elliot Lawrence; **Cast:** Faye Dunaway, William Holden, Peter Finch, Robert Duvall, Beatrice Straight, Wesley Addy, Ned Beatty, Arthur Burghardt, Bill Burrows.

UBS has the lowest ratings of the three television networks and decides to fire its longtime news anchorman (Peter Finch). The news of his dismissal unbalances the already troubled man and he announces on his live broadcast that he has found God and will commit suicide on his next program. Viewers make an idol of him and the icy cold network programmer (Faye Dunaway) convinces the evangelical chairman (Ned Beatty) and the cynical CEO (Robert Duvall) to exploit the unexpected publicity and boost the ratings. Finch becomes a prophet of sorts and gains an immense following. The film's thesis is that the networks will air anything to boost ratings. It was a provocative movie with biting humor but has lost its punch. The apprehensions of the screenwriter, Paddy Chayefsky, have materialized and gone beyond what he was warning against. It has other weaknesses as some of the characters are not fully developed and remain stereotypes. It is, however, well directed and well acted. The film won best actor, actress and supporting actress awards for Peter Finch, Faye Dunaway and Beatrice Straight respectively.

Never on Sunday

Pote Tin Kyriaki. 1960. 91 min. b.w. Greek. **Prod.** Jules Dassin; **Dir.** Jules Dassin; **Scr.** Jules Dassin; **Cin.** Jacques Natteau; **Ed.** Roger Dwyre; **Mus.** Manos Hadjidakis; **Cast:** Melina Mercouri, Jules Dassin, Georges Foundas, Tito Vandis.

Homer (Jules Dassin), an American Hellenophile, travels to Piraeus, Greece. He is in love with everything Greek. He meets Ilya (Melina Mercouri), a prostitute with a heart of gold. She only accepts customers she likes and never on Sundays when she goes to the theater to see the great plays of Sophocles and Euripides

without knowing the ancient Greek language or really understanding the meaning of the plays. She loves Medea and is certain
she didn't kill her children, and Oedipus' only problem was that he
loved his mother, maybe too much. The stodgy Homer tries to
reform the earthy Ilya but gives up. He is himself reformed and
begins to appreciate hedonistic pleasures. The film belongs to
Melina Mercouri who plays the carefree hooker to perfection.
Dassin is no actor but a good director who made some great realistic American films, *Brute Force* (1948) and *The Naked City*
(1948), and some notable films in Europe while in self-exile.

The New Land

Nybyggarna. 1972. 161 min. color. Swedish. **Prod.** Bengt Forslund; **Dir.** Jan Troell; **Scr.**
Bengt Forslund, Jan Troell (based on the novel *The Emigrants* by Vilhelm Moberg); **Cin.**
Jan Troell; **Ed.** Jan Troell; **Art D.** P.A. Lundgren; **Mus.** Bengt Ernryd, George Oddner; **Cast:**
Max von Sydow, Liv Ullmann, Eddie Axberg, Hans Alfredson, Halvar Bjork.

The New Land is the sequel to *The Emigrants* (1971), which was
the saga of the arduous journey of Oskar and Kristina from Sweden to the U.S. and their settling in the wilderness of Minnesota.
This film deals with their struggle to eke out a living in the new
land. Not as panoramic as the earlier film, but it is a worthy
sequel by the same director and the same actors.

A Night to Remember

1958. 123 min. b.w. British. **Prod.** William McQuitty; **Dir.** Roy Ward Baker; **Scr.** Eric
Ambler (based on the book by Walter Lord); **Cin.** Geoffrey Unsworth; **Ed.** Sidney Hayers;
Art D. Alex Vetchinsky; **Mus.** William Alwyn; **Cast:** Kenneth Moore, Ronald Allen, Honor
Blackman, Anthony Bushell, Robert Ayers.

By far the best film about the sinking of the *Titanic*. It is a very
factual account of what transpired on the night of 14 April 1912
when the ship struck an iceberg and 1,513 passengers and crew
members from a total of 2,224 perished. There are no heroes or

villains, only those who behaved badly and those who behaved well. Kenneth Moore stands out as Second Officer Herbert Lightoller in a film that has well over one hundred speaking parts. Although made on a relatively small budget, the film shows us the opulence of the dining rooms, lounges and Georgian suites.

None But the Lonely Heart

1944. 113 min. b.w. U.S. **Prod.** David Hempstead; **Dir.** Clifford Odets; **Scr.** Clifford Odets (based on the novel by Richard Llewellyn); **Cin.** George Barnes; **Ed.** Roland Gross; **Prod. D.** Mordecai Gorelik; **Art D.** Albert S. D'Agostino; **Mus.** Hanns Eisler; **Cast:** Cary Grant, Ethel Barrymore, Barry Fitzgerald, Jane Wyatt, Dan Duryea, George Coulouris, June Duprez, Konstantin Shayne.

A dark and brooding story of a cockney drifter (Cary Grant) from London's East End in the thirties prior to World War II. His mother (Ethel Barrymore) owns a secondhand furniture shop and disapproves of his vagabond life. When he learns that his mother is dying he settles down and helps around the shop, but he shortly backslides and gets involved with local underworld figures. His mother is reduced to dealing in stolen goods. The film gives a dramatic portrayal of slum life aided by the dark camera work of George Barnes. The acting is of a high caliber all around. Ethel Barrymore won an Academy Award as best supporting actress. Cary Grant who was shy of serious roles shows himself more than capable in this film.

Norma Rae

1979. 110 min. color. U.S. **Prod.** Tamara Asseyev, Alexandra Rose; **Dir.** Martin Ritt; **Scr.** Irving Ravetch, Harriet Frank, Jr.; **Cin.** John A. Alonzo; **Ed.** Sidney Levin; **Prod. D.** Walter Scott Herndon; **Art D.** Tracy Bousman; **Mus.** David Shire; **Cast:** Sally Field, Beau Bridges, Ron Leibman, Pat Hingle, Barbara Baxley, Gail Strickland.

The film is set in a small Southern town. Everyone is dependent for their livelihood on a textile mill, the town's only industry.

The workers are virtual slaves and are overworked under insuffer-able conditions. The noise level is unbearable. Most of the workers soon become deaf or afflicted with lung diseases. All attempts to make the owners improve working conditions and pay better wages have been fruitless. Talk of collective bargaining or unionizing is looked at as the work of communists and athe-ists. The film tells the story of Norma Rae (Sally Field), a poor young widow with two children, and a union organizer (Ron Leibman) from New York who finally prevails on Norma Rae to take the lead in unionizing the workers. But the film is more than a story of a successful attempt at forming a union. What makes it powerful is the development of an ordinary woman, without much education, into a leader. Sally Field gives the best perform-ance of her career, for which she won an Oscar. The rest of the cast is also very good, especially Leibman, and Pat Hingle and Barbara Baxley as Norma Rae's parents. The film also owes its success to the tight direction of Martin Ritt.

Nothing Sacred

1937. 75 min. color. U.S. **Prod.** David O. Selznick; **Dir.** William Wellman; **Scr.** Ben Hecht, Ring Lardner, Jr., Bud Schulberg (based on the story "Letter to the Editor" by James H. Street); **Cin.** W. Howard Greene; **Ed.** Hal C. Kern, James E. Newcom; **Art D.** Lyle Wheeler; **Mus.** Oscar Levant; **Cast:** Carole Lombard, Fredric March, Walter Connolly, Charles Winninger, Sig Rumann, Frank Fay, Maxie Rosenbloom, Margaret Hamilton.

Hazel Flagg (Carole Lombard) is a working girl from Vermont. She is diagnosed as having fatal radium poisoning. She is resigned to dying but has one last wish—to see New York City. The star reporter for a New York newspaper, Wally Cook (Fredric March), gets wind of the story and goes to Vermont. By the time Hazel and the reporter get to New York it is established that there had been a wrong diagnosis by the incompetent alcoholic doctor Enoch Downer (Charles Winninger) and Hazel is a perfectly healthy woman. The unprincipled editor, Oliver Stone (Walter Connolly), and the reporter decide to go ahead with the plans they had made in New York, hoping the publicity will boost the paper's circulation. Hazel is celebrated and feasted. She is given the key to the city and later she is designated "America's sweetheart." The public just can't hear enough of her suffering and the number of weeks or days she has left to live. Meanwhile a romance develops between the reporter and Hazel. They disappear and get married somewhere far away.

This is a very uneven movie, although the first forty-five minutes are wonderful. Brilliantly written by some of the best scriptwriters of the day—Ben Hecht, Ring Lardner, Jr., and Bud Schulberg—it is in many ways a more caustic commentary on the fourth estate than *The Front Page* (1931). It is also a showcase for the acting talents of Carole Lombard, the best comedienne of the thirties. The supporting cast is also one of the best. The last half hour runs out of steam and it becomes more an ordinary screwball romance than a sardonic look at the press.

Oblomov

1980. 146 min. color. Russian. **Dir.** Nikita Mikhalkov; **Scr.** Nikita Mikhalkov, Aleksander Adabashyan (based on the novel by Ivan Goncharov); **Cin.** Pavel Lebechev; **Mus.** Eduard Artemyev; **Cast:** Oleg Tabakov, Yuri Bogatyrev, Elena Solovei, Andrei Popov.

The film is based on the 1859 celebrated Russian novel of Ivan Goncharov. Ilya Ilych Oblomov (Oleg Tabakov) is a young man of considerable wealth. One day he gets tired of exerting himself and decides to leave his estate and 150 serfs and go to St. Petersburg. For the next twelve years he just eats and sleeps and never leaves his house. Zokar (Andrei Popov) his devoted and much abused old servant, takes care of him, washes him and feeds him. Oblomov is told he is nearly bankrupt and must return to his estate to make improvements, but he refuses to get out of bed. His childhood friend, Andrei (Yuri Bogatyrev), is finally able to enliven him and introduces him to a lovely girl. He courts her for a short while but decides to go back to his bed. The story is a satire on the Russian aristocracy; their indolence, inertia and sloth. It is a well-acted film and Tabakov brings a great deal of charm to his characterization of the world-weary Oblomov. The cinematography is first rate and the flashbacks to Oblomov's childhood and the wheat fields beside which he grew up stand out. The film suffers, however, from its length of 146 minutes.

The Old Man and the Sea

1956. 86 min. color. U.S. **Prod.** Leland Hayward; **Dir.** John Sturges; **Scr.** Peter Viertel (based on the novella by Ernest Hemingway); **Cin.** James Wong Howe, Floyd Crosby, Tom Tutwiler, Lamar Boren; **Ed.** Arthur Schmidt; **Art D.** Art Loel, Edward Carrere; **Mus.** Dimitri Tiomkin; **Cast:** Spencer Tracy, Felipe Pazos, Harry Bellaver.

Spencer Tracy plays a poor old Cuban fisherman who has had no decent catch for several months. He has become the object of derision by the villagers who think he should retire. He lives in a shack by the sea. The only person who has maintained faith in him is a young boy who brings him coffee every morning and talks with him about baseball. He sets off one day in his skiff and decides to go much farther than usual. After a monumental struggle he lands a huge marlin that is too large to bring into the boat and must be strapped to the side. The film is an account of his enormous effort to bring it back to shore while fending off the sharks that attack the bleeding fish. As he rows he establishes a communion with the fish and feels ashamed for having killed the beautiful marlin.

John Sturges, the director, did wonders for a near impossible film. He had to use a rubber fish in the Warner Brothers. water tank. James Wong Howe, one of the best cinematographers, was forced to borrow footage of the sea and fish from documentary films. The color and texture of the borrowed footage and his own shots vary and the cuts from one to the other clearly show. It is a one-actor film, and the camera had to be glued to Spencer Tracy. Yet Sturges has fashioned a moving film, remaining faithful to the Hemingway novella. Spencer Tracy gives one of his finest performances. The film has been derided by some partly because the macho Hemingway, both as a person and as a writer, no longer enjoys his former immense popularity.

Oliver Twist

1948. 105 min. b.w. British. **Prod.** Ronald Neame, Anthony Havelock-Allan; **Dir.** David Lean; **Scr.** David Lean, Stanley Haynes (based on the novel by Charles Dickens); **Cin.** Guy Green; **Ed.** Jack Harris; **Art D.** John Bryan; **Mus.** Arnold Bax; **Cast:** Alec Guinness, Robert Newton, John Howard Davies, Kay Walsh, Francis L. Sullivan, Anthony Newley, Henry Stephenson, Ralph Truman.

Although directed and produced by the same team who created *Great Expectations* (1946), *Oliver Twist* is not as good. It is, however, better than any other adaptation of a Dickens novel, including the big budget MGM production of *David Copperfield* (1935) that had a memorable performance by W. C. Fields. Where *Oliver Twist* just misses is in its scant recognition of a cruel Victorian London. Dickens' novel devotes several chapters to inhuman workhouses and orphanages, the cruelty of people running them and the abuse and misery of children. David Lean chose to compress the horrors to one or two short scenes of slums, undertaker parlors and the pervading filth. The movie ends on an upbeat note as Oliver acquires a benefactor, but it is not shown what happens to Fagin's pickpockets. However, it is still a very superior film. The opening scene nearly matches that of *Great Expectations.* A pregnant woman in a raging storm is desperately trying to reach the parish workhouse before her child is born. It is a beautifully acted film. Alec Guinness, in only his second film, as Fagin, Robert Newton as the murderous Bill Sykes, Kay Walsh as Sykes' mistress, Nancy, all stand out. Francis L. Sullivan as the cruel head of the workhouse and John Howard Davies as the young Oliver are also very good. The film had censorship problems with the character of Fagin and did not reach the U.S. until 1951, after the elimination of most of Fagin's scenes. A restored version came out in 1970.

Ossessione

Obsession. 1942. 140 min. b.w. Italian. **Prod.** Libero Solaroli; **Dir.** Luchino Visconti; **Scr.** Mario Alicata, Antonio Pietrangeli, Gianni Puccini, Giuseppe De Santis, Lucino Visconti (based on the novel *The Postman Always Rings Twice* by James M. Cain); **Cin.** Aldo Tonti, Domenico Scala; **Ed.** Mario Serandrei; **Art D.** Gino Rosati; **Mus.** Giuseppe Rosati; **Cast:** Massimo Girotti, Clara Calamai, Juan de Landa.

Luchino Visconti's first film, *Ossessione*, was made during World War II in Fascist Italy. It was an unauthorized production of James M. Cain's *The Postman Always Rings Twice,* which MGM later made in 1946, directed by Tay Garnett. Visconti transferred the California setting to the Po Valley in Italy. His film has more explicit sex scenes and the destructive force of illicit passions is better handled. However, overall the Hollywood film is more imaginative and John Garfield's performance as the drifter far outshines that of Massimo Girotti. *Ossessione* is considered by film scholars as the first neorealist film. It was badly cut by the Italian censors and was not shown in the U.S. until 1959 when the copyright issue was settled.

Othello

1952. 92 min. b.w. U.S./French/Italian. **Prod.** Orson Welles; **Dir.** Orson Welles; **Scr.** Orson Welles (based on the play by William Shakespeare); **Cin.** Anchisi Brizzi, G. R. Aldo, Georges Fanto, Oberdan Trojani, Alverto Fusi; **Ed.** Jean Sacha, John Shepridge, Renzo Lucidi, William Morton; **Art D.** Alexander Trauner; **Mus.** Angelo Francesco Lavagnino, Alberto Barberis; **Cast:** Orson Welles, Michael MacLiammoir, Suzanne Cloutier, Robert Coote, Fay Compton, Doris Dowling, Michael Laurence.

The film begins before the credits with an imaginative scene not in the play. Desdemona (Suzanne Cloutier) and Emilia (Fay Compton), Iago's wife, are being buried. Othello (Orson Welles), the Moor, is also being given a Christian burial. The wounded Iago (Michael Laurence) is in a cage being hoisted to the ramparts for all to view the devil incarnate. After the credits, events unfold as in the play. Although Welles has eliminated a number of scenes, he remains faithful to the heart of the play. For lack of money, Welles had to shoot *Othello* between acting assignments in several countries and dozens of locations. It took more than three years to complete the film. When he ran out of money he improvised. When costumes did not arrive he had a naked Cassio wounded in a Turkish bath. The film perforce suffers from the on and off shooting, changes of location, lines dubbed by changing actors and, more seriously, from the lack of sound synchronization. But there is innovative cinematography and editing, and a first-rate performance by Welles as Othello. Suzanne Cloutier as the beautiful Desdemona, Michael MacLiammoir as Iago, the epitome of evil, and Fay Compton as Emilia give credible performances. With all the difficulties and drawbacks, Welles' *Othello* is one of the better screen adaptations of a Shakespeare play, superior to Laurence Olivier's filmed 1965 stage version.

Our Man in Havana

1960. 107 min. b.w. British. **Prod.** Carol Reed; **Dir.** Carol Reed; **Scr.** Graham Greene (based on his novel); **Cin.** Oswald Morris; **Ed.** Bert Bates; **Art D.** John Box; **Mus.** Hermanos Deniz; **Cast:** Alec Guinness, Burl Ives, Maureen O'Hara, Ernie Kovacs, Noel Coward, Ralph Richardson, Gregoire Aslan, Jo Morrow.

Set in prerevolutionary Cuba, long before the Soviet presence, a British vacuum cleaner salesman in Havana, Jim Wormold (Alec Guinness), is approached by a senior British intelligence operative (Noel Coward) to keep his eyes and ears open and send reports on anything suspicious. Wormold needing the extra income agrees. As there is nothing to report, he makes up tall tales and sends drawings of giant vacuum cleaners to London that are taken for missiles. The absurdity is compounded when the Soviets, through their moles, also believe the tall tales and Wormold's life is placed in danger. On his return to the U.K. Wormold is honored with an Order of the British Empire by the Queen. Based on Graham Greene's novel, the movie is a low-key spoof of the establishment and intelligence gathering agencies. An excellent comedy, but it suffers somewhat toward the end when Wormold has to fend off a Soviet would-be assassin. There are three superb performances: Alec Guinness, Noel Coward and Ernie Kovaks as the head of the Cuban police.

Out of the Past

(a.k.a. *Build My Gallows High*). 1947. 98 min. b.w. U.S. **Prod.** Warren Duff; **Dir.** Jacques Tourneur; **Scr.** Geoffrey Homes (based on the novel *Build My Gallows High* by Geoffrey Homes); **Cin.** Nicolas Musuraca; **Ed.** Samuel E. Beetley; **Art D.** Albert S. D'Agostino; **Mus.** Roy Webb; **Cast:** Robert Mitchum, Jane Greer, Kirk Douglas, Rhonda Fleming, Steve Brodie, Paul Valentine, Dickie Moore.

The film has a convoluted plot that at times becomes unnecessarily confusing. Private detective Jeff Bailey (Robert Mitchum) is hired by Whit Sterling (Kirk Douglas), a big-time shady gambler, to find his mistress Kathie Moffett (Jane Greer), who has fled with $40,000. Jeff finds her in Mexico. She denies stealing the money. They become involved and move to northern California. He is found out by his former partner who demands money as the price for his silence. Kathie kills the blackmailer. From then on there are double-crosses and triple-crosses and by film's end all of the lead characters are dead.

A well-directed movie, *Out of the Past* has excellent camera work with low angles and dark shadows. It is a story of greed, deceit and betrayal. It is also a story of obsessive love. Every character is tainted. The film was a breakthrough for Robert Mitchum who plays the laconic central character to perfection. Jane Greer's character, a heartless killer, is not fully developed. But the film holds you and it is one of the best film noirs of the period.

Paisan

(a.k.a. *Paisà.*) 1946. 120 min. b.w. Italian. **Prod.** Roberto Rossellini; Rod E. Geiger, Mario Conti; **Dir.** Roberto Rossellini; **Scr.** Sergio Amidei, Federico Fellini, Roberto Rossellini, Annalena Limentani (based on stories by Victor Haines, Marcello Pagliero, Amidei, Fellini, Klaus Mann, Vasco Pratolini); **Cin.** Otello Martelli; **Ed.** Eraldo Da Roma; **Mus.** Renzo Rossellini; **Cast:** Carmela Sazio, Robert Van Loon, Alfonsino Pasca, Maria Michi; Renzo Avanzo, Harriet White, Dotts Johnson, William Tubbs, Dale Edmonds, Carlo Piscane.

The World War II Italian campaign is told in six separate episodes. It begins with the Allied invasion of Sicily up to a battle in the Po Valley, culminating in the liberation of Italy. It is the best depiction of the Italian experience in World War II. Poorly acted, mostly by nonprofessionals, and some segments drag. But it is still impressive moviemaking and one of the great works of neorealist cinema.

The Pajama Game

1957. 101 min. color. U.S. **Prod.** George Abbott, Stanley Donen; **Dir.** George Abbott, Stanley Donen; **Scr.** George Abbott, Richard Bissell (based on the musical by Bissell and Abbott, and the novel *Seven and a Half Cents* by Bissell); **Cin.** Harry Stradling; **Ed.** William Ziegler; **Art D.** Malcolm Bert; **Mus.** Nelson Riddle, songs by Richard Adler, Jerry Ross; **Cast:** Doris Day, John Raitt, Carol Haney, Eddie Foy, Jr., Barbara Nichols, Reta Shaw, Thelma Pelish.

This musical was described by Jean Luc Godard as the first left-wing operetta. "Babe" Williams (Doris Day) is the workers' representative in a pajama factory. She is asking for a seven and a half cent raise, but management turns it down cold. She and a delegation of workers take the matter to newly appointed superintendent Sid Sorokin (John Raitt) who at the outset is equally dismissive. Babe nearly ruins the workers' solidarity when she falls in love with Sid. Not one of the celebrated movie musicals, it is nevertheless full of movement and imaginative dance numbers.

This is one of the rare Broadway musicals transferred to the screen that does not appear stagebound. The film opens up vast spaces in an ensemble song and dance scene in a grassy field at the annual workers' picnic, "Once a Year Day." There are also other wonderful song and dance numbers: Carol Haney's "Steam Heat" and the tango "Hernando's Hideaway" both choreographed by Bob Fosse.

The Palm Beach Story

1942. 90 min. b.w. U.S. **Prod.** Paul Jones; **Dir.** Preston Sturges; **Scr.** Preston Sturges; **Cin.** Victor Milner; **Ed.** Stuart Gilmore; **Art D.** Hans Dreier, Ernst Fegte; **Mus.** Victor Young; **Cast:** Claudette Colbert, Joel McCrea, Rudy Vallee, Mary Astor, Sig Arno, William Demarest, Franklin Pangborn, Robert Warwick.

Gerry Jeffers (Claudette Colbert), wife of Tom Jeffers (Joel McCrea), a young struggling architect, has an argument with her husband and takes the train to Palm Beach seeking a divorce. She meets J. D. Hackensacker III (Rudy Vallee), the heir to a great fortune, who proposes marriage. Her husband finds her, and Hackensacker's often-married sister, Princess Centimillia (Mary Astor), falls for him. Husband and wife extricate themselves. The movie lacks the sardonic bite of Sturges' best and goes in too many directions, but it is still very enjoyable. Two episodes stand out: Colbert's encounter with the very rich hot dog czar and later, on the train, with members of the "Ale and Quail Club." There are credible performances all around, but honors go to former crooner Rudy Vallee as the billionaire and two of Sturges' perennial favorites, Demarest and Pangborn.

Panic in the Streets

1950. 93 min. b.w. U.S. **Prod.** Sol C Siegel; **Dir.** Elia Kazan; **Scr.** Richard Murphy; **Cin.** Joe MacDonald; **Ed.** Harmon Jones; **Art D.** Lyle Wheeler, Maurice Ransford; **Mus.** Alfred Newman; **Cast:** Richard Widmark, Paul Douglas, Barbara Bel Geddes, Jack Palance, Zero Mostel.

A government medical officer discovers that a murdered illegal alien who has jumped ship had been a carrier of the pneumonic plague. It is no longer enough to find the murderer. It is a race against time to find everyone who had been in contact with the murdered man to prevent an epidemic. The film is tightly directed by Elia Kazan who, as always, extracts excellent performances from his actors. A very good film noir photographed entirely in New Orleans.

The Paper Chase

1973. 111 min. color. U.S. **Prod.** Robert C. Thompson, Rodrick Paul; **Dir.** James Bridges; **Scr.** James Bridges (based on the novel by John J. Osborn, Jr.); **Cin.** Gordon Willis; **Ed.** Walter Thompson; **Art D.** George Jenkins; **Mus.** John Williams; **Cast:** Timothy Bottoms, Lindsay Wagner, John Houseman, Edward Hermann, Graham Beckel.

The film focuses on Professor Kingsfield (John Houseman) and his first year Harvard Law School students. Kingsfield teaches contracts, probably the most important course in the entire three years. He lectures that the sanctity of contract is the cornerstone of a civilized society. Once the intentions of the parties are established they are bound to faithfully carry out the provisions of the undertaking. As final exams approach students begin to form study groups of five or six, each member agreeing to prepare an outline of his strong course and pass it along to the rest. What gives the film an ironic bite is the contrast between the teachings of Kingsfield and the students' conduct. Despite the emphasis on the inviolability of a contract, the members of the study group break their word and each goes his own selfish way. An interesting film that says more than what was intended with a good cast and a majestical performance by John Houseman.

The Parallax View

1974. 102 min. color. U.S. **Prod.** Alan J. Pakula; **Dir.** Alan J. Pakula; **Scr.** David Giler, Lorenzo Semple, Jr. (based on the novel by Loren Singer); **Cin.** Gordon Willis; **Ed.** John W. Wheeler; **Prod. D.** George Jenkins; **Art D.** George Jenkins; **Mus.** Michael Small; **Cast:** Warren Beatty, Paula Prentiss, William Daniels, Hume Cronin, Anthony Zerbe, Kelly Thordsen, Chuck Waters.

A prominent senator with presidential possibilities is assassinated in the restaurant of the Seattle Space Needle. A waiter is believed to be the assassin. Within the next three years all the witnesses disappear or die in unusual circumstances. A newspaper reporter (Warren Beatty) begins an investigation and discovers that a tightly knit group running the Parallax Corporation is behind the assassinations. This well-directed film by Alan J. Pakula has the same menacing atmosphere and tension he introduced in *Klute* (1971) and later in *All the President's Men* (1976). The film suffers, however, from lackluster acting and a far-fetched plot.

A Passage to India

1984. 163 min. color. British. **Prod.** John Brabourne, Richard Goodwin; **Dir.** David Lean; **Scr.** David Lean (based on the play by Santha Rama Rau and the novel by E.M. Forster); **Cin.** Ernest Day; **Ed.** David Lean; **Prod. D.** John Box; **Art D.** Leslie Tomkins, Clifford Robinson, Ram Yedekar, Herbert Westbrook; **Mus.** Maurice Jarre; **Cast:** Judy Davis, Victor Banerjee, Peggy Ashcroft, James Fox, Alec Guinness, Nigel Havers.

The film is set in 1920s India during the Raj. It portrays the class system, cultural clashes and the restrictive British society, and tells the story of a sexually repressed young Englishwoman (Judy Davis) who has come from England to marry a British government functionary (Nigel Havers) and her disastrous encounter with a hospitable Indian doctor (Victor Banerjee). The best acting is by Victor Banerjee, Judy Davis, James Fox who administers a cultural organization and, as to be expected, by the great Peggy Ashcroft, a uniquely open-minded and wise visitor to India. Alec Guinness does not handle his difficult role well. The film is over-long and slow in parts. It is David Lean's last film and certainly not his best, but it is still an ambitious Lean picture that captures the atmosphere, time and place.

The Passenger

1975. 119 min. color. Italian. **Prod.** Carlo Ponti; **Dir.** Michelangelo Antonioni; **Scr.** Mark Peploe, Peter Wollen, Michelangelo Antonioni; **Cin.** Luciano Tovoli; **Ed.** Franco Arcalli, Michelangelo Antonioni; **Art D.** Piero Poletto; **Mus.** Ivan Vandor; **Cast:** Jack Nicholson, Maria Schneider, Jenny Runacre, Ian Hendry, Steven Berkoff.

David Locke (Jack Nicholson) is a reporter sent to an unnamed African country that is in the midst of a civil war. He is to inter-view the leader of the guerrilla movement. He travels to the desert and makes contact with a few of the rebels, but he becomes frustrated when he can't communicate with them. To make matters worse, on his way back his jeep gets stuck in the sand. He reaches his run-down hotel exhausted and angry. Stay-ing at the same hotel on the same floor is an Englishman, a Mr. Robertson, who does not divulge what he is doing in Africa. Robertson has a heart attack and dies. Locke who is angry and bored with his existence sees this as an opportunity to begin a new life. He switches passports and photos, and moves the corpse into his own room. Locke bears a slight resemblance to the dead man and he also assumes the natives can't distinguish one guest from another. He looks through Robertson's belongings and finds a diary with certain names and appointments in various cities in Europe. He leaves Africa and decides to keep the appointments. Too late he discovers that Robertson was an arms salesman. What he did not realize was that Robertson's activities had made him a target for rival factions.

The *Passenger* was the last good film of Michelangelo Antonioni, although it does not match his great films of the sixties. Jack Nicholson has one of his best roles as the alienated reporter. The cinematography of Luciano Tovoli in the first twenty minutes and the last ten minutes are innovative and dazzling. What slows the film in the middle is the gratuitous introduction of Maria Schneider and her relationship with Locke.

Pather Panchali

Song of the Road. 1955. 112 min. b.w. Indian. **Prod.** Satyajit Ray; **Dir.** Satyajit Ray; **Scr.** Satyajit Ray (based on the novel by Bibhutibhusan Bandopadhaya); **Cin.** Subrata Mitra; **Ed.** Dulal Dutta; **Art D.** Banshi Chandra Gupta; **Mus.** Ravi Shankar; **Cast:** Kanu Banerji, Karuna Banerji, Subir Banerji, Runki Banerji, Umas Das Gupta, Chunibala Devi.

Apu, a young boy, lives in near poverty with his parents, cheerful little sister and elderly frail aunt in a small village in Bengal. His father barely makes a living as a rent collector and lay priest. In a series of beautifully photographed events the film chronicles the death of Apu's aunt and the discovery of her body in the woods, the death of his undernourished sister who dies of pneumonia and the decision of his father to move to another village. *Pather Panchali* is a graceful film, the first of Satyajit Ray who wrote and directed this little gem with the background music of Ravi Shankar. India had been one of the major centers of filmmaking from the early thirties. The quality of the films had always been commonplace and in later decades declined further. They were either third rate musicals or glossy romances. The emergence of a serious socially conscious director influenced by the Italian neorealists was unexpected. *Pather Panchali* is the first part of a trilogy, followed by *Aparajito* (1956) and *The World of Apu* (1959). Both are fine films, but neither matches the originality or the impact of the first.

Patton

1970. 169 min. color. U.S. **Prod.** Frank McCarthy, Frank Caffey; **Dir.** Franklin J. Schaffner; **Scr.** Francis Ford Coppola, Edmund H. North (based on the books *Patton: Ordeal and Triumph* by Ladislas Farago and *A Soldier's Story* by General Omar Bradley); **Cin.** Fred Koenekamp; **Ed.** Hugh S. Fowler; **Art D.** Urie McCleary, Gil Parrondo; **Mus.** Jerry Goldsmith; **Cast:** George C. Scott, Karl Malden, Stephen Young, Michael Strong, Frank Latimore, James Edwards, Michael Bates, Edward Binns, John Doucette, Richard Munch.

The film opens with a very effective scene of General Patton (George C. Scott) standing against a backdrop of a huge American flag delivering a six minute address about the fighting spirit of Americans: "All Americans love the sting of battle. That's why we never lost a war." The film follows the career of General George S. Patton, Jr. from 1942, when inexperienced American troops landed in North Africa and met their initial defeat at Kasserine Pass by the forces of Field Marshal Rommel. Patton, as commander of a tank corps, puts his troops through rigid training and ultimately defeats Rommel's Afrika Korp. In the invasion of Sicily he disobeys orders and beats the ever-cautious Field Marshal Montgomery to liberate Messina. When he slaps a soldier suffering from mental fatigue at a field hospital he is almost relieved of his command. It is arranged by his superiors that he publicly apologize and he maintains his post. After D-Day he becomes head of the Third Army and relieves U.S. troops surrounded by the German army at Bastogne, bringing the last German counteroffensive to a halt. At the end of the war he seethes with anger at any suggestion that it was the Russians who broke Hitler's back, and wants to "liberate" Prague from Russian rule. At a press conference, he denigrates U.S. political parties by comparing German politicians with Democrats and Republicans. He is relieved of command and dies in a jeep accident before leaving Germany.

We don't get a clear picture of Patton. He is described as "a rebel with a cause" but the cause is never explained. After the battle in North Africa he confides to General Omar Bradley, his superior, "I love war more than anything." The film demonstrates

Patton's lust for power, glorifies war and strongly hints that Patton was the greatest Allied general of World War II. George C. Scott dominates the film. All other actors have peripheral roles. Karl Malden as General Bradley, Edward Binns as Major General Walter Bedell Smith, and Michael Bates as Field Marshal Montgomery are cardboard figures with mere walk-on roles. The eminent American historian and one-time film critic, Arthur Schlesinger, Jr., has written that U.S. military figures can be categorized as roundheads or cavaliers. The roundheads are best exemplified by George Washington, General Sherman of "War is hell!" fame, Generals Ulysses S. Grant, George Marshall and Omar Bradley. The cavaliers, who believe manhood and man's noblest instincts come to the fore in war, are the Stonewall Jacksons, Douglas MacArthurs and George Pattons.

Pelle the Conqueror

Pelle Erobreren. 1988. 160 min. color. Danish/Swedish. **Prod.** Per Holst; **Dir.** Bille August; **Scr.** Billy August (based on a novel by Martin Anderson Nexo); **Cin.** Jorgen Persson; **Ed.** Janus Billeskov Jansen; **Prod. D.** Anna Asp; **Mus.** Stefan Nilsson; **Cast:** Max von Sydow, Pelle Hvenegaard, Erik Paaske, Kristina Tornqvist, Astrid Villaume, Axel Strobye.

During a famine in Sweden in the 1880s, an aging widower, Lasse (Max von Sydow), takes his seven-year-old son, Pelle (Pelle Hvenegaard), to Denmark hoping for a better life. They get jobs as laborers on a large farm. They are worked to the bones and become virtual slaves. They encounter inexplicable wanton cruelty, which they endure because they are fed regular meals. The film recounts the abuses heaped on them and depicts the grimness of life. It ends with Pelle, now a grown man, deciding to leave and "conquer" unknown lands. It is an extremely well made film with a towering performance from von Sydow in the twilight of his career. The film at 160 minutes is perhaps some twenty minutes too long.

Pepe Le Moko

1937. 90 min. b.w. French. **Prod.** Robert Hakim, Raymond Hakim; **Dir.** Julien Duvivier; **Scr.** Julien Duvivier, Henri Jeanson, Henri La Barthe, Jacques Constant (based on the book by Henri La Barthe); **Cin.** Jules Kruger, Marc Fossard; **Ed.** Marguerite Beauge; **Prod. D.** Jacques Krauss; **Mus.** Vincent Scotto, Mohamed Yguerbouchen; **Cast:** Jean Gabin, Mirielle Balin, Gabriel Gabrio, Lucas Gridoux, Line Noro, Marcel Dalio.

A notorious jewel thief and bank robber (Jean Gabin) has been forced to flee Paris and seek refuge in the underworld of Algiers. The police are after him, but he surrounds himself with loyal men and never leaves the confines of the Casbah, a quarter where the police dare not set foot. He has a mistress of whom he is tiring. Through coincidence he comes across a beautiful Parisian tourist, Gaby Gould (Mirielle Balin), and falls in love with her. She represents the elegance and charm of his beloved Paris. He becomes careless and leaves the Casbah, and the police nab him. What distinguishes the film is the fluid camera work and the realistic sets shrouded in shadows, a forerunner of noir films to come. It is beautifully acted by Jean Gabin who established himself as the leading French actor. There were two American remakes— *Algiers* (1938) with Charles Boyer and Hedy Lamarr and a semi-musical, *Casbah* (1948) with Tony Martin and Yvonne de Carlo—both inferior to *Pepe Le Moko*.

Petulia

1968. 105 min. color. U.S/British. **Prod.** Raymond Wagner; **Dir.** Richard Lester; **Scr.** Larry Marcus, Barbara Turner (based on the novel *Me and the Arch Kook Petulia* by John Haase); **Cin.** Nicolas Roeg; **Ed.** Anthony Gibbs; **Art D.** Dean Tavoularis; **Mus.** John Barry; **Cast:** Julie Christie, George C. Scott, Richard Chamberlain, Shirley Knight, Joseph Cotton, Arthur Hill.

A touching film about relationships. It is a convoluted story of guilt-ridden people, beautifully photographed by Nicolas Roeg, but overdirected as many films of the sixties, when directors felt compelled to demonstrate their technical skill at the expense of a coherent story. Despite the flashy cutting and editing, the many flashbacks and flash-forwards the movie holds up and has excellent acting. It is probably the only comprehensible movie that Richard Lester made.

Phantom Lady

1944. 87 min. b.w. U.S. **Prod.** Joan Harrison; **Dir.** Robert Siodmak; **Scr.** Bernard C. Schoenfeld (based on the novel by Cornell Woolrich); **Cin.** Elwood Bredell; **Ed.** Arthur Hilton; **Art D.** John B. Goodman, Robert Clatworthy; **Mus.** H. J. Salter; **Cast:** Ella Raines, Franchot Tone, Alan Curtis, Thomas Gomez, Elisha Cook, Jr., Aurora Miranda, Fay Helm.

While a psychopathic serial murderer is on the loose, an innocent man is convicted on circumstantial evidence of murdering his wife. The convicted man's only alibi is a mysterious woman whose existence is denied by everyone. The dialogue is ordinary and the only competent acting is by the supporting actors, Elisha Cook, Jr., and Thomas Gomez. But this low-budget thriller has a good deal to recommend it visually: its claustrophobic sets, moody dramatic lighting and odd camera angels.

The Phenix City Story

1955. 100 min. b.w. U.S. **Prod.** Samuel Bischoff, David Diamond, **Dir.** Phil Karlson; **Scr.** Crane Wilbur, Dan Mainwaring; **Cin.** Harry Neumann; **Ed.** George White; **Art D.** Stanley Fleischer; **Mus.** Harry Sukman; **Cast:** John McIntire, Richard Kiley, Kathryn Grant, Edward Andrews.

This is the true story of the self-styled "wickedest city in the U.S." Phenix City is a small town in Alabama across the river from the army's Fort Benning, Georgia. From the beginning of World War II the town was run by criminals, with legalized, but crooked, gambling and prostitution. The film centers on the true story of Albert Patterson (John McIntire), who attempts to dislodge the crime czar of the city. After his murder, his son John (Richard Kiley), a returned veteran, took up the task when he was elected attorney general of the state. But the film ends on an incongruous note. It is not John Patterson but the U.S. army that invades the town and breaks up the criminal ring. The film is very well directed and has an almost newsreel authenticity. There are fine performances by McIntire and Kiley.

The Philadelphia Story

1940. 112 min. b.w. U.S. **Prod.** Joseph L. Mankiewicz; **Dir.** George Cukor; **Scr.** Donald Ogden Stewart, Waldo Salt (based on the play by Philip Barry); **Cin.** Joseph Ruttenberg; **Ed.** Frank Sullivan; **Art D.** Cedric Gibbons, Wade B. Rubottom; **Mus.** Franz Waxman; **Cast:** Cary Grant, Katharine Hepburn, James Stewart, Ruth Hussey, John Howard, Roland Young, John Halliday, Virginia Weidler, Mary Nash, Henry Daniell.

In a good opening scene, C. K. Dexter Haven (Cary Grant), who is being divorced for excessive drinking, is thrown out of the mansion by heiress Tracy Lord (Katharine Hepburn). She throws his golf bag after him and breaks one of the clubs over her knee. She tells him, "You can go right back to where you came from." She is to marry a stuffy, arrogant coal-mining heir. Some months later Dexter invites himself to the wedding and, before the movie ends, she remarries him. The film has dated but still retains its charm, not so much for the dialogue and wit for which it is often praised, but for the mere presence of Hepburn, Grant, Stewart and Ruth Hussey. A musical remake in 1956, *High Society,* with Bing Crosby, Grace Kelly and Frank Sinatra, should convince any viewer how superior the original was.

Pinocchio

1940. 88 min. color. Animated. U.S. **Prod.** Walt Disney; **Dir.** Ben Sharpsteen, Hamilton Luske; **Scr.** Ted Sears, Otto Englander, Webb Smith, William Cottrell, Joseph Sabo, Erdman Penner, Aurelius Battaglia (based on the story by Carlo Collodi); **Mus.** Leigh Harline, Paul J. Smith, Ned Washington; **Voices:** Dickie Jones, Christian Rub, Cliff Edwards, Evelyn Venable, Walter Catlett.

Pinocchio, the second full–length animated Disney film, is far superior to *Snow White and the Seven Dwarfs* (1937). This lovely story is about a childless wood–carver who makes puppets. The puppet Pinocchio wants to become a real boy but he must undergo trials of character before his wish is granted. This is one of the best animated films.

A Place in the Sun

1951. 122 min. b.w. U.S. **Prod.** George Stevens; **Dir.** George Stevens; **Scr.** Michael Wilson, Harry Brown (based on the novel *An American Tragedy* by Theodore Dreiser and the play by Patrick Kearney); **Cin.** William Mellor; **Ed.** William Hornbeck; **Art D.** Hans Dreier and Walter Tyler; **Mus.** Franz Waxman; **Cast:** Montgomery Clift, Elizabeth Taylor, Shelley Winters, Keefe Brasselle, Raymond Burr, Anne Revere, Fred Clark, Shepperd Strudwick, Herbert Heyes.

The film tells the story of the short life of George Eastman (Montgomery Clift), a poor boy from Chicago who is executed because the thought of murder was on his mind when his pregnant girlfriend, Alice Tripp (Shelley Winters), drowns in a lake. Slow in parts, there are some beautifully photographed scenes: George's first invitation to the home of his wealthy industrialist uncle and meeting the beautiful Angela Vickers (Elizabeth Taylor); his first night of intimacy with the plain–looking Alice, his coworker at the plant; the scenes in the woods and on the lake preceding Alice's drowning when she is babbling on relentlessly about things he doesn't want to hear: "I don't mind being poor…it's the little things in life that count…we'll scrape and save," while George is planning to marry the rich and beautiful Angela.

George Stevens has turned Theodore Dreiser's "naturalist" novel, *An American Tragedy*, into a glossy and somewhat confusing film. But it has the best acting of Clift and a convincing Elizabeth Taylor. There is also fine acting by Shepperd Strudwick as Angela's father and Anne Revere as George's missionary mother. Raymond Burr as the zealous district attorney may be too bombastic. The film won Academy Awards for best director, best original screenplay, cinematography and score, among others; and received nominations for best picture, actor and actress (Shelley Winters).

Play It Again, Sam

1972. 87 min. color. U.S. **Prod.** Arthur P. Jacobs; **Dir.** Herbert Ross; **Scr.** Woody Allen; **Cin.** Owen Roizman; **Ed.** Marion Rothman; **Prod. D.** Ed Wittstein; **Mus.** Billy Goldberg, Max Steiner; **Cast:** Woody Allen, Diane Keaton, Tony Roberts, Jerry Lacy, Susan Anspach, Jennifer Salt.

Alan Felix (Woody Allen) is a movie buff who is obsessed with the movie *Casablanca*. He dreams of being Humphrey Bogart and tries to emulate his hero. In reality he is a neurotic mess who wants to escape his boring self. When his wife leaves him he is in even worse shape. He imagines the ghost of Bogart giving him advice as to how to behave and carry himself. His dream is realized when he is placed in a *Casablanca* situation and plays the noble hero in a real-life situation. It is well acted with Jerry Lacy giving an excellent performance as Humphrey Bogart.

Playtime.

1967. 108 min. color. French. **Prod.** Rene Silvera; **Dir.** Jacques Tati; **Scr.** Jacques Tati, Jacques Lagrange, Art Buchwald; **Cin.** Jean Badal, Andreas Winding; **Ed.** Gerard Pollicand; **Prod. D.** Eugene Roman; **Mus.** Francis Lemarque, David Stein, James Campbell; **Cast:** Jacques Tati, Barbara Dennek, Jacqueline Lecomte, Valerie Camille, Henri Piccoli, George Montant.

Playtime is set in Paris of the future. Here as in *Mon Oncle* (1958), Jacques Tati, in his third film featuring Monsieur Hulot, vents his rage and frustration at the modern world and its gadgetry. He shows a sanitized ultramodern city. A group of American women tourists are in Paris for twenty-four hours. All they see are Orly Airport, the sights on the bus ride to their hotel and dinner at an unfinished, just-opened supper club. Hulot has an appointment nearby with an executive at an avant-garde office building and later his path crosses with the tourists at the supper club where chaos reigns. As in his previous films there is no dialogue, only sounds of push-button objects and gadgets. It has fewer sight gags and funny incidents than his two previous films but it has a charm of its own. It was too ambitious a film with its expensive sets and it bankrupted Tati who had invested much of his own money.

The Postman

Il Postino. 1994. 113 min. color. Italian. **Prod.** Mario Cecchi Gori, Vittorio Cecchi Gori, Gaetano Daniele; **Dir.** Michael Radford; **Scr.** Anna Pavignano, Michael Radford, Furio Scarpelli; Giacomo Scarpelli, Massimo Troisi (based on the novel *Burning Patience* by Antonio Skarmeta); **Cin.** Franco Di Giacomo; **Ed.** Roberto Perpignani; **Art D.** Lorenzo Baraldi; **Mus.** Luis Enrique Bacalov; **Cast:** Massimo Troisi, Philippe Noiret, Maria Grazia Cucinotta, Linda Moretti, Renato Scarpa, Anna Buonaiuto.

A fictionalized version of the exile of the Chilean poet Pablo Neruda (Philippe Noiret). He finds refuge with his lady friend in an island town off the coast of Naples. A postman, Mario (Massimo Troisi), is hired to handle the unprecedented amount of mail that arrives for the celebrity. He makes deliveries several times a day and an unlikely friendship develops between the two. Mario is in love with the beautiful local barmaid and wishes to woo her with poetry. The poet helps the postman, in the course of which Mario becomes obsessed with metaphors. One of the highlights of the film is a nostalgic tango danced by Neruda and his lady love to the music of a gramophone record, overseen by Mario through an open door. A bittersweet story of friendship and beauty interlaced with some politics. Noiret and Troisi are outstanding.

The Postman Always Rings Twice

1946. 113 min. b.w. U.S. **Prod.** Carey Wilson; **Dir.** Tay Garnett; **Scr.** Harry Ruskin, Niven Busch (based on the novel by James M. Cain); **Cin.** Sidney Wagner; **Ed.** George White; **Art D.** Cedric Gibbons, Randall Duell; **Mus.** George Bassman; **Cast:** Lana Turner, John Garfield, Cecil Kellaway, Hume Cronyn, Audrey Totter, Leon Ames, Alan Reed.

An itinerant, Frank Chambers (John Garfield), stops at a Twin Oaks, California, diner/gas station owned by the elderly, good-humored Nick Smith (Cecil Kellaway). There is a "Man Wanted" sign outside, but Frank has no interest in a job. One look at Nick's young wife, Cora (Lana Turner), standing in a doorway wearing shorts and decked out all in white, changes Frank's mind and he accepts the job of waiter/handyman. It takes very little time for the two to become sexually involved and plan to run away together. Cora changes her mind as she wants the security offered by her husband. They then plan to murder Nick. They are tried for first-degree murder, but the case is mishandled by the district attorney's office and they are released with suspended sentences. At the suggestion of their lawyer, Arthur Keats (Hume Cronyn), they marry, but the element of trust has disappeared from their relationship. When Cora dies in a car crash, Frank becomes a suspect.

The potboilers of James M. Cain served Hollywood well. The plot is fairly obvious and the dialogue commonplace. What elevates the film is the inspired direction of journeyman director Tay Garnett who had directed more than forty films, most quite ordinary. *The Postman Always Rings Twice* is by far his best film and he extracted the best performance from the wooden Lana Turner. Garfield is very good, as is Cronyn. There are some imaginative scenes: the film's opening with a suggestive "Man Wanted" sign; Lana Turner's first appearance where she drops her lipstick on the floor, a scene which exudes sex; and Turner and Garfield dancing to the music of a jukebox with the room lit only by the neon signs outside the diner.

Pride and Prejudice

1940. 117 min. b.w. U.S. **Prod.** Hunt Stromberg; **Dir.** Robert Z. Leonard; **Scr.** Aldous Huxley, Jane Murfin (based on the novel by Jane Austen); **Cin.** Karl Freund; **Ed.** Robert J. Kern; **Art D.** Cedric Gibbons, Paul Groesse; **Mus.** Herbert Stothart; **Cast:** Greer Garson, Laurence Olivier, Edna May Oliver, Edmund Gwenn, Mary Boland, Maureen O'Sullivan, Karen Morely, Melville Cooper, Marsha Hunt, Ann Rutherford, Frieda Inescort, Heather Angel, Bruce Lester.

This film is based on the witty and satirical Jane Austen novel about the Bennet family and their five marriageable daughters, and has an excellent screenplay by Aldous Huxley and Jane Murfin. The novel is more a commentary on early-nineteenth-century conventions and customs of middle-class provincial society than a romance. Laurence Olivier is excellent as the proud and arrogant D'Arcy and Greer Garson has one of her best roles as the prejudiced Elizabeth, the second-eldest daughter. Mary Boland as the mother hen, Mrs. Bennet, and the formidable Edna May Oliver as Lady Catherine de Bourgh, the epitome of pride, give very good performances. Robert Z. Leonard who had mostly made glossy glamor and mushy romance films does justice to the Austen novel.

Pride of the Yankees

1942. 127 min. b.w. U.S. **Prod.** Samuel Goldwyn; **Dir.** Sam Wood; **Scr.** Jo Swerling, Herman J. Mankiewicz (based on a story by Paul Gallico); **Cin.** Rudolph Maté; **Ed.** Daniel Mandell; **Prod. D.** William Cameron Menzies; **Art D.** Perry Ferguson; **Mus.** Leigh Harline; **Cast:** Gary Cooper, Teresa Wright, Walter Brennan, Dan Duryea, Elsa Janssen, Ludwig Stossel, Babe Ruth.

Pride of the Yankees is the story of one of the greatest baseball players, Lou Gehrig (Gary Cooper), nicknamed "The Iron Man" for the number of consecutive games he played. He was struck down by a rare neurological disease, now named after him. It is a quintessential American success story. A superb athlete with loving

refugee parents, Gehrig, through dedication, comes into prominence and marries a bright and charming girl (Teresa Wright).
Gary Cooper has one of his best roles, almost playing himself, as
the shy, modest Gehrig. Teresa Wright, an underrated actress, is also
ideal for her part. They are supported by the convincing performances of Walter Brennan and Dan Duryea. The film is ten to
fifteen minutes too long with too many scenes of Gehrig's loving
parents and an unnecessary scene of professional ballroom dancers
in a nightclub. The film is beautifully photographed by Rudolph
Maté and has one of Irving Berlin's loveliest songs, the simple
"Always," as background music.

The Prisoner

1955. 91 min. b.w. British. **Prod.** Vivian A. Cox; **Dir.** Peter Glenville; **Scr.** Bridget Boland
(based on her play); **Cin.** Reginald Wyer; **Ed.** Freddie Wilson; **Art D.** John Hawkesworth;
Mus. Benjamin Frankel; **Cast:** Alec Guinness, Jack Hawkins, Raymond Huntley, Wilfrid
Lawson, Kenneth Griffiths, Ronald Lewis, Gerard Heinz.

The story is based on the notorious trial of Cardinal Jozef
Mindzenty, the Primate of the Catholic Church in Hungary, who
was falsely arrested for treason, tried and sentenced to solitary
imprisonment in 1948. Alec Guinness, in one of his finest roles,
plays the tormented cardinal. Jack Hawkins plays the shrewd
inquisitor, a highly intelligent man who has been reduced to trying to pry open the cardinal's mind and obtain a false confession.
Hawkins does break the cardinal but at a cost to himself. What
mars the film is the static direction, more suitable to the stage.

The Prisoner of Zenda

1937. 101 min. b.w. U.S. **Prod.** David O. Selznick; **Dir.** John Cromwell, George Cukor, W. S. Van Dyke II; **Scr.** John Balderston, Wells Root, Donald Ogden Stewart (based on the novel by Anthony Hope and the play by Edward Rose); **Cin.** James Wong Howe; **Ed.** Hal C. Kern, James E. Newcom; **Art D.** Lyle Wheeler; **Mus.** Alfred Newman; **Cast:** Ronald Coleman, Madeleine Carroll, Douglas Fairbanks, Jr., C. Aubrey Smith, Raymond Massey, Mary Astor, David Niven, Montagu Love.

Highly enjoyable well–paced romantic/adventure nonsense set in the mythical kingdom of Ruritania. There is fine acting by the entire cast, especially Douglas Fairbanks, Jr. John Cromwell often elicited good performances from his actors: Charles Boyer in *Algiers* (1938); the entire cast of *Anna and the King of Siam* (1946) and the great performance of Kim Stanley in *The Goddess* (1958).

The Private Life of Henry VIII

1933. 97 min. b.w. British. **Prod.** Alexander Korda, Ludovico Toeplitz; **Dir.** Alexander Korda; **Scr.** Lajos Biro, Arthur Wimperis; **Cin.** Georges Perinal; **Ed.** Harold Young, Stephen Harrison; **Art D.** Vincent Korda; **Mus.** Kurt Schroeder; **Cast:** Charles Laughton, Binnie Barnes, Elsa Lanchester, Merle Oberon, Miles Mander, Wendy Barry, Robert Donat, Everley Gregg, Franklin Dyall, Lady Tree.

An amusing picture, almost entirely due to the great characterization by Charles Laughton as Henry VIII and the scene stealing of Elsa Lanchester as Anne of Cleves in her very brief scenes. Henry is depicted as a glutton who marries his six wives in part to give England a male heir. When he is about to consummate his marriage to the German Anne of Cleves, a none too pretty girl, he sighs, "The things I've done for England." After beheading two of the wives, he becomes tamed by his last marriage to Catherine Paar (Everley Gregg). Laughton won the Academy Award for best actor.

Prizzi's Honor

1985. 129 min. color. U.S. **Prod.** John Foreman; **Dir.** John Huston; **Scr.** Richard Condon, Janet Roach (based on the novel by Richard Condon); **Cin.** Andrzej Bartkowiak; **Ed.** Rudi Fehr, Kaja Fehr; **Art D.** Michael Helmy, Tracy Bousman; **Prod. D.** J. Denis Washington; **Mus.** Alex North; **Cast:** Jack Nicholson, Kathleen Turner, Robert Loggia, John Randolph, William Hickey, Lee Richardson, Michael Lombard, Anjelica Huston, George Santopietro, Lawrence Tierney.

Charley Partanna (Jack Nicholson) is a hit man for the powerful Brooklyn-based Prizzi Mafia family. The loyal and efficient Charley is the favorite of the head of the family, Don Corrado Prizzi (William Hickey), who regards Charley as a son. For Charley's initiation rites as a full-fledged member of the family, the don had mixed his own blood with Charley's. At the wedding of the don's youngest granddaughter, Charley spots the woman of his dreams, the beautiful Irene Walker (Kathleen Turner), and falls head over heels in love. Irene is said to be a tax consultant living in Los Angeles. Charley's life becomes bicoastal and he proposes marriage. Soon thereafter he discovers she is in the same profession as he—a freelance hit woman who had recently fulfilled a contract for the Prizzi family. To complicate matters, Charley finds that Irene is already married and, much worse, she and her husband recently cheated the Prizzi family out of a large sum of money. Charley's loyalties are now at issue and he doesn't know which way to turn. Should he "marry her or ice her?"

Prizzi's Honor is fully controlled by the ailing John Huston in his penultimate film. There are several subplots and some outlandish characters: William Hickey as the old don and John Randolph as Pop, Charley's father and the Prizzi's consigliere, who beams with pride at his son's accomplishments. There is also Anjelica Huston as Maerose, the don's eldest granddaughter, Charley's former fiancée, who has the best lines in the movie. When Charley tells her Irene is a hit woman, she advises him, "Just because she's a thief and a hitter, don't mean she ain't good enough in all other departments." Maerose is the more interesting of the two women and her role could have been enlarged. Anjelica Huston won an

Academy Award as best supporting actress. The film received nominations in most major categories.

The Public Enemy

1931. 84 min. b.w. U.S. **Prod.** Darryl F. Zanuck; **Dir.** William Wellman; **Scr.** Kubec Glasmon, John Bright, Harvey Thew (based on the story "Beer and Blood" by John Bright); **Cin.** Dev Jennings; **Ed.** Ed McCormick; **Art D.** Max Parker; **Mus.** David Mendoza; **Cast:** James Cagney, Jean Harlow, Eddie Woods, Beryl Mercer, Donald Cook, Joan Blondell, Mae Clarke, Leslie Fenton.

The Public Enemy is one of the early gangster films that suggests that crime is the product of social and economic conditions. It traces the career of a gangster from 1909 to the late twenties. We first see young Tom Powers (James Cagney) beaten by his brutish father. We next see him as a petty thief, soon graduating to a big-time bootlegger and murderer. James Cagney's persona was indelibly established in this film. His body movements and gestures were unique whether pushing a grapefruit in Mae Clarke's face or punching someone out. Other than Cagney, the acting of the rest of the cast is mediocre. The film is well controlled by William Wellman whose career took off after this.

Quartet

1948. 120 min. b.w. British. **Prod.** Antony Darnborough; **Dir.** Ken Annakin, Arthur Crabtree, Harold French, Ralph Smart; **Scr.** R. C. Sheriff (based on the short stories of W. Somerset Maugham); **Cin.** Ray Elton, Reg Wyer; **Ed.** A. Charles Knott, Jean Barker; **Art D.** George Provis; **Mus.** John Greenwood; **Cast:** Basil Radford, Naunton Wayne, Mai Zetterling, Ian Fleming, Jack Raine, Françoise Rosay, Dirk Bogarde, Angela Baddeley, James Robertson-Justice, George Cole, Cecil Parker, Nora Swinburne.

Four short stories by W. Somerset Maugham have been filmed by four separate directors. "Facts of Life" has a naive, gullible nineteen-year-old going to Monte Carlo for a university tennis tournament. He is cautioned by his father about gambling and loose women. The son comes back having been successful at both. The second story titled "The Alien Corn" tells of an aspiring concert pianist whose parents object to a music career and he reaches an agreement with them. A renowned concert pianist is to judge his ability. If her judgment is favorable they will withdraw their objections; if unfavorable he will abandon his aspirations. He is not judged well which results in a tragedy. The third, "The Kite," is a simple story of a young man whose principal enjoyment consist of flying kites. A rift develops between his wife and shrewish mother, but it is resolved and they all enjoy their kite flying outings. The fourth and the best is "The Colonel's Lady." A middle aged married woman publishes a book of love poems dedicated to a young man who is the subject of the poems. The book becomes widely read and praised. Her husband, a retired colonel, becomes increasingly disturbed and jealous about her presumed young lover who turns out to be himself in the early years of their marriage.

There is fine acting by all, especially Françoise Rosay as the accomplished pianist, Dirk Bogarde as the aspiring pianist, and Cecil Parker and Nora Swinburne as the colonel and his wife. This is one of the very few films of unconnected multiple segments that are uniformly good. The success of *Quartet* led to further filming of Maugham's short stories, *Trio* (1950) and *Encore* (1951) which are not as good as *Quartet* but each has one very superior story.

Radio Days

1987. 85 min. color. U.S. **Prod.** Robert Greenhut; **Dir.** Woody Allen; **Scr.** Woody Allen; **Cin.** Carlo Di Palma; **Ed.** Susan E. Morse; **Prod. D.** Santo Loquasto; **Art. D.** Speed Hopkins; **Mus.** Dick Hyman; **Cast:** Mia Farrow, Seth Green, Julie Kavner, Josh Mostel, Dianne Wiest, Danny Aiello, Tony Roberts, Diane Keaton, Kitty Carlisle Hart, Renee Lippin, Michael Tucker.

Not one of Woody Allen's best, but *Radio Days* is a highly entertaining movie. It chronicles the lives of members of a Jewish family in Brooklyn from about the time of America's entry in World War II to the end of the forties. The film's focus is on two women: Dianne Wiest, a thirtyish, unmarried Aunt Bea who is in a desperate search to find a husband; and a totally unrelated, not too bright nightclub cigarette girl (Mia Farrow) who rises to become a leading radio gossip reporter. Woody Allen is the off-screen narrator. The entire cast is good, but the real star of the movie is radio.

Raging Bull

1980. 128 min. color. b.w. U.S. **Prod.** Irwin Winkler, Robert Chartoff; **Dir.** Martin Scorsese; **Scr.** Paul Schrader, Mardik Martin (based on the book by Jake LaMotta with Joseph Carter, Peter Savage); **Cin.** Michael Chapman; **Ed.** Thelma Schoonmaker; **Cast:** Robert De Niro, Cathy Moriarty, Joe Pesci, Frank Vincent, Nicholas Colasanto, Theresa Saldana, Frank Adonis, John Turturro.

The film is a biography of Jake LaMotta (Robert De Niro) who held the middleweight championship for a short time during an era when there were great boxers in that division. The film follows his career from the mid-forties to the mid-sixties. He was close to the mob and was briefly banned from the ring because he threw a fight on their orders. He falls in love with a fifteen-year-old girl, Vickie (Cathy Moriarty), and divorces his wife to marry her. He abuses Vickie and Joey (Joe Pesci), his brother and manager, mercilessly. He beats Marcel Cerdan in 1949 and becomes middleweight champion, then loses the title in 1951 to the great Sugar Ray Robinson. His career thereafter is all downhill. He drinks heavily, adds some fifty pounds and ends up as a stand-up comic in sleazy nightclubs. The film begins when he is a comic and then a lengthy flashback follows.

Raging Bull is a fine film, masterfully directed. One of the best things about it is the black and white photography. It also has a realistic and uncompromising script, but it is an unsatisfying film. There is no respite or one calm moment in the entire 128 minutes. The pervading high pitch exhausts the viewer. Most of the violence takes place outside the ring. What makes it depressing is that it is basically a story of a sick man, not about boxing. The central character is obnoxious, and his degradation at the end neither evokes sympathy nor provides a catharsis. Robert De Niro who weighed 145 pounds, went to 160 for the fight scenes. He then added still more weight to reach 200 pounds for the nightclub scenes. De Niro won the Academy Award for best actor and the film received several nominations in major categories.

The Reckless Moment

1949. 81 mins. b.w. U.S. **Prod.** Walter Wanger; **Dir.** Max Ophuls; **Scr.** Henry Garson, Robert W. Soderberg (based on the story "The Blank Wall" by Elisabeth Sanxay Holding); **Cin.** Burnett Guffey; **Ed.** Gene Havlick; **Art D.** Cary Odell; **Mus.** Hans J. Salter; **Cast:** James Mason, Joan Bennett, Geraldine Brooks, Henry O'Neill, Shepperd Strudwick, David Blair.

A young girl (Geraldine Brooks) accidentally kills her older lover, a shady character who is after money (Shepperd Strudwick). Her mother (Joan Bennett) conceals the evidence and dumps the body in a lake to protect her daughter. A loan shark to whom the murdered man owed money gets wind of what had happened and sends his "collector" (James Mason) to blackmail the mother. The "collector" begins to respect the mother and becomes infatuated with her. An extremely well crafted, tense and suspenseful film with moody and shadowy cinematography by Burnett Guffey. James Mason is very good and it is probably the best acting of Joan Bennett who had become a better actress under the guidance of her husband, producer Walter Wanger, and the influence of the director Fritz Lang. *The Reckless Moment* together with *Letter from an Unknown Woman* (1948) are the best work of Max Ophuls during his stay in America.

The Red Inn

L'Auberge Rouge. 1951. 110 min. b.w. French. **Dir.** Claude Autant-Lara; **Scr.** Jean Aurenche, Pierre Bost; **Cin.** André Bac; **Mus.** René Cloerec; **Cast:** Fernandel, Françoise Rosay, Julien Carette, Gregoire Aslan, Marie-Claire Olivia, Lud Germain.

Set in 1853 in the Ardeche mountains of France, it is the story of an inn where almost all travelers who stop for the night disappear by the next day. A gluttonous priest (Fernandel) along with some other coach passengers stop at the inn. The innkeeper's wife (Françoise Rosay) who has not seen a priest for some time wants him to hear her confession. She tells the priest that she and her husband (Julien Carette) rob and murder every guest who stays with them. The priest is horrified. He has to urge the other guests to leave but must find a way to warn them without violating the secrecy of the confessional. It is all Fernandel's movie, who with his lugubrious face and huge mouth became the premier French comedian from the mid–forties to the late sixties. Françoise Rosay is magnificent as the proprietress of the inn. The anticlerical nature of the film delayed its release in several countries. Newcomer Yves Montand sings on the soundtrack.

The Red Shoes

1948. 133 min. color. British. **Prod.** Michael Powell, Emeric Pressburger; **Dir.** Michael Powell, Emeric Pressburger; **Scr.** Michael Powell, Emeric Pressburger, Keith Winter; **Cin.** Jack Cardiff; **Ed.** Reginald Mills; **Art D.** Hein Heckroth, Arthur Lawson; **Mus.** Brian Easdale; **Cast:** Anton Walbrook, Marius Goring, Moira Shearer, Robert Helpmann, Leonide Massine, Albert Basserman, Esmond Knight, Ludmilla Tcherina.

Gifted ballerina Victoria Page (Moira Shearer) is discovered by a Diaghilev-type impresario, Boris Lermontov (Anton Walbrook). She is to have the lead role in a new ballet, *The Red Shoes,* based on a Hans Christian Andersen fairy tale about a malevolent shoemaker who sells a pair of ballet slippers to a young girl that enables her to dance gloriously. However, once worn, the dancer cannot stop dancing. Life mimics art. The impresario slowly takes over her personal life and thwarts her romance, and ultimately she is driven to suicide.

With a very thin plot Michael Powell and Emeric Pressburger have fashioned a visually beautiful film with vibrant colors and a lovely fifteen-minute ballet sequence. The great actor Anton Walbrook has one of his best roles, and Moira Shearer, who had been a dancer with Sadler's Wells ballet company, is refreshing. There are some renowned dancers in the cast including Leonide Massine and Ludmilla Tcherina. Robert Helpmann is both the choreographer and one of the dancers. One of the film's drawbacks is the casting of the boring Marius Goring as an effete young composer, beloved by Victoria. He either sulks or overacts throughout the film. The ending is too contrived and reeks with sentimentality, but the film has not dated and is visually stunning.

Reign of Terror

(a.k.a. *The Black Book*). 1949. 89 min. b.w. U.S. **Prod.** William Cameron Menzies; **Dir.** Anthony Mann; **Scr.** Philip Yordan; **Cin.** John Alton; **Cast:** Robert Cummings, Arlene Dahl, Richard Basehart, Richard Hart, Norman Lloyd, Arnold Moss, Charles McGraw, Jess Barker, Beulah Bondi.

Reign of Terror is a little noted but superior film, well directed by an up-and-coming Anthony Mann, with effective noirish sets and camera work. The story is set during the height of the French Revolution when Robespierre's Committee of Public Safety sent thousands to the guillotine. The film is marred by the inferior acting of the two leads, Robert Cummings and Arlene Dahl, both fictitious characters inserted in the plot for commercial reasons. But Richard Basehart as Robespierre and Arnold Moss as the cunning and opportunistic Joseph Fouché, the head of police, more than redeem the movie.

Rio Bravo

1959. 141 min. color. U.S. **Prod.** Howard Hawks; **Dir.** Howard Hawks; **Scr.** Jules Furthman, Leigh Brackett (based on a story by Barbara Hawks Campbell); **Cin.** Russell Harlan; **Ed.** Folmar Blangsted; **Art D.** Leo Kuter; **Mus.** Dimitri Tiomkin; **Cast:** John Wayne, Dean Martin, Ricky Nelson, Angie Dickinson, Walter Brennan, Ward Bond, John Russell, Claude Aikins, Bob Steele, Pedro Gonzalez-Gonzalez.

John T. Chance (John Wayne) sheriff of the small town of Rio Bravo has arrested Joe Burdette (Claude Aikins) for the vicious murder of an unarmed man. He intends to deliver the murderer to the U.S. marshal. Joe's older brother, Nathan (John Russell), who owns one of the largest ranches in the territory and employs more than forty men will go to any length to free his brother. Chance has an elderly, crippled deputy Stumpy (Walter Brennan) as his only help. His chief deputy, Dude (Dean Martin), a top gun, has become a drunkard because the woman he loved turned out to be no good. A quiet young gunfighter, Colorado (Ricky Nelson), throws his lot in with the sheriff. Together they stop Burdette's gang, greatly aided by a wagon loaded with fuel and dynamite, and unexpected help from Feathers (Angie Dickinson), the saloon girl .

Rio Bravo is a highly enjoyable film, but at 141 minutes it is a little too long. It is an old-fashioned Western with several excellent sequences. It is also a very commercial film. Stumpy, the Walter Brennan character, is in the film purely for the comedy. The insertion of pop idol Ricky Nelson, a nonactor who has no more than twenty lines, is aimed at a young audience. To have him and Dean Martin sing is fun but slows the pace and lessens the tension. Howard Hawks' female leads were often beautiful women who were not necessarily accomplished actresses, not dissimilar to Joanne Dru in *Red River*. What makes the film work is Howard Hawks' years of experience and the surprisingly touching performance of Dean Martin.

Hawks and Wayne had criticized *High Noon* (1952) as an inaccurate depiction of a sheriff's behavior during a crisis. A good sheriff, they argued, would not be afraid of his adversary nor would he beg for help from the townspeople. Their answer is *Rio Bravo* where the sheriff even turns down offers of help. Whatever the merits of their argument, Hawks and Wayne had strong political differences with what they perceived as the liberal bias of the makers of *High Noon,* the writer Carl Foreman, director Fred Zinnemann and producer Stanley Kramer. It is interesting that the communist hierarchy in Europe and the U.S. also objected to *High Noon,* one man acting alone and emerging as the hero. They argued that the only meaningful solution would have been collective action by the town against the outlaws. No matter the political undertones of the two films, *High Noon* is a far better film.

The River

1951. 99 min. color. Indian. **Prod.** Kenneth McEldownery; **Dir.** Jean Renoir; **Scr.** Jean Renoir, Rumer Godden (based on the novel by Rumer Godden); **Cin.** Claude Renoir, Ramananda Sen Gupta; **Ed.** George Gale; **Mus.** M. A. Partha Sarathy; **Cast:** Nora Swinburne, Arthur Shields, Radha Shri Ram, Patricia Walters, Thomas E. Breen, Adrienne Corri, Esmond Knight, June Hillman (narrator).

Jean Renoir made only one worthwhile film, *The Southerner* (1945), during his seven-year stay in Hollywood. He was not given artistic control nor approval of the final cut. He was invited to India in 1949 by an Indian film company and given complete control to make a film of his choosing. Renoir selected *The River,* a semiautobiographical novel by Rumer Godden. The film tells the story of a serene English colonial family living in Bengal along the banks of the Ganges River during the last years of the Raj. It concentrates on one of the daughters, Harriet (Patricia Walters), who matures and comes of age during the course of the film. It was Renoir's first film in color and is beautifully photographed by his nephew, Claude Renoir. The elegantly restrained film could easily have become maudlin, but Renoir has stayed clear of sentimentality. Where the film is weak is in the mostly amateurish cast.

Rocco and His Brothers

Rocco e I Suoi Fratelli. 1960. 180 min. b.w. French/Italian. **Prod.** Giuseppe Bordogni; **Dir.** Luchino Visconti; **Scr.** Luchino Visconti, Suso Cecchi D'Amico, Pasquale Festa Campanile, Massimo Franciosa, Enrico Medioli (based on the novel *The Bridge of Ghisolfa* by Giovanni Testori); **Cin.** Giuseppe Rotunno; **Ed.** Mario Sarandrei; **Art D.** Mario Garbuglia; **Mus.** Nino Rota; **Cast:** Alain Delon, Renato Salvatori, Annie Giradot, Katina Paxinou, Claudia Cardinale, Roger Hanin, Suzy Delair, Paolo Stoppa, Spiros Focas, Max Cartier.

This is the story of a family with a domineering mother that moves from the pastoral south of Italy to the industrial north with tragic results. The film falters with its mix of melodrama and neorealism. The acting is uneven with only Katina Paxinou and Renato Salvatori showing any fire. But there are powerful scenes throughout this intense movie. Several of Visconti's films deal with the disintegration of a family as their central theme, similar to *The Leopard* (1963) and *The Damned* (1969).

Room at the Top

1959. 118 min. b.w. British. **Prod.** John Woolf, James Woolf; **Dir.** Jack Clayton; **Scr.** Neil Paterson (based on the novel by John Braine); **Cin.** Freddie Francis; **Ed.** Ralph Kemplen; **Art D.** Ralph Brinton; **Mus.** Mario Nascimbene; **Cast:** Laurence Harvey, Simone Signoret, Heather Sears, Hermione Baddeley, Donald Wolfit, Donald Houston, Raymond Huntley.

Room at the Top is the story of a cynical amoral young Yorkshire man (Laurence Harvey), born to poverty and raised on the wrong side of the tracks, who rises to the top. The film was a forerunner of the British social realism films of the sixties. It is made memorable by one of the finest screen performances by an actress. Simone Signoret's sublime scenes of passion and despair as a cast off paramour won her an Academy Award. It is well directed by Jack Clayton in his first feature film. His later works are disappointing. He never equaled this film. He mishandled *The Great Gatsby* (1973) and years later the filming of another novel, *The Lonely Passion of Judith Hearne* (1987).

Sahara

1943. 97 min. b.w. U.S. **Prod.** Harry Joe Brown; **Dir.** Zoltan Korda; **Scr.** John Howard Lawson, Zoltan Korda; **Cin.** Rudolph Maté; **Ed.** Charles Nelson; **Mus.** Miklos Rozsa; **Cast:** Humphrey Bogart, Bruce Bennett, J. Carrol Naish, Lloyd Bridges, Dan Duryea, Kurt Krueger, Rex Ingram.

The film is set in the Libyan desert in 1942 after the fall of Tobruk to Rommel's forces. The American forces were not yet fully engaged in North Africa. A few tank commanders had been sent to the British Eighth Army to gain experience and become acclimated to the desert. In this story Sergeant Joe Gunn (Humphrey Bogart), an American tank commander with a crew of two (Bruce Bennett and Dan Duryea), lose contact with the Allied forces in the withdrawal and become stranded in the desert. Along their way they pick up a Sudanese sergeant (Rex Ingram) with his Italian prisoner (J. Carrol Naish), a downed German pilot, and several British and Free French stragglers. They are short of water but they reach the ruins of an old fort that has a small water hole, full enough to sustain their small group. They are soon surrounded by a few hundred Germans who have been without water for several days and are desperate to reach the well. The movie then becomes a challenge as to whether the nine Allied soldiers can hold the fort and trick the Germans into believing there is a deep well and they can hold out indefinitely.

There are two strands in the story, one of which works to per-fection while the other merely limps along. The first is a purely exciting action film with the Allies trying to fool the Germans. John Howard Lawson, the coscriptwriter, also makes a forced wartime propaganda attempt to demonstrate the bond of human-ity among the Allies fighting Nazi Germany. The film is well directed with fine performances by Bogart and J. Carrol Naish, an Irishman who plays the Italian prisoner to perfection

Sammy Going South

(a.k.a. *A Boy Ten Feet Tall*). 1963. 118 min. color. British. **Prod.** Michael Balcon; **Dir.** Alexander Mackendrick; **Scr.** Denis Cannan; **Cin.** Edwin Hillier; **Ed.** Jack Harris; **Mus.** Tristam Cary; **Cast:** Edward G. Robinson, Fergus McClelland, Constance Cummings, Harry H. Corbett.

A ten-year-old English boy (Fergus McClelland) loses his parents in a bombing raid by British bombers over Port Said during the Suez crisis in 1956. He vaguely remembers that his only relative is an Aunt Jane in Durban, South Africa. He begins walking south on a journey of three thousand miles. He is initially helped by an Arab peddler who becomes his guide, hoping for a reward from Aunt Jane. He loses the guide in an accident. Now alone, he is helped by a wealthy American woman tourist and later by an old diamond smuggler (Edward G. Robinson). The last scene is his seeing Aunt Jane. An unpretentious charming film made on a shoestring budget. Edward G. Robinson, whose career spanned nearly fifty years, gives the performance expected from an actor of his caliber.

The Scarlet Empress

1934. 110 min. b.w. U.S. **Dir.** Josef von Sternberg; **Scr.** Manuel Komroff (based on the diary of Catherine the Great); **Cin.** Bert Glennon; **Ed.** Josef von Sternberg; **Art D.** Hans Dreier, Peter Ballbusch, Richard Kollorsz; **Mus.** Mendelssohn, Tchaikovsky, Wagner, Josef von Sternberg; **Cast:** Marlene Dietrich, John Lodge, Louise Dresser, Sam Jaffe, C. Aubrey Smith, Ruthelma Stevens.

The film narrates the life of Princess Sophia Frederica (Marlene Dietrich) who later became Catherine the Great. In 1744 she was sent from Germany to marry Grand Duke Peter (Sam Jaffe), the unbalanced and prematurely senile son of Elizabeth, Empress of Russia (Louise Dresser). Upon arrival she is ordered to change her name to Catherine and have a male child forthwith. Catherine changes from a sheltered and romantic girl to a master of intrigue at the court of Elizabeth. Her marriage to the grand duke is never consummated, but she has a male child by a handsome officer, Count Alexei (John Lodge). She discards Count Alexei when she finds he is also the lover of the empress. She takes numerous other lovers, always selected from the elite officer class who could later help in realizing her ambition to ascend the throne of Russia. Peter, within six months after becoming Csar in 1762, was assassinated by army officers instigated and encouraged by Catherine. The film shows how through sheer will she becomes the empress of Russia.

The Scarlet Empress is Josef von Sternberg's most intense film. He took certain liberties with historical facts that gave the film greater drama and impact. He telescoped events that take place over many years into a brief time span. The film is most imaginative visually with provocative sexual imagery as Catherine seduces nearly an entire regiment of the Russian officer elite. Marlene Dietrich has never been as beautiful or as well photographed. She is photographed from her best angles, under veils or behind transparent curtains. There are also several highly original scenes. To the strains of "The Ride of the Valkyries," Dietrich mounted on a horse triumphantly bounds up the steps of the palace. Sam Jaffe is very good as the imbecilic grand duke. The only shortcoming amongst the actors is Louise Dresser who lacks the needed fire and wiles as the Empress. This was the sixth collaboration of Sternberg and Dietrich, whom Sternberg had discovered. The film was not popular with the public or the critics and Sternberg made only one more film thereafter.

The Scarlet Pimpernel

1935. 95 min. b.w. British. **Prod.** Alexander Korda; **Dir.** Harold Young, Roland V. Brown, Alexander Korda; **Scr.** S. N. Behrman, Robert E. Sherwood, Arthur Wimperis, Lajos Biro (based on the novel by Baroness Orczy); **Cin.** Harold Rosson; **Ed.** William Hornbeck; **Prod. D.** Vincent Korda; **Mus.** Arthur Benjamin; **Cast:** Leslie Howard, Merle Oberon, Raymond Massey, Nigel Bruce, Bramwell Fletcher, Anthony Bushell.

The Scarlet Pimpernel is the story of an English aristocrat, Sir Percy (Leslie Howard), who saves innocent French aristocrats from the guillotine. To accomplish this he poses as a foppish, effeminate dilettante at the court of the Prince of Wales. In reality he is the ingenious and daring adventurer known as the Scarlet Pimpernel. He has fooled everyone, including his wife (Merle Oberon). A very enjoyable film with Leslie Howard in great form and Raymond Massey as Chauvelin, a fanatic bloodthirsty French revolutionary who will do anything to capture the elusive Pimpernel. One of the best adventure stories from the prolific producer Alexander Korda, whose other films include The Four Feathers (1939) and The Thief of Baghdad (1940).

Seconds

1966. 106 min. b.w. U.S. **Prod.** Edward Lewis; **Dir.** John Frankenheimer; **Scr.** Lewis John Carlino (based on the novel by David Ely); **Cin.** James Wong Howe; **Ed.** Ferris Webster, David Webster; **Art D.** Ted Haworth; **Mus.** Jerry Goldsmith; **Cast:** Rock Hudson, Salome Jens, John Randolph, Will Geer, Jeff Corey, Murray Hamilton, Richard Anderson, Karl Swenson.

The story of a married, middle-aged, successful New York businessman, Arthur Hamilton (John Randolph), who is tired of his life and wants a complete change. He is introduced to a secret organization that is engaged in rendering a service to the very well-to-do. It will provide a new identity, a new face and body through plastic surgery, and a new career. Against a hefty fee it will also stage a credible accident, supply a corpse to confirm the subject's death, and provide for the surviving relatives. Arthur

Hamilton becomes a "second" and is transformed into Tony Wilson (Rock Hudson), a bachelor abstract painter living in a California beach house. The whole experiment takes a deadly turn as Tony Wilson can't hold his liquor and talks too much, and Arthur Hamilton did not really know what he wanted.

The story is original and intriguing and works very well for the first half of the film. What could have been another of John Frankenheimer's successful gripping films falls short on several counts. Rock Hudson was the wrong choice for the lead. Frankenheimer had offered the film to Laurence Olivier who accepted, but the producers thought he was not "bankable." The realistic details are magnificently photographed by James Wong Howe, but some scenes are too long, e.g. a grape stomping scene, while too little has gone into exploring the background of Arthur Hamilton. The secondary cast of John Randolph, Will Geer, Murray Hamilton and Jeff Corey is perfect.

Sergeant York

1941. 134 min. b.w. U.S. **Prod.** Jesse L. Lasky, Hal B. Wallis; **Dir.** Howard Hawks; **Scr.** Abem Finkel, Harry Chandlee, Howard Koch, John Huston (based on *War Diary of Sergeant York* by Sam K. Cowan, *Sergeant York and His People* by Sam K. Cowan, and *Sergeant York—Last of the Long Hunters* by Tom Skeyhill); **Cin.** Sol Polito, Arthur Edeson; **Ed.** William Holmes; **Art D.** John Hughes; **Mus.** Max Steiner; **Cast:** Gary Cooper, Walter Brennan, Joan Leslie, George Tobias, Stanley Ridges, Margaret Wycherly, Ward Bond, Noah Beery, Jr., June Lockhart, Dickie Moore.

This is the story of Alvin C. York (Gary Cooper), a sharpshooter from eastern Tennessee, one of the most highly decorated soldiers in American history. He was a conscientious objector who converted when America entered World War I. He is credited with killing twenty or more German soldiers and single-handedly capturing 132 prisoners during the battle of Meuse–Argonne. The film is uneven. It has some moving scenes and excellent acting, but it also has some maudlin scenes. Among the outstanding scenes are a rain-soaked Alvin entering a church

with the parishioners singing, "Give Me That Old Time Religion," led by the pastor (Walter Brennan); and the turkey shoot,
which is pure Americana with a good deal of humor. The most
embarrassing scene is Alvin going to the mountains and leaning
against a boulder with his faithful dog at his feet, meditating on
the efficacy of war. When he comes to "render unto Caesar…" all
doubts are dispelled and he is converted to war. The scene is
beneath the sensibilities of Howard Hawks. Cooper, born to play
York, gives one of his finest performances. Margaret Wycherly is
even better as Mother York. George Tobias brings great humor to
his role as Pusher Ross, a New York subway guard become soldier. Cooper won the Academy Award for best actor and the film
received nominations in almost all major categories.

Seven Days in May

1964. 118 min. b.w. U.S. **Prod.** Edward Lewis; **Dir.** John Frankenheimer; **Scr.** Rod Ser-
ling (based on the novel by Fletcher Knebel, Charles Waldo Bailey II); **Cin.** Ellsworth
Fredricks; **Ed.** Ferris Webster; **Art D.** Cary Odell; **Mus.** Jerry Goldsmith; **Cast:** Burt Lancaster, Kirk Douglas, Fredric March, Ava Gardner, Edmond O'Brien, Martin Balsam,
George Macready, Whit Bissell, Hugh Marlowe, John Houseman.

The film details an attempted coup d'état led by the chairman
of the Joint Chiefs of Staff, General James Scott (Burt Lancaster),
to forcibly remove President Jordan Lyman (Fredric March). The
conspiracy includes several senior military men, one or more senators and an influential television commentator. The high brass is
extremely troubled by a nuclear disarmament treaty the U.S. has
concluded with the Soviet Union. Colonel Martin Casey (Kirk
Douglas), a special aide to General Scott, accidentally gets wind
of the plot and after some soul-searching alerts the president. The
coup is to take place during a military alert exercise when the
president will be relatively isolated. The rest of the film covers the
attempt by the president and his aides to expose the plotters and
abort the coup.

Based on the popular novel by Fletcher Knebel and Charles
Bailey that gets the thread of its theme from incidents during the

presidencies of Harry Truman and John Kennedy: Truman's removal of General Douglas MacArthur from command for insubordination, and a vitriolic campaign by at least one general to have President Kennedy removed. With the demise of the Soviet Union, the film has somewhat dated. It was made when John Frankenheimer was at the height of his craftsmanship. The black and white photography gives something of a documentary appearance. It is extremely well edited, with cross-cutting that moves the film at a fast pace. The set designs and art direction are near perfect. The Pentagon security system with surveillance cameras and TV monitors is very well depicted. It is also, overall, a well-acted film. Fredric March, Kirk Douglas, Edmond O'Brien, Martin Balsam and John Houseman are outstanding.

Seven Days to Noon

1950. 93 min. b.w. British. **Prod.** Roy Boulting, John Boulting; **Dir.** John Boulting; **Scr.** Roy Boulting, Frank Harvey; **Cin.** Gilbert Taylor; **Ed.** Roy Boulting, John Boulting; **Art D.** John Elphick; **Mus.** John Addison; **Cast:** Barry Jones, Olive Sloane, Andre Morell, Sheila Manahan, Hugh Cross, Joan Hickson.

An atomic scientist, Professor Willingden (Barry Jones), is disillusioned with his work. One day without warning he smuggles out a small nuclear device in a satchel and heads for London. The film begins with a postman dropping an envelope at 10 Downing Street on a Monday. The unsigned letter warns the British government that he will blow up London on the coming Sunday unless the government disposes of its entire nuclear arsenal and takes the lead in outlawing all nuclear weapons. The film is the story of the next seven days. What makes it powerful is that Willingden is presented as a sane, rational man, married with an engaging daughter. The government depicts him as a madman who has broken under the strain of his work. The film is well photographed and the scenes of crowded London, and later a deserted city, have a documentary look. Barry Jones is excellent and Olive Sloane as a former showgirl give good performances.

Seven Thieves

1960. 102 min. b.w. U.S. **Prod.** Sidney Boehm; **Dir.** Henry King; **Scr.** Sidney Boehm (based on the novel *Lions at the Kill* by Max Catto); **Cin.** Sam Leavitt; **Ed.** Dorothy Spencer; **Art D.** Lyle Wheeler, John De Cuir; **Mus.** Dominic Frontiere; **Cast:** Edward G. Robinson, Rod Steiger, Joan Collins, Eli Wallach, Alexander Scourby, Michael Dante, Sebastian Cabot, Berry Kroeger.

Seven Thieves is a well-made caper film about a perfectly executed robbery of the Monte Carlo casino with several twists. It is carried by Edward G. Robinson, a great, forceful actor who portrays the urbane mastermind. A weak ending mars the film somewhat.

The Seven-Per-Cent Solution

1976. 113 min. color. British. **Prod.** Herbert Ross; **Dir.** Herbert Ross; **Scr.** Nicholas Meyer (based on his novel); **Cin.** Oswald Morris; **Ed.** Chris Barnes; **Prod. D.** Ken Adam; **Art D.** Peter Lamont; **Mus.** John Addison; **Cast:** Alan Arkin, Nicol Williamson, Vanessa Redgrave, Robert Duvall, Laurence Olivier, Joel Grey, Samantha Eggar, Charles Gray, Jeremy Kemp, Georgia Brown.

The film is based on an imaginative novel by Nicholas Meyer who also wrote the screenplay. It brings together Sigmund Freud (Alan Arkin), a detective of the mind, and Sherlock Holmes (Nicol Williamson), a fictitious detective created by Arthur Conan Doyle. It begins in London with Dr. Watson (Robert Duvall), the devoted friend and colleague of Holmes, noticing that the erratic behavior of his friend is becoming worse. He decides Holmes needs medical and psychiatric attention. With the help of Holmes' brother Mycroft (Charles Gray), Watson tricks Holmes into traveling to Vienna and meeting Freud. Freud who had experimented with cocaine himself patiently works on Holmes' addiction and long-buried secrets. Holmes painfully sheds his addiction and in the process Freud also discovers the roots of Holmes' obsession with Professor Moriarty (Laurence Olivier). When one of Freud's patients (Vanessa Redgrave) is kidnapped by an Ottoman potentate, Holmes assists Freud in finding the girl. The first three-fourths of the film is fascinating. The last quarter, which deals with the rescue of Redgrave, is forced and too hectic and detracts from the movie. The acting of the principal actors is outstanding, although Robert Duvall with his forced British accent is miscast. The re-creation of Hapsburg Vienna and Victorian London is perfect.

The Seventh Cross

1944. 110 min. b.w. U.S. **Prod.** Pandro S. Berman; **Dir.** Fred Zinnemann; **Scr.** Helen Deutsch; **Cin.** Karl Freund; **Ed.** Thomas Richards; **Art D.** Cedric Gibbons, Leonid Vasian; **Mus.** Roy Webb; **Cast:** Spencer Tracy, Signe Hasso, Hume Cronyn, Jessica Tandy, Felix Bressart, Ray Collins, Alexander Granach, Agnes Moorehead, George Macready, Steven Geray, Kaaren Verne, George Zucco.

Set shortly before the onset of World War II, seven men, all political prisoners, have escaped from a concentration camp and the Gestapo is after them. Six are either killed or captured. The most prominent, George Heisler (Spencer Tracy), manages to flee to Holland. Heisler, a disillusioned labor activist, has his faith restored when at almost every turn he is helped by various people, some of whom he had never met before. This was Zinnemann's first full length feature film and he is ably assisted by the excellent cinematography of Karl Freund. What also gives the film credibility is the great cast where every actor gives a memorable performance.

The Shawshank Redemption

1994. 142 min. color. U.S. **Prod.** Niki Marvin; **Dir.** Frank Darabont; **Scr.** Frank Darabont (based on the story "Rita Hayworth and the Shawshank Redemption" by Stephen King); **Cin.** Roger Deakins; **Ed.** Richard Francis-Bruce; **Art D.** Terence Marsh; **Mus.** Thomas Newman; **Cast:** Tim Robbins, Morgan Freeman, Bob Gunton, William Sadler, Clancy Brown, James Whitmore.

Andy Dufresne (Tim Robbins) is a bank vice-president sentenced on circumstantial evidence to life imprisonment for the murder of his wife and her lover. His only friend is another lifer (Morgan Freeman). When it becomes known that Andy is a whiz in accounting and tax matters he is brought to work in the office of the corrupt, hypocritical warden to straighten the financial records of his crooked deals. Andy executes an ingeniously planned escape but not before exposing the warden's cruelty and corruption to the proper authorities. *The Shawshank Redemption* is a well-told and engrossing story, although some incidents drag too long. The acting is uniformly good. It is an unusual prison movie; the film that comes closest to it is *My Six Convicts* (1952).

She Done Him Wrong

1933. 66 min. b.w. U.S. **Prod.** William Le Baron; **Dir.** Lowell Sherman; **Scr.** Mae West, Harvey Thew, John Bright (based on the play *Diamond Lil* by Mae West); **Cin.** Charles Lang; **Ed.** Al Hall; **Art D.** Robert Usher; **Mus.** Ralph Rainger; **Cast:** Mae West, Cary Grant, Gilbert Roland, Noah Beery, Rochelle Hudson, Rafaela Ottiano.

Set in the naughty 1890s, Mae West plays Lady Lou, the mistress of saloon owner Gus Jordan (Noah Beery) who also runs a counterfeit ring. She is the chief attraction and lead singer of his establishment. Cary Grant plays a Salvation Army captain who is in reality a Treasury agent. He is asked by Lady Lou to "come up and see me sometime." He does and is promptly seduced. She sings the suggestive "I Like a Man Who Takes His Time." At the end she is arrested along with Jordan. Mae West made twelve films and this, her second film and first starring role, is her best.

Her films are uneven and some have dated badly, but she was always true to her famous line, "When I'm good, I'm very good. When I'm bad, I'm better." She was one of a kind and her overt sexuality influenced even the actresses of the fifties.

Ship of Fools

1965. 149 min. b.w. U.S. **Prod.** Stanley Kramer; **Dir.** Stanley Kramer; **Scr.** Abby Mann (based on the novel by Katherine Anne Porter); **Cin.** Ernest Laszlo; **Ed.** Robert C. Jones; **Prod. D.** Robert Clatworthy; **Mus.** Ernest Gold; **Cast:** Vivien Leigh, Oscar Werner, Simone Signoret, Jose Ferrer, Lee Marvin, Jose Greco, George Segal, Elizabeth Ashley, Charles Korvin, Michael Dunn, Heinz Ruhmann.

Ship of Fools is an allegory set aboard a German ship in 1933, the year Hitler came to power, traveling from Mexico to Germany. It is a serious film based on a superior novel, but there is an overcrowded big-name cast. By the time every character, including the superfluous Jose Greco's Flamenco dancers, has his moment, the movie has lost its direction. The film is also at least a half hour too long. There is, however, some compensation: Vivian Leigh in a role not too dissimilar to Blanche Dubois in *A Streetcar Named Desire* (1951) and two performances for the ages; the star-crossed lovers, Simone Signoret as a drug-addicted Spanish contessa and Oscar Werner as the disillusioned ship's doctor who is seriously ill.

Shoot the Piano Player

Tirez Sur Le Pianiste. 1960. 80 min. b.w. French. **Prod.** Pierre Braunberger; **Dir.** Francois Truffaut; **Scr.** Francois Truffaut, Marcel Moussy (based on the novel *Down There* by David Goodis); **Cin.** Raoul Coutard; **Ed.** Cecile Decugis, Claudine Bouche; **Art D.** Jacques Mely; **Mus.** Georges Delerue, Jean Constantin; **Cast:** Charles Aznavour, Marie Dubois, Nicole Berger, Michele Mercier, Albert Remy.

The film is a takeoff on the well-known sign in the old west saloons: "Don't shoot the piano player. He's doing his best." A former concert pianist, Charlie (Charles Aznavour) now plays in a cheap Paris bar. Everyone has pushed him around—his unfaithful wife, and his crooked brother and the gangsters following him. He is attracted to the local waitress who genuinely cares for him, but he has been hurt so often, he does not dare to approach her. It is Francois Truffaut's second film but completely different from the first, *The Four Hundred Blows* (1959). Here he is paying homage to the B gangster movies of the thirties. The film has no logical plot and takes whatever direction Truffaut wants. The casting of the sad-faced Aznavour, one of the most popular French singers, works very well.

The Shooting Party

1984. 108 min. color. British. **Prod.** Geoffrey Reeve; **Dir.** Alan Bridges; **Scr.** Julian Bond (based on the novel by Isabel Colegate); **Cin.** Fred Tammes; **Ed.** Peter Davies; **Art D.** Morley Smith; **Mus.** John Scott; **Cast:** James Mason, Dorothy Tutin, Edward Fox, Cheryl Campbell, John Gielgud, Gordon Jackson, Robert Hardy, Aharon Ipale, Rupert Frazer, Judi Bowker.

The film is set in the autumn of 1913, less than a year before the advent of World War I. It covers a weekend pheasant-shooting party on a large estate in southeast England. The host is Sir Randolph Nettleby (James Mason). The guests are shown to be egocentric, selfish and uncaring. There is rampant infidelity where husbands and wives have made "civilized arrangements" and each partner is free to pursue his or her pleasure. Lady Nettleby (Dorothy Tutin) had been a favorite of King Edward VII. The scenes of the pheasant shoot turn into an orgy of mindless male competition and violence portending the coming slaughter of the war. It is a well-acted film and Mason's last.

Show Boat

1936. 113 min. b.w. U.S. **Prod.** Carl Laemmle, Jr.; **Dir.** James Whale; **Scr.** Oscar Hammerstein II (based on the novel by Edna Ferber and the play by Oscar Hammerstein II and Jerome Kern); **Cin.** John Mescall; **Ed.** Ted J. Kent, Bernard W. Burton; **Art D.** Charles D. Hall; **Mus.** Jerome Kern, Oscar Hammerstein II; **Cast:** Irene Dunne, Alan Jones, Helen Morgan, Paul Robeson, Charles Winninger, Hattie McDaniel, Donald Cook.

The film follows a conventional plot of boy gets girl, boy loses girl, but in the end boy and girl are reunited. It also tangentially touches on one of the deep-rooted phobias of a segment of the American population—racial intermarriage. The film falters somewhat in its last half hour and has a maudlin ending. But it has some of the best American show tunes: "Make Believe," "Ol' Man River," "Can't Help Lovin' That Man of Mine," "Bill," "You Are Love," "Ah Still Suits Me" and "Why Do I Love You?" It is directed with great imagination by James Whale of *Frankenstein* (1931) fame, and well photographed by John Mescall despite the cheap cardboard sets. The showstopper is Paul Robeson at his peak, singing the definitive rendition of "Ol' Man River" with the camera sweeping around him against the background of the mighty Mississippi. The film also has one of the rare appearances of Helen Morgan, the original torch singer, the fine voice of Alan Jones, and a shuffle dance by the stately Irene Dunne in one of her few singing roles.

The Silence of the Lambs

1991. 118 min. color. U.S. **Prod.** Edward Saxon, Kenneth Utt, Ron Bozman; **Dir.** Jonathan Demme; **Scr.** Ted Tally (based on the novel by Thomas Harris); **Cin.** Tak Fujimoto; **Ed.** Craig McKay; **Art D.** Tim Galvin; **Mus.** Howard Shore; **Cast:** Jodie Foster, Anthony Hopkins, Scot Glen, Ted Levine, Anthony Heald, Roger Corman, Brooke Smith, Charles Napier, Diane Baker, Kasi Lemmons.

A young FBI trainee (Jodie Foster) is assigned to trace the whereabouts of a serial killer of women. She is told by her superiors to seek the help of Dr. Hannibal Lecter (Anthony Hopkins), a brilliant but deranged psychiatrist and serial killer who has been in a high-security cell for the last eight years. Lecter can offer insight into how a serial killer's mind works. In the provoking encounters between the two, Foster reveals much about herself in order to elicit information. There is too much that is distasteful in the story but it is ingenious filmmaking that holds one's attention throughout. The level of acting by the entire cast is very high.

Sitting Pretty

1948. 84 min. b.w. U.S. **Prod.** Samuel G. Engel; **Dir.** Walter Lang; **Scr.** F. Hugh Herbert (based on the novel *Belvedere* by Gwen Davenport); **Cin.** Norbert Brodine; **Ed.** Harmon Jones; **Art D.** Lyle Wheeler, Leland Fuller; **Mus.** Alfred Newman; **Cast:** Robert Young, Maureen O'Hara, Clifton Webb, Richard Haydn, Louise Allbritton, Ed Begley.

Sitting Pretty was one of the great sleepers of the forties. Lynn Belvedere (Clifton Webb), an arrogant, prissy genius of sorts, takes the job of babysitter for three unruly boys. The name Lynn on his application gave their mother (Maureen O'Hara) the impression he was a woman. He brings order to the household and also writes a book about suburbia, exposing the local gossipmongers. Clifton Webb was ideal for the part and received an Oscar nomination for best actor. Webb had appeared in a few silent films and later made a name as a singer and ballroom dancer on Broadway and in New York nightclubs. In 1944, after an absence of twenty years, he appeared in *Laura* (1944) as a sexually impotent murderer, followed by a similar role in *Dark Corner* (1946) and then as a Somerset Maugham character in *The Razor's Edge* (1946). None of the roles commended him for *Sitting Pretty*, a very funny film.

Sleuth

1972. 138 min. color. British. **Prod.** Morton Gottlieb; **Dir.** Joseph L. Mankiewicz; **Scr.** Anthony Shaffer (based on his play); **Cin.** Oswald Morris; **Ed.** Richard Marden; **Prod. D.** Ken Adam; **Art D.** Peter Lamont; **Mus.** John Addison; **Cast:** Laurence Olivier, Michael Caine.

Michael Caine, who plays the owner of several beauty salons, is invited to the country mansion of Olivier, who plays a successful writer of detective stories who likes to play elaborate games. Olivier tells Caine at the outset that he has known for some time that Caine has been having an affair with his estranged wife, but he is no longer upset. He proposes a scheme where both of them can make a lot of money. Caine is to steal his wife's jewelry; Olivier will get the insurance money and Caine will keep the jewels that Olivier's wife loves so much. Olivier has orchestrated the faked robbery. Caine agrees and the game begins. What Caine does not realize is that Olivier's motives are more complicated. He wants to humiliate Caine and regain his lost honor. The movie is a showcase for the talents of the great actor, Laurence Olivier, and Michael Caine. It is intelligently directed by Mankiewicz in this his last film. The film is never opened up and the suffocating atmosphere of the mazelike mansion with hidden rooms and passages heightens the tension.

A Slight Case of Murder

1938. 85 min. b.w. U.S. **Prod.** Samuel Bischoff; **Dir.** Lloyd Bacon; **Scr.** Earl Baldwin, Joseph Schrank (based on the play by Damon Runyon and Howard Lindsay); **Cin.** Sid Hickox; **Ed.** James Gibbon; **Art D.** Max Parker; **Mus.** M. K. Jerome, Jack Scholl; **Cast:** Edward G. Robinson, Jane Bryan, Alan Jenkins, Ruth Donnelly, Edward Brophy, Willard Parker, John Litel, Bobby Jordan, Harold Huber.

Remy Marco (Edward G. Robinson) owns a brewery and has made a fortune during Prohibition. When Prohibition is repealed and he has competition he starts losing money as no one wants his atrocious tasting beer. As a teetotaler he has never tasted it. One sip convinces him he will lose his shirt if he continues. He closes his operation and wants to go legit and mix with the swells. But there are other gangsters who are after his money and want to do away with him. A very funny farce with black humor, it is based on a play by Damon Runyon and Howard Lindsay and has the typical Runyon characters: No-nose Cohen, Blockhead Gallagher and Little Dutch. Robinson shows his talent for comedy.

The Southerner

1945. 91 mins. b.w. U.S. **Prod.** David L. Loew, Robert Hakim; **Dir.** Jean Renoir; **Scr.** Jean Renoir, Hugo Butler, William Faulkner (uncredited), Nunnally Johnson, (based on the novel *Hold Autumn in Your Hand* by George Sessions Perry); **Cin.** Lucien Andriot; **Ed.** Gregg G. Tallas; **Art D.** Eugene Lourie; **Mus.** Werner Janssen; **Cast:** Zachary Scott, Betty Fields, Beulah Bondi, Bunny Sunshine, Percy Kilbride, J. Carrol Naish, Norman Lloyd, Jay Gilpin, Charles Kemper (narrator).

The Southerner is a warm and often poetic account of one man's fight for survival. It tells of the hardships faced by a poor Southern sharecropper who is given a small plot of land by his dying uncle. He now has the chance to work his own land. Renoir made five films while in America from 1940 to 1947. The *Southerner* is his best work in Hollywood, but far from the masterpieces he directed in France.

Spellbound

1945. 111 min. b.w. U.S. **Prod.** David O. Selznick; **Dir.** Alfred Hitchcock; **Scr.** Ben Hecht, Angus Macphail (based on the novel *The House of Dr. Edwardes* by Francis Beeding-Hilary St. George Saunders, John Palmer); **Cin.** George Barnes, Rex Wimpy; **Ed.** William Ziegler, Hal C. Kern; **Prod. D.** James Basevi; **Art D.** John Ewing; **Mus.** Miklos Rozsa; **Cast:** Ingrid Bergman, Gregory Peck, Leo G. Carroll, John Emery, Michael Chekhov, Steven Geray, Rhonda Fleming.

An amnesiac (Gregory Peck) claims he is Dr. Edwardes and takes over as the head doctor at a hospital for the mentally disturbed. He is really John Ballantine, wanted by the police for the murder of Dr. Edwardes. Dr. Constance Peterson (Ingrid Bergman), a psychiatrist on the hospital staff, falls in love with him and soon realizes something is wrong. She takes him to her former teacher, Dr. Alex Brutov (Michael Chekhov), an eminent psychoanalyst, who treats him. It becomes apparent that Ballantine is suffering from a guilt complex. He has blamed himself for the death of his brother in a childhood accident. When years later Ballantine accidentally witnessed the murder of the real Dr. Edwardes he blamed himself, which led to a total loss of memory and his assuming the identity of Dr. Edwardes.

Spellbound is not one of Hitchcock's best films, but it has enough to make it interesting and enjoyable. There is the fine acting of Ingrid Bergman who puts her life and reputation in danger to protect her love, and the touching cameo role by Michael Chekhov (the nephew of Anton Chekhov). There are some original Hitchcock scenes. The first kiss by Bergman and Peck is accompanied by the camera sweeping down a corridor through some seven doors opening one after another, implying the untold pleasures the two lovers have unlocked. Other effective images are a crack of light coming from under a closed door; Peck holding a razor blade as he descends the stairs coming toward Dr. Brutov; the extremely well-done scene at the end when the gun Leo G. Carroll, playing Dr. Murchison the hospital chief, has pointed at Ingrid Bergman is turned 180 degrees and fired, and the screen turns red. There is a very good score by Miklos Rozsa. The film also has many drawbacks. Foremost is the confused "dream sequence," created by Salvador Dali. It was shot as a fifteen-minute sequence that Selznick cut to a mere two minutes. There is also the absurdity of Peck being "cured" after one session of psychoanalysis. An important drawback is the casting of a young Gregory Peck who was not convincing in the part.

The Stalking Moon

1969. 109 min. color. U.S. **Prod.** Alan J. Pakula; **Dir.** Robert Mulligan; **Scr.** Alvin Sargent; **Cin.** Charles Lang; **Ed.** Aaron Stell; **Art D.** Roland Anderson, Jack Poplin; **Mus.** Fred Karlin; **Cast:** Gregory Peck, Eva Marie Saint, Robert Forster, Noland Clay, Russell Thorson.

After a raid by the cavalry on an Indian camp, a white woman (Eva Marie Saint) is found among the Apaches. She had been kidnapped years earlier, had become the woman of the Indian chief and bore him a son. A retiring army scout (Gregory Peck) takes pity on the homeless woman and her son and takes them with him to his remote ranch. The boy's Apache father learns of their whereabouts and comes after his son. He stalks the scout like an animal. Director Robert Mulligan of *To Kill a Mockingbird* (1962) had a way with children. The boy has no dialogue, but his movements and sulking expression reveal his confusion and alienation. We never clearly see the face of the Apache stalker, only glimpses of the animal skin-clad body, which heightens the terror and tension.

Star Wars

1977. 121 min. color. U.S. **Prod.** Gary Kurtz; **Dir.** George Lucas; **Scr.** George Lucas; **Cin.** Gilbert Taylor; **Ed.** Paul Hirsch, Marcia Lucas, Richard Chew; **Prod. D.** John Barry; **Art D.** Norman Reynolds, Leslie Dilley; **Mus.** John Williams; **Cast:** Mark Hamill, Harrison Ford, Carrie Fisher, Peter Cushing, Alec Guinness, David Prowse, voice of James Earl Jones as Darth Vader.

The galaxy, which had been ruled by a senate of wise and benevolent representatives of the planets, has been taken over by the Evil Empire which imposes its will through repression and terror. Its greatest weapon is the Death Star, a gigantic interplanetary craft that houses awesome weapons of mass destruction that can obliterate any planet. A small group of rebels from various planets, headed by Princess Leia Organa (Carrie Fisher), has gained access to the details of the Death Star weapon system and its vulnerabilities. Luke Skywalker (Mark Hamill), a restless orphan youth, learns the secrets of the benevolent Force from an old retired Jedi master, Obi Wan Kenobi (Alec Guinness), and sets out to have a showdown with the masters of the Evil Empire. He is aided by Han Solo (Harrison Ford), an intergalaxial adventurer; Chewbacca (Peter Mayhew), a bearlike navigator; and two lovable droids, C-3PO and R2-D2. With Princess Leia they overthrow the Evil Empire and restore peace and tranquility to the galaxy.

The film is an imaginative take on the *Flash Gordon* serials of the thirties which were must viewing for youngsters of the time. *Star Wars* was innovative in its use of special effects, but it has dated. Its novelty has been superseded by countless imitations and sequels by George Lucas himself. The film can also be blamed for its negative effect on films from the late seventies onward. Special effects have taken over at the expense of character development and dialogue. There is little acting as such in *Star Wars,* but the mere sound of Alec Guinness' mellifluous voice and the timbre of James Earl Jones' lush bass as the evil Darth Vader give the film a certain dignity and gravitas. But the ones who steal the movie are the weird half-human characters. Lucas credits the inspiration for R2-D2 and C-3PO to two characters in Akira Kurosawa's *Hidden Fortress* (1958). He has repaid the debt by helping Kurosawa arrange financing for two of his films.

The Stars Look Down

1939. 104 min. b.w. British. **Prod.** Isadore Goldsmith; **Dir.** Carol Reed; **Scr.** J. B. Williams (based on the novel by A. J. Cronin); **Cin.** Ernest Palmer, Henry Harris, Mutz Greenbaum; **Ed.** Reginald Beck; **Art D.** James Carter; **Mus.** Hans May; **Cast:** Michael Redgrave, Margaret Lockwood, Edward Rigby, Emlyn Williams, Cecil Parker, Linden Travers, Nancy Price, Allan Jeayes.

The Stars Look Down is an early film by Carol Reed, one of the great masters of cinema. Michael Redgrave, also in one of his early films, plays a miner's son who hopes to get a university education, win a seat in Parliament, and convince the government and the mine owners to improve safety standards. He is tricked into marrying a sluttish girl (Margaret Lockwood) and is temporarily sidetracked. When his duplicitous wife leaves him he becomes free to continue his mission. A well made movie with a good cast. Redgrave was at his best when playing cerebral roles, as in *The Browning Version* (1951) and *The Dam Busters* (1955), and he is excellent as the thoughtful, idealistic miner's son. Reed shows great promise in this work. Details are always important in his films and the scenes in the mines have almost a documentary look. He went on to make such masterpieces as *Odd Man Out* (1947), *The Fallen Idol* (1948) and *The Third Man* (1949).

State of the Union

1948. 124 min. b.w. U.S. **Prod.** Frank Capra; **Dir.** Frank Capra; **Scr.** Anthony Veiller, Myles Connolly (based on the play by Howard Lindsay and Russel Crouse); **Cin.** George Folsey; **Ed.** William Hornbeck; **Art D.** Cedric Gibbons, Urie McCleary; **Mus.** Victor Young; **Cast:** Spencer Tracy, Katharine Hepburn, Angela Lansbury, Van Johnson, Adolphe Menjou, Lewis Stone, Raymond Walburn, Charles Dingle.

The Republican Party is to nominate a wealthy industrialist (Spencer Tracy) as its presidential candidate. His marital difficulty with his wife (Katharine Hepburn) is covered up and his unacceptable political convictions are adjusted for public consumption. In addition to the Tracy/Hepburn magic the film has a fine supporting cast. There is much inside humor relating to the Truman-Dewey presidential campaign of 1948. The film exposes the contrivances and shenanigans of a race for party nomination that are still relevant today, only on a grander and more sophisticated scale.

The Sting

1973. 129 min. color. U.S. **Prod.** Tony Bill, Julia Phillips, Michael Phillips; **Dir.** George Roy Hill; **Scr.** David S. Ward; **Cin.** Robert Surtees; **Ed.** William Reynolds; **Art D.** Henry Bumstead; **Mus.** Scott Joplin, John Philip Sousa; **Cast:** Paul Newman, Robert Redford, Robert Shaw, Charles Durning, Ray Walston, Eileen Brennan, Harold Gould, John Heffernan, Dana Elcar, Jack Kehoe, Robert Earl Jones.

Set in Chicago of the thirties, two petty con men (Robert Redford and Robert Earl Jones) con a delivery man for a New York mob out of the $5,000 he is carrying. The boss (Robert Shaw) has Jones killed and is after Redford. To avenge Jones' murder Redford contacts a friend of the dead man (Paul Newman), a former top-flight con artist now a drunkard. Redford convinces him to plan a sting to bankrupt the big-time racketeer and gambler. To do this they fake a big-stakes betting parlor. It is greed and arrogance that make the shrewd gangster from New York's Hell's Kitchen fall for the setup. Creating the sting operation is great fun and the final climax surprises everyone, including the audience. Redford and Newman are better than in *Butch Cassidy and the Sundance Kid* (1969), but the film belongs to the supporting cast. Robert Shaw is superb and dominates all his scenes. The rest are excellent. The photography, set designs and costumes capture the period perfectly. Marvin Hamlishch's adaptation of Scott Joplin's ragtime music set a trend. *The Sting* received awards for best picture, direction, screenplay, art direction, music and several other categories. Robert Redford was nominated as best actor.

The Story of G.I. Joe

1945. 109 min. b.w. U.S. **Prod.** Lester Cowan; **Dir.** William A. Wellman; **Scr.** Leopold Atlas, Guy Endore, Philip Stevenson (based on the book by Ernie Pyle); **Cin.** Russell Metty; **Ed.** Otho Lovering, Al Joseph; **Art D.** James Sullivan, David Hall; **Mus.** Ann Ronell, Louis Applebaum; **Cast:** Burgess Meredith, Robert Mitchum, Freddie Steele, Wally Cassell, Jimmy Lloyd, Jack Reilly, William Murphy.

The film is a foot soldier's view of war based on the dispatches of Ernie Pyle, the best known American combat correspondent of World War II. It tells the story of a platoon of raw infantrymen in Italy in 1943-44 as it slowly advances north from town to town. We see the soldiers' sheer boredom and fatigue in pouring rain and mud, and their awareness that some will not return home. The film also demonstrates that it is ultimately the foot soldier that wins battles and holds ground. It is similar to director William Wellman's later film, *Battleground* (1949), with no flag waving or sermonizing. The film is documentary-like by having a minimum of stock characters that were in almost all of Hollywood's war films. Burgess Meredith as Ernie Pyle gives a well-modulated performance. Robert Mitchum as the lieutenant, then captain, of the platoon is especially convincing, and on the strength of this role his career was launched.

The Stranger

1946. 95 min. b.w. U.S. **Prod.** Sam Spiegel; **Dir.** Orson Welles; **Scr.** Anthony Veiller, Orson Welles (based on the story by Victor Trivas, Decla Dunning); **Cin.** Russell Metty, **Ed.** Ernest Nims; **Art D.** Perry Ferguson; **Mus.** Bronislau Kaper; **Cast:** Orson Welles, Loretta Young, Edward G. Robinson, Philip Merivale, Richard Long, Martha Wentworth, Byron Keith, Konstantin Shayne.

The Stranger is not one of Orson Welles' best, nor as creative as most of his films. A former Nazi war criminal, Franz Kindler (Orson Welles), has escaped to the U.S. and settled in a small Connecticut town teaching at a prep school under an assumed name. He has married an unsuspecting local beauty (Loretta Young). An FBI agent (Edward G. Robinson) working for the Allied War Crime Commission has methodically traced Kindler who through sheer arrogance gives himself away. The script is too conventional and pat, with no surprises. The film is well photographed by Russell Metty and has some of Welles' favorite camera angles. But only the opening and concluding scenes are worthy of Orson Welles. Even his acting is uninspired. Edward G. Robinson is the dominant actor.

Straw Dogs

1971. 171 min. color. British/U.S. **Prod.** Daniel Melnick; **Dir.** Sam Peckinpah; **Scr.** David Zelag Goodman, Sam Peckinpah (based on the novel *The Siege of Trencher's Farm* by Gordon M. Williams); **Cin.** John Coquillon; **Ed.** Paul Davies, Roger Spottiswoode, Tony Lawson; **Prod. D.** Ray Simm; **Art D.** Ken Bridgeman; **Mus.** Jerry Fielding; **Cast:** Dustin Hoffman, Susan George, T. P. McKenna, Peter Ame, David Warner, Del Henney, Collin Welland, Peter Vaughn.

A young withdrawn American mathematician, David Sumner (Dustin Hoffman), and his English-born wife, Amy (Susan George), seeking to escape urban life and violence, decide to live in the small Cornwall village where Amy was born. Their marriage has difficulties from the outset. He needs to be alone to do his work; Amy needs attention and interferes. When the garage requires repairs, David hires four workers who are all related. The head of their family is Tom Hedden (Peter Vaughn), a violent man whose fierce behavior is seen early in the film. One of the workers, Charlie (Del Henney), had been intimate with Amy some years ago, before she had met David. The workers begin to loaf, mock David, and look suggestively at Amy, who encourages them by flaunting her half-naked body from the windows. They strangle Amy's cat and David does nothing about it. David, the mild-mannered pacifist, ignores their taunts and hostility, and even accepts their invitation to go bird shooting. They leave him stranded some distance from home and Charlie returns to the house and rapes Amy, not entirely against her will. Soon another of them shows up and rapes her. David learns nothing of this but a bit later, seeing no progress on the garage, fires all four. While David and Amy are driving back from a church social David knocks down Henry (David Warner), the village dolt. Not knowing that he had just strangled a young tart, a niece of the four workers, they take him home and call the local magistrate to come for the injured man. The workers and their uncle, thoroughly drunk, learn of Henry's whereabouts and lay siege to the house. The magistrate is killed when he tries to take a shotgun from Tom Hedden. David barricades the house knowing they too would be killed. The last thirty minutes of the film is an orgy of violence seldom seen on the screen until then. As the five attempt to storm the house, each is killed in carefully devised plans by David, the mathematician. One bleeds to death after having his foot shot off; another is caught in a huge steel mantrap; another by having boiling oil poured on him.

The film is a further example of Sam Peckinpah's absolute control over his films. The first ninety minutes move deliberately and a menacing atmosphere is established; then comes the orgy of violence. But *Straw Dogs* is not one of Peckinpah's best. Nothing in the film prepares us for the violence at the end. The transformation of a quiet, withdrawn mathematician into someone who enjoys violence in order to prove his manhood and defend his property and his wife is too sudden. Also, there is not one likeable character in the entire movie as there are in Peckinpah's earlier and far superior films. In *Ride the High Country* (1962), we had the character of Joel McCrea; and in *The Wild Bunch* (1969) we had the Ernest Borgnine and William Holden characters. Here, there is no one we can vaguely sympathize with. Dustin Hoffman is not entirely at ease in his role. The best acting is by Susan George and Peter Vaughn.

Summertime

1955. 99 min. color. U.S. **Prod.** Ilya Lopert; **Dir.** David Lean; **Scr.** David Lean, H. E. Bates (based on the play *The Time of the Cuckoo* by Arthur Laurents); **Cin.** Jack Hildyard; **Ed.** Peter Taylor; **Art D.** Vincent Korda; **Mus.** Alessandro Cicognini; **Cast:** Katharine Hepburn, Rossano Brazzi, Isa Miranda, Darren McGavin, Mari Aldon, Andre Morell, Jane Rose, MacDonald Parke, Gaitano Audiero.

Katharine Hepburn, an unmarried secretary from Ohio in her forties, has saved money for a trip to Venice, her as yet unseen favorite city. She meets Rossano Brazzi, the owner of an antiques shop. A romance develops and they fall in love, but soon she discovers he has a wife and grown children. She fights with herself, torn between leaving or remaining close to him. The film has the weakness of most films about famous cities. Even David Lean can't avoid its temptation and there are too many views of Venice. It must be said, however, that Venice has never been as beautifully filmed. A subplot that could have enriched the movie is dismissed with one very brief scene. Isa Miranda, a fine actress, as the proprietress of the pension where Hepburn is staying also has a story to tell. But Lean, in his anxiety for his camera to capture Venice, ignores the potential. *Summertime* is a touching and delicate story with a sensitive performance by Hepburn.

The Sundowners

1960. 133 min. color. U.S. **Prod.** Fred Zinnemann, Gerry Blattner; **Dir.** Fred Zinnemann; **Scr.** Isobel Lennart (based on the novel by Jon Cleary); **Cin.** Jack Hildyard; **Ed.** Jack Harris; **Art D.** Michael Stringer; **Mus.** Dimitri Tiomkin; **Cast:** Deborah Kerr, Robert Mitchum, Peter Ustinov, Glynis Johns, Dina Merrill, Chips Rafferty, Mervyn Johns, Chill Wills, Michael Anderson, Jr.

Set in the twenties the film tells a story of Irish–Australian sheepherders, Ida and Paddy Carmody (Deborah Kerr and Robert Mitchum) and their young son. They have no home or permanent place. They roam the land picking up odd jobs and when the sun sets, they stop for the night. They have no money but dream of the day when they can settle somewhere. Paddy takes a job to drive over a thousand head of sheep to westernmost Australia. Along the way a former naval captain (Peter Ustinov) offers to help. The arduous journey and the people they meet is the subject of this subdued Fred Zinnemann film. Working with a good script, the characters are fully developed and there are scenes of immense charm and insight into their hopes and dreams. The acting of the entire cast is superb and this often ignored film is one of Zinnemann's best.

Sunrise at Campobello

1960. 143 min. color. U.S. **Prod.** Dore Schary; **Dir.** Vincent J. Donehue; **Scr.** Dore Schary (based on his play); **Cin.** Russell Harlan; **Ed.** George Boemler; **Art D.** Edward Carrere; **Mus.** Franz Waxman; **Cast:** Ralph Bellamy, Greer Garson, Hume Cronyn, Jean Hagen, Ann Shoemaker, Alan Bunce, Tim Considine.

Sunrise at Campobello is a moving film covering three crucial years in the life of Franklin Delano Roosevelt (Ralph Bellamy). It begins in August 1921 at the small island of Campobello off New Brunswick, Canada, where Roosevelt is vacationing with his entire family. He is stricken with polio and his legs are paralyzed. FDR had been Assistant Secretary of the Navy during the latter part of the Wilson administration and the vice-presidential candidate on the Democratic ticket in 1920. Despite the wishes of his mother (Ann Shoemaker) who wants her son to abandon politics and retire to the family home in Hyde Park, New York, FDR makes an attempt at a comeback with the encouragement of his wife, Eleanor (Greer Garson), and his close aide, Louis Howe (Hume Cronyn). The best parts of the film are Roosevelt's struggles to gain at least some movement in his legs. The film ends with FDR's "Happy Warrior" speech nominating Al Smith at the Democratic National Convention in June 1924 in New York City. Taken from a stage play, it remains stagy on the screen. It is, however, distinguished by the fine acting of the entire cast. Ralph Bellamy who had been seen mostly in colorless roles as the second lead is perfect as the young FDR. Even better is Greer Garson. She somehow mastered Mrs. Roosevelt's voice and speech patterns. Hume Cronyn as Louis Howe, FDR's loyal and trusted political mentor, also shines.

Swing Time

1936. 103 min. b.w. U.S. **Prod.** Pandro S. Berman; **Dir.** George Stevens; **Scr.** Howard Lindsay, Allan Scott; **Cin.** David Abel; **Ed.** Henry Berman; **Art D.** Van Nest Poglase, Carroll Clark; **Mus.** Jerome Kern, Dorothy Fields; **Cast:** Fred Astaire, Ginger Rogers, Victor Moore, Helen Broderick, Eric Blore, Betty Furness, Landers Stevens.

Swing Time is the second-best Astaire and Rogers film after *Top Hat* (1935). In addition to the magical dancing, it has two of the best Jerome Kern songs: "The Way You Look Tonight" and "A Fine Romance." A better directed film than *Top Hat*, but the music and the dance numbers of the earlier *Top Hat* are more memorable.

The Taking of Pelham One Two Three

1974. 104 min. color. U.S. **Prod.** Gabriel Katzka, Edgar J. Scherick; **Dir.** Joseph Sargent; **Scr.** Peter Stone (based on the novel by John Godey); **Cin.** Owen Roizman; **Ed.** Jerry Greenberg, Robert Q. Lovett; **Art D.** Gene Rudolph; **Mus.** David Shire; **Cast:** Walter Matthau, Robert Shaw, Martin Balsam, Hector Elizondo, Earl Hindman, James Broderick.

A New York subway train is hijacked and eighteen passengers in one car are taken hostage. The hijack is masterminded by Robert Shaw, a former British mercenary in Africa, with three accomplices. Shaw asks for $1 million ransom in one hour, otherwise one hostage will be shot every minute. Walter Matthau is a Transit Authority detective who happens to be at the subway control center at the time and he has to negotiate with the hijackers. The film begins as a comedy when Matthau is giving a guided tour to a group of Tokyo subway officials whom he insults thinking they don't understand English. Thereafter it becomes an exciting action picture. What greatly enhances the movie is the witty dialogue by Peter Stone who also wrote the script for *Charade* (1963). There is very good editing and the outdoor scenes capture the look of New York. Matthau, Shaw and Martin Balsam give the superlative performances expected of them. The film is also enhanced by a fine jazz score.

A Tale of Two Cities

1935. 128 min. b.w. U.S. **Prod.** David O. Selznick; **Dir.** Jack Conway; **Scr.** W. P. Lipscomb, S. N. Behrman (based on the novel by Charles Dickens); **Cin.** Oliver T. March; **Ed.** Conrad A. Nervig; **Art D.** Cedric Gibbons, Frederic Hope; **Mus.** Herbert Stothart; **Cast:** Ronald Colman, Elizabeth Allen, Edna May Oliver, Reginald Owen, Basil Rathbone, Donald Woods, Blanche Yurka, Henry B. Walthall, Walter Catlett.

It is far, far better than the 1958 remake. But it is not as good as David Lean's Dickens tales, *Great Expectations* (1946) or *Oliver Twist* (1948). The film is notable and best remembered for the two women at opposite poles. Edna May Oliver as Miss Pross stands for goodness and mercy while Blanche Yurka as Madam DeFarge represents the baser instincts of cruelty and revenge. They dominate the film with their performances. With the exception of Walter Catlett, the rest of the cast, including Ronald Colman as Sydney Carton, give colorless performances. The scenes of revolutionary Paris are very well done.

The Talk of the Town

1942. 118 min. b.w. U.S. **Prod.** George Stevens; **Dir.** George Stevens; **Scr.** Irwin Shaw; Sidney Buchman; **Cin.** Ted Tetzlaff; **Ed.** Otto Meyer; **Art. D.** Lionel Banks, Rudolph Sternad; **Mus.** Frederick Hollander, **Cast:** Cary Grant, Jean Arthur, Ronald Colman, Glenda Farrell, Edgar Buchanan, Charles Dingle, Rex Ingram, Lloyd Bridges, Leonid Kinsky.

Leopold Dilg (Cary Grant), a labor activist, is on the run from a lynch mob, on trumped up charges of arson and murder. He is given refuge by Nora Shelley (Jean Arthur), a childhood friend.

What they hadn't counted on is that Nora had leased the house for the summer to Professor Michael Lightcap (Ronald Colman), the dean of a prestigious law school, while he awaits his appointment to the Supreme Court of the United States. Dilg is introduced as the gardener. Both Dilg and Lightcap learn from one another about what the law says and how it is interpreted by the courts. *The Talk of the Town* has a forced plot but an intelligent and humorous script beautifully acted by the three leads, which revitalized the career of Ronald Colman who had not made a successful film since *The Prisoner of Zenda* (1937).

Targets

1968. 90 min. color. U.S. **Prod.** Peter Bogdanovich; **Dir.** Peter Bogdanovich; **Scr.** Peter Bogdanovich; **Cin.** Laszlo Kovacs; **Ed.** Peter Bogdanovich; **Prod. D.** Polly Platt; **Mus.** Charles Greene; **Cast:** Boris Karloff, Tim O'Kelly, Nancy Hsueh, James Brown, Peter Bogdanovich, Sandy Baron.

Byron Orlok (Boris Karloff), the best-known actor of horror movies, has just completed his latest film, *The Terror,* directed by Sammy Michaels (Peter Bogdanovich). He is watching a private screening with Sammy. Sammy tells Orlok he has written the script for Orlok's next film in which he will play a real person and not a monster. Orlok says that he is through with movies and has decided to retire and go back to England. He explains that people are no longer frightened by horror movies. Real life has become more frightening with the number of murders taking place every day and someone going berserk with a gun every other week. Sammy then asks Orlok to make a final promotional appearance at the premier of *The Terror,* which is scheduled for the following night. Orlok agrees to this last favor.

Bobby Thompson (Tim O'Kelly) is a young man recently married. The couple live with Bobby's parents as he is unemployed. His wife has a night job with the telephone company and does not come home until late, when Bobby is already asleep. Bobby's father (James Brown) is an avid gun enthusiast and had taken

Bobby from childhood on his frequent hunting trips, target practice and gun shows. Bobby has become a crack shot with both
rifles and pistols. One night he has a bad dream. The next morning he very calmly shoots his wife, his mother and a delivery boy.
He leaves a note that he will kill more people until he is stopped.
Bobby has tens of guns with loads of ammunition. He drives to
the highway and from an elevation he picks off motorists. When
he hears police sirens he drives away. To elude the police he pulls
into the drive-in movie theater where Orlok is to make his
appearance that night. He hides behind the screen and waits until
dark. When the movie starts, he begins shooting everybody
within his sights. Some in the audience open the trunks of their
cars and bring out their own guns. A few approach the screen
where the gunfire had come from. Bobby tries to escape but in
his confusion he runs into Orlok who knocks the gun from his
hand and slaps him several times. Bobby submissively falls to his
knees begging for mercy. As the police take him away, however,
his last words are a boast, "I didn't miss much, did I?"

   The film is somewhat based on the Charles Whitman murder
spree at the University of Texas at Austin in 1966 when Whitman,
hiding in the University Tower, shot forty-four people, killing
fourteen, before he was gunned down by the police. *Targets* is a
direct attack on America's fascination with guns. Bogdanovich
sees any average man raised with an obsession with guns as a
potential Bobby. In an early scene, when Bobby opens the trunk
of his car, we see his large stash of firearms. At the drive-in, when
the spectators acting as vigilantes open their car trunks, we again
see several guns in each trunk. *Targets* is the first directorial effort
of Bogdanovich who also wrote the script. It was made on a
shoestring budget, greatly helped by his friend Roger Corman
for whom he had worked. Corman lent him several actors
including Boris Karloff and permission to use scenes from his
movie *Terror* (1963). The film also boasts a moving piece of acting
by Boris Karloff essentially playing himself. With the exception of
the very fine *The Last Picture Show* (1971) and *Paper Moon* (1973)
Bogdanovich's movies were not box office successes. He has,
however, made a mark as an important film historian.

They Shoot Horses, Don't They?

1969. 120 min. color. U.S. **Prod.** Irwin Winkler, Robert Chartoff, Sydney Pollack; **Dir.** Sydney Pollack; **Scr.** James Poe, Robert E. Thompson (based on the novel by Horace McCoy); **Cin.** Philip Lathrop; **Ed.** Fredric Steinkamp; **Prod. D.** Harry Horner; **Mus.** Johnny Green; **Cast:** Jane Fonda, Michael Sarrazin, Susannah York, Gig Young, Red Buttons, Bonnie Bedelia, Bruce Dern.

This is the story of a dance marathon, a phenomenon popular in the thirties at the height of the Great Depression. The film focuses on five contestants and the physical and psychological ordeal they go through. There is a farmer and his pregnant wife (Bruce Dern and Bonnie Bedelia); a sailor with a bad heart condition who is a veteran contestant (Red Buttons); a Jean Harlow look-alike (Susannah York) who is in the contest hoping to be discovered; then there is Gloria (Jane Fonda), a foul-tempered, hard-boiled girl who has had a rough life. She changes partners in midstream and selects an aimless young man (Michael Sarrazin). The master of ceremonies is a cynical barker (Gig Young) who encourages and goads the dancers to remain on the floor beyond their endurance. The prize for this orgy of self-destruction is $1,500, a fortune for the times. The film shows the ugly side of human nature and the humiliation people submit to at times of desperate need. They have no chance and will be cheated in the end. A powerful film but it is over-directed with its flash-forwards and flashbacks. The acting is also uneven. Jane Fonda, Susannah York and Gig Young, who won the Academy Award for best supporting actor, are fine, but there is a mediocre performance from Michael Sarrazin. The look of the film is its best part; the run-down, sleazy atmosphere and the glaring lights of the ballroom.

They Were Expendable

1945. 135 min. b.w. U.S. **Prod.** John Ford; **Dir.** John Ford; **Scr.** Frank Wead (based on the book by William S. White); **Cin.** Joseph August; **Ed.** Frank E. Hull, Douglas Biggs; **Art D.** Cedric Gibbons, Malcolm Brown; **Mus.** Herbert Stothart; **Cast:** Robert Montgomery, John Wayne, Donna Reed, Jack Holt, Ward Bond, Marshal Thompson, Leon Ames, Cameron Mitchell.

The film is based on the exploits of Lieutenant John Bulkeley (Robert Montgomery), commander of a squadron of torpedo boats in the aftermath of America's defeat in the Philippines in the early days of World War II. The Small PT boats were instrumental in sinking many Japanese ships and ferrying supplies, and transporting General Douglas MacArthur to Australia for regrouping. It is a poorly acted film and a little too long, but it is distinguished by some extraordinary black and white cinematography. John Ford himself was always ambivalent about this film.

The Thief of Baghdad

1940. 106 min. color. British. **Prod.** Alexander Korda; **Dir.** Ludwig Berger, Tim Whelan, Michael Powell, Zoltan Korda, William Cameron Menzies, Alexander Korda; **Scr.** Lajos Biro, Miles Malleson; **Cin.** George Perinal, Osmond Borradaile; **Ed.** William Hornbeck, Charles Crichton; **Prod. D.** Vincent Korda; **Mus.** Miklos Rozsa; **Cast:** Sabu, John Justin, June Duprez, Conrad Veidt, Rex Ingram, Miles Malleson.

Based on the *Arabian Nights*, the film features Abu (Sabu), an orphan boy who has become a street thief and is thrown into a dungeon in Baghdad. Prince Ahmad (John Justin), the heir to the throne, is overthrown by Grand Vizier Jaffar (Conrad Veidt) and joins Abu in the dungeon. The rest of the movie follows Ahmad and Abu as they attempt to defeat the evil Jaffar. They accomplish their task with the help of a beautiful princess (June Duprez) beloved by Ahmad, a magic carpet, a flying horse, a three hundred-foot-tall Djinni (Rex Ingram) and an all-seeing eye.

What makes the film memorable are the monumental sets designed by Vincent Korda, the lavish costumes by Oliver Messel, the best color photography of the period and the rousing score of Miklos Rozsa. The presence of Conrad Veidt, one of the great villains of the screen, and Sabu as the endearing street urchin adds much to the film. It is one of the most marvelous of fantasy films, ranking with the best of the Hollywood studios and Disney productions that followed. It was directed by at least six different directors in England. The advent of World War II, however, forced its completion in the U.S. This version of *The Thief of Baghdad* is completely different from the silent 1924 Douglas Fairbanks film.

The Thin Man

1934. 93 min. b.w. U.S. **Prod.** Hunt Stromberg; **Dir.** W. S. Van Dyke; **Scr.** Albert Hackett, Frances Goodrich (based on the novel by Dashiell Hammet); **Cin.** James Wong Howe; **Ed.** Robert J. Kern; **Art D.** Cedric Gibbons, David Townsend; **Mus.** William Axt; **Cast:** William Powell, Myrna Loy, Maureen O'Sullivan, Nat Pendleton, Caesar Romero, Porter Hall, Minna Gombell.

The Thin Man was the first pairing of two very charming actors, William Powell and Myrna Loy as Nick and Nora Charles. Nick Charles is a retired detective married to the wealthy Nora. They now intend to devote their entire time to taking care of each other and doing some serious drinking—bouts of six martinis each before dinner. They live in San Francisco but travel to New York for a holiday. Nick is asked by a young girl (Maureen O'Sullivan), whom he had known from her childhood, to locate her missing father who had been working on an invention. With the help of their terrier, Asta, Nick and Nora solve the case.

Based on a Dashiell Hammett novel, there is witty and radiant dialogue by the two fine actors. The pair, depicting one of the happiest marriages on film, went on to make twelve films together, including five of *The Thin Man* series. There is also smooth directing by the old pro W. S. Van Dyke. The film was made just after the repeal of Prohibition and no eyebrows were raised by the hero and heroine's heavy drinking.

This Gun for Hire

1942. 80 min. b.w. U.S. **Prod.** Richard Blumenthal; **Dir.** Frank Tuttle; **Scr.** Albert Maltz, W. R. Brurnett (based on the novel *A Gun for Sale* by Graham Greene); **Cin.** John Seitz; **Ed.** Archie Marshek; **Art D.** Hans Dreier; **Mus.** David Buttolph, **Cast:** Alan Ladd, Veronica Lake, Robert Preston, Laird Cregar, Tully Marshall, Marc Lawrence, Pamela Blake, Mikhail Rasumny.

The plot involves the sale of poison gas by an American industrial tycoon to the Nazis. The story is about a heartless hired killer (Alan Ladd) who cares only for cats. Ladd doesn't crack a smile throughout the entire film until he is dying. The love interest is Veronica Lake whose face is blank. The film made Ladd and Lake stars. It is a well-made film that, despite shortcomings, has a certain panache. This *Gun for Hire* has very little to do with Graham Greene's novel.

Tight Spot

1955. 97 min. b.w. U.S. **Prod.** Lewis J. Rachmil; **Dir.** Phil Karlson; **Scr.** William Bowers (based on the play *Dead Pigeon* by Leonard Kantor); **Cin.** Burnett Guffey; **Mus.** Morris Stoloff; **Cast:** Ginger Rogers, Edward G. Robinson, Brian Keith, Lorne Greene, Katherine Anderson.

A former gangster's moll (Ginger Rogers) has agreed to testify against the crime boss. She is being kept in a safe apartment by the D.A. (Edward G. Robinson), pending her appearance in court. Brian Keith is the policeman assigned to protect her. The gangster has informants in the police department and it is a matter of time before an attempt will be made on her life. There is great suspense and excellent direction by one of the best B-movie directors, Phil Karlson. Ginger Rogers handles her role well and there is a superlative performance by Brian Keith.

T-Men

1947. 96 min. b.w. U.S. **Prod.** Aubrey Schenck; **Dir.** Anthony Mann; **Scr.** John C. Higgins; **Cin.** John Alton; **Ed.** Fred Allen; **Art D.** Edward C. Jewell; **Mus.** Paul Sawtell; **Cast:** Dennis O'Keefe, June Lockhart, Alfred Ryder, Charles McGraw, Wallace Ford, Mary Meade, Art Smith.

An early film noir, *T-Men* is expertly crafted by Anthony Mann who had begun directing B films for RKO and Republic Studios in 1942. *T-Men* was another low-budget film for a newly formed company, Eagle-Lion. Mann showed his mastery of the medium and it foreshadowed the excellent Westerns he made with James Stewart and Gary Cooper. It is the story of a counterfeit ring that had baffled the Treasury Department for several years. Two new agents are assigned to the case and after several murders, the ring is exposed and its members are either captured or killed. The film has some well-done scenes. The opening scene has a Treasury agent murdered in cold blood by a professional assassin against a background of dark shadows. Another violent scene has a member of the mob murdered in a steam bath by the steam being turned on full blast with the doors locked. The hired killer stands outside and, through a small unbreakable window, watches the victim slowly die. The film is also notable for depicting the very thin line that separates the morality of government agents and criminals. An agent stands by while his comrade is murdered. His action is justified by the fact that the counterfeit ring is ultimately exposed. There is very good camera work by John Alton. Dennis O'Keefe as the surviving Treasury agent and the supporting cast of Wallace Ford and Charles McGraw as the vicious hit man are excellent. In an attempt to make a documentary-like film there is a continuing off-screen narration, explaining the methods used by Treasury agents and the hazards they face, which weakens the film.

To Have and Have Not

1944. 100 min. b.w. U.S. **Prod.** Howard Hawks; **Dir.** Howard Hawks; **Scr.** Jules Furthman, William Faulkner (based on the novel by Ernest Hemingway); **Cin.** Sid Hickox; **Ed.** Christian Nyby; **Art D.** Charles Novi; **Mus.** Franz Waxman; **Cast:** Humphrey Bogart, Walter Brennan, Lauren Bacall, Hoagy Carmichael, Dan Seymour, Marcel Dalio, Dolores Moran, Sheldon Leonard, Walter Sande, Walter Molnar.

The film is set circa 1940 on the Vichy-occupied island of Martinique before U.S. entry in World War II. American Harry Morgan (Humphrey Bogart) is the owner of a cabin cruiser and takes wealthy tourists on fishing trips. He is approached by a member of the French Resistance and asked to smuggle out a leader of the movement who is in hiding. Morgan is apolitical and doesn't want to take risks. However, for the love of a woman (Lauren Bacall) he has recently met who also wants to leave Martinique, he agrees to the perilous journey. Most of Howard Hawks' films have a love story at their center. Warner Brothers, the producers, wanting another box office hit insisted on changing the Hemingway novel to resemble *Casablanca* (1942). The character of Rick Blaine became Harry Morgan, Hoagy Carmichael was Dooley Wilson and hopefully Lauren Bacall would be another Ingrid Bergman. The end result is an enjoyable minor film but devoid of the magic of *Casablanca*.

In an unusual confluence of circumstances, *To Have and Have Not* is based on a novel by Ernest Hemingway and scripted by William Faulkner, both Nobel Prize winners for literature.

To Kill a Mockingbird

1962. 129 min. b.w. U.S. **Prod.** Alan J. Pakula; **Dir.** Robert Mulligan; **Scr.** Horton Foote (based on the novel by Harper Lee); **Cin.** Russell Harlan; **Ed.** Aron Stell; **Art D.** Alexander Golitzen, Henry Bumstead; **Mus.** Elmer Bernstein; **Cast:** Gregory Peck, Mary Badham, Philip Alford, John Megna, Brock Peters, Robert Duvall, Frank Overton, Rosemary Murphy.

The film is set in a small town in rural Alabama during the Great Depression. The focus is on the relationship between a widower father, Atticus Finch (Gregory Peck), a principled and courageous lawyer, and his two children. The older is a ten-year-old boy, Jem (Philip Alford), the younger is a six-year-old girl, Jean Louise (Mary Badham), nicknamed Scout. There are also themes of racial bigotry and Southern injustice when Atticus agrees to represent an innocent black man accused of raping a white woman. The film is made memorable by the acting of the two children, especially the tomboyish Scout. Gregory Peck has a role that befits his persona and won an Academy Award for best actor. Mary Badham was nominated for best supporting actress. The picture and director, Robert Mulligan, were also nominated for Oscars.

Tom Jones

1963. 131 min. color. British. **Prod.** Tony Richardson; **Dir.** Tony Richardson; **Scr.** John Osborne (based on the novel by Henry Fielding); **Cin.** Walter Lassally; **Ed.** Anthony Gibbs; **Prod. D.** Ralph Brinton; **Art D.** Ted Marshall; **Mus.** John Addison; **Cast:** Albert Finney, Susannah York, Hugh Griffith, Edith Evans, Joyce Redman, Diane Cilento, Joan Greenwood, Peter Bull, David Warner.

This is the tale of a baby left on the bed of Squire Allworthy that is assumed to be the offspring of unmarried servants in the house. The squire undertakes to raise the infant whom he names Tom Jones, played as a grown up by Albert Finney. The film covers the life and escapades of Tom who breaks many a woman's heart and is framed by evil rivals for a robbery. Just as he is to be hanged, the truth comes out and he marries the girl he loves.

John Osborne, the well-known playwright of the fifties, wrote the screenplay, condensing the massive 1749 Henry Fielding novel into a 131-minute film. It is an oddity amongst the films of the 60s and it has some marvelous scenes: a great stag hunt in the woods by a group of frenzied hunters on horseback led by Hugh Griffith; and the lascivious consuming of a multi-course dinner in total silence by Albert Finney and Joyce Redman as a prelude to sex. It is also one of the most self-conscious of films. At the end of the dinner scene, just before the two will retire to the bedroom, Tom places his hat over the camera as if a curtain has been drawn. The very opening scene, when the baby is discovered, is filmed as a silent film with title cards. There are also scenes where the action is momentarily frozen and one of the characters directly addresses the viewer. Somehow Tony Richardson was able to get the maximum effect from these scenes and they found great favor with the audience. There is good acting by the entire cast. Albert Finney is fine as the energetic, good-natured Tom. Hugh Griffith as Squire Western gives a fine performance, as do the seductive Joyce Redman, Diane Cilento and Joan Greenwood who are all after Tom. The film is also graced with one of the rare appearances of Edith Evans on film as Miss Western. *Tom Jones* won Academy Awards for best picture, director, screenplay and score and was nominated for awards in several other categories.

Topkapi

1964. 120 min. color. U.S. **Prod.** Jules Dassin; **Dir.** Jules Dassin; **Scr.** Monja Danischewsky (based on the novel *The Light of Day* by Eric Ambler); **Cin.** Henri Alekan; **Ed.** Roger Dwyer; **Art D.** Max Douy; **Mus.** Manos Hadjidakis; **Cast:** Melina Mercouri, Peter Ustinov, Maximilian Schell, Robert Morley, Akim Tamiroff, Gilles Segal, Jess Hahn.

A group of professional and amateur thieves plan and execute a daring robbery of a jewel-encrusted dagger from the Topkapi museum in Istanbul. The film is all exotic charm with a delightfully hammy cast where each upstages the other in turn. Melina Mercouri is softly emotional, Maximilian Schell is tongue-in-cheek serious, and Robert Morley, Peter Ustinov and Akim Tamiroff give great comic performances. At times it appears that director Jules Dassin is attempting a comic takeoff of his earlier film, *Rififi* (1954).

Torment

(a.k.a. *Frenzy) Hets*. 1944. 100 min. b.w. Swedish. **Dir.** Alf Sjoberg; **Scr.** Ingmar Bergman; **Cin.** Martin Bodin; **Ed.** Oscar Rosander; **Art D.** Arne Akermark; **Mus.** Hilding Rosenberg; **Cast:** Mai Zetterling, Stig Jarrel, Alf Kjellin, Gunnar Bjornstrand.

This impressive film tells the story of a serious secondary school student, Jan Erik (Alf Kjellin), who becomes emotionally and sexually involved with an alcoholic young widow, Bertha (Mia Zetterling), who has become a part-time prostitute. Jan Erik's only weak subject at school is Latin. The teacher (Stig Jarrel), a tyrannical, sadistic man, delights in tormenting his students who have named him Caligula. Unknown to Jan Erik, Caligula regularly visits Bertha who has become virtually the slave of the sadistic teacher. Bertha meets a tragic end, engulfing both Jan Eric and Caligula. This well-made film is almost a case study of a sado-masochistic relationship. There is fine acting, especially by Zetterling. Caligula has been made to bear an uncanny resemblance to Heinrich Himmler, the fiendish head of the SS in Nazi Germany. *Torment* was the first Swedish film to receive international acclaim and constituted a film renaissance in Sweden which had not produced anything notable since the advent of sound. Twenty-six-year-old Ingmar Bergman wrote the screenplay and was the assistant director. Within a year he was directing his own films. The acting and directorial careers of both Zetterling and Kjellin were also launched.

A Tree Grows in Brooklyn

1945. 128 min. b.w. U.S. **Prod.** Louis D. Lighton; **Dir.** Elia Kazan; **Scr.** Tess Slesinger, Frank Davis (based on the novel by Betty Smith); **Cin.** Leon Shamroy; **Ed.** Dorothy Spencer; **Art D.** Lyle Wheeler; **Mus.** Alfred Newman; **Cast:** Dorothy McGuire, Joan Blondell, James Dunn, Lloyd Nolan, Peggy Ann Garner, Ted Donaldson James Gleason.

The film is the saga of an impoverished Irish family living in the Williamsburg section of Brooklyn at the beginning of the twentieth century. The family breadwinner, Johnny Nolan (James Dunn), works as a singing waiter in a local restaurant. He doesn't earn enough money to support his wife, Katie (Dorothy McGuire), their early teenage daughter (Peggy Ann Garner) and young son. Their daughter's dream is to go to a better public school in another district, which by pure chance her loving father is able to arrange. A tender and beautifully acted film. Dunn won the Oscar for best supporting actor. Dorothy McGuire, one of the best actresses of her generation, brings warmth and kindness to her role. The supporting cast of Lloyd Nolan, as a policeman who marries Katie after Johnny dies, Joan Blondell as the free-spirited aunt and James Gleason as McGarrity are perfect for their parts. This was Elia Kazan's first directorial effort and as a newcomer he was wise not to overdirect or bring unnecessary flourishes to the film. Kazan's talent was to get the best performances from actors, which he ably did.

Trio

1950. 88 min. b.w. British. **Prod.** Antony Darnborough; **Dir.** Ken Annakin, Harold French; **Scr.** W. Somerset Maugham, R. C. Sherriff, Noel Langley (based on stories by W. Somerset Maugham); **Cin.** Reg Wyer, Geoffrey Unsworth; **Ed.** Alfred Roome; **Art D.** Maurice Carter; **Mus.** John Greenwood; **Cast:** James Hayter, Kathleen Harrison, Anne Crawford, Nigel Patrick, Jean Simmons, Michael Rennie.

The success of *Quartet* (1948) led to the filming of these three short stories by W. Somerset Maugham. The first is titled "The Verger." It tells the story of the verger (James Hayter) of a prominent church who is dismissed after many years of service when it is found he can neither read nor write. With his meager savings he opens a small tobacconist shop that he expands and soon becomes the proprietor of a chain of stores. The best and most subtle is the second story titled "Mr. Know It All." It is the story of an insufferable bore (Nigel Patrick) who has recently acquired British citizenship and who is a passenger on a cruise ship traveling east. He can't stop talking and soon he is shunned and avoided by all the passengers. He claims expertise in everything, including jewels. He is challenged to estimate the price and authenticity of a string of pearls worn by a married lady passenger and given to her by a friend during a lengthy absence of her husband. In an act of chivalry to protect the lady's honor, he deliberately gives a false valuation much to the delight of his fellow passengers who revel in his humiliation. The third, titled "Sanitarium," is the story of a love that develops between a young girl (Jean Simmons) and a tired man of the world (Michael Rennie). It also tells of how people react and handle the knowledge that they have an incurable disease.

Twelve O'Clock High

1949. 132 min. b.w. U.S. **Prod.** Darryl F. Zanuck; **Dir.** Henry King; **Scr.** Sy Bartlett, Beirne Lay, Jr. (based on their novel); **Cin.** Leon Shamroy; **Ed.** Barbara McLean; **Art. D.** Lyle Wheeler, Maurice Ransford; **Mus.** Alfred Newman; **Cast:** Gregory Peck, Hugh Marlow, Gary Merrill, Millard Mitchell, Dean Jagger, Paul Stewart, Robert Arthur, John Kellogg.

The film is set in the late fall of 1943 when the U.S. 8th Air Force had begun its daylight "precision bombing" of Germany. The film revolves around the 918th Bomber Group led by Colonel Keith Davenport (Gary Merrill) who has grown too attached to his men and concerned with their safe return from their missions. The 918th is underperforming and a large number of its planes have been shot down. Colonel Davenport is unceremoniously relieved and Major General Frank Savage (Gregory Peck) replaces him. Savage's task is to boost morale, enforce strict discipline and get results. The whole efficacy of daylight bombing is now at issue and if the costs are too high it will be scrapped. The U.S. Air Force will have to join its British ally in limiting bombing to nighttime. General Savage gets the desired results, but he too starts to care for the safety of his men and has a nervous breakdown.

Beginning with *Battleground,* also released in 1949, Hollywood World War II movies became more probing and intelligent. *Twelve O'Clock High* dealt with hitherto unexplored issues—the toll and psychological strains on the bomber crews as well as the commanders who send the young men to their death. The film begins with a very imaginative opening sequence. Some two or three years after the end of the war a bald-headed American tourist in London, the former Major Harvey Stoval (Dean Jagger), buys a hat. Walking down the street he finds a little statue of a one-eyed pirate in a junk shop. The statue had been the mascot of the 918th Bomber Group. He travels to the Midlands, rents a bicycle and reaches the now empty and deserted headquarters of the 918th. The background music changes to "Don't Sit Under the Apple Tree" and there is a flashback to B-17's landing and taking off. The film is well directed by the underrated Henry King and has excellent cinematography. It has one of Gregory Peck's best performances, the other being *The Gunfighter* (1950), also directed by Henry King. Millard Mitchell and Dean Jagger, who won an Academy Award as best supporting actor, are also excellent. The Twentieth Century Fox sound department won the award for best sound, and the film received a nomination for best picture.

Two Women

1961. 99 min. b.w. Italian/French. **Prod.** Carlo Ponti; **Dir.** Vittorio De Sica; **Scr.** Cesare Zavattini, Vittorio De Sica (based on the novel by Alberto Moravia); **Cin.** Gabor Pogany, Mario Capriotti; **Ed.** Adriana Novelli; **Art D.** Gastone Medin; **Mus.** Armando Trovajoli; **Cast:** Sophia Loren, Raf Vallone, Eleanora Brown, Jean-Paul Belmondo, Renato Salvatori.

Cesira (Sophia Loren), a widow, flees with her thirteen-year-old daughter from the Allied bombing of Rome. Cesira does everything she can to protect her daughter from the calamities of war, but in their final flight both mother and daughter are raped in a bombed-out church by Allied Moroccan soldiers. Vittorio De Sica has made an intense and moving film without pathos or melodrama. Sophia Loren won an Academy Award as well as prizes in France, Britain for her portrayal.

Ugetsu Monogatari

1953. 96 min. b.w. Japanese. **Prod.** Masaichi Nagata; **Dir.** Kenji Mizoguchi; **Scr.** Matsutaro Kawaguchi, Yoshikata Yoda (based on two classic stories by Akinari Ueda); **Cin.** Kazuo Miyagawa; **Ed.** Mitsuji Miyata; **Art D.** Kisaku Ito; **Mus.** Fumio Hayasaka, Ichiro Saito; **Cast:** Machiko Kyo, Masayuki Mori, Kinuyo Tanaka, Sakae Ozawa, Mitsuko Mito.

The film is set in sixteenth-century Japan in the midst of a civil war. Two peasants, both humble potters, live with their wives and children in a war-torn village. Despite the pleadings of their wives they leave home to seek fame and fortune. One wants to be a master potter and acquire wealth. The other wants to gain fame as a great samurai warrior. The first peasant meets an alluring noble lady who takes him to her spacious home where he can design and create the highest quality pottery. Soon she makes him her lover and inspires him to become a master potter. It turns out his achievements were illusory and she was merely a ghost. The other peasant takes the severed head of a famous samurai who had committed suicide and claims he had vanquished him in combat. Both peasants fulfill their foolish ambitions but at the expense of losing their families. One wife is killed by bandits and the other is raped and becomes a prostitute. As in his other films, Kenji Mizoguchi was concerned with the plight of women in Japanese society. Here, the two men are foolish dreamers while the women are earth mother symbols. One of the most original of directors, he had a painter's eye. His films have numerous intense images and long takes where the camera lingers on a face or scene.

The Umbrellas of Cherbourg

Les Parapluies de Cherbourg. 1964. 91 min. color. French/West German. **Prod.** Mag Bodard; **Dir.** Jacques Demy; **Scr.** Jacques Demy; **Cin.** Jean Rabler; **Ed.** Anne-Marie Cotret; **Art D.** Bernard Evein; **Mus.** Michel Legrand; **Cast:** Catherine Deneuve, Nino Castelnuovo, Anne Vernon, Marc Michel, Ellen Farnen.

In this a fairy-tale-like romantic musical, nineteen-year-old Genevieve (Catherine Deneuve) works in her mother's umbrella shop in Cherbourg, northern France. She is in love with Guy (Nino Castelnuovo), a garage mechanic at a nearby gas station. He is called for military service during the war of Algerian independence. After he leaves Genevieve discovers she is pregnant. She does not hear from Guy for some time. Not wanting a fatherless child, and at the urging of her ambitious mother, she marries a well-to-do merchant. Her real love comes back, but it is too late. Although influenced by Hollywood, it does not resemble the traditional Hollywood musical. All the dialogue is sung, even mundane conversation. The film is beautifully photographed with a good score by Michel Legrand and lyrics by director Jacques Demy.

Un Carnet De Bal

Life Dances On, (a.k.a. *The Dance Programme).* 1937. 135 min. b.w. French. **Dir.** Julien Duvivier; **Scr.** Julien Duvivier, Jean Sarment, Pierre Wolff, Bernard Zimmer, Henri Jeanson; **Cin.** Michel Kelber, Philippe Agostini, Pierre Levent; **Ed.** Andre Versein; **Mus.** Maurice Jaubert; **Cast:** Marie Bell, Françoise Rosay, Louis Jouvet, Raimu, Harry Baur, Fernandel, Pierre Blanchar, Pierre-Richard Willm.

A recently widowed woman (Marie Bell) comes across the dance card of her first ball some twenty years earlier. There are six names on the card. She decides to travel to the city of her birth and find out what each is doing now. One is a monk, another a hairdresser, another a seedy nightclub owner and yet another a ski instructor. She is sadly disappointed. To redeem something from her youth she decides to help the son of a deceased dance partner. Julien Duvivier was one of the most famous directors of French cinema in the thirties. During the Second World War he made films in Hollywood, without turning out any lasting work. He was known as a director of multi-actor films and continued the same trend in Hollywood with *Tales of Manhattan* (1942) and *Flesh and Fantasy* (1943). *Un Carnet De Bal* was a great success in its day but has dated a bit. It still stands out, however, for its cast of the cream of French cinema: Harry Baur, Louis Jouvet, Raimu, Fernandel and Françoise Rosay, among others.

Unfaithfully Yours

1948. 105 min. color. U.S. **Prod.** Preston Sturges; **Dir.** Preston Sturges; **Scr.** Preston Sturges; **Cin.** Victor Milner; **Ed.** Robert Fritch; **Art D.** Lyle Wheeler, Joseph C. Wright; **Mus.** Rossini, Wagner, Tchaikovsky; **Cast:** Rex Harrison, Linda Darnell, Rudy Vallee, Barbara Lawrence, Kurt Kreuger, Lionel Stander, Edgar Kennedy, Al Bridge, Julius Tannen.

Sir Alfred de Carter (Rex Harrison) is an internationally famous British conductor happily and adoringly married to Daphne (Linda Darnell). He is leaving New York for engagements in Europe and as he departs he offhandedly tells his rich, dim-witted, stuffy brother-in-law, August Henshier (Rudy Vallee), married to Daphne's sister, Barbara (Barbara Lawrence), to look after Daphne in his absence. On his return, August hands him a report from a private detective, Swceney (Edgar Kennedy), whom August had hired to follow Daphne. Sir Alfred hits the roof, almost slaps the twit, burns the report and kicks August out of the room. However, with seeds of doubt planted in his mind, Sir Alfred decides to see the private detective who shows him the original report. It appears that late one night Daphne had gone to the hotel room of the handsome Anthony (Kurt Kreuger), Sir Alfred's private secretary. Sir Alfred is now bent on revenge. That night at his concert while conducting three pieces, Rossini's "Semiramide Overture," Wagner's "Tannhauser Overture" and Tchaikowski's tone poem "Francesca De Rimini," he conjures up in his mind three scenarios to get satisfaction for what Daphne and Anthony had done: murdering Daphne and planting evidence implicating Anthony; writing a check for $1 million to Daphne freeing her to go off with Anthony; playing Russian roulette with Anthony, Daphne being the prize for the survivor. The concert ends and Sir Alfred and Daphne go back to their hotel suite. He now tries to implement his plan to commit the "perfect murder," but he is hopelessly clumsy and everything goes wrong. He soon realizes that Sweeney had mistaken Barbara for Daphne, and once again all is love.

Unfaithfully Yours is a most imaginative and funny film. It is witty and literate and has some outstanding scenes. On his way to see the private detective Sir Alfred mistakenly goes to the shop of a next door tailor (Julius Tannen). The scene is a masterpiece of bumbling wit and Preston Sturges' special brand of humor. Detective Sweeney turns out to be a big fan of Sir Alfred and loves how Sir Alfred "handles Handel." Lionel Stander as Sir Alfred's manager is great. If there are any flaws, they are minor. The scenes where Sir Alfred imagines how he will get even with Anthony and Daphne drag a little. The film was conceived by Sturges as a parody of the famous twentieth-century conductor Sir Thomas Beecham. But classical music had not reached a general audience in the forties, and the film received damning reviews and was a flop at the box office. A remake in 1984 with Dudley Moore and Nastassja Kinski is better forgotten.

Unforgiven

1992. 130 min. color. U.S. **Prod.** Clint Eastwood, **Dir.** Clint Eastwood; **Scr.** David Webb Peoples; **Cin.** Jack N. Green; **Ed.** Joel Cox; **Prod. D.** Henry Bumstead; **Art D.** Rick Roberts, Adrian Gorton; **Mus.** Lennie Niehaus, **Cast:** Clint Eastwood, Gene Hackman, Morgan Freeman, Richard Harris, Frances Fisher, Anna Thomson, Jaimz Woolvett, Saul Rubinek.

Big Whiskey, Wyoming, 1880. Two cowboys visit the local whorehouse. One of them is enraged when the girl innocently makes fun of his "little pecker." He slashes her face while his friend holds her. To the sadistic sheriff, "Little Bill" Dogette

(Gene Hackman), it is only a matter of commerce. He sets the two cowboys free when they agree to compensate the brothel owner with seven ponies by the following spring. The disfigured girl is kept on as a cleaning woman. Little Bill regards it as a passing incident, but the other girls can't forget the matter. They secretly raise $1,000 from their savings as a reward for anyone who kills the two cowboys. Word of this bounty soon reaches gunfighters as far as Texas. One of them is William Munny (Clint Eastwood), a ruthless killer in the Kansas/Missouri wars who had married a good woman, hung up his guns and started a pig farm. When his wife died two years ago his fortunes began to fail, and Munny is now destitute with two small children to feed. Together with a youngster with a fast draw, the Schofield Kid (Jaimz Woolvett), and an old cohort, Ned Logan (Morgan Freeman), he goes after the reward. He doesn't know that the sheriff has seven experienced deputies and has been warned that bounty hunters are on their way. Munny himself hasn't used a gun in eleven years, the Schofield Kid is nearsighted and can barely see his target, and Ned Logan is well past his prime. Scores are finally settled in one of the bloodiest of endings.

The film is well controlled by Eastwood's direction. For a 130-minute film with several novel themes for a Western, the pace doesn't ever slacken. Eastwood, never a good actor, is fine as Munny with his craggy, aging face and customary limited dialogue. Gene Hackman as the sadistic sheriff and Morgan Freeman as the loyal friend give the excellent performances we expect from actors of their caliber. Richard Harris as English Bob is cast well and is also excellent. What makes the film memorable is the introduction of a feminist theme, unusual in a Western. The solidarity shown by the prostitutes is very touching, and the acting of Frances Fisher and Anna Thomson plays a key part in gaining our sympathy for the abused girls in the God-forsaken frontier town. What does not work so well is the unnecessary theme of inventing legends and myths that Eastwood attempts to establish.

Eastwood's first directorial effort, *Play Misty for Me* (1971), seemed an auspicious beginning. After a series of mediocre films, he directed *White Hunter, Black Heart* (1990), which showed promise. Two years later he directed *Unforgiven*, his best work to that date. *Mystic River* (2003), his finest film, was released as this book neared completion.

Utz

1992. 94 min. color. British/German/Italian. **Prod.** John Goldschmidt; **Dir.** George Sluizer; **Scr.** Hugh Whitemore (based on the novel by Bruce Chatwin); **Cin.** Gerard Vandenberg; **Mus.** Nicola Piovani; **Cast:** Armin Mueller Stahl, Brenda Fricker, Peter Riegert, Paul Scofield, Gay Brown, Miriam Karlin.

Utz (Armin Mueller Stahl) is a man in his sixties from an upper-class Prague family that had suffered under Nazi and communist tyrannies. He now lives alone in modest circumstances with a dedicated housekeeper of many years (Brenda Fricker). He had been a womanizer but his foremost passion has been collecting porcelain figurines of exceptional quality. His collection is considered one of the very best in the world. The communist government has made a detailed inventory of the pieces, believing that they will be left to the state. Utz dies and his collection disappears. Despite searches by the state museum and the secret police nothing turns up. It is only toward the end of the film that the housekeeper reveals the fate of the world class-collection. There are several subplots and interesting characters. There is also a good deal of humor in the film and the communist government is mercilessly ridiculed. The musical score is very good. Utz is an intelligent and charming little gem with three superb performances: Armin Mueller Stahl, Brenda Fricker and Paul Scofield.

Vanya on 42nd Street

1994. 120 min. color. U.S. **Prod.** Fred Berner; **Dir.** Louis Malle; **Scr.** David Mamet (based on the play *Uncle Vanya* by Anton Chekhov); **Cin.** Declan Quinn; **Ed.** Nancy Baker; **Art D.** Eugene Lee; **Mus.** Joshua Redman; **Cast:** Wallace Shawn, Julianne Moore, Phoebe Brand, George Gaynes, Larry Pine, Brooke Smith, Jerry Mayer, Andre Gregory, Lynn Cohen, Mahdur Jaffrey.

A small group of actors come to the dilapidated cavernous Amsterdam Theatre in New York City to rehearse a production of David Mamet's adaptation of Chekhov's *Uncle Vanya*. They are sitting around the bare stage with some chairs and tables. Soon, without our being aware, the rehearsal becomes the play. Although this is basically a filmed stage play, it works to perfection. There is superlative acting by Julianne Moore as Yelena, the young second wife of a wealthy, aging, pompous professor. Equally good is Wallace Shawn as the unfulfilled and tormented Vanya. *Uncle Vanya*, the best and most difficult of Chekhov's plays, has far more contemporary themes and relevance than his other three full-length plays. This was the last film of Louis Malle who died shortly afterward. His body of work is uneven but he directed several memorable films, most notably *Lacombe Lucien* (1975), *Atlantic City* (1981) and *Au Revoir Les Enfants* (1990).

Village of the Damned

1960. 78 min. b.w. British. **Prod.** Ronald Kinnoch; **Dir.** Wolf Rilla; **Scr.** Wolf Rilla, Stirling Silliphant, George Barclay (based on the novel *The Midwich Cuckoos* by John Wyndham); **Cin.** Geoffrey Faithfull; **Ed.** Gordon Hales; **Art D.** Ivan King; **Mus.** Ron Goodwin; **Cast:** George Sanders, Barbara Shelley, Michael Gwynne, Laurence Naismith, John Phillips.

Through a strange phenomenon all the inhabitants of a small English village are put in a trance for twenty-four hours. All women capable of bearing children are impregnated. In due course some twelve children are born. They all look alike, are highly intelligent, emotionless and possess telepathic powers. They are adored by their mothers. When they reach school age, a physicist (George Sanders), whose wife is the mother of one of the children, agrees to the job of educating them. He soon realizes that the children were fathered by aliens and their purpose is to take over the planet, but he is helpless as the children can read his mind. A very modest film made for less than $300,000, it becomes melodramatic towards the end, losing some of its impact. However, it is well made with an eerie atmosphere.

The Virgin Spring

Jungfrukallan. 1960. 88 min. b.w. Swedish. **Prod.** Ingmar Bergman, Allan Ekelund; **Dir.** Ingmar Bergman; **Scr.** Ulla Isaksson (based on the fourteenth-century ballad *Tores Dotter I Vange)*; **Cin.** Sven Nykvist, Rolf Halmquist; **Ed.** Oscar Rosander; **Art D.** P. A. Lundgren; **Mus.** Erik Nordgren; **Cast:** Max von Sydow, Brigitta Valberg, Gunnel Lindblom, Brigitta Pettersson, Axel Duberg, Tor Isedal, Ove Porath.

Set in fourteenth-century Sweden the film recounts a medieval tale about the rape and murder of a fifteen-year-old innocent girl on her way to church to light candles for the Virgin. She stops to share her lunch with three goatherds who violate and kill her. Her father (Max von Sydow) exacts his revenge and slays the goatherds who, by chance, have come to sell her belongings and dress. A spring gushes from the spot where the young virgin's body was found and the father vows to build a church beside it. *The Virgin Spring* is a minor Bergman film but well told with excellent cinematography by Sven Nykvist.

I Vitelloni

1953. 104 min. b.w. Italian. **Prod.** Mario de Vecchi; **Dir.** Federico Fellini; **Scr.** Federico Fellini, Ennio Flaiano, Tullio Pinelli; **Cin.** Otello Martelli, Luciano Trasatti, Carlo Carlini; **Ed.** Rolando Benedetti; **Art D.** Mario Chiari; **Mus.** Nino Rota; **Cast:** Franco Interlenghi, Franco Fabrizi, Alberto Sordi, Leopoldo Trieste, Riccardo Fellini, Leonora Ruffo, Lida Baarova.

This is the first of Federico Fellini's semi-autobiographical films, which was followed by *Amarcord* (1974). Both are set in the

seaside town of Rimini, his birthplace. It is the story of five aimless young men in their mid to late twenties who have remained
adolescent daydreamers and cannot accept responsibility. Only
one of them, probably Fellini himself, sees no future in the small
town and leaves. It is Fellini's second collaboration with Nino
Rota who composed a beautiful nostalgic score.

Viva Zapata!

1952. 113 min. b.w. U.S. **Prod.** Darryl F. Zanuck; **Dir.** Elia Kazan; **Scr.** John Steinbeck
(based on the novel *Zapata the Unconquered* by Edgcumb Pichon); **Cin.** Joseph MacDonald; **Ed.** Barbara McLean; **Art D.** Lyle Wheeler, Leland Fuller; **Mus.** Alex North; **Cast:**
Marlon Brando, Jean Peters, Anthony Quinn, Joseph Wiseman, Arnold Moss, Alan Reed,
Harold Gordon, Margo, Mildred Dunnock.

The film covers the Mexican civil wars of 1911 to 1919, leading
to the overthrow of Porfirio Diaz; the installation of the reformer
Francisco Madero as president; the brief assumption of power by
Emiliano Zapata and his assassination. It has one of Marlon
Brando's best performances as the illiterate and brooding Zapata.
Anthony Quinn as Emiliano's brother also gives what is probably
his best performance resulting in an Academy Award for best supporting actor. Harold Gordon as Madero, and Alan Reed as
Pancho Villa are credible. As in all Elia Kazan's films, he gets the
best from almost every actor. The exception here is Joseph Wiseman who, as a Judas figure, is let loose by Kazan and overacts. What
weighs the film down is the ponderous script by John Steinbeck
that becomes a meditation on the corrupting nature of power.

Walkabout

1971. 95 min. color. Australian. **Prod.** Si Litvinoff; **Dir.** Nicolas Roeg; **Scr.** Edward Bond (based on the novel by James Vance Marshall); **Cin.** Nicholas Roeg; **Ed.** Anthony Gibbs, Alan Pattillo; **Prod D.** Brian Eatwell; **Art D.** Terry Gough; **Mus.** John Barry; **Cast:** Jenny Agutter, Lucien John, David Gulpilil, John Meillon, Peter Carver, John Illingsworth.

An architect drives his six-year-old son (Lucien John) and four-teen-year-old daughter (Jenny Agutter) from Sydney to the Australian desert for a picnic. They have immigrated to Australia from Barbados. He has been a failure in his profession and has become suicidal. He stops the car at the edge of the desert and lets the children out. He attempts to shoot his son but misses. He then pours gasoline over himself and shoots himself, dying in flames. The daughter having witnessed the entire event takes her brother into the desert. They have no food or water and nearly die of thirst. They find an oasis and a quandong tree that sustains them for a while. Fortunately their path crosses with a seventeen-year-old aborigine boy (David Gulpilil) who is on a "walkabout," a ritual for boys to prove their manhood by being able to survive in the desert for several weeks. He becomes a brother to the boy and acts as their guide. He kills animals for food and finds water in the unlikeliest holes. The young boy learns to communicate with the aborigine in sign language. The aborigine boy, obviously attracted to the girl, does a lengthy ritual mating dance. She ignores him entirely. Having been rejected, he hangs himself. The girl shields her brother from the sight and they continue on their journey until they are rescued. We next see the girl years later when she has married a hard-driving businessman. The film closes as she appears to be daydreaming about the time she was in the desert.

Walkabout is about the wonder of growing up. There is a resemblance to the early Hemingway short stories. But whereas in Hemingway the focus is always on a young boy, here we have a girl in her early teens. In her final reverie she is begrudgingly acknowledging her attraction to the aborigine boy who killed himself for love. *Walkabout* is Nicolas Roeg's second film and was made in the Red Desert near Alice Spring. There is superlative photography of the desert and its creatures. The score by John Barry uses aborigine instruments with some music from Stockhausen. Roeg's seven-year-old son, Lucien John, who had never acted before, and the seventeen-year-old Gulpilil are fine.

War and Peace

Voyna I Mir. 1966–1967. 373 min. color. Russian. **Dir.** Sergei Bondarchuk; **Scr.** Vasili Solovyov, Sergei Bondarchuk (based on the novel by Leo Tolstoy); **Cin.** Anatoli Petritsky; **Ed.** Tatyana Likhacheva; **Art D.** Mikhail Bogdanov, Gennadi Myasnikov; **Mus.** Vyacheslav Ovchinnikov; **Cast:** Ludmila Savelyeva, Vyacheslav Tikhonov, Hira Ivanova-Golovko, Sergei Bondarchuk, Anatoli Ktorov, Boris Smirnov, Anastasia Vertinskaya, Irina Skobotseva, Boris Zakhava, V. Stanitsyn, Vladislav Strzhelchik.

War and Peace, the definitive film of Tolstoy's great novel, is the story of Napoleon's ill-fated campaign in Russia and how it changes the lives and fortunes of two aristocratic families. It stands out for the mammoth size of the production. Nothing was spared in making the film that took nearly five years. In the two battle scenes there are probably more than fifty thousand extras and there is a magnificent ballroom scene that dwarfs any Hollywood effort. *War and Peace* was released in the USSR in four parts totalling about eight hours. The English Version was reduced to just over six hours. Viewing a six-hour film in one session, however, is a problem even for a serious movie buff.

Way Out West

1937. 65 min. b.w. U.S. **Prod.** Stan Laurel; **Dir.** James W. Horne; **Scr.** Charles Rogers, Felix Adler, James Parrott; **Cin.** Art Lloyd, Walter Lundin; **Ed.** Bert Jordan; **Art D.** Arthur I. Royce; **Mus.** Marvin Hatley, LeRoy Shield, Egbert Van Alstyne, J. L. Hill, Nathaniel Shilkret, Irving Berlin, Franz Von Suppe; **Cast:** Stan Laurel, Oliver Hardy, Sharon Lynn, James Finlayson, Rosina Lawrence.

Way Out West is Laurel and Hardy's best full-length film. They are to deliver a gold mine deed to the daughter of their partner who had recently died. They are conned by a saloon keeper, Mickey Finn (James Finlayson), and deliver the deed to a loud and brassy saloon girl, Lola Marcel (Sharon Lynn), who poses as the daughter. The two dumb guys are happy to have met their obligation. In the end they retrieve the deed and give it to the rightful girl.

Unlike their other feature films, here the comedy is sustained throughout. The pair also show their vaudeville experience, most notably in the duets they sing, one being "In the Blue Ridge Mountains of Virginia," and a lovely soft-shoe routine in front of the saloon. The best line in the movie comes when Ollie, trying to make conversation with a fellow stagecoach passenger, says, "A lot of weather we've been having lately." Laurel and Hardy are nearly forgotten today. They were overshadowed by the talents of Chaplin and Keaton. But Stanley as a dumb guy and Ollie, though unaware, an even dumber guy were great fun.

Weekend

(a.k.a. *Week-end*). 1967. 103 min. color. French. **Dir.** Jean-Luc Godard; **Scr.** Jean-Luc Godard; **Cin.** Raoul Coutard; **Ed.** Agnes Guillemot; **Mus.** Antoine Duchamel, Mozart; **Cast:** Mireille Darc, Jean Yanne, Jean-Pierre Kalfon, Jean-Pierre Leaud, Yves Beneyton.

Jean-Luc Godard's last film before he withdrew from mainstream cinema, *Weekend* has some of the nastiest and greediest people. Its focus is on a scheming Parisian couple on their journey by car to the wife's mother to get or extort some money from her. On the road we see every conceivable crime including murder, rape and cannibalism, the hallmarks of an acquisitive consumer society. It is Godard's vision of hell on earth and the descent of the bourgeois society to the edge of the abyss. Godard's only remedy is a Maoist revolution that can uproot the existing structure and wash and cleanse everything on its way. It is a flawed film with some incomprehensible passages but will be remembered for a ten minute sequence of a monumental traffic jam. Hereafter Godard's films become even more personal and devoid of any conventional form.

Whisky Galore

(a.k.a. *Tight Little Island*). 1949. 82 min. b.w. British. **Prod.** Michael Balcon; **Dir.** Alexander Mackendrick; **Scr.** Compton Mackenzie, Angus MacPhail (based on the novel by Compton Mackenzie); **Cin.** Gerald Gibbs, Chick Waterson; **Ed.** Joseph Sterling; **Mus.** Ernest Irving; **Cast:** Basil Radford, Joan Greenwood, James Robertson Justice, Gordon Jackson, John Gregson, Wylie Watson, Finlay Currie (narrator).

The film is set in 1943, during World War II, in the Outer Hebrides on the small island of Todday. A cargo ship, the SS *Politician*, bound for the U.S. with a cargo of fifty thousand cases of scotch whiskey, is near sinking after running onto rocks near the shoreline. The entire crew has abandoned the ship. Due to wartime restrictions, all alcoholic beverages have been rationed, and the quota for Todday had run out some six months earlier. Of late, the villagers have become less civil to each other and a general gloom has descended. The parched villagers are now even willing to risk their lives to salvage as many cases as possible. Problems arise when the overly conscientious commander of the Home Guard, Captain Waggett (Basil Radford), a Colonel Blimp-type Englishman who resides on the island, decides to salvage the sinking cargo for His Majesty's Customs. It becomes a race as to who can get to the *SS Politician* first, and where to hide the cargo once it is brought on shore.

The film is a minor gem by Alexander Mackendrick, who was to direct two other great comedies at Ealing Studios: *The Man in the White Suite* (1951) and *The Ladykillers* (1955). The film also hosts some of the best of British supporting actors.

The White Balloon

Badkonak-e Sefid. 1995. 85 min. color. Iranian. **Dir.** Jafar Panahi; **Scr.** Abbas Kiarostami; **Cin.** Farzad Jowdat; **Ed.** Jafar Panahi; **Cast:** Aida Mohammadkhani, Mohsen Kalifi, Fereshteh Sadr Orfani, Anna Borkowska, Mohammad Shahani, Mohammad Bakhtiari.

The film takes place in real time. In eighty-five minutes, when the sun crosses the equator on the first day of spring, the new Iranian year begins. A lower-income family—husband, wife and two children—are preparing for the arrival of the new year. It is the custom to have several objects on the table at the time, including a live goldfish. Their seven-year-old daughter, Razieh (Aida Mohammadkhani), wants not just any fish but a chubby one with feathery tail fins she has seen at a local store. After Razieh sulks and cries her mother gives her last five hundred tomans (seventy-five cents) to the girl to buy the goldfish. She sets out accompanied by her older brother. They are soon separated and it is her first time alone in the streets of Tehran. The film now becomes Razieh's odyssey. She loses and finally finds the five hundred toman note. In the interim she encounters all sorts of people—two snake charmers anxious to separate her from her money, an exasperated shopkeeper, a kindly old Polish lady, a soldier from the provinces and a young Afghan boy who sells balloons. She is reunited with her brother and gets her goldfish. The film ends with the tolling of the new year. A charming, well made-film scripted by the notable filmmaker Abbas Kiarostami. The director, Jafar Panahi, brings in tension and an element of suspense. We are never certain about Razieh's safety. The film is told entirely from the child's perspective, her bewilderment in a crowded city and her determination, with superlative acting by the young girl. A modest film that works very well.

White Mischief

1987. 107 min. color. British. **Prod.** Simon Perry; **Dir.** Michael Radford; **Scr.** Michael Radford, Jonathan Gems (based on the book by James Fox); **Cin.** Roger Deakins; **Ed.** Tom Priestley; **Art D.** Roger Hall; **Mus.** George Fenton; **Cast:** Sara Miles, Joss Ackland, John Hurt, Greta Scacchi, Charles Dance, Susan Fleetwood, Geraldine Chaplin, Trevor Howard, Jacqueline Pearce, Hugh Grant.

Based on an actual happening, the film depicts the rich and titled British colonials in East Africa during the early days of World War II. The opening scene shows the aristocracy drinking champagne in a London underground shelter during an air raid. The film then moves to Happy Valley in Kenya with the arrival of recently married wealthy and knighted Jack (Joss Ackland) and his beautiful young wife Diana (Greta Scacchi). She soon takes a lover, Erroll (Charles Dance), a peer, which becomes the talk of Happy Valley. Erroll is murdered. Jack is tried but acquitted. A well-acted kinky movie showing the decadence of British colonials while London is burning. The film gains much by excellent production design illustrating the life of the idle rich.

Wilson

1944. 154 min. color. U.S. **Prod.** Darryl F. Zanuck; **Dir.** Henry King; **Scr.** Lamar Trotti; **Cin.** Leon Shamroy; **Ed.** Barbara McLean; **Art D.** Wiard Ihnan, James Basevi; **Mus.** Alfred Newman; **Cast:** Alexander Knox, Charles Coburn, Geraldine Fitzgerald, Thomas Mitchell, Ruth Nelson, Cedric Hardwicke, Vincent Price, William Eythe, Mary Anderson, Sidney Blackmer.

The film is an ambitious biography of Woodrow Wilson (Alexander Knox), the twenty-eighth president of the U.S. It begins with Wilson's appointment as president of Princeton University, then election as governor of New Jersey, followed by his election to the presidency in 1912. He succeeds on the domestic front, leading a campaign against trusts and monopolies. He was re-elected in 1916 having kept the U.S. out of the world war that had started in 1914. After the German U-boat campaign sank several American ships, Congress declared war in 1917. The entry of fresh U.S. troops in France turned the tide and Germany and Austria sued for peace. Wilson was celebrated across the world and hailed as a savior. He annunciated his Fourteen Points to make the world safe for democracy. But he was frustrated at the Paris Peace Conference in 1919. The colonial powers, Britain, France and Italy, carved up Asia and Africa. His hopes for U.S. membership in the League of Nations were dashed by the Republican-dominated senate led by Senator Henry Cabot Lodge (Cedric Hardwicke). Vigorously campaigning for his ideals, Wilson suffered a stroke and was incapacitated for the remainder of his term. Far from a great movie, *Wilson* is still the best screen biography of a U.S. president. There is a first-rate cast and the relatively unknown Alexander Knox as Wilson gives the best performance of his career. Thomas Mitchell as Joseph Tumulty, his press secretary, and Geraldine Fitzgerald as Edith Wilson, his second wife, are outstanding. Despite its length of 154 minutes, the film moves well under the direction of the experienced Henry King.

Winchester '73

1950. 92 min. b.w. U.S. **Prod.** Aaron Rosenberg; **Dir.** Anthony Mann; **Scr.** Robert L. Richards, Borden Chase; **Cin.** William Daniels; **Ed.** Edward Curtiss; **Art D.** Bernard Herzbrun, et al. **Mus.** Joseph Gershenson; **Cast:** James Stewart, Shelley Winters, Dan Duryea, Stephen McNally, Charles Drake, Millard Mitchell, John McIntire, Will Geer, Jay C. Flippen.

The film begins in Dodge City on the Fourth of July in the 1870s. Lin McAdam (James Stewart) has been pursuing his brother (Stephen McNally) who had killed their father. There is a shooting contest and first prize is a rare Winchester 1873 model rifle. By sheer coincidence the two brothers are contestants. Lin wins the rifle, but his brother ambushes him and steals it. The rifle changes hands several times and at the end there ˙ a dramatic shoot-out between the brothers. This was th˙

collaboration of James Stewart and director Anthony Mann. It is a superior Western with psychological dimensions. As in all of Mann's Westerns there is spectacular outdoor photography. It is finely acted by James Stewart with an excellent supporting cast. Only Shelley Winters appears miscast. An equally well-made film by Anthony Mann also with James Stewart, *The Naked Spur* (1953) has similar themes.

The Winslow Boy

1948. 117 min. b.w. British. **Prod.** Anatole de Grunwald; **Dir.** Anthony Asquith; **Scr.** Terence Rattigan, Anthony Asquith, Anatole de Grunwald (based on the play by Terence Rattigan); **Cin.** Freddie Young, Osmond Borradaile; **Ed.** Gerald Turney-Smith; **Prod. D.** Andre Andrejew; **Mus.** William Alwyn; **Cast:** Robert Donat, Margaret Leighton, Cedric Hardwicke, Francis L. Sullivan, Basil Radford, Wilfrid Hyde-White, Kathleen Harrison, Marie Lohr, Jack Watling, Neil North.

Based on an actual 1912 case, a fourteen-year-old boy, Ronnie Winslow (Neil North), is expelled after a perfunctory investigation from the Royal Naval College for stealing a five shilling postal order. The boy's father (Cedric Hardwicke) believes in his innocence but can do nothing as the sovereign is immune from any lawsuit. He seeks the assistance of Britain's most outstanding barrister (Robert Donat) to test the archaic principle that the king can do no wrong. It was a landmark case in English jurisprudence that resulted in citizens being granted the right to initiate legal proceedings against the crown (government). The boy is found to be innocent. The film is based on a play and therefore stagy but what makes it work is the flawless acting by a cast of some of the finest British actors.

Woman in the Window

1944. 99 min. b.w. U.S. **Prod.** Nunnally Johnson; **Dir.** Fritz Lang; **Scr.** Nunnally Johnson (based on the novel *Once Off Guard* by J. H. Wallis); **Cin.** Milton Krasner; **Ed.** Marjorie Johnson, Gene Fowler, Jr.; **Art D.** Duncan Cramer; **Mus.** Arthur Lange; **Cast:** Joan Bennett, Edward G. Robinson, Dan Duryea, Raymond Massey, Bobby (Robert) Blake, Dorothy Peterson, Edmund Breon, Thomas Jackson, Arthur Loft.

A highly respected professor of psychology, Richard Manley (Edward G. Robinson), has seen his family off for their summer vacation. He is to join them after delivering a scheduled series of lectures. On his first night alone he goes to his club to have dinner with two friends. After dinner, he takes a short nap in a chair and then leaves. He stops in front of an art gallery that is exhibiting the portrait of a beautiful woman in its window. As he turns, he finds the subject of the painting standing beside him. They introduce themselves. She is Alice Reed (Joan Bennett), an unmarried woman living alone. He compliments her beauty. She is touched by his remarks and invites him for a drink to her nearby apartment. He is unaware that she is the mistress of a prominent financier, Claude Mazard (Arthur Loft). Unexpectedly Mazard comes in and, in a rage, tries to strangle Manley. Alice is able to give Manley a pair of scissors with which he stabs and kills Mazard. Instead of calling the police, Manley panics and hauls the body out and leaves it in a wooded area. The next day the police find the body and begin their investigation. Soon Mazard's bodyguard, Heidt (Dan Duryea), who had followed his boss on the evening of the murder, attempts to blackmail Manley and Alice. The story ends with a most unusual twist.

The film embodies two of director Fritz Lang's often-used themes: the vagaries of fate, and how an upright and intelligent man has his life turned around by one inadvertent mistake: Manley's chance encounter with an alluring woman and his failure to call the police after the stabbing. The film is tightly controlled by Lang and the atmospheric camera work of Milton Krasner maintains the high suspense. The ending, although imaginative, lessens both the impact of the film as well as the main thrust of the script. Lang used the same excellent cast of Robinson, Bennett and Duryea and a similar theme of fate a year later in *Scarlet Street* (1945).

The Wrong Man

1957. 105 min. b.w. U.S. **Prod.** Alfred Hitchcock; **Dir.** Alfred Hitchcock; **Scr.** Maxwell Anderson, Angus MacPhail (based on *The True Story of Christopher Emmanuel Balestrero* by Maxwell Anderson); **Cin.** Robert Burks; **Ed.** George Tomasini; **Art D.** Paul Sylbert, William L. Kuehl; **Mus.** Bernard Herrmann; **Cast:** Henry Fonda, Vera Miles, Anthony Quayle, Harold J. Stone, Nehemiah Persoff, Esther Minciotti, Charles Cooper.

Christopher "Manny" Balestrero (Henry Fonda), a married man with two sons, plays the bass fiddle in the famed Stork Club dance orchestra. He is a quiet, gentle, mild-mannered man in financial difficulty. His salary barely pays for daily expenses. He has borrowed from several sources and the only course left to him is to borrow on his wife's insurance policy. He goes to the neighborhood insurance and loan bank to make inquiries. He is identified by several office girls as the man who had robbed the company recently. The next day he is arrested. Thereafter, his life becomes a nightmare. Bail is denied as the police have been after a man who has perpetrated several other holdups. His wife, Rose (Vera Miles), cannot cope with the ordeal and goes into a deep depression. As her condition worsens she is placed in a hospital. After a lapse of almost a year his trial begins. During the preliminary hearings the real culprit is caught while robbing a store and Manny is absolved.

Hitchcock, after making three glossy films in the mid-fifties—*To Catch a Thief* (1955) and *The Trouble with Harry* (1955), and a remake of *The Man Who Knew Too Much* (1956)—decided on a true story of a man caught in a nightmare of "justice," solely on circumstantial evidence. The film was made in stark black and white in documentary style, free from any Hitchcock flourish and macabre humor. It is probably his most gloomy and somber film. Lives have been ruined and at the end the protagonists face a dark future. They turn to religion for solace. *The Wrong Man* was Hitchcock's second "Catholic film" and far superior to the first, *I Confess* (1953). The details of police procedure and especially the final brief confrontation between Manny and the actual robber are very well done. The acting is also superior. Fonda, Miles, Anthony Quayle as Manny's lawyer, and Harold J. Stone as a police lieutenant are all very good. What detracts from the film is the sudden shift of focus from Manny to Rose, without any preparation or groundwork.

Yankee Doodle Dandy

1942. 126 min. b.w. U.S. **Prod.** William Cagney; **Dir.** Michael Curtiz; **Scr.** Robert Buckner, Edmund Joseph; **Cin.** James Wong Howe; **Ed.** George Amy; **Art D.** Carl Jules Weyl; **Mus.** Heinz Roemheld, Ray Heindorf, songs by George M. Cohan; **Cast:** James Cagney, Joan Leslie, Walter Huston, Irene Manning, Rosemary De Camp, Richard Whorf, Jeanne Cagney, S. Z. Sakall, Walter Catlett, Frances Langford, Eddie Foy, Jr., George Tobias.

This is a biography of a forgotten entertainer and songwriter, George M. Cohan, who wrote such memorable World War I songs as "Over There" and "Give My Regards to Broadway." It is a slick film typical of those manufactured by the big studios in the thirties through the mid-fifties. There are many super-patriotic numbers that were well received when the movie was released shortly after Pearl Harbor. What makes this dated film enjoyable is the presence of James Cagney, who singlehandedly lifts it above the run-of-the mill Hollywood musical of the time. Cagney, who appeared mostly as villains and gangsters, showed his talents as a song-and-dance man. His style of acting and mannerisms stood in stark contrast to other actors of his day. Here we see his dancing, which was also unique.

Yojimbo

1961. 110 min. b.w. Japanese. **Dir.** Akira Kurosawa; **Scr.** Akira Kurosawa, Ryuzo Kikushima, Hideo Oguni; **Cin.** Kazuo Miyagawa; **Art D.** Yoshiro Muraki; **Mus.** Masaru Sato; **Cast:** Toshiro Mifune, Eijiro Tono, Seizaburo Kawazu, Isuzu Yamada, Hiroshi Tachikawa, Kyu Sazanka, Kamatari Fujiwara, Takashi Shimura.

Sanjuro Kuwabatake (Toshiro Mifune), an unemployed and impoverished samurai, is traveling on foot. When he reaches a crossroad he picks up a stick and throws it into the air. How it falls will determine the way he goes. He reaches a village terrorized by two factions. On one side stands a silk merchant, Tazaemon (Kamatari Fujiwara), and on the other a sake merchant, Tokuemon (Takashi Shimura). Sanjuro soon realizes both are greedy, evil men and their followers are cutthroats. Still he is hungry and needs lodging and food. At first both sides are suspicious, but each needs an experienced samurai. He is first hired by Tazaemon as a yojimbo (bodyguard). Soon he switches sides. He begins manipulating the two factions with the intention of having them destroy each other. He is caught, tortured and thrown into a dungeon. He escapes, and when he recovers his health he returns to the village where he instigates a battle between the two factions that leaves most of their warriors dead. Finally peace comes to the village.

Yojimbo is among Kurosawa's most enjoyable films. It is well photographed and the battle scenes are well staged. Mifune's mannered and eccentric acting lends weight to the film. It is slow in parts, however, and the comedy scenes weaken the film. *Yojimbo* was popular in Japan and Kurosawa made a similar film, *Sanjuro* (1962), a year later that is not as good. *Yojimbo* was later made as a spaghetti Western, *A Fistful of Dollars* (1964), and influenced U.S. filmmakers in mixing violence and comedy.

Young Frankenstein

1974. 105 min. b.w. U.S. **Prod.** Michael Gruskoff; **Dir.** Mel Brooks; **Scr.** Gene Wilder, Mel Brooks (based on the characters from the novel *Frankenstein* by Mary Wollstonecraft Shelley); **Cin.** Gerald Hirschfeld; **Ed.** John C. Howard; **Art D.** Dale Hennesy; **Mus.** John Morris; **Cast:** Gene Wilder, Peter Boyle, Marty Feldman, Teri Garr, Madeline Kahn, Cloris Leachman, Kenneth Mars, Gene Hackman, Richard Haydn.

Dr. Frederick Frankenstein (Gene Wilder), a brain surgeon and lecturer at a medical school, learns that he has inherited his grandfather's Transylvanian estate. He bids farewell to his fiancée, Elizabeth (Madeline Kahn) and leaves. He is met by the servant Igor (Marty Feldman), Inga (Teri Garr) who will be his research assistant and Frau Blucher (Cloris Leachman), a hideous old woman who had been his grandfather's housekeeper, modeled after Mrs Danvers in *Rebecca* (1940). He soon finds his grandfather's secret library and comes across the sole copy of the book he had written: *How I Did It*. The young doctor becomes intent on creating a new and better monster. But once again the brain of an "abnormal man" is used and the result is a gentler but incoherent monster (Peter Boyle). Frederick's fiancée finds sexual satisfaction with the monster and marries him, and Frederick gets together with Inga. There are several scenes of hilarity: Frankenstein takes his creation to a medical convention in Bucharest and in white tie and tails they do a soft-shoe routine and sing "Puttin' on the Ritz"; an encounter between the monster and a blind hermit (Gene Hackman); Frankenstein insisting his name be pronounced "Frank-en-*steen*"; Igor insisting his name is "Eye-gore"; the mere mention of Frau Blucher's name making the horses neigh with fright. *Young Frankenstein* and *The Producers* (1967) are the best of Mel Brooks. But even in the best of Brooks some of the intended gags don't work.

Young Mr. Lincoln

1939. 100 min. b.w. U.S. **Prod.** Kenneth MacGowan; **Dir.** John Ford; **Scr.** Lamar Trotti; **Cin.** Bert Glennon, Arthur Miller; **Ed.** Walter Thompson; **Art D.** Richard Day, Mark-Lee Kirk; **Mus.** Alfred Newman; **Cast:** Henry Fonda, Alice Brady, Marjorie Weaver, Arleen Whelan, Eddie Collins, Pauline Moore, Donald Meek, Richard Cromwell, Milburn Stone, Ward Bond.

The film begins in 1832 when Abraham Lincoln moved from Kentucky to Springfield, Illinois. He is aware of his lack of formal education and becomes a voracious reader. He loses the love of his life, Ann Rutledge; sets up a legal practice; and soon becomes known as Honest Abe. He marries the ambitious Mary Todd and defends two young men accused of murder, which helps to open up a political career. Henry Fonda makes a perfect young Abe. (Although, the tall and gaunt Raymond Massey bore a closer resemblance to the future president in *Abe Lincoln in Illinois* in 1940.) As in most John Ford films there are comic scenes that only partially work. Nineteen thirty-nine was a rewarding year for admirers of John Ford. He made three near great films: *Stagecoach, Young Mr. Lincoln* and *Drums Along the Mohawk. Young Mr. Lincoln* is the best representation of a young Lincoln on film.

Zero De Conduite

Zero for Conduct. 1933. 45 min. b.w. French. **Prod.** Jean Vigo; **Dir.** Jean Vigo; **Scr.** Jean Vigo; **Cin.** Boris Kaufman; **Ed.** Jean Vigo; **Mus.** Maurice Jaubert; **Cast:** Jean Daste, Robert Le Flon, Louis Lefevre, Gilbert Pruchon, Gerard de Bedarieux, Constantine Kelber.

Jean Vigo's father, a militant anarchist, had been murdered while in prison. Jean, a sickly child with tuberculosis had been sent to various state-run boarding schools. The film is a remembrance of those days by the now twenty-eight-year-old Vigo. It is the story of a revolt by boys in a boarding school against arbitrary authority and their takeover of the school. It is beautifully photographed by Boris Kaufman, who twenty-one years later would be the cinematographer of *On the Waterfront* (1954). The scene of the start of the revolt is by far the best of the entire movie. The boys overturn their beds and rip open the pillows, creating a rain of feathers. The film was banned and not shown until after the war in 1945. Vigo made his masterpiece, *L'Atalante* (1934), and died shortly thereafter of leukemia at age twenty-nine. *Zero De Conduite* is a bold and imaginative film that influenced other filmmakers. Lindsay Anderson's *If* (1965) is almost a remake of *Zero De Conduite,* although far more violent.

Zorba the Greek

1964. 146 min. b.w. U.S./Greek. **Prod.** Michael Cacoyannis; **Dir.** Michael Cacoyannis; **Scr.** Michael Cacoyannis (based on the novel by Nikos Kazantzakis); **Cin.** Walter Lassally; **Ed.** Michael Cacoyannis; **Art D.** Vassele Fotopoulos; **Mus.** Mikis Theodorakis, **Cast:** Anthony Quinn, Alan Bates, Irene Papas, Lila Kedrova, George Foundas, Eleni Anousaki.

An English writer (Alan Bates) comes to Greece seeking his identity and to work a lignite mine he has inherited from his Greek father. Zorba (Anthony Quinn), a lusty local peasant, attaches himself to the inhibited Englishman. He helps him attempt to open the mine, which fails, but above all teaches him to live without repression and with fatalistic humor. Irene Papas is expressively effective as a silent widow to whom Bates is attracted. Lila Kedrova as an aging French courtesan cared for by Zorba is very good. Alan Bates holds his own well against Quinn's larger-than-life portrayal for which he won an Oscar. Other awards included best picture, supporting actress (Kedrova), and director.

Zulu

1964. 138 min. color. British. **Prod.** Stanley Baker, Cy Endfield; **Dir.** Cy Endfield; **Scr.** John Prebble, Cy Endfield; **Cin.** Stephen Dade; **Ed.** John Jympson; **Art D.** Ernest Archer; **Mus.** John Barry; **Cast:** Stanley Baker, Jack Hawkins, Michael Caine, Ulla Jacobsson, Nigel Green, James Booth, Ivor Emmanuel, Paul Daneman. Richard Burton (narrator).

Set at Rorke's Drift, Natal, South Africa, on 22 January 1879, 105 men of the 24th Regiment of South Wales are warned by a Dutch missionary that they are in imminent danger. Another contingent of some 300 British soldiers had just been wiped out by Zulu warriors who were only days away from Rorke's Drift. There are only two officers at the outpost and neither has had any combat experience. Lieutenant John Chard of the Royal Engineers (Stanley Baker), by reason of a few months seniority over Lieutenant Gonville Bromhead (Michael Caine), assumes command and orders the troops to dig in. In extended ferocious battles over several days, the vastly outnumbered 24th Regiment holds off the Zulus, even inflicting heavy casualties. On the third day, suffering from exhaustion and being greatly reduced in number, the British fear the Zulus will make a final assault and overrun their position. A seemingly endless line of Zulus appears on the horizon, but instead of charging they slowly withdraw with a chant celebrating warriors as brave as themselves.

Zulu is the best of the colonial movies made from the thirties through the fifties. However, as always, nineteenth-century British colonialism is disguised and *Zulu* is presented as a test of bravery between two opposing forces. Nevertheless, the film has everything else going for it: an historical battle beautifully photographed by Stephen Dade; the excellent screenplay of John Prebble and Cy Endfield that brings to life some ten characters; and the stellar performances of the two leads, Stanley Baker and Michael Caine in his screen debut. There is also fine acting by Nigel Green as Color Sergeant Bourne, James Booth as Private Henry Hook, Jack Hawkins as Reverend Witt and Ulla Jacobsson as his sex-starved daughter. The Welsh voices bravely raised in song is moving and John Barry's rousing score gives added force to the battle scenes. The film came from a most unexpected source, a virtually unknown Cy Endfield who had been a minor Hollywood director in the late forties. Endfield had been black-listed in the early fifties and had moved to England, working under assumed names in small productions. *Zulu* was the only movie of note Enfield directed. His *Sands of the Kalahari* (1969) about the survivors of a plane crash in the desert has its moments but it fails. *Zulu* was made in collaboration with Stanley Baker, a Welshman who was a novice at movie production. As the film was about a Welsh regiment, Richard Burton, also a Welshman, did the voice narration, which is very effective.

BIBLIOGRAPHY

Bergan, Ronald and Robyn Karney. *The Holt Foreign Film Guide*. New York, 1988.

Fox, Ken et al., ed. *The Movie Guide*. New York, 1998.

Katz, Ephraim. *The International Film Encyclopedia*. London, 1982.

Maltin, Leonard. *Movie and Video Guide*. New York, 2003.

Pym, John, ed. *Time Out Film Guide*. London, 1999.

Thomson, David. *The New Biographical Dictionary of Film*. New York, 2002.

Variety Movie Guide. New York, 2001

Wilhelm, Elliot. *Video Hound's World Cinema*. Michigan, 1999.

INDEX OF FILM TITLES